OS X® Mavericks

Ben Harvell

Teach Yourself VISUALLY™ Complete OS X® Mavericks

Published by
John Wiley & Sons, Inc.
10475 Crosspoint Boulevard
Indianapolis, IN 46256

www.wiley.com

Published simultaneously in Canada

Wiley publishes in a variety of print and electronic formats and by print-on-demand. Some material included with standard print versions of this book may not be included in e-books or in print-on-demand. If this book refers to media such as a CD or DVD that is not included in the version you purchased, you may download this material at http://booksupport.wiley.com. For more information about Wiley products, visit www.wiley.com.

Library of Congress Control Number: 2013952427

ISBN: 978-1-118-73676-0

Manufactured in the United States of America

10 9 8 7 6 5 4 3 2 1

Trademark Acknowledgments

Contact Us

For general information on our other products and services please contact our Customer Care Department within the U.S. at 877-762-2974, outside the U.S. at 317-572-3993 or fax 317-572-4002.

For technical support please visit www.wiley.com/techsupport.

Sales | Contact Wiley at (877) 762-2974 or fax (317) 572-4002.

Credits

Acquisitions Editor
Aaron Black

Project Editor
Lynn Northrup

Technical Editor
Dennis Cohen

Copy Editor
Kim Heusel

Director, Content Development & Assembly
Robyn Siesky

Vice President and Executive Group Publisher
Richard Swadley

About the Author

Ben Harvell is a freelance writer based in Bournemouth, United Kingdom. Formerly the editor of iCreate magazine, Ben has written several consumer technology books with a focus on Apple products, including *Make Music with your iPad* and *Teach Yourself Visually Facebook,* also published by Wiley. He blogs at www.benharvell.com, tweets as @benharvell, and provides a professional copywriting service for mobile app developers at www.pocket-copy.com.

Author's Acknowledgments

As with all of the books I write for Wiley, my involvement is just one cog in a finely tuned, well-oiled machine. My thanks and immense appreciation go out to the masters of production, proofing, and patience who work behind the scenes to turn the text I provide into the legible form you hold in your hands.

Special thanks go to Lynn Northrup for her unwavering calm in the face of a scatterbrained British writer, and to Dennis Cohen for knowing more than is healthy about tech and using this superpower to ensure this book's factual accuracy.

My thanks, as always, also go to acquisitions editor Aaron Black for asking me to work on this project, our third in as many years.

How to Use This Book

Who This Book Is For

This book is for the reader who has never used this particular technology or software application. It is also for readers who want to expand their knowledge.

The Conventions in This Book

1 Steps

This book uses a step-by-step format to guide you easily through each task. Numbered steps are actions you must do; bulleted steps clarify a point, step, or optional feature; and indented steps give you the result.

2 Notes

Notes give additional information — special conditions that may occur during an operation, a situation that you want to avoid, or a cross reference to a related area of the book.

3 Icons and Buttons

Icons and buttons show you exactly what you need to click to perform a step.

4 Tips

Tips offer additional information, including warnings and shortcuts.

5 Bold

Bold type shows command names, options, and text or numbers you must type.

6 Italics

Italic type introduces and defines a new term.

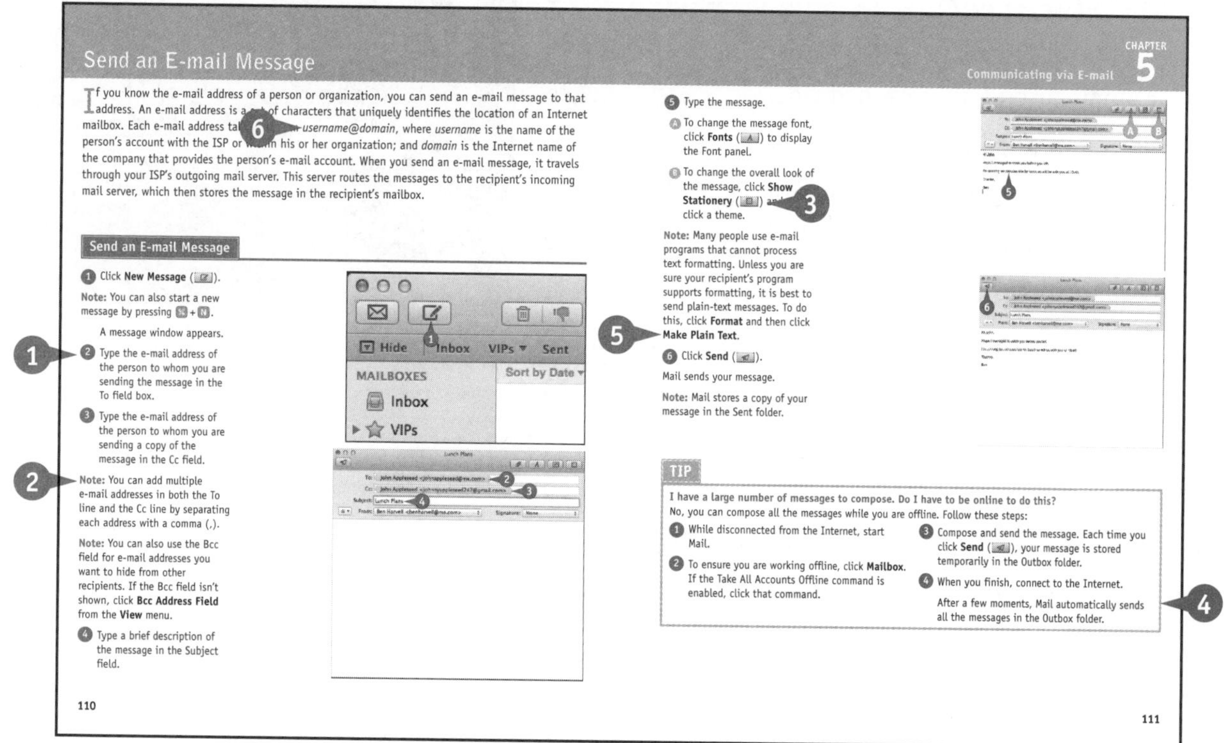

Send an E-mail Message

CHAPTER 5 Communicating via E-mail

If you know the e-mail address of a person or organization, you can send an e-mail message to that address. An e-mail address is a set of characters that uniquely identifies the location of an Internet mailbox. Each e-mail address takes the form *username@domain*, where *username* is the name of the person's account with the ISP or within his or her organization; and *domain* is the Internet name of the company that provides the person's e-mail account. When you send an e-mail message, it travels through your ISP's outgoing mail server. This server routes the messages to the recipient's incoming mail server, which then stores the message in the recipient's mailbox.

Send an E-mail Message

1 Click **New Message** ( ).

Note: You can also start a new message by pressing ⌘+N.

A message window appears.

2 Type the e-mail address of the person to whom you are sending the message in the To field box.

3 Type the e-mail address of the person to whom you are sending a copy of the message in the Cc field.

Note: You can add multiple e-mail addresses in both the To line and the Cc line by separating each address with a comma (,).

Note: You can also use the Bcc field for e-mail addresses you want to hide from other recipients. If the Bcc field isn't shown, click **Bcc Address Field** from the **View** menu.

4 Type a brief description of the message in the Subject field.

5 Type the message.

A To change the message font, click **Fonts** ( ) to display the Font panel.

B To change the overall look of the message, click **Show Stationery** ( ) and then click a theme.

Note: Many people use e-mail programs that cannot process text formatting. Unless you are sure your recipient's program supports formatting, it is best to send plain-text messages. To do this, click **Format** and then click **Make Plain Text**.

6 Click **Send** ( ).

Mail sends your message.

Note: Mail stores a copy of your message in the Sent folder.

TIP

I have a large number of messages to compose. Do I have to be online to do this?

No, you can compose all the messages while you are offline. Follow these steps:

1 While disconnected from the Internet, start Mail.

2 To ensure you are working offline, click **Mailbox**. If the Take All Accounts Offline command is enabled, click that command.

3 Compose and send the message. Each time you click **Send** ( ), your message is stored temporarily in the Outbox folder.

4 When you finish, connect to the Internet.

After a few moments, Mail automatically sends all the messages in the Outbox folder.

110

111

Table of Contents

Chapter 1 Reviewing What You Can Do with OS X

Chapter 2 Learning Basic OS X Program Tasks

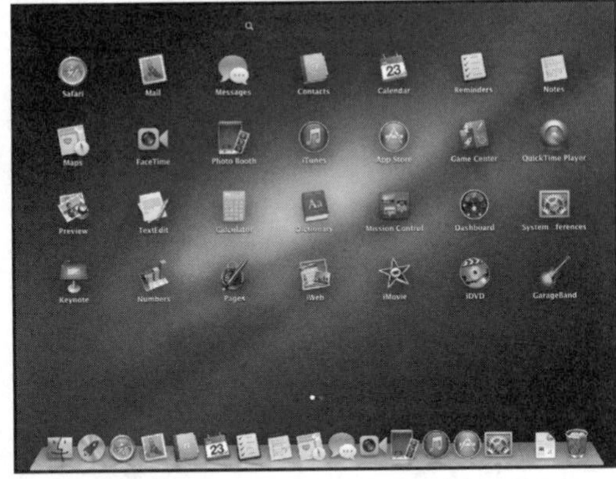

Chapter 3 Working with Files and Documents

Chapter 4 Browsing the World Wide Web

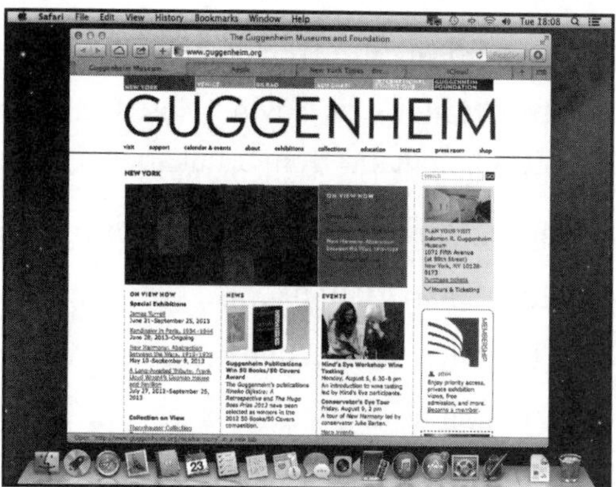

Table of Contents

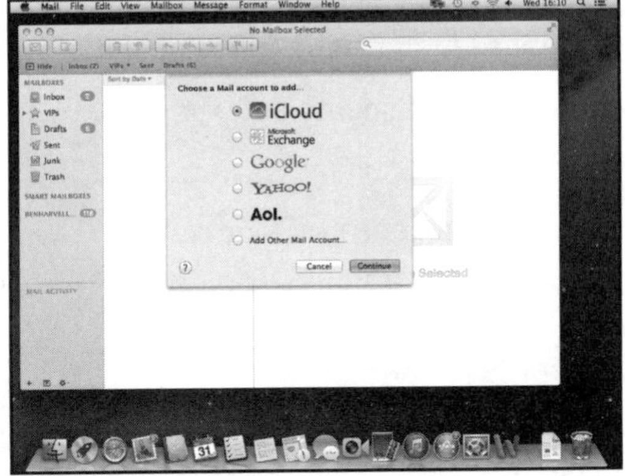

Chapter 6 Talking via Messages and FaceTime

Chapter 7 Tracking Contacts and Events

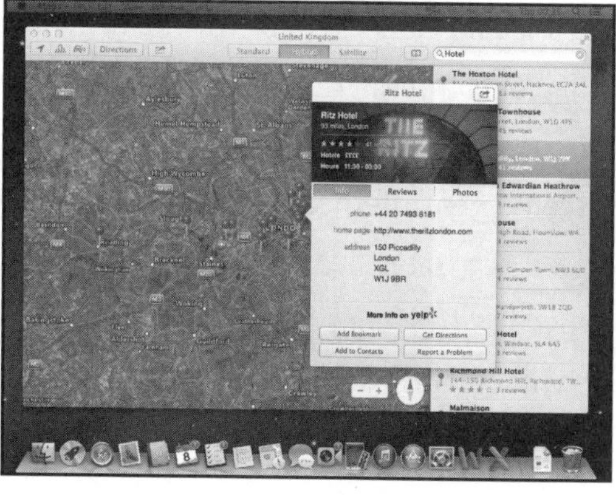

Table of Contents

Chapter 8 Playing and Organizing Music

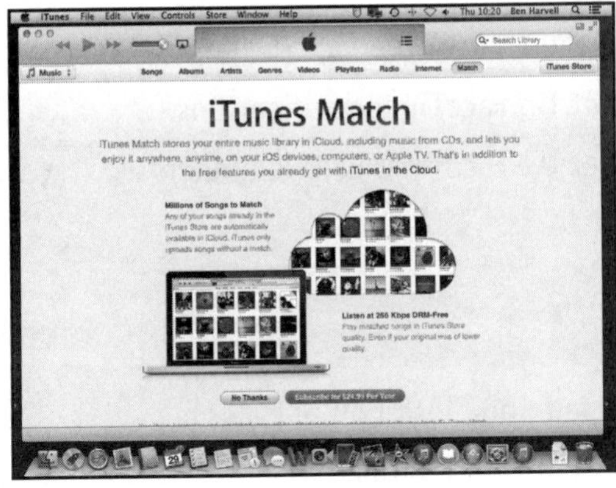

Chapter 9 Learning Useful OS X Tasks

Chapter 10 Viewing and Editing Photos

Table of Contents

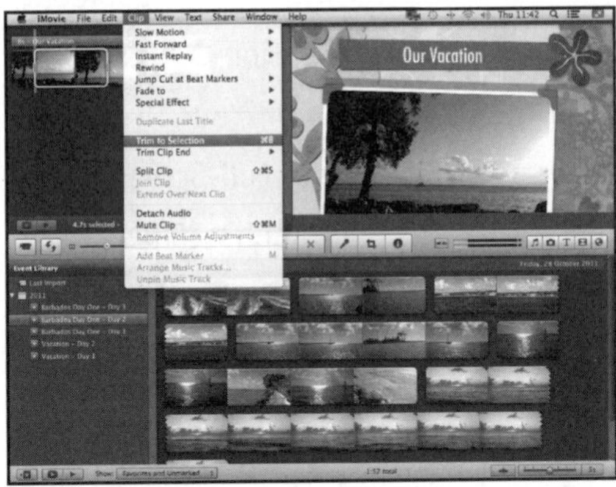

Chapter 12 Viewing and Editing Documents with Preview

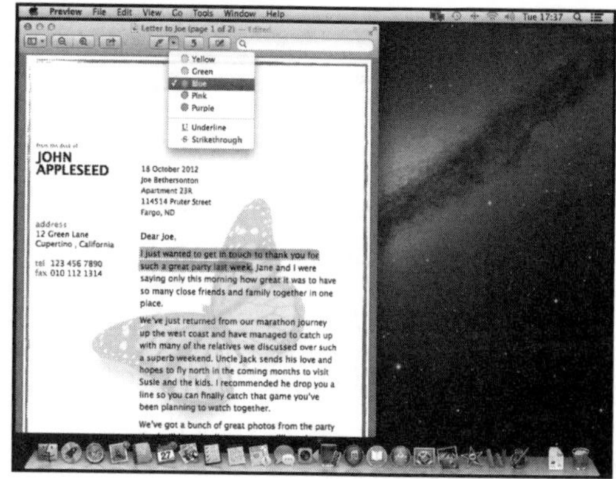

Chapter 13 Customizing OS X

Table of Contents

Chapter 14 Maintaining OS X

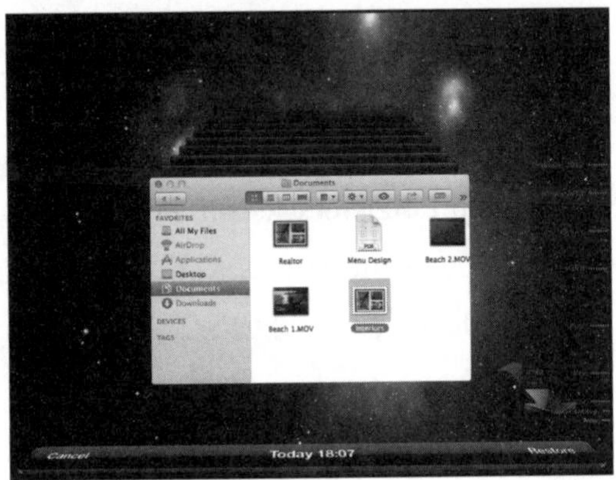

Chapter 15 Working with Your iCloud Account

Chapter 16 Networking with OS X

Chapter 17 Downloading New Software

Table of Contents

Chapter 18 Playing Games on Your Mac

CHAPTER 1

Reviewing What You Can Do with OS X

Are you ready to learn about what you can do with OS X? In this chapter, you find out about the wide variety of tasks you can perform with OS X, including creating documents; playing music; organizing photos, contacts, and appointments; and surfing the web.

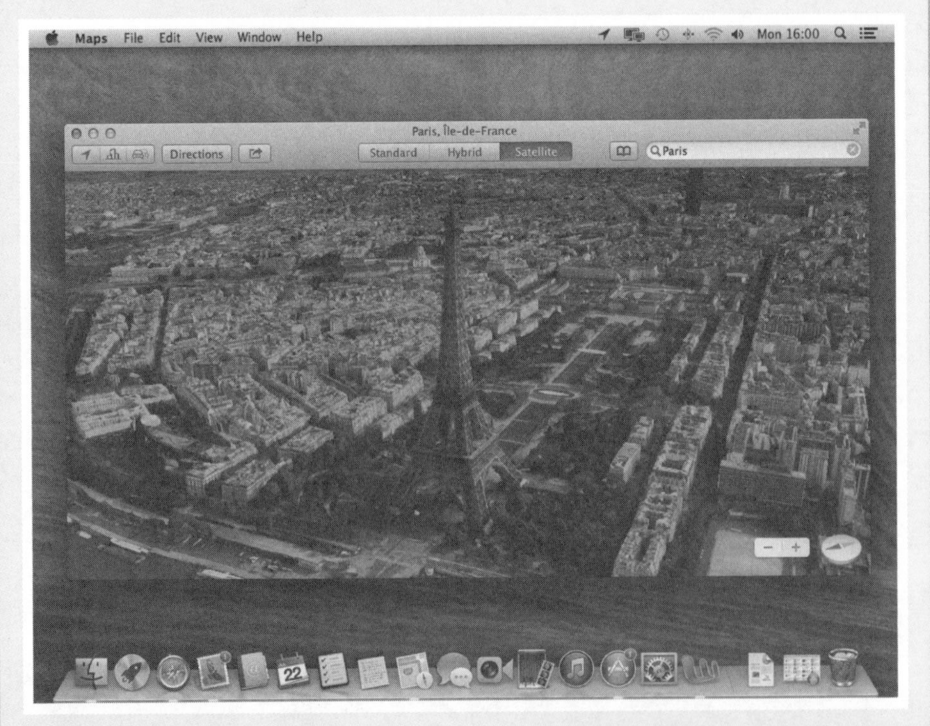

Create Documents

Whether you use your Mac at home, at the office, or on the road, you can use OS X to create a wide variety of documents. In general terms, a *document* is a file that contains information that is usually text, but it may also consist of pictures, charts, lines, and other non-text items. With OS X, you can create documents such as lists, letters, memos, budgets, forecasts, presentations, and web pages.

Text Documents

You can use text-editing software on OS X to create simple documents such as lists, notes, instructions, and other items that do not require fonts, colors, or other types of formatting. With OS X, you can use the TextEdit application to create plain text documents, and the Stickies application to create electronic sticky notes.

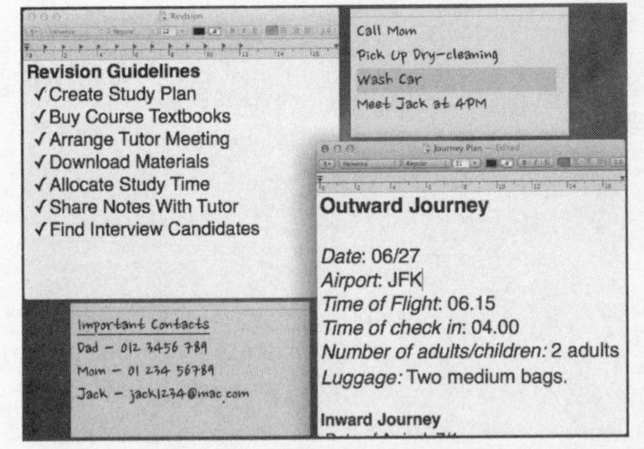

Word Processing Documents

You can use word processing software on OS X to create letters, resumes, memos, reports, newsletters, brochures, business cards, menus, flyers, invitations, and certificates. Anything that you use to communicate on paper, you can create using OS X. You can also use TextEdit to create formatted documents. Other examples include Microsoft Word for the Mac and Apple iWork Pages.

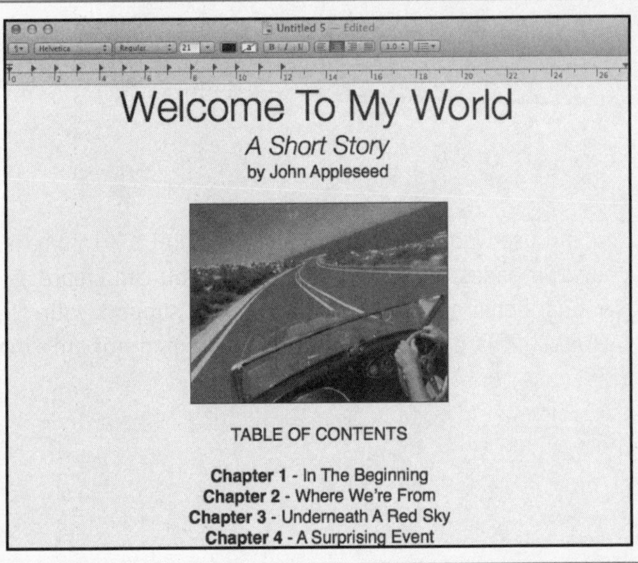

Spreadsheets

A spreadsheet application is a software program that enables you to manipulate numbers and formulas to quickly create powerful mathematical, financial, and statistical models. Apple also sells iWork Numbers for Mac, while another example is Microsoft Excel for the Mac.

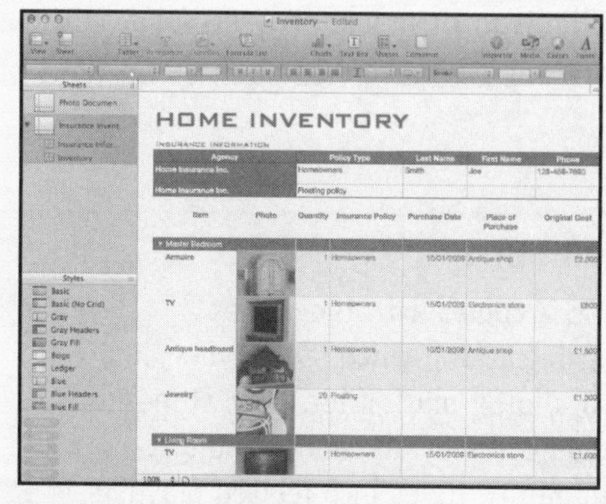

Presentations

A presentation program enables you to build professional-looking slides that you can use to convey your ideas to other people. Apple sells the Keynote application both separately and as part of the iWork suite, while another example is Microsoft PowerPoint for the Mac.

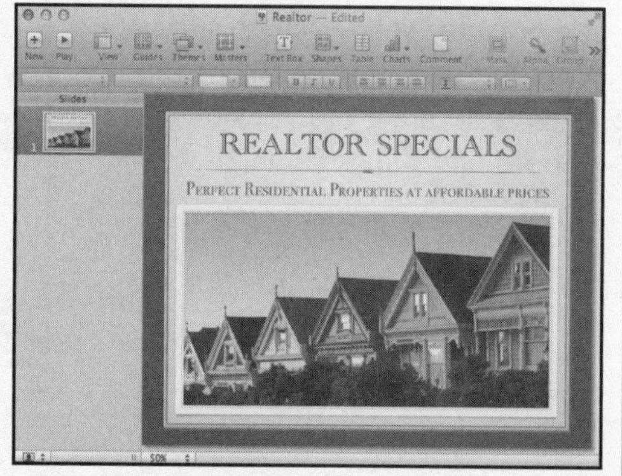

Web Pages

You can use web-page editing software on OS X to create your own pages to publish to the web. You can create a personal home page, a blog, or pages to support your business. OS X does not come with a program for creating web pages, but the App Store contains several excellent apps, including TextWrangler, BBEdit, and Web Form Builder Lite.

Play and Record Music

OS X is a veritable music machine that you can use to build, organize, play, and share your digital music collection. You can get music onto your Mac by copying it from audio CDs, or by purchasing music online. If you are musically inclined, you can record or compose new tunes using an application called GarageBand (sold both separately and as part of the Apple iLife suite). After you have a collection of music on your Mac, you can use OS X to create custom music CDs, or copy some or all of the music to a device such as an iPod or iPad.

iTunes

OS X comes with the iTunes application, which stores your library of digital music files. With iTunes, you can play albums and songs, organize tunes into related playlists, download and edit track information, and organize your music to suit your style. You can also use iTunes to listen to Internet-based radio stations and iTunes Radio.

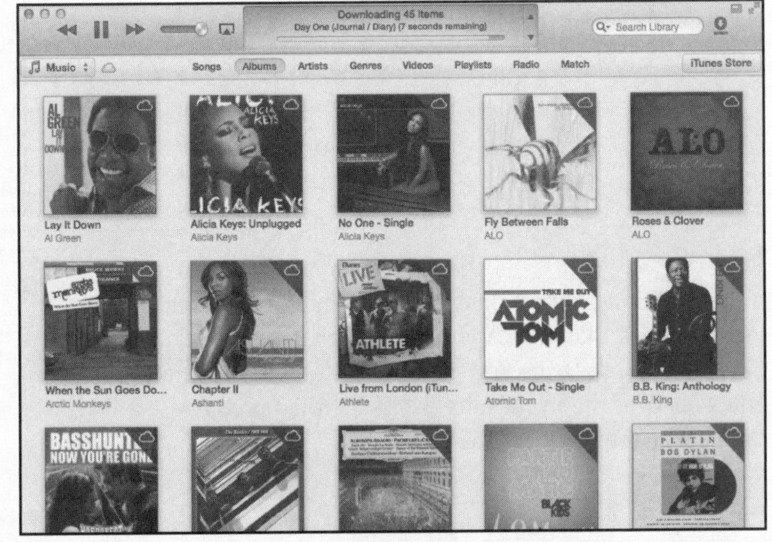

iTunes Store

You can use the iTunes application to connect directly to the online iTunes Store, where you can purchase individual songs, usually for 99 cents per song, or entire albums, usually for $9.99 per album. OS X downloads the purchased music to your iTunes library, and you can listen to the music on your Mac or add the music to your iPod, iPhone, or iPad. You can also pay to sync your music with iTunes in the cloud and access your entire library wherever you are.

Import Music from a CD

You can add tracks from a music CD to the iTunes library. This enables you to listen to an album without having to put the CD into a CD or DVD drive each time. In iTunes, the process of copying tracks from a CD to your Mac is called *importing* or *ripping*.

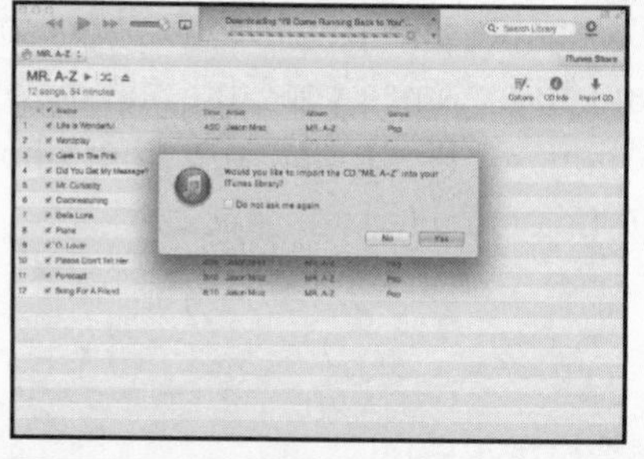

Record Music

If your Mac came with the iLife suite, or if you purchase it separately from the App Store, you can use the GarageBand program to record or compose your own tunes. You can attach an instrument such as a guitar or keyboard to your Mac and record your playing. You can also use GarageBand to add accompanying instruments such as drums, bass, piano, or another guitar.

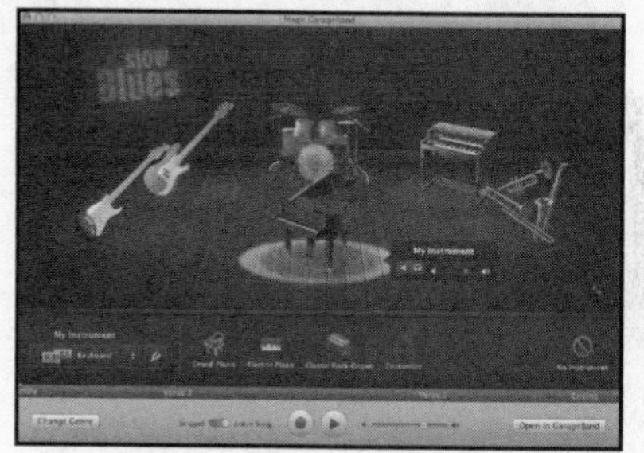

Burn Music to a CD

You can copy, or *burn*, music files from your Mac onto a CD if you have a Mac with a built-in optical drive or if you are using an external drive. Burning CDs is a great way to create customized CDs that you can listen to on the computer or in a portable device. You can burn music files using the iTunes application.

Synchronize with an iPod, iPhone, or iPad

You can use the iTunes application to copy some or all your music library to an iPod, iPhone, or iPad; this enables you to play your music wherever you are on another audio device that connects to the device. When you attach the iPod, iPhone, or iPad to your Mac, iTunes automatically synchronizes the device according to the settings you specify.

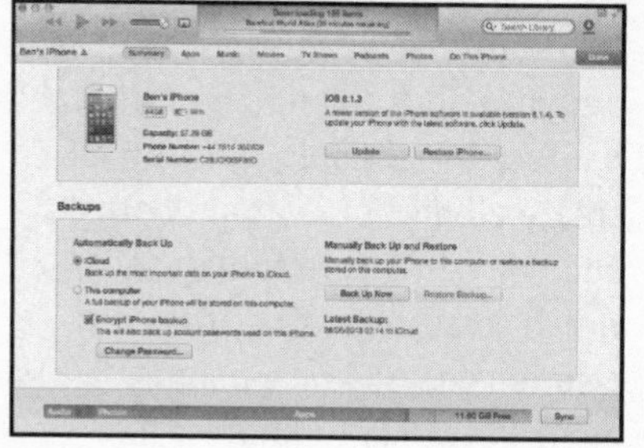

View and Organize Your Photos

Your Mac is perfect for showing your digital photos in their best light. OS X comes with tools that enable you to view individual photos and to run slide shows of multiple photos. OS X also enables you to organize your digital photos, import images from a digital camera or similar device (such as an iPhone or iPad), and edit your photos. Many Macs also come with a built-in camera that you can use to take simple snapshots.

View Photos

OS X gives you many ways to view your digital photos. You can view photos within Finder using the Cover Flow view, or by selecting the photos and pressing Spacebar. You can also double-click a photo file to open it using the Preview application, or you can open a file using the iPhoto application if it is installed on your Mac. Also, Preview, iPhoto, and Quick Look enable you to run photo slide shows.

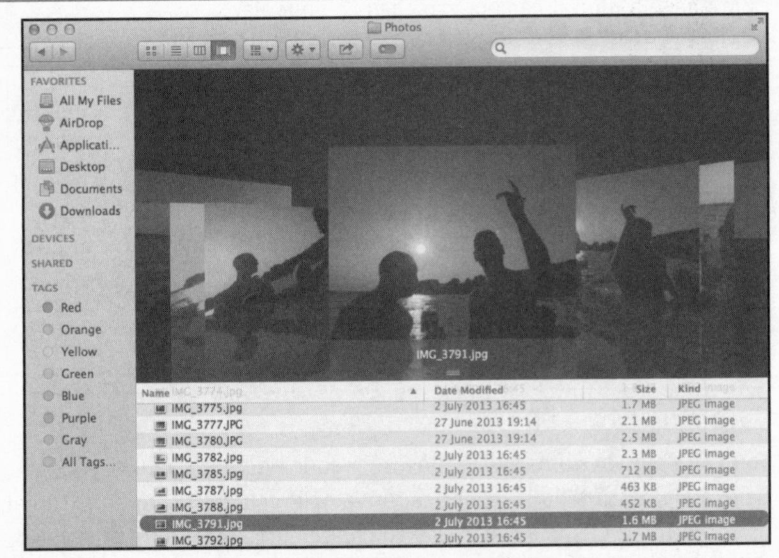

Organize Photos

If your Mac comes with iPhoto, or you have purchased iPhoto from the App Store, part of the Apple iLife suite, you can use it to organize your collection of digital photos. For example, you can create albums of related photos, and you can create folders in which to store photos. You can also rename and rate photos, apply keywords to photos, flag important photos, and sort photos in various ways.

Import Photos to OS X

If you have a digital camera attached to your Mac, you can use either the Image Capture application or the iPhoto application, part of the Apple iLife suite, to import some or all of the camera's images to OS X.

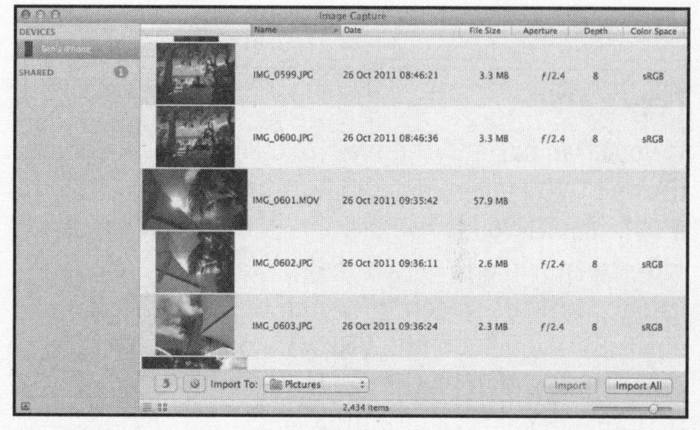

Take Snapshots

If your Mac includes an iSight or FaceTime HD camera or has a digital video camera connected, you can use the Photo Booth application to take snapshots of whatever subject is currently displayed in the camera. You can also apply various effects to the photos.

Edit Photos

If your Mac comes with the iPhoto application, you can use it to edit your digital photos. You can rotate, crop, or straighten a photo; you can modify a photo's exposure, contrast, and sharpness; you can fix problems such as red eye and blemishes; and you can apply special effects to a photo.

Play and Make a Movie or Slide Show

Your Mac's solid graphical underpinnings mean that it is a great tool for video playback. For example, OS X comes with tools that enable you to watch movies on DVD. You can play digital video such as movies, TV shows, and podcast files that you download from the Internet, or digital video that you import from a camera. You can also use OS X to create your own digital movies and your own photo slide shows.

Play a DVD

If your Mac has a DVD drive, you can use the DVD Player application to play a DVD movie. You can either use full-screen mode to watch the movie using the entire screen, or watch the movie in a window while you work on other things. DVD Player has features that enable you to control the movie playback and volume.

Play a Video File

OS X comes with an application called QuickTime BHPlayer that enables you to open video files and control the playback and volume. QuickTime Player also includes many extra features, including the ability to record movies and audio, cut and paste scenes, and publish your videos on services such as YouTube and Facebook.

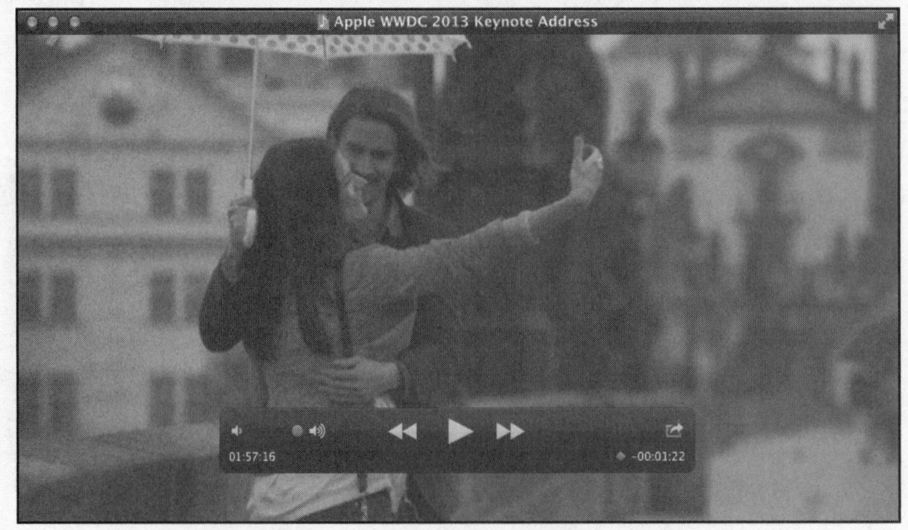

Play a Movie, TV Show, or Podcast

You most often use iTunes to play music, but you can also use it to play movies, video files stored on your Mac, and TV shows that you purchase from the iTunes Store, as well as podcasts that you download from the iTunes Store or subscribe to online.

Make a Movie

Most Macs come with an application called iMovie, part of the Apple iLife suite (it can also be purchased separately), which enables you to make your own digital movies. You can import clips from a video camera or video file, add clips to the movie, and rearrange and trim those clips as needed. You can also add transitions between scenes, music and sound effects, titles, and more.

Make a Slide Show

You can use OS X to create your own photo slide shows. Using the iPhoto application, part of the Apple iLife suite, you can create a slide show of your photos that includes animation effects, transition effects, and music. You can enhance the slide show with photo titles and sophisticated background and text themes.

Take Advantage of the Web

You can use OS X to connect to your Internet account. Once the connection has been established, you can use the built-in web browser to access almost any site that is available on the web. This means you can use your Mac to search for information, read the latest news, research and purchase goods and services, sell your own items, socialize with others, and more.

Surf the Web

OS X comes with a browser application called Safari that you use to surf the web. Safari offers several ways to load and navigate web pages. You can also use Safari to save your favorite web pages as bookmarks, view multiple pages in a single window using tabs, download files to your Mac, and much more.

Search for Information

If you need information on a specific topic, free websites called *search engines* enable you to quickly search the web for pages that have the information you require. You can search the web either by going directly to a search engine site or by using the search feature built in to Safari.

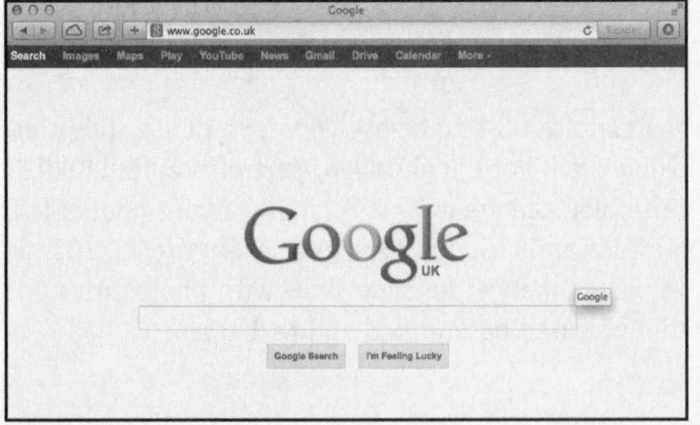

Read News

The web is home to many sites that enable you to read the latest news. For example, many print sources have websites, some magazines exist only online, and there are more recent innovations such as blogs and RSS feeds. Some media sites require that you register to access the articles, but on most sites, the registration is free.

Buy and Sell

E-commerce — the online buying and selling of goods and services — is a big part of the web. You can use web-based stores to purchase books, theater tickets, and even cars, which gives you the convenience of shopping at home, easily comparing prices and features, and having goods delivered to your door. Many sites also enable you to sell or auction your products or household items.

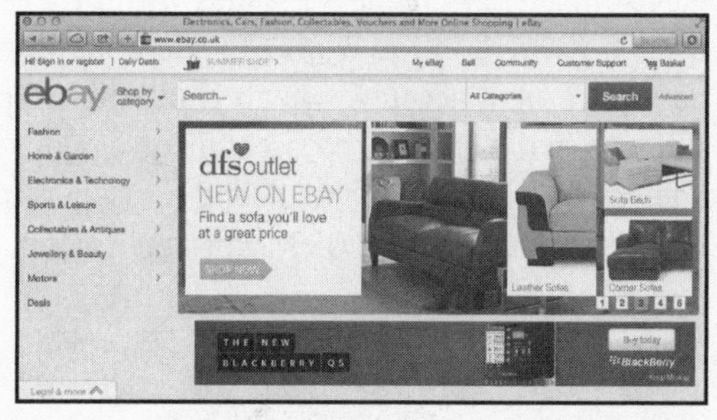

Socialize

The web offers many opportunities to socialize, whether you are looking for a friend or a date, or you just want some good conversation. However, it is a good idea to observe some common-sense precautions. For example, arrange to meet new friends in public places, supervise all online socializing done by children, and do not give out personal information to strangers.

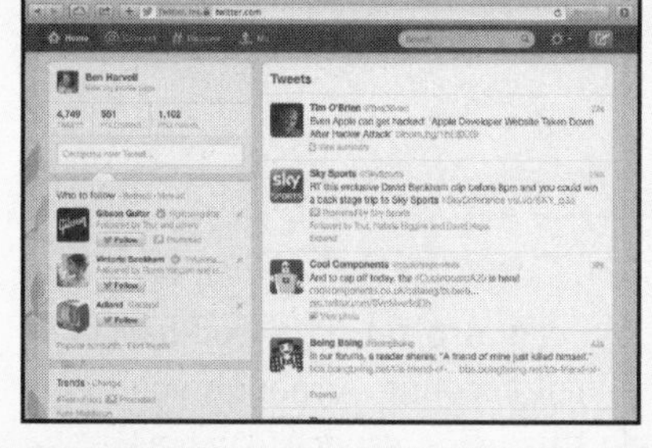

Take Advantage of iCloud

You can use OS X to set up a free web-based iCloud account that enables you to perform many activities online, including exchanging e-mail, maintaining contacts, and tracking appointments. You can also use your iCloud account to synchronize data between your Mac and other Macs; Windows PCs; and devices such as iPod touch, iPhone, and iPad.

Communicate with Others

You can use OS X to communicate with other people using online and wireless technologies. For example, once you connect your Mac to the Internet, you can start sending and receiving e-mail, using either your Internet service provider (ISP) account or a web-based account. You can also use your Internet connection to exchange instant messages and perform audio and video chats. If you have a camera attached to your Mac, you can also place video calls to other people through your wired or wireless network.

Exchange E-mail

E-mail is the Internet system that enables you to electronically exchange messages with other Internet users anywhere in the world. To use e-mail, you must have an e-mail account, which is usually supplied by your ISP or e-mail service. The account gives you an e-mail address to which others can send messages. You then set up that account in the OS X Mail application.

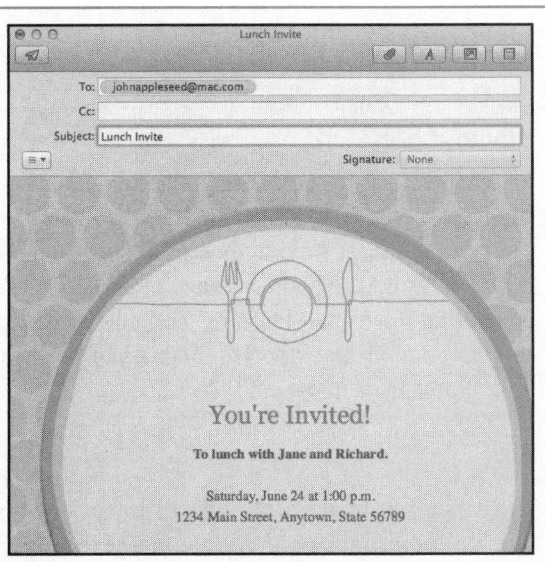

Exchange E-mail over the Web

You can also set up a web-based e-mail account. Although you can do this using services such as Hotmail.com and Yahoo.com, many Mac users create iCloud accounts, which include web-based e-mail. A web-based account is convenient because it enables you to send and receive messages from any computer that has access to the Internet.

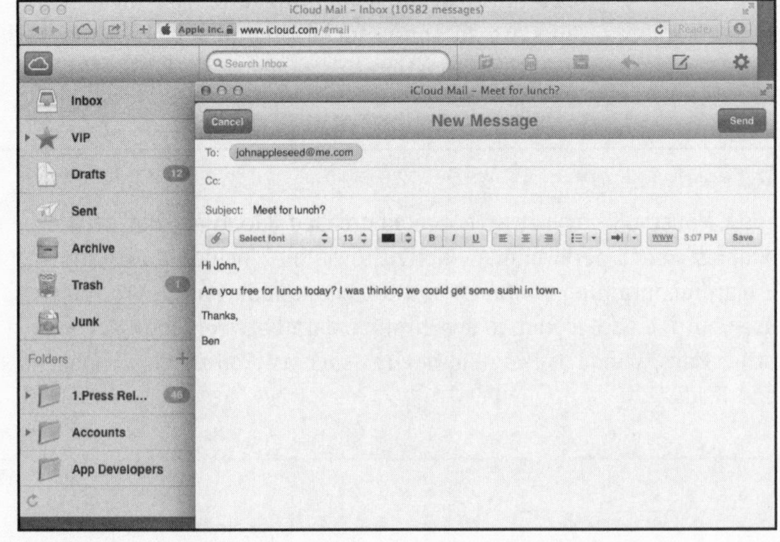

Exchange Instant Messages

Instant messaging allows you to contact other people who are online, thus enabling you to have a real-time exchange of messages. Communicating in real time means that if you send a message to another person who is online, that message appears on the person's computer right away. If that person sends you a response, it appears on your computer right away. In OS X Mavericks, you use the Messages application to exchange instant messages.

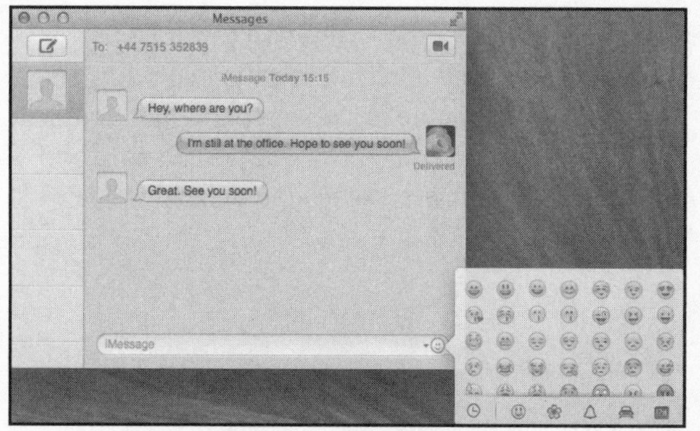

Share via Twitter and Facebook

If you have an account on Twitter, Facebook, or both, you can configure OS X with your account credentials. You can then share information with your Twitter followers and Facebook friends by sending tweets or updates from a number of OS X applications, including Safari and iPhoto. You can also use the Photo Booth application to take your picture, and then use that photo as your Twitter or Facebook profile picture. You can also update your social network accounts from the Notification Center pane in OS X.

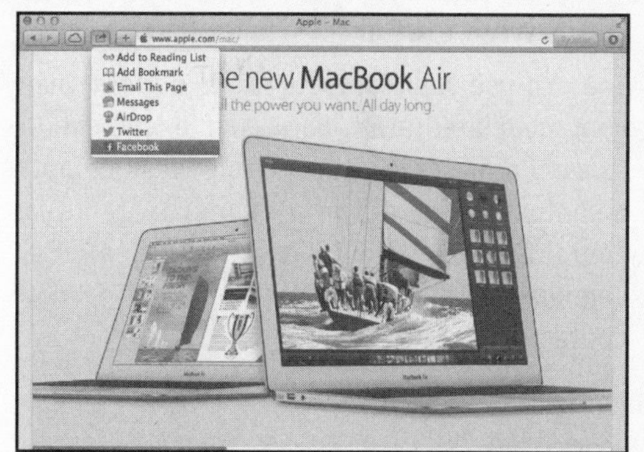

Place Video Calls

OS X Mavericks comes with a program called FaceTime that enables you to make video calls to other people. With a video call, your image is captured by a video camera — such as the FaceTime HD camera built in to many Macs — and a microphone captures your voice. Both the video and audio streams are sent to the other person, who could be using FaceTime on a Mac, an iPhone 4 or later, an iPad 2 or later, or a fourth-generation or later iPod touch. The other person can also see and hear you.

Organize Your Contacts and Appointments

You can use OS X to help you organize various aspects of your life. For example, OS X comes with tools that enable you to enter, edit, organize, and work with your contacts, which means you can maintain a convenient digital version of your address book. Other OS X tools enable you to schedule events such as appointments, meetings, and trips. You can even configure OS X to synchronize your contacts and schedule among multiple devices.

Maintain Your Contact List

OS X comes with an application called Contacts that enables you to store information about your contacts. For each contact, you can store data such as the person's name, address, telephone number, e-mail address, and birthday.

Work with Contacts

You can use your Contacts list to perform many contact-related tasks. For example, you can use Mail to send a message either to individual contacts or to a contact group, which is a Contacts item that contains multiple contacts. Also, you can use Calendar to set up a meeting with one or more contacts.

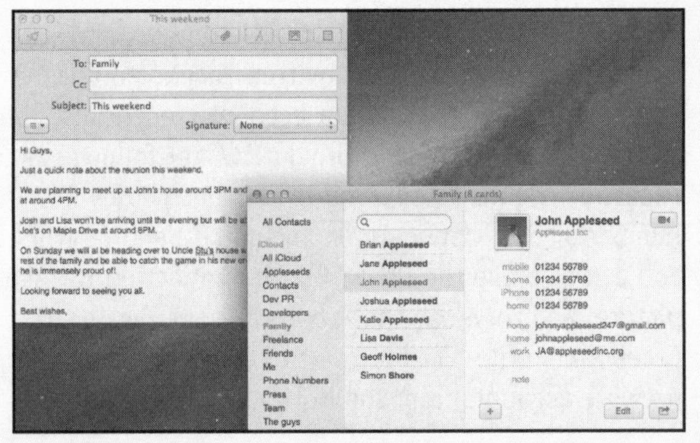

Schedule an Appointment

You can help organize your life by using OS X to record your appointments on the date and time they occur. You do this using the Calendar application, which uses an electronic calendar to store your appointments. You can even configure Calendar to display a reminder or two before an appointment occurs.

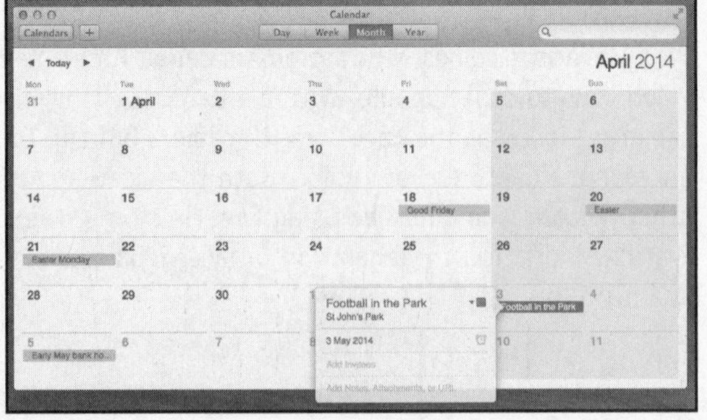

Schedule an All-Day Event

If an appointment has no set time — for example, a birthday, anniversary, or multiple-day event such as a sales meeting or vacation — you can use Calendar to set up the appointment as an all-day event.

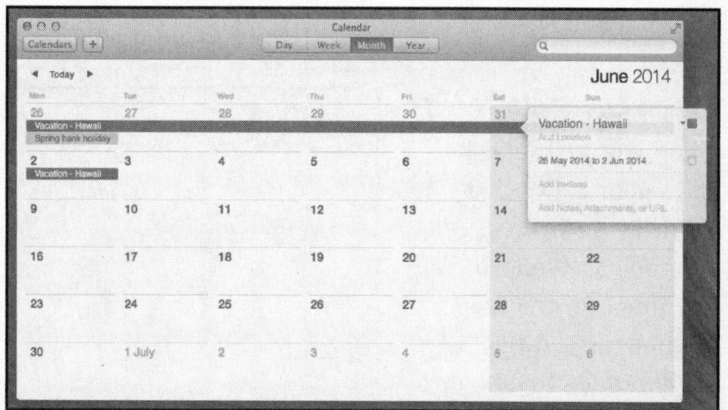

Schedule a Repeating Appointment

If an event occurs regularly — for example, once a week or once every three months — you do not need to schedule every event manually. Instead, you can use Calendar to configure the activity as a repeating event, where you specify the repeat interval. Calendar then creates all the future events automatically.

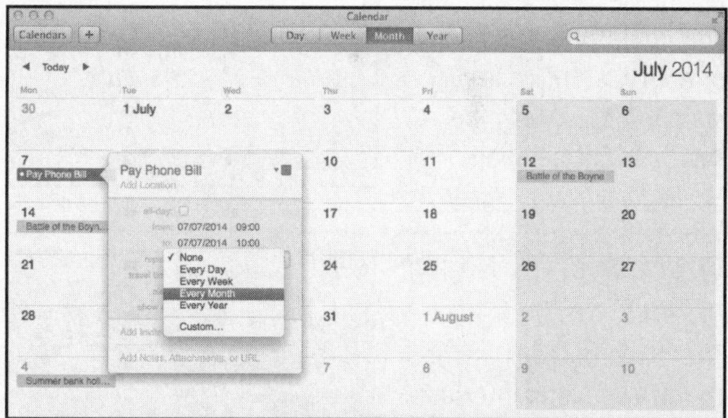

Synchronize with iCloud

If you have an iCloud account, you can synchronize your OS X contacts and events so that they also appear in the iCloud Contacts and Calendar. If you have an iPod touch, iPhone, or iPad, you can use iCloud to sync those same contacts and events to your device. If you have a second Mac or a Windows PC, you can use iCloud to keep your contacts and events in sync on both computers.

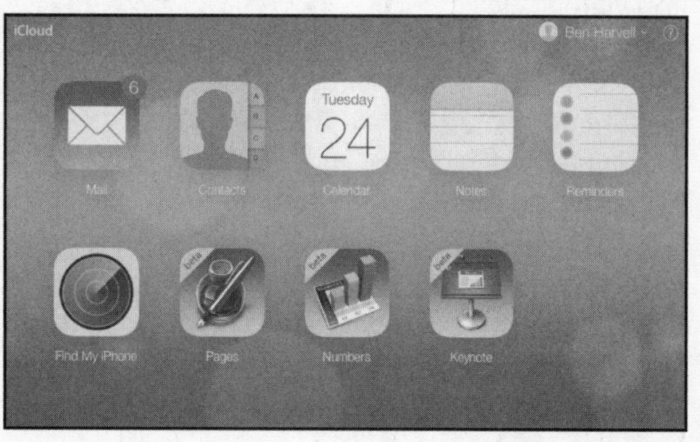

Plan Journeys

OS X includes the Maps application that allows you to look up locations worldwide, get directions, and more. The app shows maps in a standard display or as satellite images, and you can also view both styles at once. Certain locations include 3-D models of buildings that allow you to get a better view of the area and scroll around the location. The Maps app also allows you to send directions to other devices so you don't have to enter the start and end points for your journey on your iOS device as well as on your Mac.

Find Locations

When you first launch Maps your current location is shown as a blue dot on the map. You can then use the search field at the top right of the interface to look up specific areas or businesses. For example, you could type the name of a city, a ZIP code, or simply a business type such as "Coffee Shop."

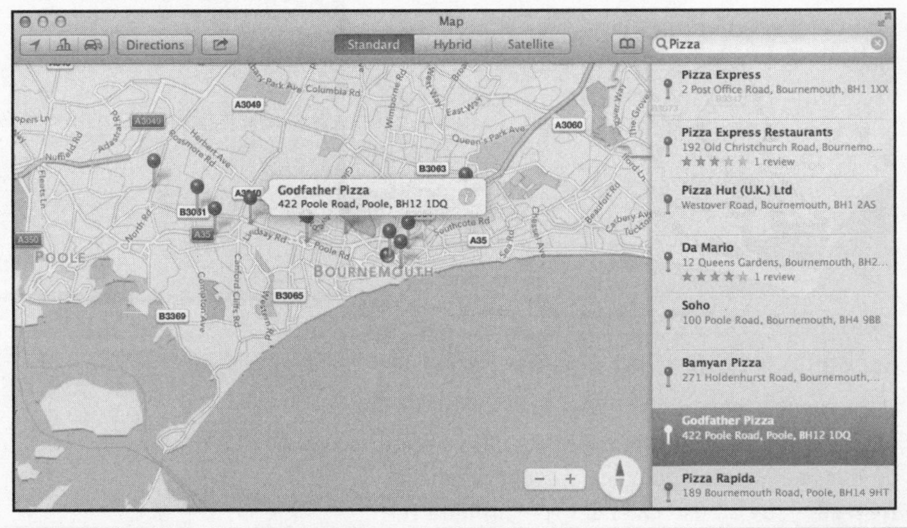

View Different Map Types

The three buttons at the top of the Maps interface allow you to change the map view. Standard shows a simple map, while Satellite uses satellite photos to show locations. Clicking the **Hybrid** option shows the Satellite combined with the Standard map view so you can view road names and locations.

Use Flyover

Certain locations in Maps can be viewed in 3-D with a feature called Flyover. Flyover angles the map view and shows buildings and other structures in three dimensions. When viewing maps in 3-D you can zoom in and rotate to get a better view.

Get Directions

By clicking **Directions** you can quickly plan a route between two locations. Typing a starting point and an end point for your journey and then clicking **Directions** displays one or more suggested routes, and you can switch between routes for walking or driving.

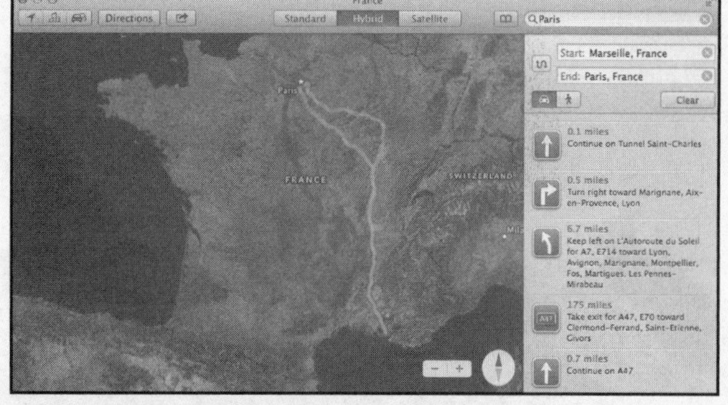

Share Directions

When you plan a route in the Maps application, you can send it to one of your other devices such as an iPad or an iPhone. You can also send directions via e-mail or upload them to Facebook or Twitter. You also have the option to bookmark directions so you can access them later.

CHAPTER 2

Learning Basic OS X Program Tasks

One of the most crucial OS X concepts is the application (also sometimes called a program), because it is via applications that you perform all other OS X tasks. Therefore, it is important to have a basic understanding of how to start and manage applications in OS X.

Explore the OS X Screen

Before you can begin to understand how the OS X operating system works, you should become familiar with the basic screen elements. These elements include the OS X menu bar, the desktop, desktop icons, and the Dock. Understanding where these elements appear on the screen and what they are used for will help you work through the rest of the tasks in this book and will help you navigate OS X and its applications on your own.

A Menu Bar

The menu bar contains the pull-down menus for OS X and most Mac software.

B Desktop

This is the OS X work area, where you work with your applications and documents.

C Mouse Pointer

When you move your mouse or move your finger on a trackpad, the pointer moves along with it.

D Desktop Icon

An icon on the desktop represents an application, a folder, a document, or a device attached to your Mac, such as a hard drive, a CD or DVD, or an iPod.

E Dock

The Dock contains several icons, each of which gives you quick access to some commonly used applications.

Tour the Dock

The Dock is the strip that runs along the bottom of the Mac screen. The Dock is populated with several small images, which are called *icons*. Each icon represents a particular component of your Mac — an application, a folder, a document, and so on — and clicking the icon opens the component. This makes the Dock one of the most important and useful OS X features because it gives you one-click access to applications, folders, and documents. The icons shown here are typical, but your Mac may display a different arrangement.

A Finder

Work with the files on your computer.

B Launchpad

View, organize, and start your applications.

C Safari

Browse the World Wide Web on the Internet.

D Mail

Send and receive e-mail messages.

E Contacts

Store and access people's names, addresses, and other contact information.

F Calendar

Record upcoming appointments, birthdays, meetings, and other events.

G Reminders

Set reminders for upcoming tasks.

H Notes

Record to-do lists and other short notes.

I Maps

Get directions and find locations on a map.

J Messages

Send instant messages to other people.

K FaceTime

Place video calls to other FaceTime users.

L Photo Booth

Take a picture using the camera on your Mac.

M iTunes

Play music and other media and add media to your iPod, iPhone, or iPad.

N App Store

Install new applications and upgrade existing ones.

O System Preferences

Customize and configure your Mac.

P Downloads

Display the contents of your Downloads folder.

Q Trash

Delete files, folders, and applications.

Start an Application

To perform tasks of any kind in OS X, you use one of the applications installed on your Mac. The application you use depends on the task you want to perform. For example, if you want to surf the World Wide Web, you use a web browser application, such as the Safari program that comes with OS X. Before you can use an application, however, you must first tell OS X which application you want to run. OS X launches the application and displays it on the desktop. You can then use the application's tools to perform your tasks.

Start an Application

1. In the Dock, click the **Finder** icon (🙂).

Note: If the application that you want to start has an icon in the Dock, you can click the icon to start the application and skip these steps.

The Finder window appears.

2. Click **Applications.**

Note: You can also navigate to Applications in any Finder window by pressing Shift+⌘+A or by choosing Go and then clicking **Applications**.

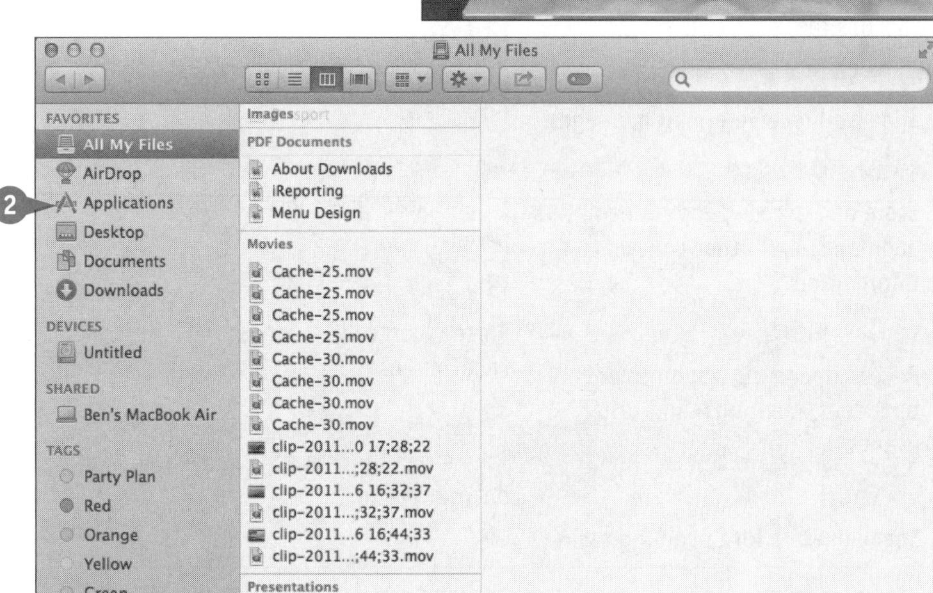

The Applications window appears.

3 Double-click the application that you want to start.

Note: If you see a folder icon (📁), it means that the application resides in its own folder, which is a storage area on the computer. Double-click 📁 to open the folder and then double-click the application icon.

A The application appears on the desktop.

B OS X adds an icon for the application to the Dock.

C The menu bar displays the menus associated with the application.

Note: Another common way to launch an application is to use Finder to locate a document you want to work with, and then double-click that document.

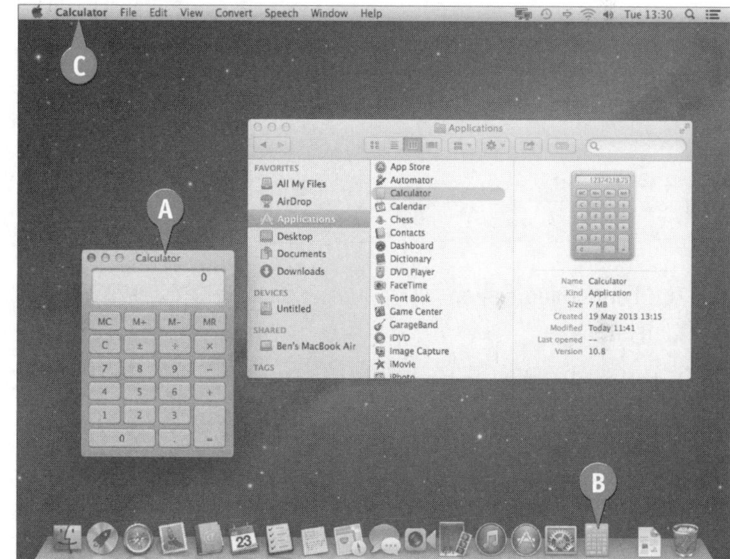

TIPS

How do I add an icon to the Dock for an application I use frequently?
First, start the application as described in steps 1 to 3. Right-click the application's Dock icon, click **Options**, and then click **Keep in Dock**.

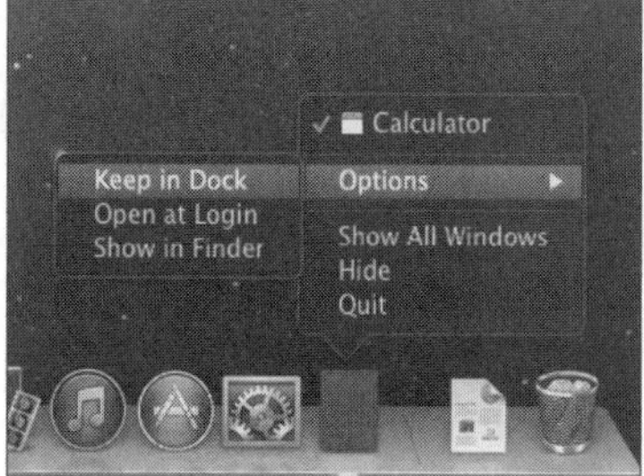

How do I shut down a running application?
The easiest way is to right-click the application's Dock icon and then click **Quit**. Alternatively, you can switch to the application and press ⌘+Q.

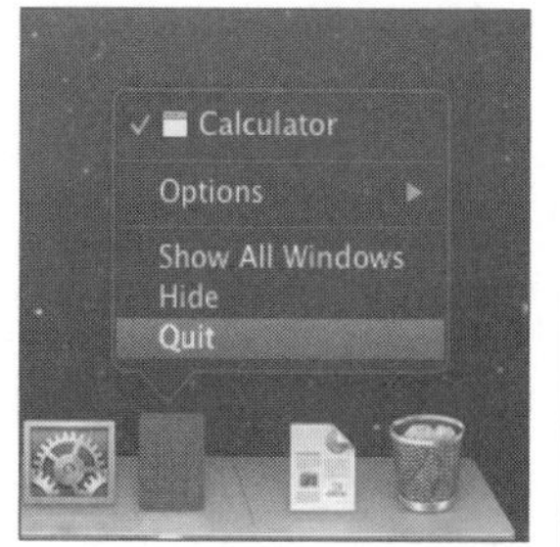

Start an Application Using Launchpad

You can start an application using the Launchpad feature. This is often faster than using the Applications folder. Launchpad is designed to mimic the Home screens of the iPhone, iPad, and iPod touch. So if you own one or more of these devices, then you are already familiar with how Launchpad works.

Start an Application Using Launchpad

1. In the Dock, click the **Launchpad** icon (■).

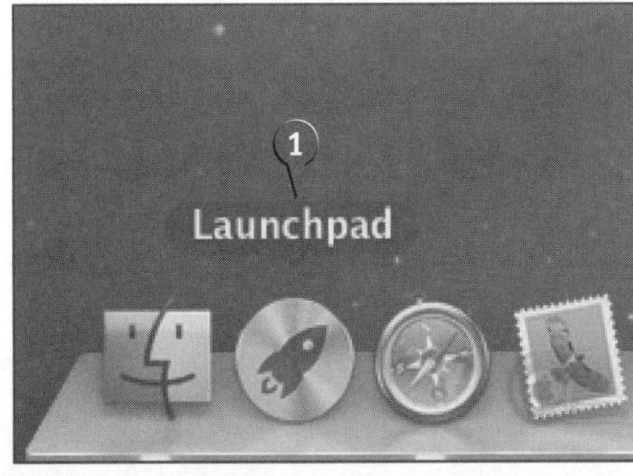

The Launchpad screen appears.

2. If the application you want to start resides in a different Launchpad screen, click the dot that corresponds to the screen or scroll through the screens until you find it.

Launchpad switches to the screen and displays the applications.

3 If the application you want to start resides within a folder, click the folder.

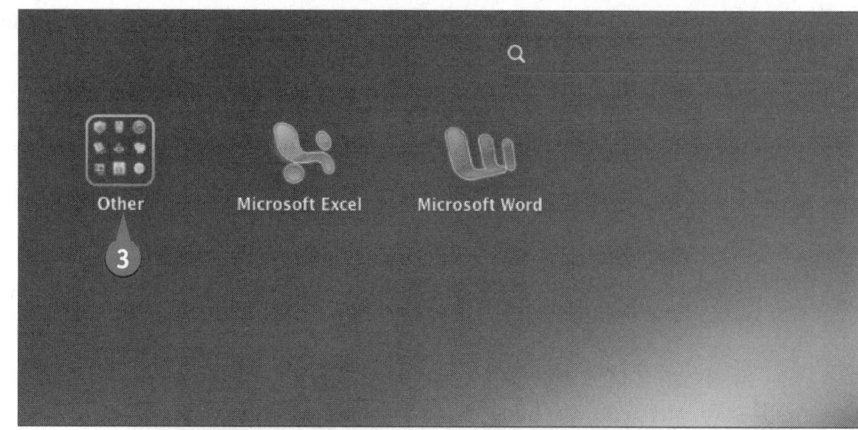

Launchpad opens the folder.

4 Click the icon of the application you want to start.

OS X starts the application.

TIP

The dots that represent each Launchpad screen are quite small, making them hard to click with the mouse. Is there an easier way to navigate the Launchpad screens?

Yes. As mentioned earlier, Launchpad looks somewhat similar to the Home screens of the iPhone, iPad, and iPod touch. Another similarity is how you navigate the screens. On an iPhone, iPad, and iPod touch, you navigate the Home screens by using a finger to swipe the screen right or left. With your Mac, you can also navigate the Launchpad screens by swiping. In this case, however, you must use two fingers, and you swipe right or left on either the trackpad or the surface of a Magic Mouse. You can also use the arrow keys on your keyboard to navigate left and right across Launchpad screens.

Note, too, that you can also use a trackpad gesture to open Launchpad: Place four fingers lightly on the trackpad and pinch them together.

Switch Between Applications

If you plan on running multiple applications at the same time, you need to know how to easily switch from one application to another. In OS X, after you start one application you do not need to close that application before you open another one. OS X supports a feature called *multitasking*, which means running two or more applications at once. This is handy if you need to use several applications throughout the day. For example, you might keep your word processing application, your web browser, and your e-mail application open all day.

Switch Between Applications

1. Click the Dock icon of the application that you want to switch to.

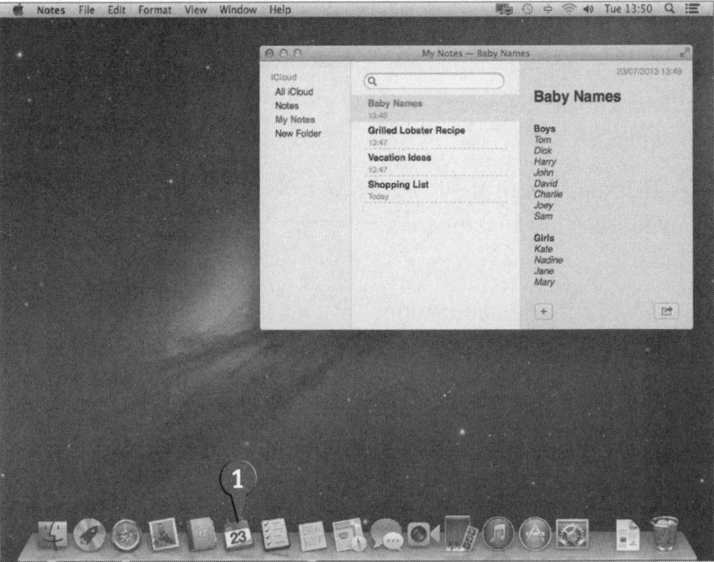

Ⓐ OS X brings the application window(s) to the foreground.

Ⓑ The menu bar displays the menus associated with the application.

Note: To switch between applications from the keyboard, press and hold ⌘ and repeatedly press Tab until the application that you want is highlighted in the list of running applications. Release ⌘ to switch to the application.

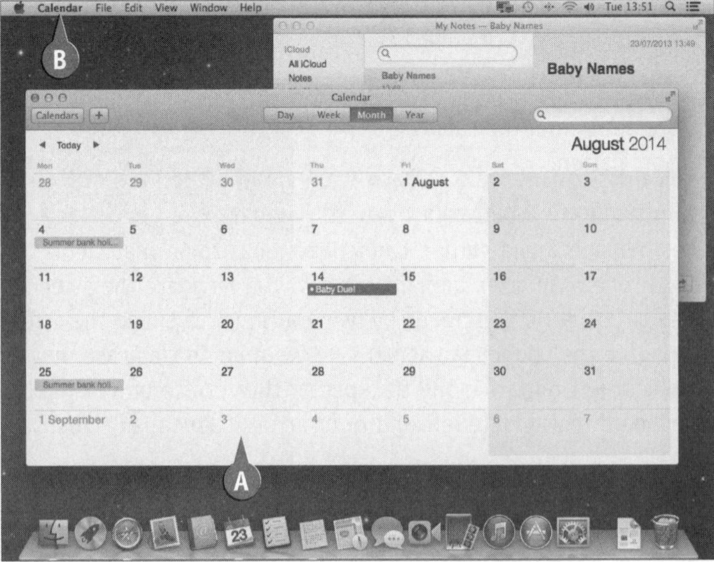

View Running Applications with Mission Control

CHAPTER 2

The Mission Control feature makes it easier for you to navigate and locate your running applications. OS X allows you to open multiple applications at once, and the only real limit to the number of open applications you can have is the amount of memory contained in your Mac. In practical terms, this means you can easily open several applications, some of which may have multiple open windows. To help locate and navigate to the window you need, use the Mission Control feature.

View Running Applications with Mission Control

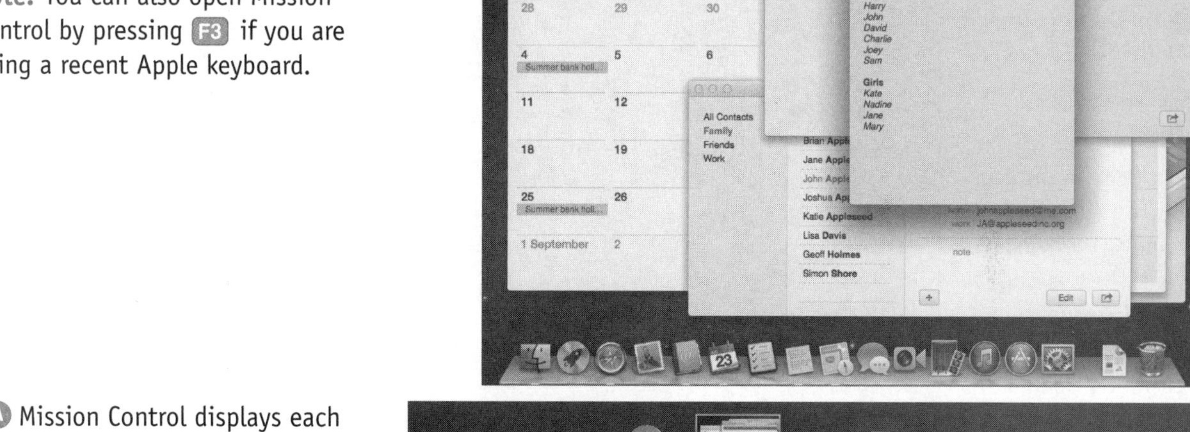

1. Open multiple windows and applications, then place three fingers on the trackpad of your Mac and swipe up.

Note: You can also open Mission Control by pressing F3 if you are using a recent Apple keyboard.

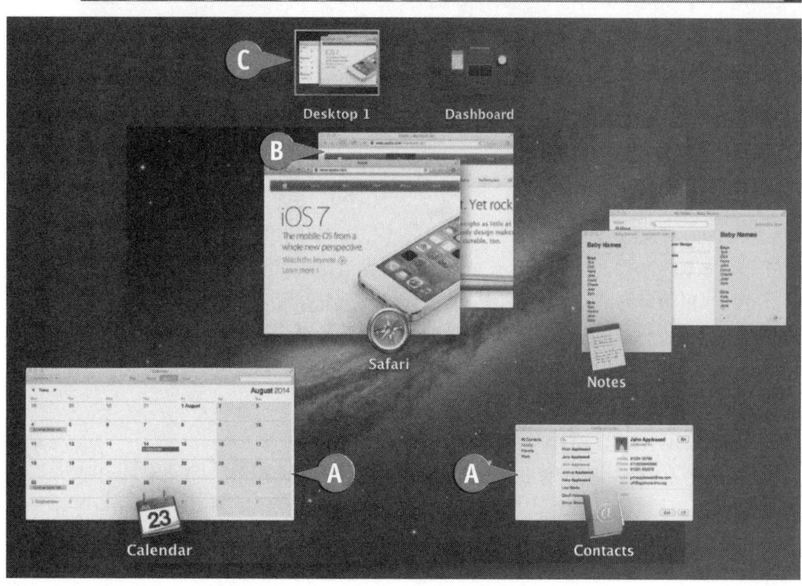

A. Mission Control displays each open window.

B. Mission Control groups windows from the same application.

   To switch to a particular window, click it.

C. To close Mission Control without selecting a window, click **Desktop** or press Esc.

Tour an Application Window

When you start an application, it appears on the OS X desktop in its own window. Each application has a unique window layout, but almost all application windows have a few features in common. To get the most out of your applications and to start working quickly and efficiently in an application, you need to know what these common features are and where to find them within the application window.

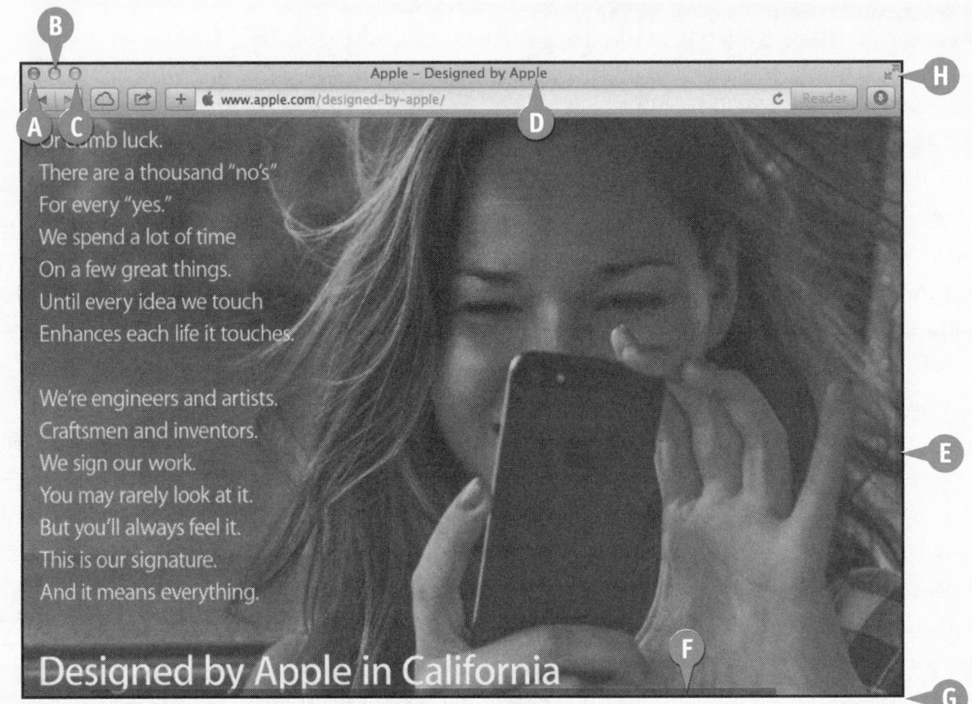

Ⓐ Close Button

Click the **Close** button (◉) to remove the application window from the desktop, usually without exiting the application.

Ⓑ Minimize Button

Click the **Minimize** button (◉) to remove the window from the desktop and display an icon for the currently open document in the right side of the Dock. The window is still open, but not active.

Ⓒ Zoom Button

Click the **Zoom** button (◉) to enlarge the window so that it can display all of its content, or as much of its content as can fit the screen. If you have already zoomed into the window or all of the window content is shown, click the **Zoom** button (◉) again to shrink the window.

Ⓓ Toolbar

The toolbar contains buttons that offer easy access to common application commands and features, although not all applications have toolbars. To move the window, click and drag the toolbar.

Ⓔ Vertical Scroll Bar

Click and drag the vertical scroll bar to navigate up and down in a document.

Ⓕ Horizontal Scroll Bar

Click and drag the horizontal scroll bar to navigate left and right in a document.

Ⓖ Resize Control

Click and drag any edge or corner of the window to make the window larger or smaller.

Ⓗ Full Screen Button

When this button is visible it can be clicked to show an application in full-screen mode.

Run an Application Full Screen

You can maximize the viewing and working areas of an application by running that application in full-screen mode. When you switch to full-screen mode, OS X hides the menu bar, the application's status bar, the Dock, and the top section of the application window (the section that includes the Close, Minimize, and Zoom buttons). OS X then expands the rest of the application window so that it takes up the entire screen. Not all programs are capable of switching to full-screen mode.

Run an Application Full Screen

1. Click **View**.
2. Click **Enter Full Screen**.

   You can also press Ctrl+⌘+F.

A. You can also click **Full Screen** (⤢).

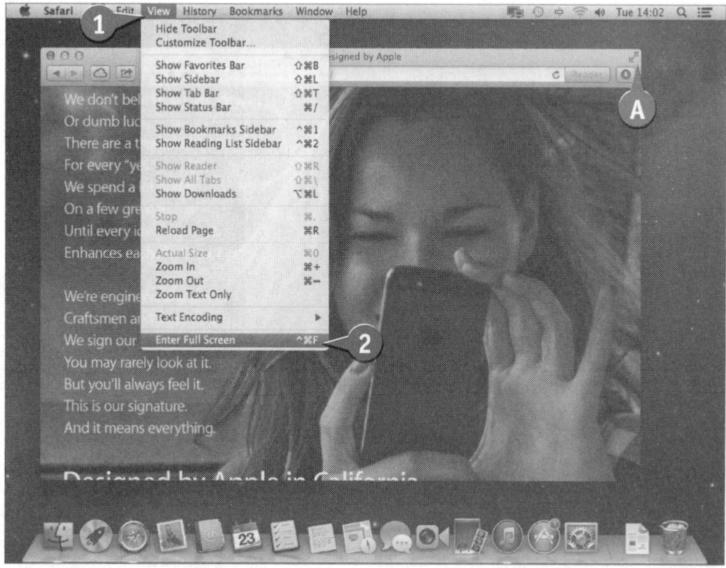

OS X expands the application window to take up the entire screen.

Note: To exit full-screen mode, move the mouse (↖) up to the top of the screen to reveal the menu bar, click **View**, and then click **Exit Full Screen**. You can also press Ctrl+⌘+F or press Esc.

Select a Command from a Pull-Down Menu

When you are working in an application, you can use the menu bar to access the application's commands and features. Each item in the menu bar represents a *pull-down menu*, a collection of commands usually related to each other in some way. For example, the File menu commands usually deal with file-related tasks such as opening and closing documents. The items in a menu are either commands that execute an action in the application, or features that you can turn on and off.

Select a Command from a Pull-Down Menu

Execute Commands

1. Click the name of the menu that you want to display.

   A. The application displays the menu.

2. Click the command that you want to invoke.

   The application executes the command.

   B. If a command is followed by an ellipsis (...), it means the command displays a dialog.

   C. If a command is followed by an arrow (▶), it means the command displays a submenu. Click the command to open the submenu and then click the command that you want to run.

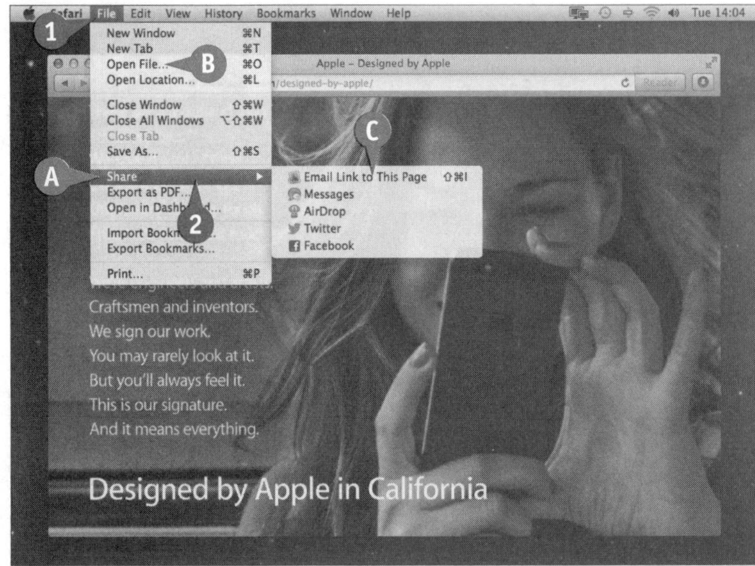

Turn Features On and Off

1. Click the name of the menu that you want to display.

   D. The application displays the menu.

2. Click the menu item.

   You may have to click for a submenu if your command is not on the main menu.

   The application turns the feature either on or off.

Select a Command Using a Toolbar

You can access many application commands faster by using the toolbar. Many applications come with a toolbar, which is a collection of buttons, lists, and other controls displayed in a strip, usually across the top of the application window. Because the toolbar is always visible, you can always use it to select commands, which means that the toolbar often gives you one-click access to the application's most common features. This is faster than using the menu bar method, which often takes several clicks, depending on the command.

Select a Command Using a Toolbar

Turn Features On and Off

1. Click the toolbar button that represents the feature you want to turn on.

A. The application turns the feature on and indicates this state by highlighting the toolbar button.

B. When a feature is turned off, the application does not highlight the button.

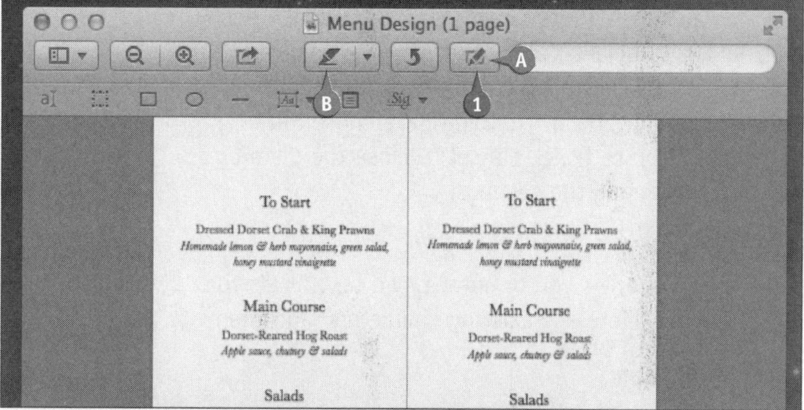

Execute Commands

1. Click the toolbar button that represents the command that you want.

2. If the button displays a menu, click the command on the menu.

The application executes the command.

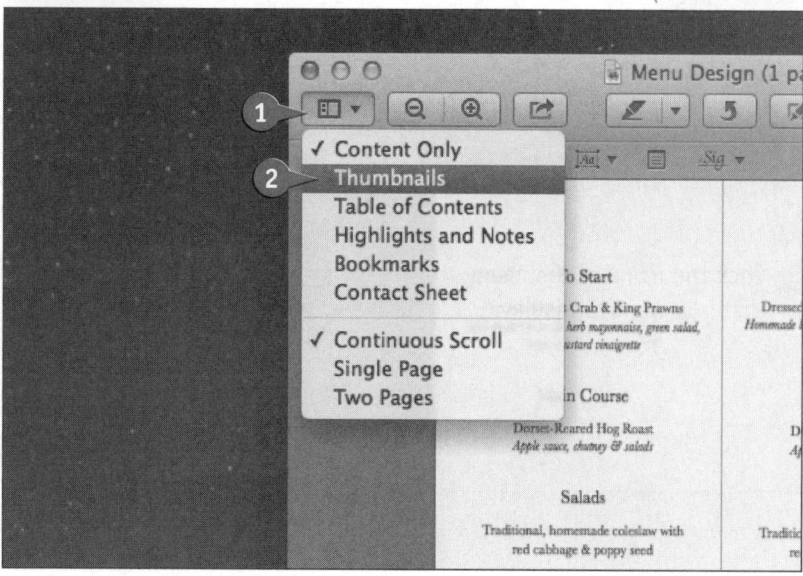

Select Options with Dialog Controls

You often interact with an application by selecting options or typing text using a dialog. A *dialog* is a window that appears when an application has information for you or needs you to provide information. For example, when you select the File menu's Print command to print a document, you use the Print dialog to specify the number of copies that you want to print.

You provide that and other information by accessing various types of dialog controls. To provide information to an application quickly and accurately, you need to know what these dialog controls look like and how they work.

A Command Button

Clicking a command button executes the command printed on the button face. For example, you can click **Save** to apply settings that you have chosen in a dialog, or you can click **Cancel** to close the dialog without changing the settings.

B Text Box

A text box enables you to enter typed text. Press the Del key to delete any existing characters, and then type your text.

C List Box

A list box displays a list of choices from which you select the item you want.

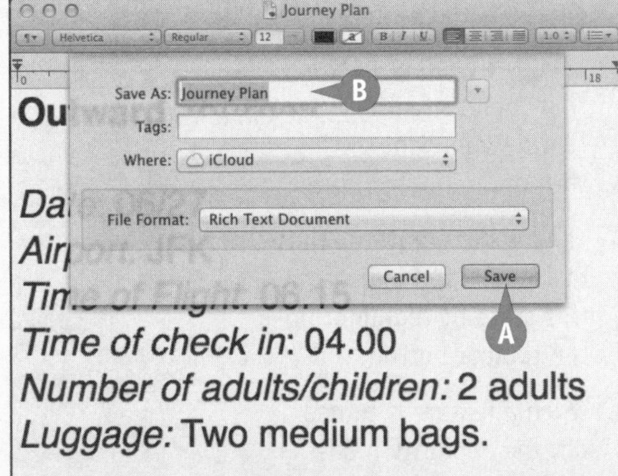

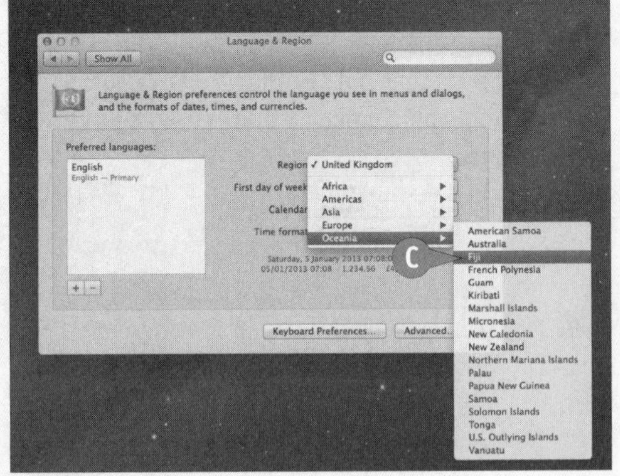

D Tabs

Many dialogs offer a large number of controls, so related controls appear on different tabs, and the tab names and icons appear across the top of the dialog. Click a tab to see its pane.

E Pop-Up Menu

A pop-up menu displays a list of choices from which you select the item you want. Click the up-down arrows (⬍) to pop up the menu, and then click the item that you want to select.

F Check Box

Selecting or deselecting a check box toggles an application feature on or off. If you are turning on a feature, the check box changes from ☐ to ☑; if you are turning off the feature, the check box changes from ☑ to ☐.

G Radio Button

Clicking a radio button turns on an application feature. Only one radio button in a group can be turned on at a time. When you click a radio button that is currently off, it changes from ○ to ◉; a radio button that is on changes from ◉ to ○.

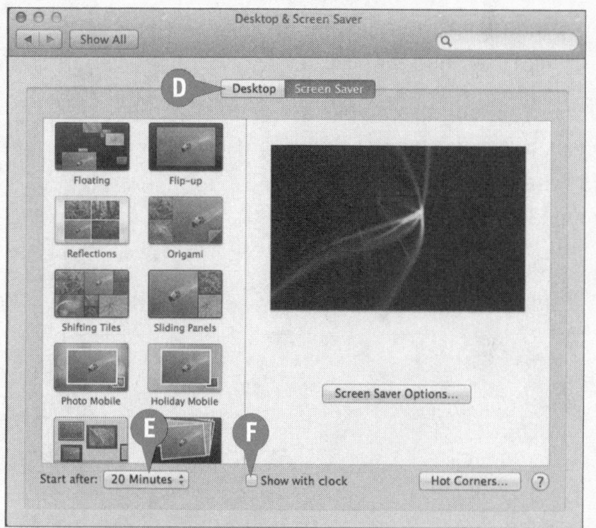

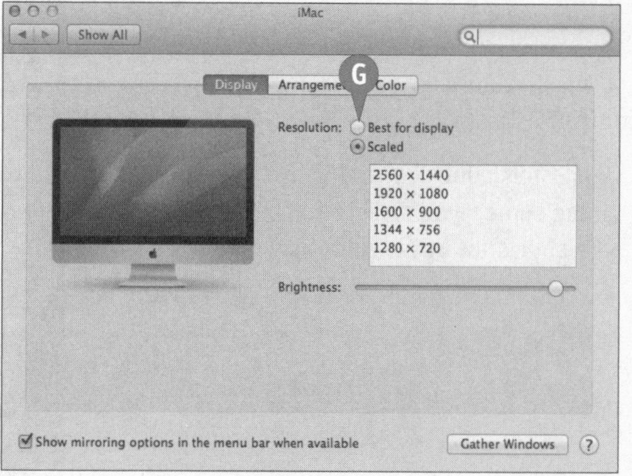

Move Windows Between Screens

Using Mission Control to move open documents, applications, and other windows between desktops helps you to quickly access the windows you need and organize your workspace. This is an especially useful trick if you are working with full-screen apps or programs with multiple windows, allowing you to drag a window from one desktop and drop it onto another.

Move Windows Between Screens

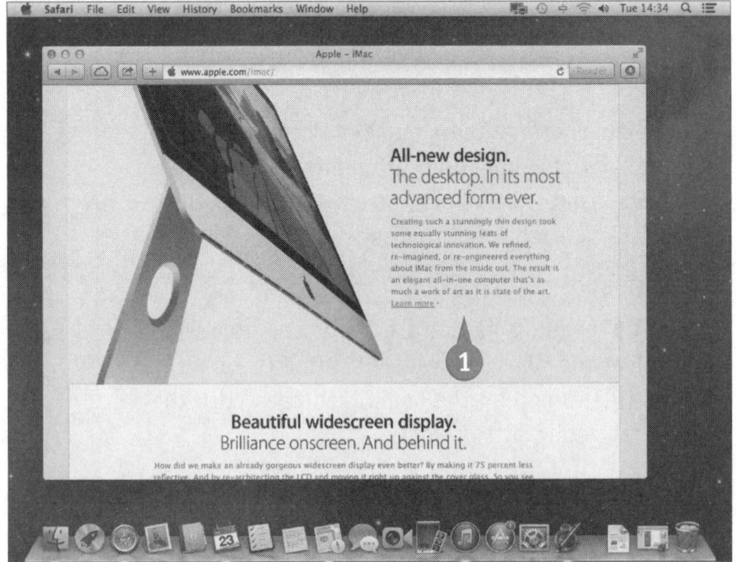

1 Launch one or more applications, then place three fingers on the trackpad of your Mac and swipe up.

Note: You can also invoke Mission Control by pressing F3 if you are using a recent Apple keyboard, or press Ctrl+↑.

The Mission Control screen appears.

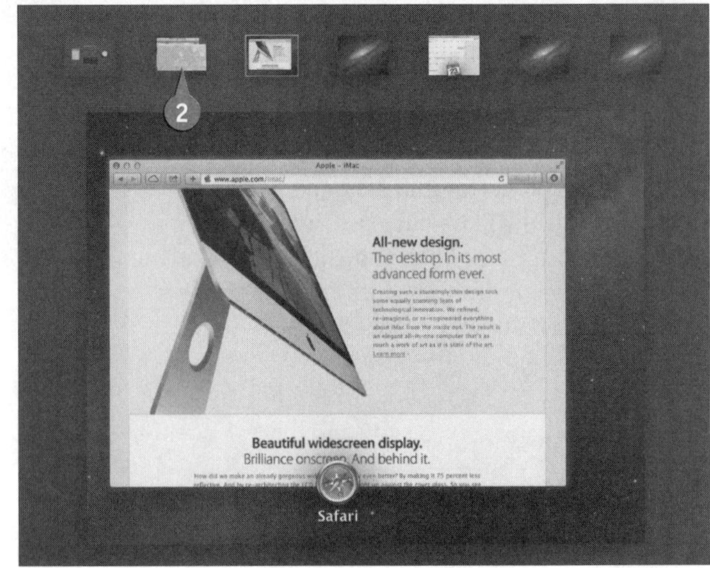

2 Click a desktop to select it.

Note: After you select a desktop, you must relaunch Mission Control.

Mission Control switches to the screen you selected and displays all open windows.

3 Click and drag a window from the selected desktop to another desktop at the top of the screen.

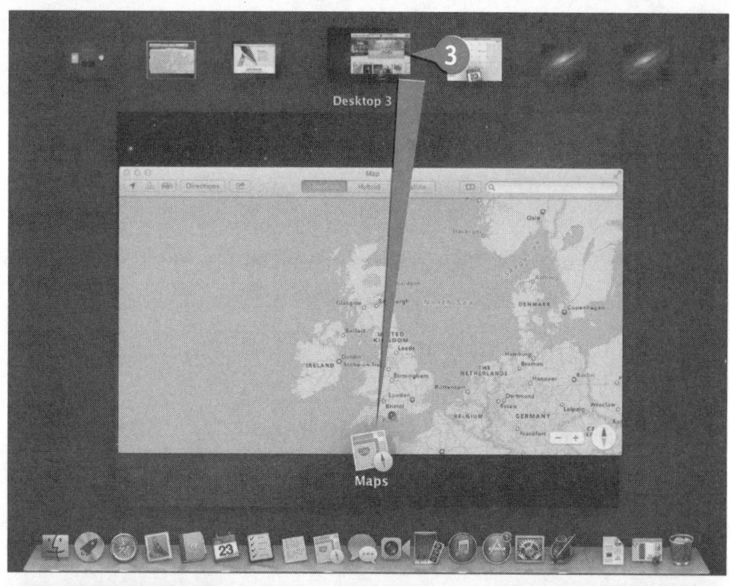

The window is moved to its new location.

4 Click the desktop where you moved the window to access it in its new location.

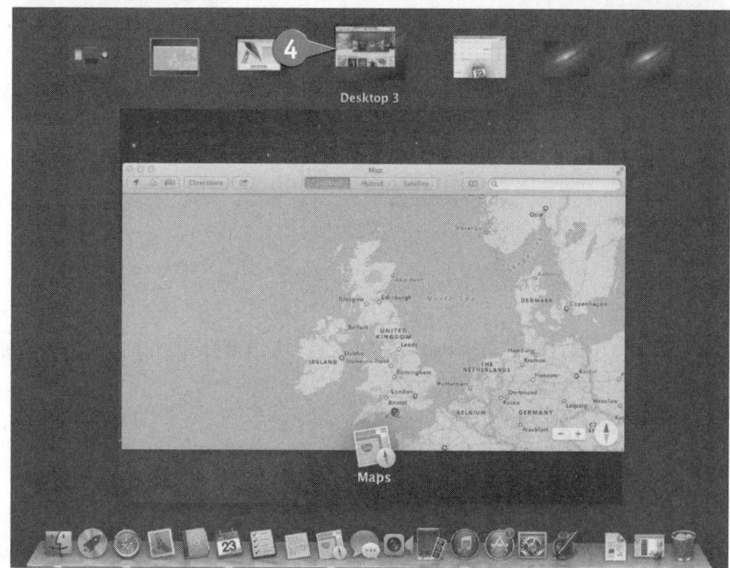

TIP

Can I drag full-screen apps between desktops using Mission Control?

No. When an app is running in full-screen mode it becomes its own desktop in Mission Control. You can, however, drag full-screen applications and desktops into new locations within Mission Control by simply clicking and dragging them across. You can even drag the Dashboard screen to a new location rather than its default position to the left of your currently running applications and desktops. To move an application to a different screen, you must first bring it out of full-screen mode by clicking the **Full Screen** button ( ).

Add Special Characters and Accents When Typing

When certain keyboard keys are held down when typing in Mac OS X, the letter doesn't repeat until you release the key as you might expect. Instead, a small menu appears above the letters E, Y, U, I, O, A, S, L, Z, C, N, and M, allowing you to use different accents and special characters in your text. This can be handy for foreign words commonly used in English, such as "cliché."

Add Special Characters and Accents When Typing

1. Launch an application in which you type text, such as TextEdit, Notes, or Mail.

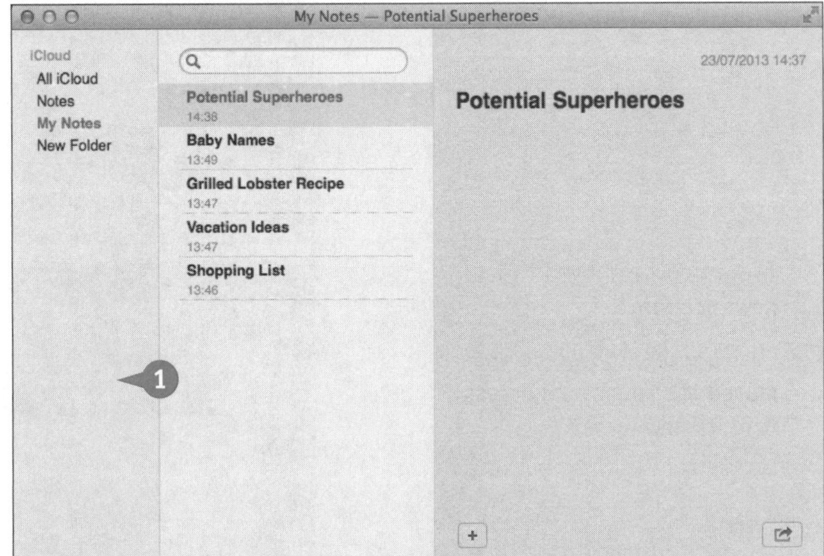

2. Click within the text editing area to select the document if it is not already selected.

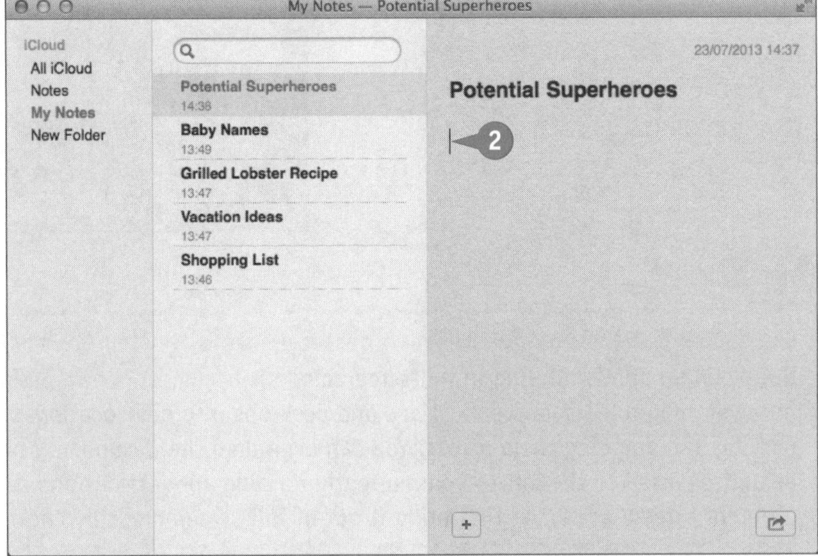

A cursor appears to show where you will begin typing.

3. Tap and hold a keyboard key for roughly 3 seconds.

Note: Only the letters E, Y, U, I, O, A, S, L, Z, C, N, and M work for this technique when using a U.S. keyboard.

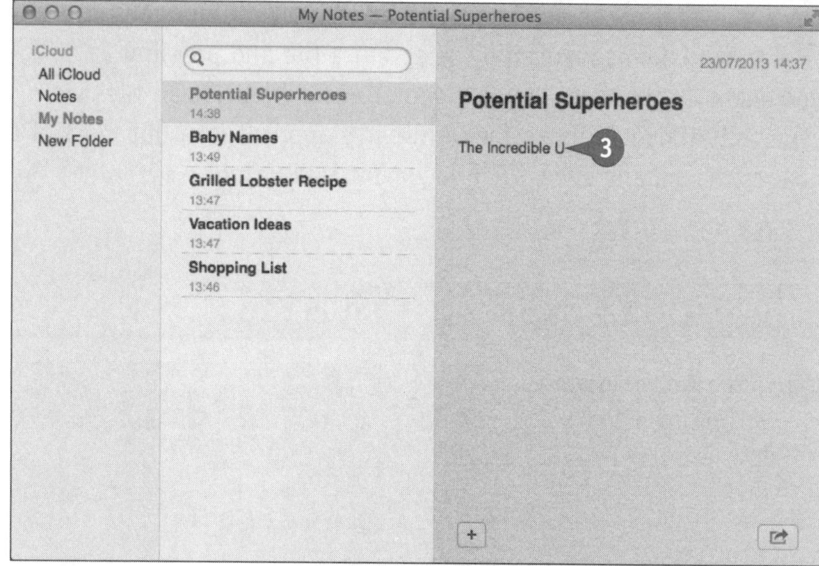

A pop-up menu appears.

4. Click the character you want to use from the menu or, alternatively, press the corresponding number key shown below the character.

A special character appears.

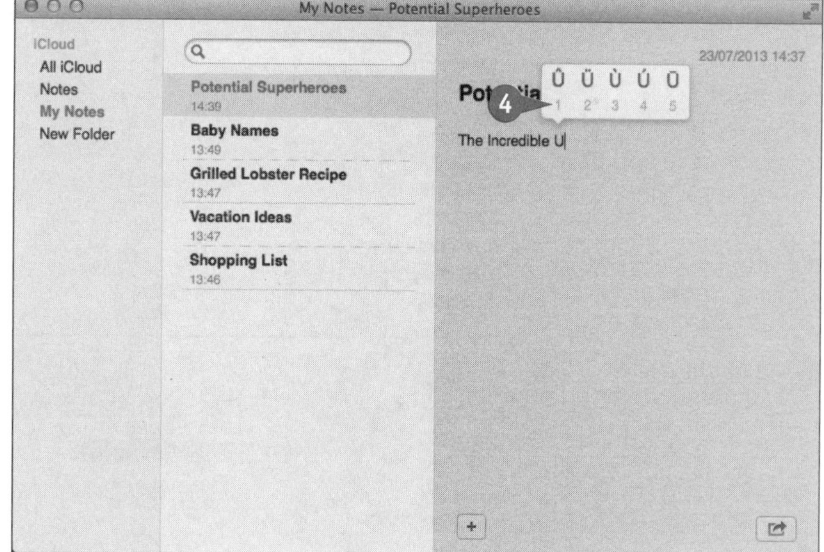

TIPS

What other special characters can I use when typing in an application?
You can access standard punctuation marks such as exclamation points, brackets, and asterisks by holding down the Shift key and pressing the corresponding number key, such as Shift + 1 for an exclamation point.

Can I adjust the characters at all?
Most lowercase characters with accent options can also be used in the same way but with the Shift key held down to capitalize the letter. The process of applying an accent or special character remains the same.

Using Quick Look to Preview Documents

Wherever you can select a file in OS X, you can normally use Quick Look to preview its contents. Quick Look is invoked by selecting a file and pressing Spacebar to show the contents of a document, a photo, or play a video or audio file. Not all files work with Quick Look, however, especially those designed for third-party applications, but most of the popular formats such as images, MP3s, and even Word documents work fine.

Using Quick Look to Preview Documents

1. In the Finder, locate a file you want to preview.

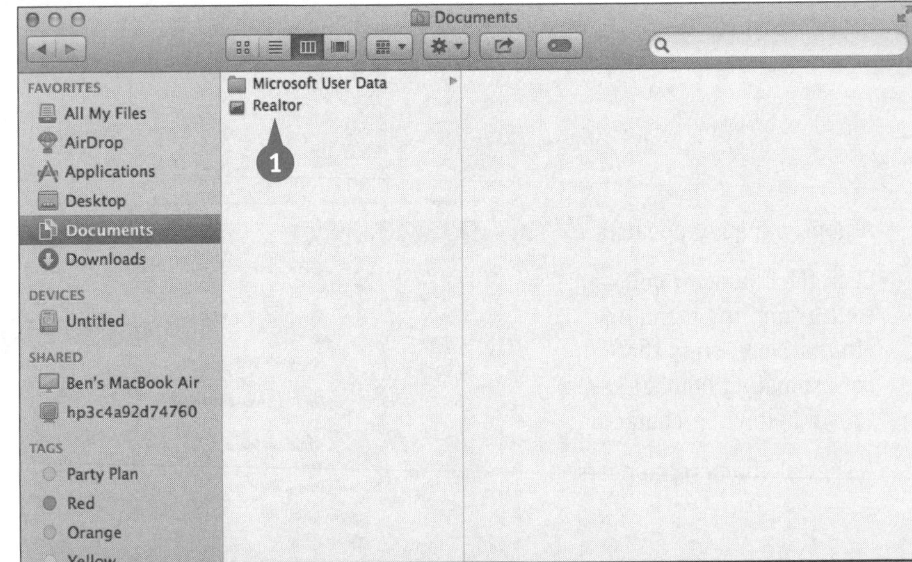

2. Click the file to select it.

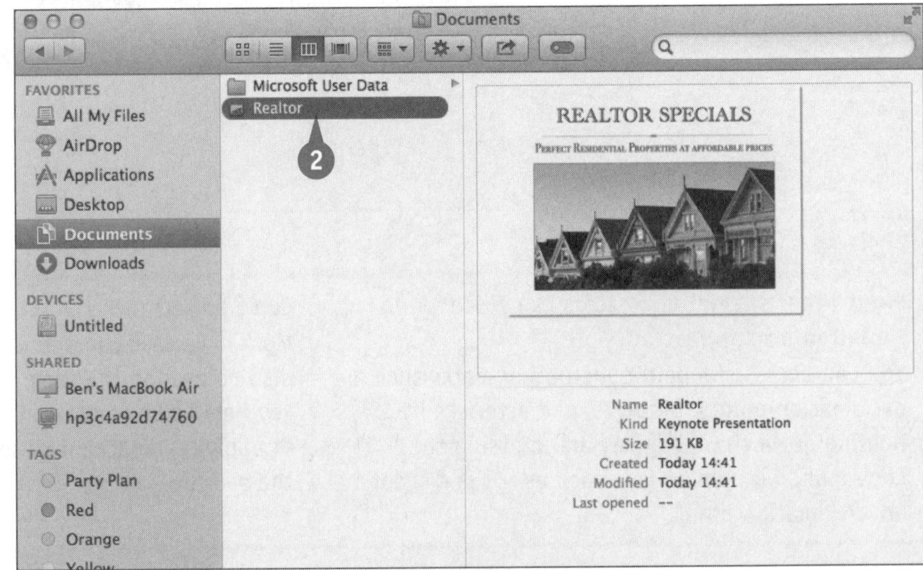

The file is highlighted.

3 Right-click or ctrl+click the file and select Quick Look from the menu that appears.

Note: You can also press Spacebar to use Quick Look, or click the **Quick Look** button from the Finder window toolbar. You can also choose Quick Look from the Finder window's Action toolbar menu.

A preview of the file appears.

4 Click **Open with...** at the top right of the Quick Look preview to open the document in its target application, or press ◉ to close the preview.

TIPS

What happens if a file isn't compatible with Quick Look?
Files that can't be previewed in Quick Look simply show a screen with information about the file and its icon. You may also be able to access the Open with... button to launch the application associated with that file type.

Can I edit documents with Quick Look?
No. You can only preview a document with Quick Look. You must launch the file in its native application to edit it. You can, however, use the OS X Share button (◉) that appears on the Quick Look preview to share the file via Mail, Messages, or AirDrop.

CHAPTER 3

Working with Files and Documents

Much of the work you do in OS X will involve documents, which are files that contain text, images, and other data. These tasks include saving, opening, printing, and editing documents, as well as copying and renaming files.

Save a Document

After you create a document and make changes to it, you can save the document to preserve your work. When you work on a document, OS X stores the changes in your computer's memory. However, OS X erases the contents of the Mac's memory each time you shut down or restart the computer. This means that the changes you have made to your document are lost when you turn off or restart your Mac. However, saving the document preserves your changes on your Mac's hard drive. Some applications automatically save documents you are working on at preset intervals, so you may be able to recover work after a power failure or crash.

Save a Document

1 Click **File**.

2 Click **Save**.

In most applications, you can also press ⌘ + S.

If you have saved the document previously, your changes are now preserved, and you do not need to follow the rest of the steps in this section.

If this is a new document that you have never saved before, the Save As dialog appears.

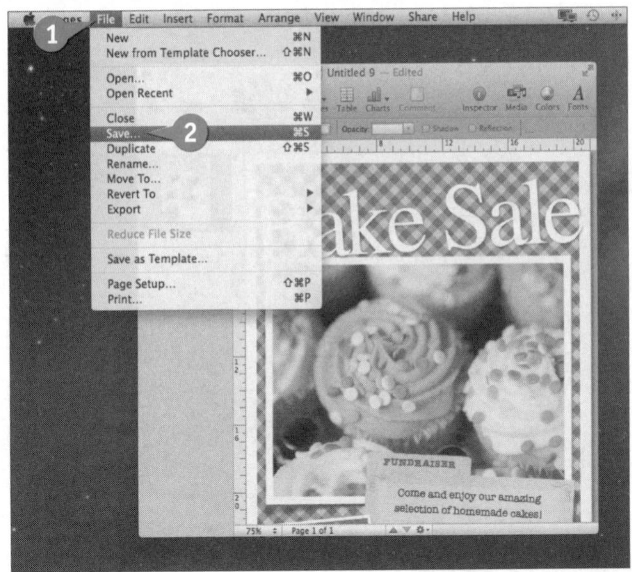

3 Type the filename you want to use in the Save As text box.

A To store the file in a different folder, you can click the **Where** pop-up menu (⇳) and then select the location that you prefer from the menu.

4 Click **Save**.The application saves the file.

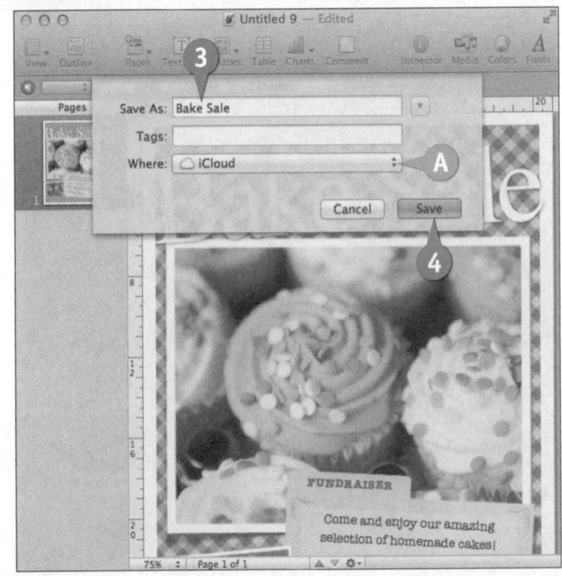

Open a Document

To work with a document that you have saved in the past, you can open it in the application that you used to create it. When you save a document, you save its contents to your Mac's hard drive, external drive, server, or online using services like iCloud or Dropbox. Those contents are stored in a separate file. When you open the document using the same application that you used to save it, OS X loads the file's contents into memory and displays the document in the application. You can then view or edit the document as needed.

Open a Document

1. Start the application that you want to work with.
2. Click **File**.
3. Click **Open**.

   In most applications, you can also press ⌘ + O.

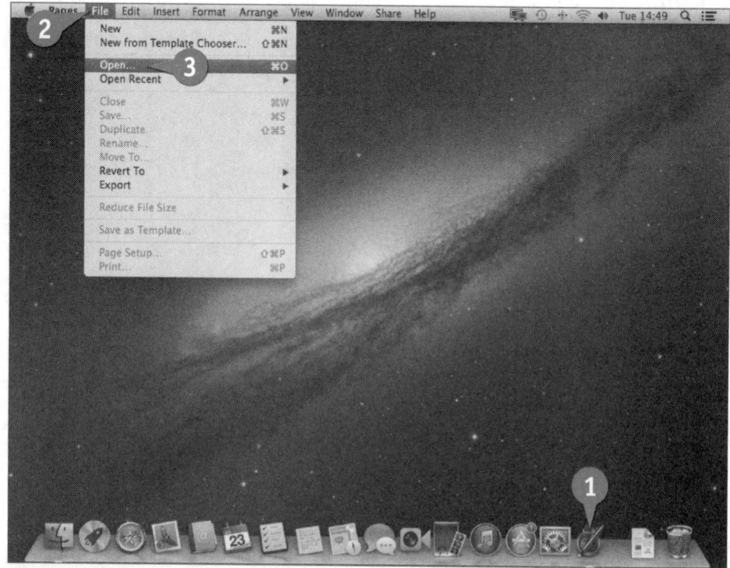

The Open dialog appears.

Ⓐ Click either **iCloud** for files stored online or **On My Mac** for files stored on your Mac's hard drive.

4. Click the document you want to open.
5. Click **Open**.

   The document appears in a window on the desktop.

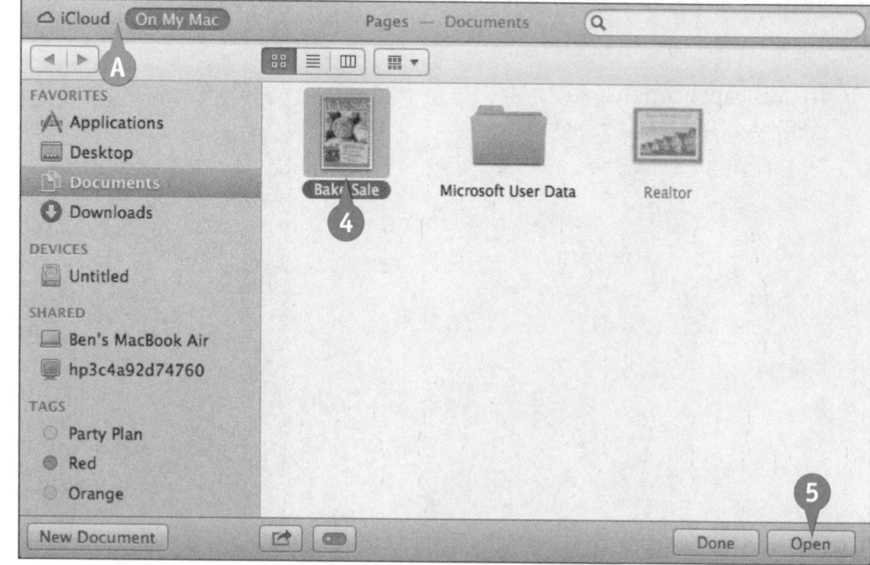

Print a Document

When you need a hard copy of your document, either for your files or to distribute to someone else, you can send the document to your printer. Most applications that deal with documents also come with a Print command. When you run this command, the Print dialog appears. You use the Print dialog to choose the printer you want to use, as well as to specify how many copies you want to print. Most Print dialogs also enable you to see a preview of your document before printing it.

Print a Document

1 Turn on your printer.

2 Open the document that you want to print.

3 Click **File**.

4 Click **Print**.

In most applications, you can select the Print command by pressing ⌘ + P.

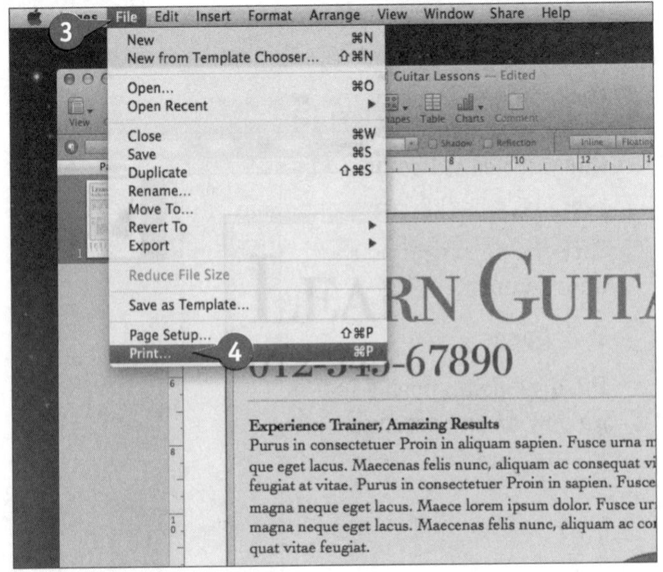

The Print dialog appears.

The layout of the Print dialog varies from application to application. The version shown here is a typical example.

5 If you have more than one printer, click ⬍ in the Printer list to select the printer that you want to use.

6 To print more than one copy, use the **Copies** text box to type the number of copies to print.

7 Click **Print**.

OS X prints the document.

A The printer's icon appears in the Dock while the document prints.

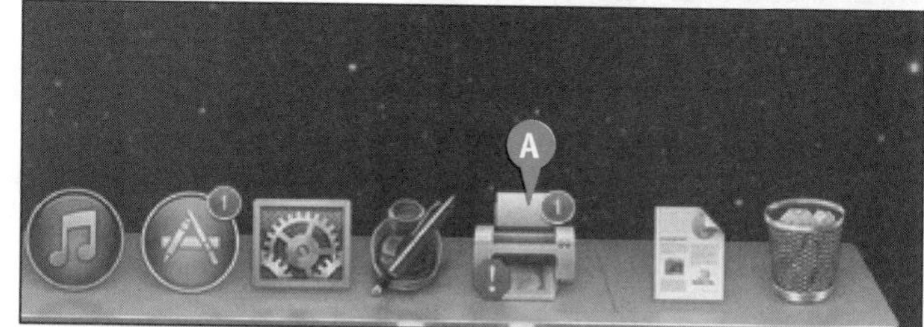

TIP

Can I print only part of my document?

Yes, although the options vary from application to application. In most applications, you can print a range of pages by selecting the **From** option (◯ changes to ◉) and then using the two text boxes to type the numbers of the first and last pages you want to print.

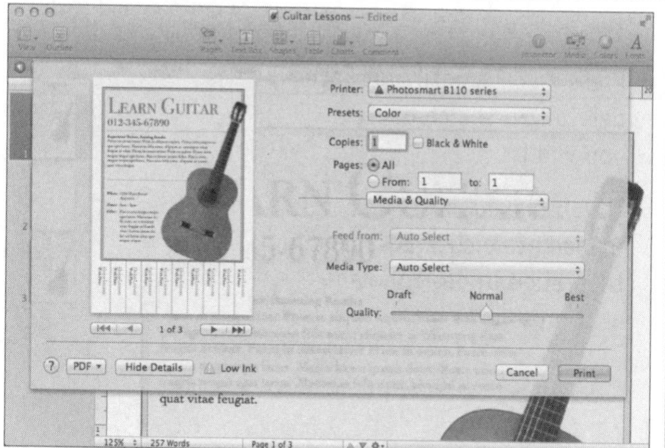

If you just want to print one page, click anywhere within the page before running the Print command; then select the **Current Page** option (◯ changes to ◉) or click **From** (◯ changes to ◉) and type the page number in both text boxes.

If you just want to print a section of the document, select the text before running the Print command, and then select the **Selection** option (◯ changes to ◉).

The Current Page and Sele3ction options are not available in all applications, but are present in default OS X software.

Edit Document Text

When you work with a character-based file, such as a text or word processing document or an e-mail message, you need to know the basic techniques for editing, selecting, copying, and moving text. It is rare that any text you type into a document is perfect the first time through. It is far more likely that the text contains errors that require correcting, or words, sentences, or paragraphs that appear in the wrong place. To get your document text the way you want it, you need to know how to edit text, including deleting characters, selecting the text with which you want to work, and copying and moving text.

Edit Document Text

Delete Characters

1. In a text document, click immediately to the right of the last character that you want to delete.

   A The cursor appears after the character.

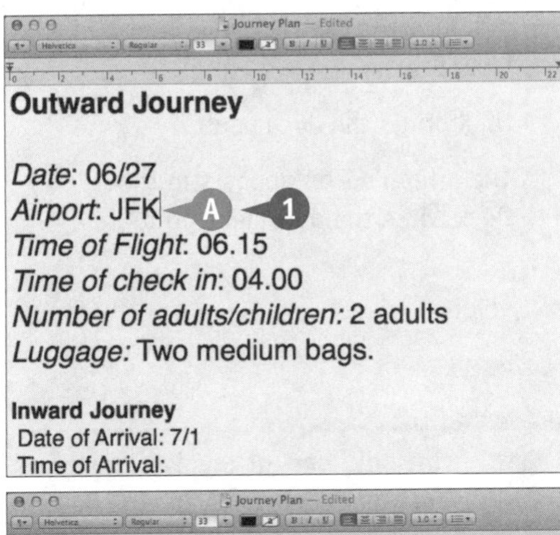

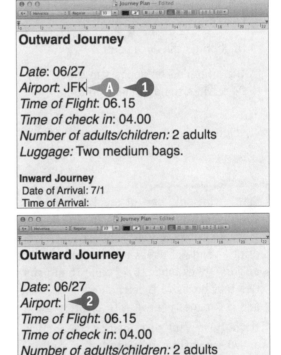

2. Press Delete until you have deleted all the characters you want.

   If you make a mistake, immediately click **Edit**, and then click **Undo**. You can also press ⌘ + Z.

Journey Plan — Edited
Outward Journey
Date: 06/27
Airport:
2
Time of Flight: 06.15
Time of check in: 04.00
Number of adults/children: 2 adults
Luggage: Two medium bags.
Inward Journey
Date of Arrival: 7/1
Time of Arrival:

Select Text for Editing

1 Click and drag across the text that you want to select and release the mouse button when done.

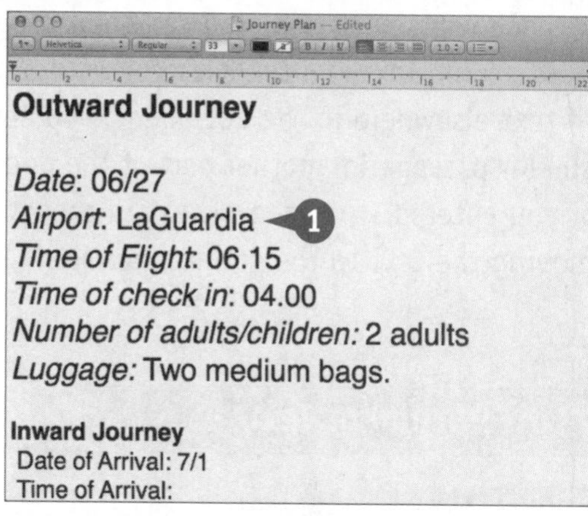

B The application highlights the selected text.

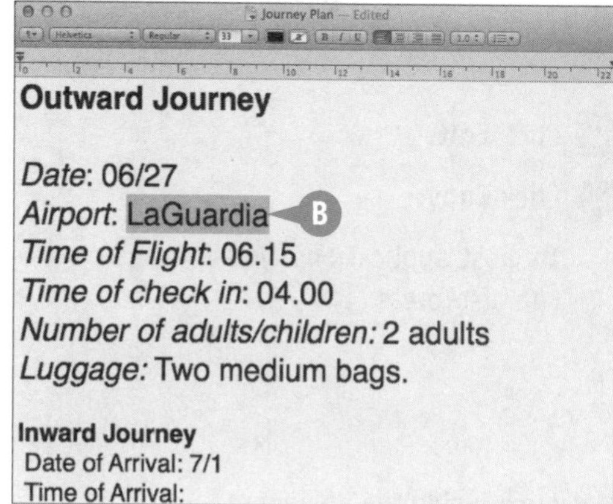

TIP

Are there any shortcut methods for selecting text?

Here are the most useful ones:

- Double-click a word to select it.
- Hold down Shift and press → or ← to select entire words.
- Hold down Shift and ⌘ and press → to select to the end of the line, or ← to select to the beginning of the line.
- Hold down Shift and ⌘ and press ↓ to select the next line, or ↑ to select the previous line.
- Triple-click inside a paragraph to select it.
- Click **Edit** and then click **Select All**, or press ⌘ + A to select the entire document.

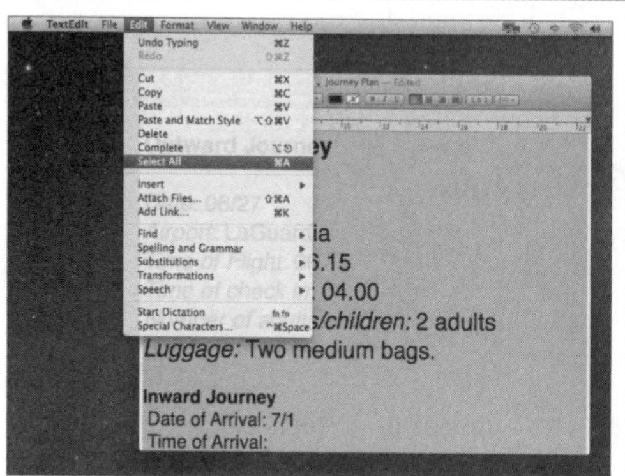

continued ▶

Once you select text, you can then copy or move the text to another location in your document. Copying text is often a useful way to save work. For example, if you want to use the same passage of text elsewhere in the document, you can copy it instead of typing it from scratch. If you need a similar passage in another part of the document, copy the original and then edit the copy as needed. If you entered a passage of text in the wrong position within the document, you can fix that by moving the text to the correct location.

Edit Document Text (continued)

Copy Text

1. Select the text that you want to copy.
2. Click **Edit**.
3. Click **Copy**.

   In most applications, you can also press ⌘ + C.

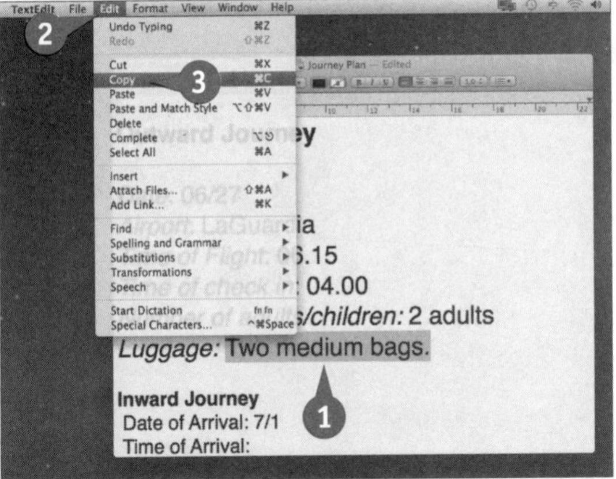

4. Click inside the document where you want the copied text to appear.

   The cursor appears in the position where you clicked.
5. Click **Edit**.
6. Click **Paste**.

   In most applications, you can also press ⌘ + V.

Ⓒ The application inserts a copy of the selected text at the cursor position.

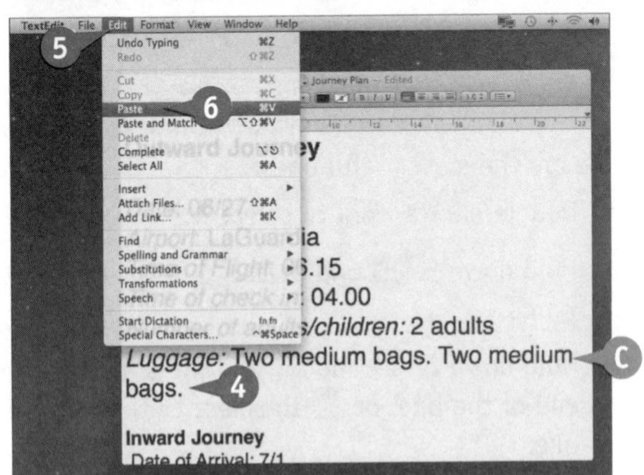

Move Text

1. Select the text that you want to move.
2. Click **Edit**.
3. Click **Cut**.

   In most applications, you can also press ⌘ + X.

   The application removes the text from the document.

4. Click inside the document where you want to move the text.

   The cursor appears at the position where you clicked.

5. Click **Edit**.
6. Click **Paste**.

   In most applications, you can also press ⌘ + V.

D The application inserts the text at the cursor position.

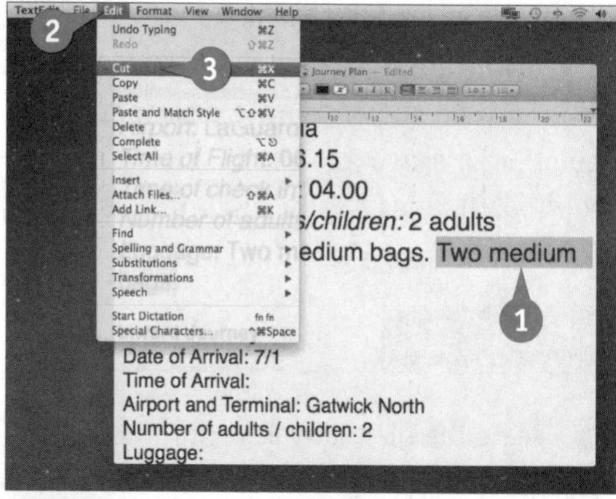

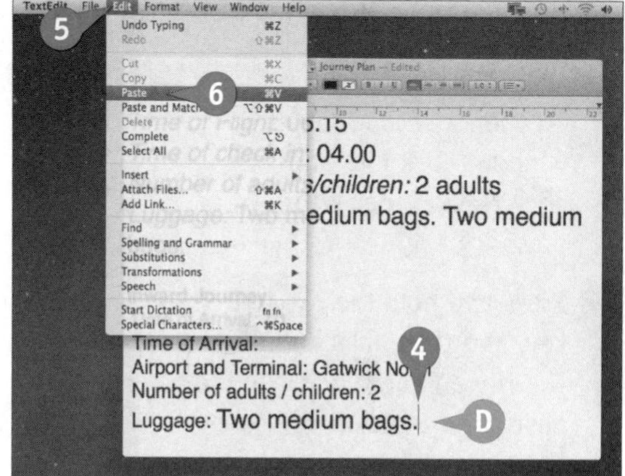

TIP

How do I move and copy text with my mouse?

First, select the text that you want to move or copy. To move the selected text, position the mouse pointer over the selection and then click and drag the text to the new position within the document.

To copy the selected text, position the mouse pointer over the selection, press and hold the Option key, and then click and drag the text (the mouse ↖ changes to ↖) to the new position within the document.

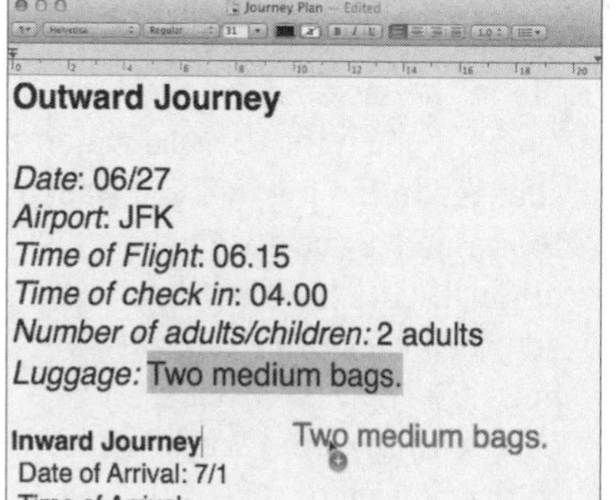

Copy a File

You can use OS X to make an exact copy of a file. This is useful when you want to make an extra copy of an important file to use as a backup. Similarly, you might require a copy of a file if you want to send the copy on a disk to another person. Finally, copying a file is also a real timesaver if you need a new file very similar to an existing file: You copy the original file and then make the required changes to the copy. You can copy either a single file or multiple files. You can also use this technique to copy a folder.

Copy a File

1. Locate the file that you want to copy.
2. Open the folder to which you want to copy the file.

   To open a second folder window, click **File** and then click **New Finder Window**, or press ⌘ + N.
3. Press and hold the Option key, and then click and drag the file and drop it inside the destination folder.

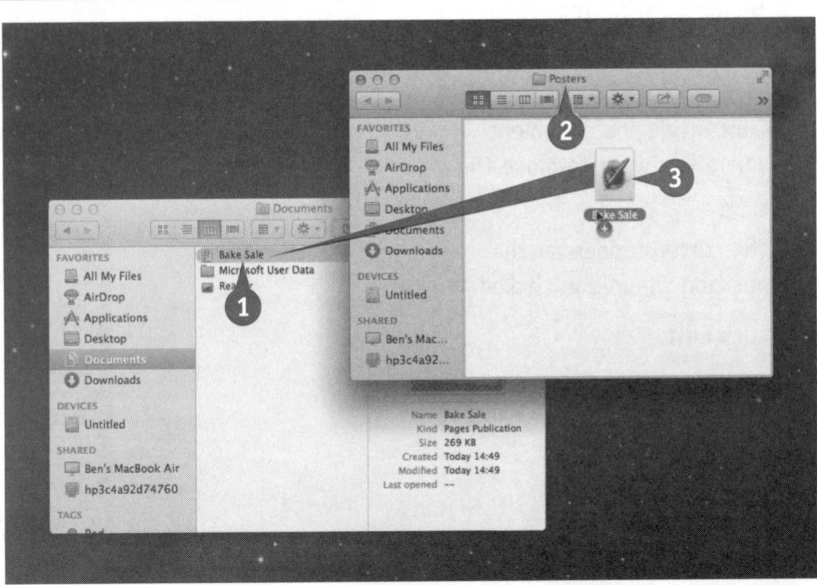

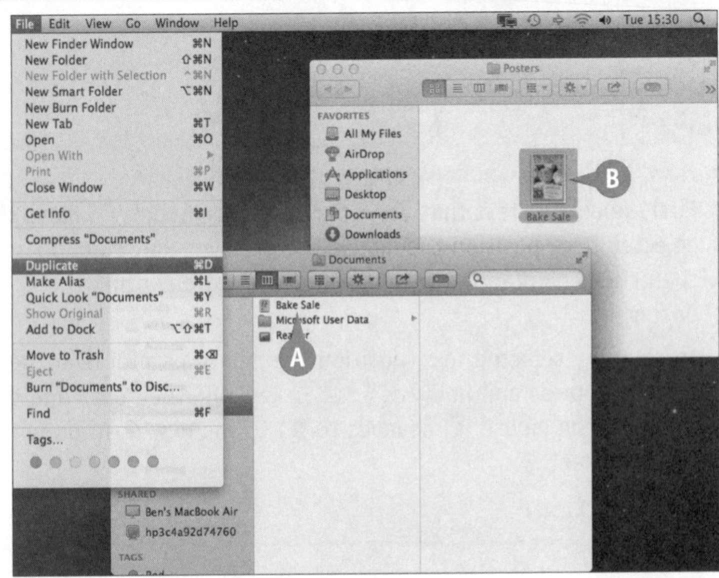

A. The original file remains in its folder.

B. A copy of the original file appears in the destination folder.

You can also make a copy of a file in the same folder, which is useful if you want to make major changes to the file and you want to preserve a copy of the original. Click the file, click **File**, and then click **Duplicate**, or press ⌘ + D. OS X creates a copy with the word "copy" added to the filename.

Move a File

When you need to store a file in a new location, the easiest way is to move the file from its current folder to another folder on your Mac. When you save a file for the first time, you specify a folder on your Mac's hard drive. This original location is not permanent, however. Using the technique in this section, you can move the file to another location on your Mac's hard drive. You can use this technique to move a single file, multiple files, and even a folder.

Move a File

1. Locate the file that you want to move.
2. Open the folder you want to move the file to.

   To create a new destination folder in the current folder, click **File** and then click **New Folder**, or press Shift + ⌘ + N.
3. Click and drag the file and drop it inside the destination folder.

Note: If you are moving the file to another drive, you must hold down ⌘ while you click and drag the file. If not, the file is simply copied to the other drive.

- A The file disappears from its original folder.
- B The file moves to the destination folder.

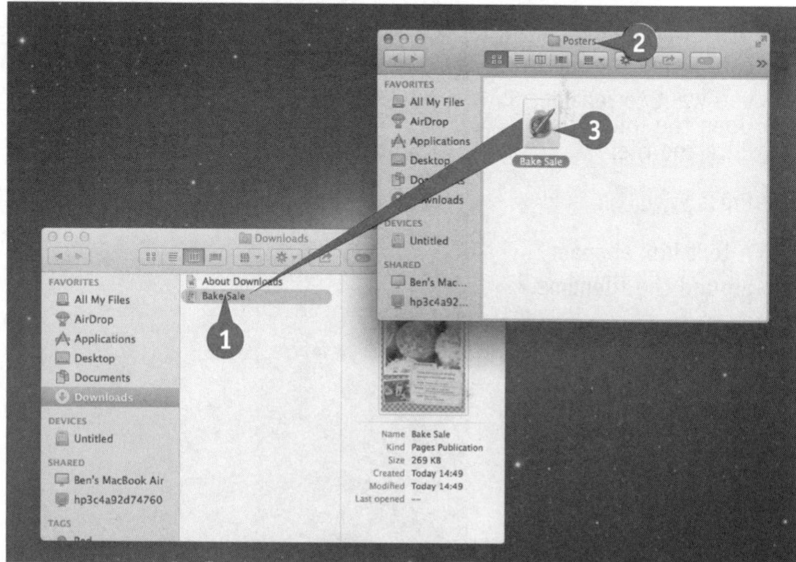

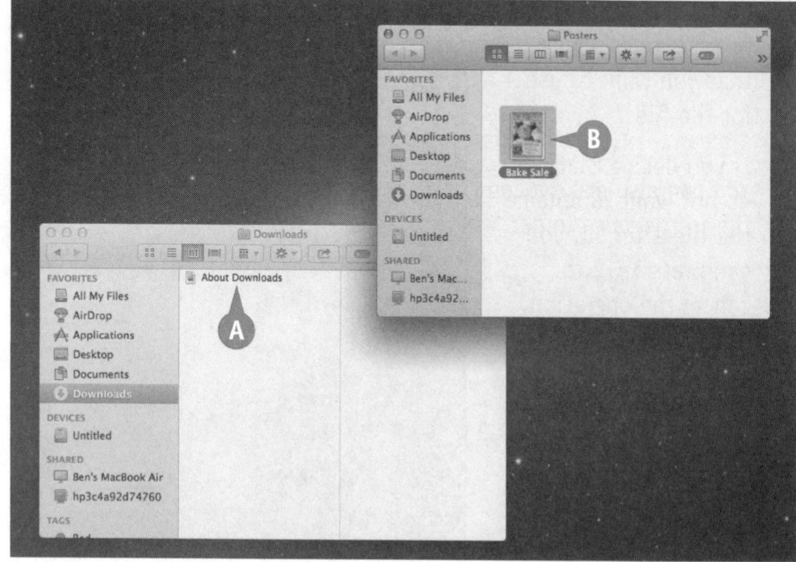

Rename a File

You can change the name of a file, which is useful if the current filename does not accurately describe the contents of the file. By giving your document a descriptive name, you make it easier to find the file later. You should rename only those documents that you have created or that have been given to you by someone else. Do not try to rename any of the OS X system files or any files associated with your applications, or your computer may behave erratically, or even crash.

Rename a File

1. Open the folder containing the file that you want to rename.
2. Click the file.
3. Press Return.

Ⓐ A text box appears around the filename.

You can also rename any folders that you have created.

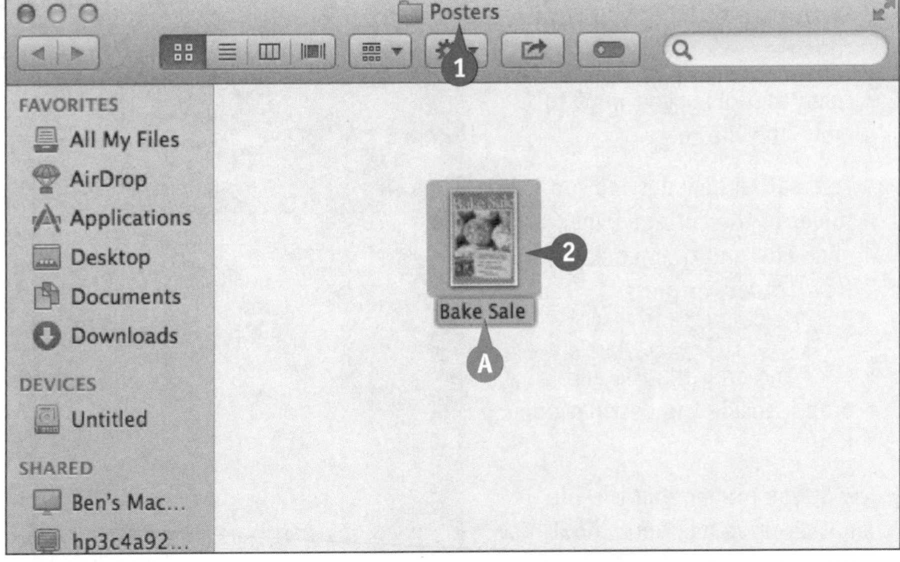

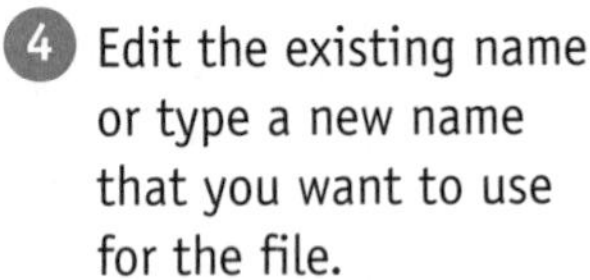

4. Edit the existing name or type a new name that you want to use for the file.

If you decide that you do not want to rename the file after all, you can press Esc to cancel the operation.

5. Press Return or click an empty section of the folder.

The new name appears under the file icon.

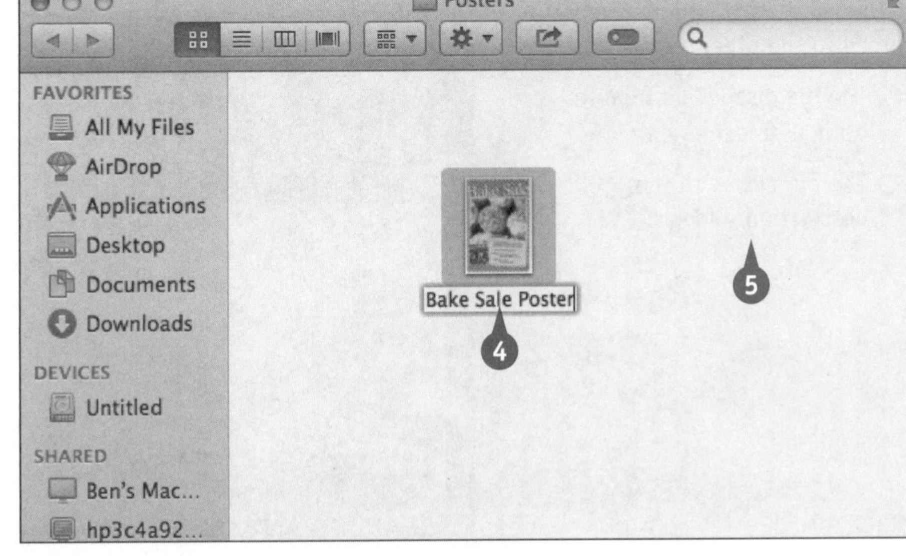

Delete a File

When you no longer need a file, you can delete it. This helps to prevent your hard drive from becoming cluttered with unnecessary files. You should ensure that you delete only those documents that you have created or that have been given to you by someone else. Do not delete any of the OS X system files or any files associated with your applications, or your computer may behave erratically, or even crash.

Delete a File

1. Locate the file that you want to delete.
2. Click and drag the file and drop it on the Trash icon in the Dock.

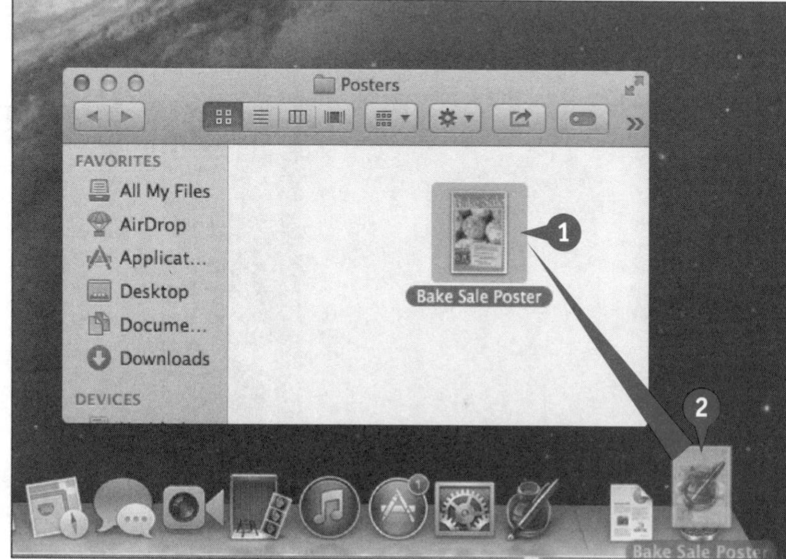

A. The file disappears from the folder.

You can also delete a file by clicking it and then pressing ⌘ + Delete.

If you delete a file accidentally, you can restore it. Click the Dock's **Trash** icon to open the Trash window. Click and drag the file from the Trash window and drop it back in its original folder. You can also hold down ⌘, click a file, and select **Put Back** from the menu that appears.

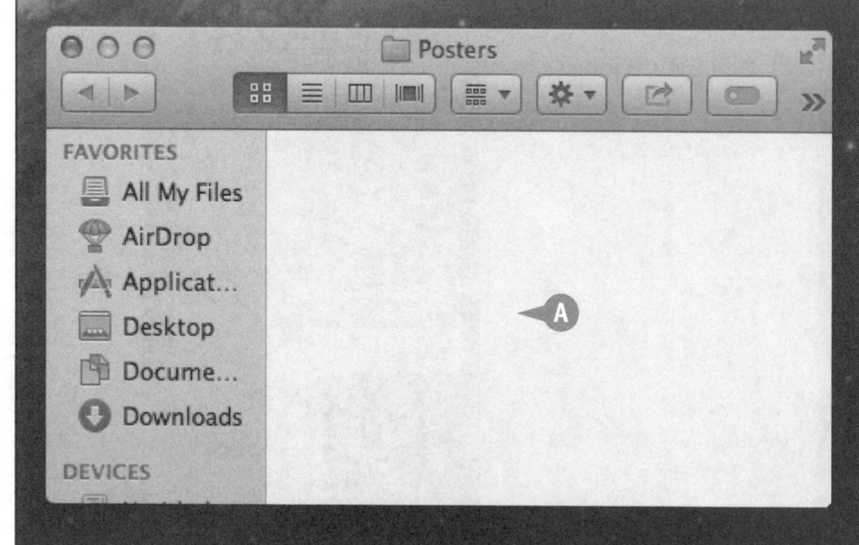

Using Finder Tabs

Finder Tabs allow you to have multiple locations open within one Finder window. Rather than have a cluttered desktop with multiple Finder windows open, Finder Tabs make it easy to access files and folders in multiple locations from a single window. Finder Tabs are flexible, too, allowing you to rearrange tabs on the fly and even drag and drop files between them.

Using Finder Tabs

1. Open a group of Finder windows by clicking the **Finder** icon (![Finder icon]) in the Dock and then pressing ⌘ + N.

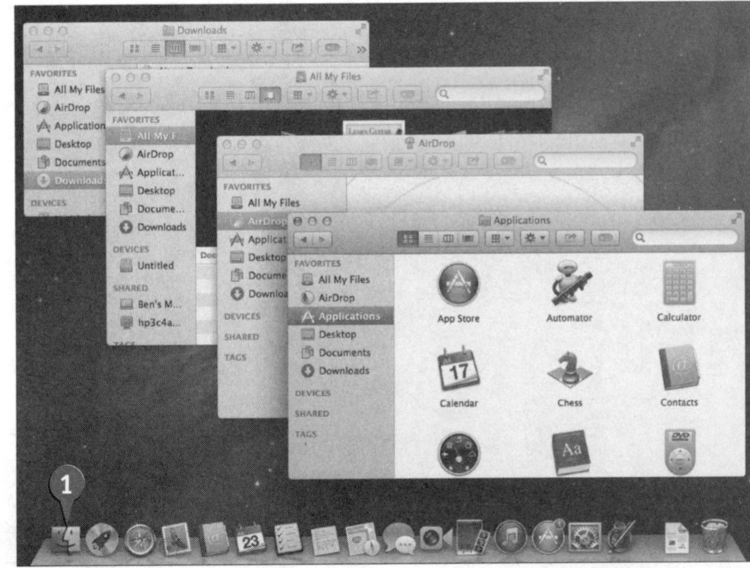

2. Click **Window**.
3. Click **Merge All Windows**.

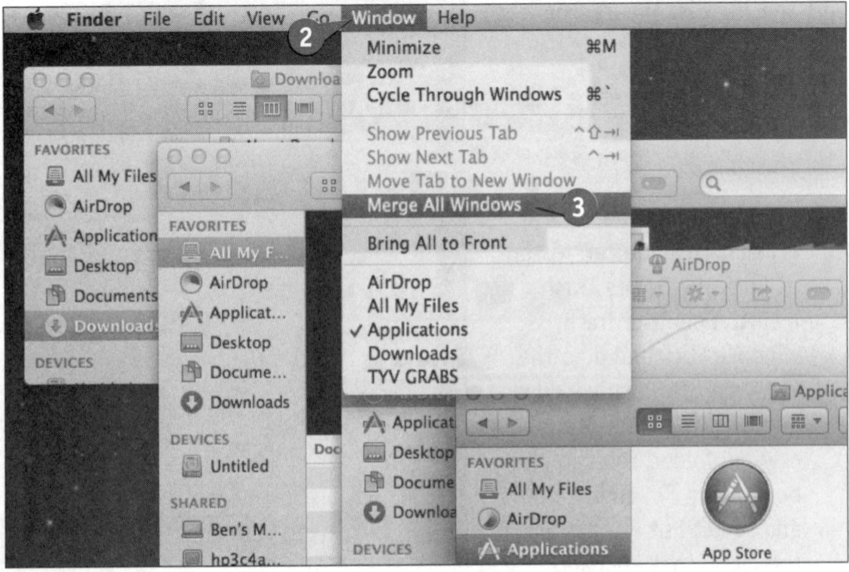

All open Finder windows appear as tabs in a single window.

4 Click a Finder tab to view the location's contents.

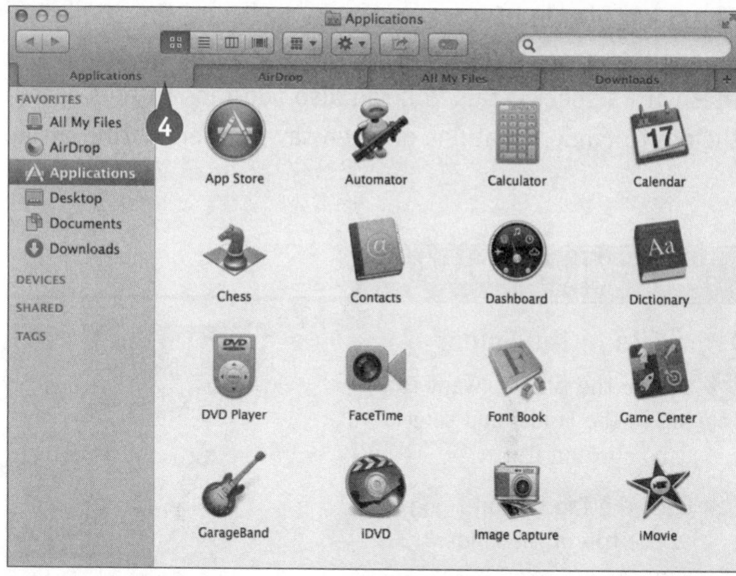

A You can add a new tab by clicking the **Plus** button (+).

B Clicking and dragging a tab moves its position in the tab list.

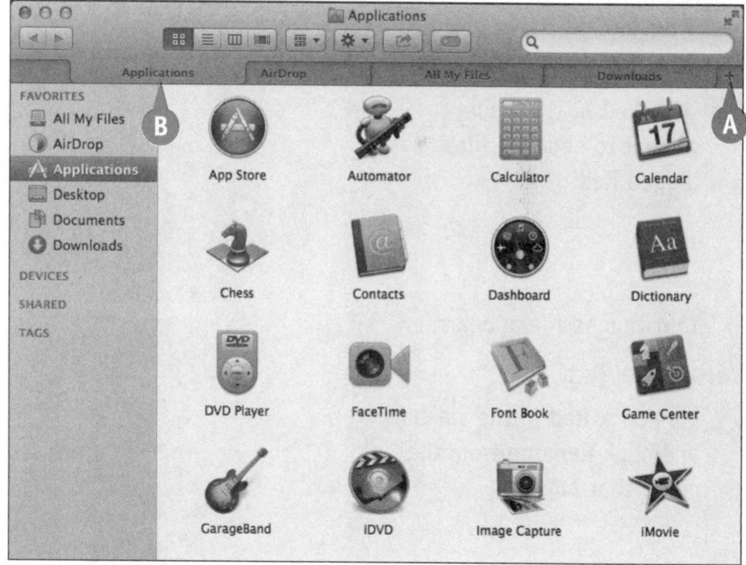

TIPS

Can I set different view settings for each Finder tab?

Yes. Simply click the tab you want to change the view of and then choose one of the four view buttons from the toolbar at the top of the window. You have a choice of showing items as icons, in a list, in columns, or with Cover Flow.

How do I close a Finder tab?

Hover the cursor over the tab you want to close until an X (☒) appears to the left of the tab's title. Click the X to close the tab.

Tag Documents and Files

Tagging files in OS X makes it easy to locate specific items in the Finder as well as within applications. You can add tags to any OS X file and then use shortcuts in the Finder to view all files with a specific tag. You can also add tags to files within the Finder by dragging and dropping them into Finder locations or when saving them within an Application's Save dialog.

Tag Documents and Files

Tag a File in the Finder

1. Locate the file you want to tag in the Finder and select it by clicking it.
2. Click the **Tag** button (▭) at the top of the Finder window and select a tag color or create a new tag. Here, Red is selected.
3. Click **Red** in the Finder sidebar to show all files tagged Red.

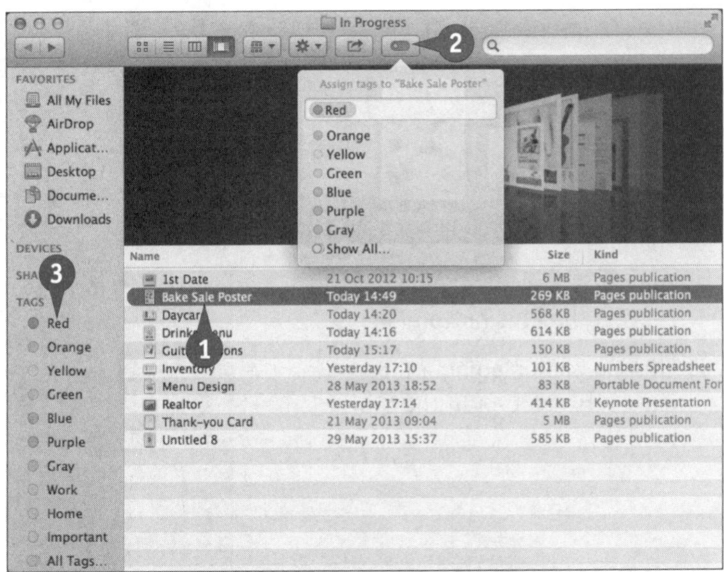

Your tagged file appears.

Rename a Tag

1. ⌘+click **Red** in the sidebar and click **Rename** from the menu that appears.

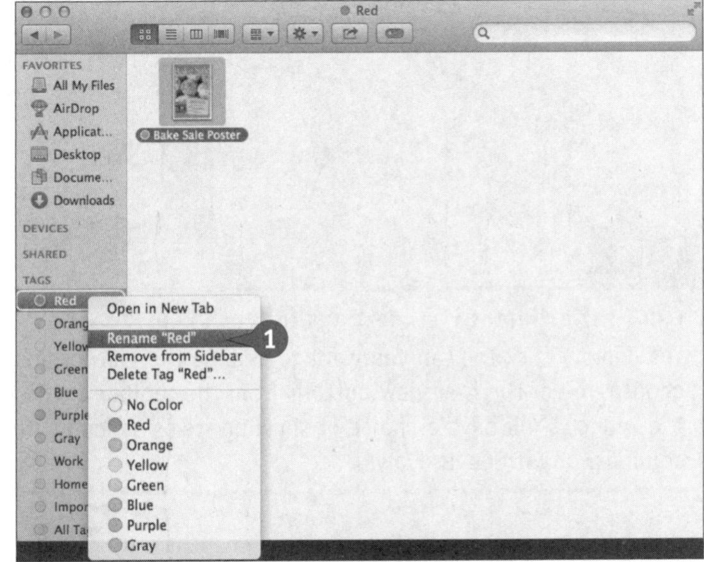

2 Type a new name for the Red tag and press Return.

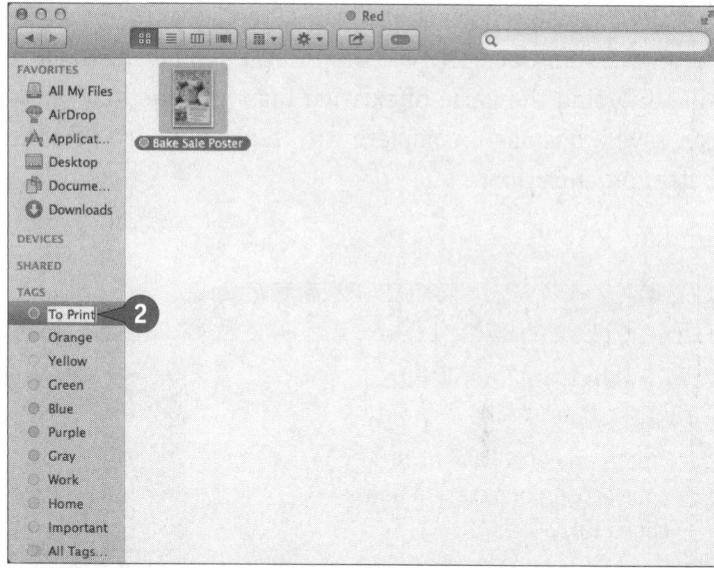

A You can drag more files into the Tags view in the Finder to tag them as well.

B You can also add tags when saving documents in Applications like Pages or TextEdit.

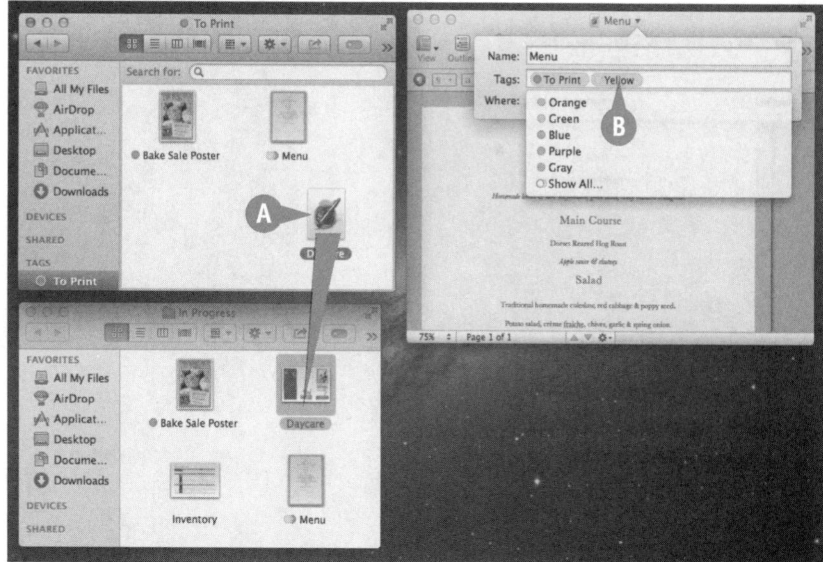

TIPS

Can I apply multiple tags to a single file?
Yes. Simply repeat step 2 and choose a different tag from the menu that appears. You can also add multiple tags when saving a document in an application like Pages or TextEdit.

Does tagging move my file to a different location?
No. When you tag a file it stays in the same location on your Mac but also appears within the Tags section of the sidebar. The files you see within the Tags area of the Finder can be opened files from this view or moved and duplicated.

Add Tags When Saving a Document

When saving a document in OS X, the Save dialog provides fields to type the name you want to save your document as, the location you want to save it in, and the option to add tags. By simply typing the name of existing tags into the field provided, or creating new tags on the fly, you can save a document complete with tags so you can find it more easily or group it with other files for better organization.

Add Tags When Saving a Document

Apply Existing Tags When Saving a Document

1. Create a new document in your chosen application and click **File**.
2. Click **Save.**

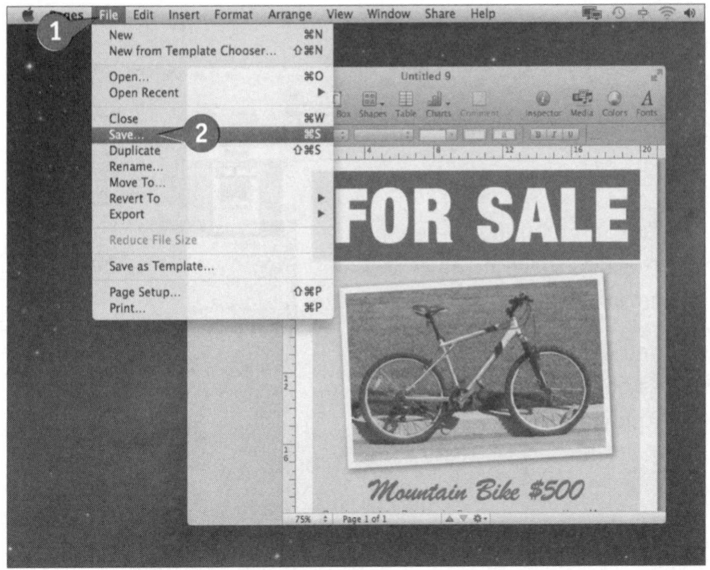

The Save dialog appears.

3. Type a name for your document in the Save As field.
4. Click the **Tags** field and select a Tag from the menu to apply it to your document.

Create a New Tag

1. Type a name for your new tag in the Tags field.
2. Click **Create new tag** to add your new tag.

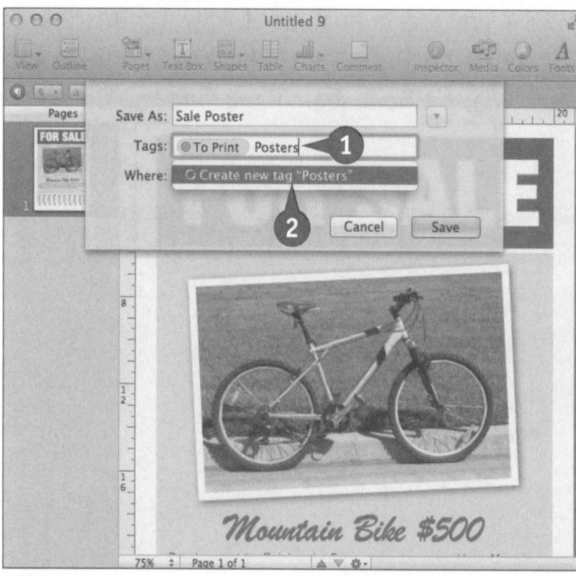

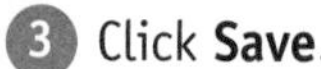

3. Click **Save**.

TIP

How do I add tags to a document I have already saved?

If you have already saved a document, clicking **Save** from the File menu simply saves the document in its current state without showing the Save dialog. In most Apple applications you can still add tags by clicking the small triangle next to the title of the document at the top of the application window. This shows a dialog where you can rename the document, add or remove tags, and change the save location. If the application you are using does not have this dialog, you can still locate the file in the Finder, ⌘+click it, and select **Tags** from the menu that appears.

Search for Documents and Files

OS X provides a number of ways to locate specific files on your Mac either via the Finder or using Spotlight. Both the Finder and Spotlight allow you to search by filename, content, or tags to help you to narrow your search and find the documents or files you are looking for quickly.

Search for Documents and Files

Search for Files with Spotlight

1. Click the **Spotlight** button (🔍).

2. Type your search in the field that appears.

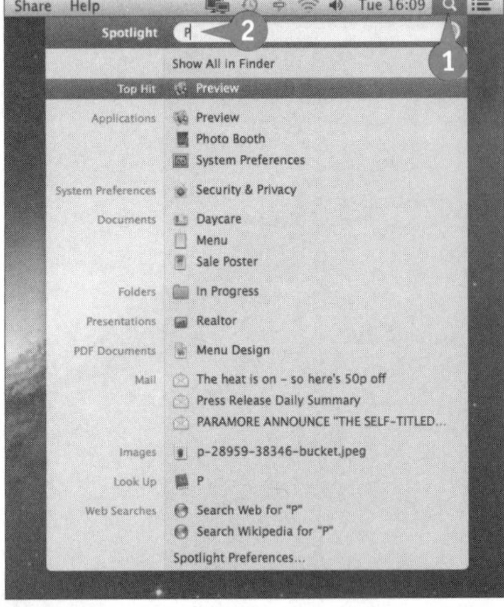

A list of files matching your search terms appears.

A You can hover the cursor over a file to view a preview.

3. Click the file to launch it in its native application.

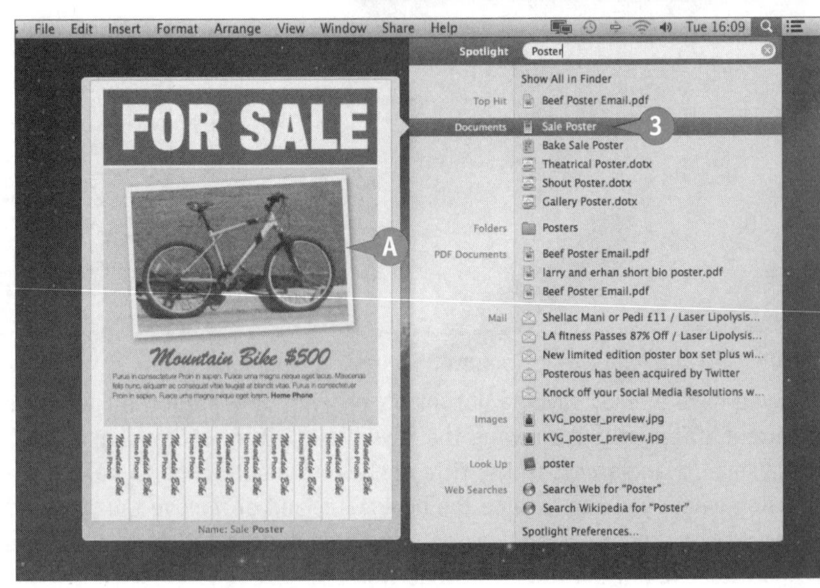

Search for Files in the Finder

1. In the Dock, click the **Finder** icon ( ) to open a new Finder window.
2. Click **All My Files** in the Finder sidebar.
3. Type a search term in the search field at the top right of the Finder window.

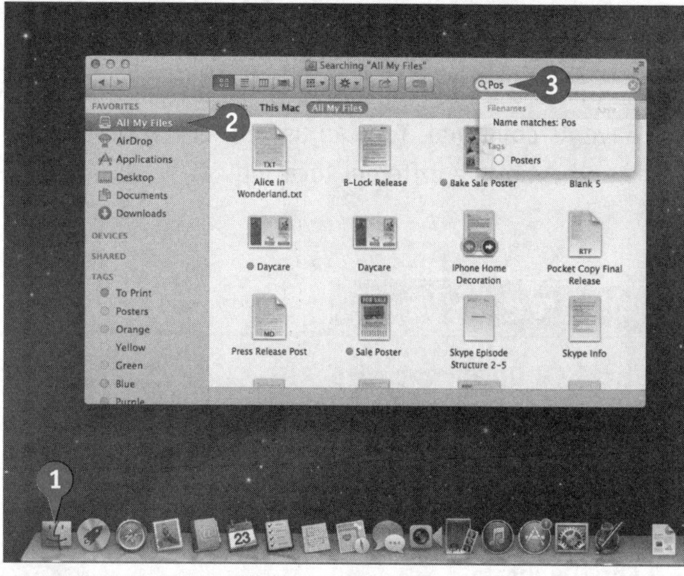

All files on your computer that match your search term appear.

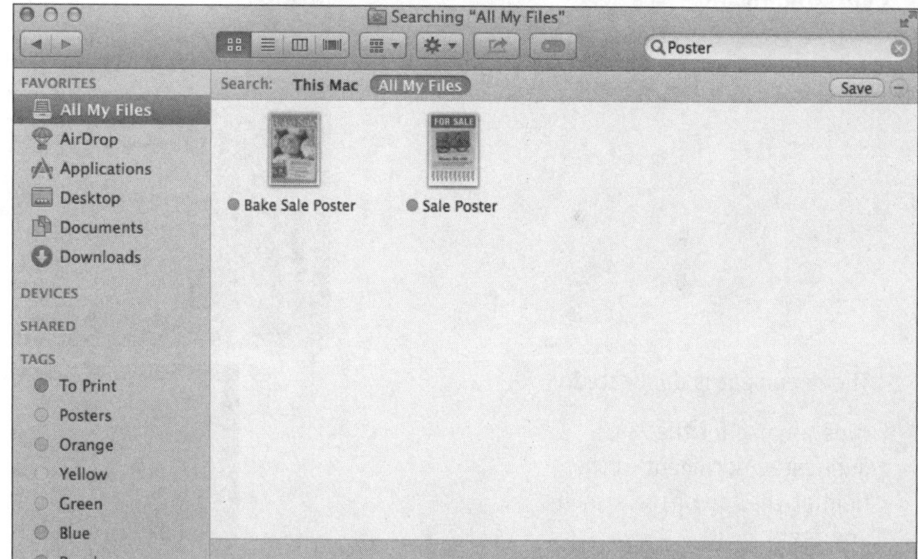

TIP

Can I search using tags?

Yes. If you type the name of a tag in the Finder search field, an option appears at the bottom of the search results to show all files tagged with that name. This is roughly the same process as clicking a tag name from the Finder sidebar to show all files associated with a specific tag. You can, however, use the Finder search field to specify a tag as well as a filename so you can narrow the search results within a set of tagged files.

Duplicate a Document

Duplicating a document is a useful way to continue working on it without the risk of overwriting or editing the original. Documents can be duplicated in a number of ways in OS X, but the easiest method is to use the Duplicate command from the File menu in most applications or, in some cases, the Save As command. You can use either option to save a copy of your document under a different name and even in a different location.

Duplicate a Document

Duplicate a Document with the Duplicate Command

1. Open a document in an application like Pages or TextEdit and click **File**.
2. Click **Duplicate**.

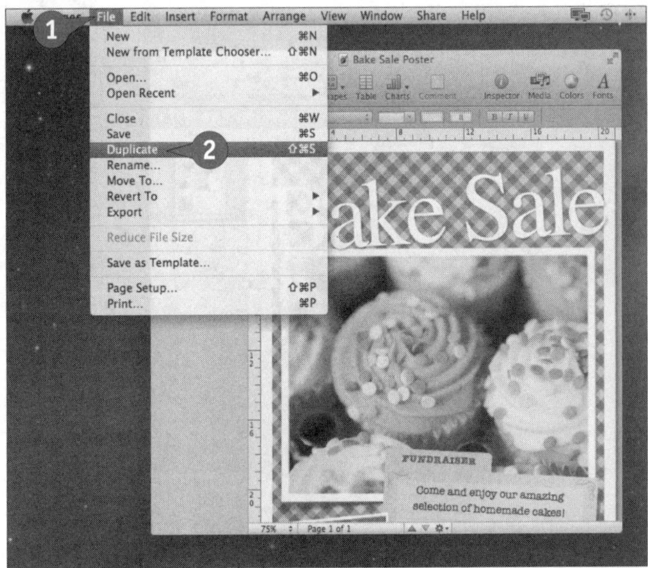

The document is duplicated.

3. Type a name for the duplicated document in the field at the top of the screen and press Return.

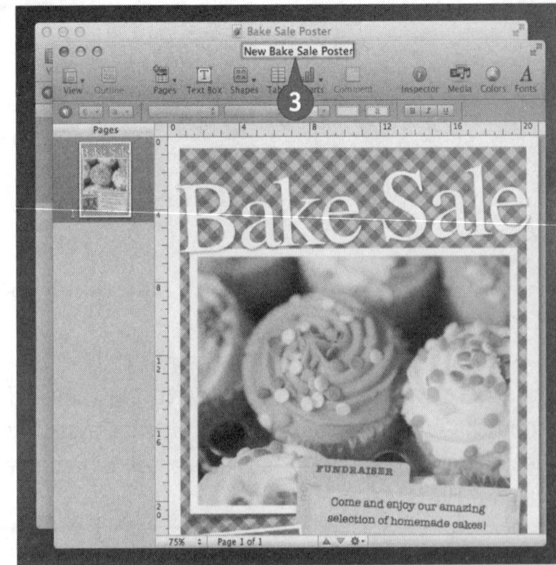

Duplicate a Document with the Save As Command

1. Open a document in an application like Pages or TextEdit and click **File**.
2. If there is a Save As option, click it. If not, hold down Option and the Duplicate option changes to **Save As**.

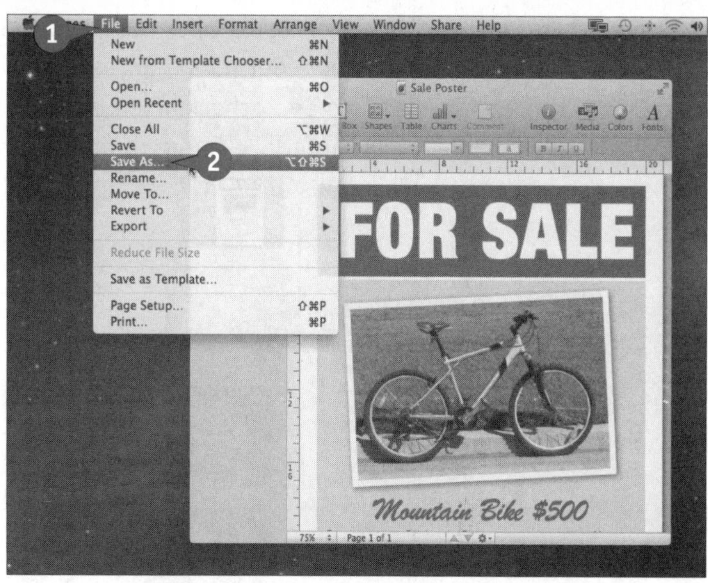

The Save dialog appears.

3. Type a name for the duplicated document and adjust the save location if required.
4. Click **Save**.

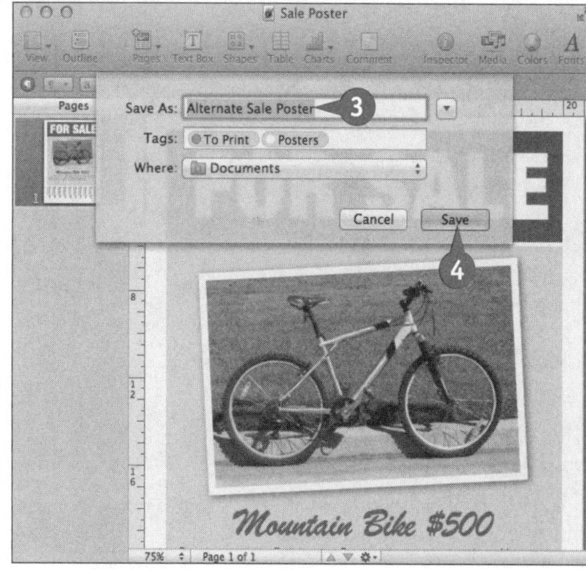

TIPS

What happens to the original file when I duplicate it?

The original file is untouched when you duplicate it or save it with another name. It is a good idea, however, to save the duplicate file with a name that is noticeably different from the original so you don't edit the wrong version.

What if I change my mind and choose not to duplicate a file?

From the Save dialog that appears when you use the Duplicate command, you can click the **Cancel** button to go back to the duplicate document, or you can click the **Delete Copy** button to delete the duplicate you just made.

Store a Document in iCloud

When saving a document in an Apple application such as Pages, Keynote, or Numbers, you can store the file online through your iCloud account so that it is available on all of your iCloud-connected devices. You can also add other documents to your iCloud storage by simply dragging and dropping them into the iCloud interface found in many Apple apps. This example uses TextEdit, but you can use any of the iWork apps or even Preview.

Store a Document in iCloud

1. Open an iCloud-compatible app such as TextEdit.

All of your iCloud documents are shown in a window.

2. Locate a file on your Mac and drag it onto the window.

Note: The file you upload must be compatible with the application you are using. A Word, TXT, or Pages document will work with Pages and PDFs, and image files will work with Preview.

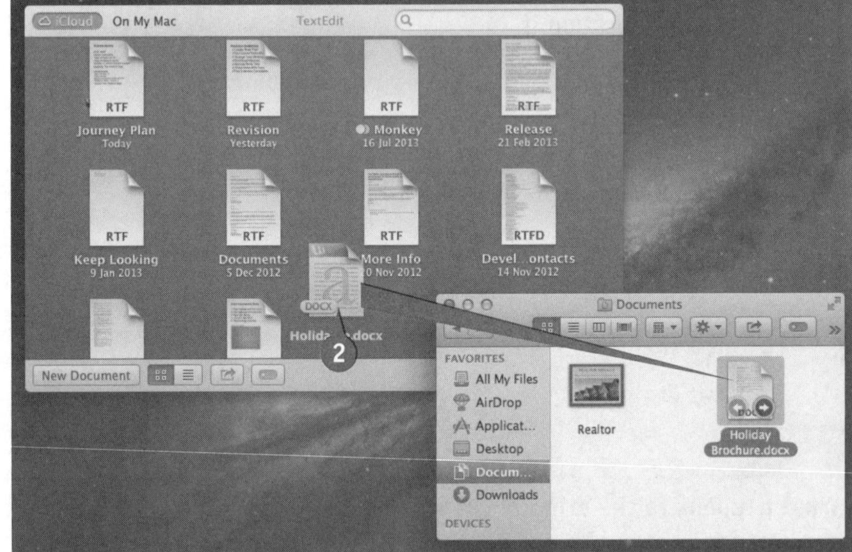

The file is uploaded to iCloud.

3. Click the document and then click **Open**.

   The file opens in your chosen application.

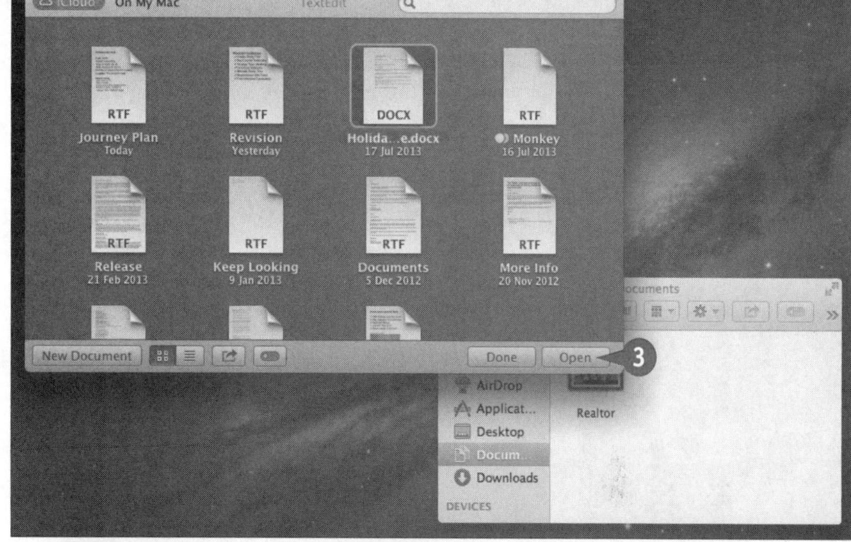

4. Edit the document as you wish and click **File**.

5. Click **Save**.

   The changes to your document are stored in the cloud and can be accessed on all of your iCloud-connected devices.

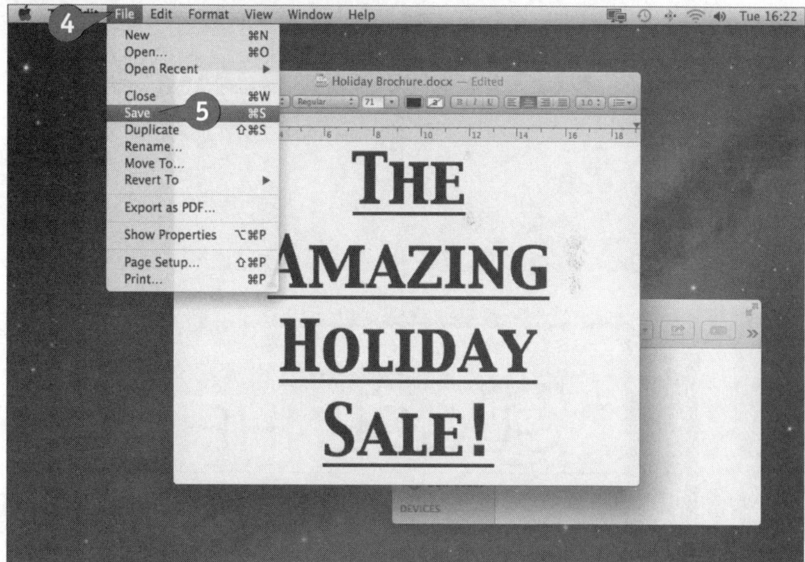

TIPS

Can I access the file I uploaded to iCloud without using this interface?

Yes. Spotlight allows you to search for files both on your Mac and those stored in iCloud. Simply click the **Spotlight** button (🔍) and type the name of the document you want to access. When the document appears in the search results, you can hover the cursor over it to preview it and then click it to open it.

What happens if I drag a file out of the iCloud interface?

If you drag a file from the iCloud interface to another location on your Mac it is moved to that location and is not available via iCloud or accessible by your other iCloud-connected devices.

CHAPTER 4

Browsing the World Wide Web

The *World Wide Web* is a massive storehouse of information that resides on computers all over the world. If your Mac is connected to the Internet, you can use the Safari browser to navigate — or *surf* — websites.

Open and Close Safari

To access websites and view web pages, you can use a web browser program. In OS X, the default web browser is Safari, which you can use to surf websites when your Mac is connected to the Internet.

The Safari application offers a number of features that make it easier to browse the web. For example, you can open multiple pages in a single Safari window, you can save your favorite sites for easier access, and you can perform Internet searches from the Safari window. To use these features, you must know how to start the Safari application. When you finish surfing the web, you need to know how to shut down Safari to save system resources on your Mac.

Open and Close Safari

Open Safari

1. In the Dock, click the **Safari** icon ( ).

   The Safari window appears.

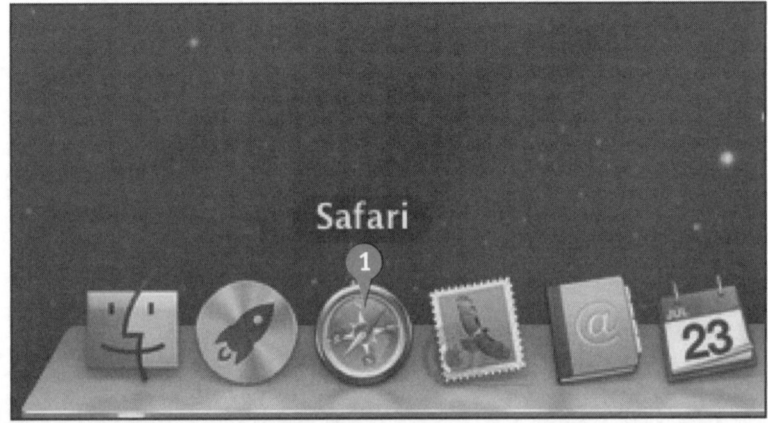

Note: The initial web page you see depends on how your version of Safari is configured. In most cases, you see the Apple.com Start page or the Top Sites page.

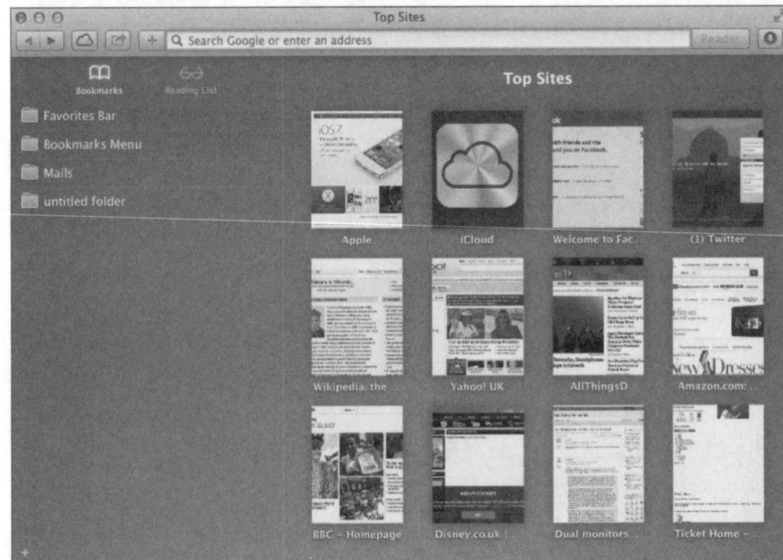

Close Safari

1 Click **Safari**.

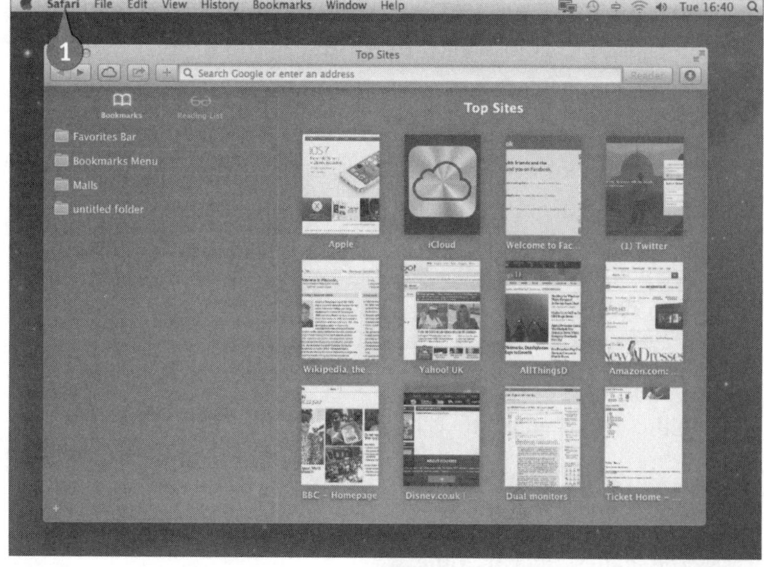

2 Click **Quit Safari**.

The Safari window closes.

TIPS

Are there other methods I can use to open Safari?

If you have removed the Safari icon (◉) from the Dock, there are a couple of other quick methods you can use to start Safari. If you have used Safari recently, click the **Apple** icon (), click **Recent Items**, and then click **Safari**. You can also click **Spotlight** (🔍), type **safari**, and then click **Safari** in the search results.

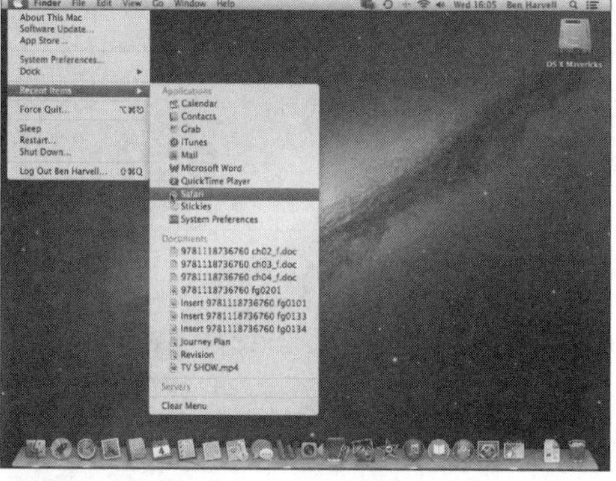

Are there faster methods I can use to close Safari?

Probably the fastest method you can use to quit Safari is to right-click its icon (◉) on the Dock and then click **Quit**. If your hands are closer to the keyboard than to the mouse, you can quit Safari by switching to the application and then pressing ⌘+Q.

Select a Link

Almost all web pages include links to other pages that contain related information. When you select a link, your web browser loads the other page. Web page links come in two forms: text and images. Text links consist of a word or phrase that usually appears underlined and in a different color from the rest of the page text. However, web page designers can control the look of their links, so text links may not always stand out in this way. Therefore, knowing which words, phrases, or images are links is not always obvious. The only way to tell for sure is to position the mouse over the text or image; if the changes to , you know the item is a link.

Select a Link

1. Position the mouse over the link (changes to).

   A The status bar shows the address of the linked page.

Note: The address shown in the status bar when you point at a link may be different from the one shown when the page is downloading. This occurs when the website redirects the link. Pay attention to this to avoid being redirected to potentially dangerous websites.

2. If the address looks right, click the text or image.

Note: If you do not see the status bar, click **View** and then click **Show Status Bar**.

The linked web page appears.

B The web page title and address change after the linked page is loaded.

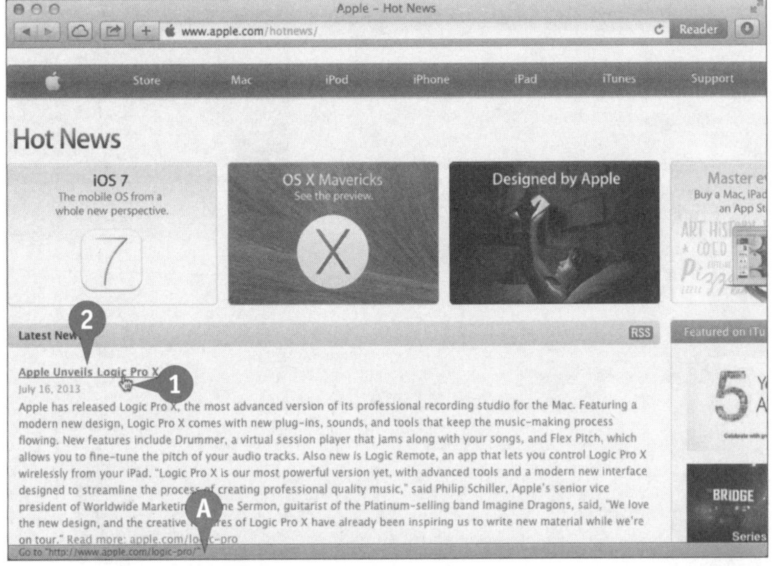

Enter a Web Page Address

If you know the address of a specific web page, you can type it into the web browser to display the page. Every web page is uniquely identified by an address called the Uniform Resource Locator, or URL (pronounced *yoo-ar-ell* or *erl*).

The URL is composed of four basic parts: the *transfer method* (usually HTTP, which stands for Hypertext Transfer Protocol), the website *domain name*, the *directory* where the web page is located on the server, and the *web page filename*. The website domain name suffix most often used is .com (commercial), but other common suffixes include .gov (government), .org (nonprofit organization), .edu (education), .biz (business), and country domains such as .ca (Canada).

Enter a Web Page Address

1. Click inside the address bar and press Delete to delete the existing address.
2. Type the address of the web page you want to visit and press Return.

Ⓐ You can also click the site if it appears in the list of suggested sites.

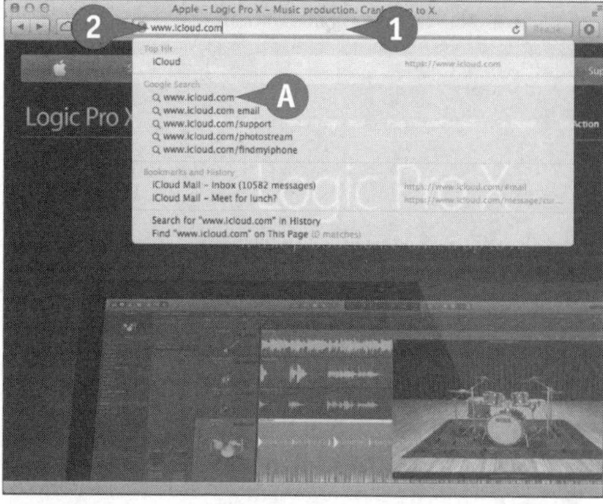

The web page appears.

Ⓑ The web page title changes after the page is loaded.

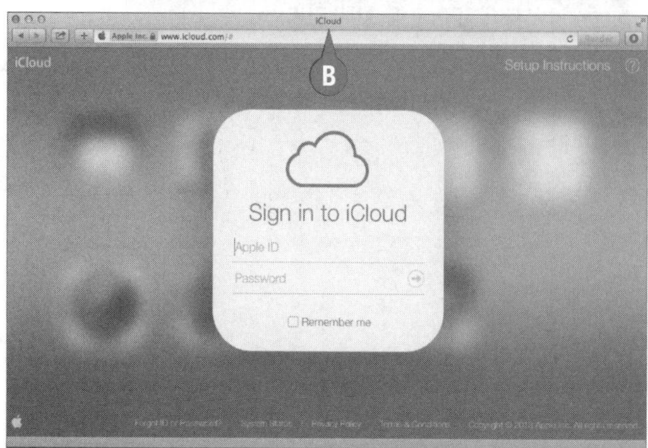

Open a Web Page in a Tab

You can make it easier to work with multiple web pages and sites simultaneously by opening each page in its own tab. As you surf the web, you may come upon a page that you want to keep available while you visit other sites. Instead of leaving the page and trying to find it again when you need it, Safari lets you leave the page open in a special section of the browser window called a *tab*. You can then use a second tab to visit your other sites. To resume viewing the first site, you need only click its tab.

Open a Web Page in a Tab

Open a Link in a New Tab

1. Right-click the link you want to open.
2. Click **Open Link in New Tab**.

Ⓐ A new tab appears with the page title.

3. Click the tab to display the page.

Create a New Tab

1. Click **File**.
2. Click **New Tab**.

B If you already have one or more tabs open, you can also click the **Create a new tab** icon (+).

Note: If the tab bar is hidden, the Create a new tab icon only appears if two or more tabs are open.

C Safari creates a new tab.

3. Type the address of the page you want to load into the new tab and press Return.

Safari displays the page in the tab.

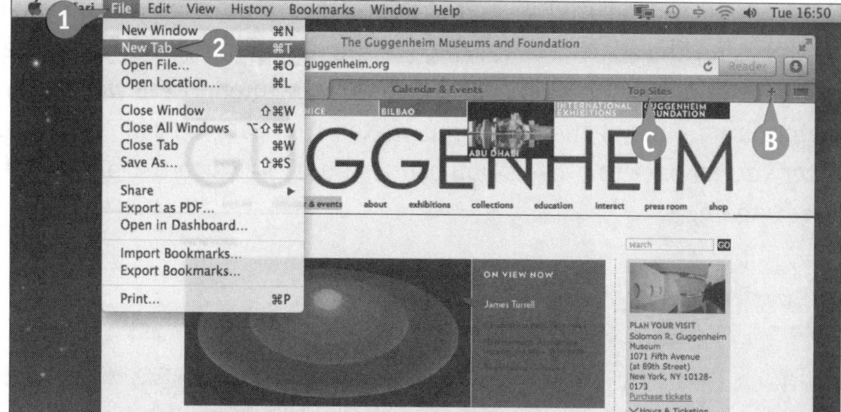

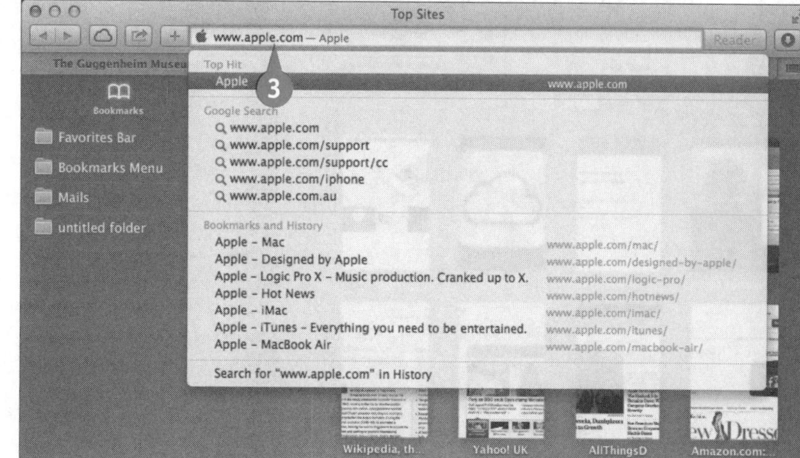

TIP

Are there any shortcuts I can use to open web pages in tabs?

Yes, here are some useful keyboard techniques you can use:

- Press and hold ⌘ and click a link to open the page in a tab.
- Press and hold ⌘ + Shift and click a link to open the page in a tab and display the page.
- Type an address and then press ⌘ + Return to open the page in a new tab.
- Type an address and then press Shift + ⌘ + Return to open the page in a new foreground tab.
- Press Shift + ⌘ +] or Shift + ⌘ + [to cycle through the tabs.
- Press ⌘ + W to close the current tab.
- Press Option and click ☒ to close every tab but the one you clicked.

Navigate Web Pages

After you have visited several pages, you can return to a page you visited earlier. Instead of retyping the address or looking for the link, Safari gives you some easier methods. When you navigate from page to page, you create a path through the web. Safari keeps track of this path by maintaining a list of the pages you visited. You can use that list to go back to a page you visited. After you go back to a page, you can also use the same list of pages to go forward through the pages again.

Navigate Web Pages

Go Back One Page

1. Click the **Previous Page** icon (◀).

   The previous page you visited appears.

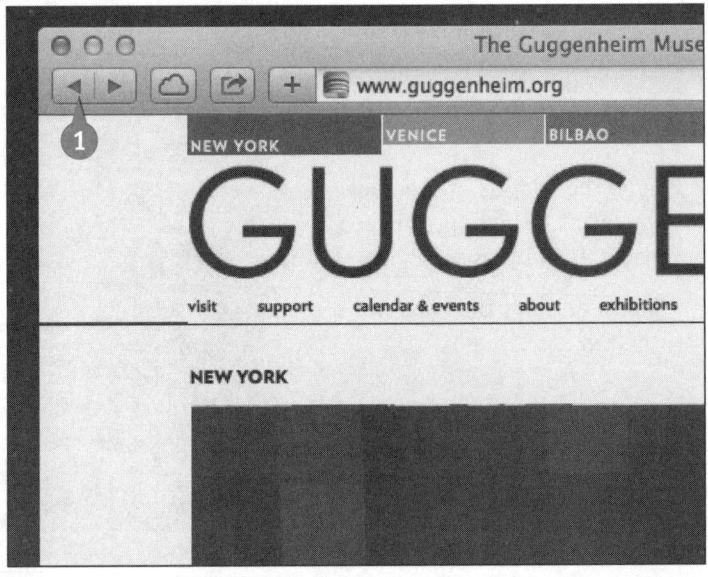

Go Back Several Pages

1. Click and hold down the cursor on the **Previous Page** icon (◀).

Note: The list of visited pages is different for each tab that you have open. If you do not see the page you want, you may need to click a different tab.

   A list of the pages you have visited appears.

2. Click the page you want to revisit.

   The page appears.

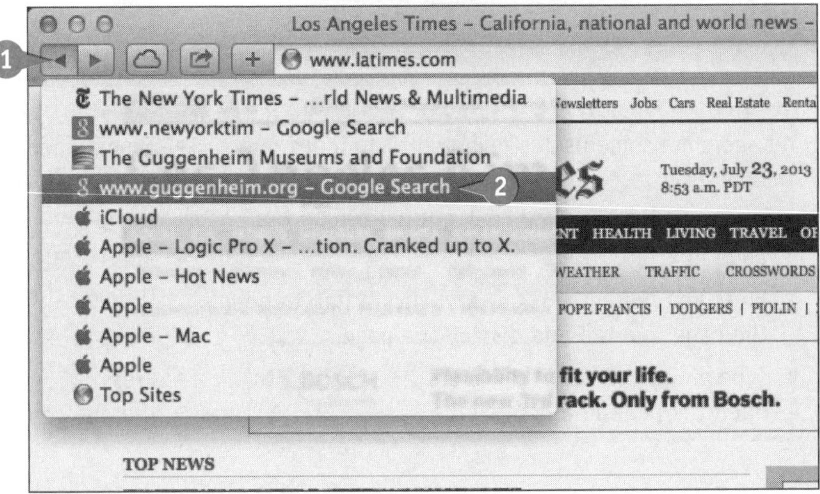

Go Forward One Page

1. Click the **Next Page** icon (▶).

   The next page appears.

Note: If you are at the last page viewed up to that point, the Next Page icon (▶) is not active.

Go Forward Several Pages

1. Click and hold the cursor on the **Next Page** icon (▶).

   A list of the pages you have visited appears.

Note: The list of visited pages is different for each tab that you have open. If you do not see the page you want, you may need to click a different tab.

2. Click the page you want to revisit.

   The page appears.

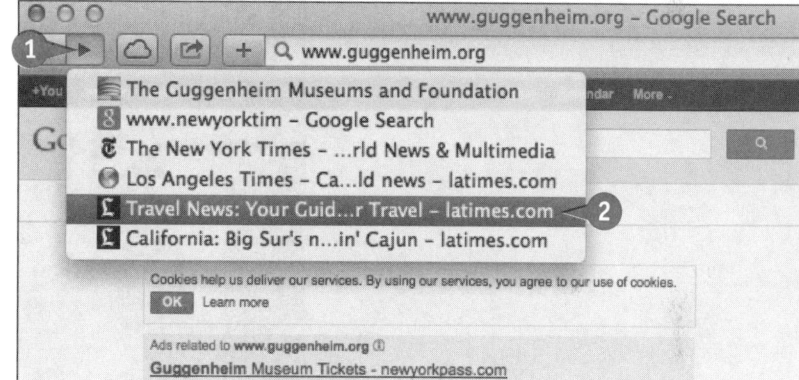

TIP

Are there any shortcuts I can use to navigate web pages?

Yes. Here are a few useful keyboard shortcuts:

- Press ⌘ + [to go back one page.
- Press ⌘ +] to go forward one page.
- Press Shift + ⌘ + H to return to the Safari home page (the first page you see when you open Safari).

Navigate with the History List

The Previous Page (◄) and Next Page (►) buttons enable you to navigate pages in the current browser session. To redisplay sites that you have visited in the past few days or weeks, you need to use the History list, which is a collection of the websites and pages you have visited over the past month, or however long you have your Preferences set to track your browsing history.

If you visit sensitive places such as an Internet banking site or your corporate site, you can increase security by clearing the history list so that other people cannot see where you have been.

Navigate with the History List

Load a Page from the History List

1 Click **History**.

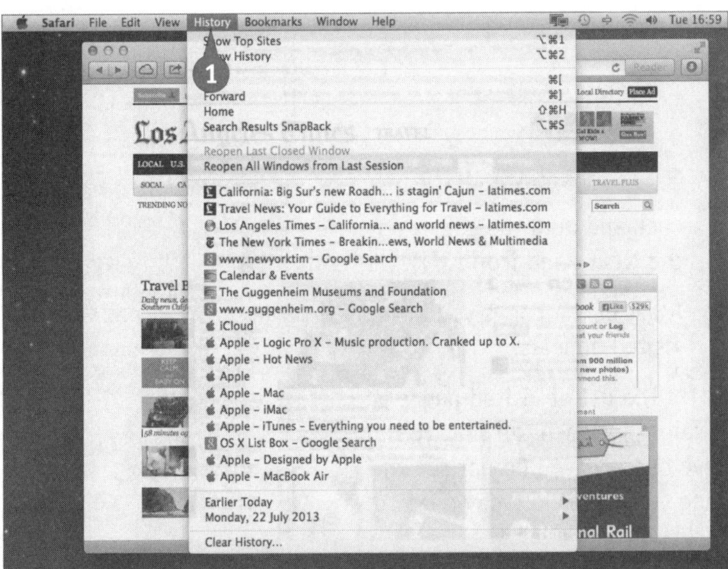

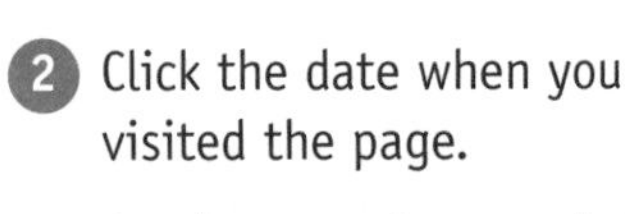

2 Click the date when you visited the page.

A submenu of pages that you visited during that day appears.

3 Click the page you want to revisit.

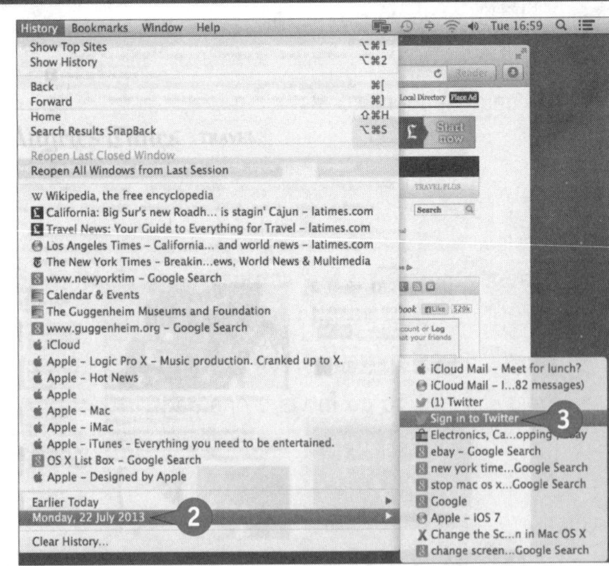

Ⓐ The page appears.

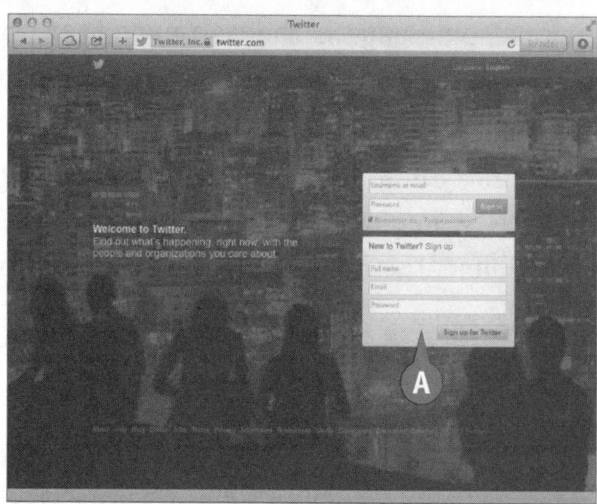

Clear the History List

1. Click **History**.
2. Click **Clear History**.

   Safari deletes all the pages from the history list.

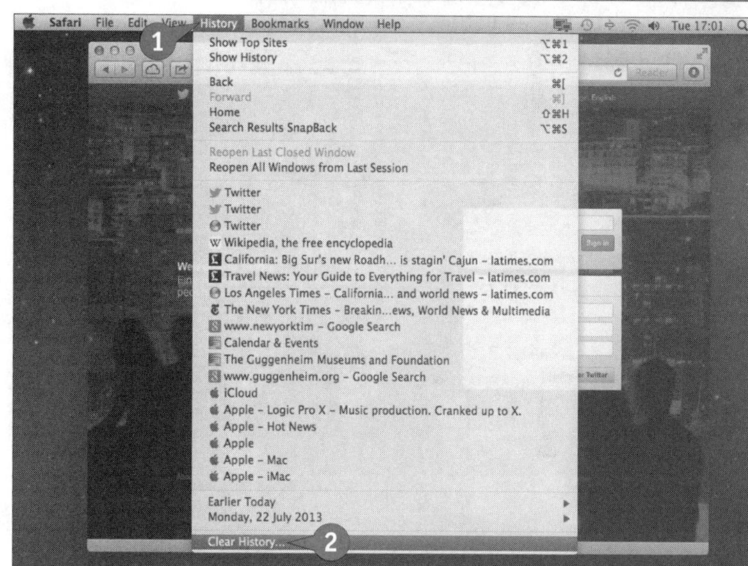

TIP

Can I control the length of time that Safari keeps track of the pages I visit?

Yes, by following these steps:

1. In the menu bar, click **Safari**.
2. Click **Preferences**.
3. Click **General**.
4. Click the **Remove history items** (⇕) and then select the amount of time you want Safari to track your history.
5. Click the **Close** button (●).

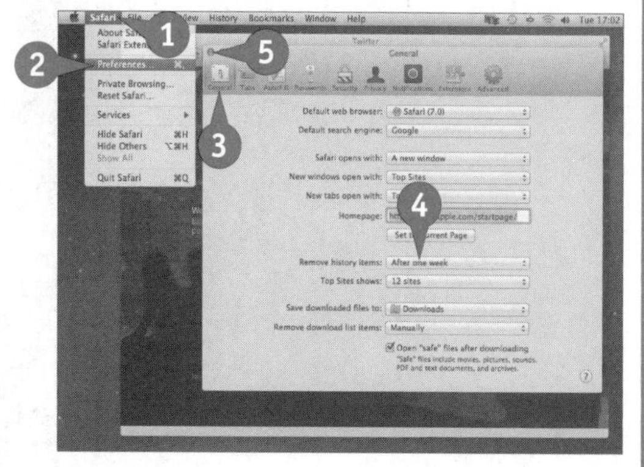

Change Your Home Page

Your home page is the web page that appears when you first start Safari. The default home page is usually the Apple.com Start page, but you can change that to any other page you want, or even to an empty page. This is useful if you do not use the Apple.com Start page, or if there is another page that you always visit at the start of your browsing session. For example, if you have your own website, it might make sense to always begin there. Safari also comes with a command that enables you to view the home page at any time during your browsing session.

Change Your Home Page

Change the Home Page

1. Display the web page that you want to use as your home page.

2. Click **Safari**.
3. Click **Preferences**.

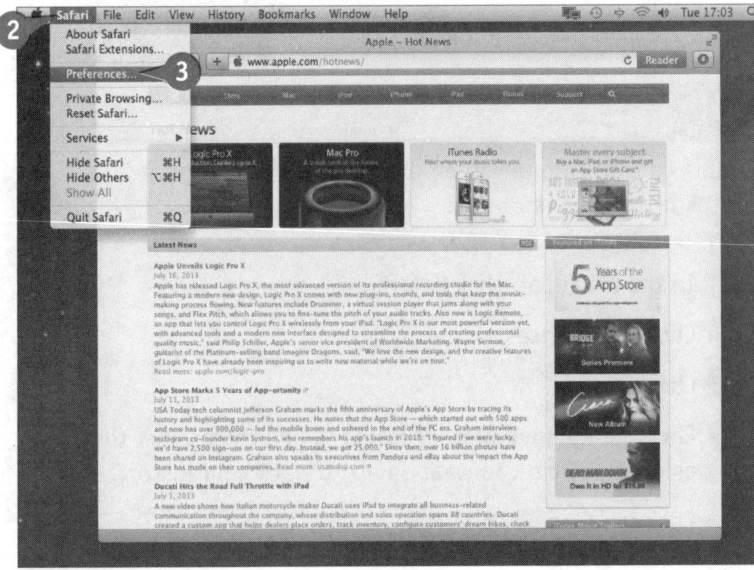

4 Click **General**.

5 Click **Set to Current Page**.

A Safari inserts the address of the current page in the Homepage text box.

Note: If your Mac is not currently connected to the Internet, you can also type the new home page address manually using the Homepage text box.

6 Click the **Close** button (◉).

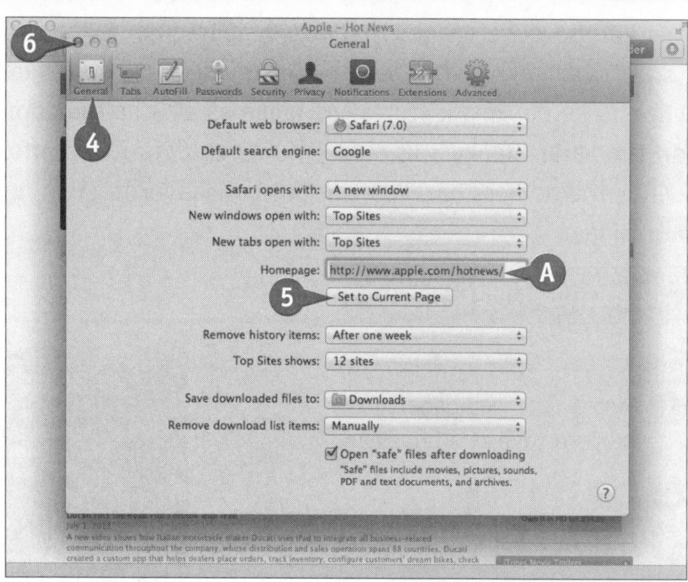

View the Home Page

1 Click **History**.

2 Click **Home**.

Note: You can also display the home page by pressing Shift + ⌘ + H.

Safari displays the home page.

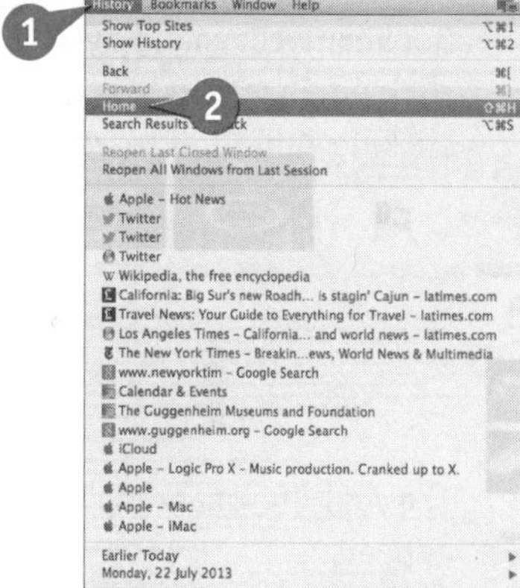

TIP

Can I get Safari to open a new window without displaying the home page?

Yes. Follow these steps:

1 In the menu bar, click **Safari**.

2 Click **Preferences**.

3 Click **General**.

4 Click the **New windows open with** ⬍ and then select **Empty Page** from the pop-up menu.

5 Click the **Close** button (◉).

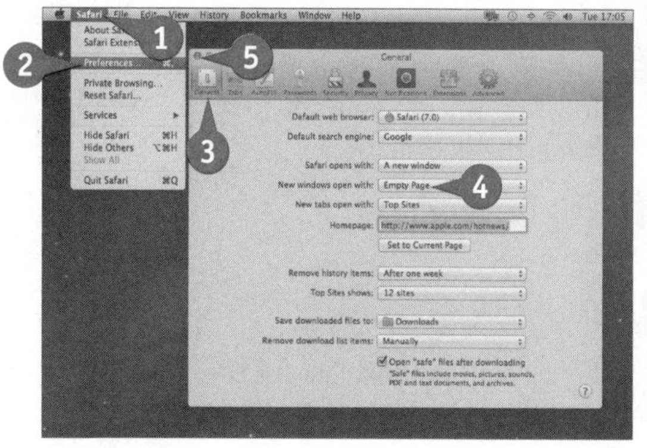

Bookmark Web Pages

If you have web pages that you visit frequently, you can save yourself time by storing those pages as bookmarks within Safari. This enables you to display the pages with just a couple of mouse clicks. The bookmark stores the name as well as the address of the page. Most bookmarks are stored on the Safari Bookmarks menu. However, Safari also offers the Bookmarks bar, which appears just below the address bar. You can put your favorite sites on the Bookmarks bar for easiest access.

Bookmark Web Pages

Bookmark a Web Page

1. Display the web page you want to save as a bookmark.
2. Click **Bookmarks.**
3. Click **Add Bookmark.**

Ⓐ You can also run the Add Bookmark command by clicking **Share** (⎘) and then clicking **Add Bookmark**.

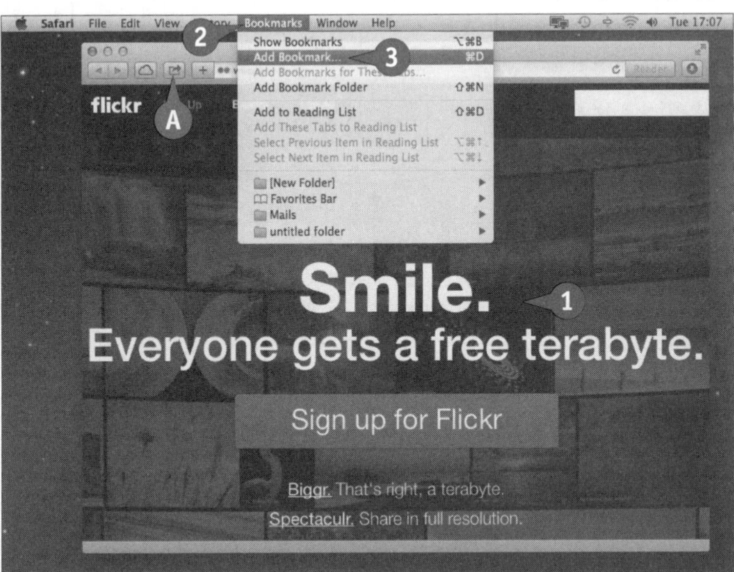

The Add Bookmark dialog appears.

Note: You can also display the Add Bookmark dialog by pressing ⌘ + D.

4. Click ⬍ and then click the location where you want to store the bookmark.
5. Edit the page name, if necessary.
6. Click **Add**.

Safari adds a bookmark for the page.

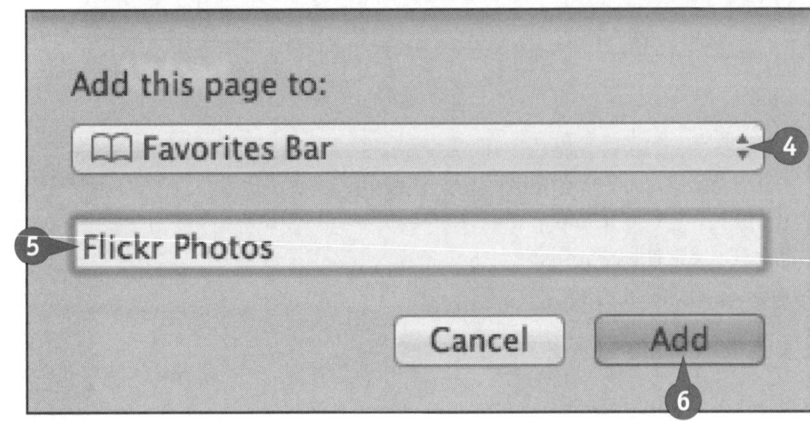

Display a Bookmarked Web Page

1. Click the **Show all bookmarks** button (📖).

B If you added the bookmark to the Bookmarks bar, click the page name.

C If you added the bookmark to a folder, click the folder and then click the page name.

The Bookmarks window appears.

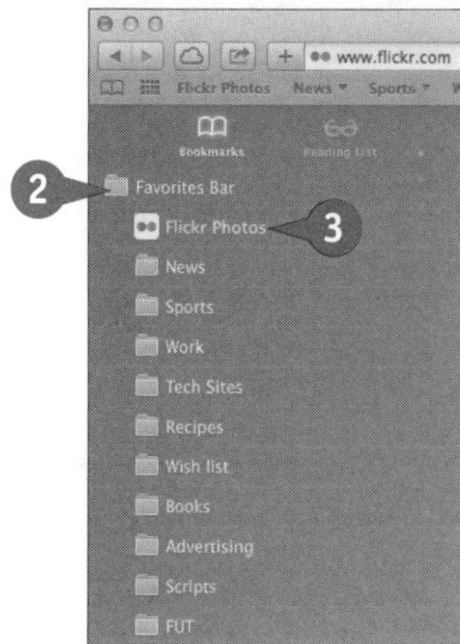

2. Click the folder that contains the bookmark you want.

All bookmarks in the folder are shown.

3. Click the bookmark.

The web page appears.

TIPS

I use my Bookmarks bar a lot. Is there an easier way to display these pages?

Yes. Safari automatically assigns keyboard shortcuts to the first nine bookmarks, counting from left to right and not including folders. For example, you display the left-most bookmark by pressing ⌘ + 1. Moving to the right, the shortcuts are ⌘ + 2, ⌘ + 3, and so on.

How do I delete a bookmark?

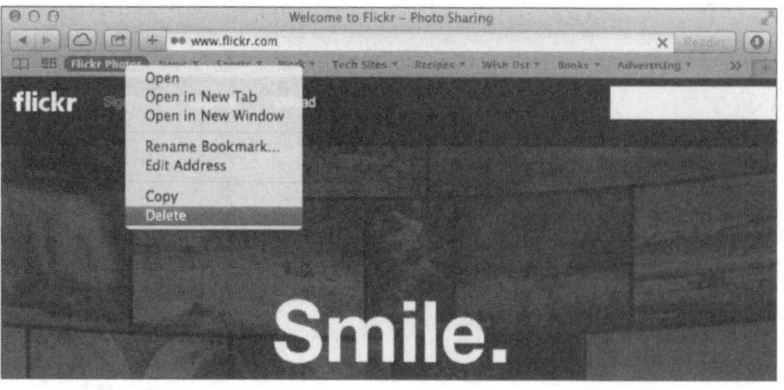

If the site is on the Bookmarks bar, right-click the bookmark and then click **Delete**, or hold down ⌘ and drag it off the bar. For all other bookmarks, click 📖 to display the Bookmarks window. Click within the folder or Collection the bookmark is in, locate the bookmark you want to remove, right-click the bookmark, and then click **Delete**. You can also click the bookmark and then press Delete.

Search for Sites

If you need information on a specific topic, Safari has a built-in feature that enables you to quickly search the web for sites that have the information you require. The web has a number of sites called *search engines* that enable you to find what you are looking for. By default, Safari uses the Google search site (www.google.com). Simple, one-word searches often return tens of thousands of *hits*, or matching sites. To improve your searching, type multiple search terms that define what you are looking for. To search for a phrase, enclose the words in quotation marks.

Search for Sites

1. Click in the Address box.
2. Delete the address.

3. Type a word, phrase, or question that represents the information you want to find and press Return.

Ⓐ If you see the search text you want to use in the list of suggested searches, click the text.

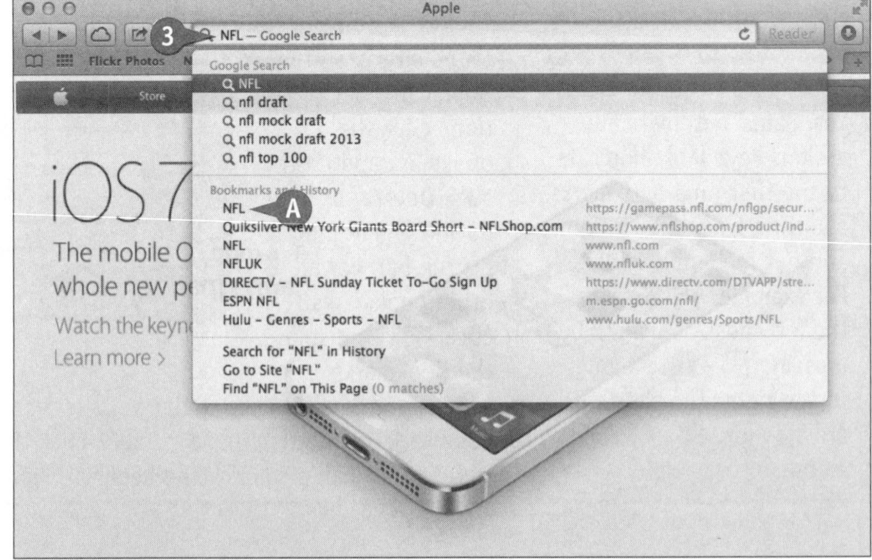

B A list of pages that match your search text appears.

4 Click a web page.

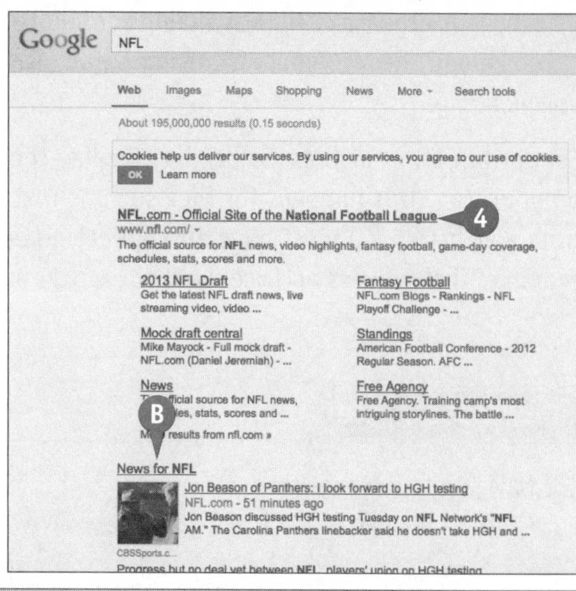

The page appears.

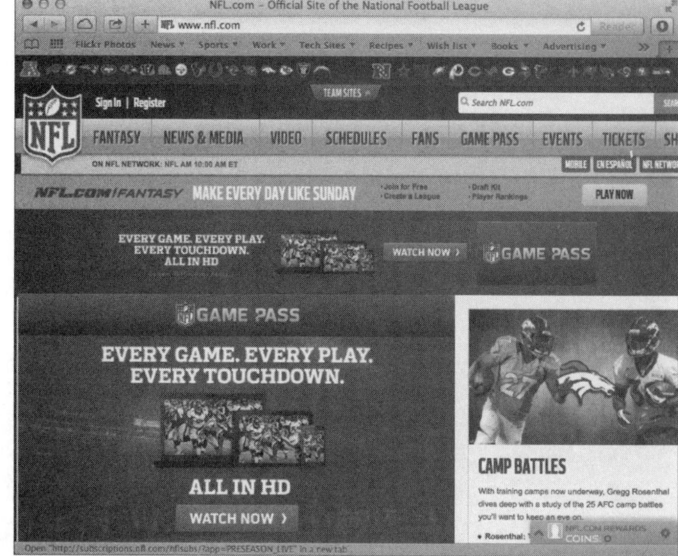

TIP

Is there an easy way that I can rerun a recent search?

1 Click **History**.

2 Click **Search Results Snapback**.

You can also press Option + ⌘ + S.

Safari sends the search text to Google.

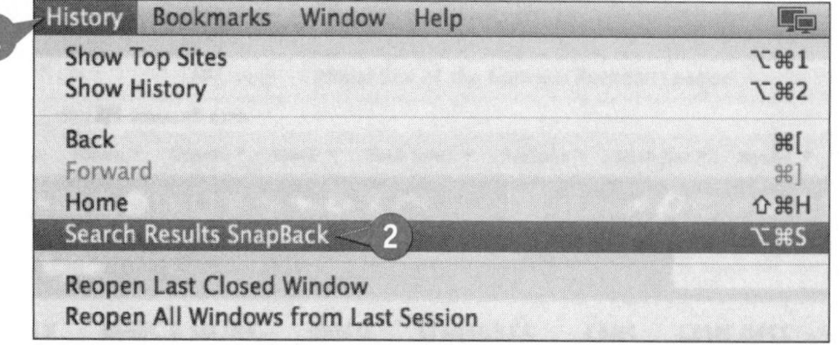

Download a File

Some websites make files available for you to open on your Mac. To use these files, you can download them to your Mac using Safari. Saving data from the Internet to your computer is called *downloading*.

For certain types of files, Safari may display the content right away instead of saving it to a location on your Mac. This happens for files such as text documents and PDF files. In any case, to use a file from a website, you must have an application designed to work with that particular file type. For example, if the file is an Excel workbook, you need either Excel for the Mac or a compatible program.

Download a File

1. Navigate to the page that contains the link to the file.

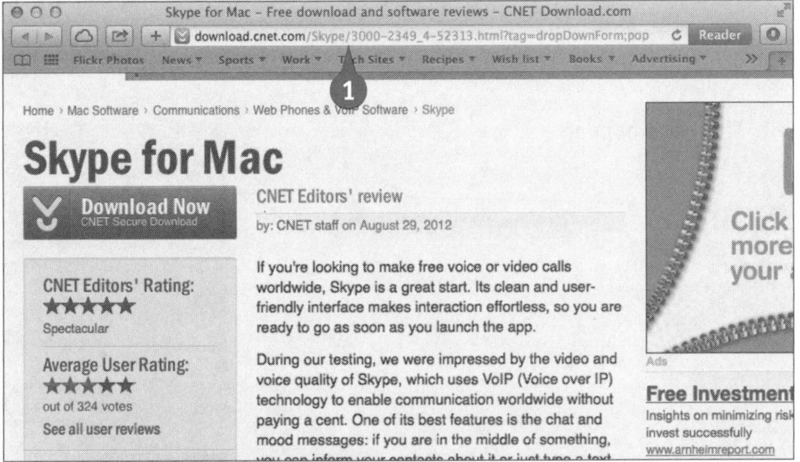

2. Click the link to the file.

   Safari downloads the file to your Mac.

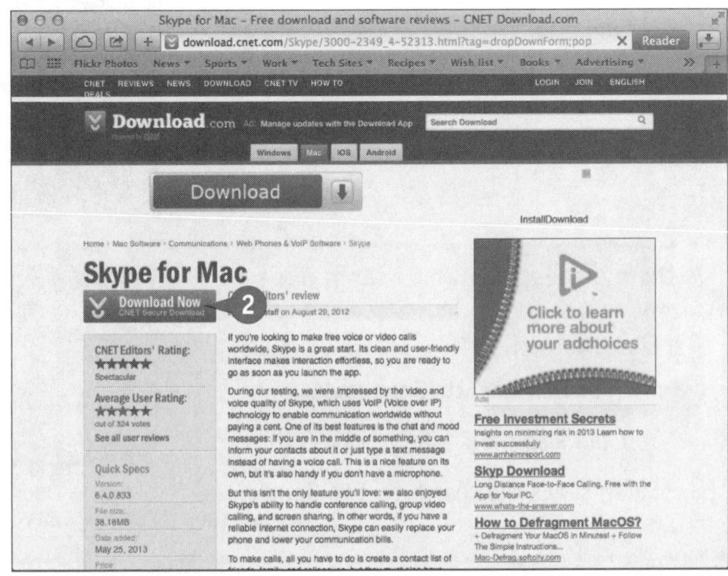

Ⓐ A status bar appears on the file in the Downloads folder on the Dock.

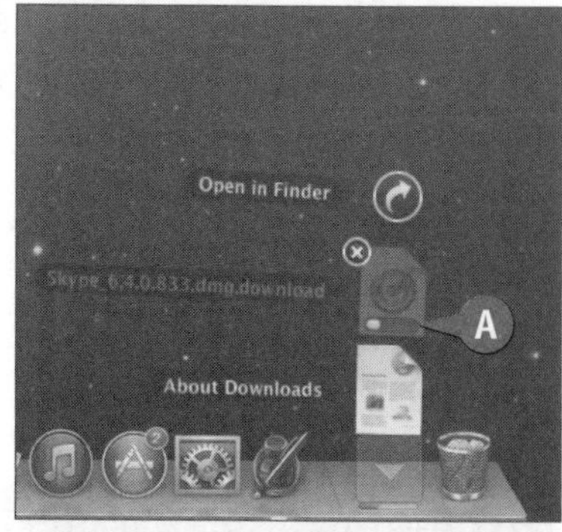

3 When the download is complete, click the **Downloads** folder on the Dock.

4 Click the file to open it.

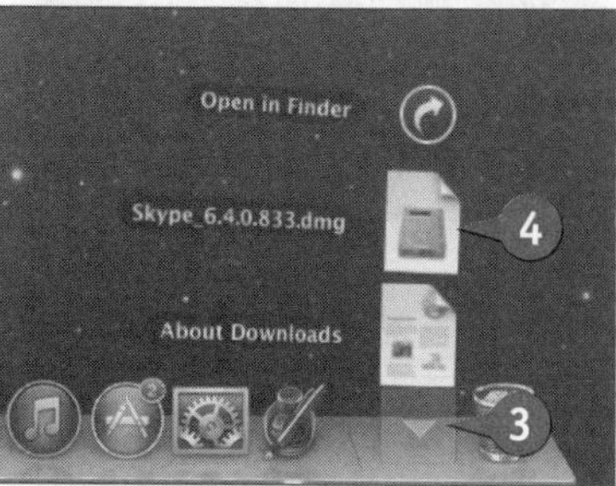

The file opens in the corresponding application or as a folder or disk image.

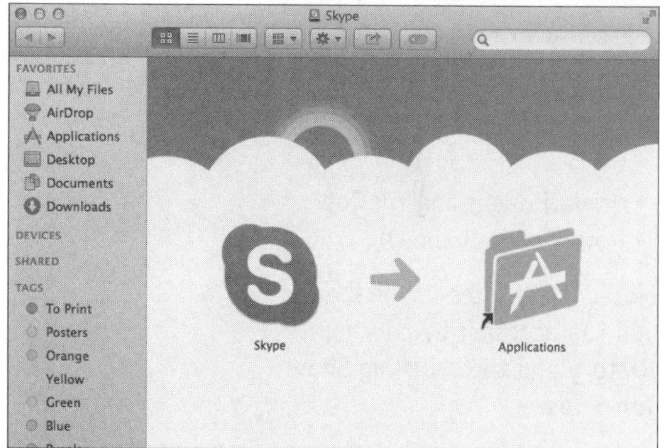

TIPS

If Safari displays the file instead of downloading it, how do I save the file to my Mac?

Click **File** and then click **Save As**. Type a name for the new file, choose a folder, and then click **Save**.

Is it safe to download files from the web?

Yes, as long as you only download files from sites you trust. If you ever notice that Safari is attempting to download a file without your permission, cancel the download immediately because it is likely the file contains a virus or other malware. If you do not completely trust a file you have downloaded, use an antivirus program — such as ClamXav; see www.clamxav.com — to scan the file before you open it.

Using Top Sites in Safari

The Top Sites screen might be the first page you see when you launch Safari unless you have already set a default home page. The page is populated with websites that you visit frequently shown in a grid, and you can edit the layout to show your favorite sites in a more prominent position, pin sites to the page so that they can't be removed, and delete them if required. If new posts or updates are added to one of the sites included on your Top Sites page, a star appears over the website preview.

Using Top Sites in Safari

Access Top Sites

1. In the Dock, click the **Safari** icon (■).

Safari opens and the Top Sites page is shown.

Note: If Top Sites is not shown, you can access it by clicking **History** and then clicking **Show Top Sites**.

- A Click any of the website previews to visit the page.
- B Hover over a website preview and click the **Pin** (■) to keep the site in Top Sites permanently.

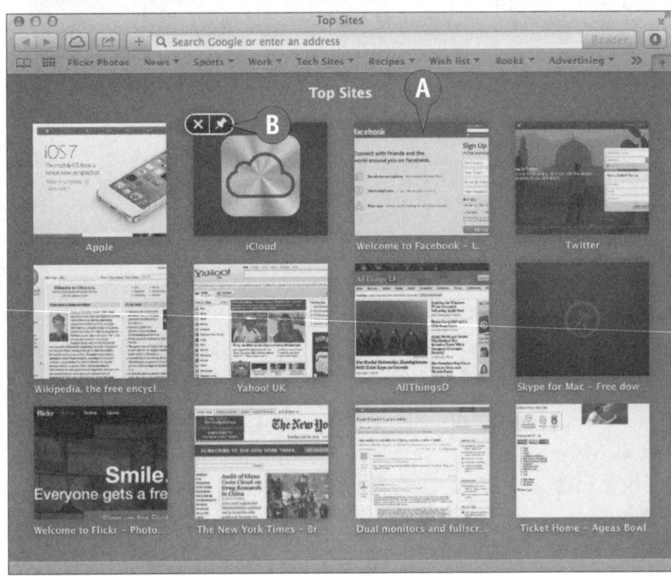

Delete and Move Top Sites

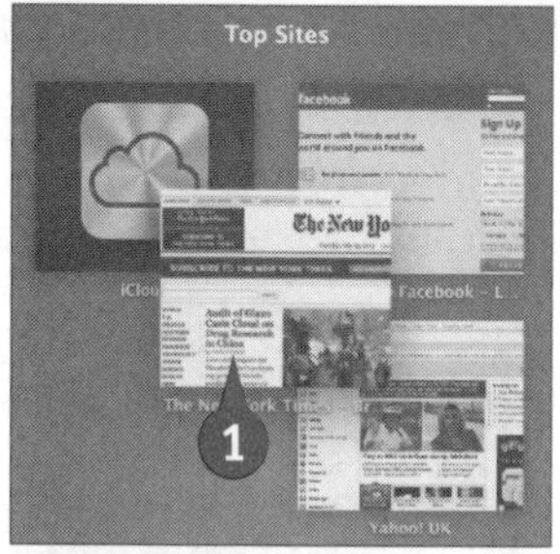

1. Click a site preview in Top Sites and drag it to a new position.

The other previews move out of the way and the preview slots into position when you drop it.

2. Hover the cursor over a site preview and click the X that appears.

The page is removed from Top Sites.

TIPS

How do I control which sites are shown in Top Sites?
The Top Sites screen is populated by the websites that you visit most often. When you first launch Safari, however, Top Sites will include suggested sites that you can choose to keep or remove as required.

How can I keep the same sites in Top Sites?
Over time, if you visit certain sites more than those in Top Sites they will begin to replace the existing sites. To prevent this from happening, click the **Pin** button (📌) that appears when you hover over a website preview with the cursor. This pins the site to the Top Sites page and prevents it from being replaced.

Using the Safari Sidebar

The Safari sidebar is a convenient addition to web browsing, as it allows you to find links you have saved as well as discover new websites and stories through social networks. The Safari sidebar is divided into three sections: Bookmarks, Reading List, and Shared Links. Bookmarks contain links you have saved, Reading List contains pages as they were at the time you saved them, and Shared Links pulls websites shared by friends from your linked social media accounts. When viewing links from the sidebar you can also scroll through each story one by one without having to click a link each time.

Using the Safari Sidebar

Access the Safari Sidebar

1. In the Dock, click the **Safari** icon (◉).
2. Click **View**.
3. Click **Show Sidebar**.

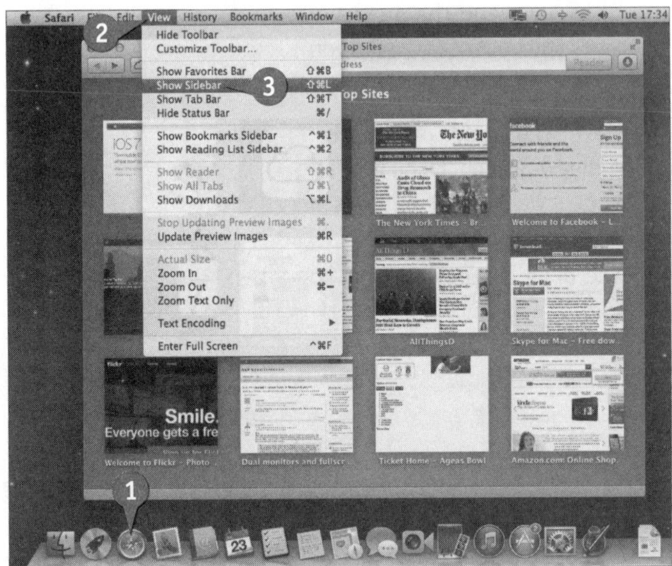

The sidebar appears.

Ⓐ Click **Bookmarks** to show your stored links.

Ⓑ Click **Reading List** to show pages you have saved to read later.

Ⓒ Click **Shared Links** to show pages shared by friends on social media accounts.

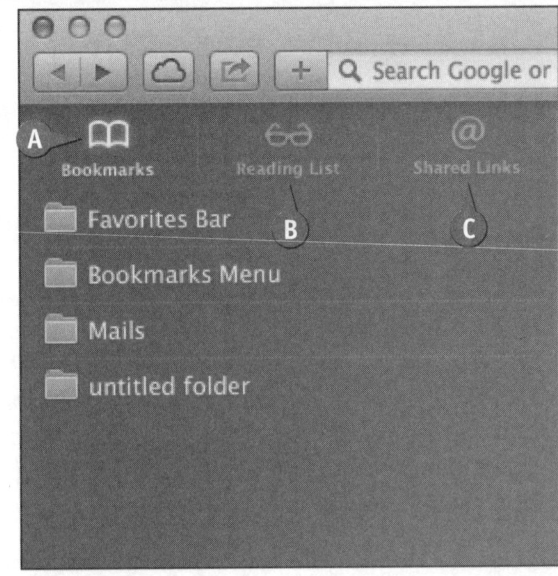

Scroll Through Sidebar Links

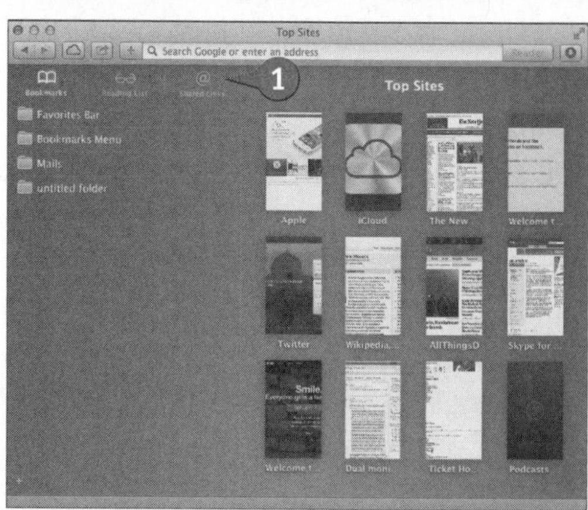

1 Click **Shared Links** in the sidebar.

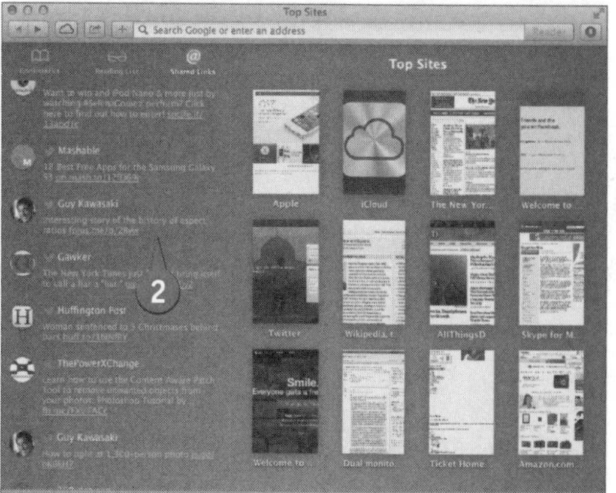

Links from your social media accounts appear.

2 Click a link you want to read.

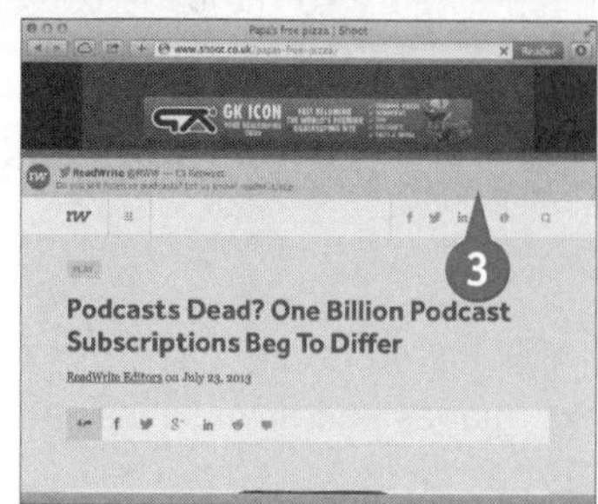

The website appears.

3 Scroll down the page using your mouse or trackpad. When you reach the end of the page, the next link loads automatically.

TIPS

How do I remove sites from my Reading List?
When you hover the cursor over a Reading List item in the Safari sidebar, an X appears. Click the X to remove the link from your Reading List.

What do the sidebar bookmark folders do?
Folders shown in the sidebar under the Bookmarks section contain links to websites. If you have already created bookmark folders they will appear in this section, and you can also add a new folder by clicking the plus button at the bottom left of the sidebar.

Share Links with the Share Button

Using the Safari Share button, you can quickly send links to a variety of locations with a couple of clicks. Whether you want to store links to websites in your Bookmarks or save pages in your Reading List, send them in an e-mail, via Messages, to social networks, or other Macs using AirDrop, you simply need to navigate to the page and click the **Share** button. From the menu that appears you can then choose the option you want to use to share the link.

Share Links with the Share Button

1. In the Dock, click the **Safari** icon (![icon]).

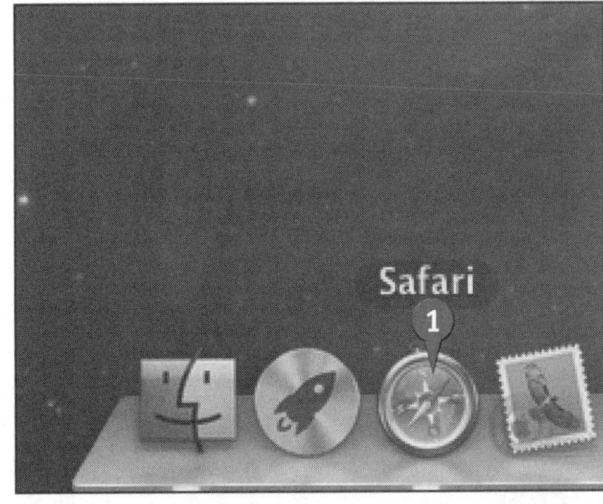

Safari appears.

2. Navigate to the page you want to share.
3. Click the **Share** button (![icon]).

The Share menu appears.

4 Click your chosen sharing method.

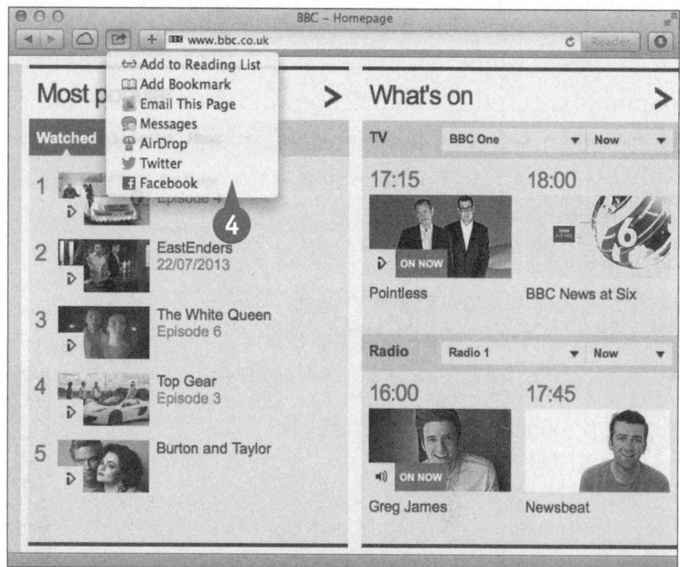

An interface for your chosen application appears.

Note: If you choose **Add to Reading List**, the page is added automatically and no interface appears.

Note: Different applications and services may provide a different button to share the link. Facebook, for example, has a Post button and Twitter has a Send button.

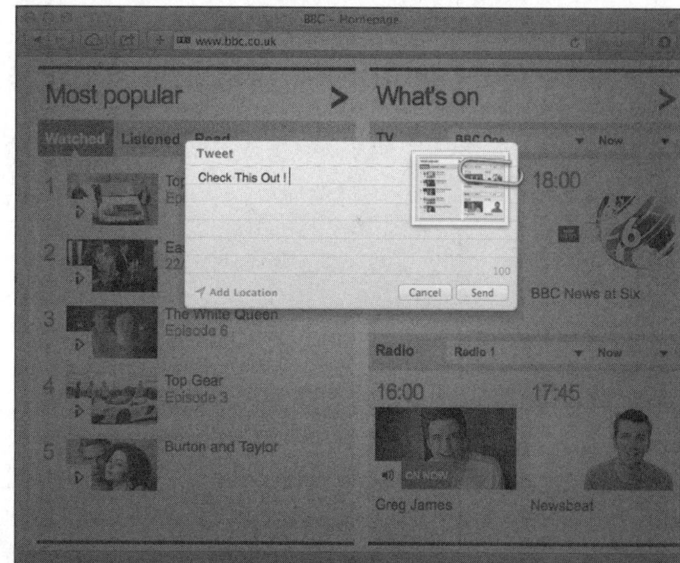

TIP

I don't have the option to post to Twitter or Facebook. Why?

Social media accounts need to first be set up within the System Preferences pane under the Internet Accounts section. Add a new account by clicking the relevant logo and typing your username and password. You can do this for as many accounts as you want. When you return to Safari, the accounts you have added will be available, and you won't need to type your username and password each time.

Turn On Private Browsing

Private Browsing is a Safari feature that prevents any information about your browsing being recorded while it is turned on. This can be very useful if you use a shared computer or are planning a surprise for someone who may access your computer, as no history or search information is stored in Safari as it would be normally. Information you enter into fields such as usernames and passwords are also not recorded.

Turn On Private Browsing

Turn Private Browsing On

1. In the Dock, click the **Safari** icon (◙).

Safari appears.

2. Click **Safari**.
3. Click **Private Browsing**.

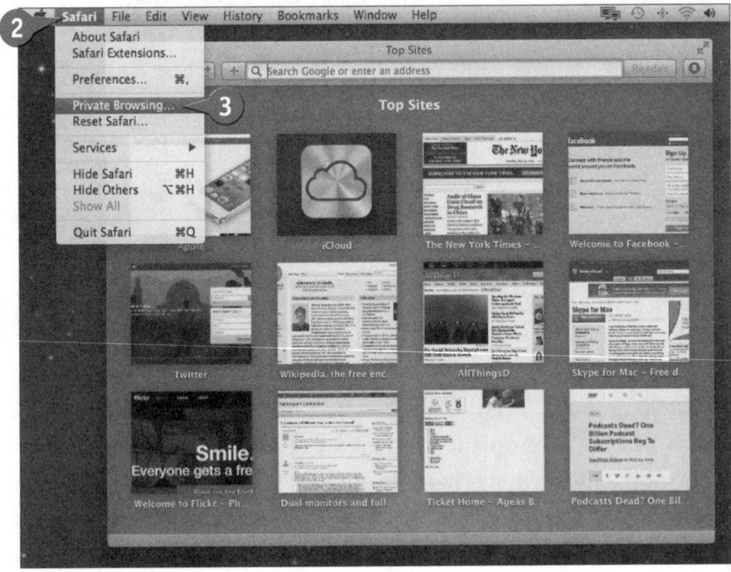

A pop-up window appears.

4 Click **OK**.

Private browsing is now turned on.

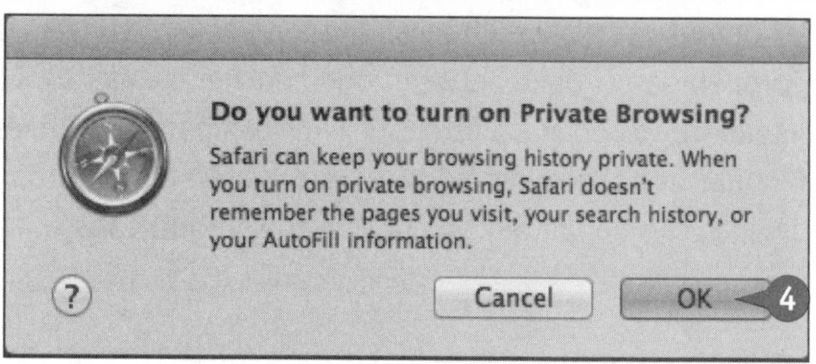

Turn Private Browsing Off

1 Click **Private** in the search bar.

A popup menu appears.

2 Click **OK**.

Private Browsing is now turned off.

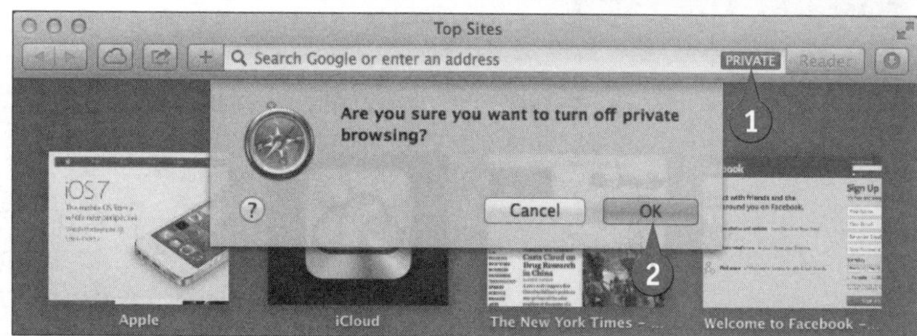

TIP

What does Private Browsing prevent?
Private Browsing prevents websites from tracking your information and also stops web pages from being added to the history list. It also prevents downloaded items from being included on the download list and stops searches from being added to the address and search pop-up menus. With Private Browsing turned on, no other computer connected to the same iCloud account can view your iCloud tabs or your Reading List and Bookmarks. Cookies are also not collected, nor is AutoFill information from fields on websites such as searches, credit card details, and contact forms.

Access iCloud Tabs

Computers, iPads, iPhones, and iPod touch devices connected to the same iCloud account can share open Safari links between one another thanks to iCloud tabs. In order for the feature to work, iCloud must be set up on all of your compatible devices via the Settings app on iOS devices like iPhones and iPads and within System Preferences on a Mac. Once set up, all open web pages on all devices can be viewed by clicking the **iCloud Tabs** button.

Access iCloud Tabs

1. In the Dock, click the **Safari** icon (🧭).

Safari appears.

2. Click the **iCloud Tabs** button (☁).

A menu listing all web pages open on your iCloud devices appears.

Ⓐ The website icon appears next to each site if available.

Ⓑ Sites are divided into sections based on which device they are on.

3 Click the link you want to view on your Mac.

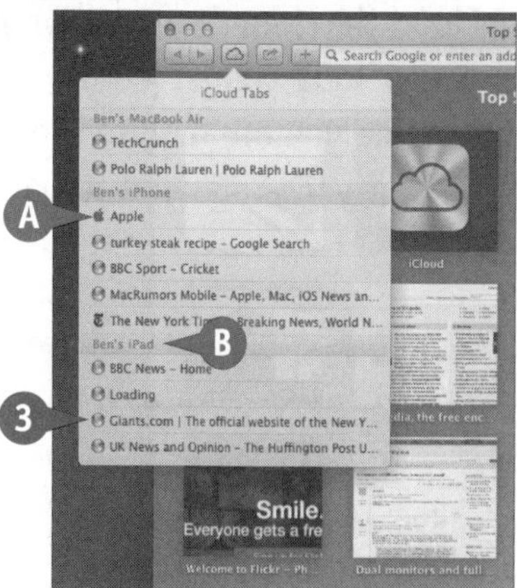

The website loads in Safari.

TIP

Why can't I see sites loaded on my iPhone, iPad, iPod touch, or Mac?

iCloud Tabs syncing is not always instant. You may have to wait a little while before you see sites you recently loaded on another device. If you want to speed up the process, try closing Safari on your Mac by pressing ⌘ + Q and then launch it again to force it to check for new pages. Also check to make sure that the same iCloud account is in use on all of your devices and that each device is connected to the Internet via either Wi-Fi or cellular data.

Sync Passwords Between Devices

iCloud Keychain keeps all of your passwords stored securely online and syncs them between all of your iCloud connected devices. So, for example, if you type a password in Safari on your iPad, the next time you are required to type the password on your Mac, Safari remembers it and autofills the fields for you. You need to have iCloud set up on all of your devices for iCloud Keychain to work.

Sync Passwords Between Devices

1 In the Dock, click the **System Preferences** icon ().

2 Click **iCloud**.

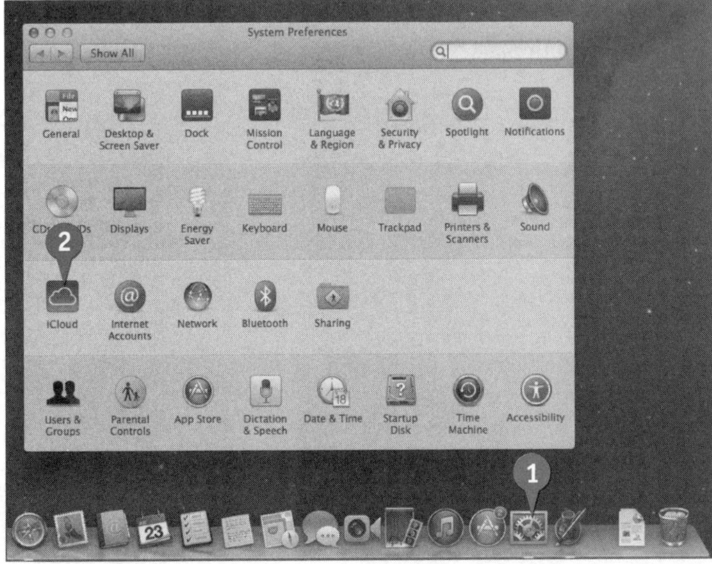

The iCloud dialog appears.

3 Scroll down to Keychain and select the check box next to it (changes to).

Note: If iCloud isn't set up already, you need to type your iCloud account details or create an account.

4. Type your iCloud password into the field that appears.
5. Click **OK**.

6. Type a memorable security code into the fields provided.
7. Click **Next**.

8. Type your country's telephone code into the first field.
9. Type your cell phone number into the second field.
10. Click **Next**.

iCloud Keychain is now set up.

TIP

Is it safe to sync information in this way?

Passwords and banking details stored with iCloud Keychain are only sent to devices you have previously approved and that have iCloud Keychain turned on. Your information is protected with powerful AES 256-bit encryption that is highly difficult to crack, and this encryption is in place when passwords are stored on your devices and when they are transferred between devices for maximum security. iCloud Keychain does not store your credit card security codes, either, so even if someone was able to access your information, he would be unable to use your bank details to make purchases.

Using the Password Generator

When iCloud Keychain is set up and turned on, it can be used to create unique, strong passwords that remain in sync across all of your iCloud-connected devices. When you come to type a password on your Mac, a suggested password is generated and automatically added to your iCloud Keychain if you choose to use it. This provides an easy way to create secure passwords without having to remember them each time you log in.

Using the Password Generator

1. In the Dock, click the **Safari** icon (◉).

Safari appears.

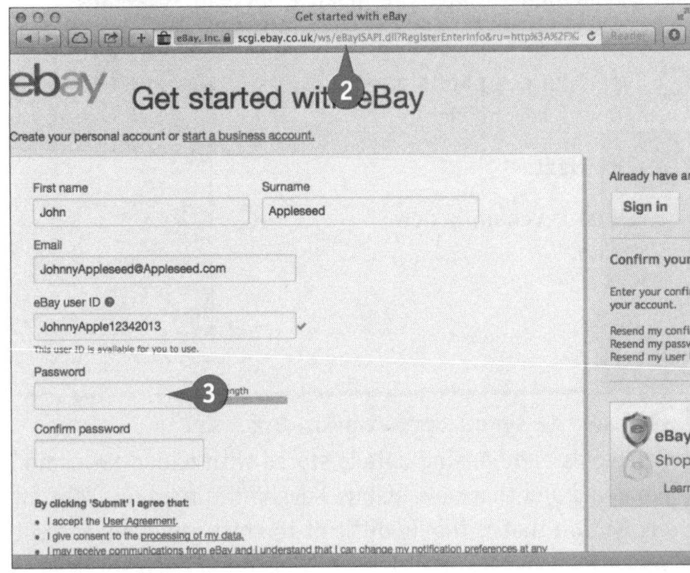

2. Navigate to the signup page for the service for which you want to create a password.
3. Type your information into the fields, and then click the Password field.

A suggested password appears.

4 Click the password to use it with this service.

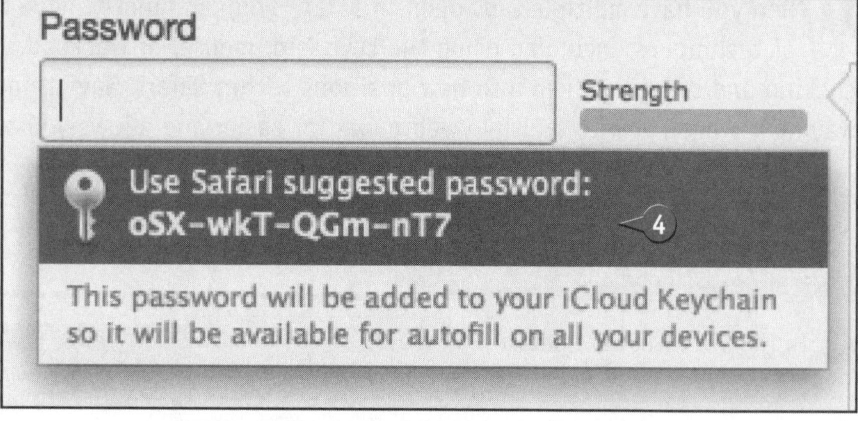

The password is added to both the Password field and the Confirm password field and stored in your iCloud Keychain.

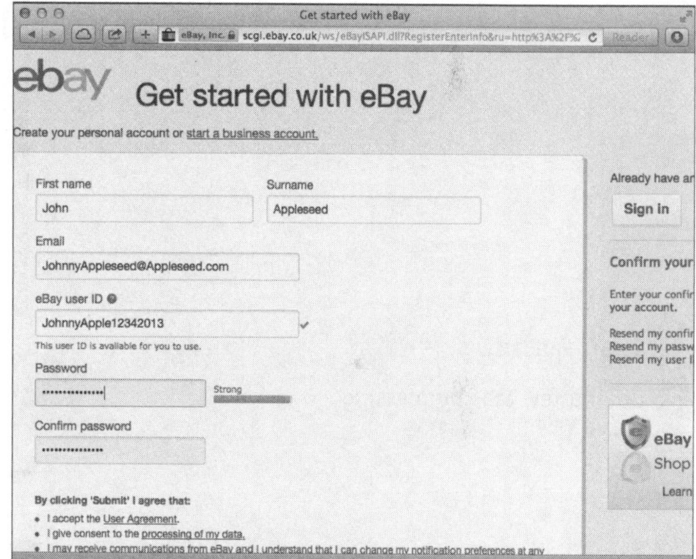

TIP

How will I be able to remember such a complex password?

You don't have to remember the password. Because iCloud Keychain stores the suggested password automatically, it is entered automatically when it is required when using any of your iCloud-connected devices. The only time you need to remember your password is if you log in to a site from a shared computer or device, or one that is not connected to your iCloud account. If there are services that you regularly use outside of your iCloud devices it may be best to choose a more memorable password rather than use iCloud Keychain.

Navigate Open Tabs in Safari

When you have multiple tabs open in Safari, you can quickly move between them using a number of techniques, including using the keyboard, mouse, or trackpad. You can also reposition tabs by clicking and dragging them into new positions within Safari. Navigating and organizing tabs in this way makes dealing with multiple web pages far easier and allows you to browse much faster.

Navigate Open Tabs in Safari

1. In the Dock, click the **Safari** icon (🧭).

Safari appears.

2. Open a few tabs by pressing ⌘+T.

3 Pinch two fingers together on the trackpad to show all open tabs.

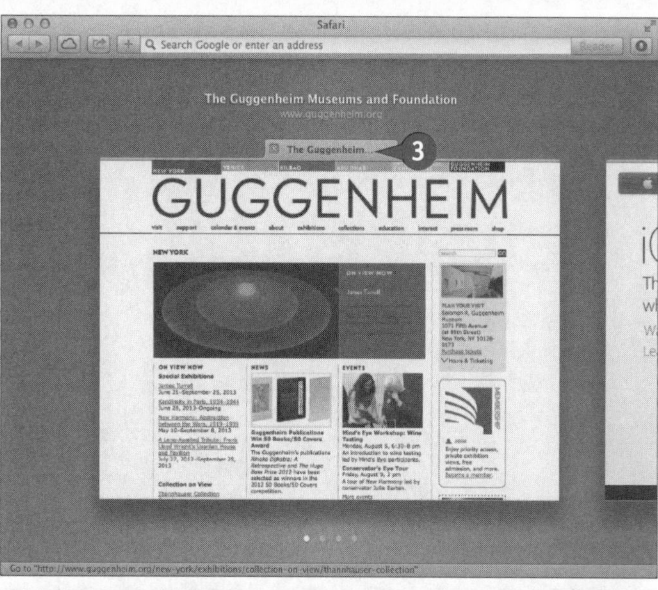

All open tabs are shown.

4 Swipe across the trackpad with two fingers to move between different tabs.

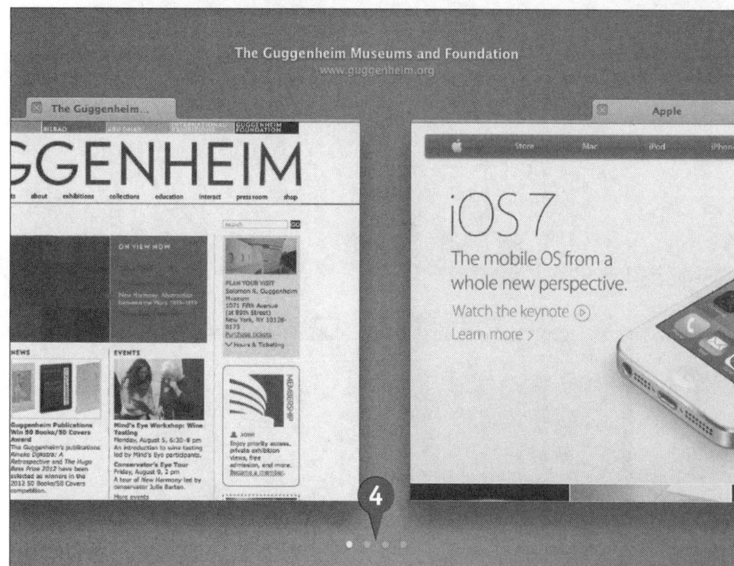

TIP

How else can I switch between tabs?

You can jump between tabs in the normal manner by clicking the name of the tab you want to view or, alternatively, you can use the keyboard to move to the Previous Tab by pressing Shift + Ctrl + Tab, or the next tab by pressing Ctrl + Tab. If you are using a Magic Mouse you can click **Show All Tabs** from the View menu and then swipe left or right to move between tabs.

CHAPTER 5

Communicating via E-mail

OS X comes with the Apple Mail application that you can use to exchange e-mail messages. After you type your account details into Mail, you can send e-mail to friends, family, colleagues, and even total strangers almost anywhere in the world.

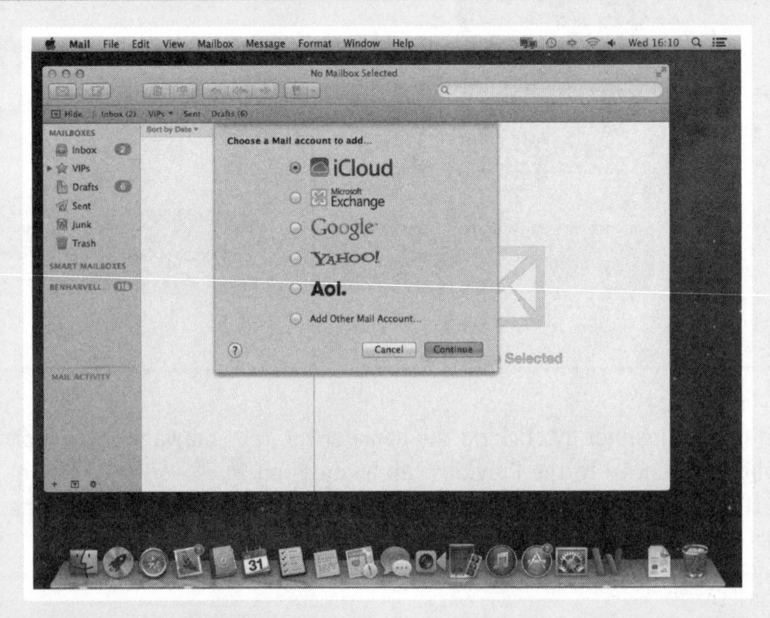

Open and Close Mail

OS X includes the Apple Mail application to enable you to use an e-mail account to exchange and manage e-mail messages. E-mail is one of the most popular Internet services because it offers three main advantages: it is universal, fast, and convenient. E-mail is universal because nearly anyone who can access the Internet has an e-mail address. E-mail is fast because messages are generally delivered within a few minutes. E-mail is convenient because you can send messages at any time of day, and your recipient does not need to be at the computer in order to receive it. Before you can send or receive e-mail messages, you must know how to start the Mail application.

Open and Close Mail

Open Mail

1. In the Dock, click the **Mail** icon (■).

Note: If the Welcome to Mail dialog appears, see the section "Add an E-mail Account" to learn how to set up your first e-mail account in Mail.

The Mail window appears.

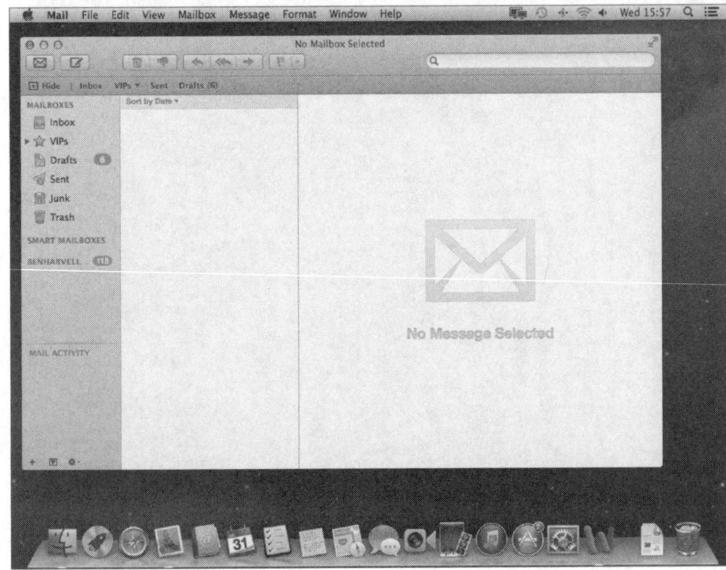

Close Mail

1 Click **Mail**.

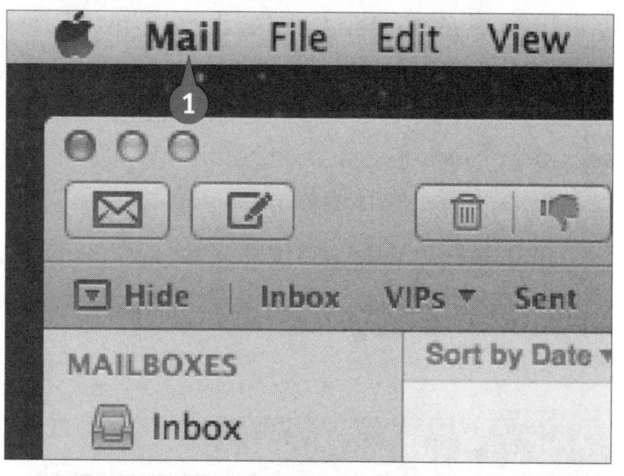

2 Click **Quit Mail**.

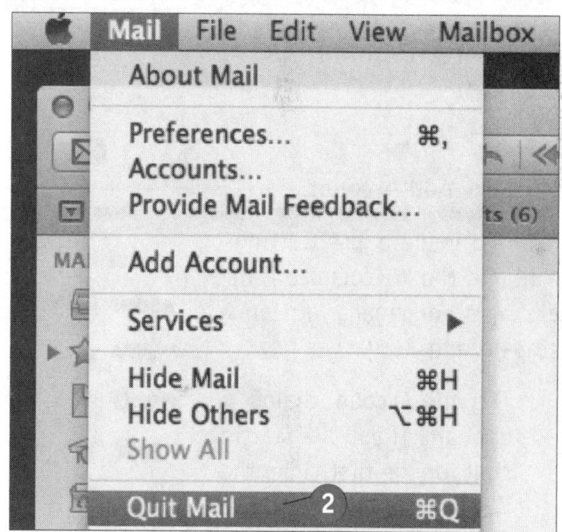

TIPS

Are there other methods I can use to open Mail?

If you have removed the icon from the Dock, there are a couple of other quick methods you can use to start Mail. If you have used Mail recently, click the **Apple** icon ( ), click **Recent Items**, and then click **Safari**. You can also click **Spotlight** ( ), type **Mail**, and then click **Mail** in the search results.

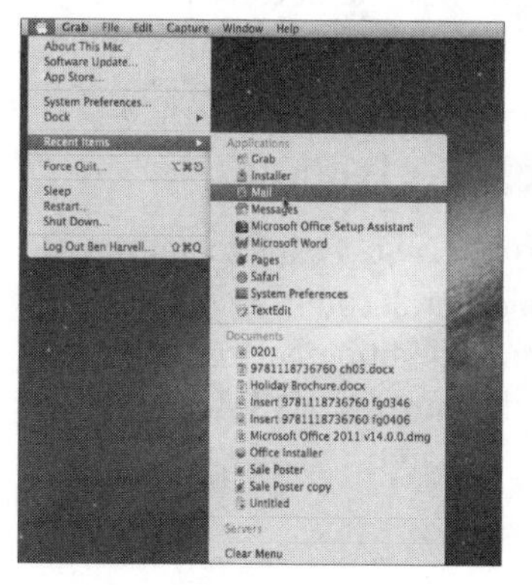

Are there faster methods I can use to close Mail?

Probably the fastest method you can use to quit Mail is to right-click its icon ( ) in the Dock and then click **Quit**. If your hands are closer to the keyboard than to the mouse, you can quit Mail by switching to the application and then pressing ⌘ + Q.

Add an E-mail Account

Before you can send and receive e-mail messages, you must add your e-mail account to the Mail application. Your e-mail account is usually a POP (Post Office Protocol) account supplied by your Internet service provider, which should have supplied you with the POP account details. You can also set up web-based e-mail accounts with services such as Hotmail and Gmail. A web-based account is convenient because it enables you to send and receive messages from any computer.

If you have an Apple ID — that is, an account for use on the Apple iCloud service (www.icloud.com) — you can also set up Mail with your Apple account details.

Add an E-mail Account

Get Started Adding an Account

1 Click **Mail**.

2 Click **Add Account.**

Note: If you are just starting Mail and the Welcome to Mail dialog is on-screen, you can skip steps 1 and 2.

The Add Account dialog appears. If you are starting Mail for the first time, the Welcome to Mail dialog is identical.

Add an iCloud Account

1 Click the button next to iCloud on the Add Account screen (◯ changes to ◉).

2 Click **Continue**.

Note: If you want to set up another account type, click the corresponding button or select **Add Another Mail Account** (◯ changes to ◉).

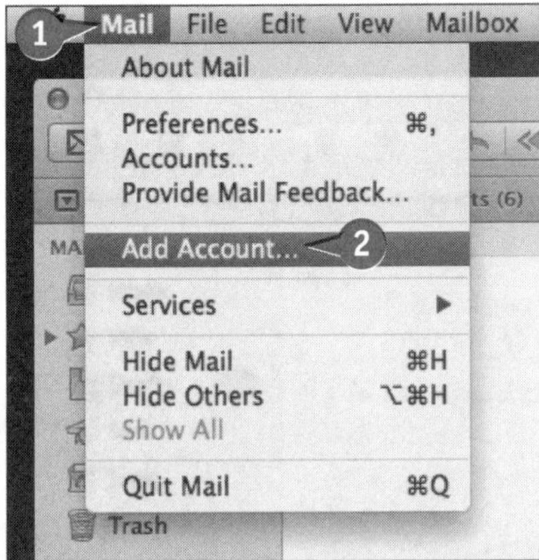

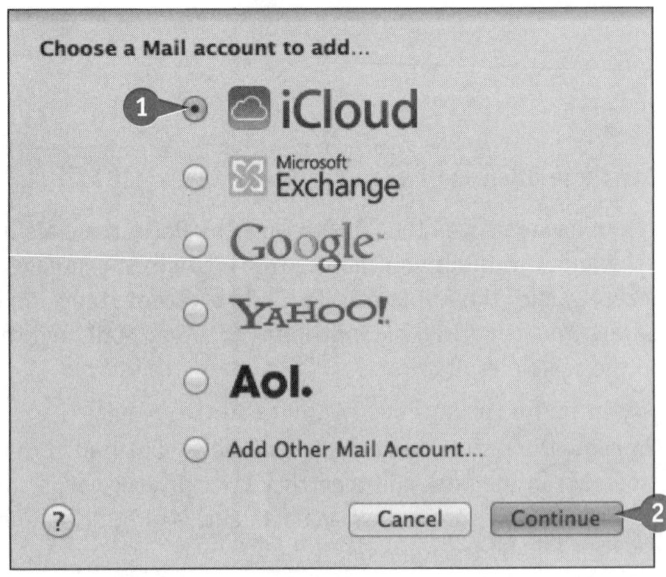

The iCloud Mail setup pane appears.

3 Type your e-mail address and password.

Note: If you don't have an Apple ID or iCloud account, click **Create Apple ID...**

4 Click **Sign In**.

5 Click **Add Account**.

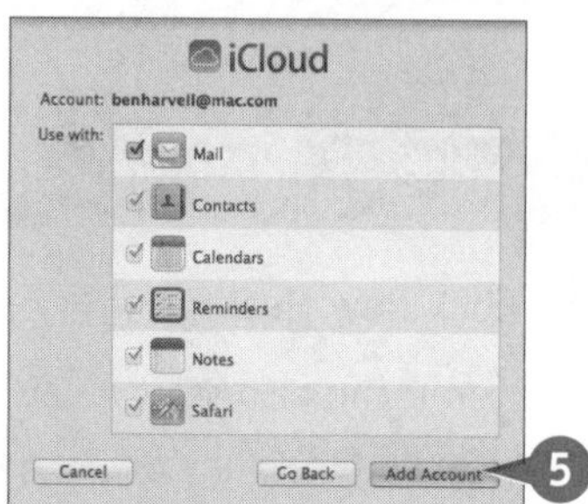

Your iCloud account is added to Mail.

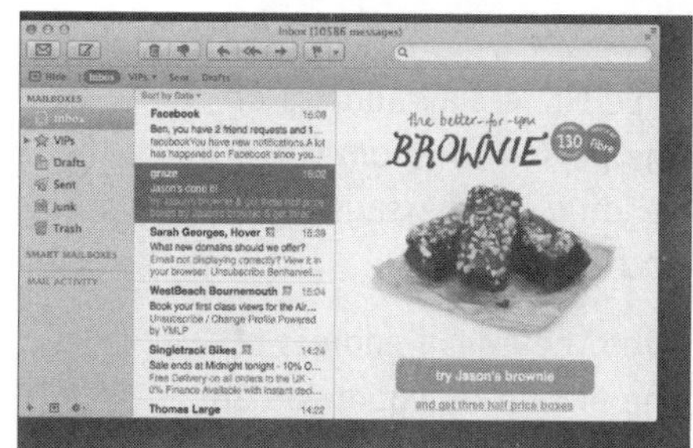

TIP

How many mail accounts can I add?

You can add as many accounts as you like by clicking **Mail** and then clicking **Add Account**. If you add multiple accounts of the same type, it is best to add a unique description for each account so that you can tell them apart in the sidebar. If not, you may find it difficult to differentiate between multiple accounts of the same type, such as iCloud, Gmail, or Yahoo!.

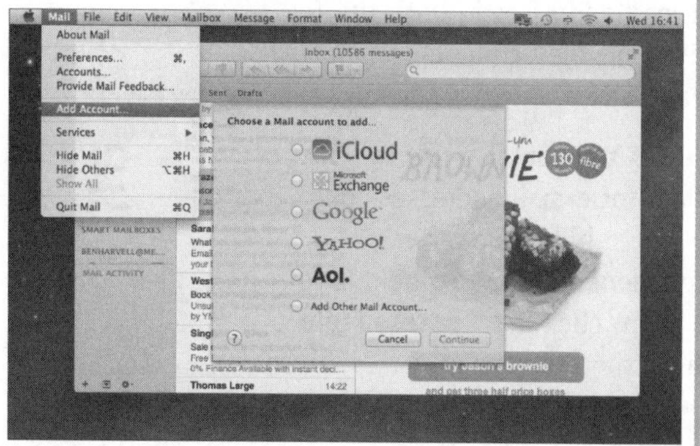

If you know the e-mail address of a person or organization, you can send an e-mail message to that address. An e-mail address is a set of characters that uniquely identifies the location of an Internet mailbox. Each e-mail address takes the form *username@domain*, where *username* is the name of the person's account with the ISP or within his or her organization; and *domain* is the Internet name of the company that provides the person's e-mail account. When you send an e-mail message, it travels through your ISP's outgoing mail server. This server routes the messages to the recipient's incoming mail server, which then stores the message in the recipient's mailbox.

Send an E-mail Message

1. Click **New Message** ( ).

Note: You can also start a new message by pressing ⌘ + N.

A message window appears.

2. Type the e-mail address of the person to whom you are sending the message in the To field box.

3. Type the e-mail address of the person to whom you are sending a copy of the message in the Cc field.

Note: You can add multiple e-mail addresses in both the To line and the Cc line by separating each address with a comma (,).

Note: You can also use the Bcc field for e-mail addresses you want to hide from other recipients. If the Bcc field isn't shown, click **Bcc Address Field** from the **View** menu.

4. Type a brief description of the message in the Subject field.

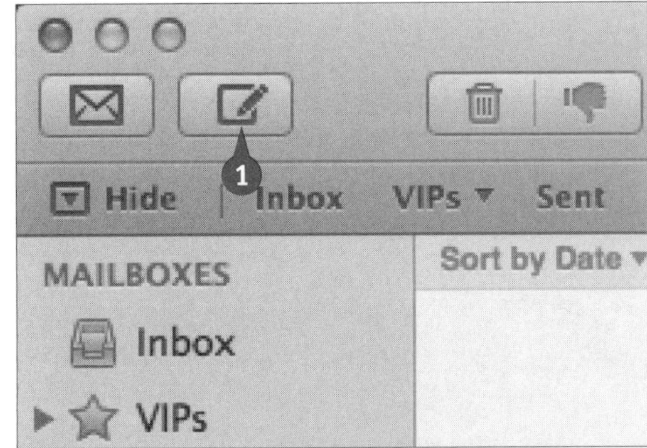

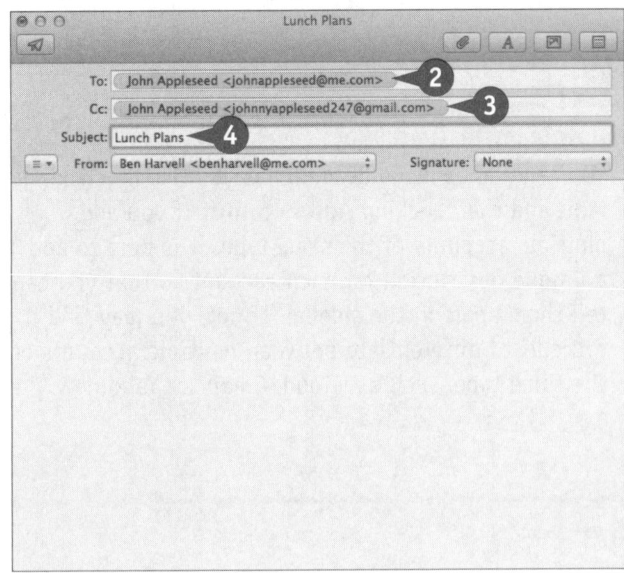

5 Type the message.

A To change the message font, click **Fonts** (A) to display the Font panel.

B To change the overall look of the message, click **Show Stationery** (▤) and then click a theme.

Note: Many people use e-mail programs that cannot process text formatting. Unless you are sure your recipient's program supports formatting, it is best to send plain-text messages. To do this, click **Format** and then click **Make Plain Text.**

6 Click **Send** (✈).

Mail sends your message.

Note: Mail stores a copy of your message in the Sent folder.

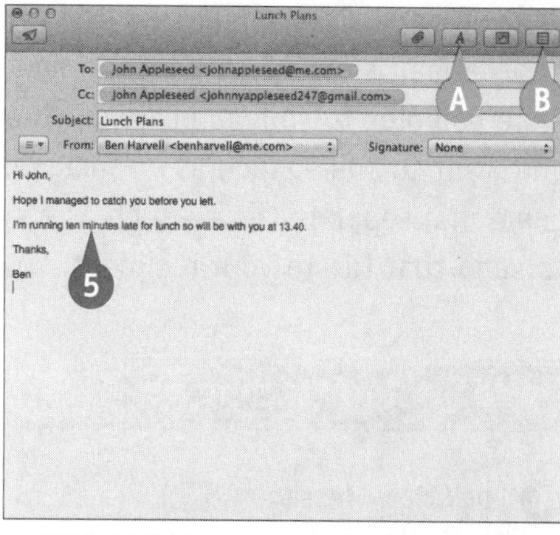

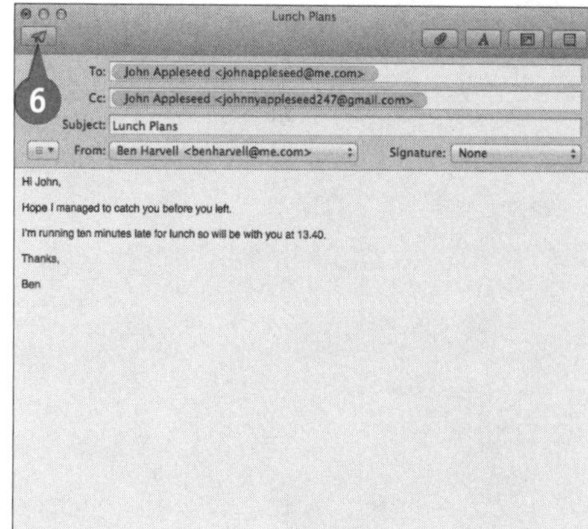

TIP

I have a large number of messages to compose. Do I have to be online to do this?

No, you can compose all the messages while you are offline. Follow these steps:

1 While disconnected from the Internet, start Mail.

2 To ensure you are working offline, click **Mailbox**. If the Take All Accounts Offline command is enabled, click that command.

3 Compose and send the message. Each time you click **Send** (✈), your message is stored temporarily in the Outbox folder.

4 When you finish, connect to the Internet.

After a few moments, Mail automatically sends all the messages in the Outbox folder.

Add a File Attachment

If you have a document that you want to send to another person, you can attach the document to an e-mail message. A typical e-mail message is fine for short notes, but you may have something more complex to communicate, such as budget numbers or a slide show, or some form of media that you want to share, such as an image or a song. Because these more complex types of data usually come in a separate file — such as a spreadsheet, presentation file, or picture file — it makes sense to send that file to your recipient. You do this by attaching the file to an e-mail message.

Add a File Attachment

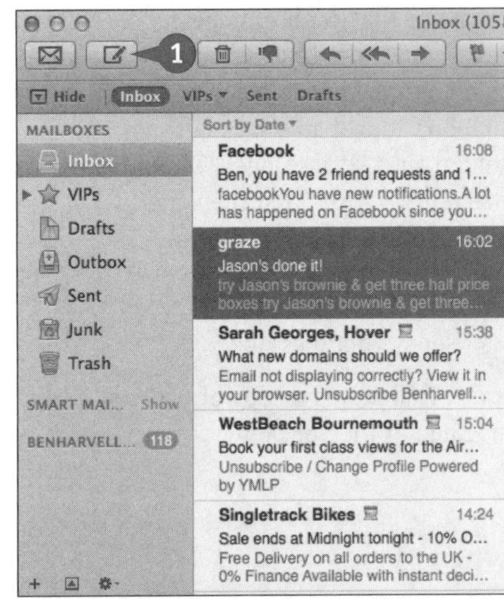

1. Click **New Message** (✎).

   A message window appears.

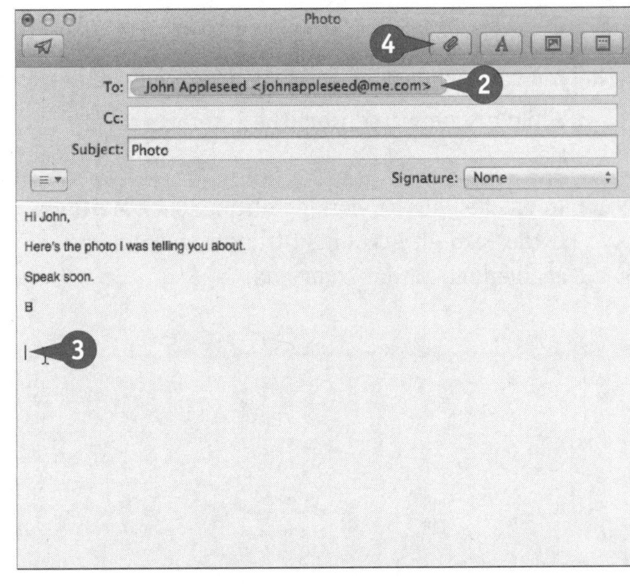

2. Fill in the recipients, subject, and message text as described in the previous section.
3. Press Return two or three times to move the cursor a few lines below your message.
4. Click **Attach** (📎).

   A file selection dialog appears.

5. Click the file you want to attach.
6. Click **Choose File**.

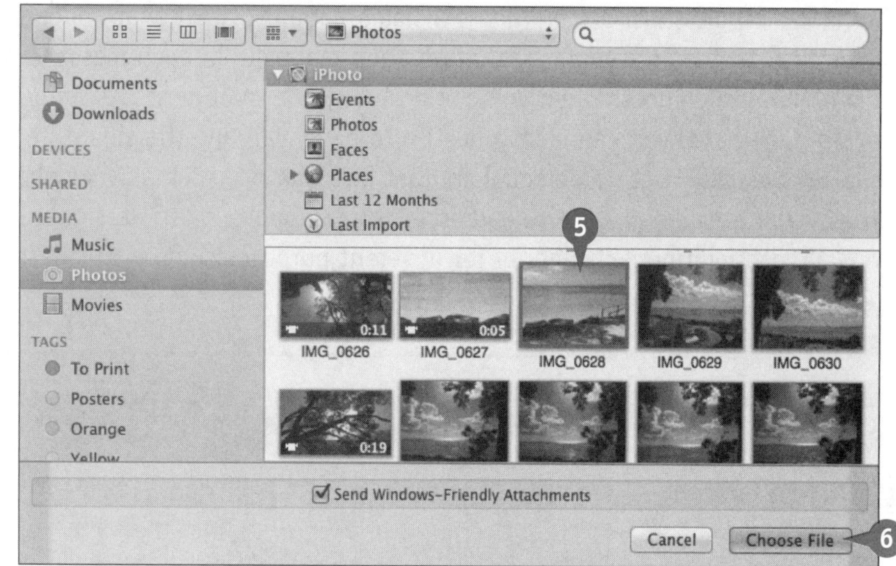

A. Mail attaches the file to the message.

Note: Another way to attach a file to a message is to click and drag the file from Finder and drop it inside the message.

7. Repeat steps **4** to **6** to attach additional files to the message.

Note: To reduce the size of your e-mail when sending photos and other images, you can use the Image Size menu to adjust how large the attached photos are. The size of the e-mail is shown above the message.

8. Click **Send** (![send icon]).

   Mail sends your message.

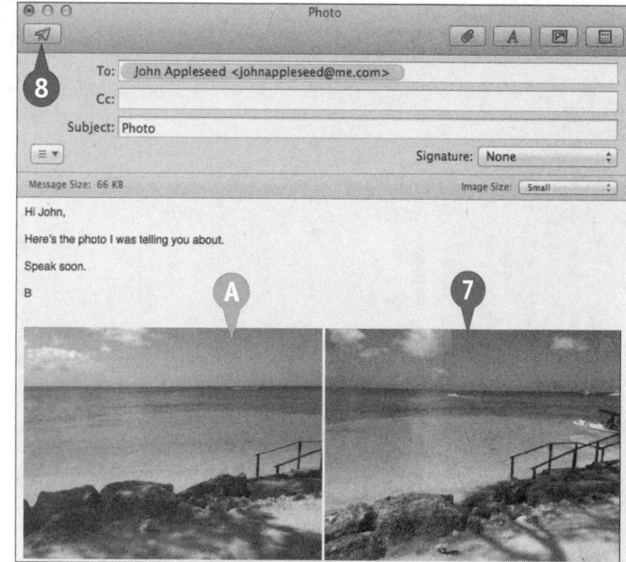

TIP

Is there a limit to the number of files I can attach to a message?

The number of files you can attach to the message has no practical limit. However, you should be careful with the total *size* of the message, including attachments, you send to someone. If either of you has a slow Internet connection, then sending or receiving the message can take an extremely long time. Also, many ISPs place a limit on the size of a message's attachments, which is usually between 2MB and 5MB. In general, use e-mail to send only a few small files at a time.

Add a Signature

In an e-mail message, a *signature* is a small amount of text that appears at the bottom of the message. Instead of typing this information manually in each message, you can save the signature in your Mail preferences. When you compose a new e-mail message, reply to an existing message, or forward a message, you can click a button to have Mail add the signature to your outgoing message. Signatures usually contain personal contact information, such as your phone numbers, business address, and e-mail and website addresses. Mail supports multiple signatures, which is useful if you use Mail with multiple accounts or for different purposes such as business and personal.

Add a Signature

Create a Signature

1. Click **Mail**.
2. Click **Preferences**.

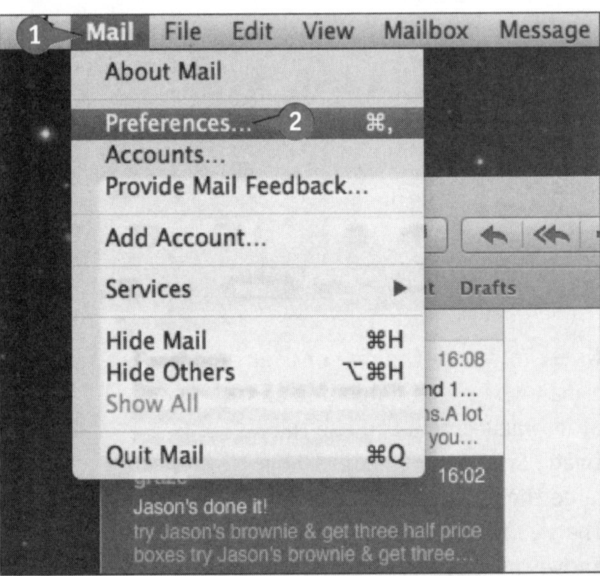

The Mail preferences appear.

3. Click **Signatures**.
4. Click the account for which you want to use the signature.
5. Click the **Plus** button.

Mail adds a new signature.

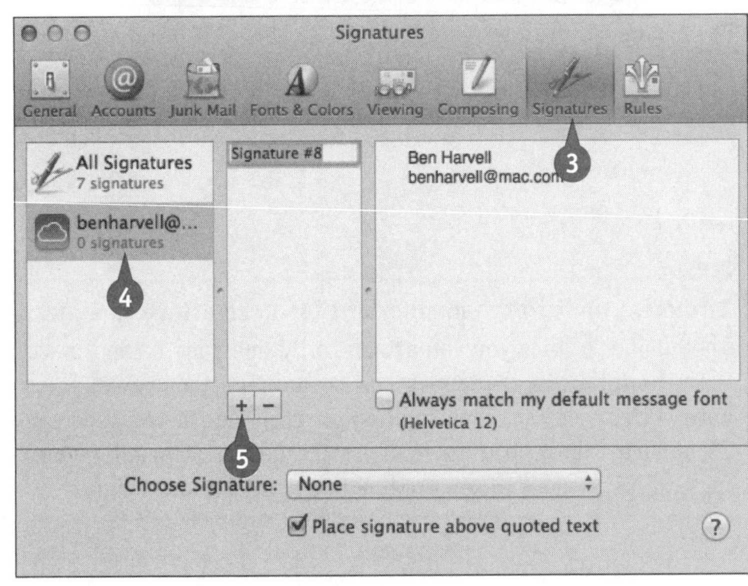

6 Type a name for the signature.

7 Type the signature text.

Repeat steps 4 to 7 to add other signatures, if required.

Note: You can add as many signatures as you want.

8 Click **Close** (●).

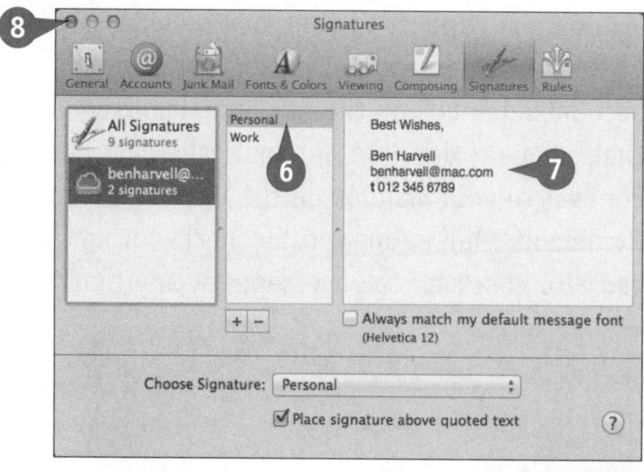

Insert the Signature

1 Click **New Message** (✎) to start a new message.

Note: To start a new message, see the section "Send an E-mail Message."

2 In the message text area, move the insertion point to the location where you want the signature to appear.

3 Click the **Signature** ⬍ and then click the signature you want to insert.

A The signature appears in the message.

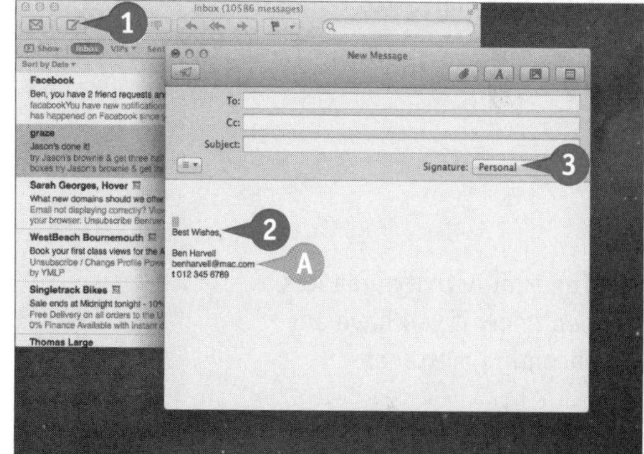

TIP

When I have multiple signatures, how can I choose which of them Mail adds automatically?

1 Follow steps 1 to 4 to display the signature preferences and choose an account.

2 Click ⬍ and then click the signature you want to insert automatically into each message.

A If you prefer to add a signature manually, click **None** instead of a signature.

3 Click **Close** (●).

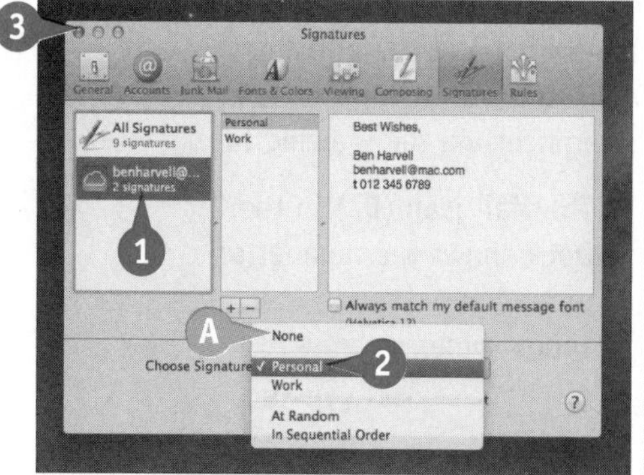

Receive and Read E-mail Messages

You must connect to your mail provider's incoming mail server to retrieve and read messages sent to you. When another person sends you an e-mail message, that message ends up in your e-mail account's mailbox on the incoming mail server maintained by your ISP or e-mail provider. However, that company does not automatically pass along that message to you. Instead, you must use Mail to connect to your mailbox on the incoming mail server and then retrieve any messages waiting for you. By default, Mail automatically checks for new messages every 5 minutes while you are online, but you can also check for new messages at any time or set another automatic interval.

Receive and Read E-mail Messages

Receive E-mail Messages

1 Click **Get Mail** (✉).

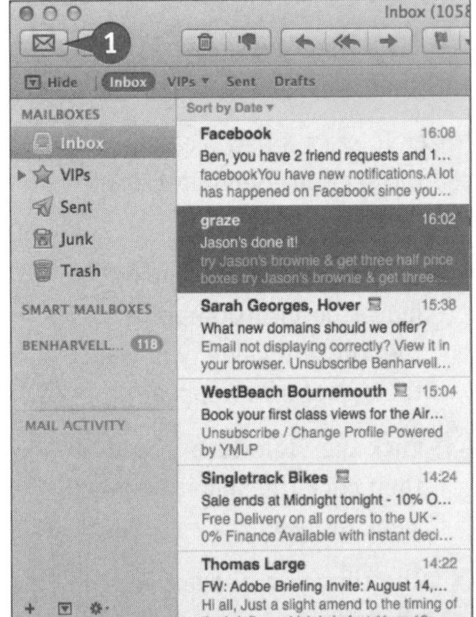

A The Mail Activity area lets you know if you have any incoming messages.

B If you have new messages, they appear in your Inbox folder with a blue dot in this column.

Note: For a simpler layout, you can use the classic Mail layout, where all e-mails are listed at the top of the screen with the preview pane at the bottom. This can be turned on in Mail Preferences via the Viewing tab.

C The Mail icon (✉) in the Dock shows the number of unread messages in the Inbox folder.

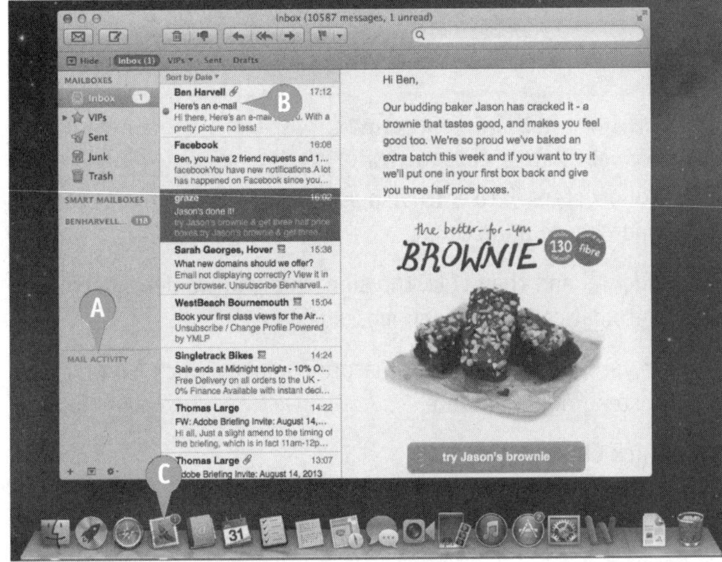

Read a Message

1 Click the message.

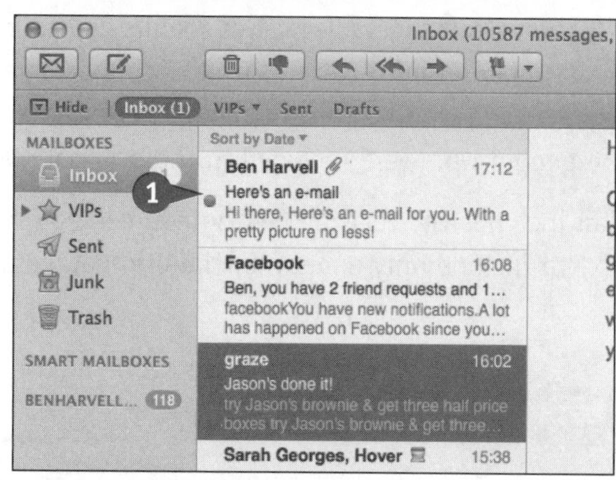

2 Read the message text in the preview pane.

Note: If you want to open the message in its own window, double-click the message.

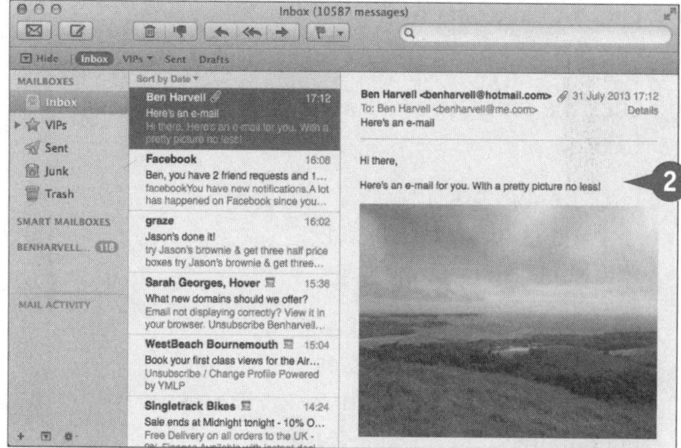

TIP

Can I change how often Mail automatically checks for messages?

Yes, by following these steps:

1 Click **Mail**.

2 Click **Preferences**.

The Mail preferences appear.

3 Click the **General** tab.

4 In the Check for new messages pop-up menu, click ⬍ and then click the time interval that you want Mail to use when checking for new messages automatically.

A If you do not want Mail to check for messages automatically, click **Manually** instead.

5 Click **Close** (⊗).

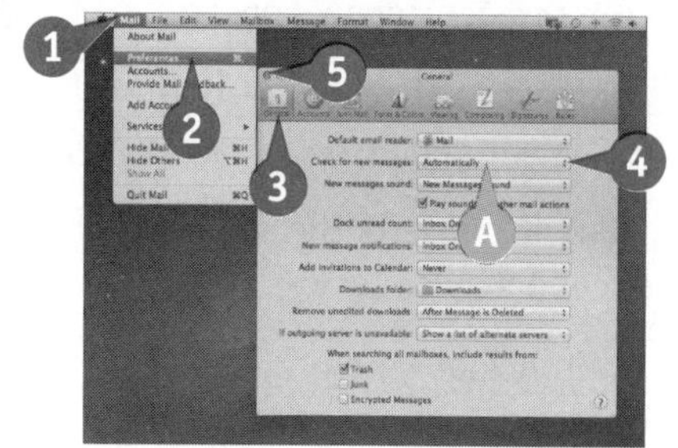

Reply to a Message

When a message you receive requires some kind of response — whether it is answering a question, supplying information, or providing comments — you can reply to that message. Most replies go only to the person who sent the original message. However, it is also possible to send the reply to all the people who were included in the original message's To and Cc lines.

Mail includes the text of the original message in the reply, but you should edit the original message text to include only enough of the original message to put your reply into context.

Reply to a Message

1. Click the message to which you want to reply.
2. Click the reply type you want to use.

   Click **Reply** ( ) to respond only to the person who sent the message.

   Click **Reply All** ( ) to respond to all the addresses in the message's From, To, and Cc lines.

   A message window appears.

A. Mail automatically inserts the recipient addresses.

B. Mail also inserts the subject line, preceded by Re:.

C. Mail includes the original message text at the bottom of the reply.

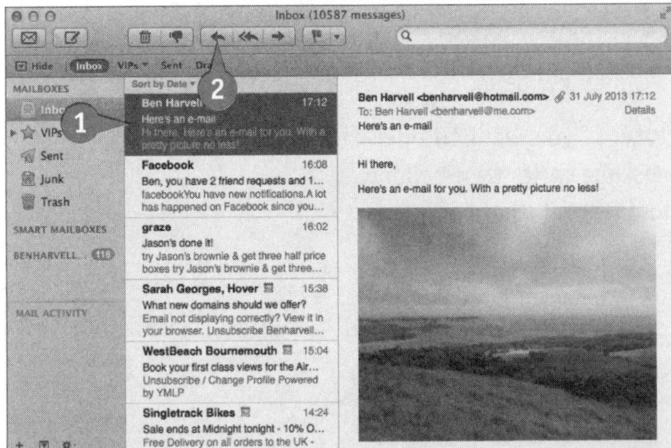

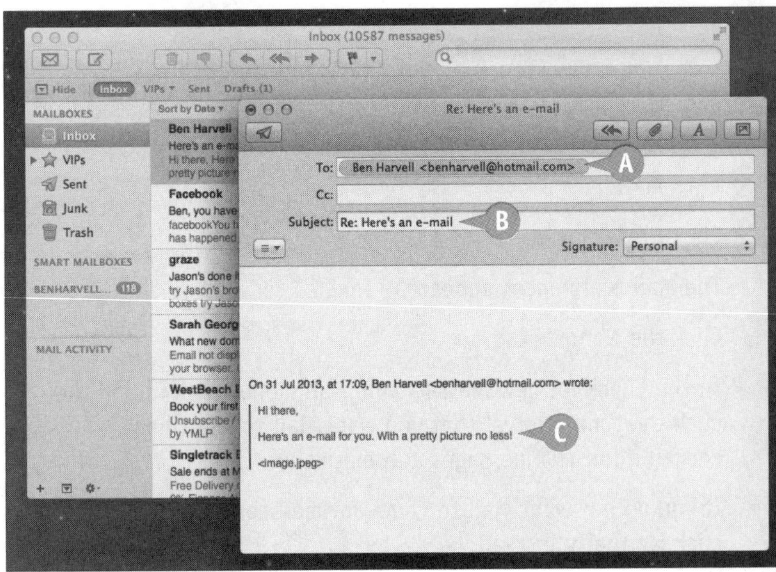

3 Edit the original message to include only the text that is relevant to your reply.

Note: You can also select text in the original message before clicking **Reply** to quote only that passage.

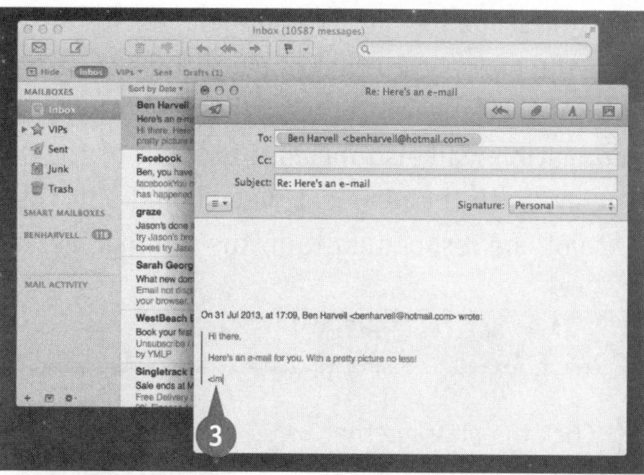

4 Click the area above the original message text and type your reply.

5 Click **Send** ( ).

Mail sends your reply.

Note: Mail stores a copy of your reply in the Sent folder.

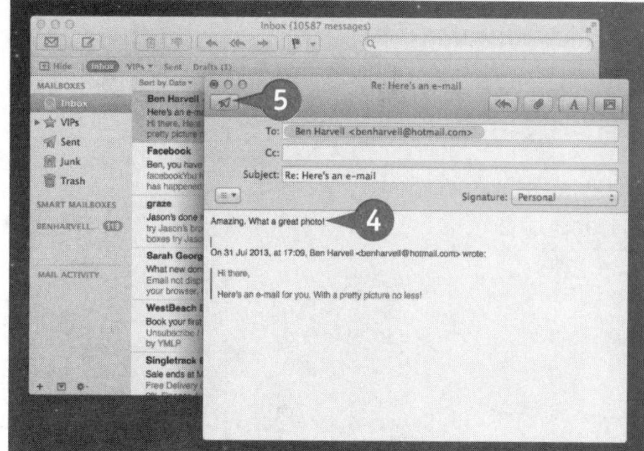

TIPS

I received a message inadvertently. Is there a way that I can pass it along to the correct recipient?

Yes. Mail comes with a feature that enables you to pass along inadvertent messages to the correct recipient. Click the message that you received inadvertently, click **Message**, and then click **Redirect** (or press Shift + ⌘ + E). Type the recipient's address and then click **Send**. Replies to this message will be sent to the original sender, not to you.

How much of the original message should I include in my reply?

If the original message is fairly short, you usually do not need to edit the text. However, if the original message is long, and your response deals only with part of that message, you will save the recipient time and confusion by deleting everything except the relevant portion of the text. Also, rather than editing the original text within the reply, first select the text you want to keep and then click **Reply** (or **Reply All**), which tells Mail to only include the selected text in the reply.

Forward a Message

If a message has information relevant to or that concerns another person, you can forward a copy of the message to that person. You can also include your own comments in the forward. In the body of the forward, Mail includes the original message's addresses, date, and subject line. Below this information Mail also includes the text of the original message. However, if only part of the message is relevant to the recipient, you should edit the original message accordingly, or simply select the text you are responding to in the original message before clicking **Reply** to quote it in your response.

Forward a Message

1. Click the message that you want to forward.
2. Click **Forward** (➡).

Note: You can also press Shift + ⌘ + F.

A message window appears.

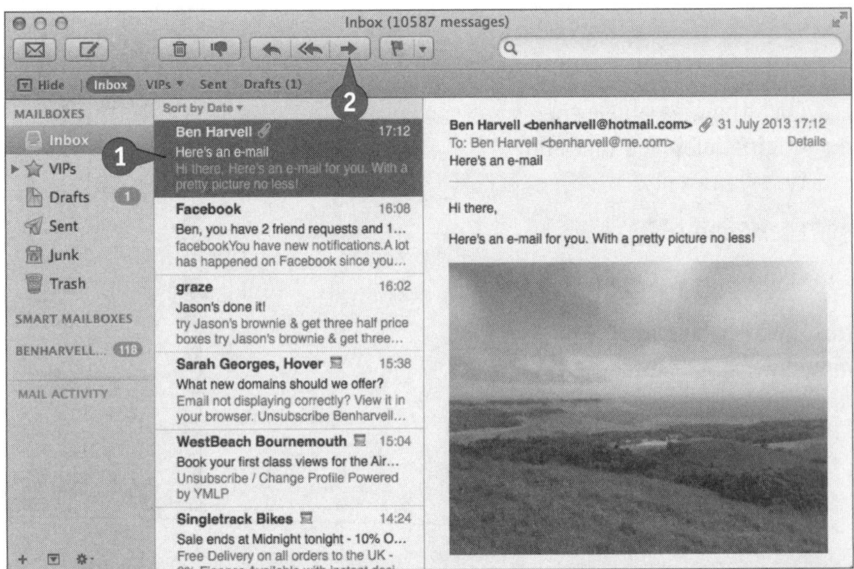

Ⓐ Mail inserts the subject line, preceded by Fwd:.

Ⓑ The original message's addressees (To and From), date, subject, and text are included at the top of the forward.

3. Type the e-mail address of the person to whom you are forwarding the message.
4. To send a copy of the forward to another person, type that person's e-mail address in the Cc line.

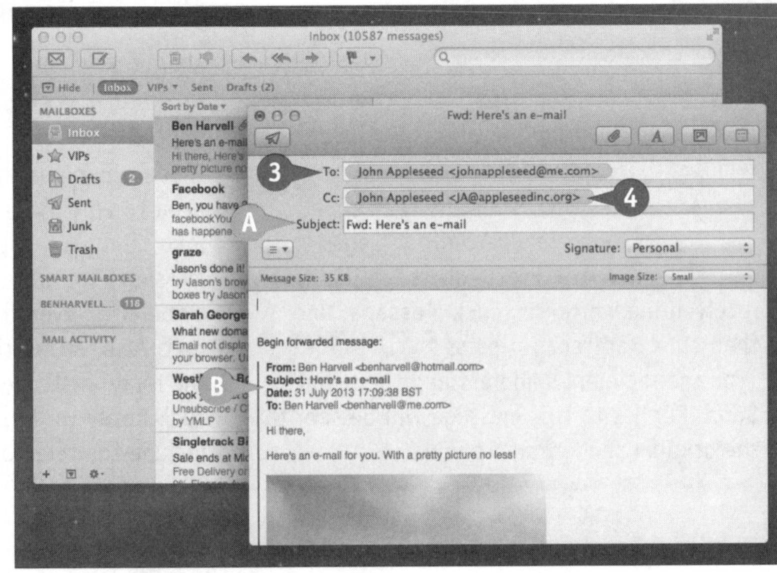

5. Edit the original message to include only the text that is relevant to your forward.
6. Click the area above the original message text and type your comments.
7. Click **Send** (✈).

   Mail sends your forward.

Note: Mail stores a copy of your forward in the Sent folder.

Note: You can forward someone a copy of the actual message instead of just a copy of the message text. Click the message, click **Message**, and then click **Forward As Attachment**. Mail creates a new message and includes the original message as an attachment.

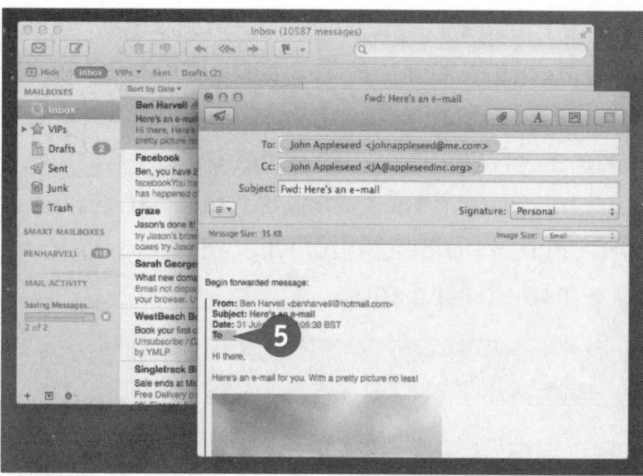

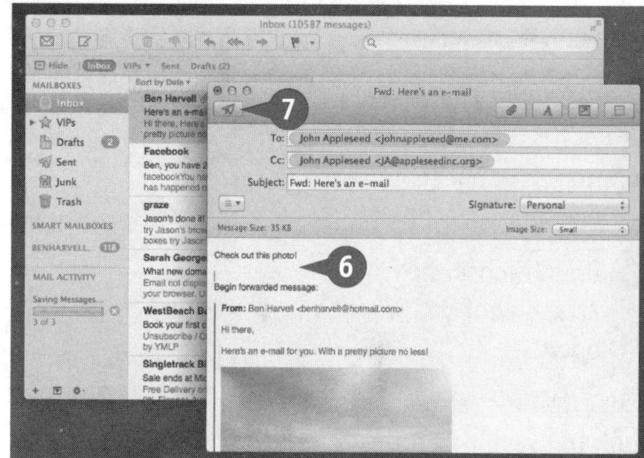

TIP

Mail always formats my replies as rich text, even when the original message is plain text. How can I fix this problem?

You can configure Mail to always reply using the same format as the original message. Follow these steps:

1. Click **Mail**.
2. Click **Preferences**.

   The Mail preferences appear.
3. Click the **Composing** tab.
4. Select the **Use the same message format as the original message** check box (☐ changes to ☑).
5. Click **Close** (●).

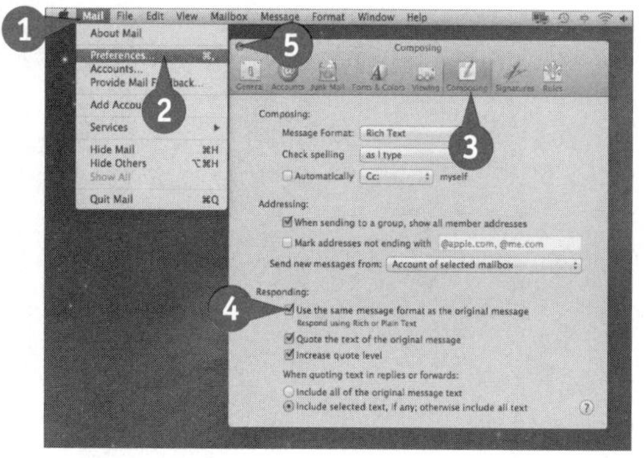

Open and Save an Attachment

If you receive a message that has a file attached, you can open the attachment to view the contents of the file. You can also save the attachment as a file on your Mac. Some files that you receive as e-mail attachments only require a quick viewing, so you can open these files and then close them when you are done. Other attachments may contain information that you want to keep, so you should save these files to your Mac's hard drive so that you can open them later without having to launch Mail. Be careful when dealing with attached files. Computer viruses are often transmitted by e-mail attachments.

Open and Save an Attachment

Open an Attachment

1. Click the message that has the attachment, as indicated by the Attachment symbol (📎).

   A. An icon appears for each message attachment.

2. Double-click the attachment you want to open.

Note: You can also use Quick Look to preview certain attachments, such as text documents.

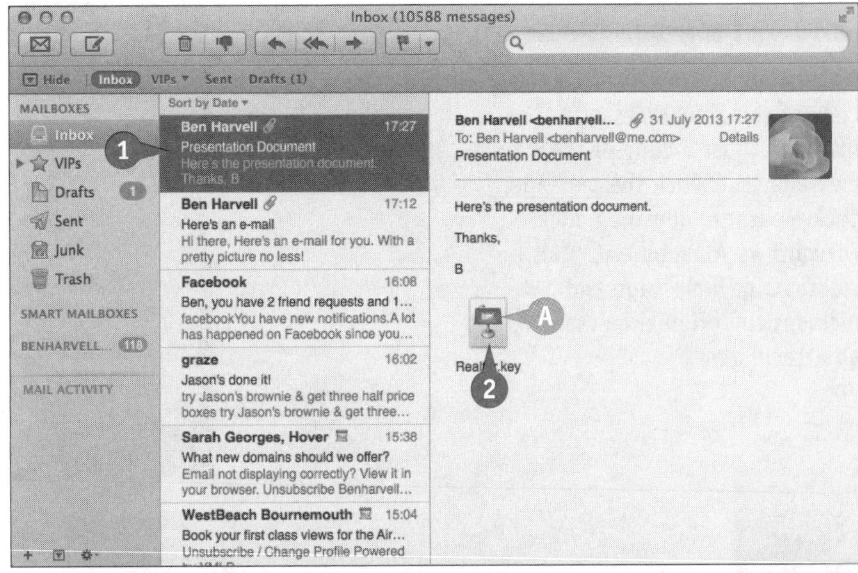

The file opens in the associated application.

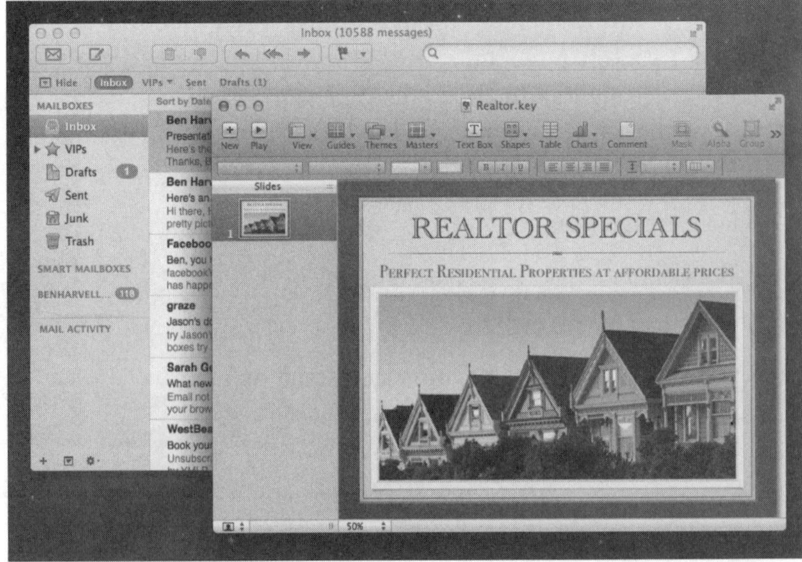

Save an Attachment

1. Click the message that has the attachment, as indicated by the Attachment symbol (📎).
2. Right-click the attachment you want to save.
3. Click **Save Attachment.**

   Mail prompts you to save the file.

4. Click in the **Save As** text box and edit the filename, if desired.
5. Click the arrows (⬍) and select the folder into which you want the file saved.
6. Click **Save.**

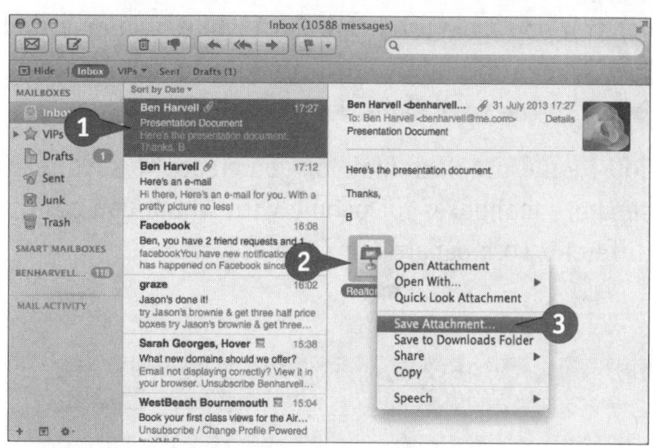

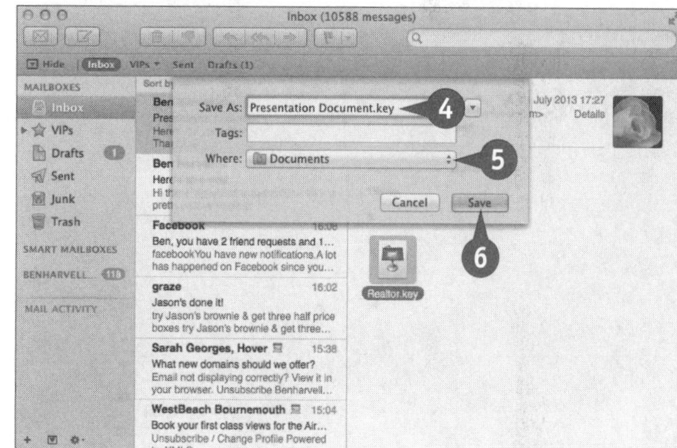

TIP

Can I open an attachment using a different application?

In most cases, yes. OS X usually has a default application that it uses when you double-click a file attachment. However, it also usually defines one or more other applications that are capable of opening the file. To check this out, right-click the icon of the attachment you want to open and then click **Open With**. In the menu that appears, click the application that you prefer to use to open the file.

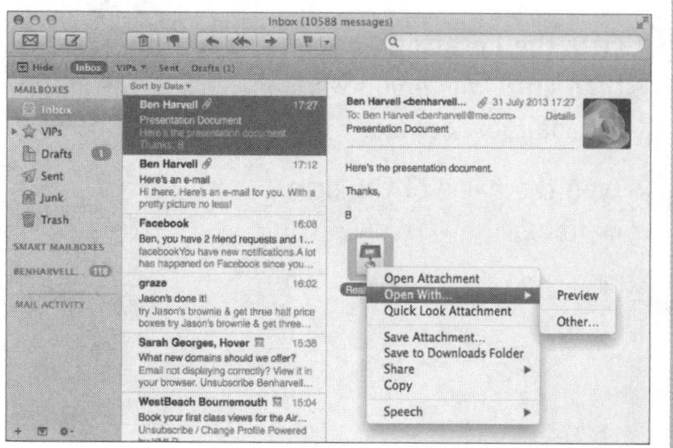

Create a Mailbox for Saving Messages

After you have used Mail for a while, you may find that you have many messages in your Inbox. To keep the Inbox uncluttered, you can create new mailboxes and then move messages from the Inbox to the new mailboxes.

You should use each mailbox you create to save related messages. For example, you could create separate mailboxes for people with whom you correspond regularly, projects you are working on, different work departments, and so on.

Create a Mailbox for Saving Messages

Create a Mailbox

1. Click **Mailbox**.
2. Click **New Mailbox**.

The New Mailbox dialog appears.

3. Click the **Location** ⇕ and then click where you want the mailbox located.
4. Type the name of the new mailbox.
5. Click **OK**.

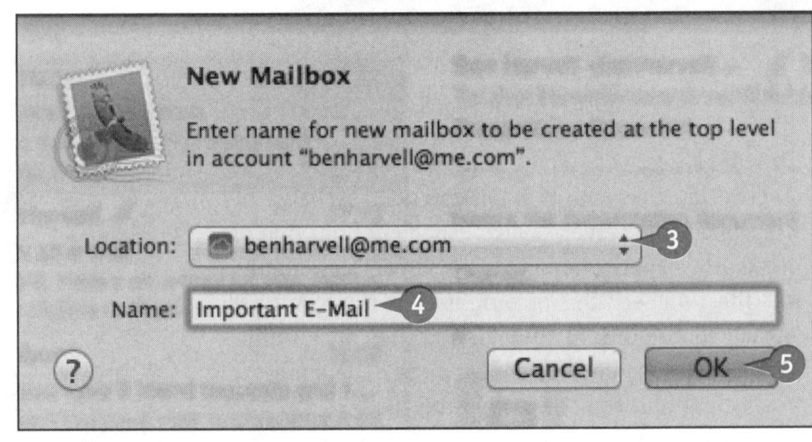

Ⓐ The new mailbox appears in the Mailbox list.

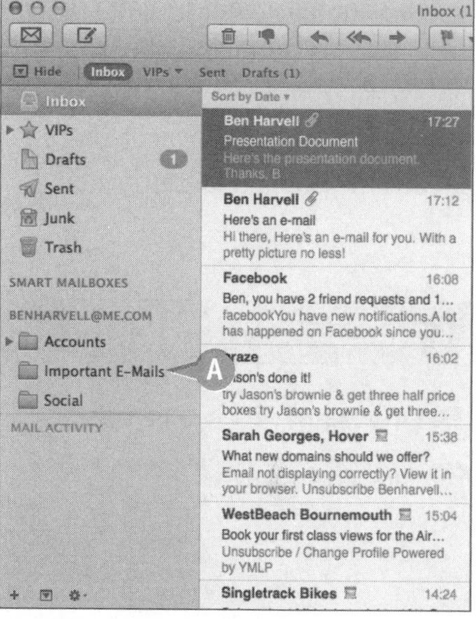

Move a Message to Another Mailbox

1. Position the mouse over the message you want to move.
2. Click and drag the message and drop it on the mailbox to which you want to move it.

   Mail moves the message.

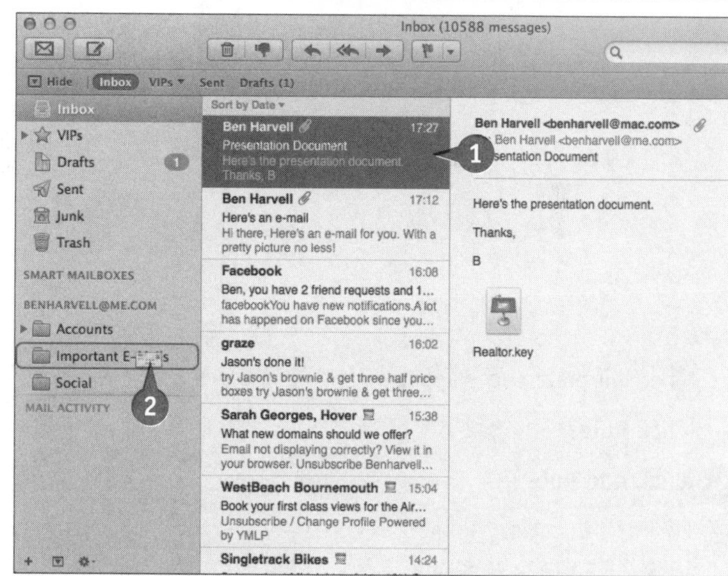

TIPS

How do I rename a mailbox?

Right-click the mailbox and then click **Rename Mailbox.** Type the new name and then press Return. Note that Mail does not allow you to rename any of the built-in mailboxes, including Inbox, Drafts, and Trash.

How do I delete a mailbox?

Right-click the mailbox and then click **Delete.** When Mail asks you to confirm the deletion, click **Delete.** Note that Mail does not allow you to delete any of the built-in mailboxes, including Inbox, Drafts, and Trash. Remember, too, that when you delete a mailbox you also delete any messages stored in that mailbox.

Create Rules to Filter Incoming Messages

You can make your e-mail chores faster and more efficient if you create *rules* that handle incoming messages automatically. A rule combines a condition and an action. The condition is one or more message criteria, such as the address of the sender or words in the subject line. Mail only applies the rule to messages that meet these criteria. The action is what happens to a message that satisfies the condition. Example actions include moving the message to another folder or sending a reply.

Create Rules to Filter Incoming Messages

1 Click **Mail.**

2 Click **Preferences.**

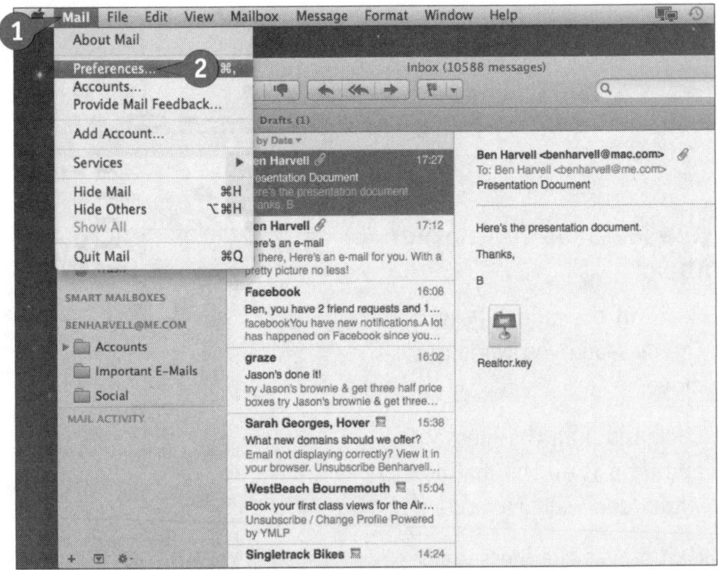

The Mail preferences appear.

3 Click **Rules.**

4 Click **Add Rule.**

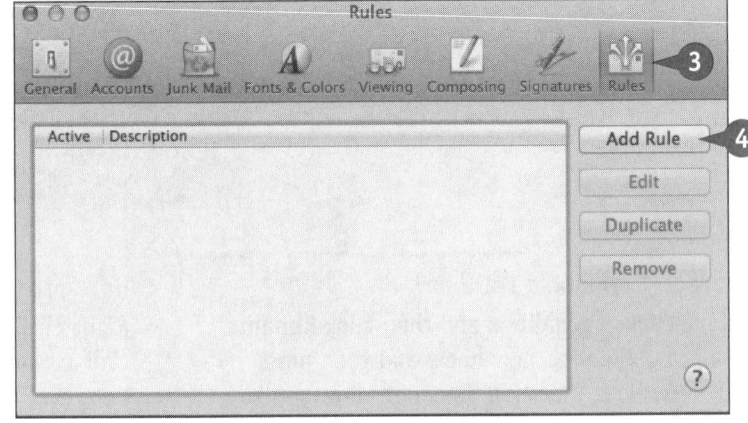

Mail begins a new rule.

5 Type a name for the rule.

6 Click the arrows (⇕) and select the object of the condition from the pop-up menu.

7 Click the arrows (⇕) and select an operator from the pop-up menu.

8 Type the value you want to match in the text box.

Note: Not all conditions require an operator or a value.

9 To add another condition, click the **Add** button (⊕) and repeat steps 6 to 8.

10 Click the arrows (⇕) and select the type of action from the pop-up menu.

11 Click the arrows (⇕) and select the specific action from the pop-up menu.

Note: Not all conditions require a specific action.

12 To add an action, click the **Add** button (⊕) and repeat steps 10 and 11.

13 Click **OK**.

A The rule is added to the Rules tab and turned on.

14 Click **Close** (●).

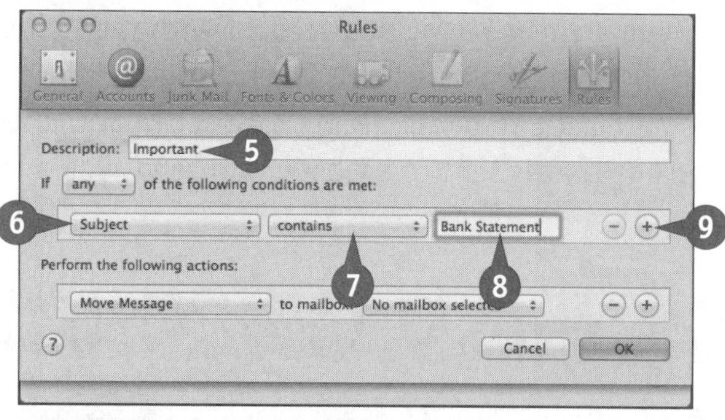

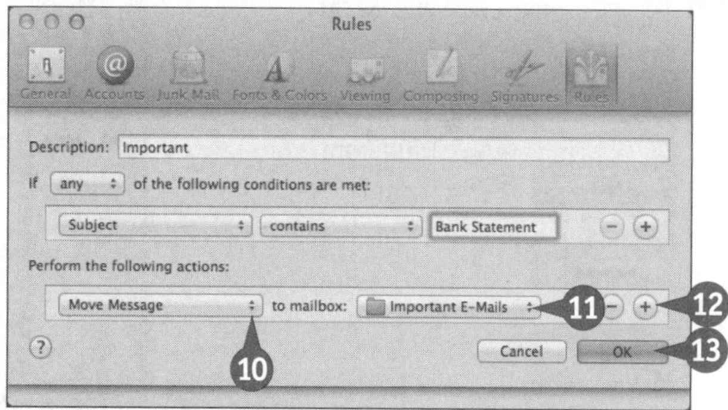

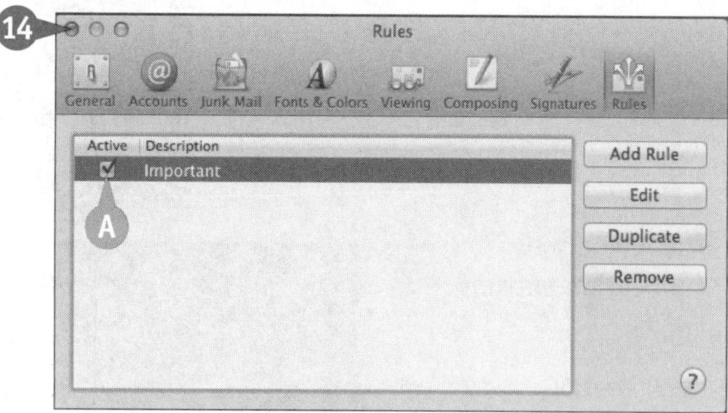

TIP

Can I create a rule that looks for messages that meet all of the conditions I specify?

Yes. By default, Mail applies a rule on messages that meet any one of the conditions you add. However, you can create more specific rules by telling Mail to only match those messages that satisfy all the criteria you add. In the new rule dialog, click the **If** ⇕ and then click **all**.

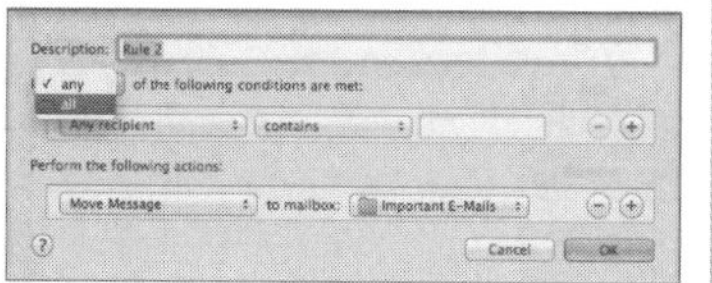

Set an Out-of-Office Auto Reply with iCloud

If you are using an iCloud account with the Mail app in OS X, you can set an out-of-office message to use when you are away from your e-mail for a period of time, such as a holiday or business trip. The automatic response needs to be set from the iCloud Mail application online and can include a message that is sent to anybody who sends you an e-mail while the out-of-office reply is turned on.

Set an Out-of-Office Auto Reply with iCloud

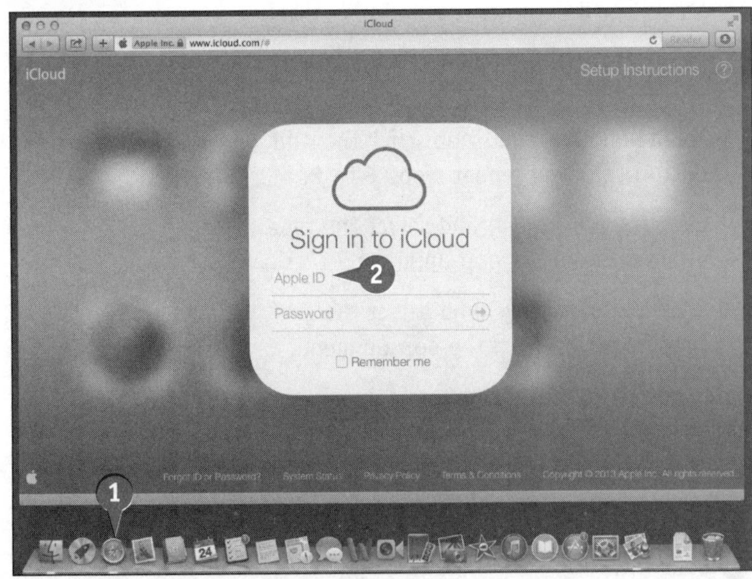

1. In the Dock, click the **Safari** icon (◎).
2. Log in to your iCloud account by visiting www.icloud.com and typing your account details.

The iCloud web application buttons appear.

3. Click **Mail**.

The web version of the Mail app appears.

4 Click the **Settings** button (⚙).

5 Click **Preferences** on the menu that appears.

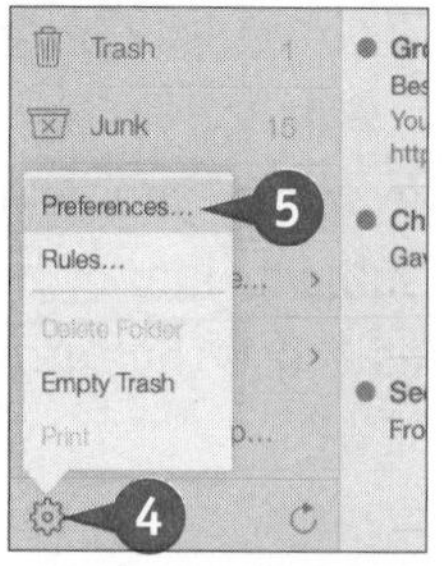

The Preferences pane appears.

6 Click **Vacation**.

7 Select the **Automatically reply to messages when they are received** check box (☐ changes to ☑).

The Auto-response is now turned on.

8 Type an out-of-office message into the field.

9 Click **Done**.

Your message will be sent to anyone who sends an e-mail to your iCloud e-mail account.

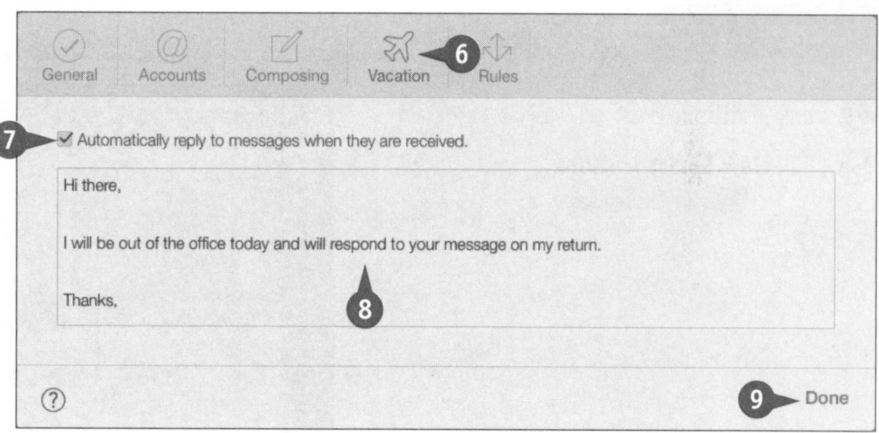

TIPS

Will the Auto-response keep sending e-mails to people who send more than one e-mail?
No. Once a person has sent an e-mail to your iCloud account and received a response, a second auto-response is not sent.

How do I turn the Auto-response off?
Follow steps 1 to 6 again, but this time deselect the **Auto-response** check box (☑ changes to ☐) and then click **Done**. The Auto-response is now turned off.

Create a Smart Mailbox

Smart Mailboxes offer a convenient way to sort messages in your inbox automatically. Similar to mailbox rules, Smart Mailboxes pull in messages that fulfill certain criteria and store them. For example, you could create a Smart Mailbox to store messages from a specific address, with a specific subject line, or both. Smart Mailboxes collect messages that already exist in your mail account as well as those that arrive once the Smart Mailbox is set up.

Create a Smart Mailbox

1. Click **Mailbox.**
2. Click **New Smart Mailbox.**

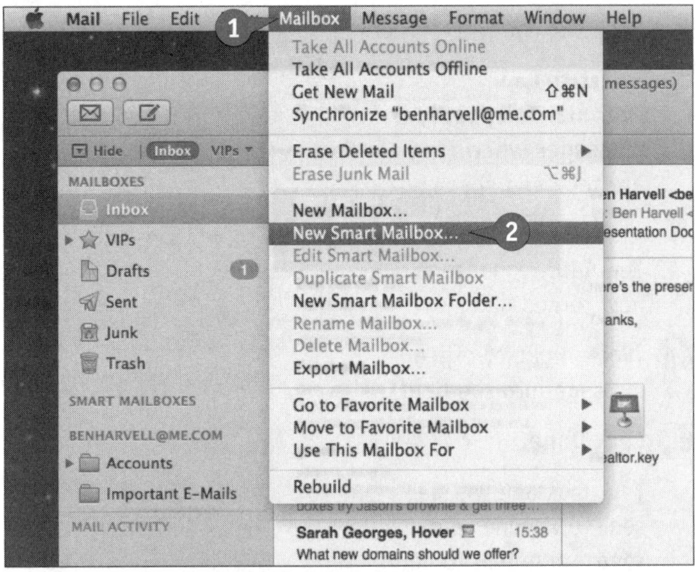

The Smart Mailbox Pane Appears.

3. Type a name for your Smart Mailbox in the first field.
4. Click the on the conditions pop-up menu and select **all** or **any**.

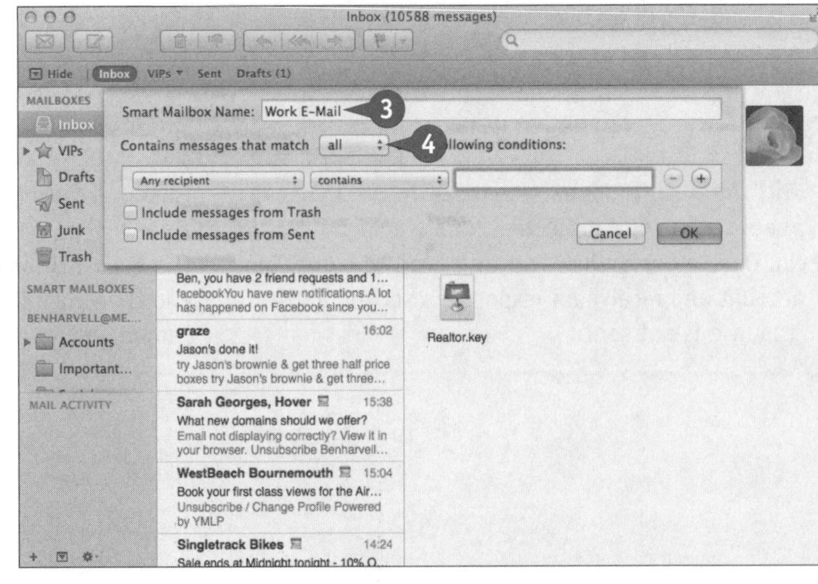

5. Click the arrows (⇕) and select the object of the condition from the pop-up menu.
6. Click the arrows (⇕) and select an operator from the pop-up menu.
7. Type the value you want to match in the text box.

Note: Not all conditions require an operator or a value.

8. To add another condition, click the **Add** button (⊕) and repeat steps **6** to **8**.
   - **A** Select this box (☐ changes to ☑) to include messages from the Trash.
   - **B** Select this box (☐ changes to ☑) to include messages from the Sent folder.
9. Click **OK**.

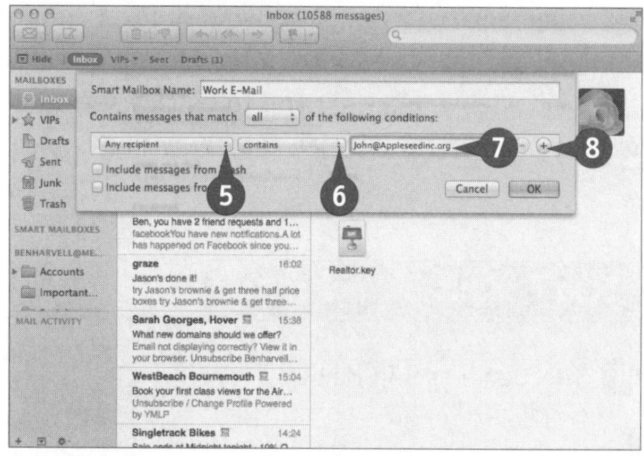

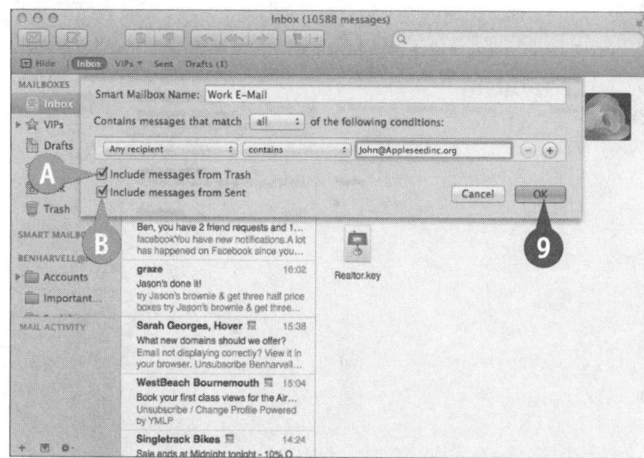

Mail creates the Smart Mailbox and messages matching the criteria you applied are added to it.

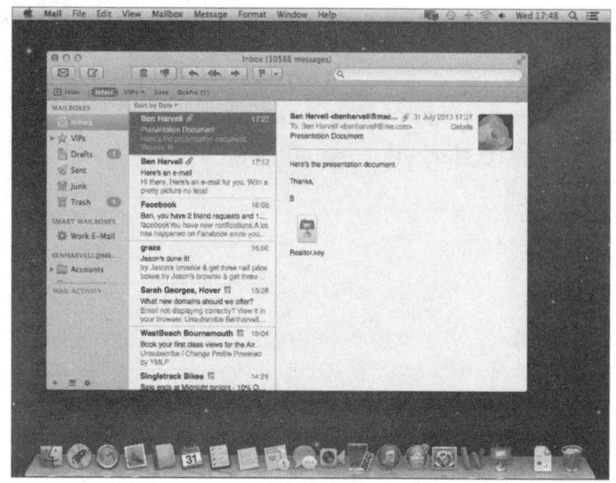

TIP

Where does my new Smart Mailbox appear?

Your Smart Mailbox will appear in the Smart Mailboxes section of the sidebar in Mail. Click the name of your Smart Mailbox to view its contents or Ctrl+click the name of your Smart Mailbox to view more options such as renaming it.

Flag E-mails in Your Inbox

To help you better organize your inbox and remember important messages, Mail allows you to highlight messages with different colored flags. These flags can then be used to sort e-mails from the Mail sidebar, allowing you to quickly see all e-mails flagged with a specific color. Flags can be quickly added from the Mail toolbar with a choice of seven flag colors available.

Flag E-mails in Your Inbox

1. Select an e-mail in Mail by clicking it.
2. Click the submenu arrow (▶) next to the Flag button on the toolbar.

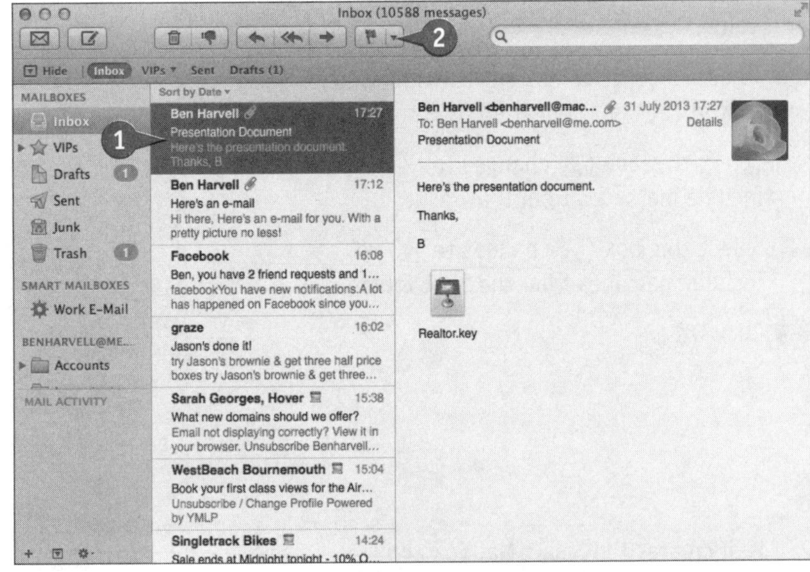

The Flag menu appears.

3. Click the color you want to use to flag your e-mail.

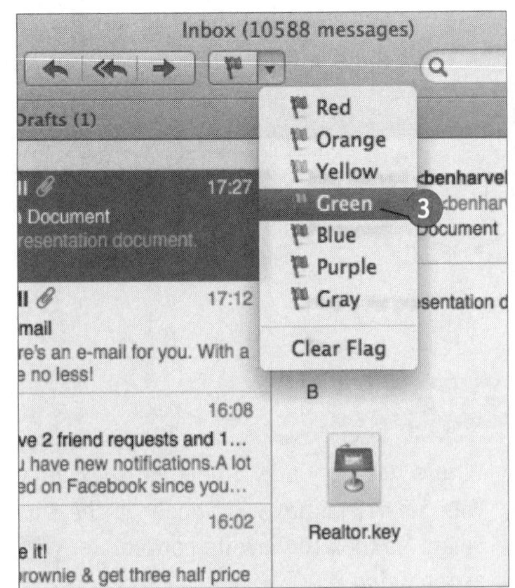

The flag color is added to the message.

4. Click the submenu arrow (▶) next to Flagged in the sidebar.

Note: If there is no submenu arrow, only one flag color is in use. Click **Flagged** instead.

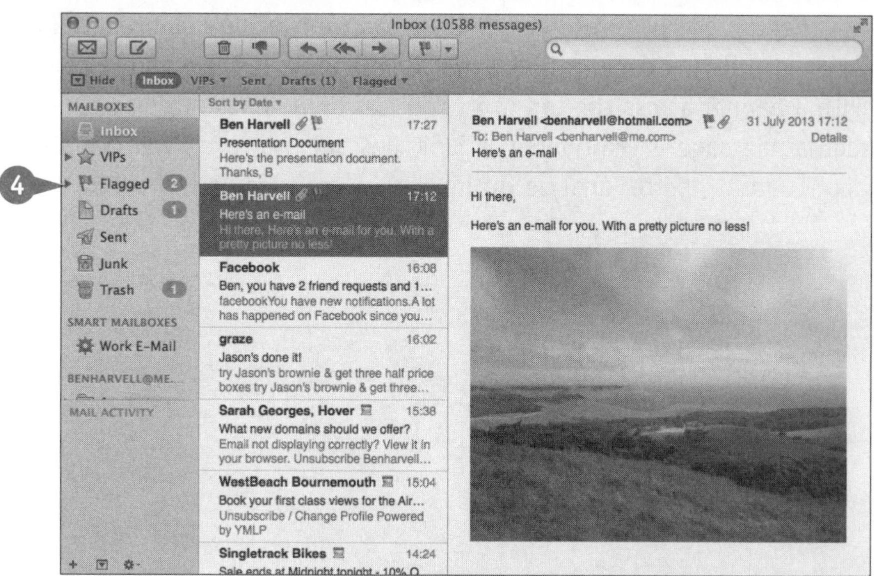

The flag color you chose is shown as well as any others you may have used.

A Click a flag to show all messages flagged with that color.

B The number next to each flag denotes how many messages are flagged with that color.

TIPS

Can I change the color I used to flag a message?
Yes. Simply select the message again and choose a new color from the Flag menu. You can also choose the Clear Flag option from the same menu.

Can I use multiple flag colors for one message?
No. You can only apply one flag color to a message. If you add a new flag color to a message the existing flag color will be replaced.

Mark E-mails as Junk

When an e-mail is received in Mail, the application analyzes it and determines whether it is junk mail. If Mail decides that a message is junk, it changes the color of the message to brown with a banner across the top of it. You can then choose to mark the e-mail as junk or accept it as a regular message. If Mail misses a junk message, however, you can mark it as such, which helps the application to better analyze future spam e-mail messages.

Mark E-mails as Junk

1. Click a message in Mail to select it.
2. Click the **Junk** button (👎) on the toolbar.

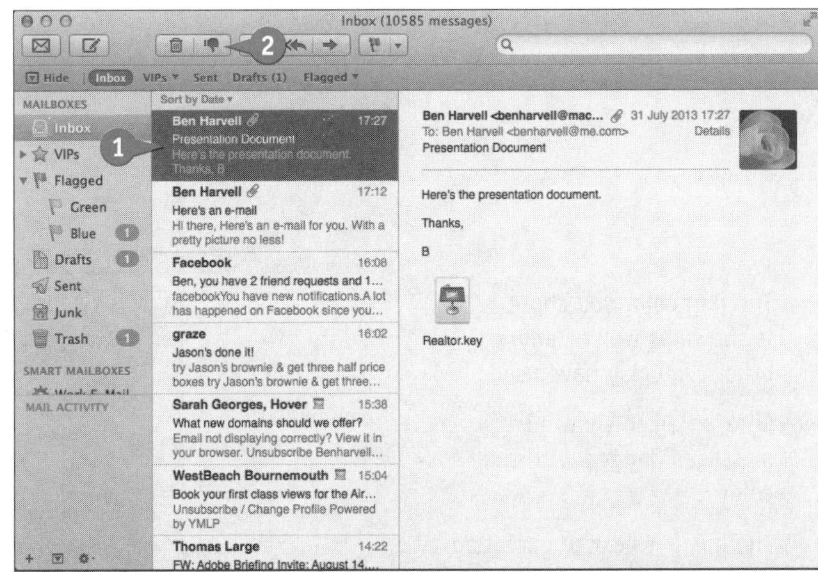

The message is marked as junk.

Ⓐ If you change your mind, click **Not Junk**.

3. Click **Junk** in the sidebar.

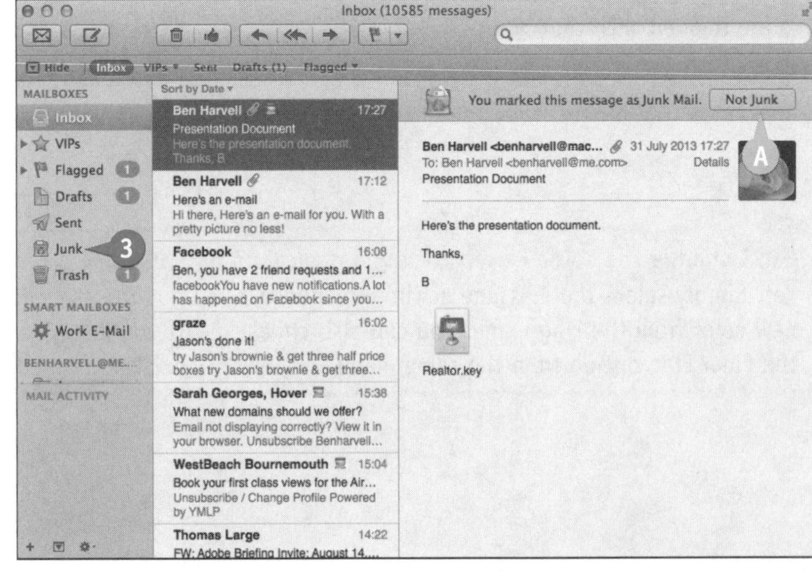

Junk messages that have been added to the Junk folder are shown.

4 Click a message to select it.

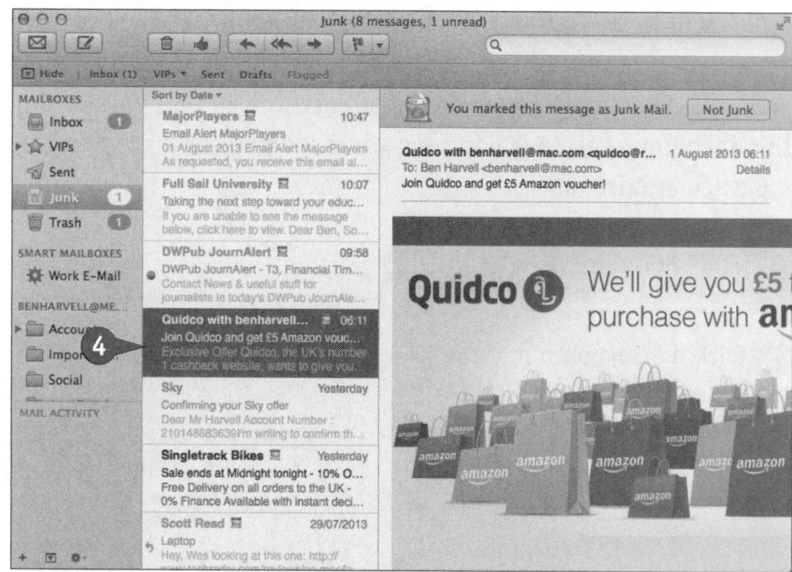

B If you decide that the message is not junk, click **Not Junk**.

5 Click and drag the message back to your inbox to remove it from the Junk folder.

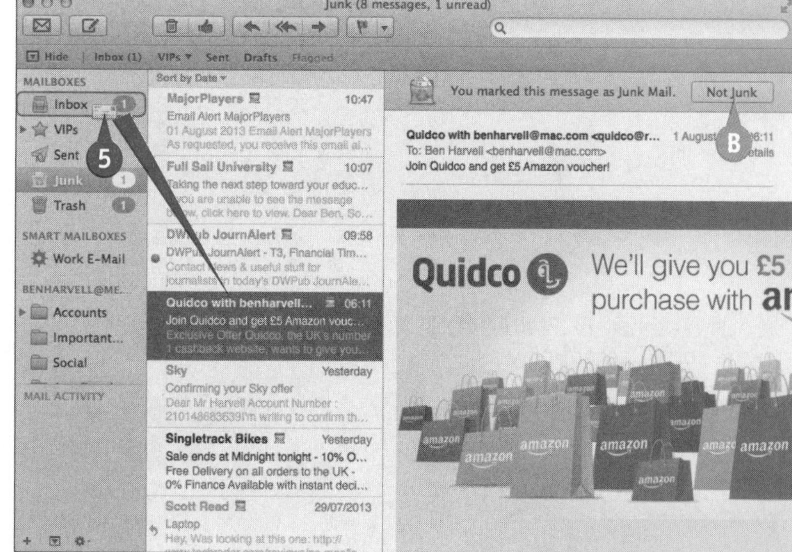

TIP

Can I turn off junk mail filtering?

Yes. In Mail Preferences under the Junk Mail tab, deselect the **Enable junk mail filtering** check box (☑ changes to ☐). From this pane you can also set Mail to move all junk messages to your Junk mailbox rather than leave them in your inbox by clicking the **Move it to the Junk mailbox** radio button (○ changes to ◉).

Sort E-mails in Your Inbox

The Mail inbox can be sorted to show different types of messages as well as order messages in a variety of ways. By sorting e-mail in your inbox, you can quickly see e-mails you have yet to read, and order them by date, name, or subject line. If you have a large number of e-mails in your inbox, this technique can save you time when looking for a specific message or a group of messages that fits a particular criteria.

Sort E-mails in Your Inbox

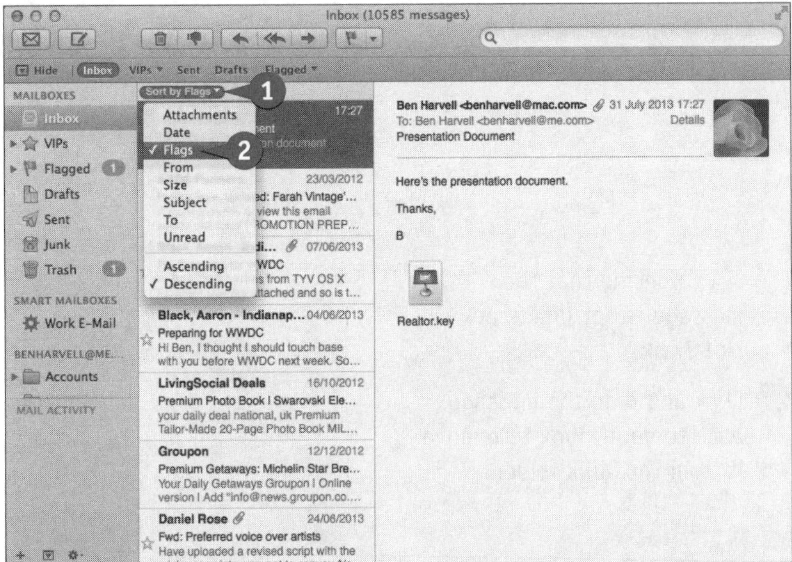

1. Click the **Sort** button at the top of your Inbox or currently selected Mailbox.
2. Click the sorting method you want to use.

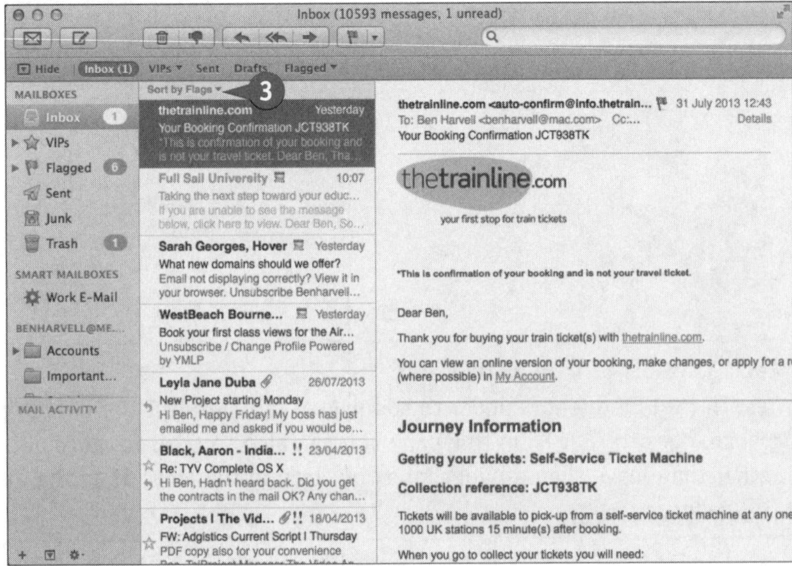

The messages in your mailbox are sorted accordingly.

3. Click the **Sort** button again.

4 Click **Ascending** or **Descending** to set the sort direction.

Note: The Ascending and Descending options change for different sorting options. A-Z and Most Recent/Oldest are other options.

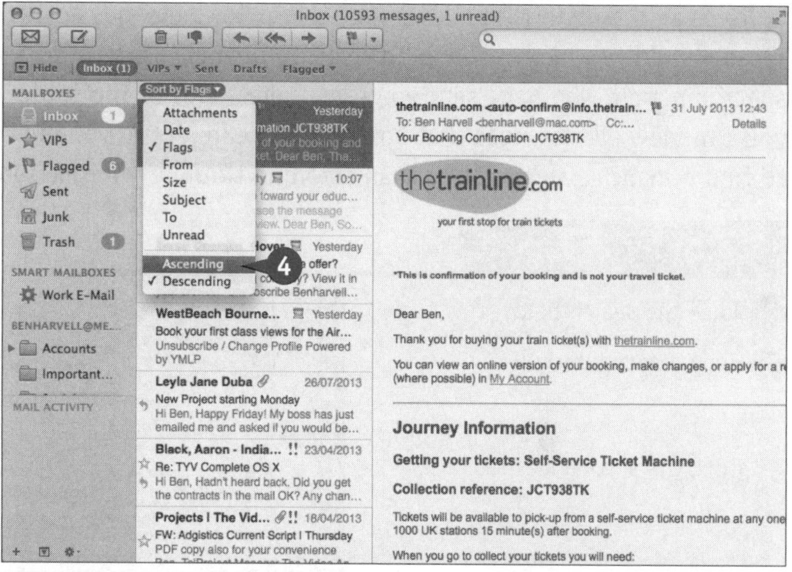

Your messages are sorted in ascending or descending order.

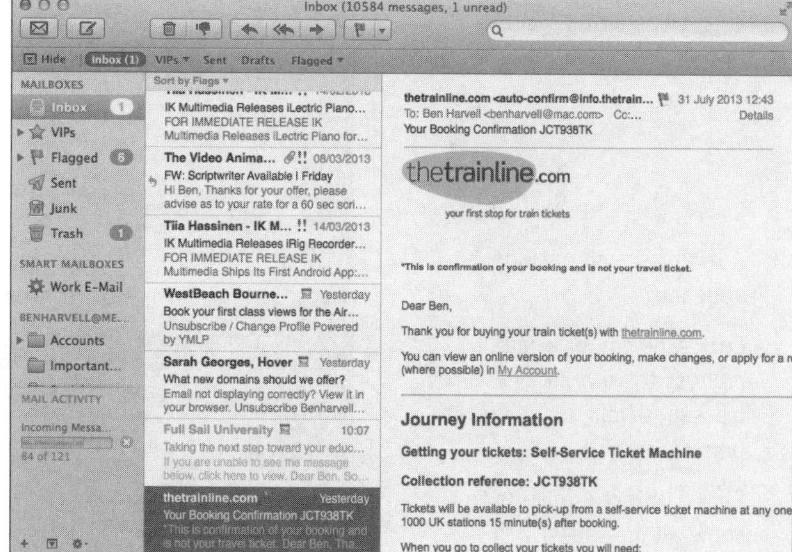

TIP

What types of sorting are available?

From the Sort menu you can choose to sort e-mails by whether they contain an attachment, by date, whether the e-mail is flagged and the color of the flag, who the message is from, the subject line of the message, or who the message is addressed to. You can also sort messages by mailbox, size, or whether they have been read.

Search for an E-mail

The Search field in Mail allows you to look for messages across all of your mailboxes using specific search criteria. The results allow you to further focus your search by narrowing the results to specific people who have sent you e-mail messages or the subject line of the message. Alternatively, you can view all messages that contain the search term you entered. Using the search field helps you to find e-mail messages faster than scrolling through your mailboxes looking for a specific message.

Search for an E-mail

1. Click the search field.
2. Type a search term.

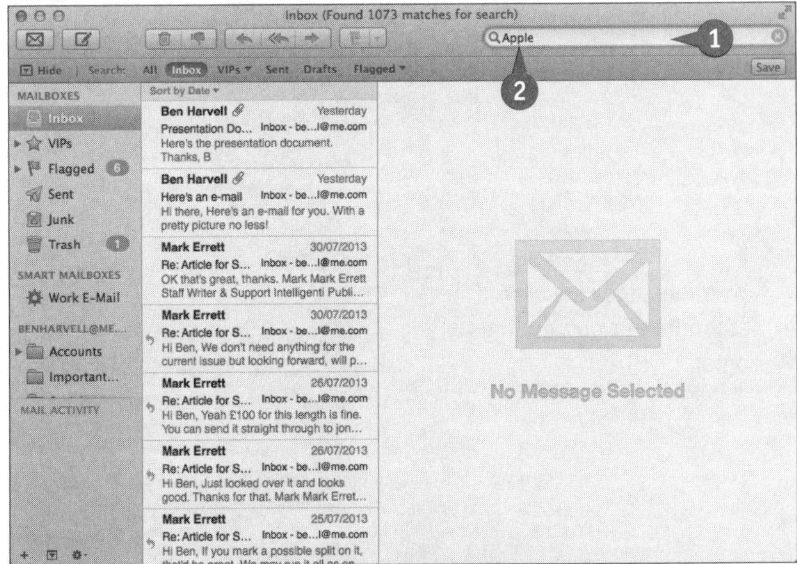

A list of search options appears.

A. Click a person or e-mail address to view all messages from a specific person.

B. Click **Subject Contains** to show all messages with your search term in the subject line.

C. Click a specific subject line to show all messages with that subject.

D. Click a mailbox name to show all mailboxes that match your search term.

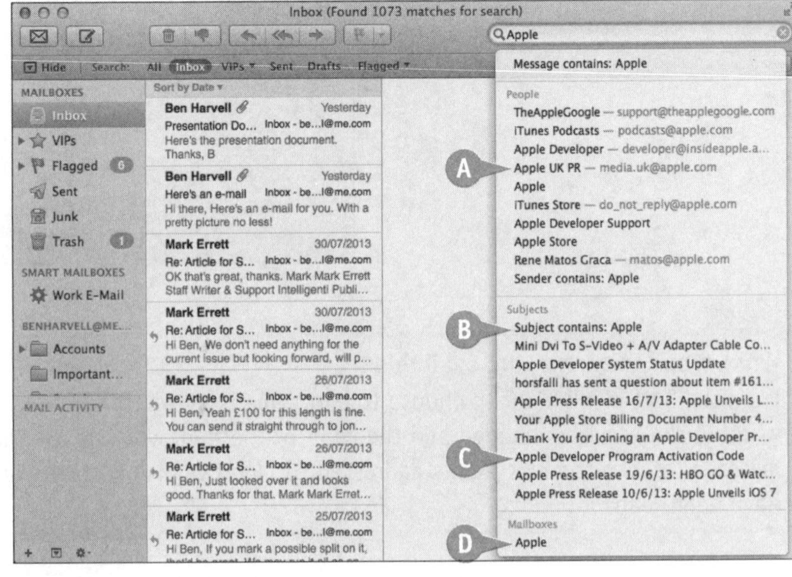

Messages matching your search are shown.

3 Click **Save**.

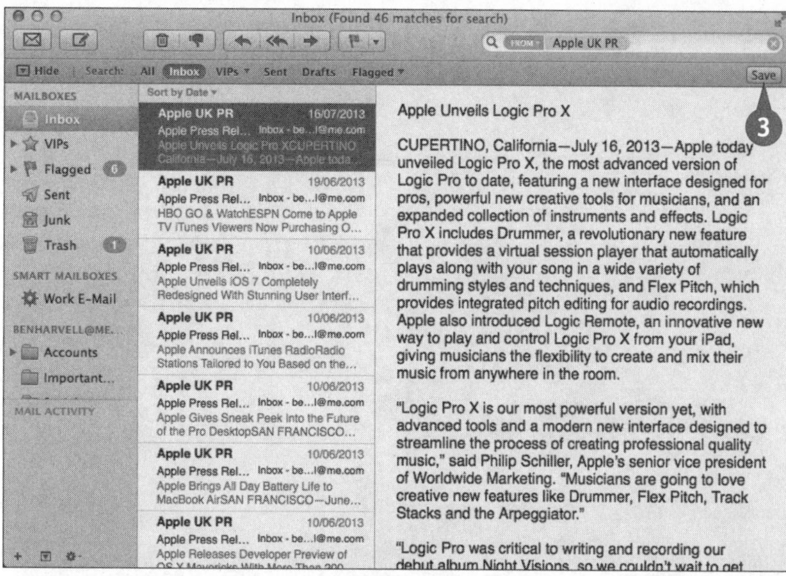

The Smart Mailbox Pane appears.

4 Click **OK** to save the search as a Smart Mailbox.

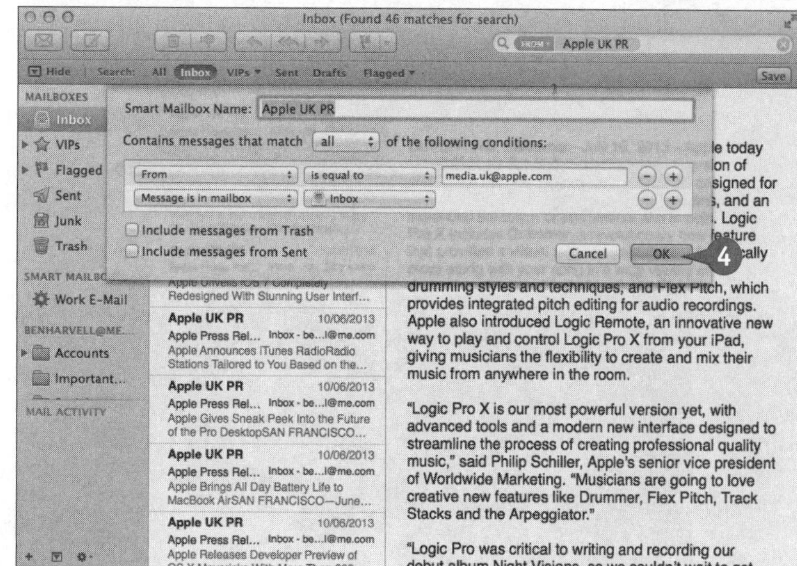

TIP

Can I adjust my search once I have made it?

Yes. If you select to view all messages that have a subject line that matches your search query, you can click **Subject** next to your search in the Search pane. A menu appears with the option to search in a different way, such as for messages that include your search term anywhere in the e-mail, including the body of the message and the subject line.

CHAPTER 6

Talking via Messages and FaceTime

OS X Mavericks comes with the Messages application, which you use to exchange instant messages with other users of OS X Mavericks, as well as anyone with an iPhone, iPad, or iPod touch. You can also use FaceTime to make video calls to other people.

Configure Messages

OS X Mavericks includes the Messages application to enable you to exchange instant messages with other people who are online. The first time you open Messages, you must run through a short configuration process to set up your account. This process involves signing in with your Apple ID and deciding whether you want Messages to send out notifications that tell people when you have read the messages they send to you.

Configure Messages

1. Click **Messages** ().

The iMessage setup dialog appears.

2. Type your Apple ID and Password.
3. Click **Sign In**.

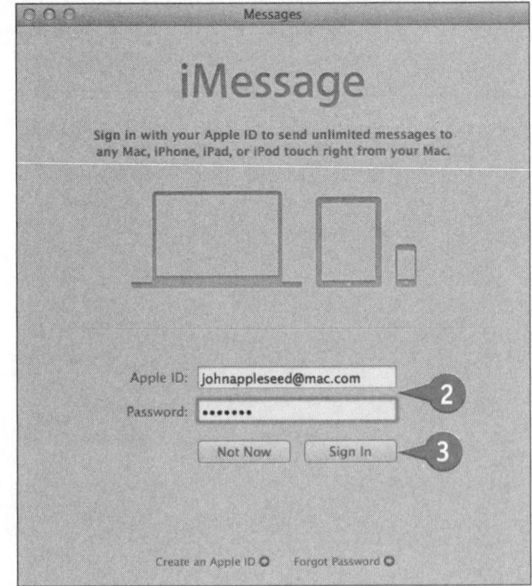

4. Select the check boxes next to e-mail addresses and phone numbers you want to use with iMessage (☐ changes to ☑).

A. Select the check box next to Send read receipts (☐ changes to ☑) to notify others when you have read their messages.

5. Click **Done**.

The Messages interface appears.

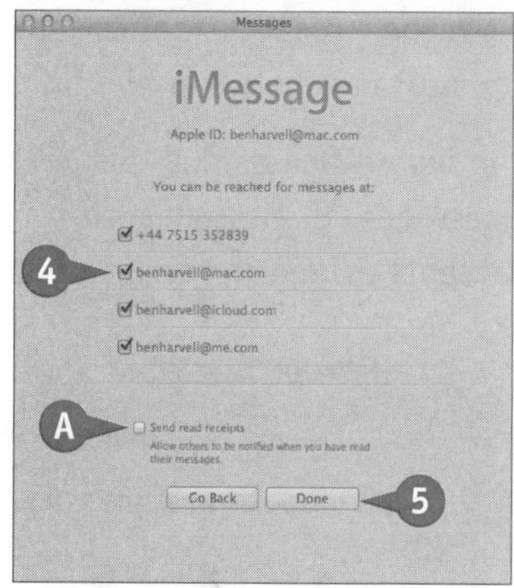

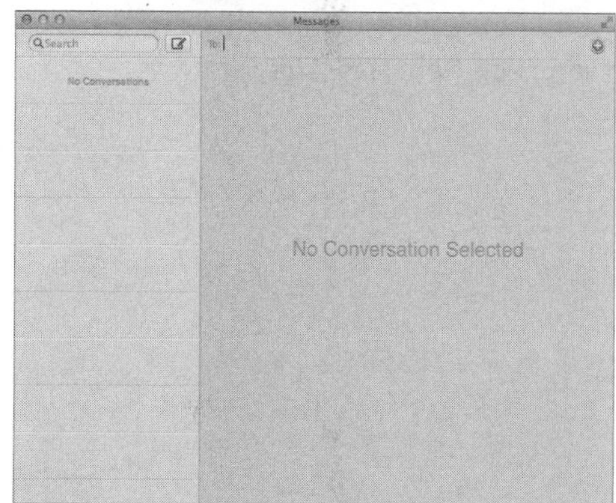

B. Conversations are shown in the left column.

C. Messages are shown in the right column.

D. Messages are typed in the field at the bottom of the interface.

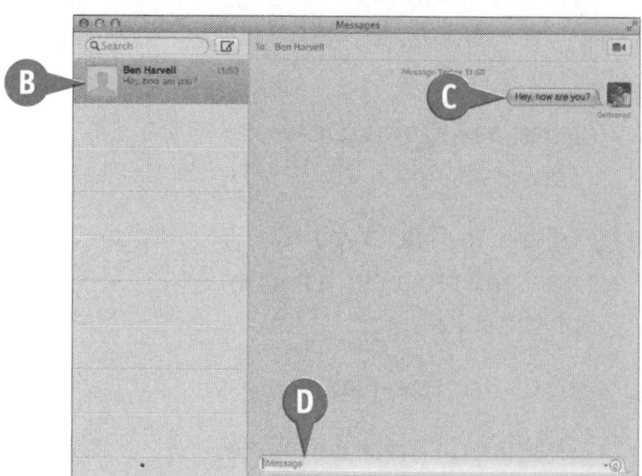

TIP

What if I do not have an Apple ID?

You can create a new Apple ID during the configuration process. Follow steps 1 and 2 to open the iMessage setup dialog, and then click **Create Apple ID**. In the dialog that appears, type your name, the e-mail address you want to use as your Apple ID, and the password you want to use. You must also choose a secret question and specify your birthday. Click **Create Apple ID** to complete the operation.

Send a Message

In the Messages application, an instant messaging conversation is most often the exchange of text messages between two or more people who are online and available to chat.

An instant messaging conversation begins by one person inviting another person to exchange messages. In Messages, this means sending an initial instant message, and the recipient either accepts or rejects the invitation.

Send a Message

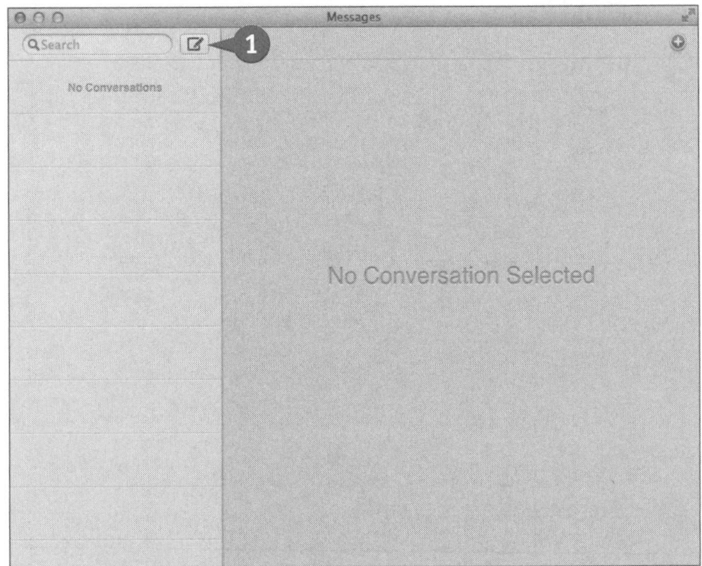

1 Click **Compose new message** (☑).

Note: You can also click **File** and then click **New Message**, or press ⌘+N.

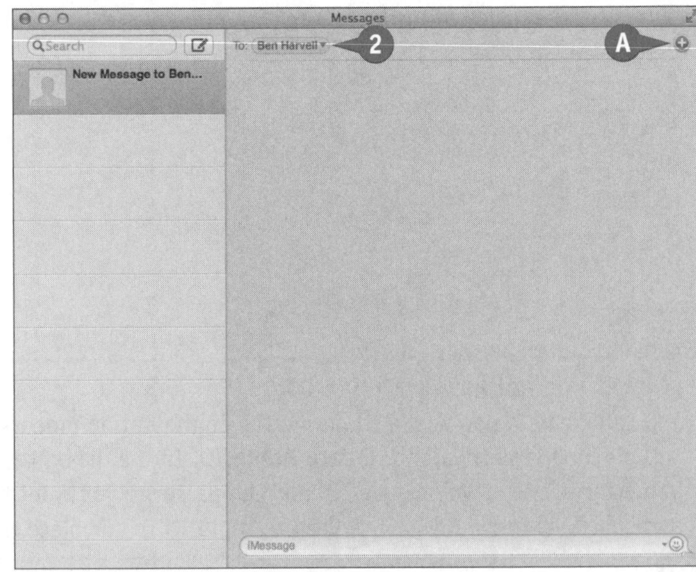

Messages begins a new conversation.

2 In the To field, type the message recipient using one of the following:

The person's e-mail address.

The person's mobile phone number.

The person's name, if that person is in your Contacts list.

A You can also click **Add Contact** (⊕) to select a name from your Contacts list.

3 Type your message.

B You can also click the **Emoticon** button (☺) if you want to insert a smiley-face symbol into your message.

4 Press Return.

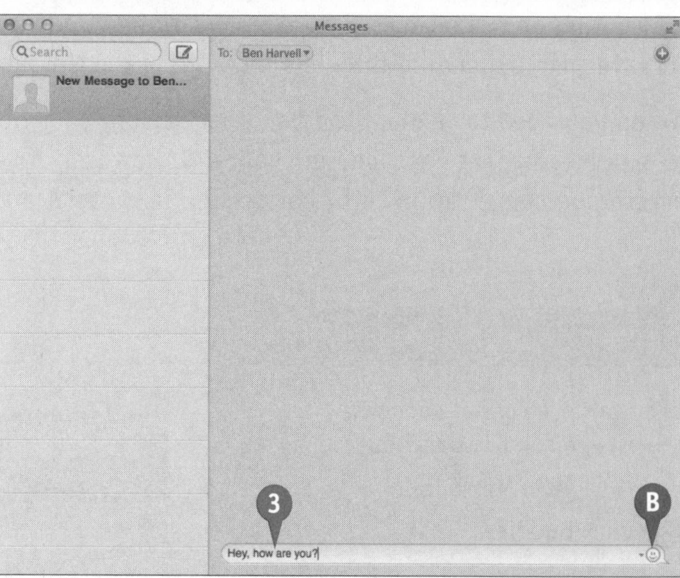

Messages sends the text to the recipient.

C The recipient's response appears in the transcript window.

D You see the ellipsis symbol (…) when the other person is typing.

5 Repeat steps 3 and 4 to continue the conversation.

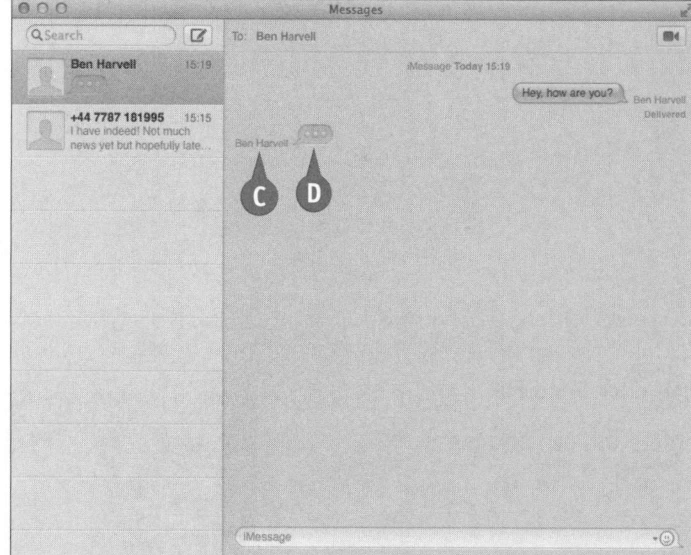

TIP

Can I change my picture?

Yes. Click **Messages** and then click **Change My Picture**. In the Edit Picture dialog that appears, select a category (such as Defaults for the OS X default account images, or Other to choose one of your own images), select the picture, and then click **Done**. If your Mac or Apple display has a built-in camera or if you have a connected webcam, you can also take a photo of yourself to use as your picture.

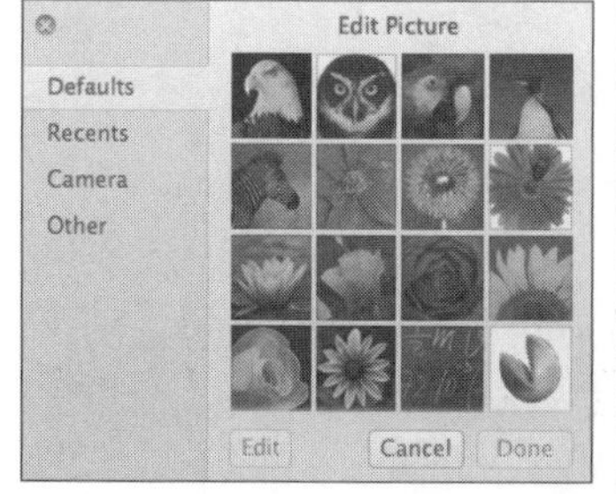

Send a File in a Message

If during an instant messaging conversation you realize you need to send someone a file, you can save time by sending the file directly from the Messages application.

When you need to send a file to another person, your first thought might be to attach that file to an e-mail message, as described in Chapter 5. However, if you happen to be in the middle of an instant messaging conversation with that person, it is easier and faster to use Messages to send the file.

Send a File in a Message

1. Start the conversation with the person to whom you want to send the file.
2. Click **Buddies**.

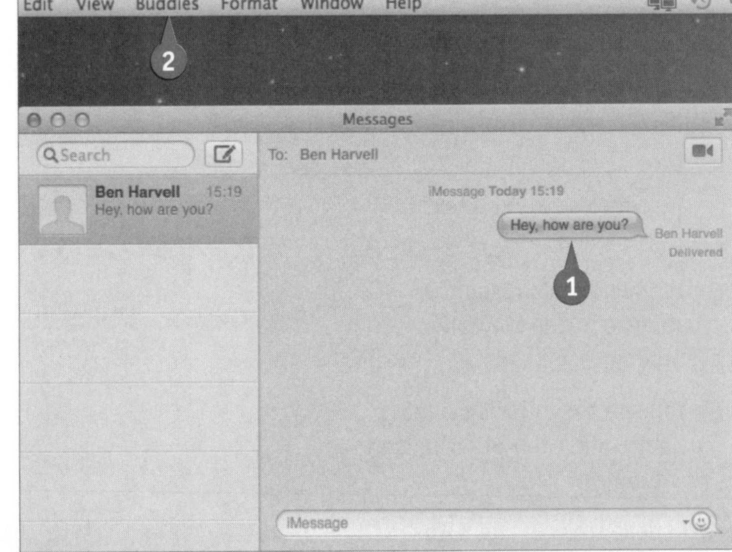

3. Click **Send File**.

Note: You can also press Option + ⌘ + F.

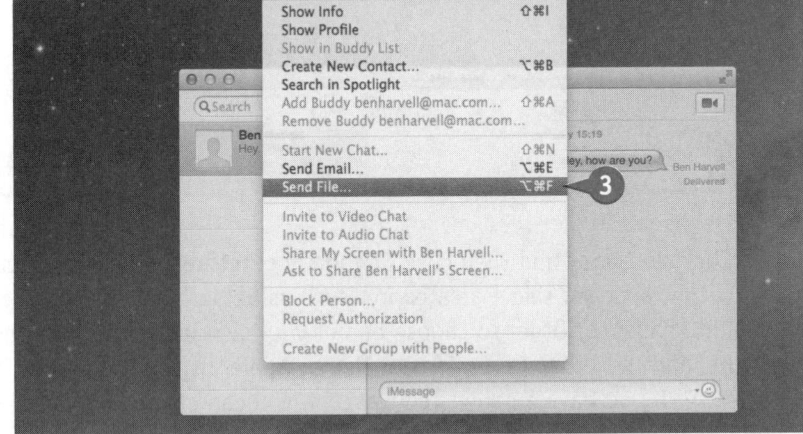

Messages displays a file selection dialog.

4 Click the file you want to send.

5 Click **Send**.

Note: You can also drag a file from the Finder into the message field to share it with the contact you are chatting with.

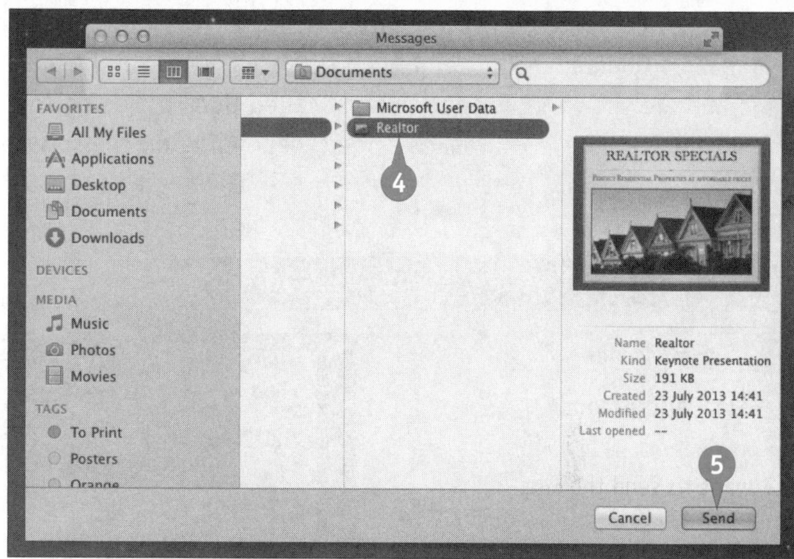

A Messages adds an icon for the file to the message box.

6 Type your message and press Return.

Messages sends the message and adds the file as an attachment.

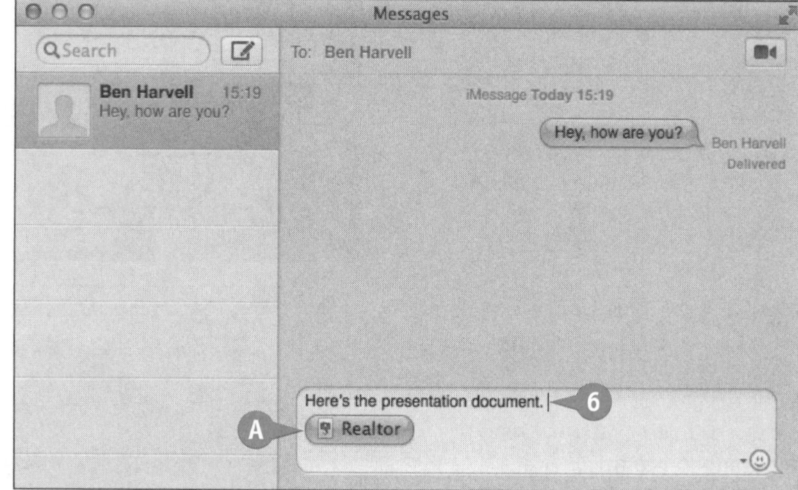

TIP

How do I save a file that I receive during a conversation?

When you receive a message that has a file attachment, the message shows the name of the file, with the file-type icon to the left and a downward-pointing arrow to the right. Click the arrow to save the file to your Downloads folder. Messages saves the file and then displays the Downloads folder.

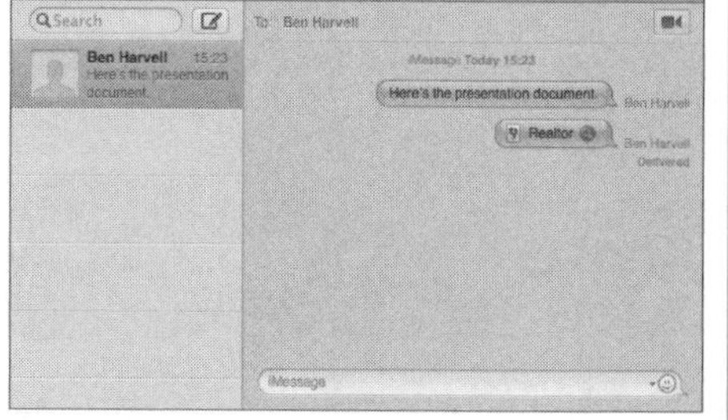

Add Non-iCloud Accounts to Messages

As well as working with iCloud accounts, the Messages app is compatible with other chat services such as Google, Yahoo!, and AOL. These accounts can be added through the Messages preference pane and are shown in a separate pane called Buddies. Using this pane you can make voice calls, video calls, and share your Mac's screen, depending on the service you are using.

Add Non-iCloud Accounts to Messages

1. Click **Messages**.
2. Click **Add Account**.

3. Click the type of account you want to add (◯ changes to ◉).

Note: You can also click **Other Messages account...** (◯ changes to ◉) if your account type is not listed.

4. Click **Continue.**

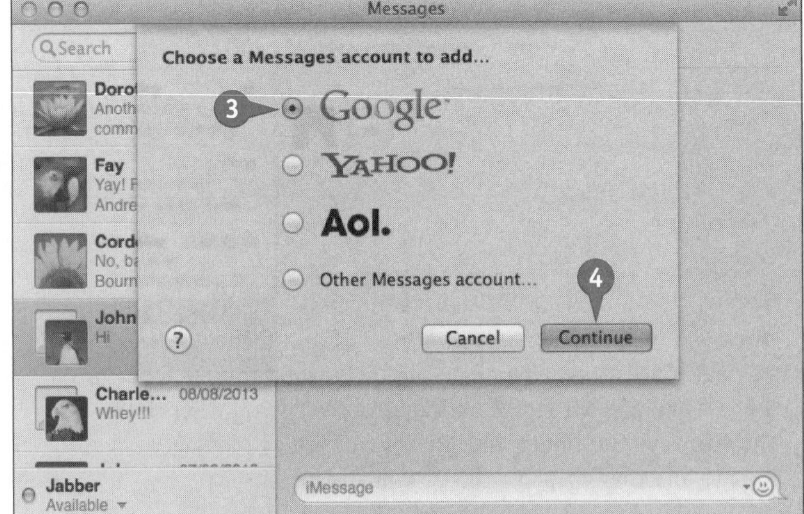

5 Type your name in the first field.

6 Type your e-mail address in the second field.

7 Type the password for your account in the third field.

8 Click **Set Up**.

Note: Depending on the account you chose, you may be asked which services to use your new account with.

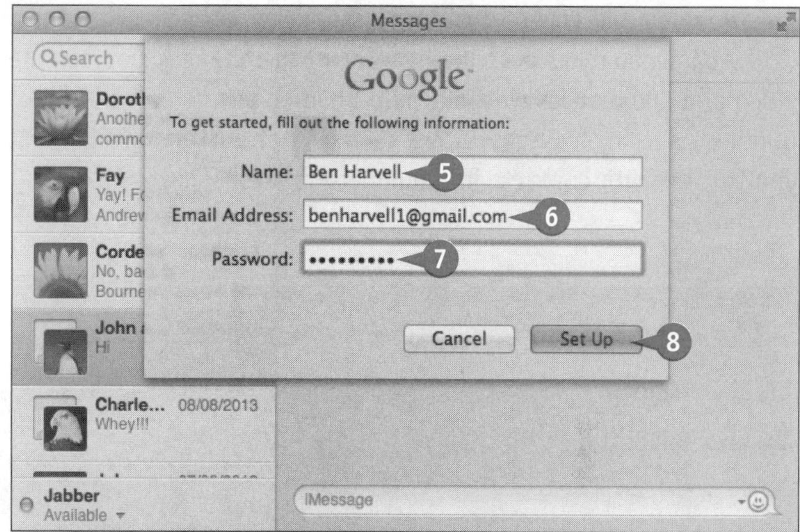

Your account is added.

9 Click **Window**.

10 Click **Buddies**.

A Contacts for your new account are shown in the Buddies window.

TIP

How do I contact AIM users through Messages?

You can use an existing @me.com or @mac.com e-mail address as an AIM account in Messages. This allows you to add buddies who are using AIM accounts and make voice and video calls as well as use text chat. Use the **Other Messages account...** option when adding a new account and select AIM from the menu that appears.

Using an AIM Account with Messages

When you add an AOL Instant Messenger account to Messages or add your mac.com account as an AIM account, as described earlier in the chapter, you can make use of additional features like video and audio chats with multiple buddies and screen sharing. These features are available from the Buddies pane in Messages with a selection of buttons available at the bottom of the pane that allow you to chat with contacts in a number of ways.

Using an AIM Account with Messages

1. Click **Window**.
2. Click **Buddies**.

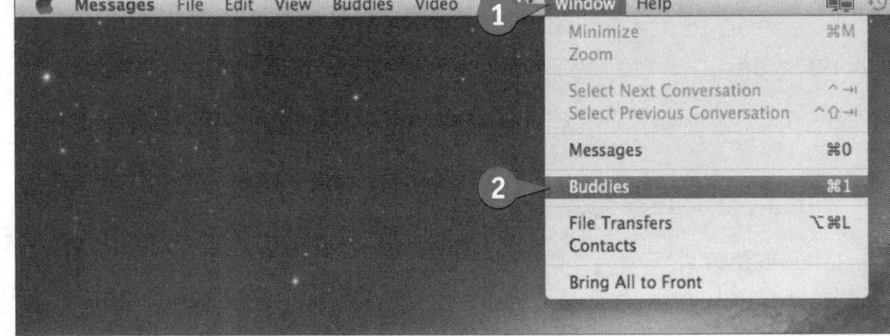

The Buddies pane appears.

3. Click a contact on the Buddies pane.

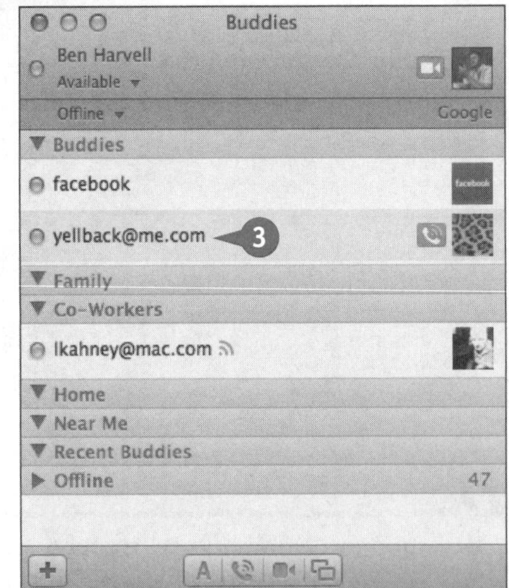

Ⓐ Click the **Text Chat** button (A) to begin a chat in Messages.

Ⓑ Click the **Audio Chat** button (📞) to invite the contact to a voice call.

Ⓒ Click the **Video Chat** button (📹) to invite the contact to a video call.

Note: You can also click the icon next to a contact's profile picture to begin an audio or video chat.

4 Click the **Screen Sharing** button (⧉).

5 Click an option from the menu that appears.

Screen sharing between you and your contact is initiated once the contact accepts the invitation.

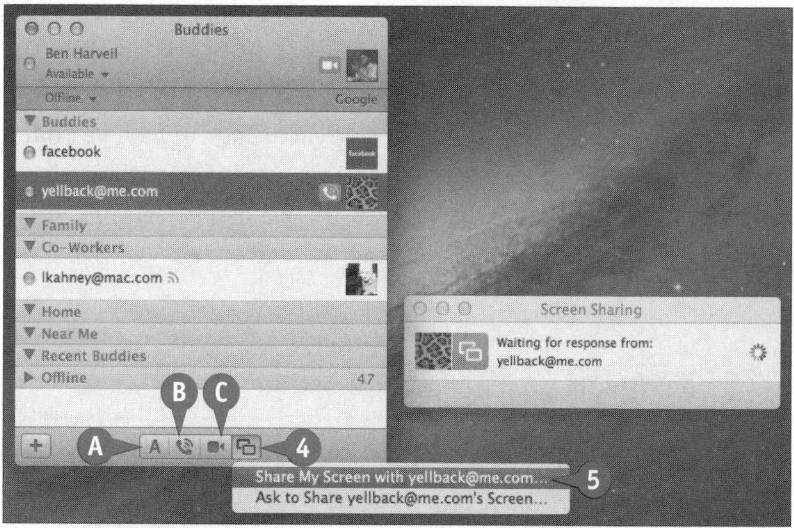

TIP

What are the benefits of Screen Sharing?

Screen sharing allows you to show a contact exactly what is on your Mac's screen at any time. This is useful for collaborating on a project or for explaining something visually. When Screen Sharing is active, an audio chat is also enabled so you can speak to the contact as you show him or her the contents of your screen.

Open and Close FaceTime

OS X Mavericks comes with a video chat feature called FaceTime that enables you to see and speak to another person over the Internet. To use FaceTime, you and your friend must have the right type of equipment. If either or both of you are using a Mac, you must have a web camera attached to the computer, such as the iSight or FaceTime HD camera that comes with many Macs, and you must have a microphone attached to the computer, such as the built-in microphone that is part of the iSight camera. After you have all the necessary equipment, you must learn how to open and close FaceTime.

Open and Close FaceTime

Open FaceTime

1. In the Dock, click the **FaceTime** icon (📹).

The FaceTime window appears.

Close FaceTime

1 Click **FaceTime**.

2 Click **Quit FaceTime**.

OS X shuts down the FaceTime application.

TIP

Are there other methods I can use to open FaceTime?

Yes. If you do not have (FaceTime icon) in the Dock, there are a couple of methods you can use to open FaceTime. If you have used FaceTime recently, a reasonably fast method is to click the **Apple** icon ( ), click **Recent Items**, and then click **FaceTime**. Alternatively, click **Spotlight** ( ), type **facetime**, and then click **FaceTime** in the search results. If you want to switch an instant messaging conversation to a FaceTime conversation, click the **FaceTime** icon ( ) in the Messages window.

Sign In to FaceTime

To use FaceTime to conduct video chats with your friends, you must each first sign in using your Apple ID. This could be an iCloud account that uses the Apple me.com address, or it could be your existing e-mail address. After you create your Apple ID, you can use it to sign in to FaceTime. Note that you only have to do this once. In subsequent sessions, FaceTime automatically signs you in.

Sign In to FaceTime

1. In the Dock, click the **FaceTime** icon (📹).

   The FaceTime window appears.

2. Type your Apple ID e-mail address.
3. Type your Apple ID password.

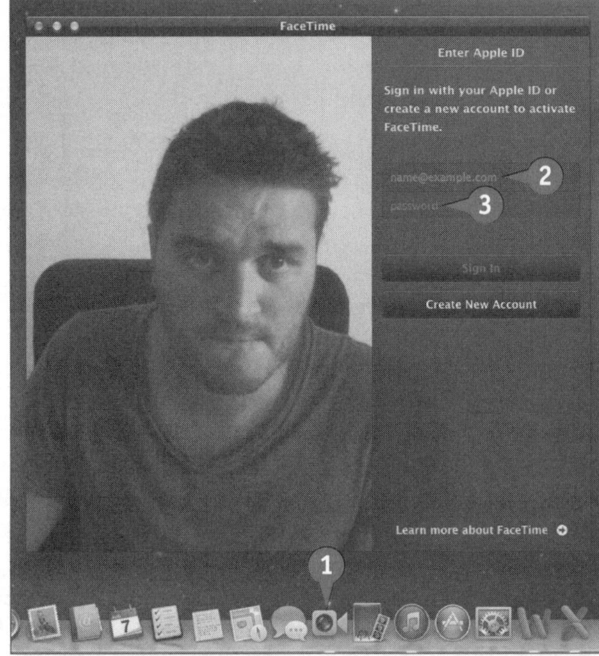

4. Click **Sign In**.

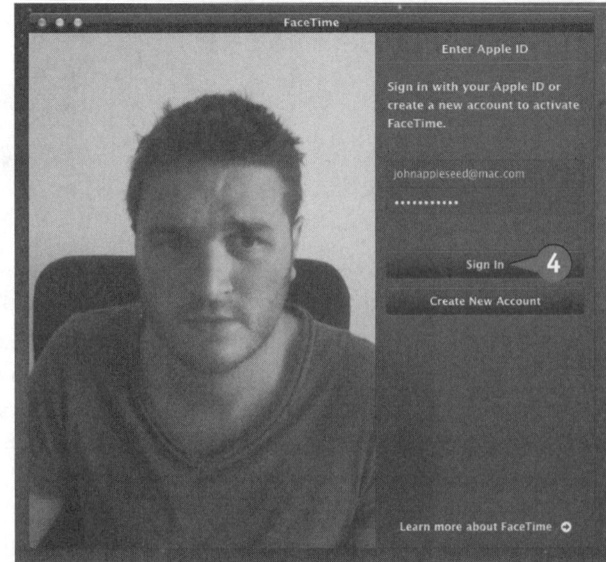

FaceTime prompts you to specify an e-mail address that people can use to contact you via FaceTime.

5 If the address you prefer to use is different from your Apple ID, click the address you want to use.

6 Click **Next**.

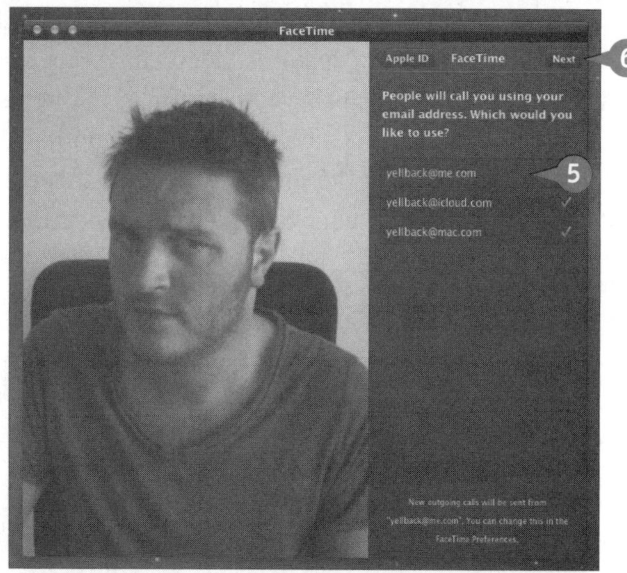

FaceTime verifies your Apple ID and then displays a list of contacts.

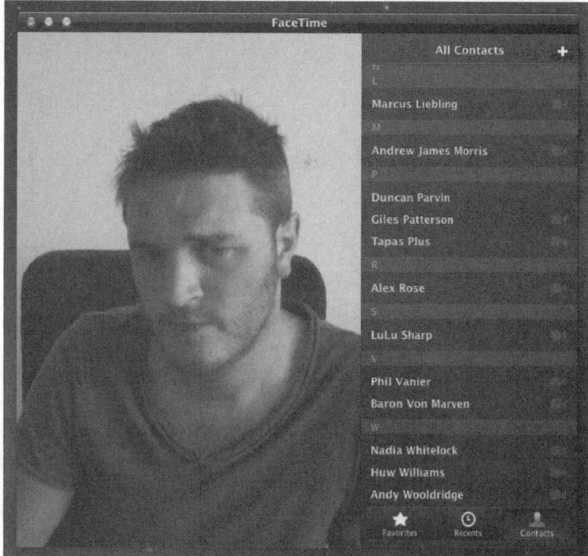

TIP

Which devices support FaceTime?

You can use the FaceTime application on any Mac that is running OS X 10.6.6 or later. For OS X Snow Leopard (10.6.6), FaceTime is available through the App Store for 99 cents. For OS X Mavericks (10.9), Mountain Lion (10.8), and OS X Lion (10.7), FaceTime is installed by default. The FaceTime software is also available as an app that runs on the iPhone 4 and later, the iPad 2 and later, and the iPod touch fourth generation and later.

Connect Through FaceTime

Once you sign in with your Apple ID, you can use the FaceTime application to connect with another person and conduct a video chat. How you connect with the other person depends on what device he or she is using for FaceTime. If the person is using a Mac, an iPad, or an iPod touch, you can use whatever e-mail address the person has designated as his or her FaceTime contact address, as described in the previous section. If the person is using an iPhone 4 or later, you can use that person's mobile number to make the connection.

Connect Through FaceTime

1. Click **Contacts**.
2. Click the contact you want to call.

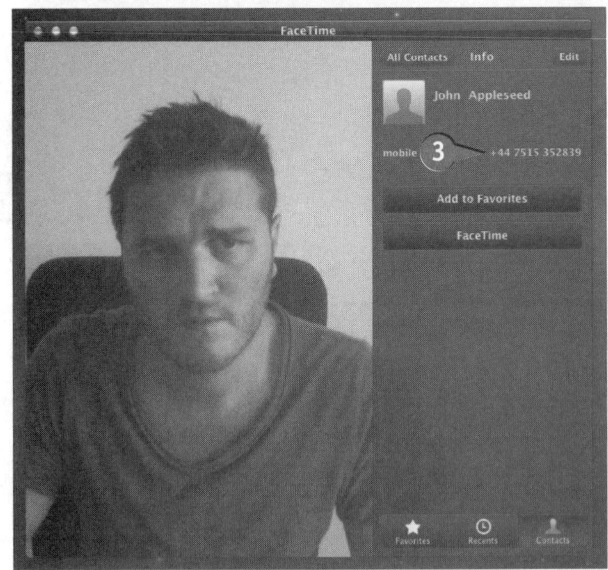

FaceTime displays the contact's data.

3. Click the phone number (for an iPhone) or e-mail address (for a Mac, iPad, or iPod touch) that you want to use to connect to the contact.

FaceTime sends a message to the contact asking if he wants a FaceTime connection.

4 The other person must click or tap **Accept** to complete the connection.

FaceTime connects with the other person.

A The other person's video takes up the bulk of the FaceTime screen.

B Your video appears in the picture-in-picture (PiP) window.

Note: You can click and drag the PiP to a different location within the FaceTime window.

5 When you finish your FaceTime call, click **End**.

TIP

Are there easier ways to connect to someone through FaceTime?

Yes. If you have connected with a person through FaceTime recently, that person may appear in the FaceTime Recents list. In the FaceTime window, click **Recents** and then click the person you want to contact. Alternatively, if you connect with someone frequently, you can add that person to the FaceTime Favorites list. Use the Contacts list to click the person, and then click **Add to Favorites**. To connect with a favorite, click **Favorites** and then click the person.

Make a FaceTime Call Through Messages

As well as using the FaceTime application, you can make FaceTime calls from elsewhere in OS X. One of the easiest places to make a FaceTime call is via the Messages app, one of the applications in which you may already be chatting with friends and family. Using the FaceTime button within Messages allows you to check whether someone is available to chat before calling by sending a message first.

Make a FaceTime Call Through Messages

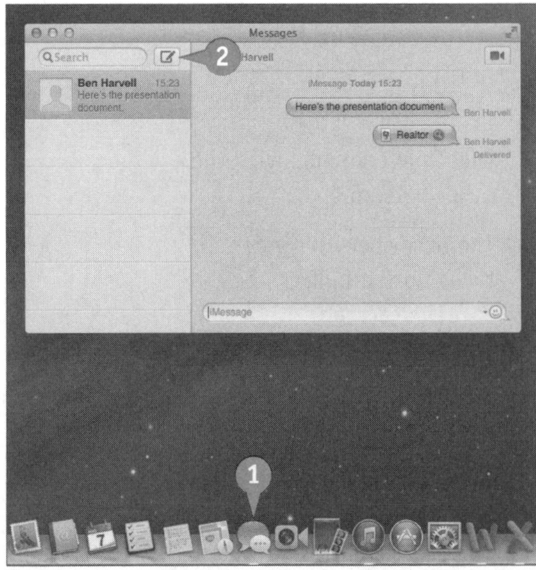

1. In the Dock, click the **Messages** icon ( ).

   The Messages application appears.

2. Click the **Compose New Message** button ( ).

Note: You can also click a previous conversation in the Messages sidebar. If you do, skip steps 2, 3, and 4.

3. Click the **Add Contact** button ( ).

Note: You can also type the name of a contact into the To: field at the top of the interface.

4. Click a contact or search for one using the search field.

Note: Make sure that the contact you select is compatible for use with FaceTime, such as an iCloud e-mail address or iPhone phone number.

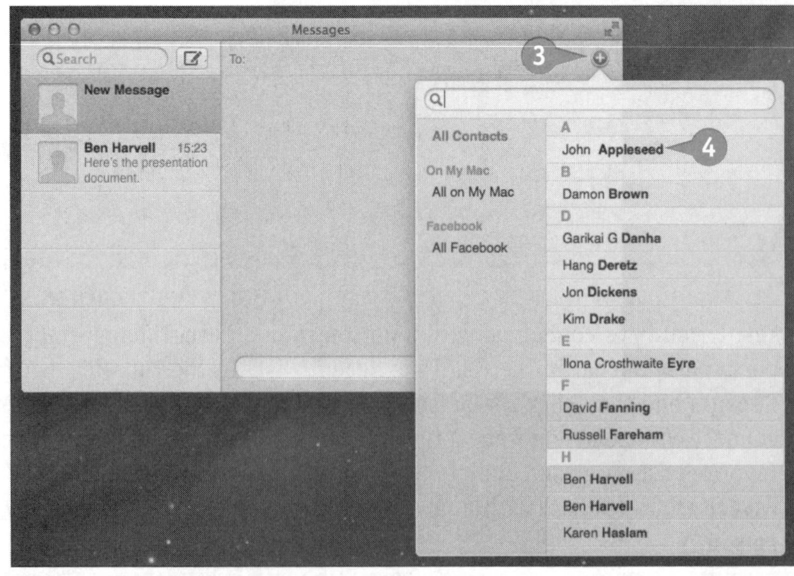

5 Type a message into the message field and press Return to send it.

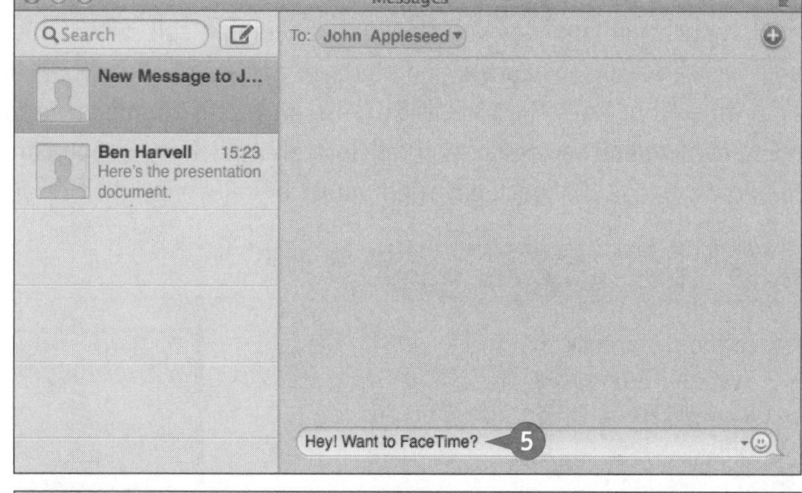

The message is sent and the FaceTime button (■◀) appears.

6 Click the **FaceTime** button (■◀) and select the number or e-mail address to call if required.

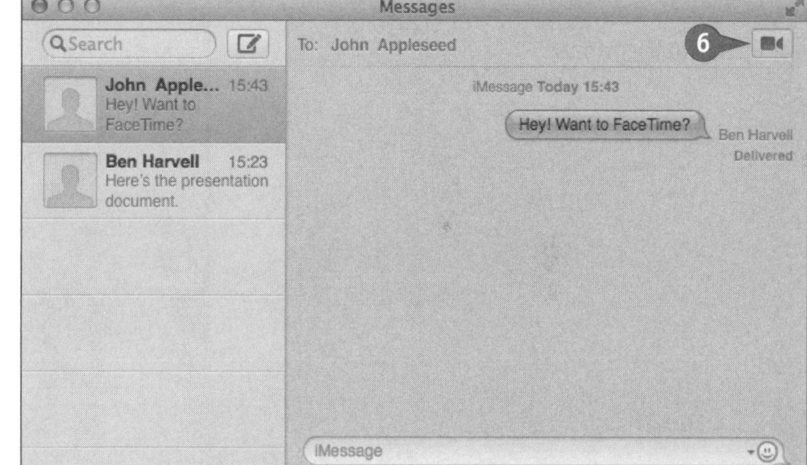

TIP

What is the difference between calling a phone number and an e-mail address?

You can make FaceTime calls to an iPhone using the telephone number assigned by a contact's carrier and also use an iCloud e-mail address. If you want to FaceTime a contact using a Mac, iPad, or iPod touch, you need to use the contact's iCloud e-mail address to make a FaceTime call.

Set Up FaceTime Notifications

When you receive a FaceTime call you can be notified in a number of ways. The FaceTime application launches and shows the incoming call, which you can choose to answer or decline, and you can also set banners and alerts to appear to show you when you miss a FaceTime call when away from your Mac. These notifications can be set to appear in different ways and even to appear on the screen when the display is off or locked. Additionally, you can set the FaceTime icon in the Dock to show a badge that includes the number of calls missed since you last used FaceTime.

Set Up FaceTime Notifications

1. In the Dock, click the **System Preferences** icon ( ).

   The System Preferences pane appears.

2. Click **Notifications**.

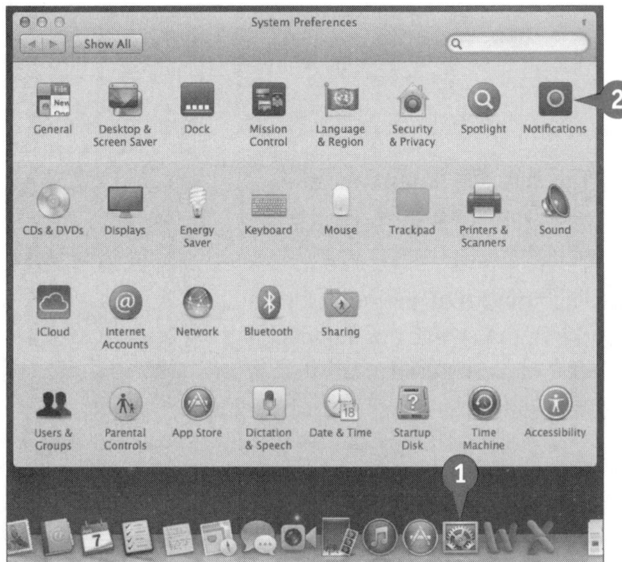

3. Click **FaceTime**.

   A. Click **None** to show no alerts from FaceTime.

   B. Click **Banners** to show a notification at the top corner of the screen that disappears after a short period of time.

   C. Click **Alerts** to show a notification that stays on the screen and allows you to interact with it.

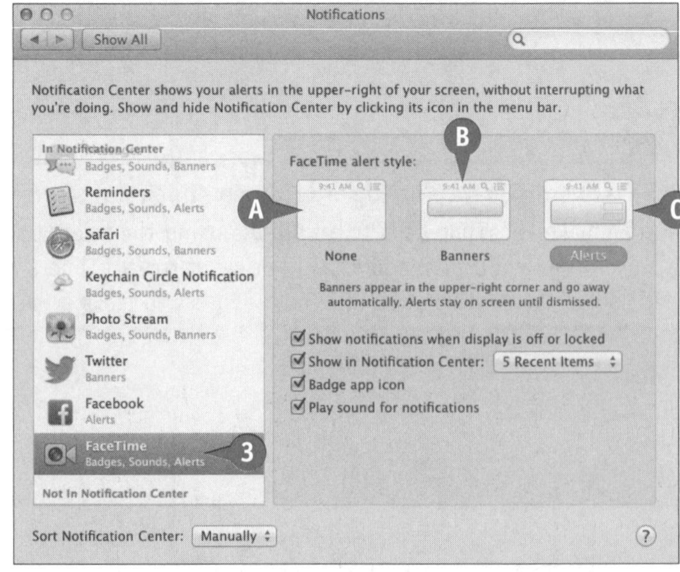

D Select the **Show notifications** check box (☐ changes to ☑) to show notifications when the screen is locked or off.

E Select the **Badge app icon** check box (☐ changes to ☑) to show the number of missed calls on the FaceTime Dock icon.

F Select the **Play sound** check box (☐ changes to ☑) to play an audio alert for an incoming FaceTime call.

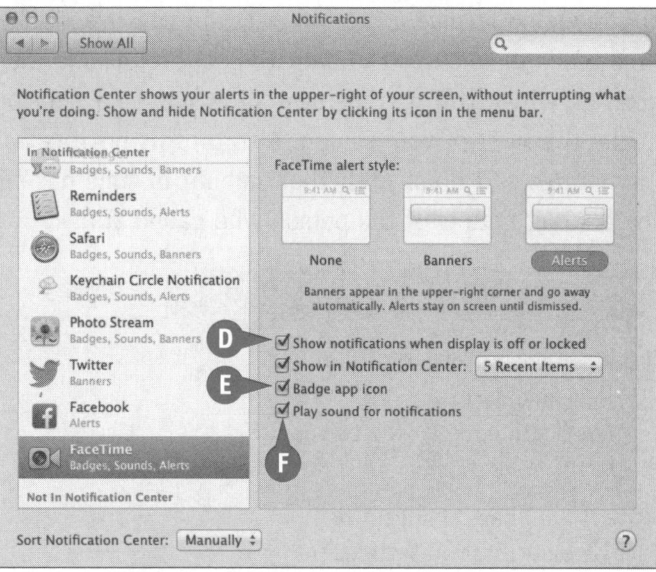

4 Select the **Show in Notification Center** check box (☐ changes to ☑).

5 Click ⬍ next to Show in Notification Center and select how many recent FaceTime items are shown in Notification Center from the pop-up menu.

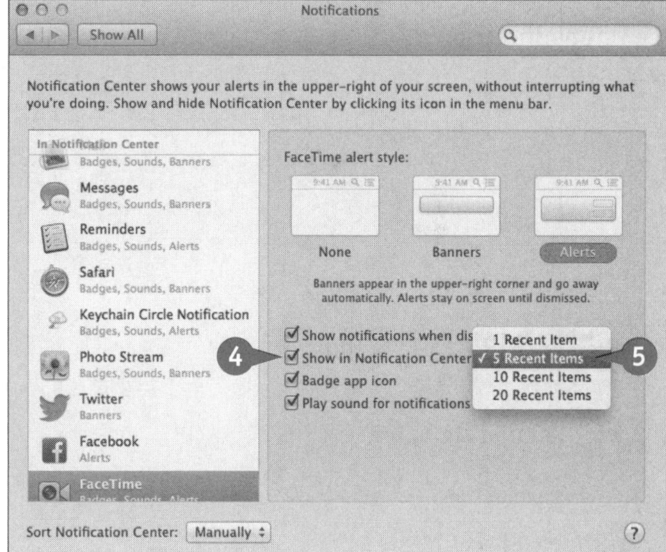

TIP

What is the difference between a banner and an alert?

A banner appears as a small notification at the top right of the OS X screen you are currently viewing and provides information about an activity or message from within an app. The banner will show for a short period of time and then slide out of view. An alert looks the same as a banner but requires an action before it is dismissed. You can interact with an alert in many ways, such as dismissing it or replying to a message from within the notification if you wish.

Set Up FaceTime Call Reminders

When you receive a FaceTime call on your Mac but you do not have time to answer it, you can set a reminder to call back the contact at another time. This can be done when using Alert notifications with FaceTime that allow you to accept or decline an incoming call from a notification at the top right of your screen. Also on this notification is the option to set a reminder for 15 minutes or 1 hour. After that amount of time has elapsed, a reminder appears that includes the contact details of the person who called you.

Set Up FaceTime Call Reminders

1. When you receive an incoming FaceTime call notification, hover the cursor over the alert.

Note: If you have changed the FaceTime notification settings in System Preferences you may not see this notification.

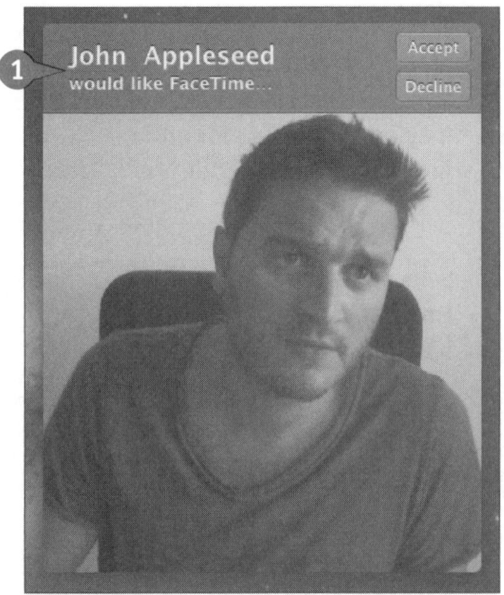

The Remind Me Later button appears.

2. Click **Remind Me Later**.

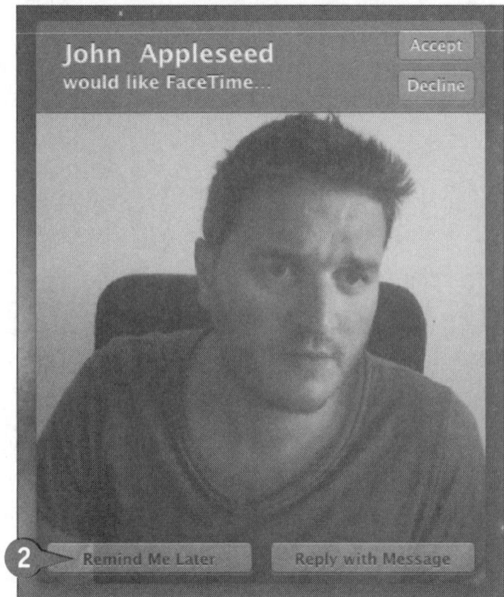

3 Select **In 15 minutes** or **In one hour** from the menu that appears.

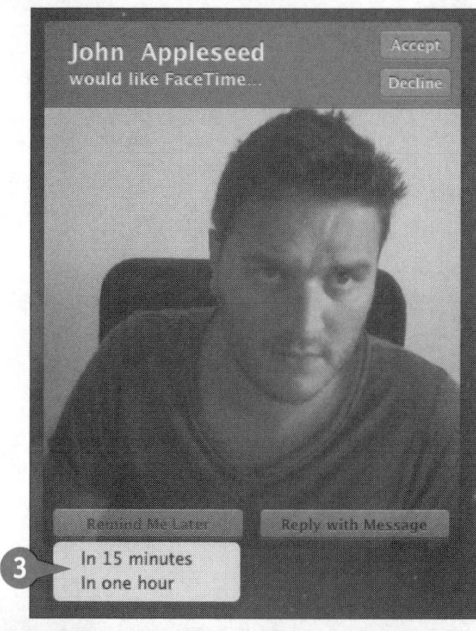

A reminder is added to the Reminders app and a notification is shown at the time you set.

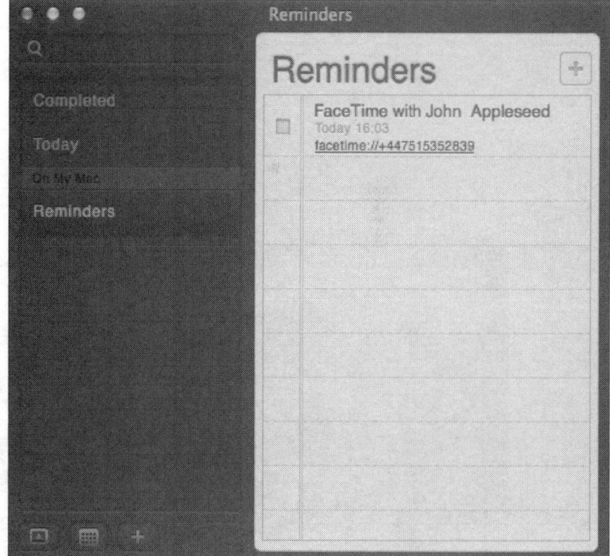

TIP

What happens to the call when I set a reminder?

The FaceTime call automatically ends and the person calling is told that you are currently busy. To stop all incoming FaceTime calls for a certain period, you can set FaceTime to Off from the FaceTime Preferences screen or use the Do Not Disturb feature in Notification Center to prevent incoming messages and alerts from appearing for a certain period of time.

CHAPTER 7

Tracking Contacts and Events

OS X comes with two applications that can help you manage your busy life. You use the Contacts application to manage your contacts by storing information such as phone numbers, e-mail addresses, street addresses, and much more. You use the Calendar application to enter and track events and to-do items.

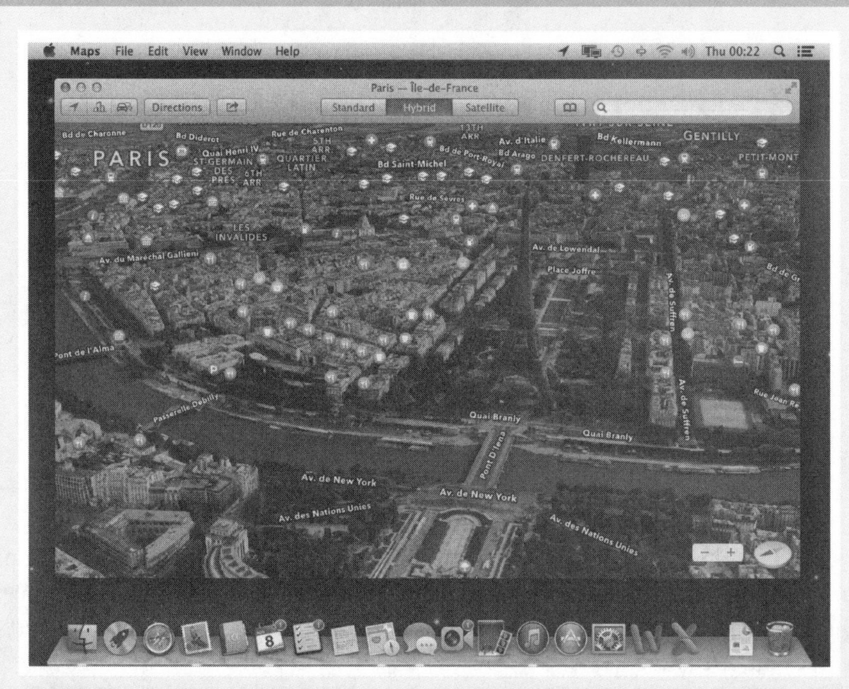

Open and Close Contacts

OS X includes the Contacts application to enable you to manage information about the people you know, whether they are colleagues, friends, or family members. The Contacts app refers to these people as *contacts*, and you store each person's data in an object called a *card*.

Before you can add to or work with your contacts, you must know how to start the Contacts application. When you finish with Contacts, you should close it to reduce desktop clutter and save system resources.

Open and Close Contacts

Open Contacts

1. In the Dock, click the **Contacts** icon (■).

The Contacts window appears.

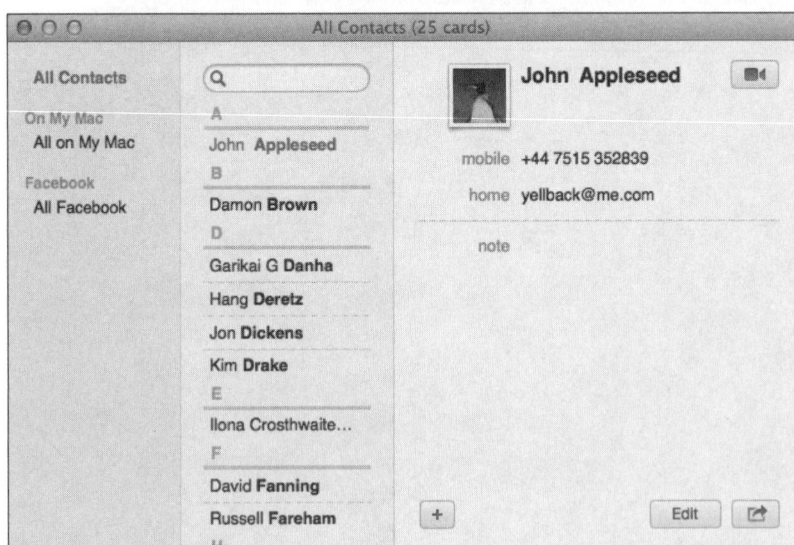

Close Contacts

1 Click **Contacts**.

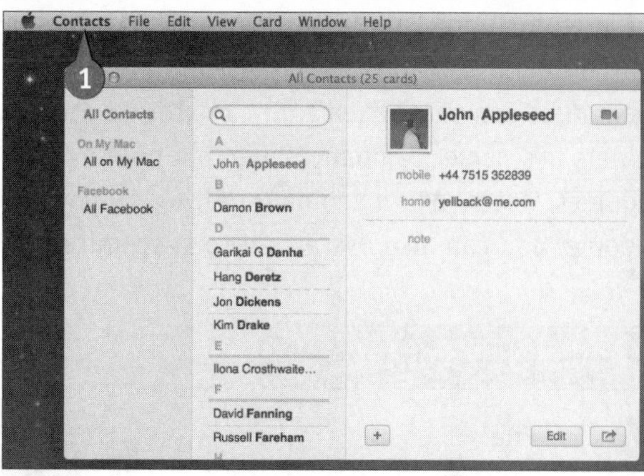

2 Click **Quit Contacts**.

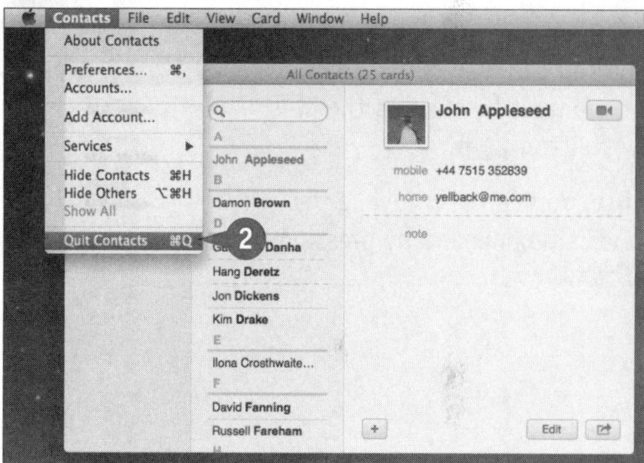

TIPS

Are there other methods I can use to open Contacts?

Yes. If you have used Contacts recently, click the **Apple** icon (), click **Recent Items**, and then click **Contacts.** You can also click **Spotlight** (), type **contacts**, and then click **Contacts** in the search results.

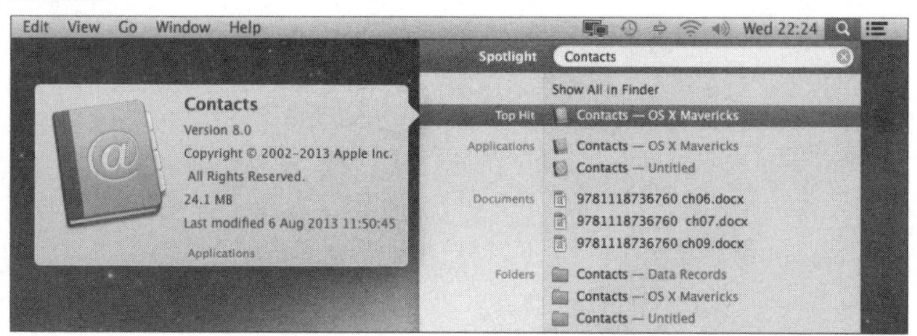

Are there faster methods I can use to close Contacts?

Yes. Probably the fastest method you can use to quit Contacts is to right-click its icon () and then click **Quit.** If your hands are closer to the keyboard than to the mouse, you can quit Contacts by switching to the application and then pressing ⌘+Q.

Add a New Contact

To store contact information for a particular person, you first need to create a new contact within Contacts. You do that by creating a new card, which is a Contacts item that stores data about a person or company. Each card can store a wide variety of information. For example, you can store a person's name, company name, phone numbers, e-mail address, instant messaging data, street address, notes, and much more. Although you will mostly use Contacts cards to store data about people, you can also use a card to keep information about companies.

Add a New Contact

1. Click **File**.
2. Click **New Card**.

Ⓐ You can also begin a new contact by clicking the plus button (+).

Note: You can also invoke the New Card command by pressing ⌘+N.

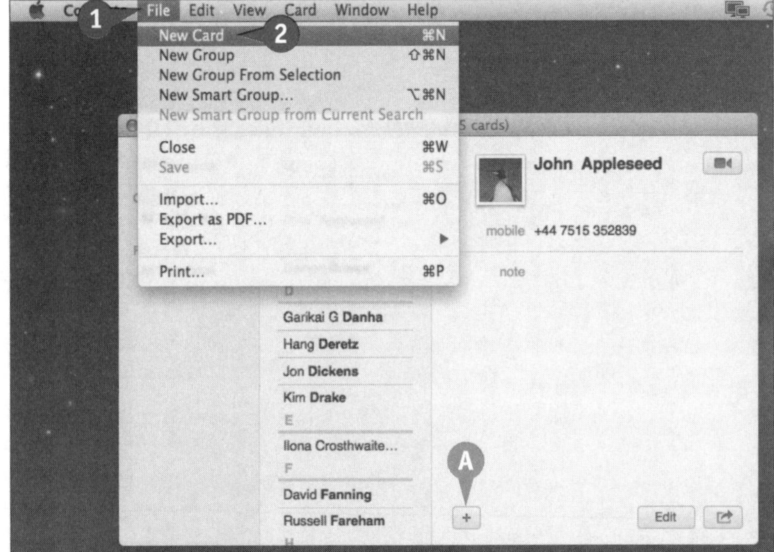

Ⓑ Contacts adds a new card.

3. In the First field, type the contact's first name.
4. In the Last field, type the contact's last name.
5. In the Company field, type the contact's company name.
6. If the contact is a company, select the **Company** check box (☐ changes to ☑).

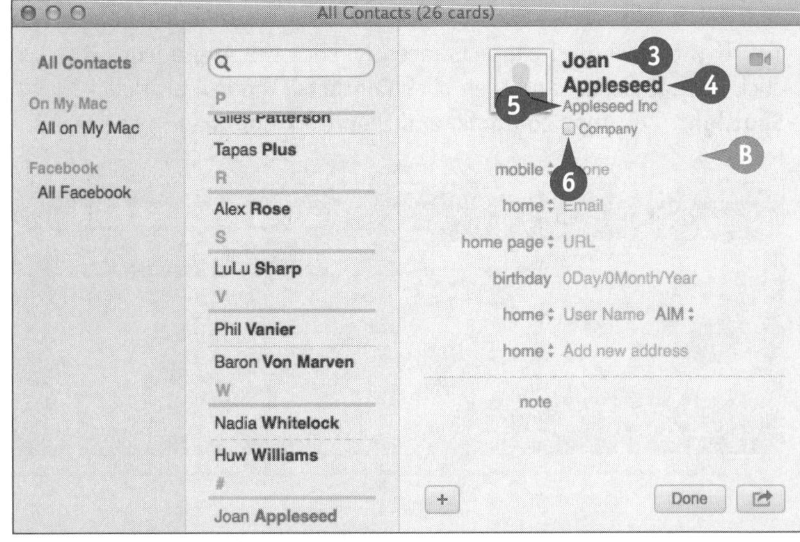

7. In the first Phone field, click ⬍ and then click the category you want to use.
8. Type the phone number.
9. Repeat steps **7** and **8** to enter data in some or all of the other fields.

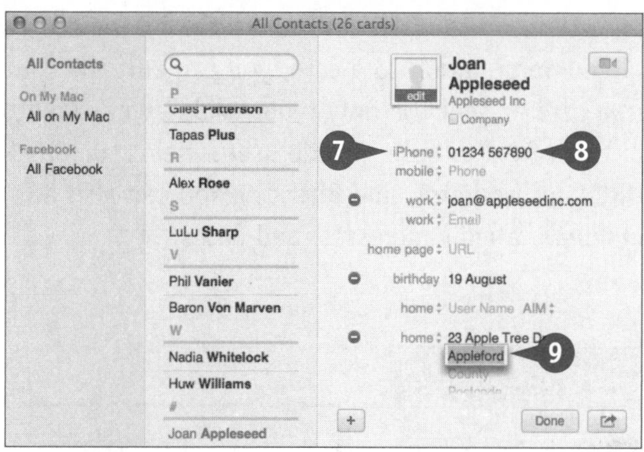

Note: To learn how to add more fields to the card, see the section "Edit a Contact."

10. Click **Done**.

Contacts saves the new card.

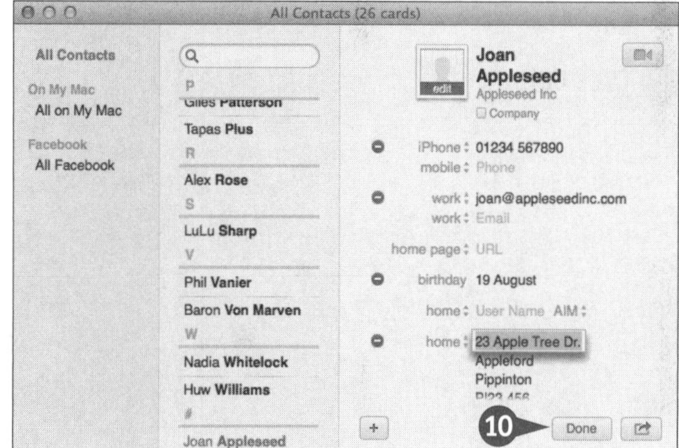

TIP

If I include a contact's e-mail address, is there a way to send that person a message without having to type the address?

Yes. Follow these steps:

1. Click the contact's card.
2. Click the e-mail address category.
3. Click **Send Email**.

   Apple Mail displays a new e-mail message with the contact already added in the To line.

   A new Mail window appears with the contact added in the To: field.

4. Fill in the rest of the message as required.
5. Click **Send**.

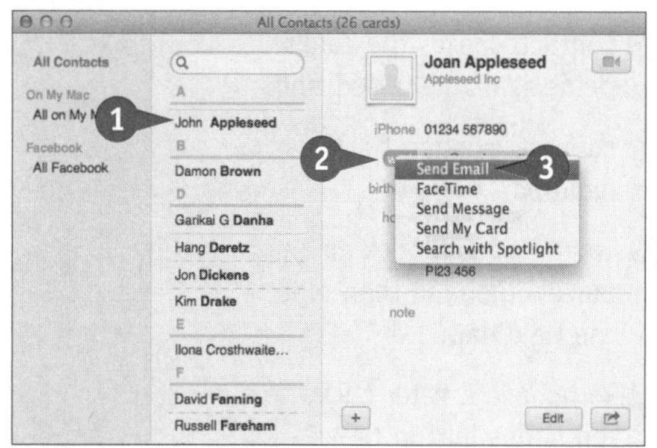

Edit a Contact

If you need to make changes to the information already in a contact's card, or if you need to add new information to a card, you can edit the card from within Contacts. The default fields you see in a card are not the only types of data you can store for a contact. Contacts offers a large number of extra fields. These include useful fields such as Middle Name, Nickname, Job Title, Department, URL (web address), and Birthday. You can also add extra fields for common data items such as phone numbers, e-mail addresses, and dates.

Edit a Contact

1. Click the card you want to edit.
2. Click **Edit**.

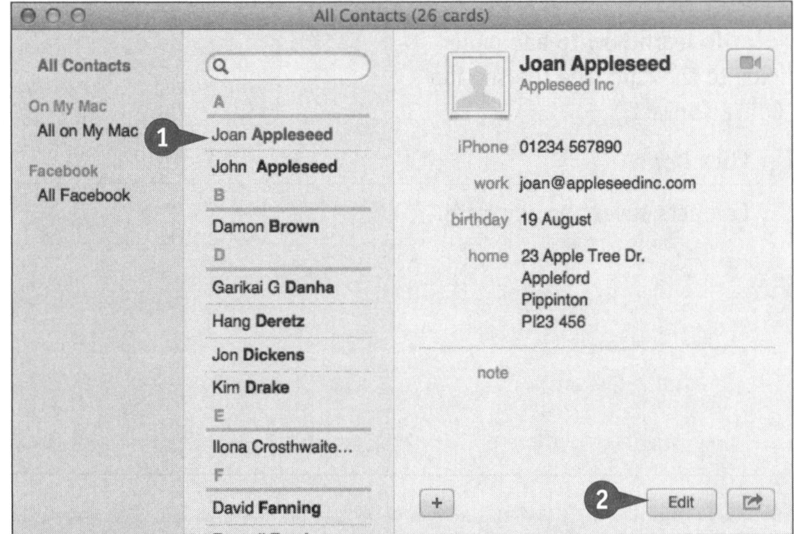

A. Contacts makes the card's fields available for editing.

3. Edit the existing fields as required.
4. To add a field, click an empty placeholder and then type the field data.
5. To remove a field, click the red minus button (⊖).

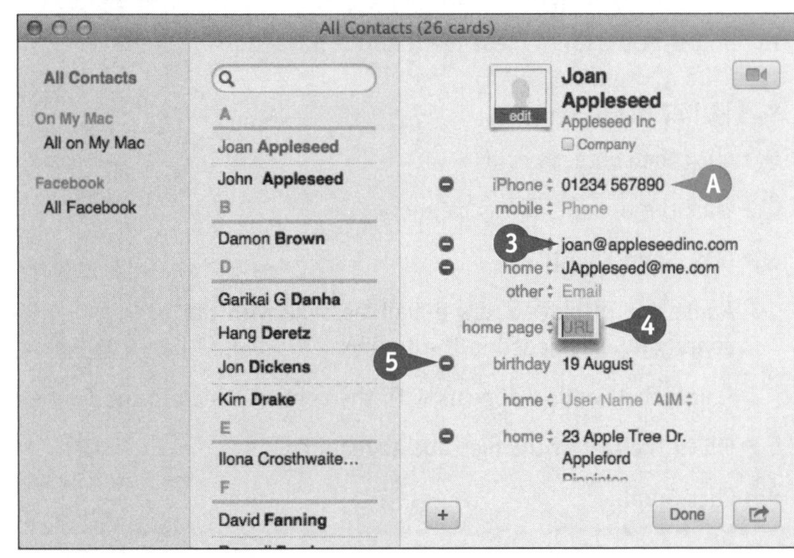

6 To add a new field type, click **Card**.

7 Click **Add Field**.

8 Click the type of field you want.

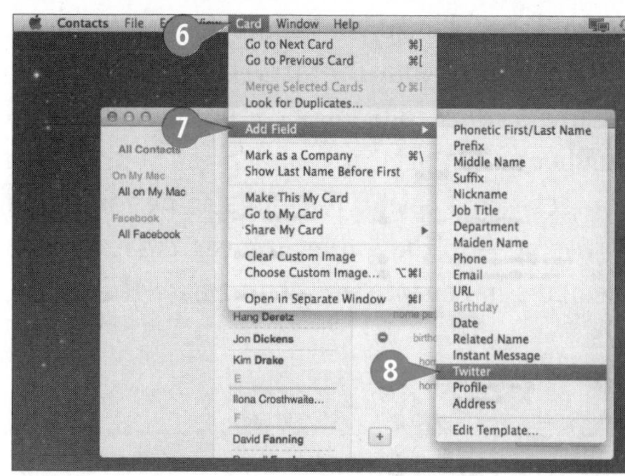

B Contacts adds the field to the card.

9 When you complete your edits, click **Done**.

Contacts saves the edited card.

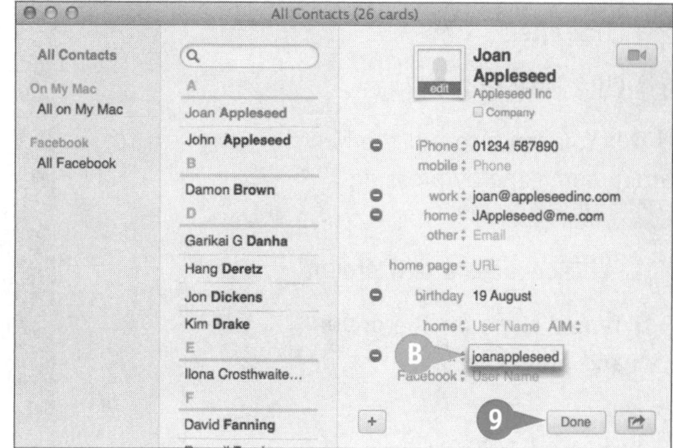

TIP

How do I add a picture for the new contact?

Follow these steps:

1 Click the contact's card.

2 Double-click the picture box.

3 Click the type of picture you want to add.

4 Click the picture.

5 Click **Done**.

6 Click **Done**.

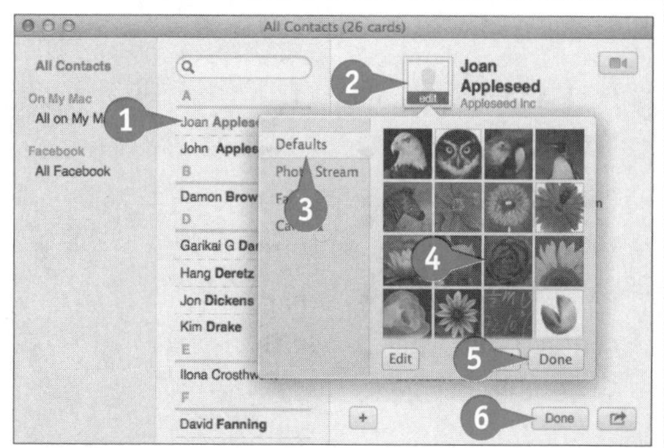

Create a Contact Group

You can organize your contacts into one or more groups, which is useful if you want to view just a subset of your contacts. For example, you could create separate groups for friends, family members, work colleagues, or business clients. Groups are particularly handy if you have a large number of contacts in your address book. By creating and maintaining groups, you can navigate your contacts more easily. You can also perform groupwide tasks, such as sending a single e-mail message to everyone in the group. You can create a group first and then add members, or you can select members in advance and then create the group.

Create a Contact Group

Create a Contact Group

1. Click **File**.
2. Click **New Group**.

Note: You can also run the New Group command by pressing Shift + ⌘ + N.

A Contacts adds a new group.

3. Type a name for the group and press Return.

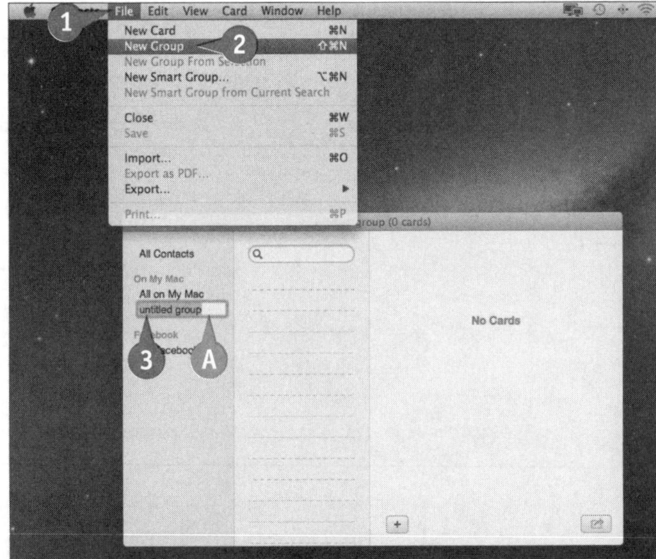

4. Click and drag a contact to the group.

   Contacts adds the contact to the group.

5. Repeat step 4 for the other contacts you want to add to the group.

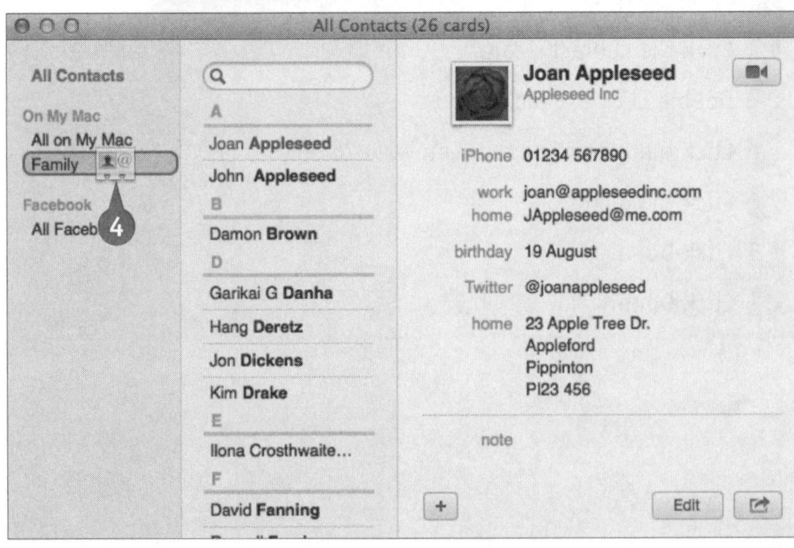

Create a Group of Selected Contacts

1. Select the contacts you want to include in the new group.

Note: To select multiple contacts, press and hold ⌘ and click each card.

2. Click **File**.
3. Click **New Group From Selection**.

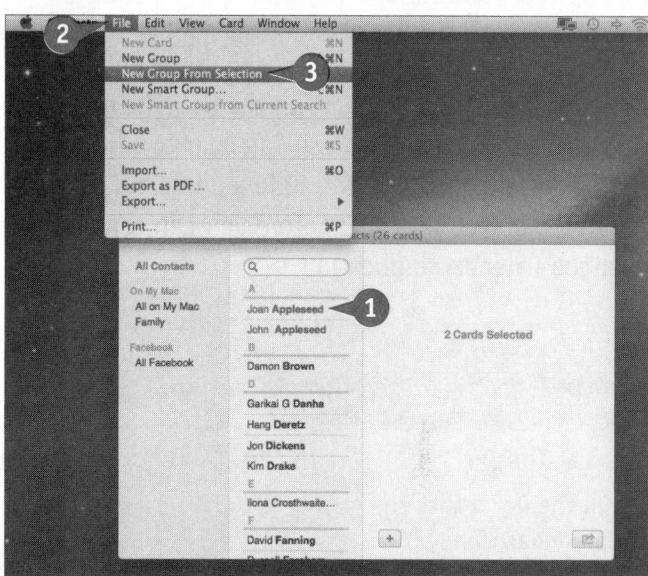

- B Contacts adds a new group.
- C Contacts adds the selected contacts as group members.

4. Type a name for the group and press Return.

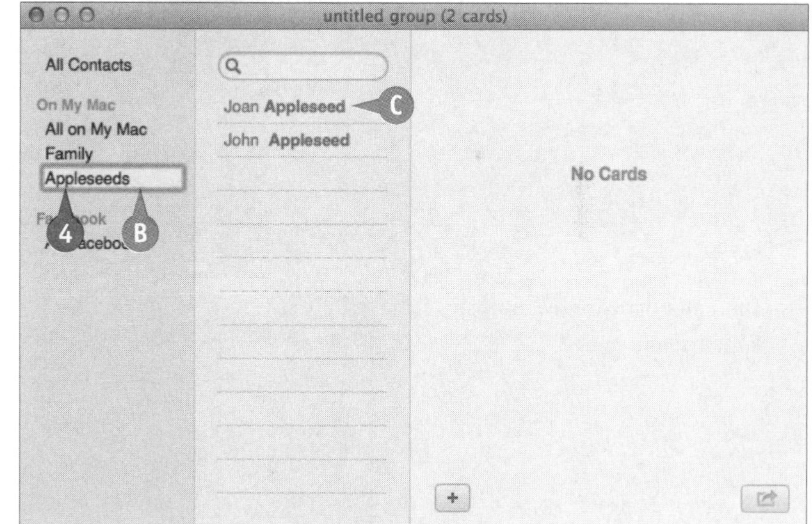

TIPS

Can I send an e-mail message to the group?

Yes. Normally, sending an e-mail message to multiple contacts involves typing or selecting multiple addresses. With a group, you send a single message to the group, and Mail automatically sends a copy to each member. Right-click the group and then click **Send Email to *"Group,"*** where *Group* is the name of the group.

What is a Smart Group?

A *Smart Group* is a special group where each member has one or more fields in common, such as the company name, department name, city, or state. When you create the Smart Group, you specify one or more criteria, and then Contacts automatically adds members to the group if they meet those criteria. To create a Smart Group, click **File**, click **New Smart Group**, and then type your group criteria.

Open and Close Calendar

Your Mac comes with the Calendar application to enable you to manage your schedule. Calendar enables you to create and work with events, which are either scheduled appointments such as meetings, lunches, and visits to the dentist, or all-day activities, such as birthdays, anniversaries, or vacations. You can also use Calendar to send event invitations and to accept or decline any event invitations that you receive. Before you can add or work with events (appointments, meetings, all-day activities, and so on), and before you can send or accept event invitations, you must know how to start the Calendar application.

Open and Close Calendar

Open Calendar

1. In the Dock, click the **Calendar** icon (📅).

The Calendar window appears.

Close Calendar

1. Click **Calendars**.

2. Click **Quit Calendar**.

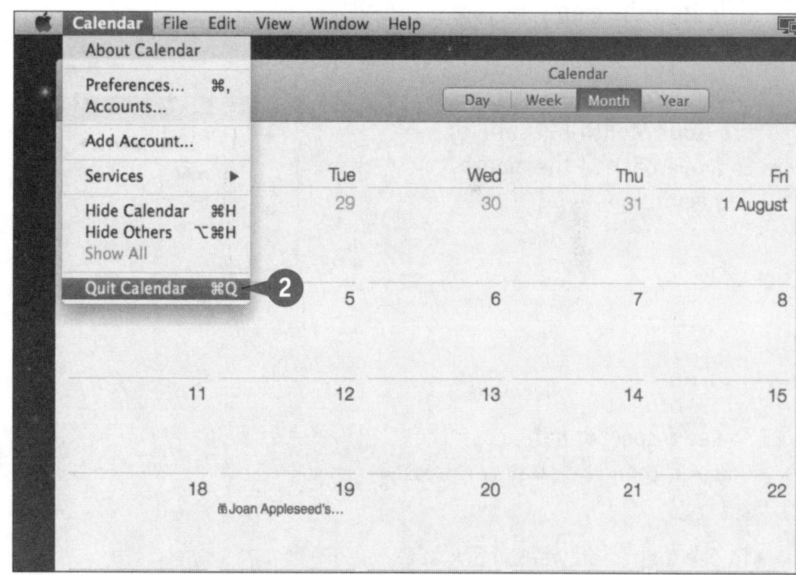

TIP

Are there other methods I can use to open Calendar?

Yes. If you have removed the Calendar icon from the Dock, there are a couple of other quick methods you can use to start Calendar. If you have used Calendar recently, a reasonably fast method is to click the **Apple** icon (), click **Recent Items**, and then click **Calendar**. You can also click **Spotlight** (), type **cal**, and then click **Calendar** in the search results.

Navigate the Calendar

Before you create an event such as an appointment or meeting, or an all-day event such as a conference, birthday, anniversary, or trip, you must first select the date on which the event occurs. You can do this in Calendar by navigating the built-in calendar or by specifying the date that you want. Calendar also lets you change the calendar view to suit your needs. For example, you can show just a single day's worth of events if you want to concentrate on that day's activities. Similarly, you can view a week's worth of events if you want to get a larger sense of what your overall schedule looks like.

Navigate the Calendar

Use the Calendar

1. Click **Month**.
2. Click the **Next Month** button (▶) until the month of your event appears.

A. If you go too far, click the **Previous Month** button (◀) to move back to the month you want.

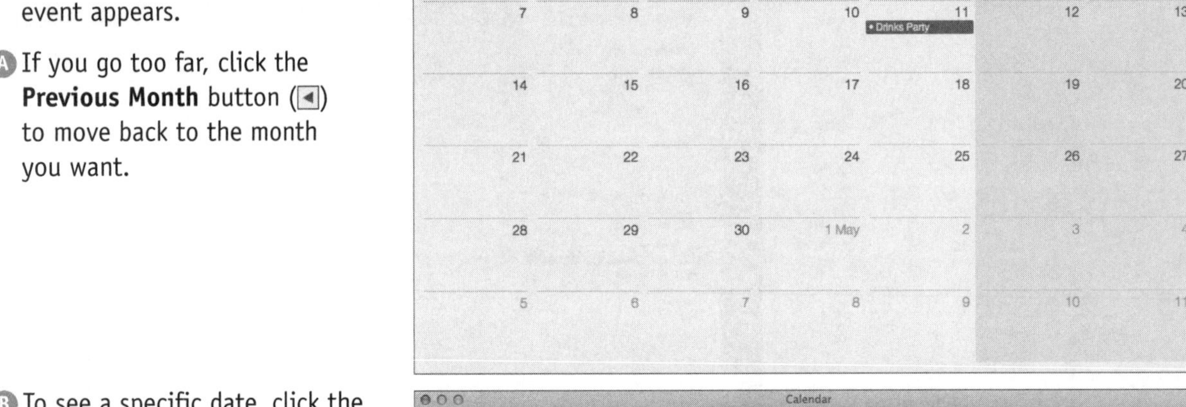

B. To see a specific date, click the day and then click **Day** (or press ⌘+1).

C. To see a specific week, click any day within the week and then click **Week** (or press ⌘+2).

D. To return to viewing the entire month, click **Month** (or press ⌘+3).

E. If you want to return to today's date, click **Today** (or press ⌘+T).

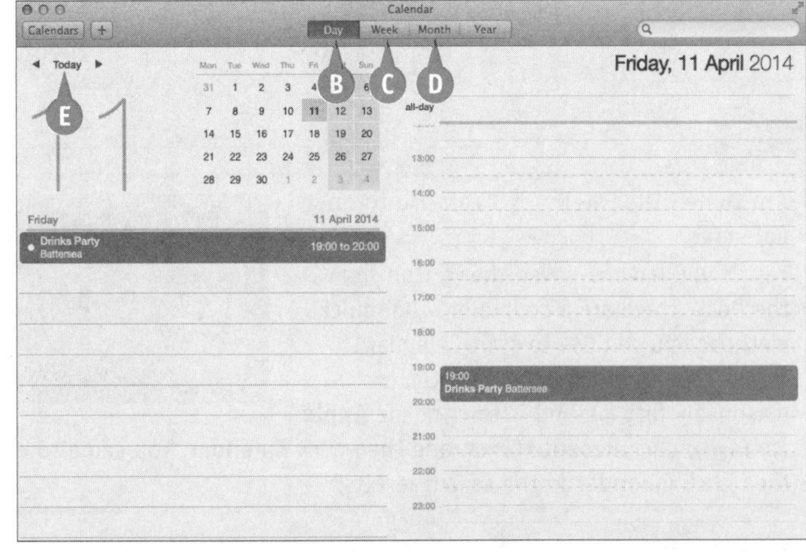

Go to a Specific Date

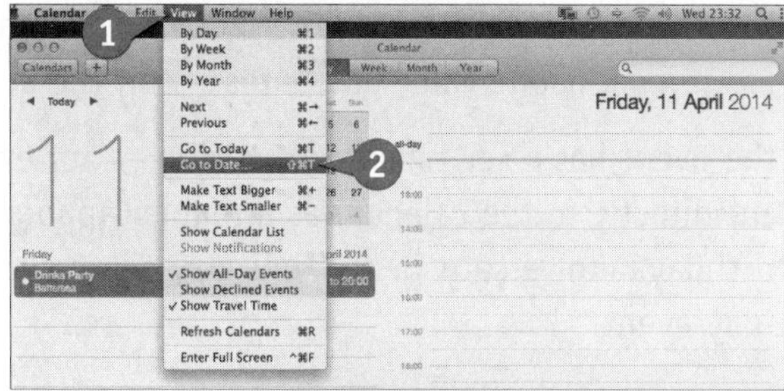

1. Click **View**.
2. Click **Go to Date**.

Note: You can also select the Go to Date command by pressing Shift + ⌘ + T.

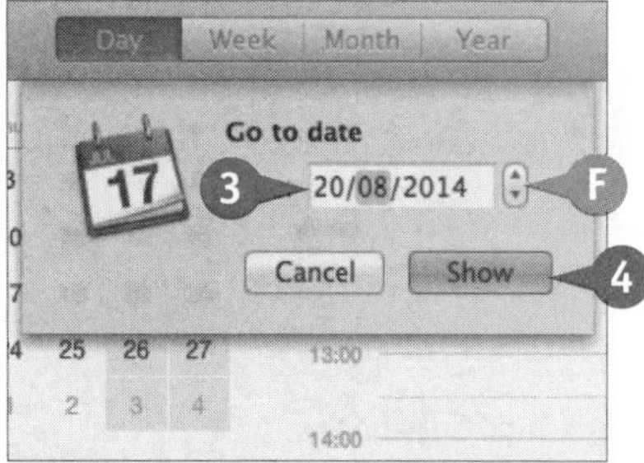

The Go to date dialog appears.

3. In the Date text box, type the date you want using the format mm/dd/yyyy.

F. You can also click the month, day, or year and then click ⬍ to increase or decrease the value.

4. Click **Show**.

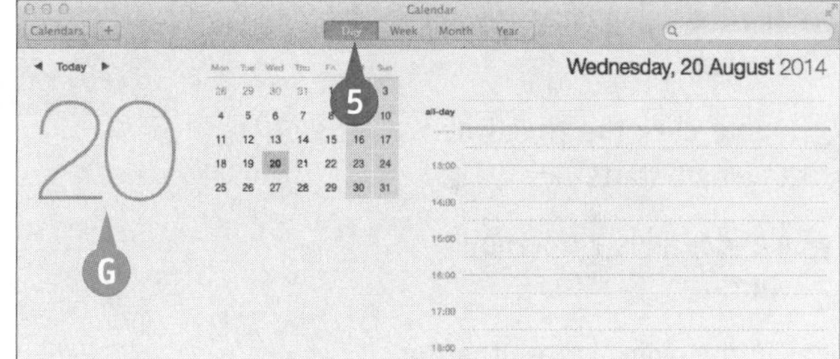

5. Click **Day.**

G. Calendar displays the date.

TIP

In the Week view, the week begins on Sunday. How can I change this to Monday?

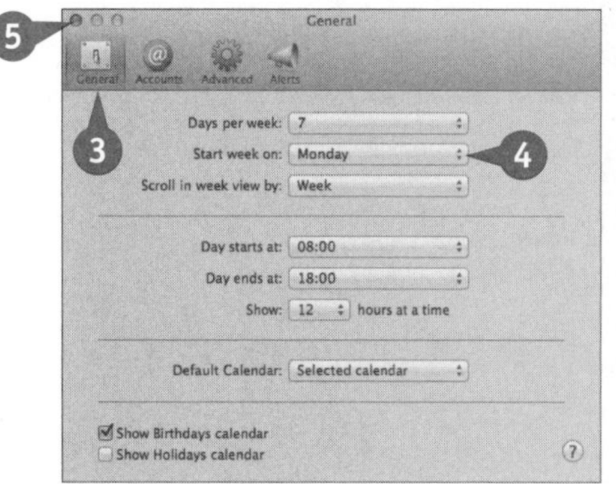

Calendar's default Week view has Sunday on the left and Saturday on the right. To display the weekend days together, with Monday on the left signaling the start of the week, follow these steps:

1. Click **Calendar** in the menu bar.
2. Click **Preferences**.
3. Click the **General** tab.
4. Click the **Start week on** ⬍ and select **Monday** from the pop-up menu.
5. Click **Close** (●).

Create an Event

You can help organize your life by using Calendar to record your events — such as appointments, meetings, phone calls, and dates — on the date and time they occur.

If the event has a set time and duration — for example, a meeting or a lunch date — you add the event directly to the calendar as a regular appointment. If the event has no set time — for example, a birthday, anniversary, or multiple-day event such as a convention or vacation — you can create an all-day event.

Create an Event

Create a Regular Event

1. Navigate to the date when the event occurs.
2. Click **Calendars**.
3. Click the calendar you want to use.
4. Double-click the time when the event starts.

A. Calendar adds a one-hour event.

Note: If the event is less than or more than an hour, you can also click and drag the mouse over the full event period.

5. Type the name of the event and press Return.

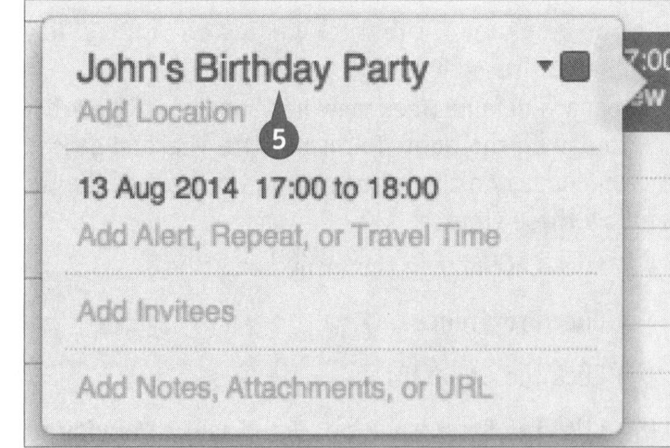

Create an All-Day Event

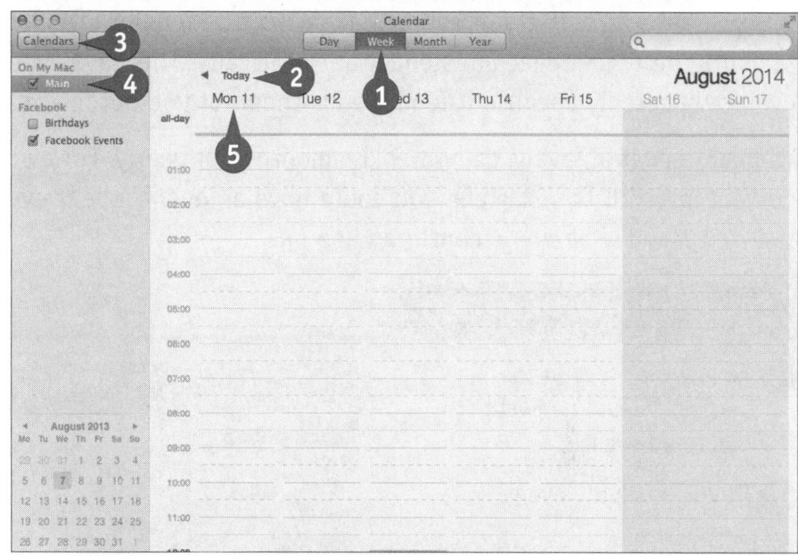

1. Click **Week**.
2. Navigate to the week that includes the date when the event occurs.
3. Click **Calendars**.
4. Click the calendar you want to use.
5. Double-click anywhere inside the event date's all-day section.

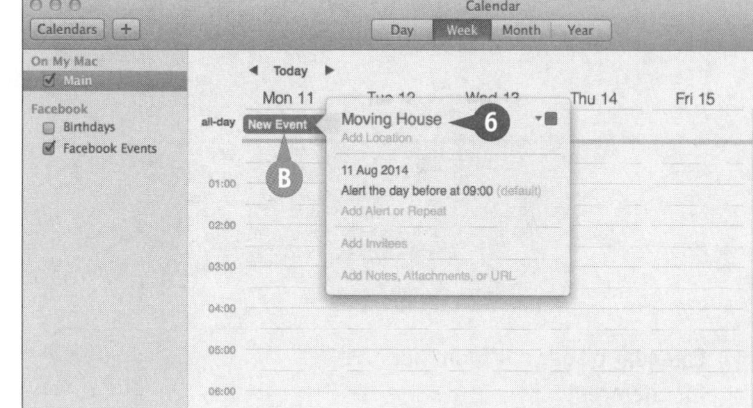

Ⓑ Calendar adds a new all-day event.

6. Type the name of the event and press Return.

TIP

How can I specify event details such as the location and a reminder message?

Double-click an existing event or follow the steps in this section to create an event. On the event info pane, click **Location** below the event title and type a location. You can also click the **alert** and set a specific time when you would like to be reminded about the event.

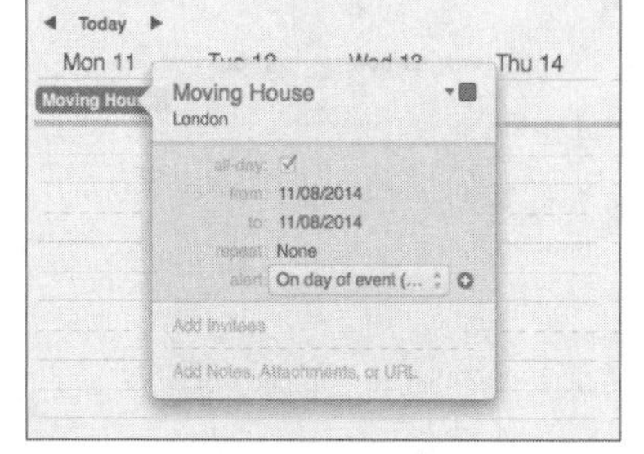

Create a Repeating Event

If you have an activity or event that recurs at a regular interval, you can create an event and configure it to repeat in Calendar automatically. This saves you from having to add the future events repeatedly because Calendar adds them for you automatically.

You can repeat an event daily, weekly, monthly, or yearly. For even greater flexibility, you can set up a custom interval. For example, you could have an event repeat every five days, every second Friday, on the first Monday of every month, and so on.

Create a Repeating Event

1. Follow the steps in the section "Create an Event" to create an event.
2. Double-click the event.

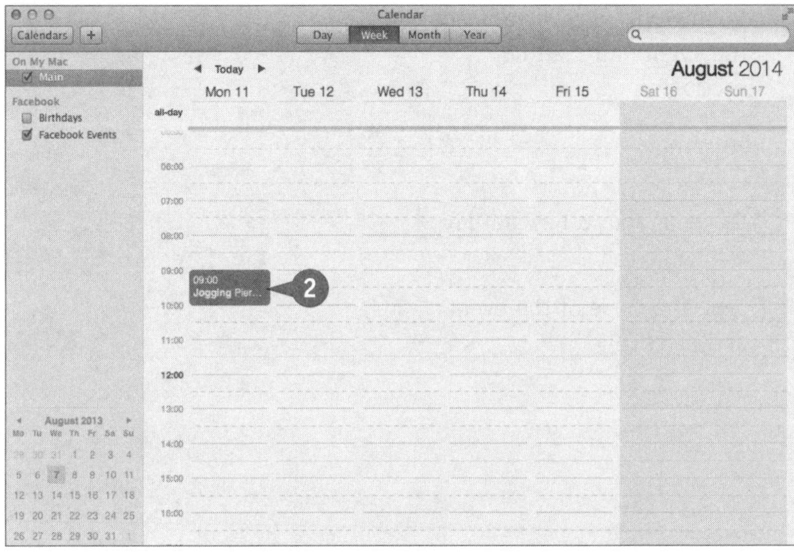

Calendar displays information for the event.

3. Click the time and date of the event.

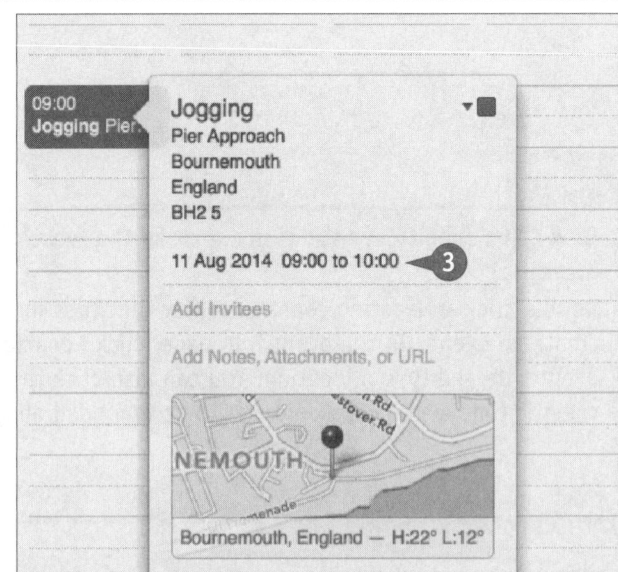

4 Beside the repeat label, click the **None** .

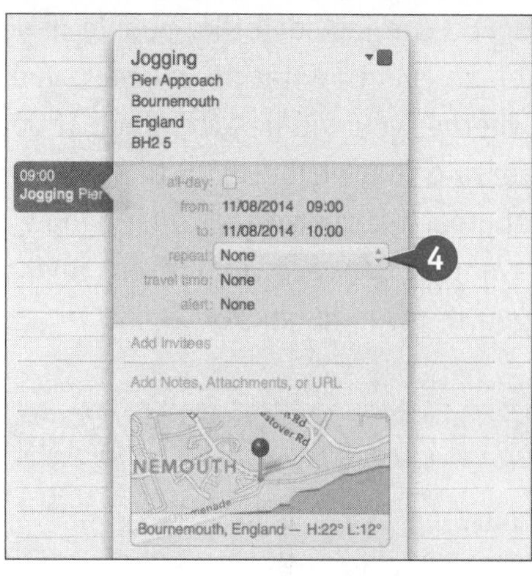

5 Click the interval you want to use.

A If you want to specify a custom interval such as every two weeks or the first Monday of every month, click **Custom** and configure your interval in the dialog that appears.

Calendar adds the repeating events to the calendar.

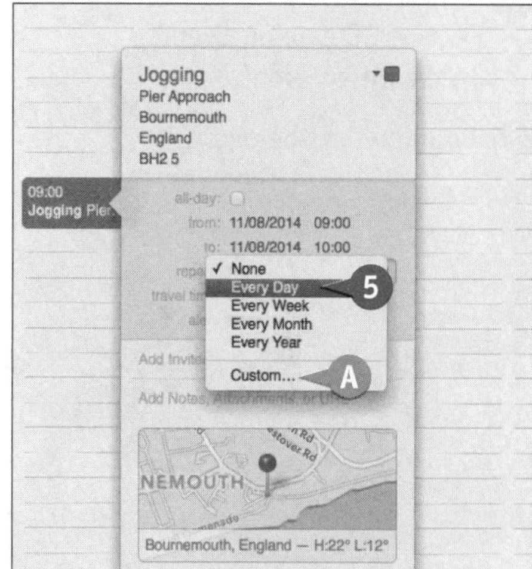

TIPS

How do I configure an event to stop after a certain number of occurrences?

Set a custom repeat time and enter the number of weeks, days, or years you want the event to repeat in the field below the frequency.

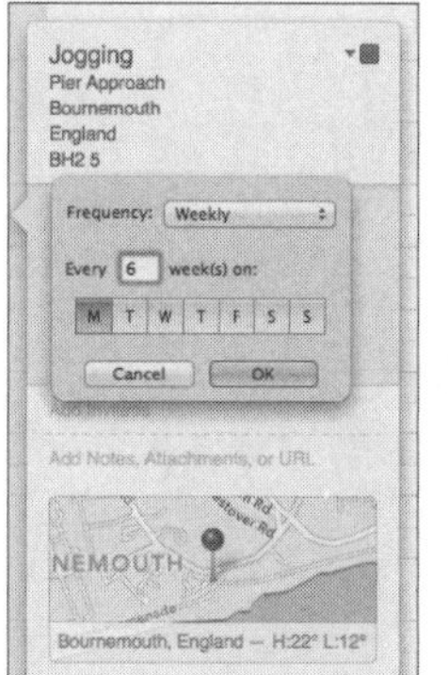

Can I delete a single occurrence from a recurring series of events?

Yes, you can delete one occurrence from the calendar without affecting the rest of the series. Click the occurrence you want to delete, and then press Delete. Calendar asks whether you want to delete all the occurrences or just the selected occurrence. Click **Delete Only This Event**.

Send or Respond to an Event Invitation

You can include other people in your event by sending them invitations to attend. If you receive an event invitation yourself, you can respond to it to let the person organizing the event know whether you will be attending. If you have an event that requires other people, Calendar has a feature that enables you to send invitations to other people who use Calendar. The advantage of this approach is that when other people respond to the invitation, Calendar automatically updates the event. If you receive an event invitation yourself, the Calendar inbox contains buttons that enable you to respond quickly.

Send or Respond to an Event Invitation

Send an Event Invitation

1. Follow the steps in the section "Create an Event" to create an event.

2. Double-click the event.

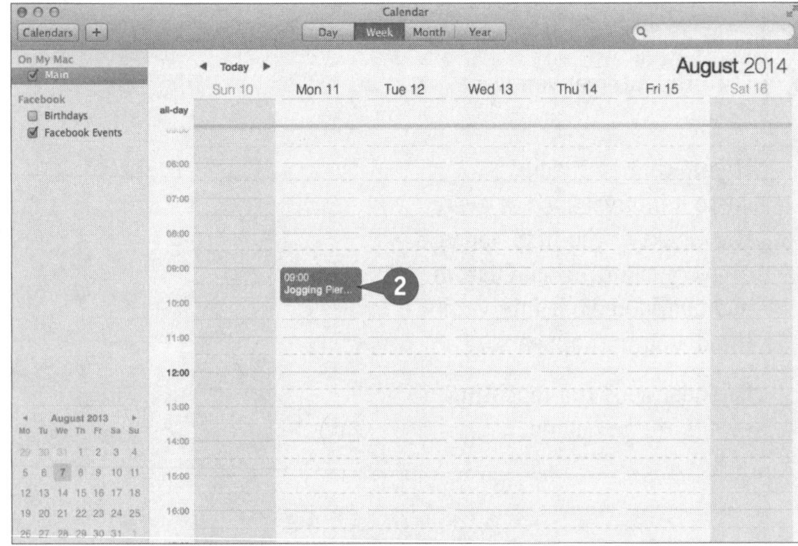

3. Click **Add invitees**.

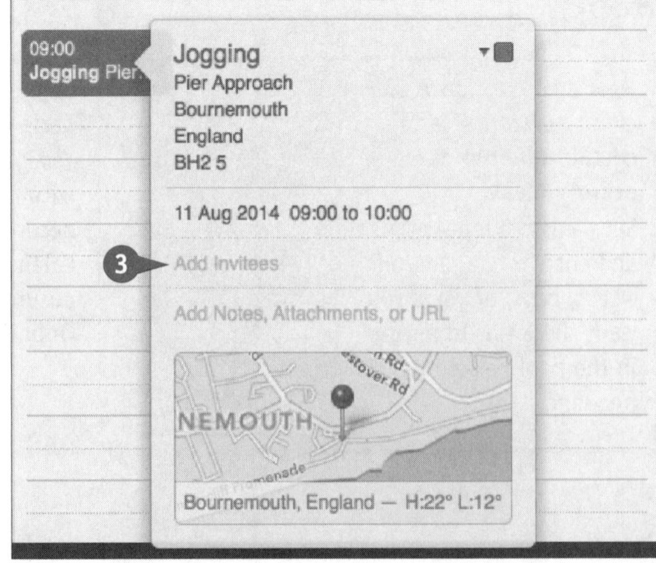

4 Begin typing the name of a person you want to invite and click the person you want to invite.

5 Repeat steps 3 and 4 to add more invitees.

6 Click **Send**.

Calendar sends the invitation.

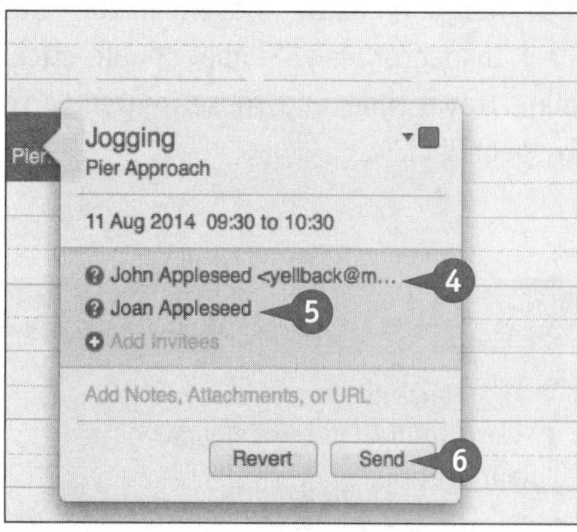

Handle an Event Invitation

1 In Calendar, click the **Inbox** button (![inbox]).

2 Click the button that represents your reply to the invitation:

A Click **Accept** if you can attend the event.

B Click **Decline** if you cannot attend the event.

C Click **Maybe** if you are currently not sure whether you can attend.

Your response is sent.

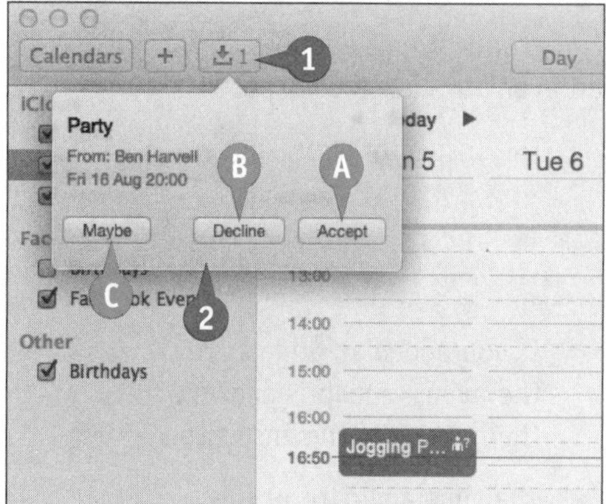

TIP

What happens if I make changes to the event I created?
If you adjust any of the details of your event, such as the time, date, or location, or you add or remove invitees, you need to update the event to let everyone invited know about the changes. Simply make the changes required and then click **Update** on the event info pane. You can also click **Revert** to cancel the changes you have made.

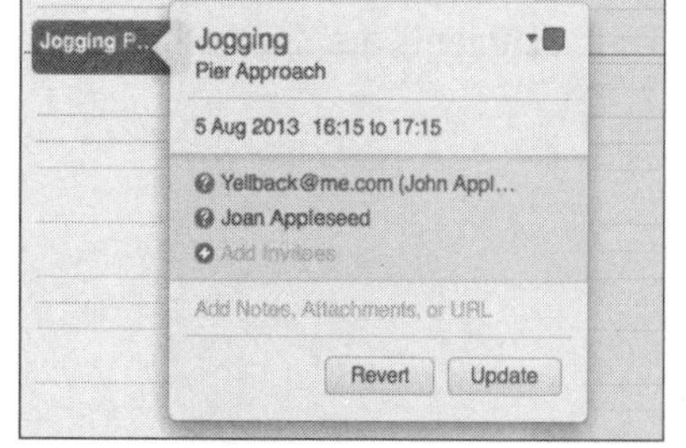

Using the Inspector to View Event Information

When you create an event in the Calendar application, you can view detailed information with the Inspector view. Simply double-clicking an event in the Calendar provides information such as a map, travel time, and those invited to the event, and you can even edit information from within the Inspector view.

Using the Inspector to View Event Information

1. Ctrl+click the event you want to view in the Calendar application.
2. Click **Get Info**.

Note: You can also double-click an event to view the Inspector.

The Inspector pane appears.

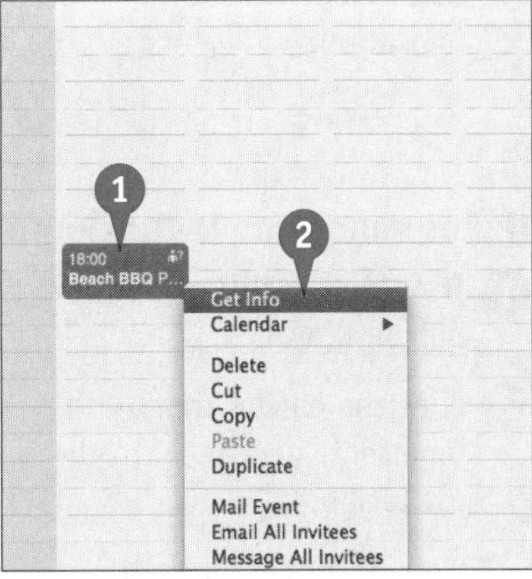

A If you added an address to the event, a map is shown at the bottom of the Inspector.

B The time and date of the event are shown below the address, and travel times are also shown if they were added.

C People invited to the event are shown here.

D Notes, URLs, and attachments are shown here.

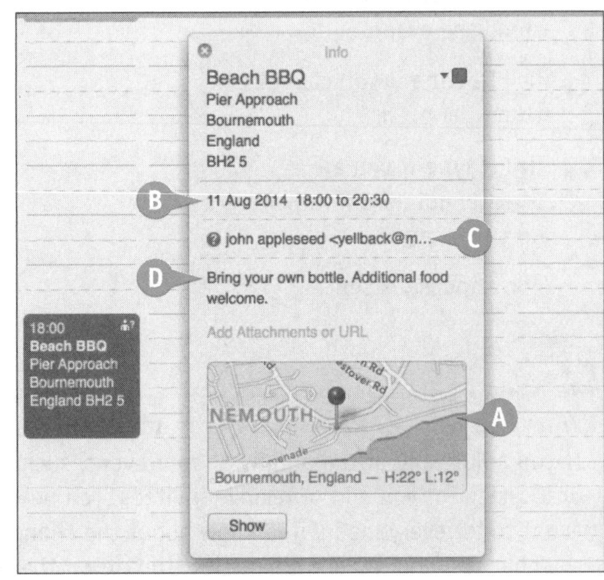

3 Click the map.

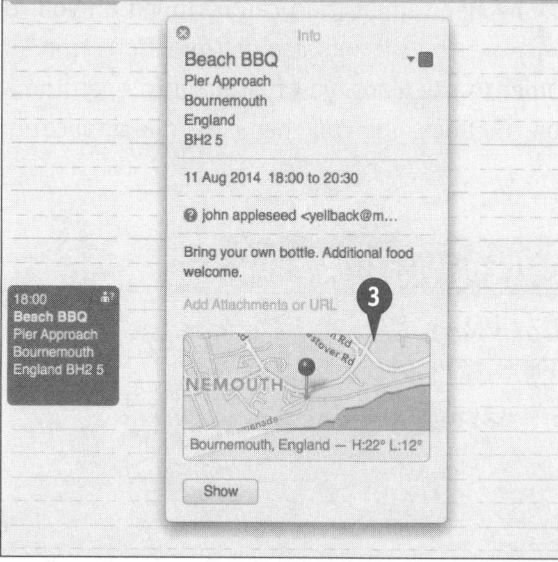

The Maps application opens and shows directions to the event from your current location.

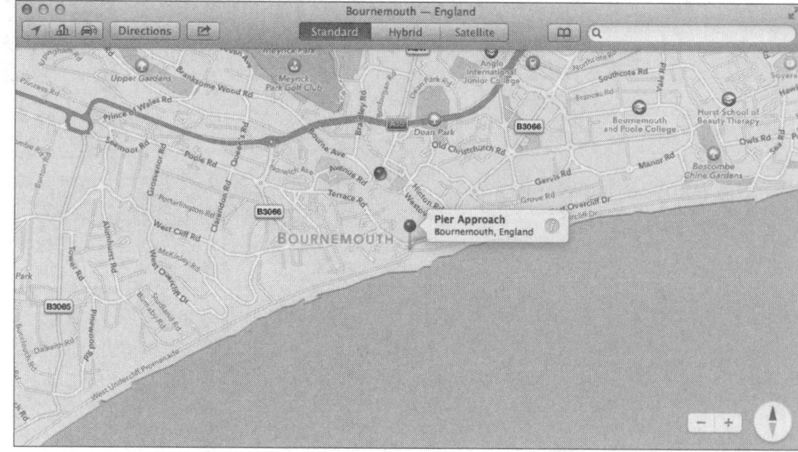

TIP

Can I edit the event information from the Inspector?

Yes. When you view event information in the Inspector view, you can click any of the information added to make changes as you wish. You can also click the colored square at the top of the Inspector to add the event to a different calendar or invite more people to the event by typing their e-mail addresses into the Invitees section.

Open and Close Maps

The Maps application can be found on your Dock and provides a handy way to look up locations you want to visit and also get directions from one place to another or from your current location. In order to use Maps, you first need to open the application, which can be done by clicking the Maps icon on the Dock. You can then close the application by using the Quit command from the Maps menu.

Open and Close Maps

Open Maps

1 In the Dock, click the **Maps** icon ( ).

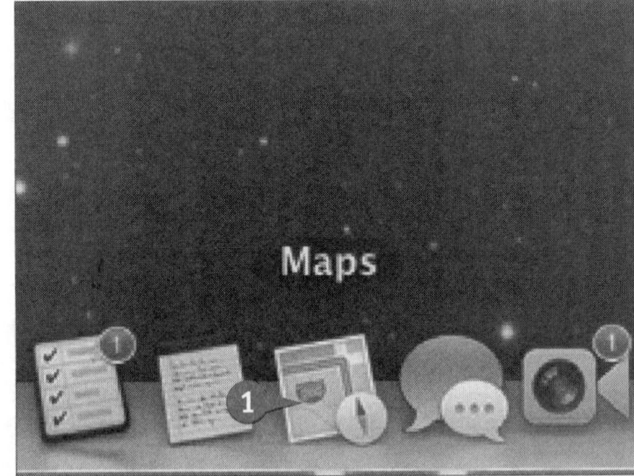

The Maps window appears.

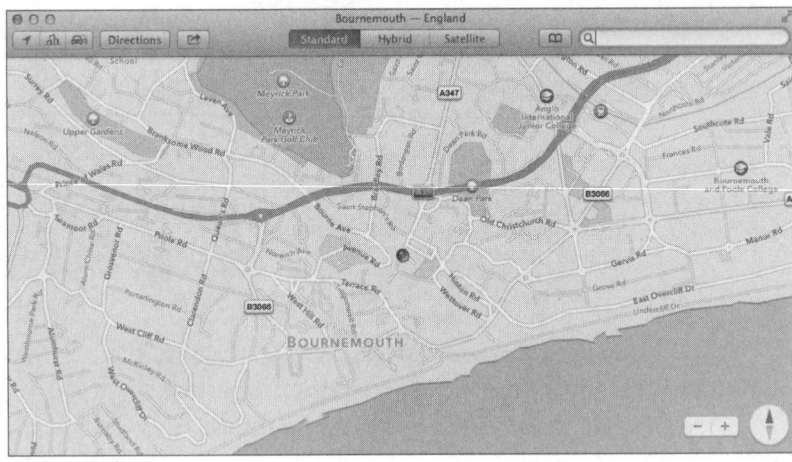

Close Maps

1 Click **Maps**.

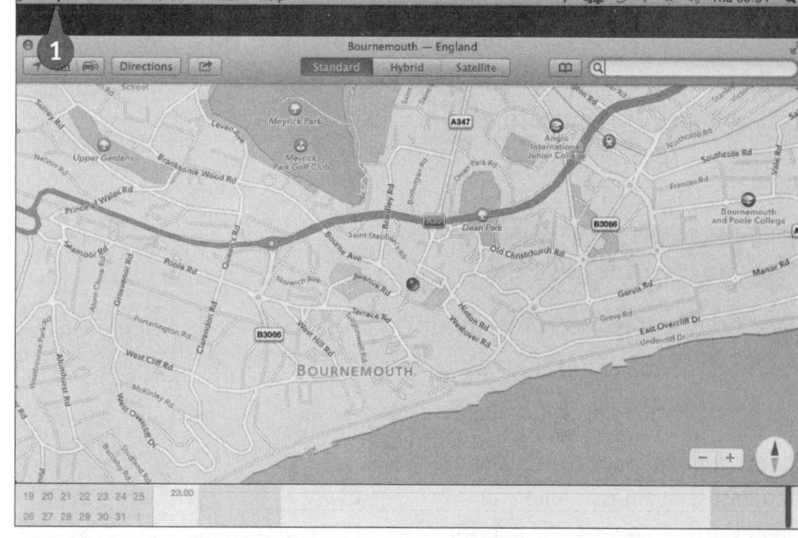

2 Click **Quit Maps**.

The Maps application closes.

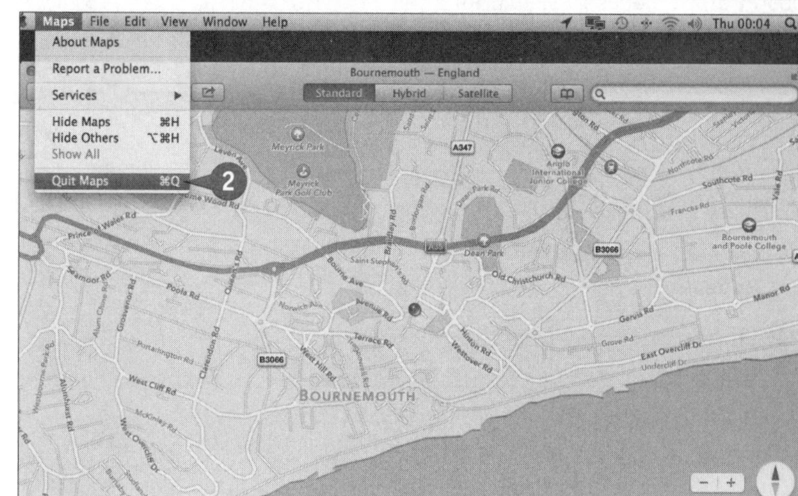

TIP

Are there other methods I can use to open Maps?

Yes. If you have removed the icon from the Dock, there are a couple of other quick methods you can use to start Maps. If you have used Maps recently, a reasonably fast method is to click the **Apple** icon ( ), click **Recent Items**, and then click **Maps**. You can also click **Spotlight** ( ), type **Maps**, and then click **Maps** in the search results.

Search for a Location

Searching for a location in the Maps application offers a quick way to pinpoint a place in your local area or anywhere in the world. Simply type the location you are looking for into the Search field and view the suggestions provided. You can also search by the name of a business or a ZIP or postal code to find exact locations.

Search for a Location

1. Click the Maps search field.
2. Type the location you want to find into the Search field.

Note: You can use street names, addresses, business names, or postal or ZIP codes to search for locations.

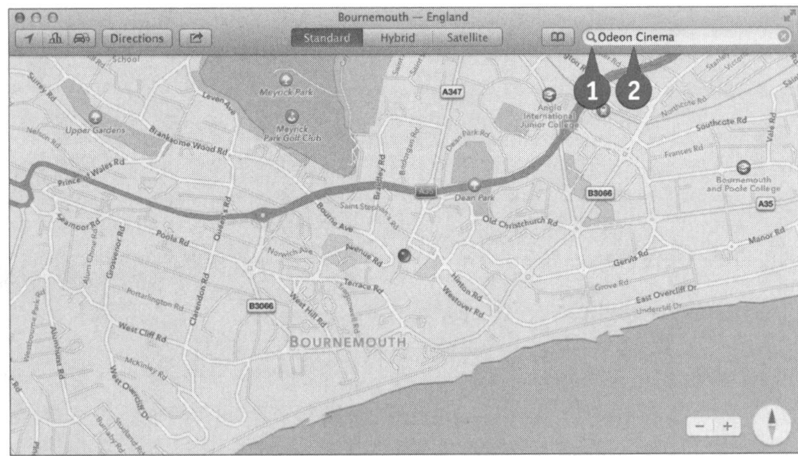

A list of suggested locations appears.

3. Click a suggestion from the list.

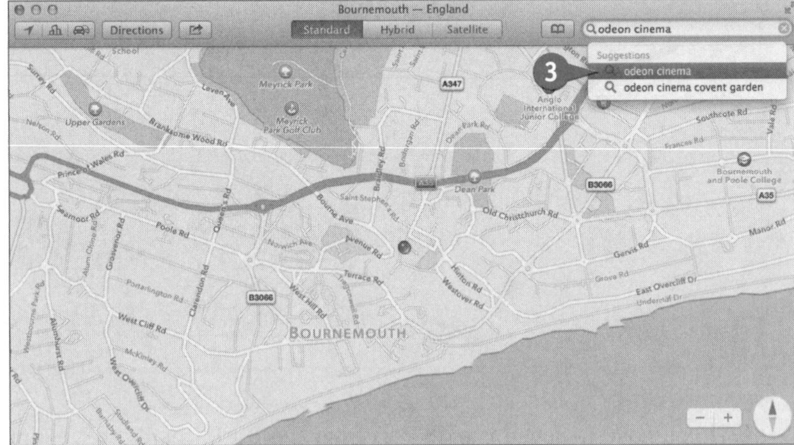

The location is shown on the map with a red drop pin.

4 Click the pin.

The location name is shown.

5 Click the **Show Info** button (ⓘ).

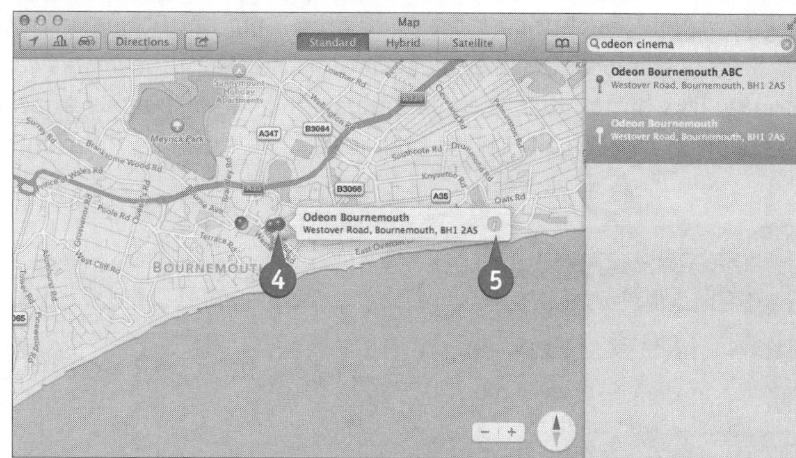

Information about the location is shown.

A Click the **Share** button (share icon) to send the location to yourself or another person.

B Click **Add Bookmark** to add the location to your Bookmarks.

C Click **Get Directions** to get directions to or from the location.

D Click **Add to Contacts** to assign the location to a contact.

E Click **Report a Problem** to notify Apple of mistakes regarding this location.

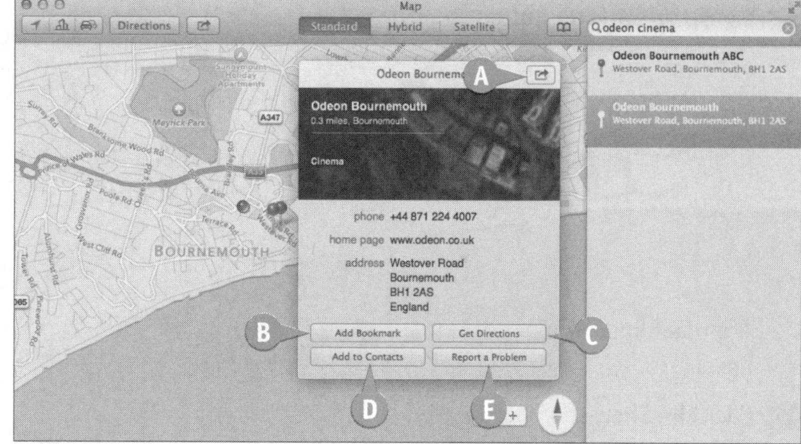

TIP

Why can't I find the location I am looking for?

By default, Maps looks for locations near to you and suggests them first based on your search terms. If you are looking for a location that is not in your local area, try to add as much information as possible such as the state or country, separating each piece of information with a comma (for example: Westminster, London, England).

Bookmark a Location

When you search for a location or drop a pin onto the map in the Maps application, you can store the location as a bookmark for use later. Bookmarks can then be accessed by clicking the **Bookmarks** button on the Maps toolbar. You can also apply a location to a contact in the Contacts application so you can use the contact's name to find a location in future searches.

Bookmark a Location

Store a Location Bookmark

1. Hover the cursor over the location you want to bookmark and hold down the mouse or trackpad button.

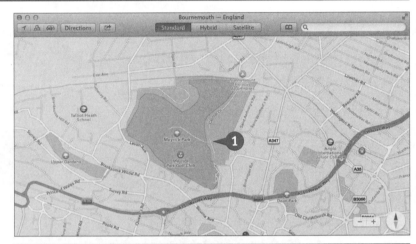

A purple dropped pin appears.

2. Click the **Show Info** button (◙).

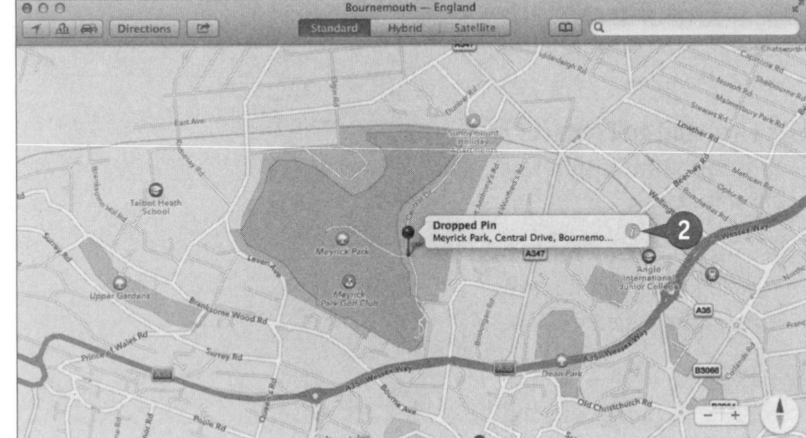

The information pane for the location appears.

3 Click **Add Bookmark**.

The bookmark is added.

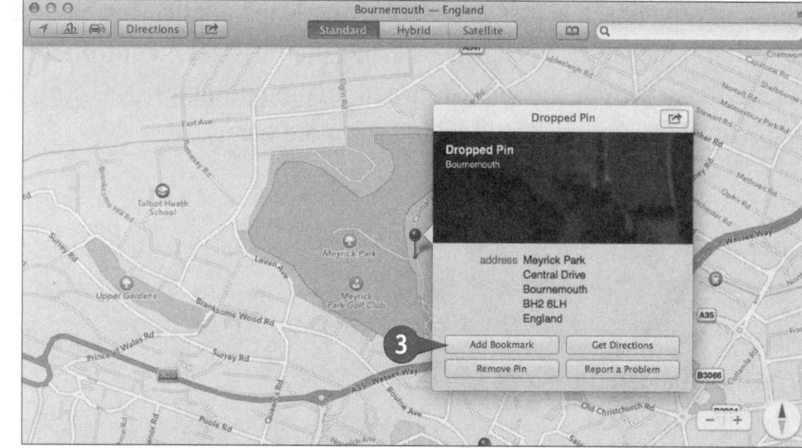

Access Stored Location Bookmarks

1 Click the **Bookmarks** button (📖).

The Bookmarks menu appears.

2 Click the bookmark you want to view.

The location appears in Maps.

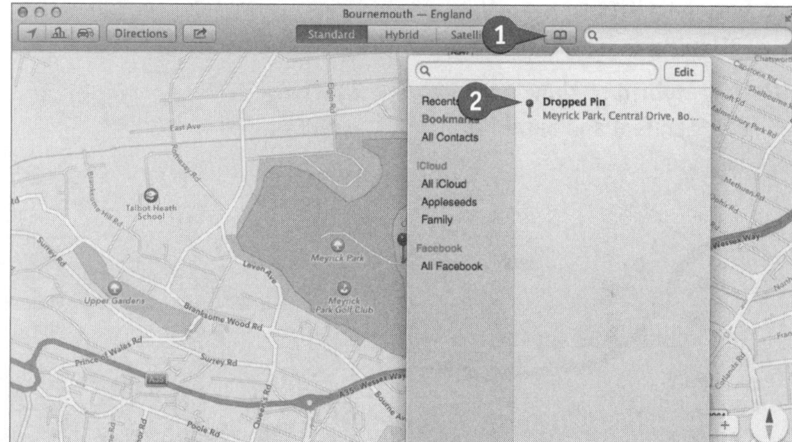

TIP

How do I add a location as a contact?

Simply follow steps 1 and 2, but click **Add to Contacts**. The location is automatically added to a new card in the Contacts application. You can then name the card as you wish and provide additional information such as e-mail addresses and phone numbers.

Change the Map View

You can navigate across the map in the Maps application in a number of ways, including scrolling using a mouse or trackpad, or using the on-screen controls to zoom in and out or rotate the map. You can also switch the view between a standard map, satellite photography, or a hybrid of both to help you find what you are looking for more easily.

Change the Map View

Change the Map Type

Ⓐ Click **Standard** to show a regular map view.

Ⓑ Click **Satellite** to show the satellite photography view.

❶ Click **Hybrid** to show both the Standard and Satellite map views at once.

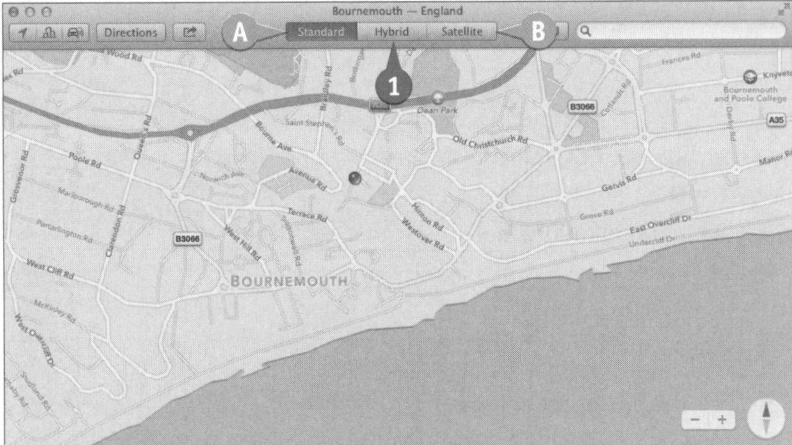

The Hybrid view appears.

Zoom, Rotate, and Tilt

A Click the minus button to zoom out of the map.

B Click the plus button to zoom in to the map.

C Click and drag left and right on the compass to rotate the map.

Click and drag across the map to adjust the location.

1 Click the **Current Location** button (![icon]).

The map moves to your current location.

TIP

What other methods can I use to control the map?
A trackpad allows you to perform navigation more quickly than when using a mouse or the compass display in the Maps application. Swiping two fingers on the trackpad moves the map up, down, left, or right. Pinching two fingers together zooms out of the map, while doing the reverse zooms in.

Using Flyover

The Maps application includes a feature called Flyover, which allows you to view 3-D representations of selected locations on the map. Not all locations can be used with Flyover, but major cities like New York, Paris, and London, as well as landmarks like Niagara Falls and the Eiffel Tower, can be viewed in this way. Flyover can be used in the Standard map view as well as in the Hybrid and Satellite views.

Using Flyover

1. Search or navigate to a location on the map.
2. Click the map view you want to use.

3. Click the **Flyover** button (![]).

The map tilts and Flyover is turned on.

4. Double-click the location you want to view to zoom in to it.

Note: You can also zoom using a mouse or trackpad or by clicking the plus button (+) at the bottom right of the map.

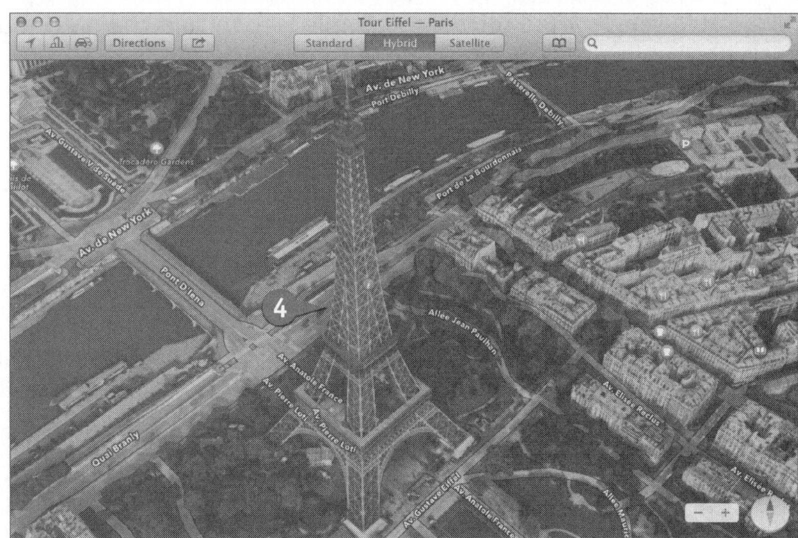

5. Click and drag forward or back on the compass to adjust the viewing angle, and drag left or right to rotate the view around a location.

The Flyover view moves accordingly.

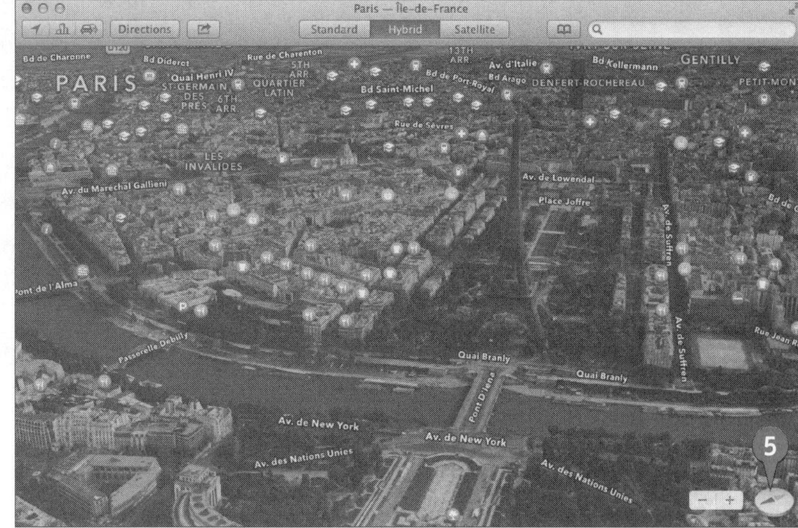

TIP

What are some good locations to test Flyover in the Maps application?

There are a number of great places on the map to use Flyover, such as central London, New York, and Chicago. For impressive landmarks, try the Colosseum in Rome, the Golden Gate Bridge in San Francisco, the Sydney Harbour Bridge and the Sydney Opera House in Australia, or even Apple's corporate headquarters in Cupertino, California.

Get Directions

The Maps application provides a simple way to find the ideal route between two locations, and can even help you to determine whether a journey would be easier on foot or where there is likely to be congestion. Directions can be found between any two locations on the map, or you can choose to set the start or end point as your current location.

Get Directions

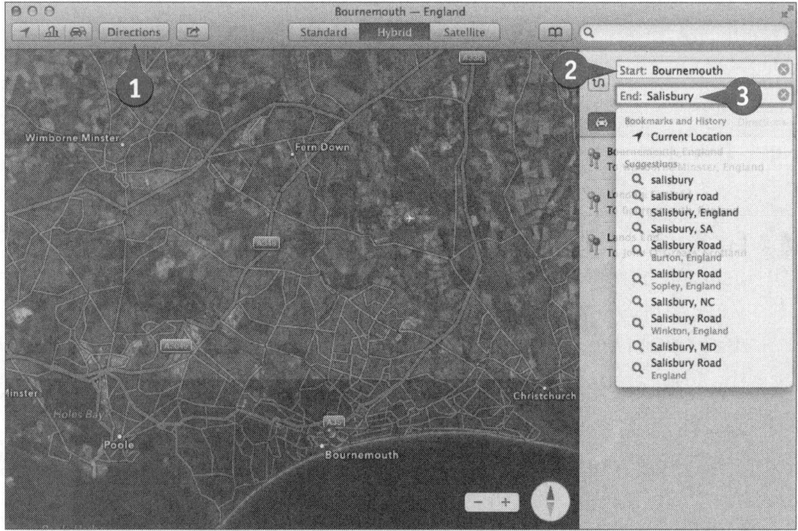

1. Click **Directions**.

   The Directions pane appears.

2. Type a Start location.
3. Type an End location.

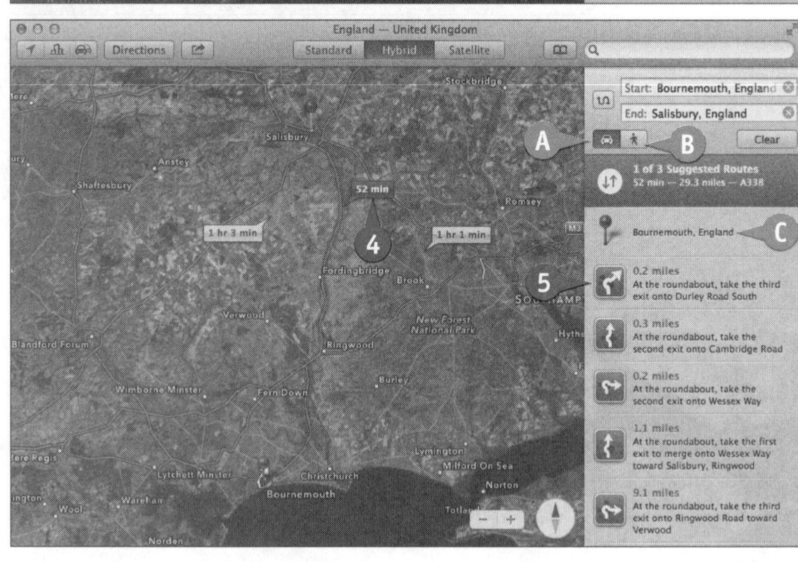

All available routes are shown on the map.

- **A** Click the **Driving** button (🚗) to show driving directions.
- **B** Click the **Walking** button (🚶) to show walking directions.

4. Click the route you want to follow.

- **C** Directions are shown to the right of the Maps interface.

5. Click the first direction on the list.

6 Click the **Traffic** button (🚗).

The map zooms in to that position and shows the direction in which you should be travelling.

TIP

What do the different colored and styled traffic highlights mean?

Traffic is shown on the map as orange dots and red dashes. Orange dots show areas that are prone to heavy traffic and therefore may slow down your journey at busy times. Red dashes indicate stop-and-start traffic, which means you may get caught in traffic jams when travelling along that route.

Find and View Suggested Locations

If you are looking to arrange a meeting or a gathering with friends and family and are creating an event in the Calendar application, you can use Maps to suggest nearby locations for you to meet. By typing a location and a type of business, activity, or food type, you are shown a list of suggestions that fit your criteria. For example, you could type your location and then type **pizza** or **bowling** to see businesses that match the criteria in the area.

Find and View Suggested Locations

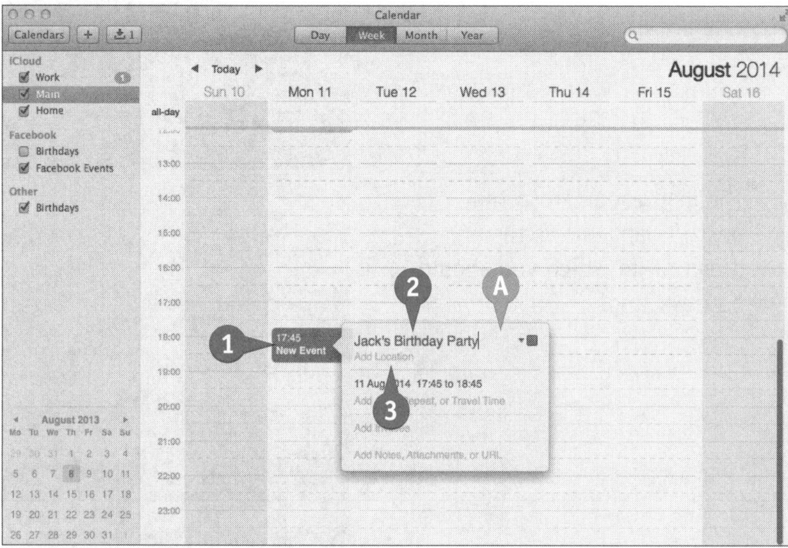

1. Double-click a date in the Calendar.

   A. A new event is created.

2. Type a name for your event in place of the New Event text.

3. Click **Add Location**.

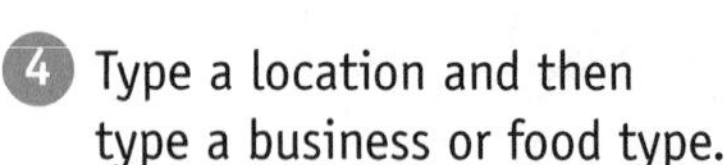

4. Type a location and then type a business or food type.

A list of suggested locations appears.

5 Click the suggestion you want to use as the location.

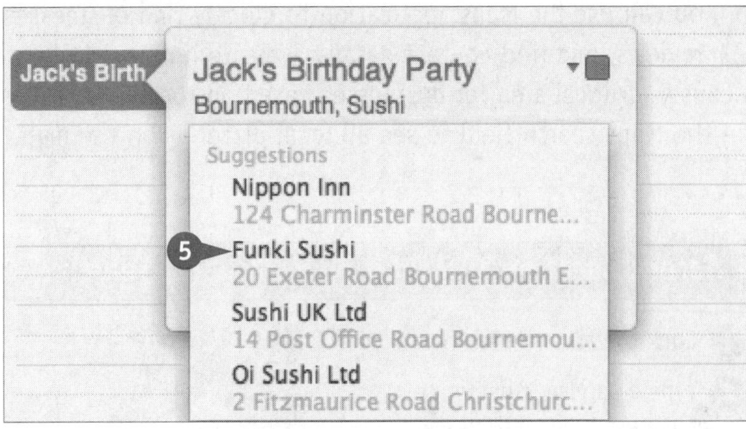

The address of the location is added to the event.

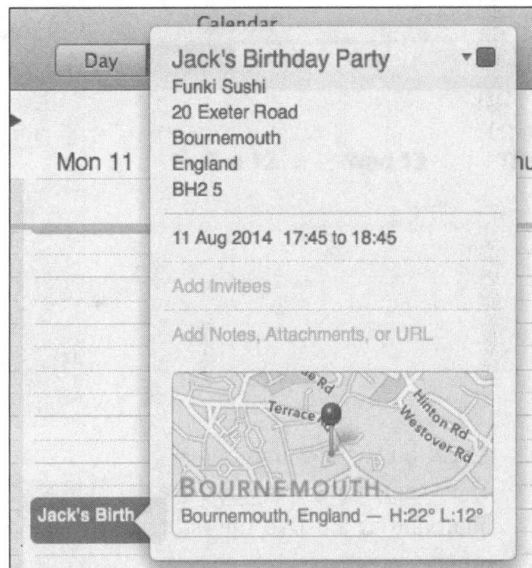

TIP

Can I find out more information about a suggested location?

Yes. Once you add the suggested location to your event, you can click the map image within the Event Inspector to be taken to the Maps application. Click the pin on the map and then click the **Show Info** button (ⓘ) to view the address and contact details if they have been added. Some businesses may also include more information from the Yelp recommendation service as well as photos.

Access Location Information with Local Search

You can use the Maps application to quickly find businesses and services near your location, read reviews, and find contact details, website links, and photos. The feature, called Local Search, scans your local area for businesses based on the search terms you provide. For example, type **pizza** in the Maps search field to see all local pizzerias on the map.

Access Location Information with Local Search

1. Click the Maps search field.
2. Type a service, cuisine, or business type, and press Return.

Local businesses matching your search are shown on the map and as a list to the right of the screen.

3. Click the name of a business or a pin on the map.
4. Click the **Show Info** button (ⓘ).

Information about the business appears.

Ⓐ Click **Info** to show contact, address, and website information.

Ⓑ Click **Reviews** to show recent reviews from Yelp.

Ⓒ Click **Photos** to show a gallery of photos.

Note: Not all businesses have Yelp reviews or photos included.

5 Click **More Info on yelp**.

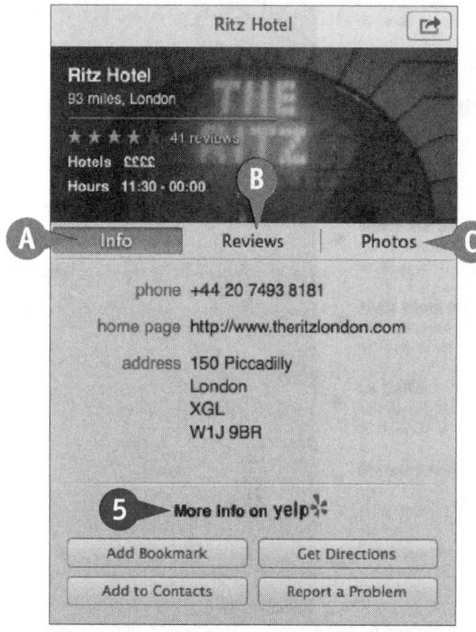

The Yelp website loads in Safari and shows more information about the business you selected.

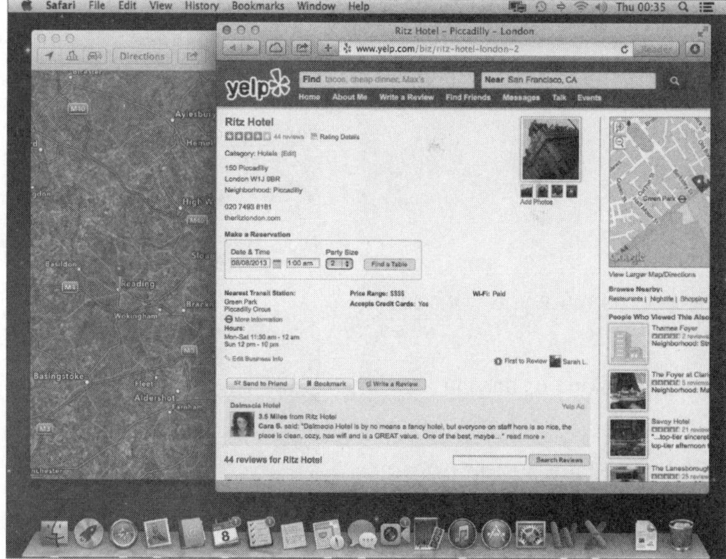

TIP

What else can I do from the Information pane?

When viewing information about a local business, you can send the information card to yourself or others by clicking the **Share** button (), or click the URL for the business to launch Safari and view the company's website. You can also open multiple information cards and drag them out of the Maps interface for reference while you browse.

Send Directions to an iOS Device

When you find directions to a location and are ready to start your journey, you can send the directions to your iOS device for turn-by-turn navigation as you travel. The directions appear on the lock screen of your iPhone or iPad and immediately launch in the iOS Maps application when you unlock the device.

Send Directions to an iOS Device

1. Follow the steps in the section "Get Directions" to get directions to a location.

2. Select the route you want to take.
3. Select walking or driving directions.
4. Click the **Share** button (□).

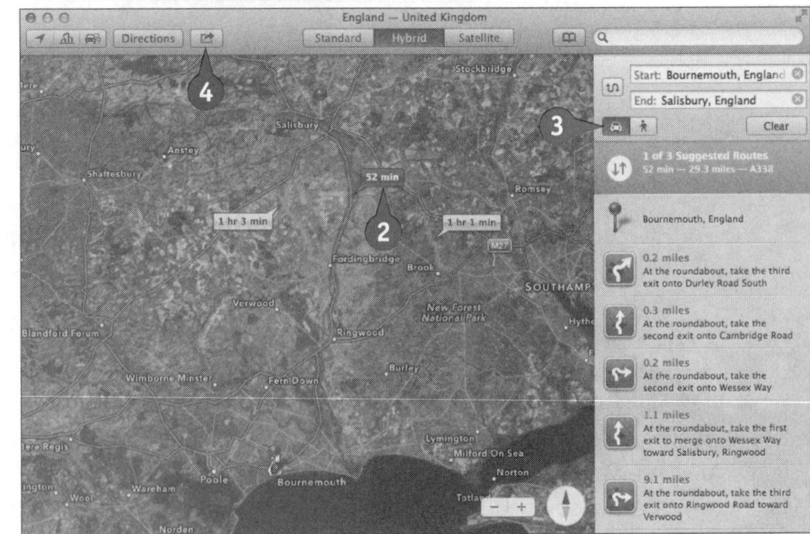

5 Click the name of your iOS device from the menu that appears.

The directions appear on the Home screen of your iOS device.

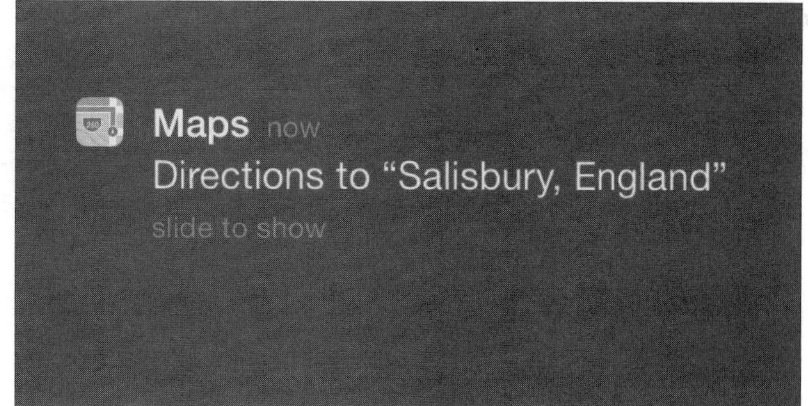

TIP

Why does my iPhone or iPad not appear when I click the Share button?

Only devices linked to the same iCloud account as your Mac will appear on the Share menu. Make sure that the iOS device you want to send directions to is set up with the same iCloud information you are using on your Mac, and that it has a working Internet connection via cellular data or a Wi-Fi network.

Turn On Location Services

Location Services is a feature of OS X that allows your computer to determine its current location based on information from local Wi-Fi networks. Once turned on, Location Services allows applications and websites to privately and securely use your location to provide suggestions based on your surrounding area. The Maps application is one such example of a program that uses Location Services to find your current location.

Turn On Location Services

1. In the Dock, click the **System Preferences** icon (▣).

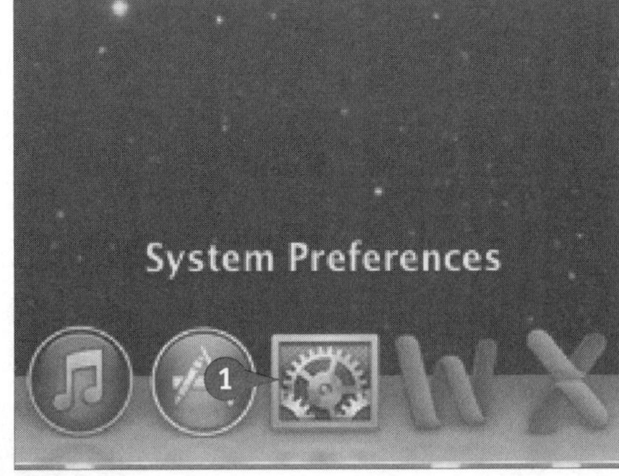

The System Preferences pane appears.

2. Click **Security & Privacy**.

3. Click the **Privacy** tab.
4. Click **Location Services**.
5. Click the lock at the bottom of the pane.
6. Type your password.
7. Click **Unlock**.

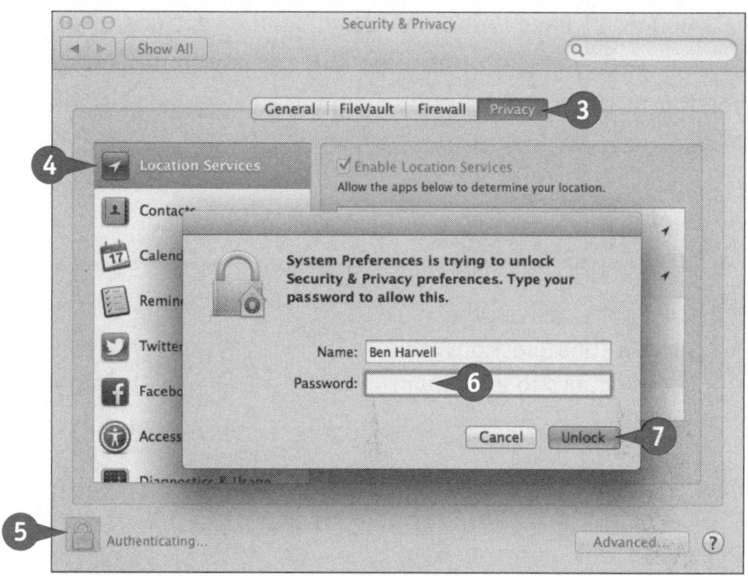

8. Select the **Enable Location Services** check box (☐ changes to ☑).
9. Select the check box next to each application you would like to allow to determine your location (☐ changes to ☑).

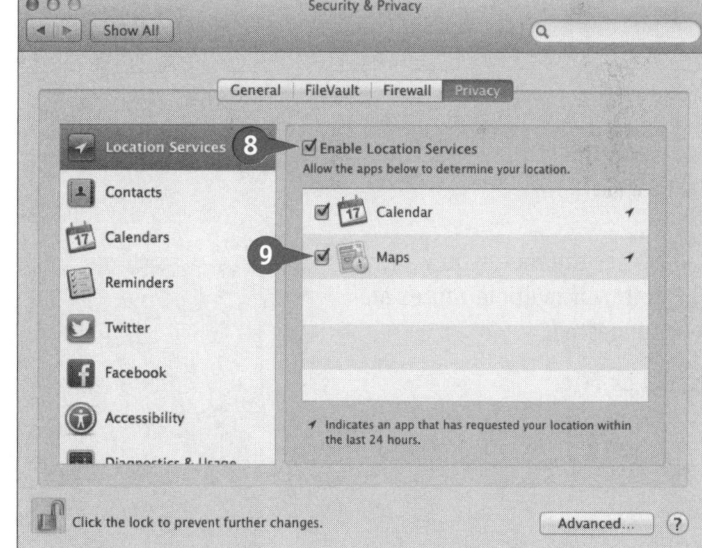

TIP

What does the arrow next to an application on the Location Services pane mean?

An arrow to the right of an application listed in the Privacy pane under Location Services indicates that that application has used Location Services to request your location within the last 24 hours. By deselecting the check box next to an application name (☑ changes to ☐) you can prevent the application from accessing your location information.

Print Directions

If you don't have an iOS device to send directions to or you prefer using a printout of the directions you need, you can print directions for any route you set in the Maps application. The printed version of the route contains diagrams as well as a list of each step of the journey for you to follow.

Print Directions

1. Follow the steps in the section "Get Directions" to get directions to a location.

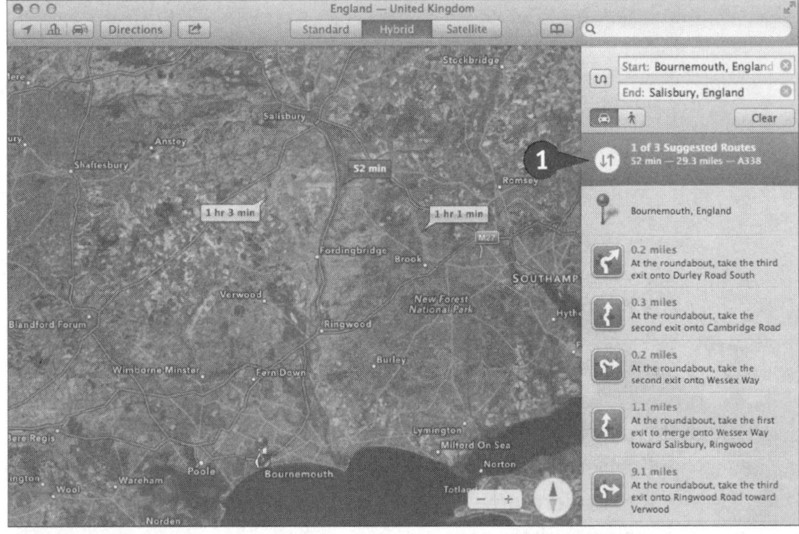

2. Select the route you want to follow if multiple routes are suggested.
3. Click **File**.

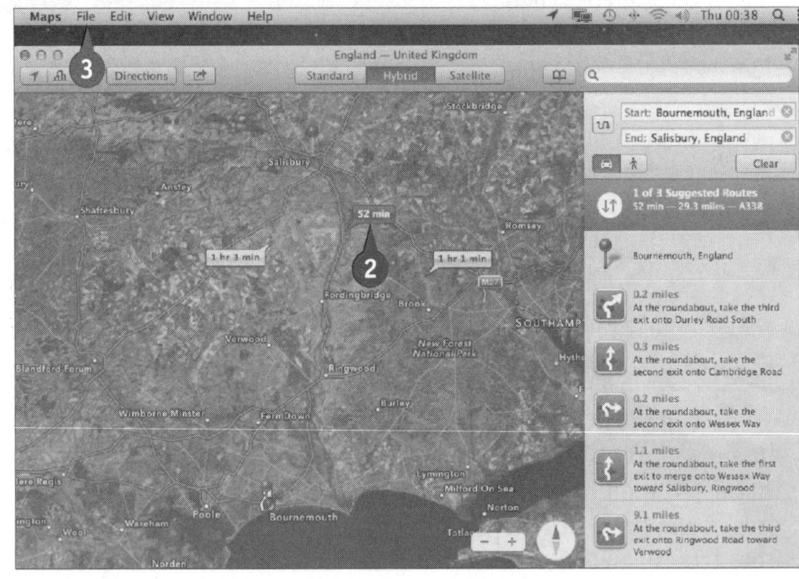

4 Click **Print**.

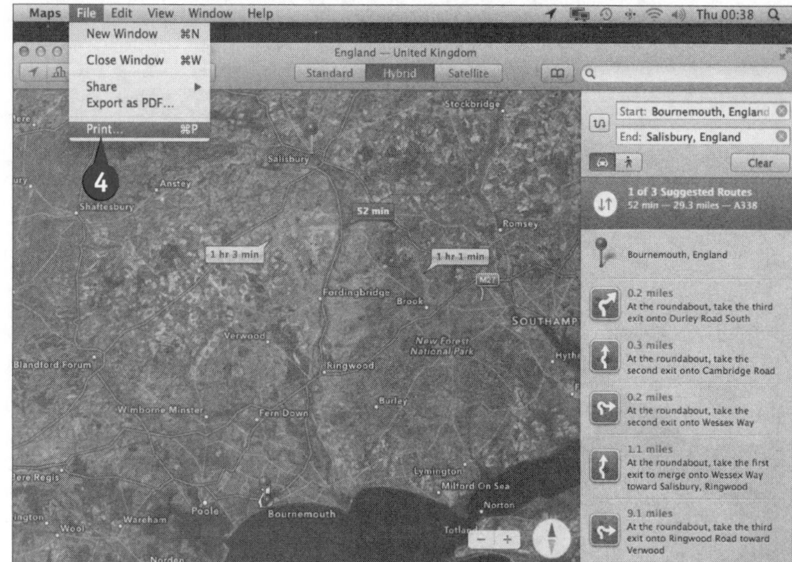

The print dialog appears.

5 Click the **Printer** ⬍ and select your printer from the menu.

6 Click **Print**.

The printer prints your selected route.

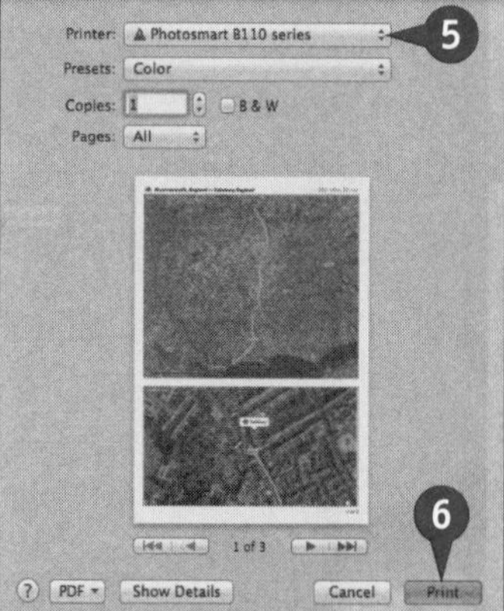

TIP

How do I print return directions for the journey home?
When you have selected your route, click the **Reverse** button next to the Start and End locations to make the End location the Start location, and vice versa. The route is recalculated in the opposite direction and you can print the directions as before.

CHAPTER 8

Playing and Organizing Music

Using iTunes, you can create a library of music and use that library to play songs, albums, and collections of songs called playlists. You can also listen to music CDs and more.

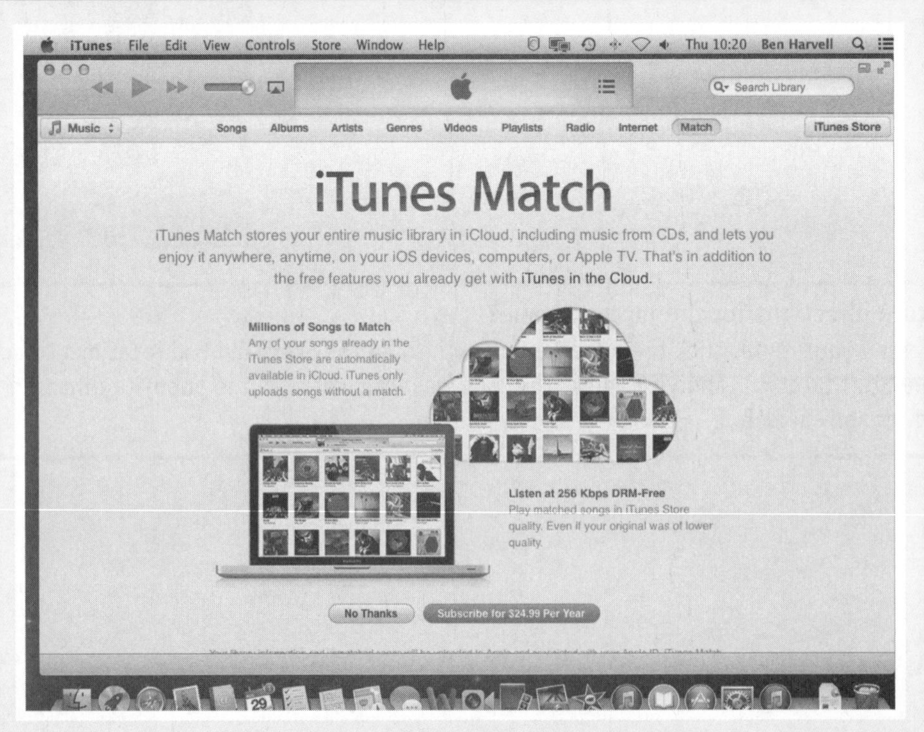

Open and Close iTunes

Your Mac includes iTunes to enable you to play back and manage various types of audio files. iTunes also includes features for organizing and playing videos, watching movies and TV shows, and syncing media to iPhones, iPads, and iPods, but this chapter focuses on the audio features in iTunes. To begin using the program, you must first learn how to find and open the iTunes window. When you finish using the program, you can close the iTunes window to free up computer processing power.

Open and Close iTunes

Open iTunes

1. In the Dock, click **iTunes** ().

The iTunes window appears.

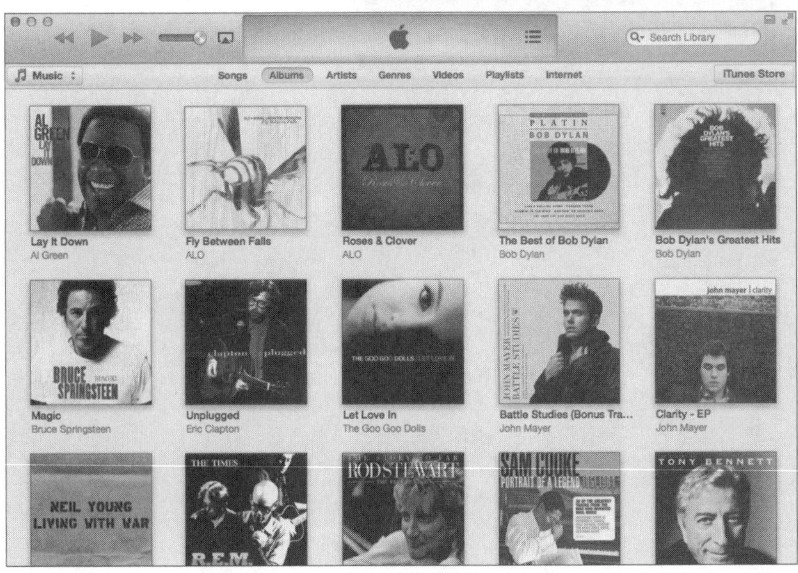

Close iTunes

1. Click **iTunes**.

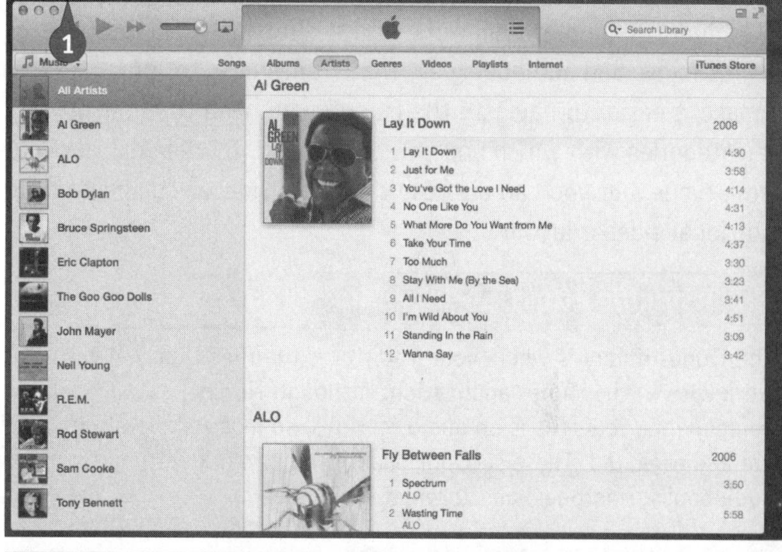

2. Click **Quit iTunes**.

   iTunes closes.

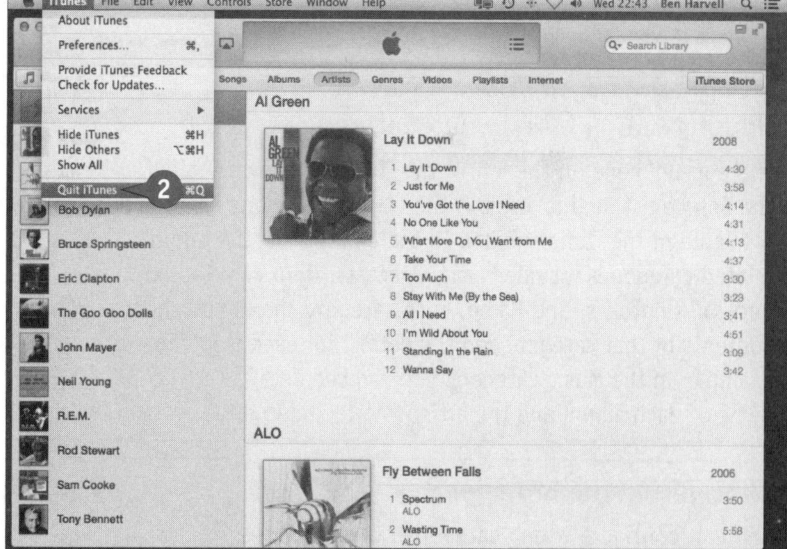

TIP

Are there other methods I can use to open iTunes?
Yes. If you have removed the iTunes icon from the Dock, there are a couple of other quick methods you can use to start iTunes. If you have used iTunes recently, a reasonably fast method is to click the **Apple** icon (), click **Recent Items**, and then click **iTunes**. You can also click **Spotlight** (🔍), type **itunes**, and then click **iTunes** in the search results.

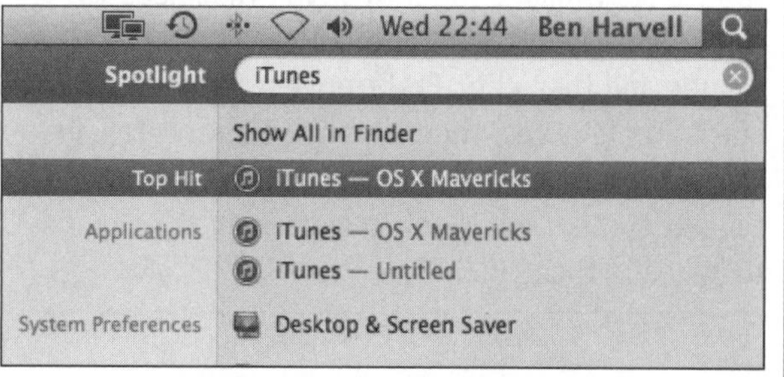

Understanding the iTunes Library

Most of your iTunes time will be spent in the Library folder, so you need to understand what the Library is and how you work with it. In particular, you need to understand the various categories — such as music and audiobooks — that iTunes uses to organize the Library's audio content. In addition, to make it easier to navigate the Library, you need to know how to configure the Library to show only the categories with which you will be working. By default, iTunes uses a pop-up menu to switch between media types, but you can also use the Show Sidebar command from the View menu to revert to the traditional sidebar layout.

Understanding the iTunes Library

The iTunes library is where your Mac stores the files that you can play and work with in the iTunes application. Although iTunes has some video components, its focus is on audio features, so most of the library sections are audio-related. These sections enable you to work with music, podcasts, audiobooks, ringtones, and Internet radio.

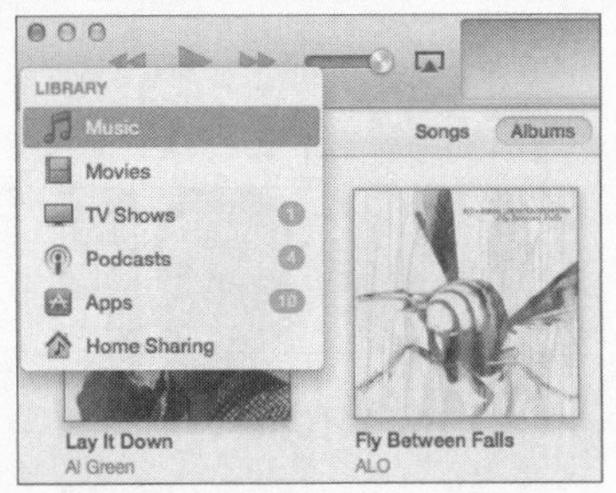

Understanding Library Categories

The pop-up menu on the left of the iTunes window is called the Source list, and it displays the various categories that are available in the iTunes library. In the Library list, the audio-related categories include Music, Podcasts, Books (for audiobooks), Ringtones, and Radio. Each category shows you the contents of that category and the details for each item. For example, in the Music category, you can see details such as the name of each album and the artist who recorded it.

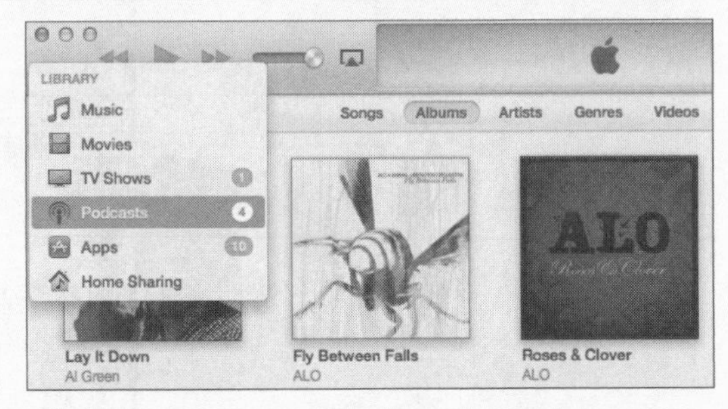

Configuring the Library

You can configure which categories of the iTunes library appear in the Library list on the left side of the iTunes window. To do this, you first need to select **Show Sidebar** from the View menu. Click **iTunes** and then click **Preferences** to open the iTunes preferences; then click the **General** tab. In the Show section, select the check box for each type of content you want to work with (☐ changes to ☑), and then click **OK**.

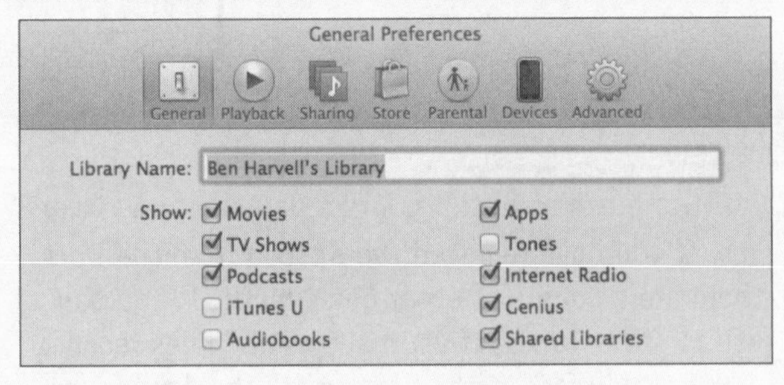

Navigate the iTunes Window

Familiarizing yourself with the various elements of the iTunes window is a good idea so that you can easily navigate and activate elements when you are ready to play audio files, music CDs, or podcasts; import and burn audio CDs; create your own playlists; or listen to iTunes Radio. In particular, you need to learn the iTunes playback controls, because you will use them to control the playback of almost all music with which you work in iTunes. It is also worthwhile to learn the different View options, because these often come in handy when navigating the iTunes library.

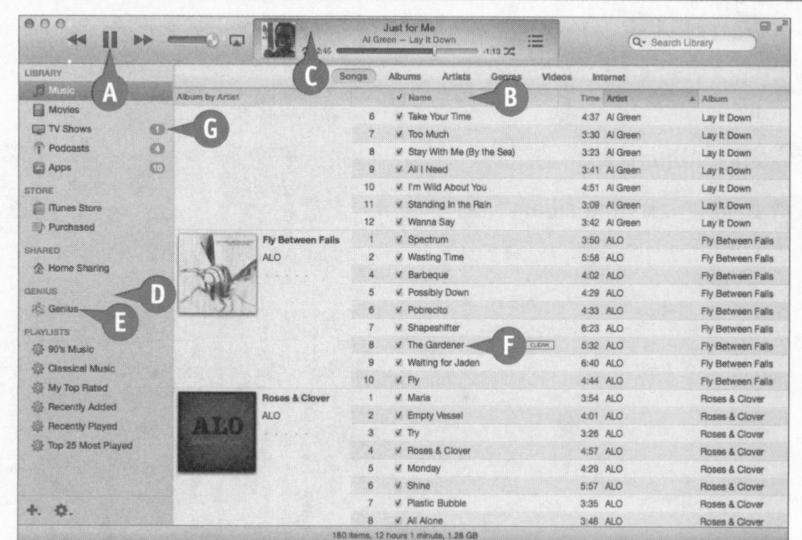

A Playback Controls

These buttons control media playback and enable you to adjust the volume.

B Sort Buttons

These buttons sort the contents of the current iTunes category.

C Status Area

This area displays information about the item that is currently playing or the action that iTunes is currently performing.

D Source Pane

From the View menu you can choose a number of different ways to see content in iTunes, including replacing the Source menu with the Sidebar that was popular in previous versions of iTunes, by selecting **Show Sidebar**.

E Genius

The Genius feature suggests songs based on music in your iTunes library. Click **Store** and then click **Turn On Genius** to use this feature.

F Contents

The contents of the current iTunes library source appear here.

G Categories

This area displays the iTunes library categories that you can view. You can also use the Source menu to view categories.

Play a Song

You use the Music category of the iTunes library to play a song that is stored on your computer. Although iTunes offers several methods to locate the song you want to play, the easiest method is to display the albums you have in your iTunes library, and then open the album that contains the song you want to play. Alternatively, you can use the iTunes search field to pinpoint the song, artist, or album you are looking for. While the song is playing, you can control the volume to suit the music or your current location. If you need to leave the room or take a call, you can pause the song currently playing.

Play a Song

1. Click **Music** on the Source menu.
2. Click **Albums**.
3. Double-click the album that contains the song you want to play.

4. Click the song you want to **play**.
5. Click the **Play** button (▶).

   iTunes begins playing the song.

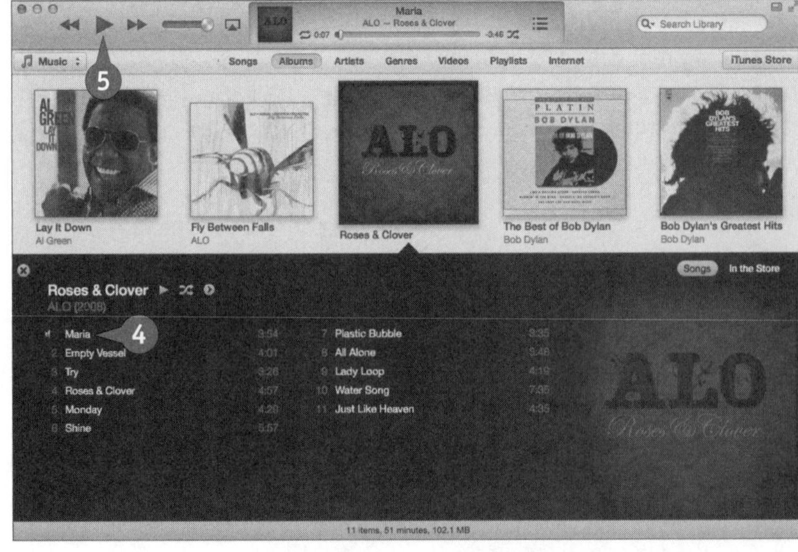

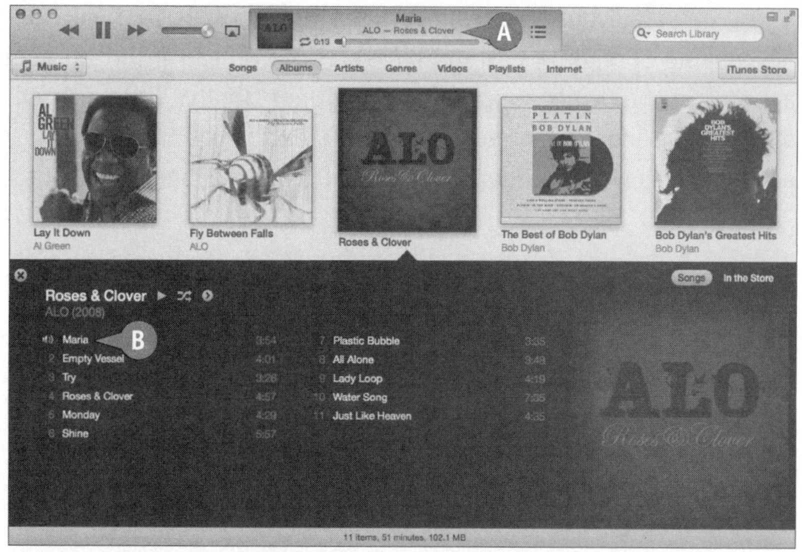

Ⓐ Information about the song playback appears here.

Ⓑ iTunes displays a speaker icon (🔊) beside the currently playing song.

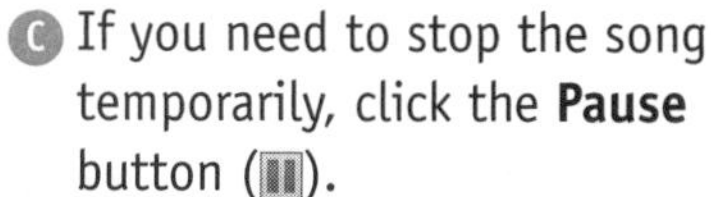

Ⓒ If you need to stop the song temporarily, click the **Pause** button (⏸).

Note: You can also pause and restart a song by pressing the Spacebar.

Ⓓ You can use the Volume slider to adjust the volume. See the Tip at the end of this task.

Note: See the section "Play a Music CD" to learn more about the playback buttons.

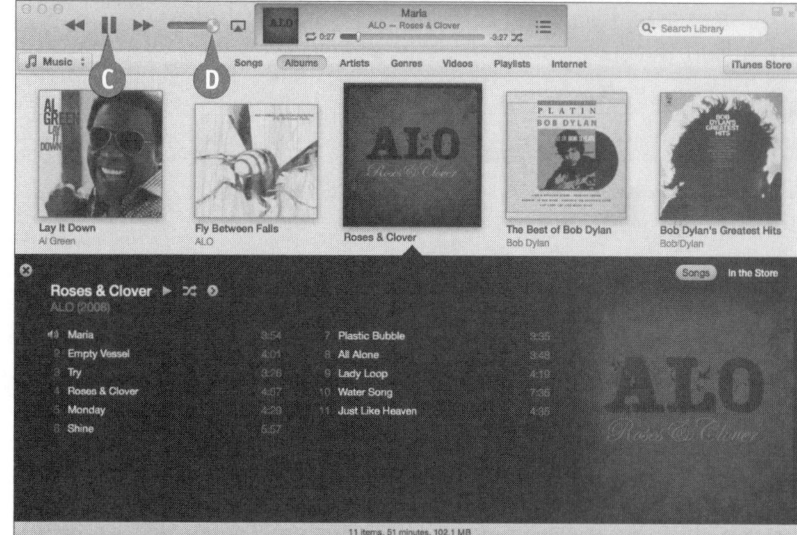

TIP

How do I adjust the volume?

To turn the volume up or down, click and drag the **Volume** slider to the left (to reduce the volume) or to the right (to increase the volume). You can also press ⌘+↓ to reduce the volume, or ⌘+↑ to increase the volume. To mute the volume, either drag the **Volume** slider all the way to the left, or press Option+⌘+↓. To restore the volume, adjust the **Volume** slider or press Option+⌘+↑.

Play a Music CD

You can play your favorite music CDs in iTunes. If your Mac has an optical drive (that is, a drive capable of reading CDs and DVDs), then you can insert an audio disc in the drive and the CD appears in the Devices section of the iTunes library. When you click the CD, the iTunes contents area displays the individual tracks on the CD, and if you have an Internet connection, you see the name of each track as well as other track data. During playback, you can skip tracks, pause, and resume play.

Play a Music CD

Play a CD

1. Insert a music CD into your Mac's optical drive. The music CD appears in the iTunes Source menu.

   iTunes asks if you want to import the CD.

2. Click **No**.

Note: To learn how to import a CD, see the section "Import Tracks from a Music CD."

A. If you have an Internet connection, iTunes shows the contents of the CD.

Note: iTunes shows the contents for most CDs, but it may not show the correct information for some discs, particularly noncommercial mixed CDs.

3. Double-click the first track on the CD.

   iTunes begins playing the CD from the first track.

Skip a Track

1. Click the **Next** button (⏩) to skip to the next track.

Note: You can also skip to the next track by pressing ⌘+→.

2. Click the **Previous** button (⏪) to skip to the beginning of the current track; click ⏪ again to skip to the previous track.

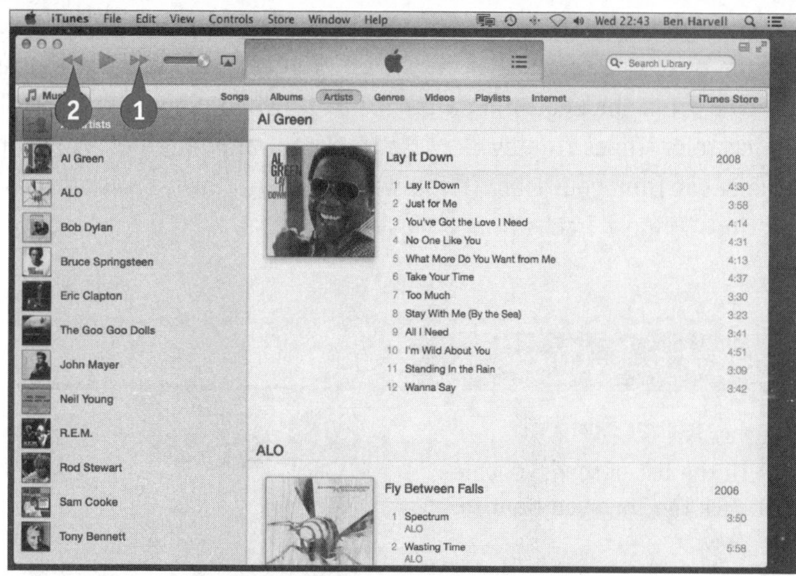

Pause and Resume Play

1. Click the **Pause** button (⏸) (⏸ changes to ▶).

   iTunes pauses playback.

   Click the button again to resume playback.

TIPS

Can I change the CD's audio levels?

Yes, iTunes has a graphic equalizer component that you can use to adjust the levels. To display the equalizer, click **Window** and then click **Equalizer** (or press Option+⌘+2). In the Equalizer window, use the sliders to set the audio levels, or click the pop-up menu (⬍) to choose an audio preset.

Can I display visualizations during playback?

Yes. You can click **View** and then click **Show Visualizer** (you can also press ⌘+T). To change the currently displayed visualizer, click **View**, click **Visualizer**, and then click the visualization you want to view.

continued ▶

Play a Music CD (continued)

iTunes gives you more options for controlling the CD playback. For example, you can easily switch from one song to another on the CD. You can also use the Repeat feature to tell iTunes to start the CD over from the beginning after it has finished playing the CD. iTunes also offers the Shuffle feature, which tells iTunes to play the CD's tracks in random order. When the CD is done, you can use iTunes to eject it from your Mac. If you want to learn how to import music from the CD to iTunes, see the section "Import Tracks from a Music CD."

Play a Music CD (continued)

Play Another Song

1. In the list of songs, double-click the song you want to play.

   iTunes begins playing the song.

Repeat the CD

1. Click the **Repeat** button (changes to).

   iTunes restarts the CD after the last track finishes playing.

   To repeat just the current song, click again.

Play Songs Randomly

1. Click the **Shuffle** button (⤮ changes to ⤮).

   iTunes shuffles the order of play.

Eject the CD

1. Click the **Eject** button (⏏) beside the album name.

Note: You can also eject the CD by pressing and holding the ⏏ key on the keyboard.

   iTunes ejects the CD from your Mac's optical drive.

TIP

Why do I not see the song titles after I insert my music CD?

When you play a music CD, iTunes tries to gather information about the album from the Internet. If you still see only track numbers, you may not have an Internet connection established, or you may have inserted a noncommercial mixed CD or commercial CD that is not recognized by the GraceNote database, which iTunes uses to retrieve song information. Connect to the Internet, click **Advanced**, and then click **Get CD Track Names**.

Import Tracks from a Music CD

You can add tracks from a music CD to the iTunes library. This enables you to listen to an album without having to put the CD into your Mac's optical drive each time. The process of adding tracks from a CD is called *importing,* or *ripping,* in OS X. After you import the tracks from a music CD, you can play those tracks from the Music category of the iTunes library. You can also use the tracks to create your own playlists and to create your own custom CDs.

Import Tracks from a Music CD

1. Insert a CD into your Mac's CD or DVD drive.

   iTunes asks if you want to import the CD.

2. Click **No**.

   A. If you want to import the entire CD, click **Yes** and skip the rest of the steps in this section.

   B. iTunes shows the contents of the CD.

3. Deselect the check box next to each CD track that you do not want to copy (☑ changes to ☐).

4. Click **Import CD**.

   iTunes shows the Import Settings dialog.

C Select an audio format.

D Select a quality level.

E Select this check box if you want to use error correction (☐ changes to ☑).

5 Click **OK**.

The CD is imported track by track.

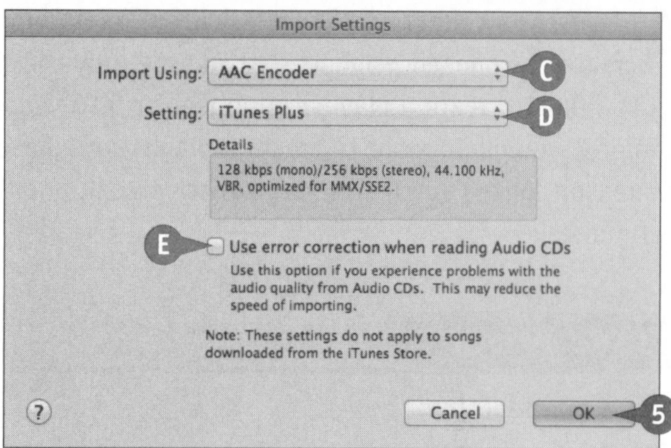

F A status bar shows the import progress of each track.

G Click **Stop Importing** if you want to cancel the import.

TIPS

I ripped a track by accident. How do I remove it from the library?

Click the **Music** category, open the album you imported, right-click the track that you want to remove, and then click **Delete** from the shortcut menu. When iTunes asks you to confirm the deletion, click **Remove.** When iTunes asks if you want to keep the file, click **Move to Trash**.

Can I specify a different quality when importing?

Yes, by changing the *bit rate*, which is a measure of how much of the CD's original data is copied to your computer. Click **Import Settings** to open the Import Settings dialog. In the **Setting** pop-up menu, click ⬍, click **Custom**, and then use the Stereo Bit Rate pop-up to click the value you want. You can also change the encoding type, which produces different file types such as MP3, AIFF, or WAV.

Create a Playlist

A *playlist* is a collection of songs that are related in some way. Using your iTunes library, you can create customized playlists that include only the songs that you want to hear. For example, you might want to create a playlist of upbeat or festive songs to play during a party or celebration. Similarly, you might want to create a playlist of your current favorite songs to burn to a CD. Whatever the reason, once you create the playlist you can populate it with songs using a simple drag-and-drop technique.

Create a Playlist

Create the Playlist

1. Click **File**.
2. Click **New**.
3. Click **Playlist**.

Note: You can also choose the New Playlist command by pressing ⌘+N.

A. iTunes creates a new playlist.

4. Type a name for the new playlist and press Return.

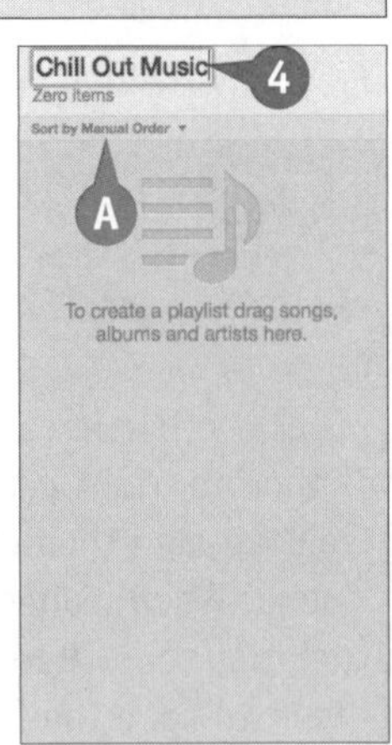

Add Songs to the Playlist

1. Click **Music** on the iTunes Source menu.
2. Open an album that has one or more songs you want to add to the playlist.
3. Click a song that you want to add to the playlist.

Note: If you want more than one song from the album's playlist, hold down ⌘ and click each of the songs you want to add.

4. Drag the selected track and drop it on your playlist.
5. Repeat steps 2 to 4 to add more songs to the playlist.
6. Click **Done**.

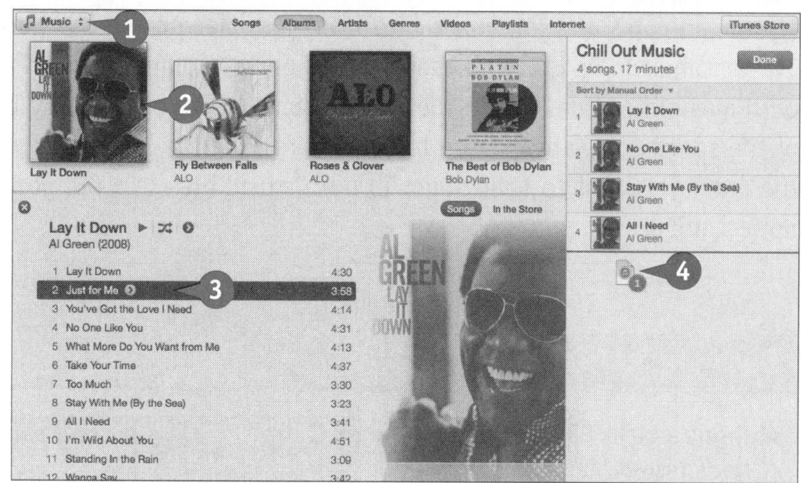

TIPS

Is there a faster way to create and populate a playlist?

Yes. First, click **Music** to open the Music category of the iTunes library. Press and hold the ⌘ key and then click each song that you want to include in your playlist. When you are done, click **File** and then click **New Playlist from Selection**. (You can also press Shift + ⌘ + N.) Type the new playlist name and then press Return.

Is there any way to make iTunes add songs to a playlist automatically?

Yes, you can create a *Smart Playlist* where the songs that appear in the list have one or more properties in common, such as the genre, rating, artist, or text in the song title. Click **File** and then click **New Smart Playlist**. (You can also press Option + ⌘ + N.) Use the Smart Playlist dialog to create one or more rules that define which songs you want to appear in the playlist. However, making changes to a song, such as changing its rating or tag, may cause it to be removed from a Smart Playlist.

Burn Music Files to a CD

You can copy, or *burn*, music files from your Mac onto a CD. Burning CDs is a great way to create customized CDs that you can listen to on the computer or on any device that plays CDs. You can burn music files from within the iTunes window. The easiest way to do this is to create a playlist of the songs you want to burn to the CD. You then organize the playlist by sorting the tracks in the order you want to hear them. To burn music files to a CD, your Mac must have a recordable optical drive.

Burn Music Files to a CD

1. Insert a blank CD into your Mac's recordable disc drive.

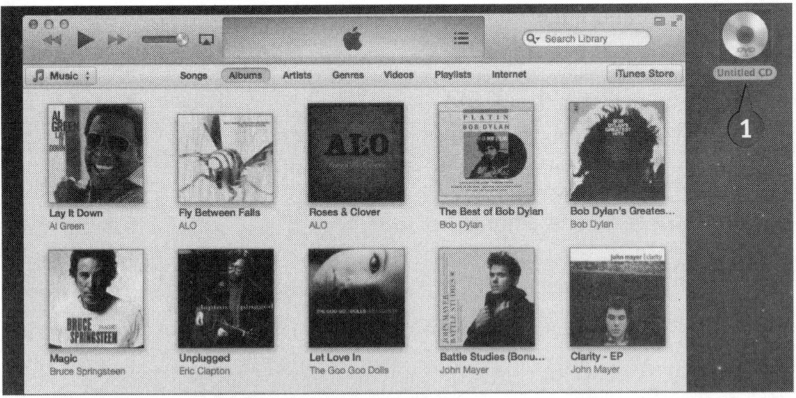

2. Create a playlist for the songs you want to burn to the disc.

Note: See the section "Create a Playlist" to learn how to build an iTunes playlist.

3. Click the playlist that you want to burn.

4 To modify the play order, click and drag a song and drop it on a new position in the playlist.

5 Repeat step 4 to get the songs in the order in which you want them to appear on the CD.

6 Click **File**.

7 Click **Burn Playlist to Disc**.

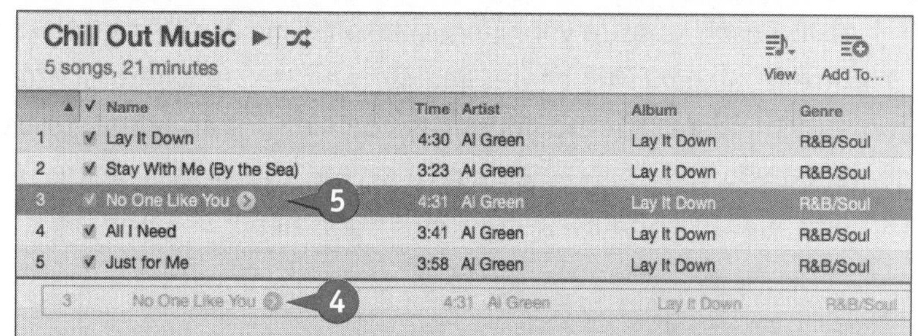

The Burn Settings dialog appears.

8 Click **Burn**.

iTunes burns the songs to the CD.

TIPS

Can I control the interval between songs on the CD?
Yes. By default, iTunes adds 2 seconds between each track on the CD. You can change that in the Burn Settings dialog. In the Gap Between Songs pop-up menu, click ⬍, and then click the interval you want to use: None, or any time between 1 second and 5 seconds.

What happens if I have more music than can fit on a single disc?
You can still add all the music you want to burn to the playlist. iTunes fills the first disc and then adds the remaining songs to further discs. After iTunes finishes burning the first disc, it prompts you to insert the next one.

Edit Song Information

Within each song in your library or on a music CD, metadata is stored that includes the song title, artist, album title, genre, and more. If a song's information contains errors or omissions, you can edit the data. For example, it is common for an album to be categorized under the wrong music genre, so you can edit the album to give it the correct genre. You can edit one song at a time, or you can edit multiple songs, such as an entire album or music CD.

Edit Song Information

Edit a Single Song

1. Click the song you want to edit.
2. Click **File**.
3. Click **Get Info**.

Note: You can also press ⌘+I. Alternatively, right-click the song and then click **Get Info**.

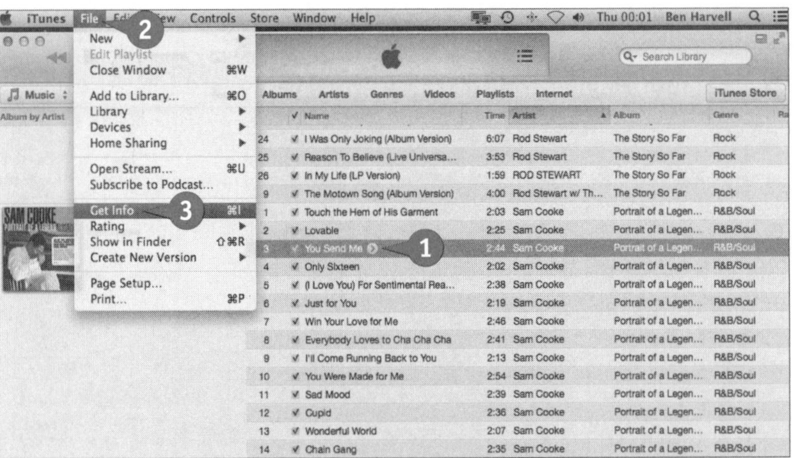

4. Click **Info**.
5. Edit or add information to the fields.

   A. If you want to edit another song, click **Previous** or **Next** to display the song you want.

6. Click **OK**.

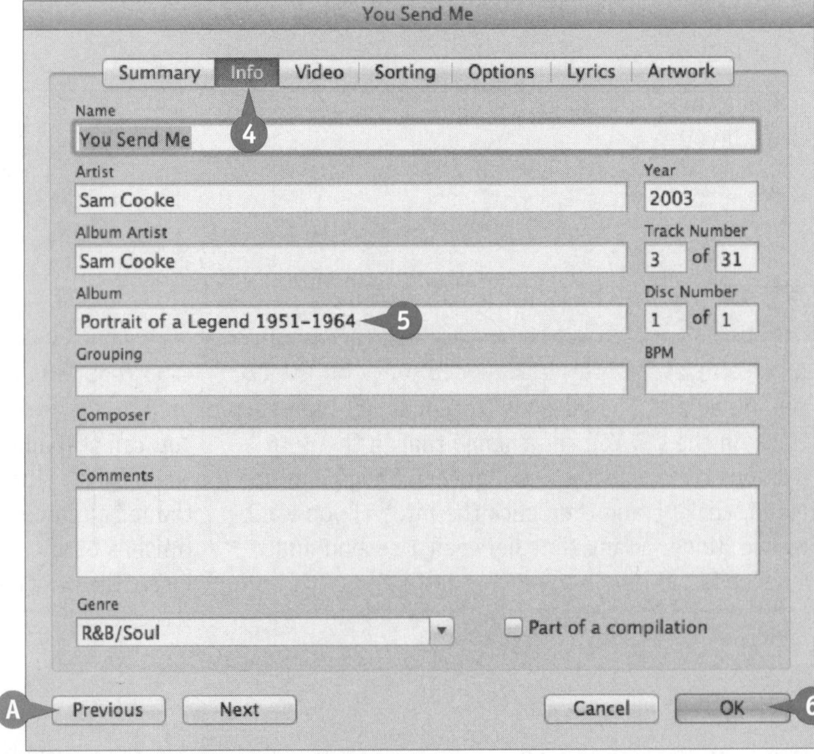

Edit Multiple Songs

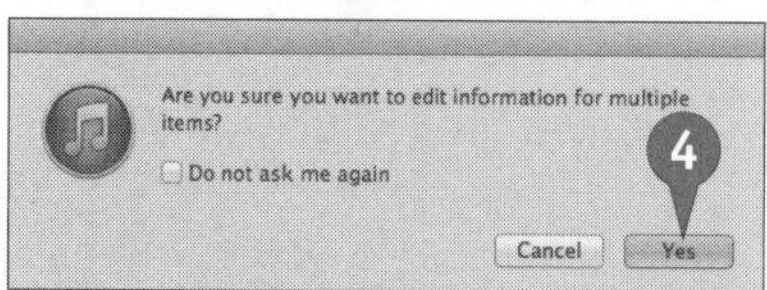

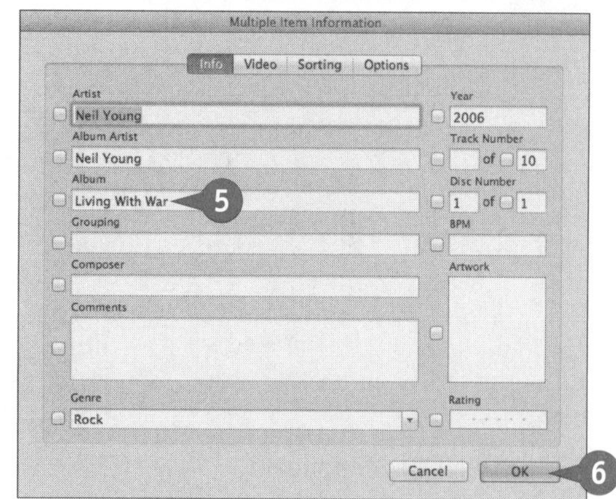

1. Select all the songs that you want to edit.

Note: To select individual songs, press and hold ⌘ and click each song; to select all songs (on a music CD, for example), press ⌘+A.

2. Click **File**.
3. Click **Get Info**.

Note: You can also press ⌘+I. Alternatively, right-click any selected song and then click **Get Info**.

iTunes asks you to confirm that you want to edit multiple songs.

4. Click **Yes**.

The Multiple Item Information dialog appears.

5. Edit or add information to the fields.
6. Click **OK**.

iTunes applies the edits to each selected song.

TIP

When I edit multiple songs, why do I not see all the fields in the Multiple Item Information dialog?
When you are editing multiple songs, you can only modify fields containing data that is common to all the songs, apart from the song title Name field. This makes sense because any changes you make apply to all the selected songs. For example, each song usually has a different title, so you would not want to give every song the same title. You see fields that are common to all the selected songs. For example, on a music CD, data such as the artist, album title, and genre are usually the same for all the songs.

Purchase Music from the iTunes Store

You can add music to your iTunes library by purchasing songs or albums from the iTunes Store. iTunes downloads the song or album to your computer and then adds it to both the Music category and the Purchased playlist. You can then play and manage the song or album just like any other content in the iTunes library. To purchase music from the iTunes Store, you must have an Apple ID, which you can obtain from https://appleid.apple.com. You can also use an AOL account, if you have one.

Purchase Music from the iTunes Store

1. Click **iTunes Store**.

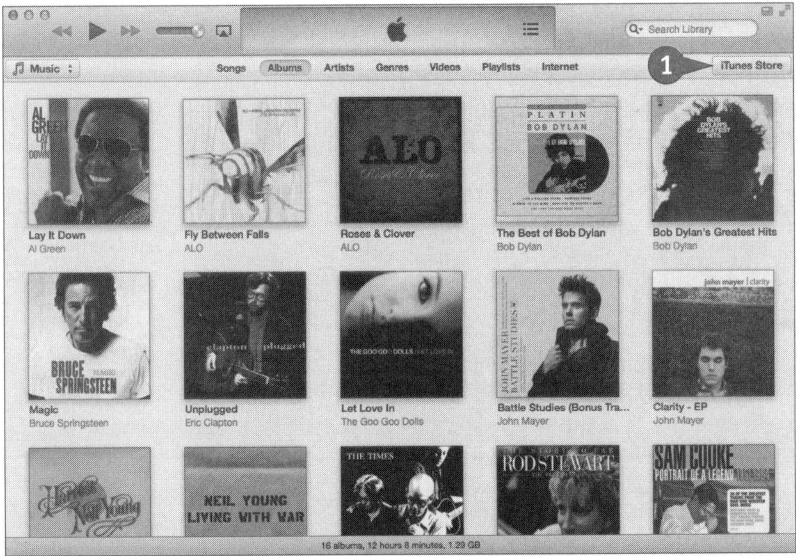

The iTunes Store appears.

2. Click **Music**.
3. Locate the music you want to purchase.

A You can use the Search box to search for an artist, album, or song.

4. Click **Buy**.

B If you want to purchase just a song, click the price button next to the song instead.

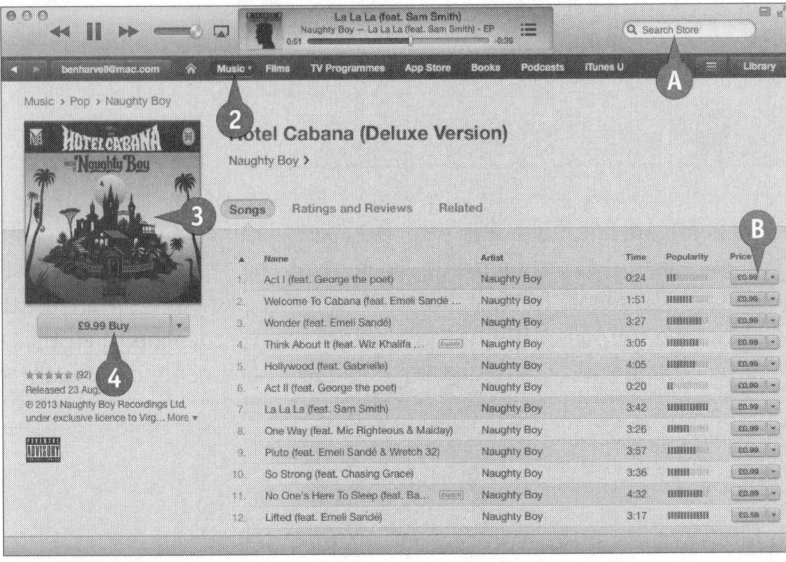

iTunes asks you to sign in to your iTunes Store account.

5. If you have not signed in to your account, you must type your Apple ID.

6. Type your password.

7. Click **Buy**.

C. Music you have purchased appears in the Purchased section in your iTunes library.

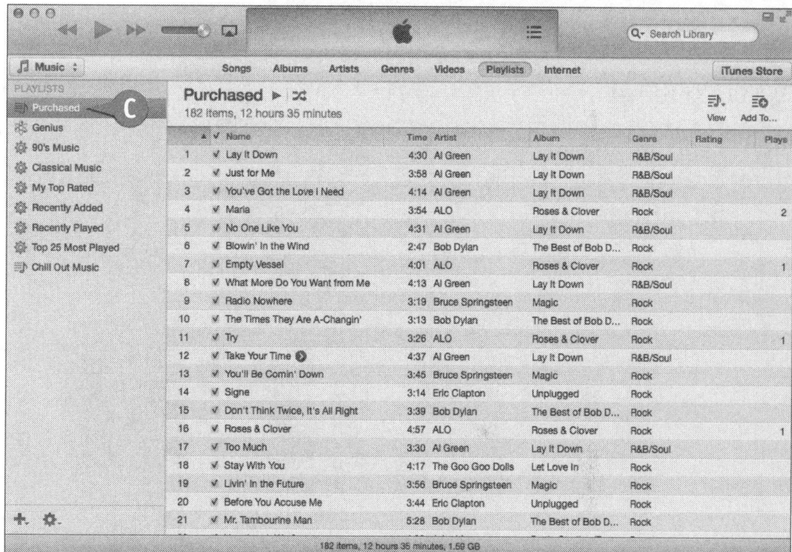

TIPS

Can I use my purchased music on other computers and devices?

Yes. Although many iTunes Store media, particularly movies and TV shows, have digital rights management (DRM) restrictions applied to prevent illegal copying, the songs and albums in the iTunes Store are DRM-free, and so do not have these restrictions. This means you can play them on multiple computers and media devices (such as iPods, iPads, and iPhones), and burn them to multiple CDs.

How do I avoid having many $0.99 or $1.99 charges on my credit card bill when purchasing multiple songs?

To avoid many small iTunes charges, purchase an iTunes gift card from an Apple Store or retailer that sells gift cards. On the back of the card, scratch off the sticker that covers the redeem code. In iTunes, access the iTunes Store and click **Redeem** at the bottom of the store. Type in the redeem code and then click **Redeem**.

Listen to an Internet Radio Station

The Internet offers a number of radio stations to which you can listen. iTunes maintains a list of many of these online radio stations, so it is often easier to use iTunes to listen to Internet radio. Just like a regular radio station, an Internet radio station broadcasts a constant audio stream, except you access the audio over the Internet instead of over the air. iTunes offers several radio stations in each of its more than two dozen genres, which include Blues, Classic Rock, Classical, Folk, Hip Hop, Jazz, and Pop.

Listen to an Internet Radio Station

1 Click **Internet**.

Note: If you do not see the Internet category, see the first Tip in this section.

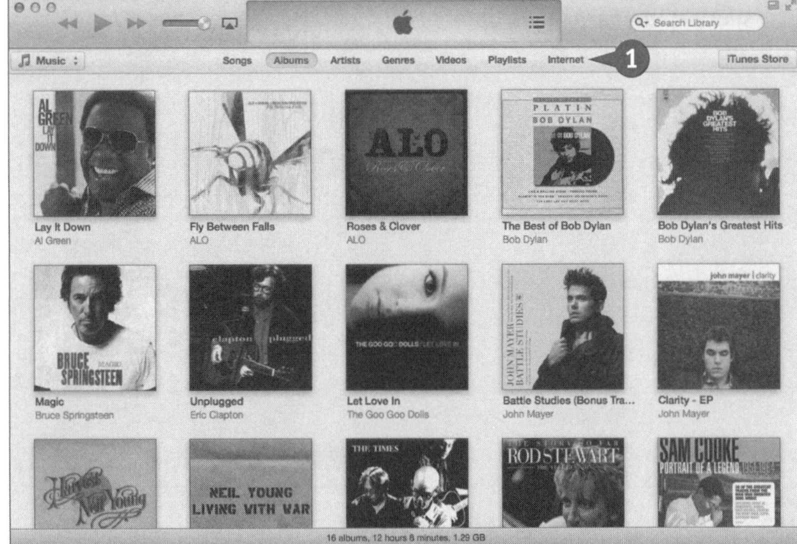

iTunes displays a list of radio genres.

2 Click ▶ to open the genre you want to listen to (▶ changes to ▼).

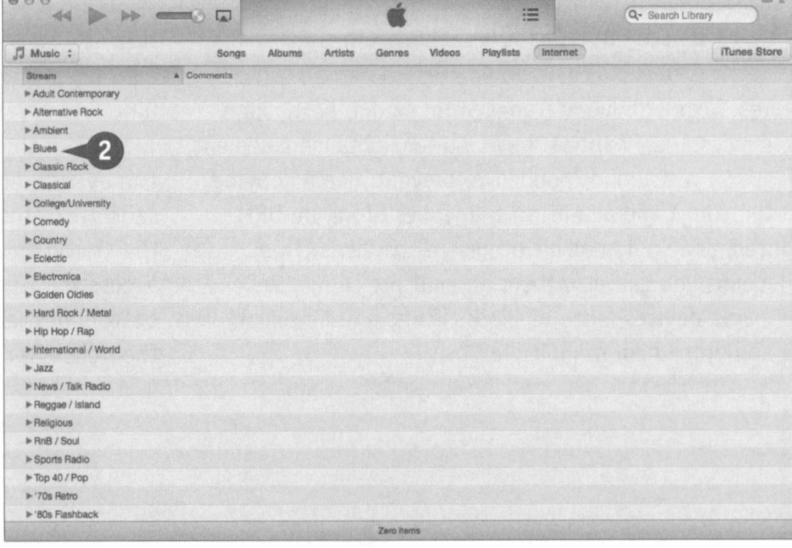

iTunes displays a list of radio station streams in the genre.

3 Double-click the station you want to play.

iTunes plays the radio station stream.

A The name of the station and the name of the currently playing track usually appear here.

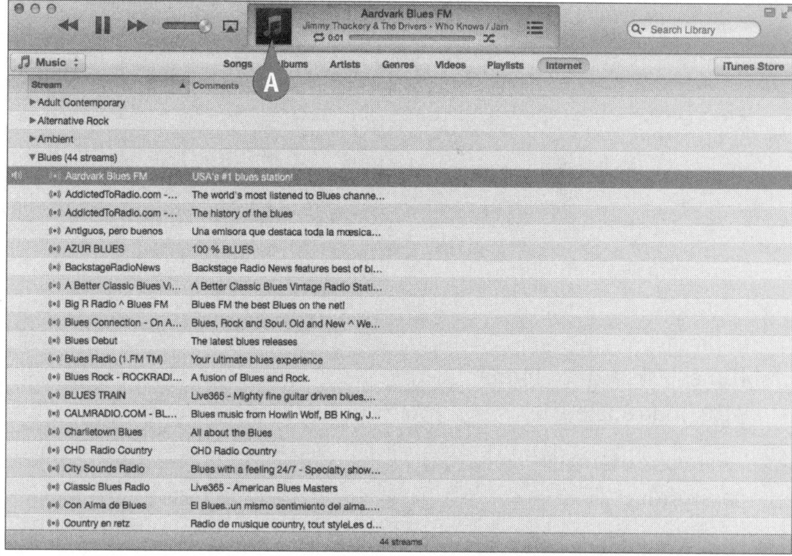

TIPS

The Radio section of the iTunes library does not appear. Can I still listen to Internet radio?

Yes. By default, iTunes does not show all of the available library categories and sources. To display the Internet source, click **iTunes** and then click **Preferences** to open the iTunes preferences. Click the **General** tab, select **Internet** (☐ changes to ☑), and then click **OK**.

Is it possible to use iTunes to save or record a song from a radio station stream?

No, an Internet radio stream is "listen-only." iTunes does not give you any way to save the stream to your Mac hard drive or to record the stream as it plays.

Listen to iTunes Radio

iTunes Radio is a music streaming service provided by Apple that plays selections of songs like a personalized radio station. iTunes Radio is available on iOS devices as well as Macs, PCs, and Apple TVs. The service is free but ad-supported, and you can remove the ads by subscribing to iTunes Match for an annual fee. Because iTunes Radio is personalized to your music tastes, the more music you listen to, the more tailored to you it becomes, similar to other radio services like Pandora.

Listen to iTunes Radio

1. Click **Radio**.

   iTunes displays the iTunes Radio welcome screen.

2. Click **Start Listening**.

   iTunes asks you to log in with your Apple ID.

3. Type your username and password.
4. Click **Sign In**.

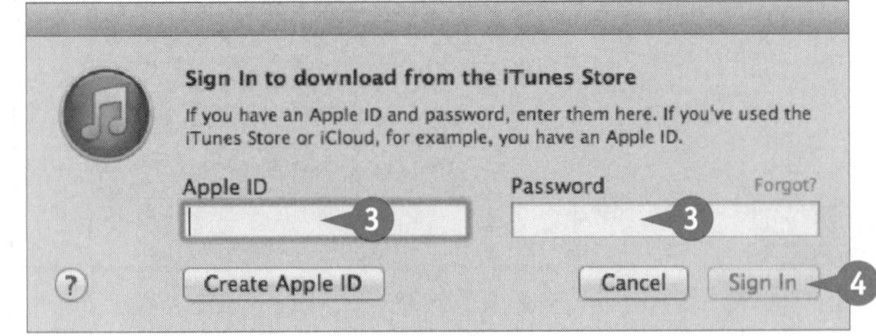

The iTunes Radio interface appears.

A Click one of the default radio stations to begin playing iTunes radio.

5 Click the **Add** button.

6 Type a song title or artist name into the field that appears.

iTunes suggests radio stations, songs and artists based on your entry.

7 Double-click any of the stations suggested.

A new radio station is created and begins playing.

B Click **Add an artist or song...** to further personalize the station.

C Click **Add an artist or song...** to block particular songs and artists from playing on this station.

D To buy the currently playing song, click the price button.

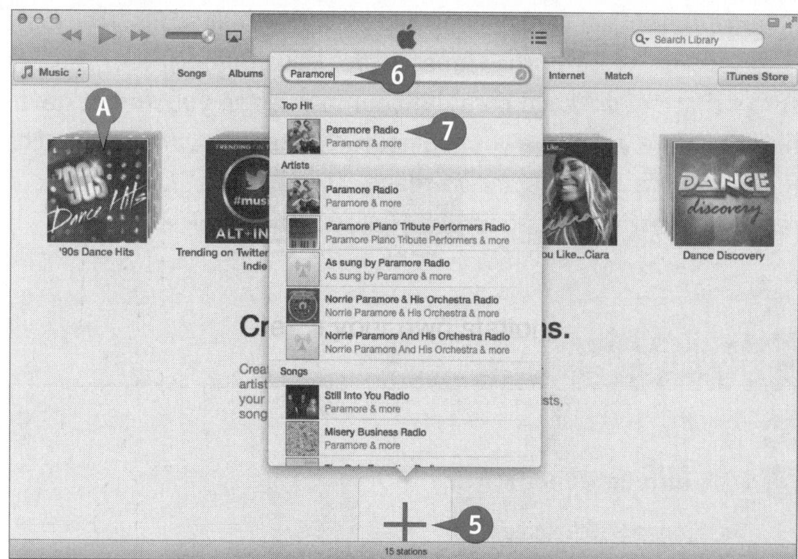

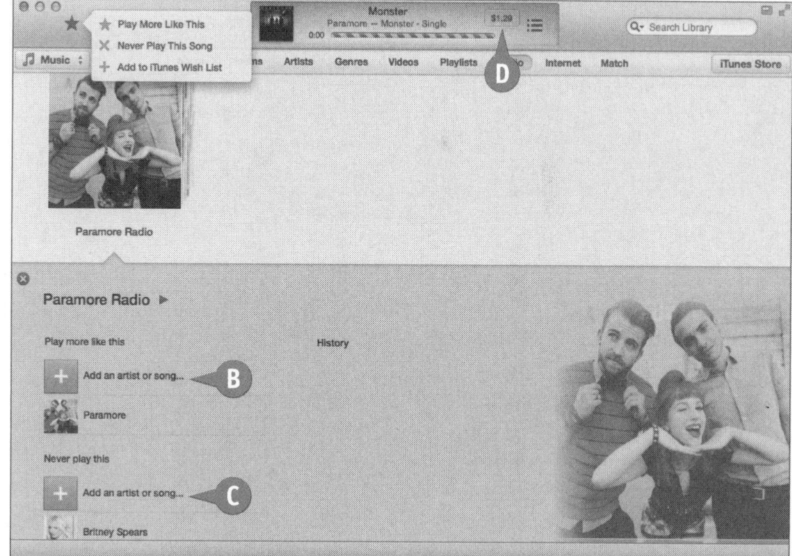

TIPS

How else can I personalize my iTunes Radio stations?
Click the star (★) next to the playback controls to access a menu on which you can tell iTunes to play more songs like the one currently playing, to never play the currently playing song again, or to add it to your iTunes Wish List so you can purchase it at a later date.

How do I create a new iTunes Radio Station?
Click **Radio** and then click the plus button next to My Stations on the iTunes Radio screen. You can now enter artists or albums to create a radio station based on the music you select.

Subscribe to iTunes Match

iTunes Match is a service provided by Apple that scans your existing music library and matches the songs with those in the iTunes Store. For an annual fee, you can then listen to and download the songs that are matched on all of your devices so you do not have to worry about syncing your entire library before you leave your computer. Songs that are not matched with iTunes are uploaded to iCloud, so you can also access them. iTunes Match subscriptions are limited to 25,000 songs and also remove advertisements from the iTunes Radio service.

Subscribe to iTunes Match

1. Click **Store**.
2. Click **Turn On iTunes Match**.

   The iTunes Match screen appears.

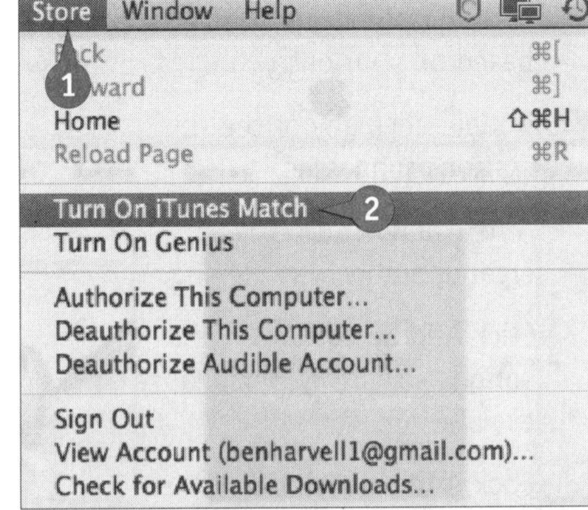

3. Click the **Subscribe** button.

Note: The Subscribe button also features the price of iTunes Match in your local currency.

Note: You will need to sign in with your Apple ID or iTunes Store account.

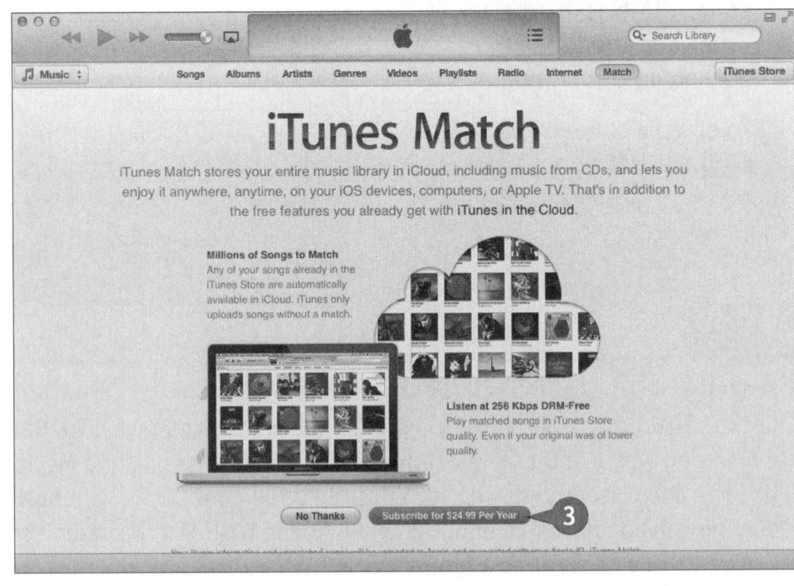

iTunes Match scans your library and matches the music it finds with music on the iTunes Store.

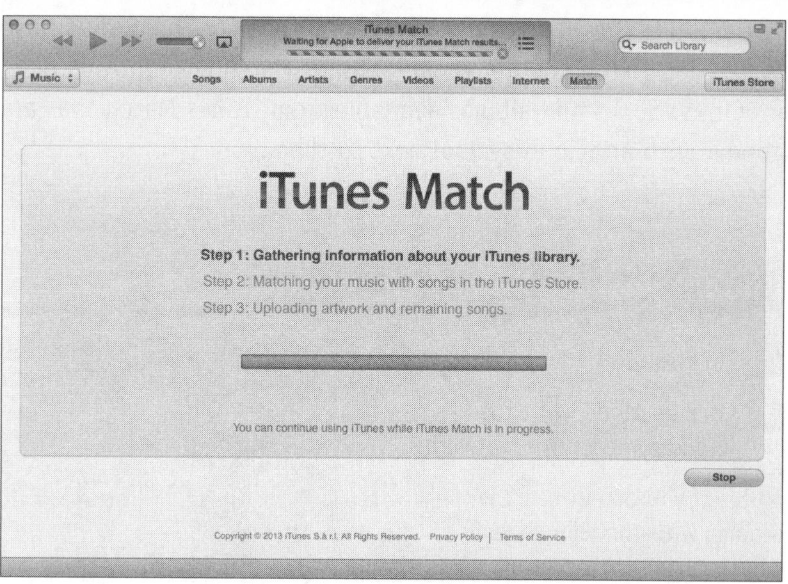

iTunes Match uploads any songs to iCloud that it can't match with music on iTunes.

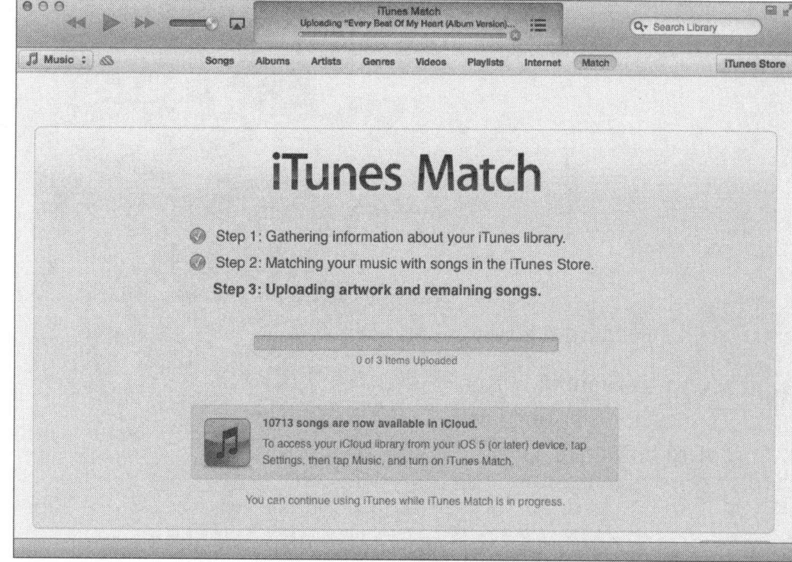

TIPS

Do the songs uploaded to iCloud count toward my available iCloud storage?

No. Any music uploaded by iTunes Match to iCloud does not use up your iCloud storage. Music is uploaded when no match for a song can be found on iTunes so you can still access the music on all of your devices.

Why is the iTunes Match setup taking so long?

If you have a large iTunes library, a number of songs that couldn't be matched with songs on iTunes, a slow Internet connection or a mixture of all of these, the initial iTunes Match setup may take a few hours to complete. It is best to leave it running and come back to it later.

Download Music with iTunes Match

If you use iTunes on a different computer than the one you used to set up iTunes Match, you can add that computer to your iTunes Match account and download the songs you have stored in iCloud. Songs and albums available from iTunes Match that are not stored in your iTunes Library appear with an iCloud symbol next to them.

Download Music with iTunes Match

1. Click **Albums**.
2. Click an album with the iCloud symbol on its artwork.

Note: If you do not see any albums with the iCloud symbol, see the Tip in this section.

iTunes displays the album.

3. Click the **Download** button (⬇) next to the song you want to download.

iTunes downloads the song.

Ⓐ The status of the download appears next to the song.

Ⓑ The status of the download also appears at the top of the interface.

Ⓒ To view all downloads, click here.

The song is added to your library.

4 Repeat steps **2** and **3** to add more music to your library from iTunes Match.

TIP

I have music in an iTunes Match subscription on another computer. How do I access it on the computer I am currently using?

Click **Store** and then click **Turn On iTunes Match**. When the iTunes Match screen appears, click the **Add This Computer** button to add the computer you are currently using to your iTunes Match account. Sign in with your Apple ID and iTunes Match will add this computer and make any existing iTunes Match music available in your library.

Listen to iTunes Match Songs

You don't have to download songs from iTunes Match in order to listen to them on another computer. Songs available in iTunes Match can be played from within your iTunes Library as a stream by simply double-clicking the title of the song. You can listen to individual songs or entire albums in this way if you want.

Listen to iTunes Match Songs

1 Click **Songs**.

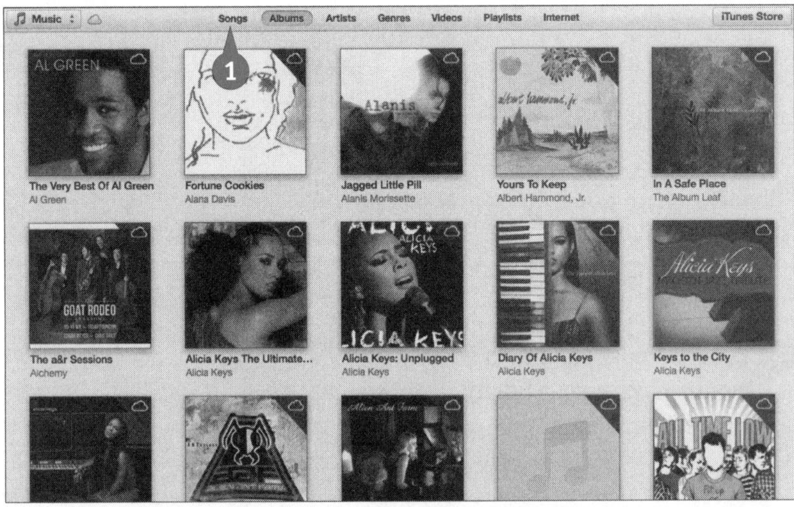

iTunes displays songs in your library and those stored in iCloud.

2 Locate a song stored in iCloud.

Note: You can tell which songs are stored in iCloud because they have the Download button (⬇) next to them.

3 Double-click the song.

iTunes begins streaming the song.

A The buffering status of the stream is shown at the top of the screen by a gray line.

TIP

Can I download a whole album stored by iTunes Match in iCloud?

Yes. Click **Albums** and locate the album stored in iCloud that you want to download. Click the **iCloud** symbol at the top right of the album artwork to download the album from iCloud to your iTunes library. The album begins to download and a download status symbol appears next to each download.

Set the Audio Output

If you have access to AirPlay speakers or an Apple TV, you can stream music from iTunes to them. Your Mac and speakers or Apple TV need to be on the same wireless network and within range of your router. The AirPlay icon that appears at the top of the iTunes interface allows you to select which speaker or device to stream to and even allows you to stream to multiple speakers if you want.

Set the Audio Output

1 Click the **AirPlay** button (▣).

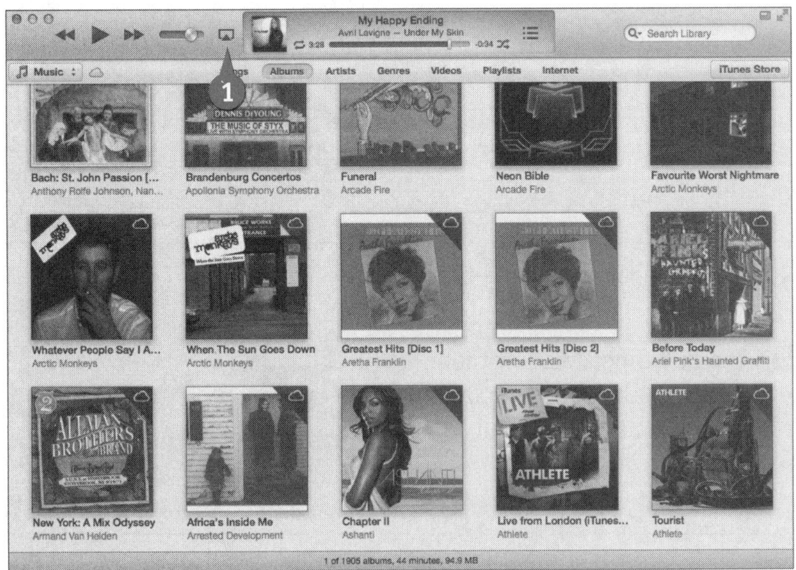

iTunes displays a list of available speakers.

A Click **Single** to stream audio to one speaker or device.

B Click **Multiple** to stream audio to more than one speaker or device.

2. Click the name of the device or devices you want to stream to.
3. Click **Play** (▶).

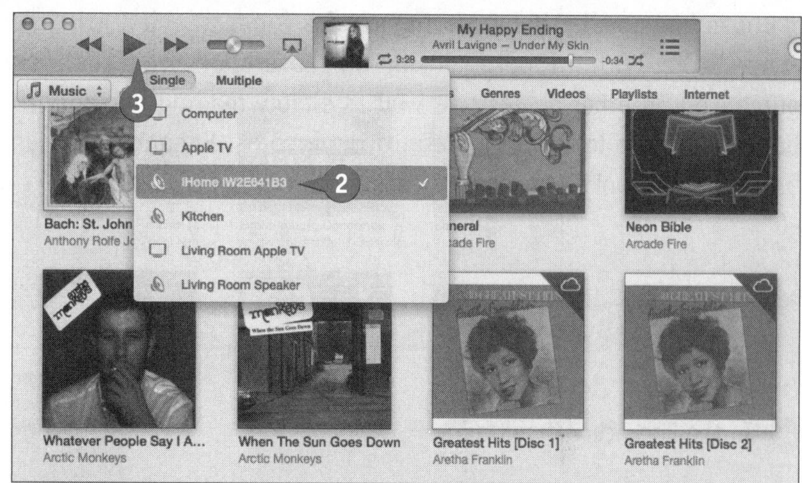

iTunes streams the currently playing music to the devices you selected.

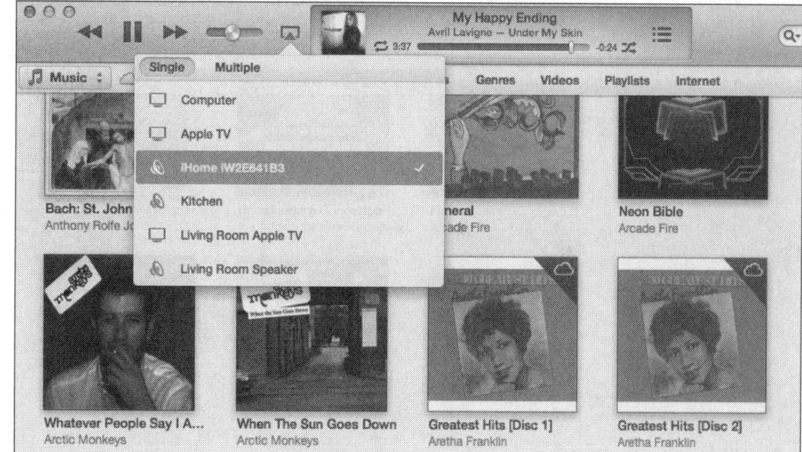

TIP

Can I adjust the volume level on speakers I stream music to?

Yes. Click **Multiple** on the AirPlay menu, even if you are only streaming to one speaker or device. Click the devices you want to stream to. A volume control for each device you are streaming to is shown next to the device name.

Open and Close iBooks

iBooks is a popular book reading application available for iOS devices and for OS X via the Mac App Store. Within iBooks you can purchase books from the iBooks Store and sync books you have purchased on other devices. As well as simply reading books in iBooks, you can also make notes, add bookmarks, and look up the definition of words. Enhanced iBooks with interactive features, normally built in the iBooks Author application, can only be used on Macs and iPads.

Open and Close iBooks

Open iBooks

1 In the Dock, click **iBooks** (📖).

iBooks opens.

Close iBooks

1 Click **iBooks**.

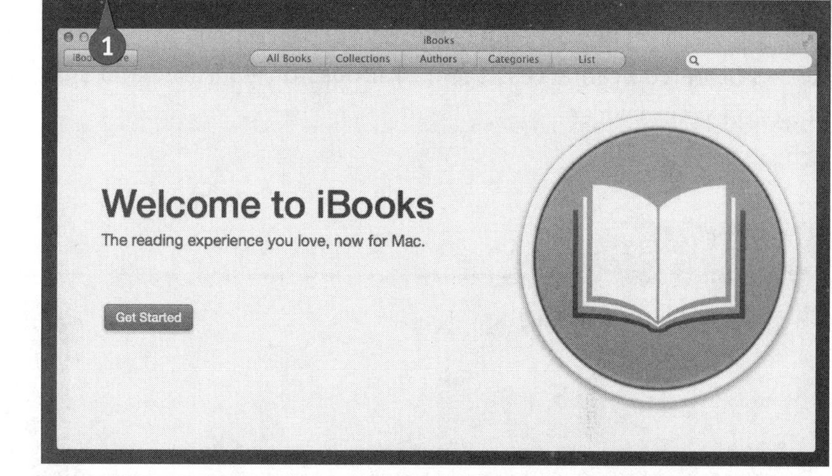

2 Click **Quit iBooks**.

iBooks closes.

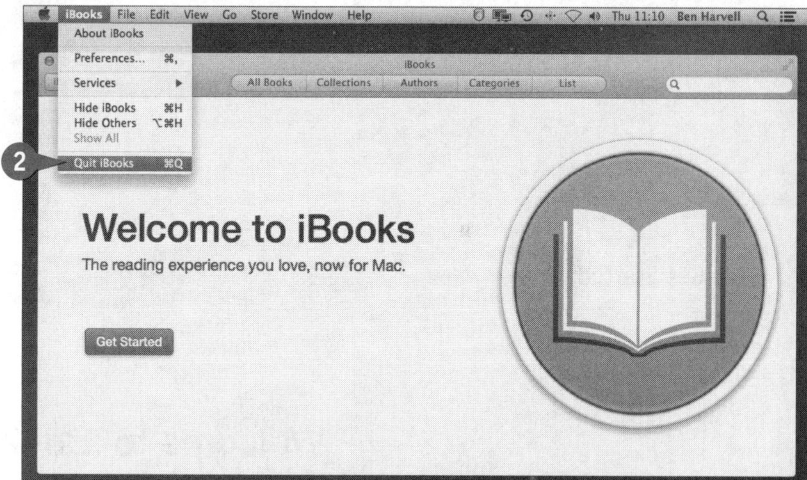

TIP

Are there other methods I can use to open and close iBooks?

If you have hidden the Dock (as described in Chapter 13) or removed the iBooks icon from the Dock, you can click **Spotlight** (🔍) and type **iBooks**. You can then click **iBooks** in the search results. Alternatively, you can double-click the **iBooks** icon in the Applications folder.

Set Up iBooks

In order to buy books and sync books between devices in iBooks, you need to sign in with your Apple ID or iTunes Store account. If you have purchased books on other devices through the iBooks Store you can access them in iBooks on your Mac and sync bookmarks and notes between books on your devices.

Set Up iBooks

1. In the Dock, click **iBooks** (📖).

2. Click **Get Started**.

3. Type your Apple ID.
4. Type your password.
5. Click **Sign In**.

A. Any books you have purchased through iBooks on other devices appear.

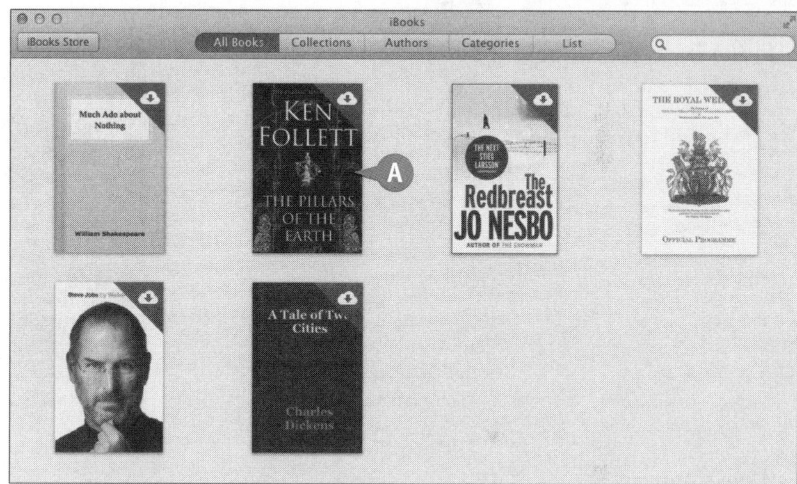

TIP

Why is there a cloud icon at the corner of my books?

These are books that you have purchased from the iBooks Store previously but not downloaded to this version of iBooks. To download a book, double-click its cover and it begins to download. When the download is complete the book is available to read in iBooks on your Mac.

Browse the iBooks Store

The iBooks Store, part of the iTunes Store and accessed via iBooks, allows you to browse books by category and popularity. You can also view new releases, bestsellers, and authors as well as free books that are available to download from the store. There are many categories available on the iBooks Store and specially curated sections to help you find new books of interest.

Browse the iBooks Store

1. In the Dock, click **iBooks** (▢).

iBooks appears.

2. Click **iBooks Store**.

The iBooks Store appears.

- **A** Exclusives, special offers, and recommendations appear here.
- **B** New and popular books appear here.
- **C** Select a category of book from this menu.

3. Click **Top Charts**.

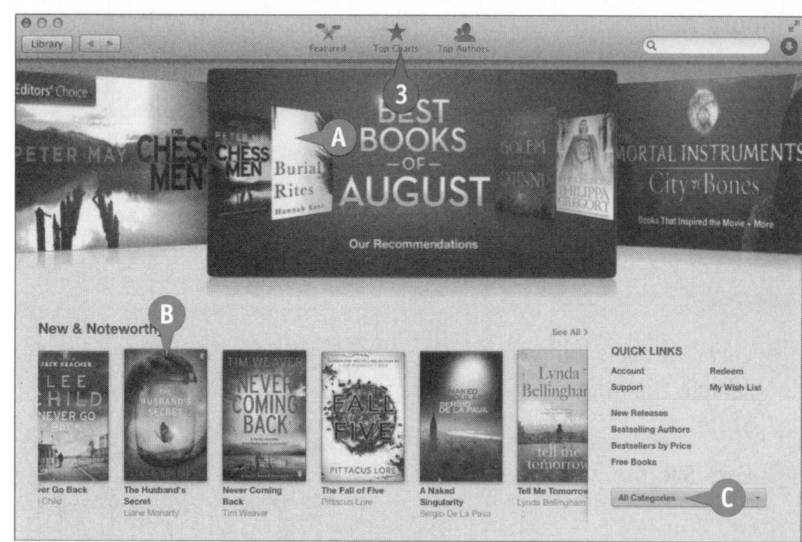

The Top Paid Books page appears.

- **D** Click **Free** to show the top free books chart.
- **E** Click **All Genres** to select a chart for a specific book category.

TIP

Why are there free books in the iBooks Store?

There are a number of reasons why a book is offered for free on iBooks. Some authors and publishers choose to make a book available at no cost, while other books are run as part of the iBooks Free Book of the Week promotion. Classic books are also available for free, such as titles by Shakespeare and Dickens.

Preview and Buy an iBook

iBooks allows you to preview a book before you buy it by downloading a sample. The sample includes a small portion, normally the opening few chapters, of the whole book to help you decide if it is right for you. iBooks allows you to return to the iBooks Store page for a book from within a sample book so you do not have to browse the iBooks Store again in order to find and download it.

Preview and Buy an iBook

1. Locate a book you want to sample from the iBooks Store.
2. Click **Sample**.

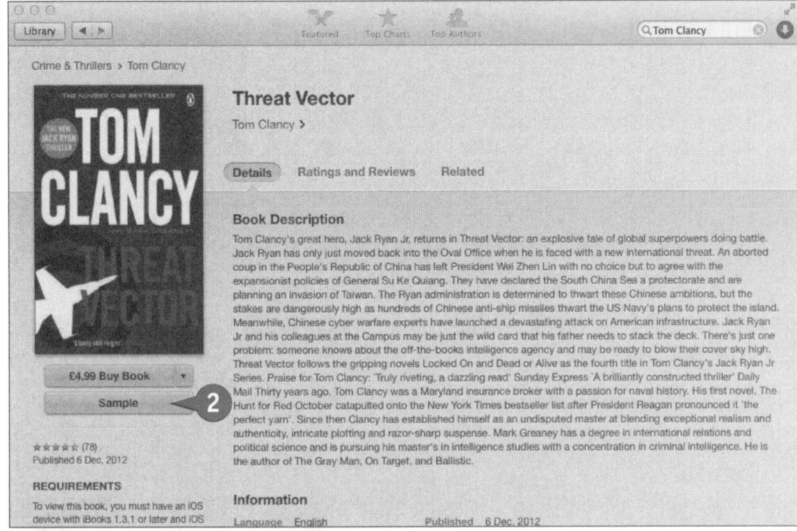

The book sample downloads to your iBooks library.

3. Click **Read**.

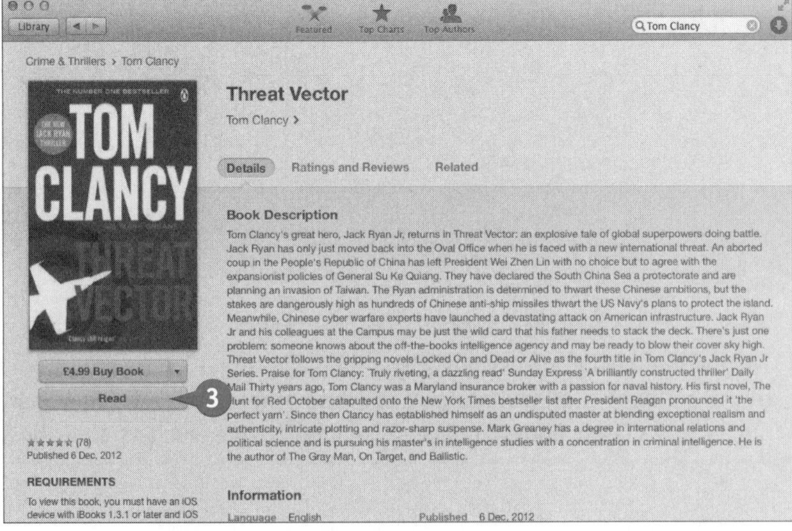

The book opens in iBooks.

4 Read the sample and then move the cursor to the top of the screen to show the toolbar.

5 Click **Buy**.

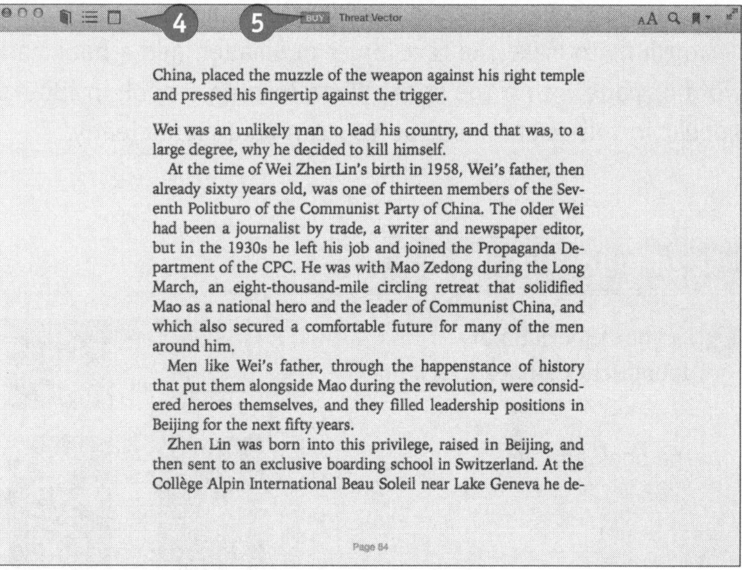

You are returned to the iBooks Store.

6 Click **Buy Book**.

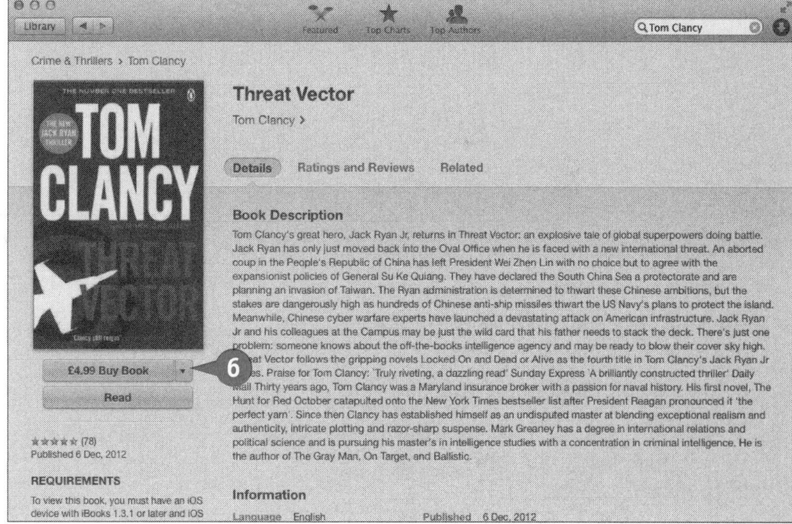

TIP

Is it possible to save a book in iBooks to buy later?

Yes. Next to the Buy Book button is a downward-facing arrow. Click this to show a menu on which you find various sharing options and the option to add to the book to your iBooks Wish List. You can access your Wish List at any time from the Feature page of the iBooks Store under Quick Links on the right of the page.

Read a Book in iBooks

Reading a book in iBooks is much the same as reading a book in iBooks on iOS devices. There are options to make the text larger or smaller, add a bookmark to a page, or search for a particular word or page within the book. When reading a book in iBooks you can also make the application appear in full-screen mode so you can read more clearly.

Read a Book in iBooks

1. In your iBooks library, double-click a book you want to read.

   The book appears.

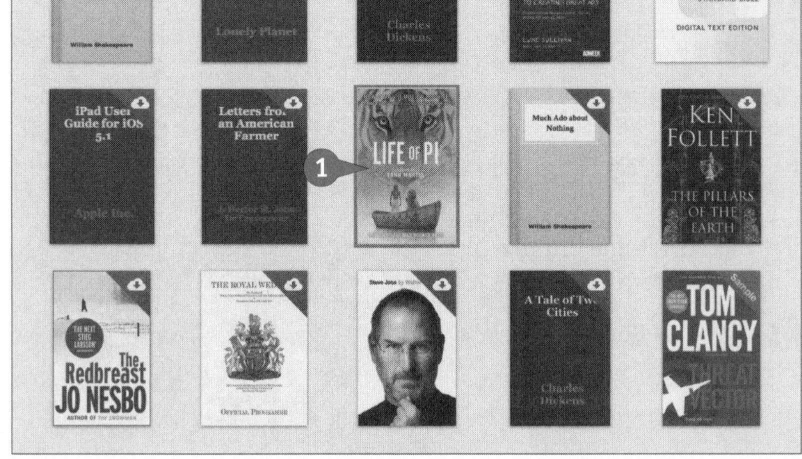

Ⓐ To move between pages, swipe left or right on a trackpad or Magic mouse (or use the scroll ball on your mouse if you have one). You can also click and drag to turn pages, use the arrow keys on your keyboard, or click the **Next** or **Previous Page** button.

2. Move the cursor to the top of the interface to show the toolbar.

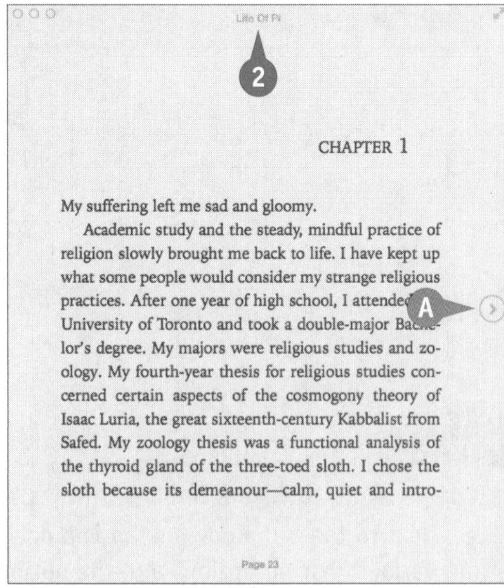

CHAPTER 1

My suffering left me sad and gloomy.

Academic study and the steady, mindful practice of religion slowly brought me back to life. I have kept up what some people would consider my strange religious practices. After one year of high school, I attended University of Toronto and took a double-major Bachelor's degree. My majors were religious studies and zoology. My fourth-year thesis for religious studies concerned certain aspects of the cosmogony theory of Isaac Luria, the great sixteenth-century Kabbalist from Safed. My zoology thesis was a functional analysis of the thyroid gland of the three-toed sloth. I chose the sloth because its demeanour—calm, quiet and intro-

The toolbar appears.

B Click the **Library** button (📕) to be returned to your iBooks library.

C Click the **Table of Contents** button (☰) to be taken to the book's table of contents.

D Click the **Notes** button (☐) to make notes.

E Click the **Search** button (🔍) to search for a word, page, or phrase.

F Click the **Bookmark** button (🔖) to bookmark a page.

G Click the **Full Screen** button (⤢) to view the book in full-screen mode.

3 Click the **Appearance** button (AA).

The appearance menu appears.

H Click the small A or large A to decrease or increase the size of the text.

I Click **White**, **Sepia**, or **Night** to change the book's background color.

J Click a font to change the default font.

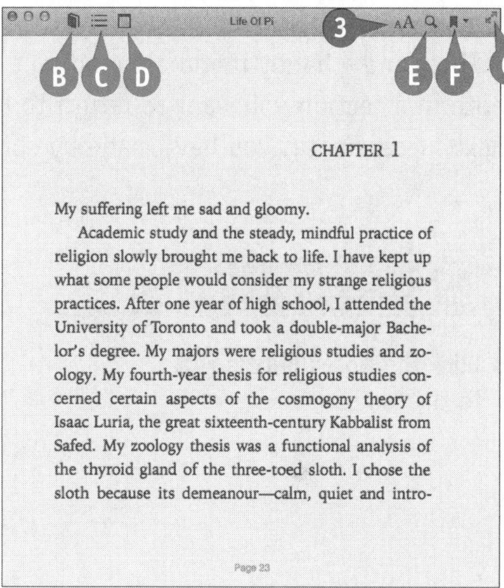

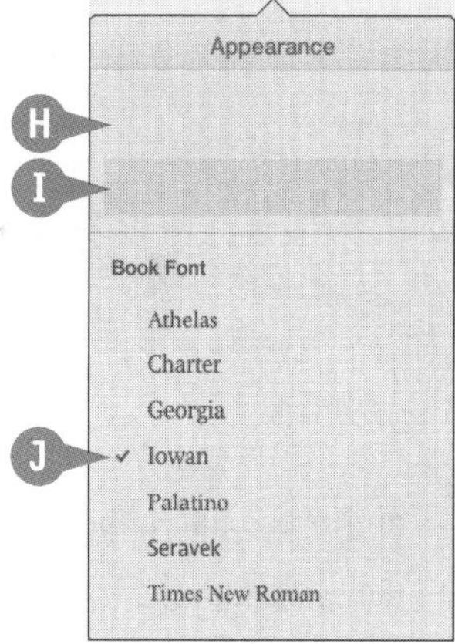

TIP

I bookmarked some pages before. How do I get back to them?

Click the arrow next to the Bookmark button to show all of the previous bookmarks you have created. Click a bookmark to be taken to the page you bookmarked. Bookmarks are stored within your iTunes Store account and can be accessed on all of the devices connected to the iBooks account you are currently using.

Take Notes in iBooks

As well as simply reading books, you can also highlight text in a book in iBooks and make notes. This can be handy if you are reading a book as part of your studies or if you simply want to make a note in a section you want to return to later. You can highlight text in a number of colors and quickly access notes you have made by clicking the Notes button at the top of the interface.

Take Notes in iBooks

1 Click the **Notes** button (▣) in the toolbar.

The Notes pane appears.

2 Click and drag over a section of text.

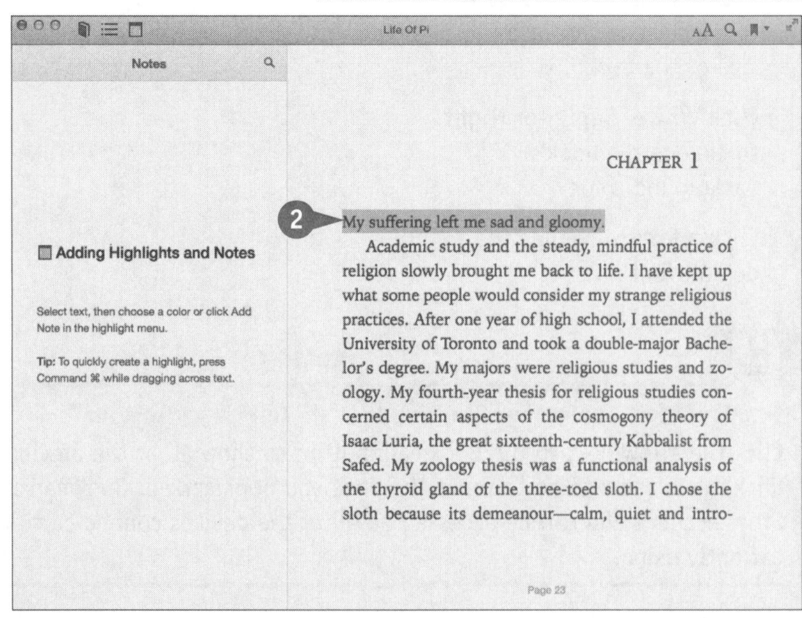

A menu appears.

Ⓐ Click a color to highlight the text.

Ⓑ Click the **Underline** button (a) to underline the selected text.

3 Click **Add Note.**

The text is highlighted and a new entry appears in the Notes pane.

4 Type your note below the highlighted text in the Notes pane.

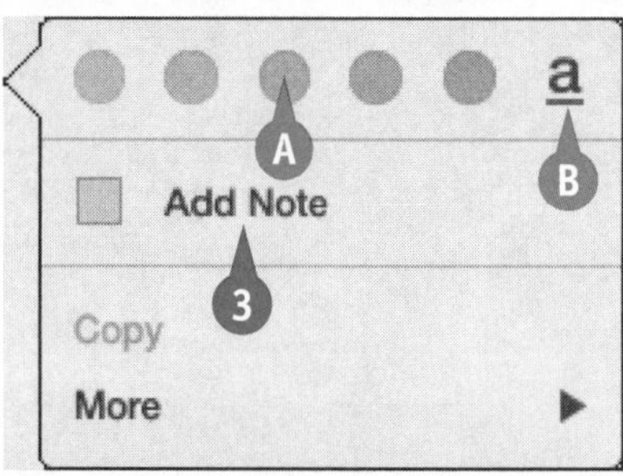

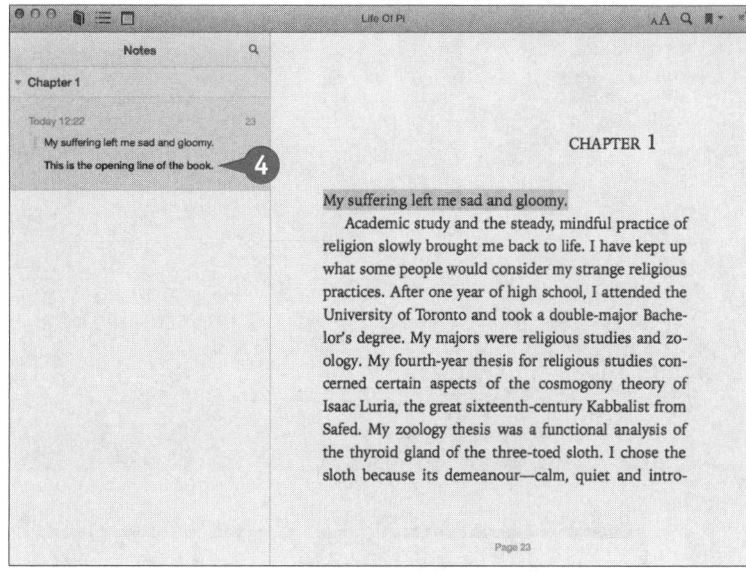

TIP

Can I search for a Note in iBooks?

Yes. iBooks sorts notes you have made by chapter, so you can show and hide notes within a chapter to get a clear view and find what you are looking for more quickly. You can also click the **Search** button on the Notes pane and type into the field that appears in order to find notes you have made.

CHAPTER 9

Learning Useful OS X Tasks

OS X Mavericks comes with many tools that help you accomplish everyday tasks. In this chapter, you learn how to connect and synchronize iOS devices, work with notes and reminders, and more.

Connect an iPod, iPhone, or iPad

Before you can synchronize data between OS X and your iPod, iPhone, or iPad, you need to connect the device to your Mac. To connect an iPod, iPhone, or iPad, you need the USB cable that came as part of the device package. You connect one end of that cable to your Mac, so you need to make sure that your Mac has a free USB port for the connection. You can also connect an iPod, iPhone, or iPad using an optional dock.

Connect an iPod, iPhone, or iPad

Connect the iPod, iPhone, or iPad

1. Using the device cable, attach the USB connector to a free USB port on your Mac.
2. Attach the other end of the cable to the port on the device or dock.

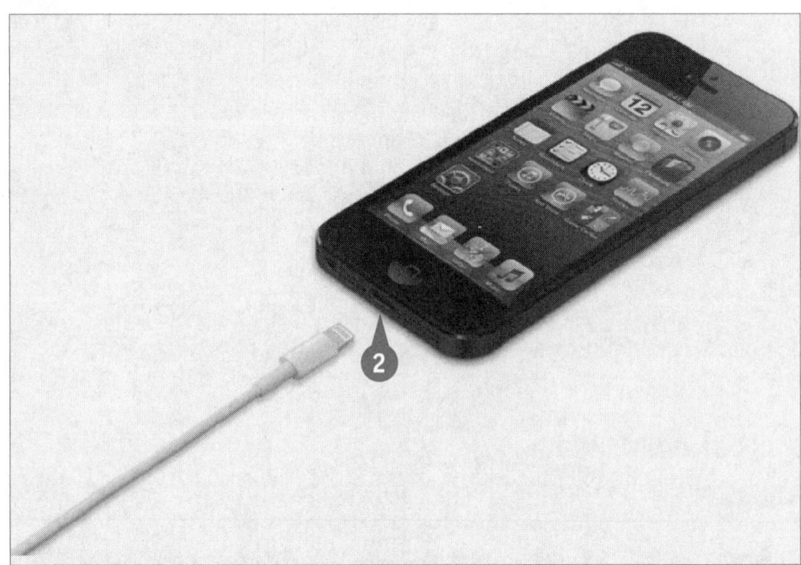

OS X launches iTunes and automatically begins synchronizing the device.

Note: You can prevent iTunes from launching when you connect a device in iTunes Preferences.

Ⓐ Your device appears as a button at the top right of the iTunes interface.

Note: If you have enabled View Sidebar from the iTunes view menu, your device appears in the sidebar to the left of the interface.

Note: Mac OS X usually also launches iPhoto to synchronize photos from the iPhone, iPad, or iPod touch. Either quit iPhoto or switch to iTunes.

Downloading 17 items
iMedia Player (11 seconds remaining)

Search Library

Music | Songs | Albums | Artists | Genres | Videos | Playlists | Radio | Match | iPhone | iTunes Store

A

✓	Name	Time	Artist	Album	Genre	Rating	Plays
✓	Lay It Down	4:30	Al Green	Lay It Down	R&B/Soul		
✓	Just for Me	3:58	Al Green	Lay It Down	R&B/Soul		
✓	You've Got the Love I Need	4:14	Al Green	Lay It Down	R&B/Soul		
✓	No One Like You	4:31	Al Green	Lay It Down	R&B/Soul		
✓	What More Do You Want fro...	4:13	Al Green	Lay It Down	R&B/Soul		
✓	Take Your Time	4:37	Al Green	Lay It Down	R&B/Soul		
✓	Too Much	3:30	Al Green	Lay It Down	R&B/Soul		
✓	Stay With Me (By the Sea)	3:23	Al Green	Lay It Down	R&B/Soul		
✓	All I Need	3:41	Al Green	Lay It Down	R&B/Soul		
✓	I'm Wild About You	4:51	Al Green	Lay It Down	R&B/Soul		
✓	Standing In the Rain	3:09	Al Green	Lay It Down	R&B/Soul		
✓	Wanna Say	3:42	Al Green	Lay It Down	R&B/Soul		
✓	Spectrum	3:50	ALO	Fly Between Falls	Rock		1
✓	Wasting Time	5:58	ALO	Fly Between Falls	Rock		1
✓	Barbeque	4:02	ALO	Fly Between Falls	Rock		1
✓	Possibly Down	4:29	ALO	Fly Between Falls	Rock		1
✓	Pobrecito	4:33	ALO	Fly Between Falls	Rock		1
✓	Shapeshifter	6:23	ALO	Fly Between Falls	Rock		1
✓	The Gardener CLEAN	5:32	ALO	Fly Between Falls	Rock		1
✓	Waiting for Jaden	6:40	ALO	Fly Between Falls	Rock		1

Disconnect the iPod, iPhone, or iPad

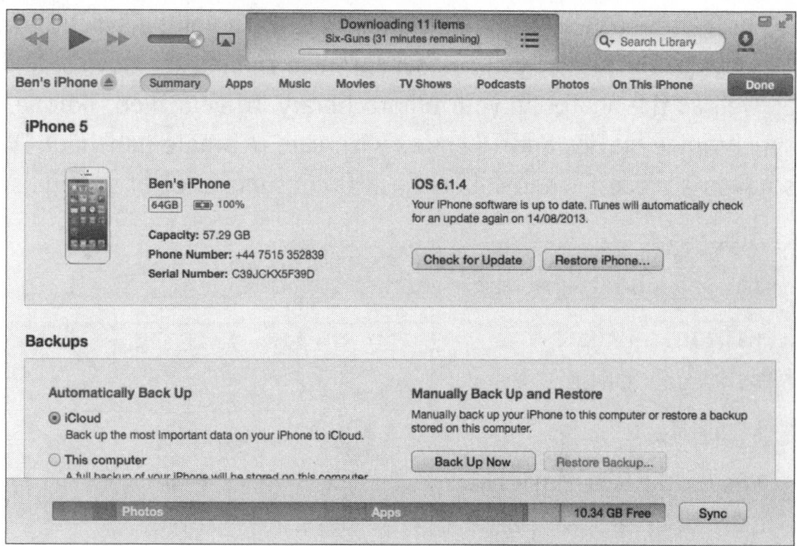

1. In iTunes, click the **Eject** button (⏏) beside your device's name.

   iTunes begins releasing the device.

Note: See the tips in this section to learn when it is safe to disconnect the cable from an iPod.

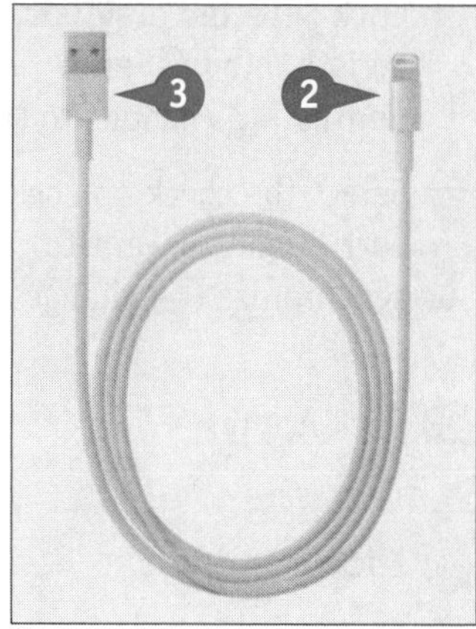

2. Pull the connector away from the device.
3. Disconnect the cable from the Mac's USB port.

   Your device is now disconnected from iTunes.

Note: If your Mac has two or more free USB ports and you synchronize your device frequently, consider leaving the cable plugged in to a USB port for easier connections in the future.

TIPS

Is there a way to prevent iTunes from starting the synchronization automatically when I connect my device?

Yes. In iTunes, click **iTunes** and then click **Preferences** to open the iTunes preferences window. Click the **Devices** tab and then select the **Prevent iPods, iPhones, and iPads from syncing automatically** check box (☐ changes to ☑). Click **OK**.

Do I have to use the USB cable to sync my device?

No. If you have an iPhone, iPad, or iPod touch, you can sync with your current settings over Wi-Fi. Connect your device as described in this section, click the Summary tab, and then select the **Sync with the *device* over Wi-Fi** check box (☐ changes to ☑), where *device* is the iPhone, iPad or iPod. To sync over Wi-Fi, on your device tap **Settings**, tap **General**, tap **iTunes Wi-Fi Sync**, and then tap **Sync Now**.

Synchronize an iPod, iPhone, or iPad

You can take your media and other data with you by synchronizing that data from OS X to your device. For media, you can synchronize the music, movies, and TV shows in your iTunes library, as well as the photos in your iPhoto library, to your iPod, iPhone, or iPad. However, you should synchronize movies and TV shows with care. A single half-hour TV episode may be as large as 650MB, so even a modest video collection will consume a lot of storage space on your device.

Synchronize an iPod, iPhone, or iPad

Synchronize Music

1. Click your device.
2. Click **Music**.
3. Select the **Sync Music** check box (☐ changes to ☑).
4. Click **Selected playlists, artists, albums, and genres** (○ changes to ◉).
5. Select the check box beside each item you want to synchronize (☐ changes to ☑).
6. Click **Apply**.

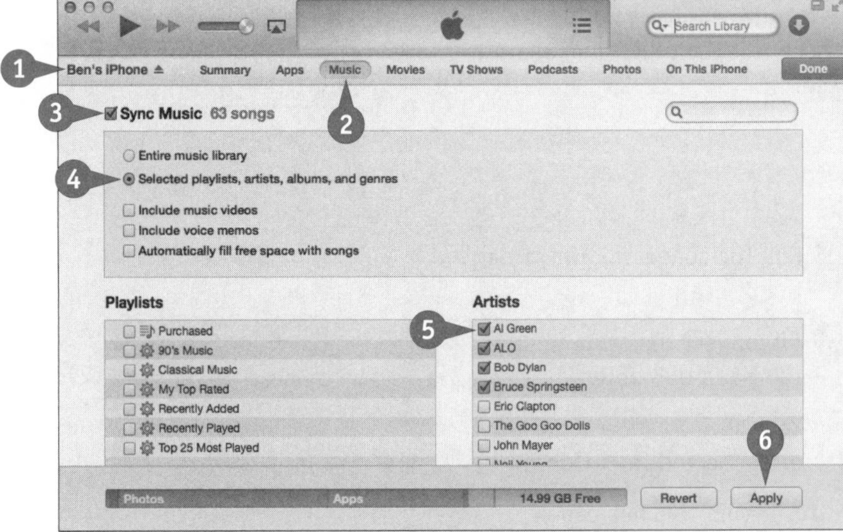

Synchronize Photos

1. Click your device.
2. Click **Photos**.
3. Select the **Sync Photos from** check box (☐ changes to ☑).
4. Click **Selected albums, Events, and Faces, and automatically include** (○ changes to ◉).
5. Select the check box beside each item you want to synchronize (☐ changes to ☑).
6. Click **Apply**.

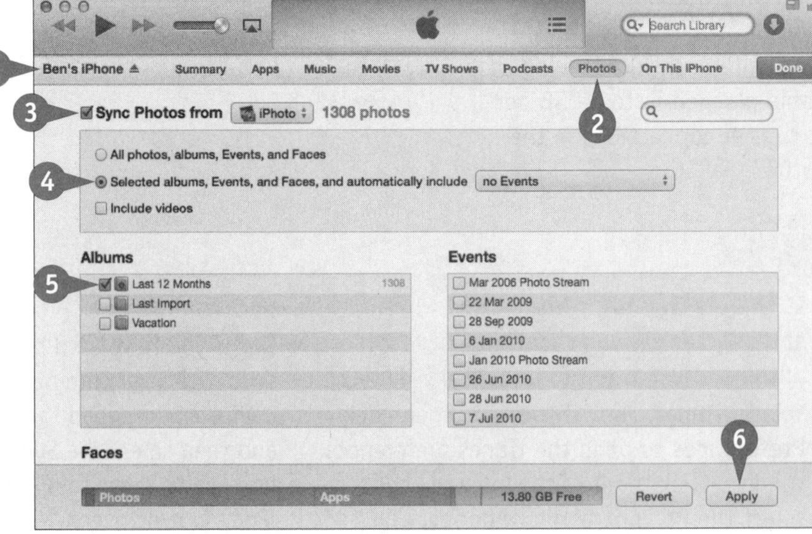

Synchronize Movies

1. Click your device.
2. Click **Movies.**
3. Select the **Sync Movies** check box (☐ changes to ☑).
4. Select each movie you want to synchronize (☐ changes to ☑).
5. Click **Apply**.

Synchronize TV Shows

1. Click your device.
2. Click **TV Shows.**
3. Select the **Sync TV Shows** check box (☐ changes to ☑).
4. Select each TV show you want to synchronize (☐ changes to ☑).
5. Click **Apply**.

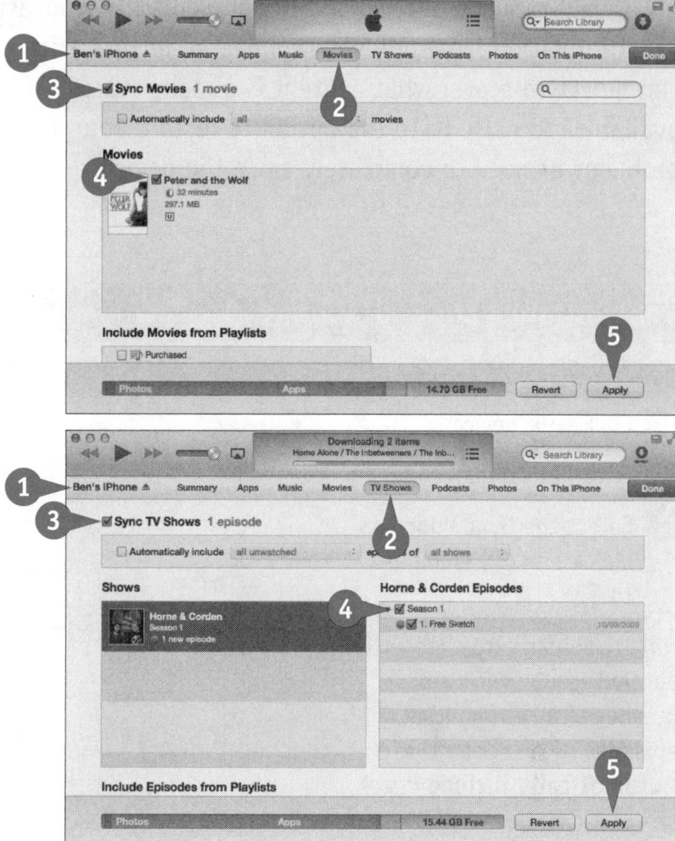

TIPS

Is there a way to control which music is synchronized to my iPod shuffle?

Yes. Although by default iTunes uses a feature called Autofill to send a selection of songs to the iPod shuffle, you can configure iTunes to send a playlist instead. Connect your iPod shuffle, click it in the Devices section, and then click the **Contents** tab. Click the **Autofill From** ⬍, click the playlist you want to send to the device, and then click **Autofill**.

How do I get my photos from my device to my Mac?

If you have used a camera device to take pictures, you can view and work with those pictures on your Mac by using iPhoto to import them from your device. In iPhoto, click your device, then press and hold ⌘ and click each photo you want to import. Use the Event Name text box to type a name for this event, and then click **Import Selected**. If you do not have iPhoto installed, you can use Aperture or Photoshop Elements if either application is installed; if not, use the default Image Capture application that comes with OS X.

continued ►

Synchronize an iPod, iPhone, or iPad (continued)

As well as synchronizing additional media like podcasts and apps, iTunes also allows you to view information regarding your connected device. With your device connected to your Mac you can quickly discover what content is already stored on it as well as check if software updates are available. You also have the option to restore your device to its default settings if you encounter problems or need to completely erase the device.

Synchronize an iPod, iPhone, or iPad (continued)

Synchronize Podcasts

1. Click your device.
2. Click **Podcasts**.
3. Select the **Sync Podcasts** check box (☐ changes to ☑).

Note: You can also choose to automatically sync a set number of recent podcast episodes by selecting the **Automatically include** check box (☐ changes to ☑).

4. Select each Podcast you want to synchronize (☐ changes to ☑).
5. Click **Apply**.

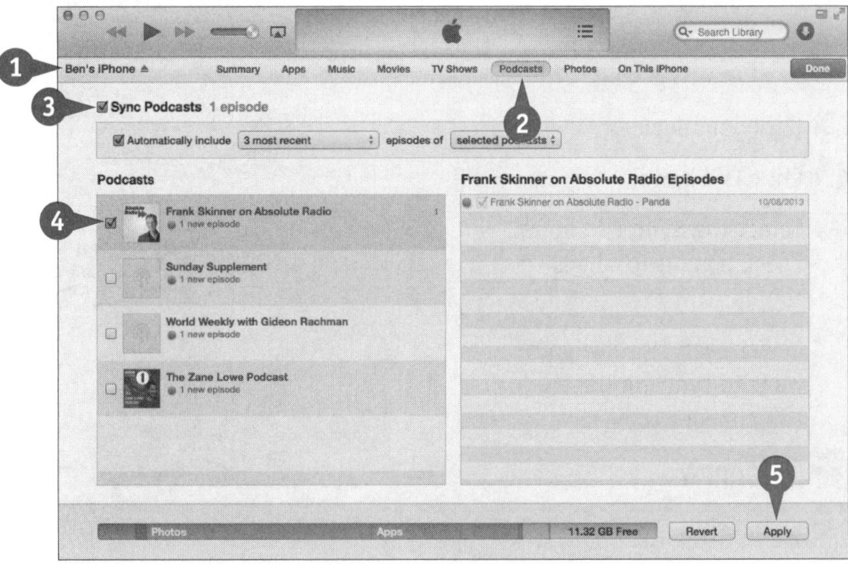

Update iPhone, iPad, and iPod Software

1. Click your device.
2. Click **Summary**.
3. Click **Check for Update**.

iTunes checks your device software and lets you know if an update is available.

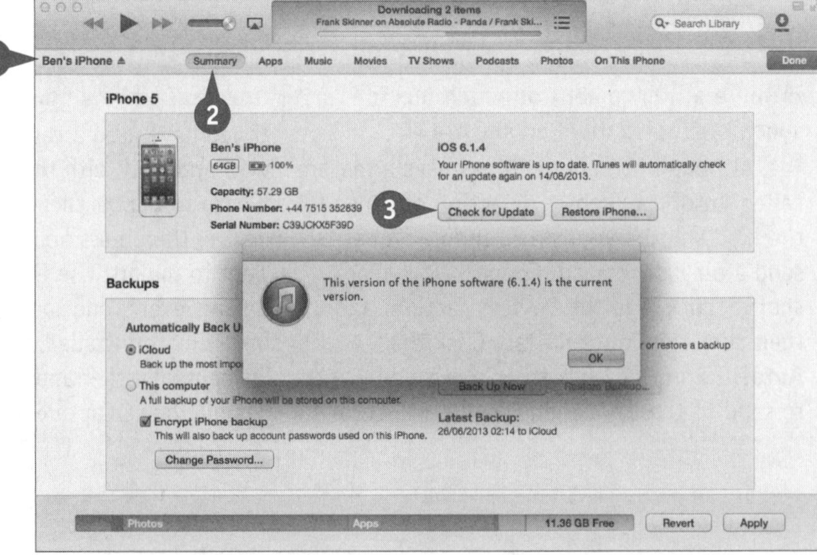

View Content

1. Click your device.
2. Click **On This iPhone**.

Note: The tab name changes depending on the device connected.

3. Click the media type from the pane on the left to view the content stored on your device.

Ⓐ The files stored on your device are shown in the main window.

Ⓑ The amount of storage for each media type is shown at the bottom of the screen.

4. Click **Done**.

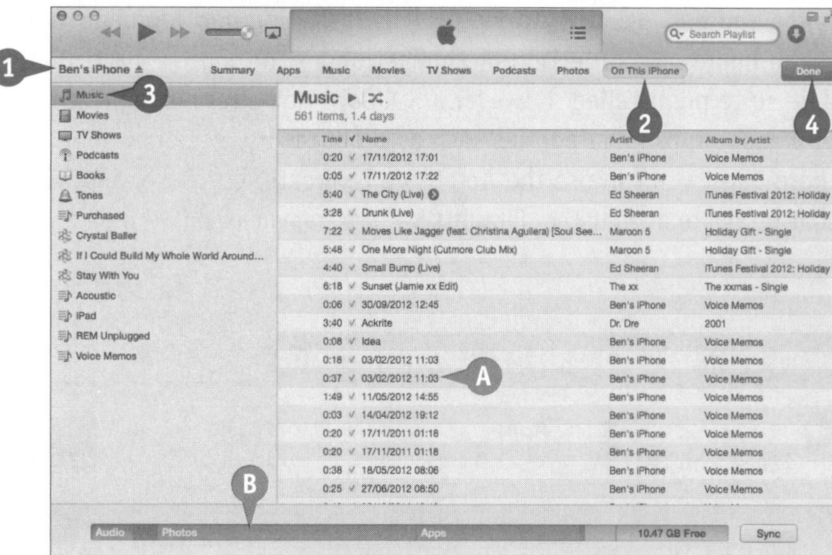

Synchronize Apps

1. Click your device.
2. Click **Apps**.
3. Click the **Install** button beside each app you want to add to your device.
4. Click the **Remove** button beside each app you want to delete from your device.

Ⓒ You can also click and drag apps to new locations on your device Home screen using the preview window.

5. Click **Apply**.

TIP

How can I restore my device to its factory settings?

Click your device in iTunes and then click **Summary**. Click **Restore** to erase all content from your device and restore it to its factory settings.

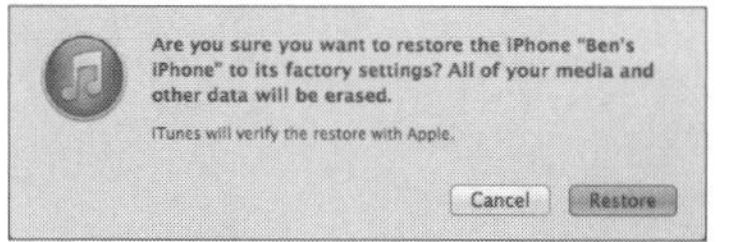

Install a Program Using the App Store

You can enhance and extend OS X by installing new programs from the App Store. OS X comes with an impressive collection of applications — or *apps* — particularly if your Mac comes with the iLife suite preinstalled. However, OS X does not offer a complete collection of apps. For example, OS X lacks apps in categories such as productivity, personal finance, and business tools. To fill in these gaps, you can use the App Store to locate, purchase, and install new programs, or look for apps that go beyond what the default OS X programs can do.

Install a Program Using the App Store

1. In the Dock, click the **App Store** icon (▣).

The App Store window appears.

2. Locate the app you want to install.
3. Click the **Free** button.

Note: If the app is a paid app, the button shows the price instead of the word Free.

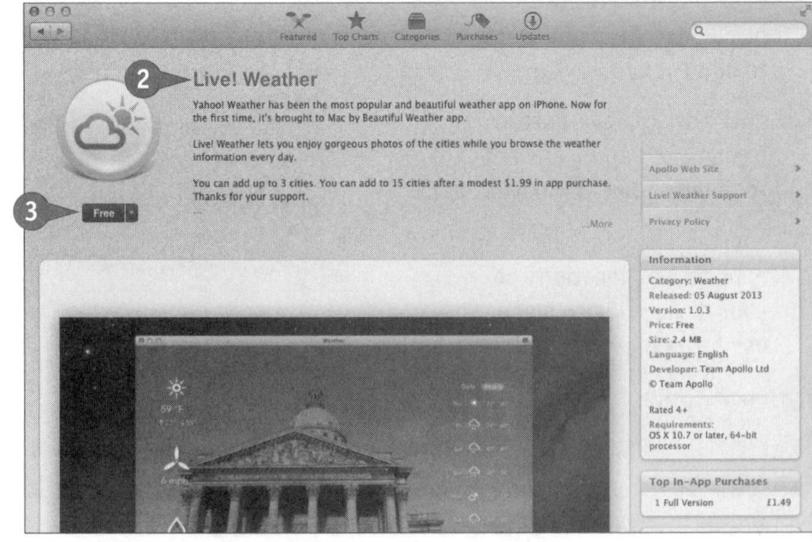

The price button changes to a Buy App button, or the Free button changes to an Install App button.

4 Click **Buy App** (or **Install App**).

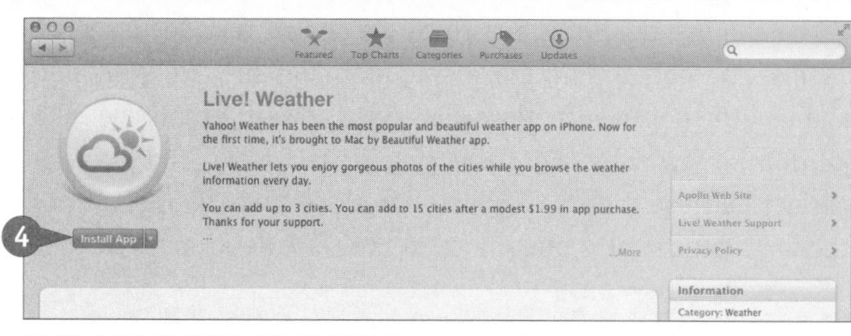

The App Store prompts you to log in with your Apple ID.

5 Type your Apple ID.

6 Type your password.

7 Click **Sign In**.

The App Store begins downloading the app. When the progress meter disappears, your app is installed.

8 Click **Launchpad** (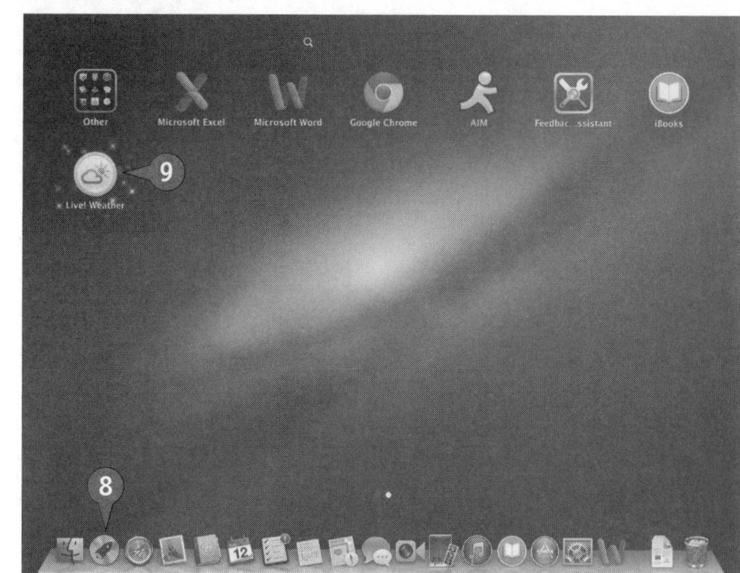).

9 Click the app icon to run it.

OS X runs your newly installed app.

TIP

How do I use an App Store gift card to purchase apps?

If you have an App Store or iTunes gift card, you can redeem the card to give yourself store credit in the amount shown on the card. Scratch off the sticker on the back to reveal the code. Click the App Store icon to open the App Store, click **Redeem**, type the code, and then click **Redeem**. In the App Store window, the Account item shows your current store credit balance. If your gift card has a box around the code, you can also use your Mac's built-in camera to redeem a gift card.

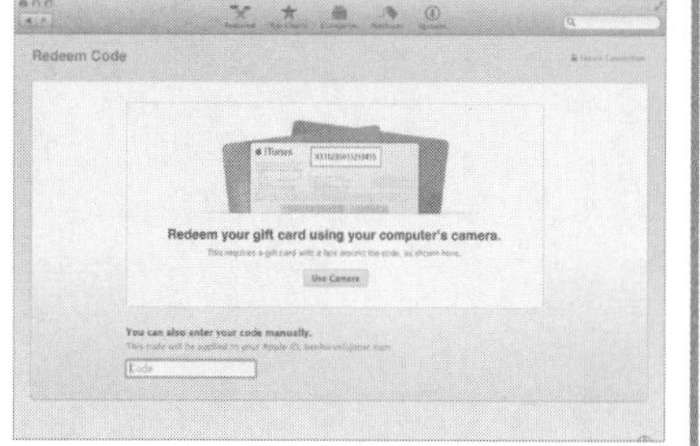

Write a Note

You can use the Notes app to create simple text documents for things such as to-do lists and meeting notes. Word processing programs such as Word and Pages are useful for creating complex and lengthy documents. However, these powerful tools feel like overkill when all you want to do is jot down a few notes. For these simpler text tasks, the Notes app that comes with OS X Mavericks is perfect because it offers a simple interface that keeps all your notes together. As you see in the next section, you can also pin a note to the OS X desktop for easy access.

Write a Note

Create a New Note

1. In the Dock, click the **Notes** icon (▣).

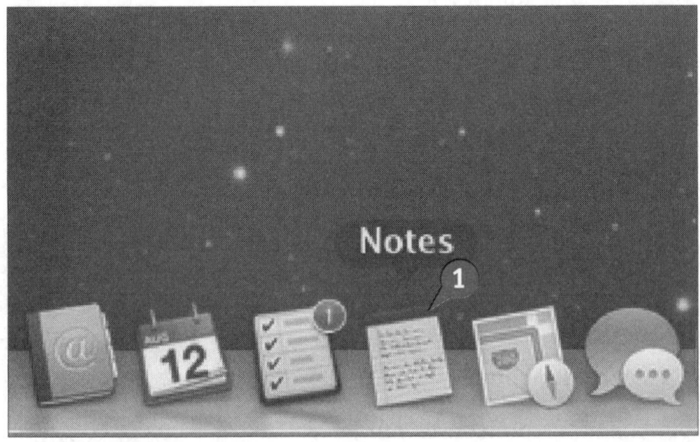

The Notes window appears.

2. Click **New Note** (+).

Note: You can also click **File** and then click **New Note**, or press ⌘+N.

A The Notes app creates the new note.

3 Type your note text.

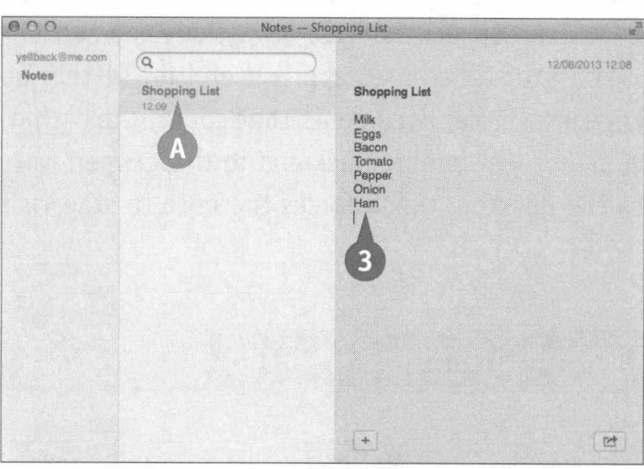

Delete a Note

1 Click the note you want to delete.

2 Click **Edit.**

3 Click **Delete.**

Note: You can also press Backspace to delete a selected note.

The Notes app deletes the note.

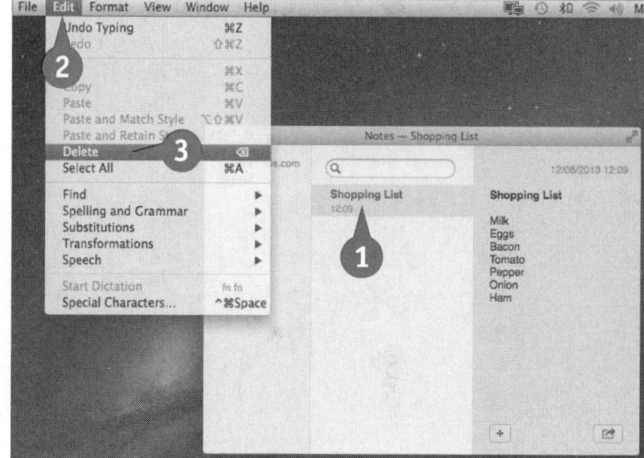

TIPS

Can I synchronize my notes with my iPod touch, iPhone, or iPad?

Yes, as long as you have an iCloud account and you have set up that account in OS X, as described in Chapter 14. To create a new note using iCloud, click **View**, click **View Folders List**, and then click **Notes** under the iCloud folder.

How do I create a bulleted or numbered list?

Position the cursor where you want the list to begin, click **Format**, and then click **Lists.** In the menu that appears, click **Insert Bulleted List**, **Insert Dashed List**, or **Insert Numbered List.**

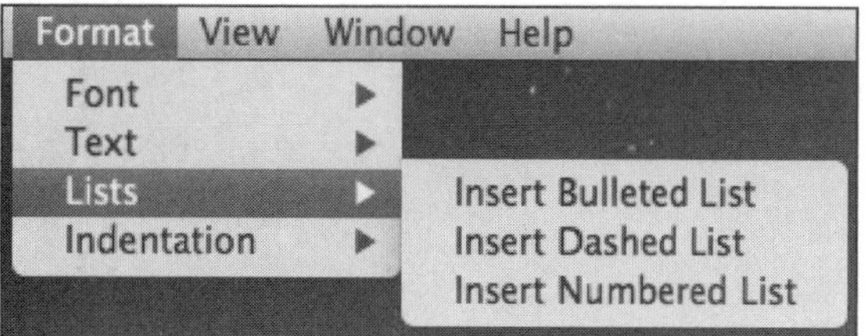

Pin a Note to the Desktop

You can ensure that you always see the content of a note by pinning that note to the OS X desktop. The Notes app is useful for setting up to-do lists, jotting down things to remember, and creating similar documents that contain text that you need to refer to while you work. Rather than constantly switching back and forth between Notes and your working application, you can pin a note to the desktop, which forces the note to stay visible, even when you switch to another application.

Pin a Note to the Desktop

1. Double-click the note you want to pin.

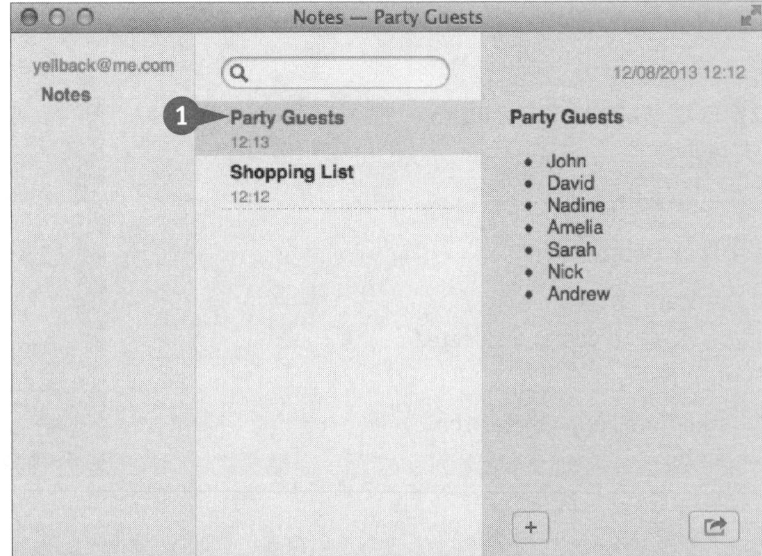

The Notes app opens the note in its own window.

2. Click and drag the note title to the position you want.

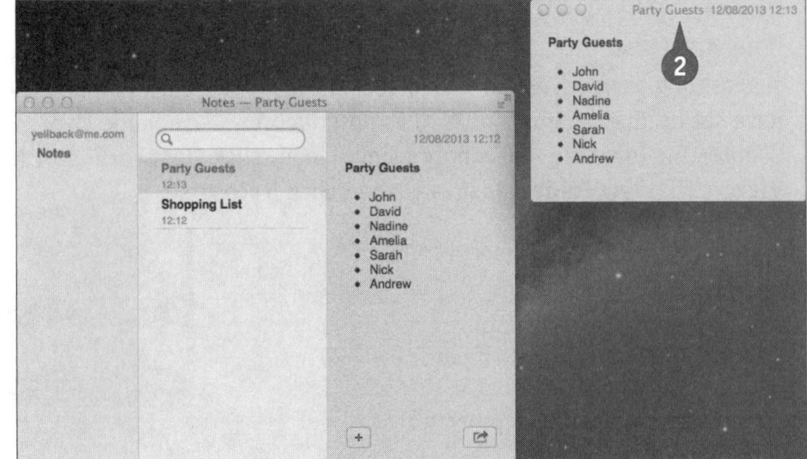

3 Click **Window**.

4 Click **Float on Top**.

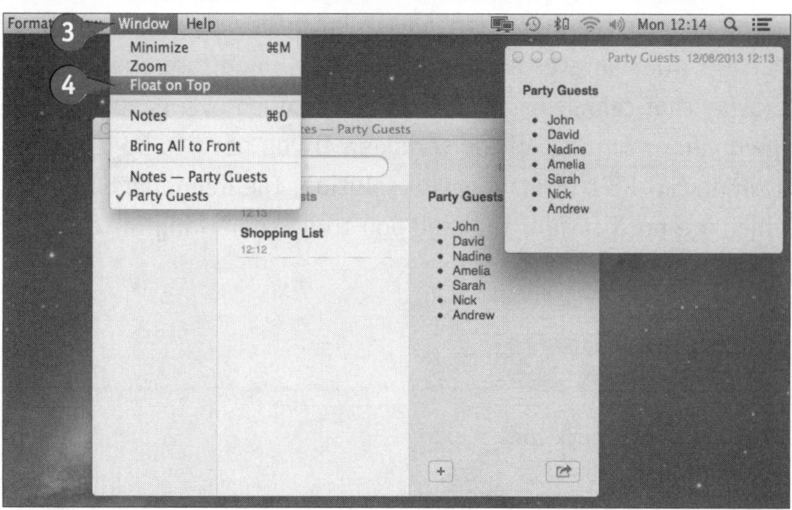

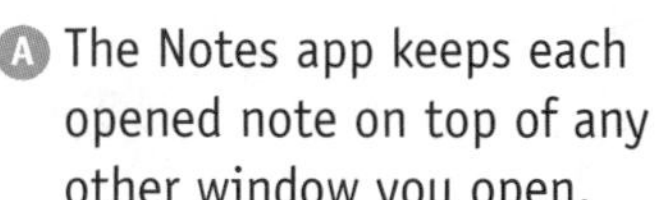

A The Notes app keeps each opened note on top of any other window you open.

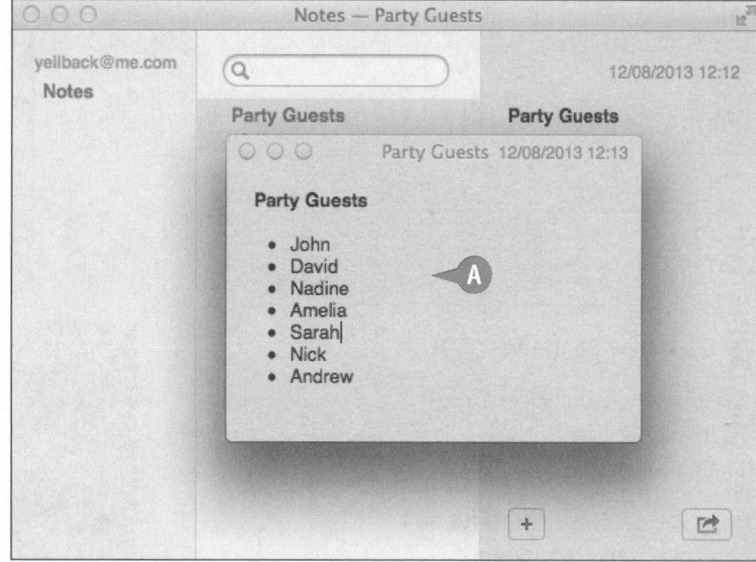

TIPS

Is it possible to pin the Notes app window to the desktop so that it always remains in view?

No, OS X does not allow you to keep the Notes window on top of other windows on your desktop. The pinning technique you learned in this section applies only to open note windows.

Am I only able to pin one note at a time to the desktop?

No, the Notes app enables you to pin multiple notes to the OS X desktop. This is useful if you have different notes that apply to the same task that you are working on in another application. However, you need to exercise some caution as the pinned notes take up space on the desktop.

Create a Reminder

You can use the Reminders app to have OS X display a notification when you need to perform a task. You can use Calendar to schedule important events, but you likely have many tasks during the day that cannot be considered full-fledged events such as returning a call, taking clothes out of the dryer, or turning off the sprinkler. If you need to be reminded to perform such tasks, Calendar is overkill, but OS X offers a better solution: the Reminders app. You use this app to create reminders, which are notifications that tell you to do something or to be somewhere.

Create a Reminder

1. In the Dock, click the **Reminders** icon (▣).

   The Reminders app appears.

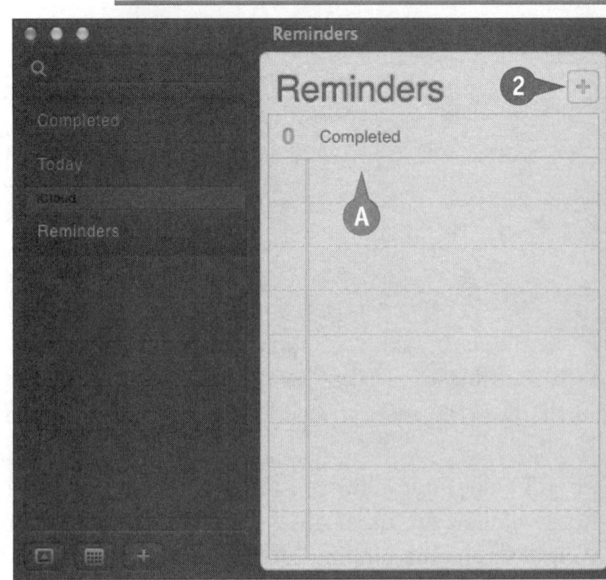

2. Click **New Reminder** (+).

   A You can also click the next available line in the Reminders list.

Note: You can also click **File** and then click **New Reminder**, or press ⌘+N.

3 Type the reminder title.

4 Click **Show Info** (ⓘ).

The Reminders app displays the reminder details.

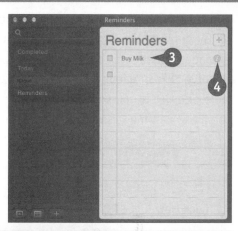

5 Select the **On a Day** check box (☐ changes to ☑).

6 Specify the date and time you want to be reminded of.

7 Click **Done**.

The Reminders app adds the reminder to the list.

B When you complete the reminder, select its check box (☐ changes to ☑).

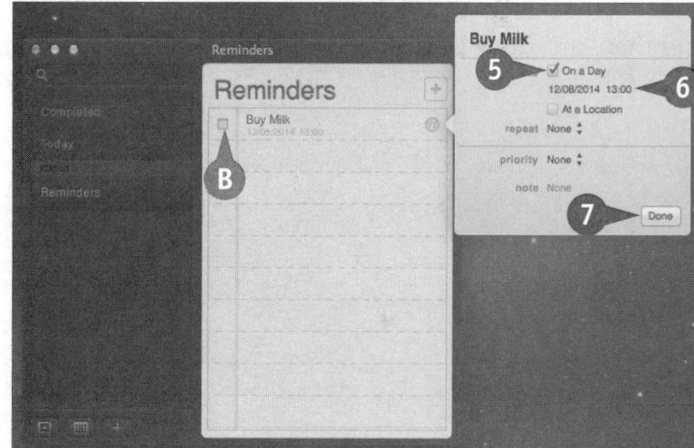

TIP

What does the At a Location option do?

The At a Location option allows the Reminders app to display a notification for a task when you arrive at or leave a location. If Reminders on your Mac is synced with Reminders on an iPhone or iPad, an alert appears on the device when it recognizes, via GPS or Wi-Fi triangulation, that you are at the location you set. To set this up, follow steps 1 to 4, select the **At a Location** check box (☐ changes to ☑), then type the address or choose a contact that has a defined address. Click either **Leaving** or **Arriving** (○ changes to ◉), and then click **Done**.

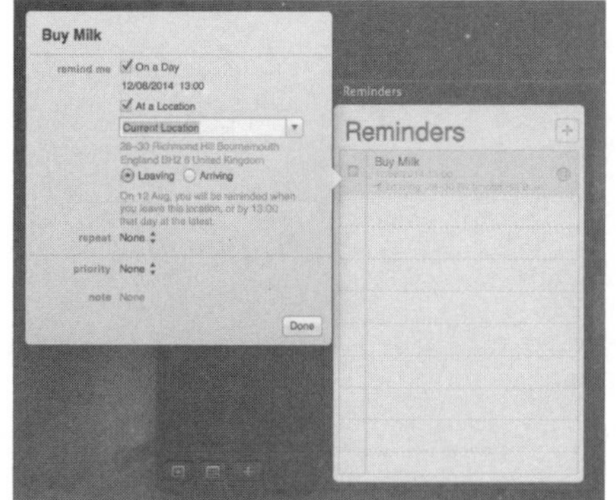

Create a New Reminder List

You can organize your reminders and make them easier to locate by creating new reminder lists. By default, the Reminders app comes with a single list called Reminders. However, if you use reminders frequently, the Reminders list can become cluttered, making it difficult to locate reminders. To solve this problem, you can organize your reminders by creating new lists. For example, you could have one list for personal tasks and another for business tasks. After you create one or more new lists, you can move some or all of your existing reminders to the appropriate lists.

Create a New Reminder List

Create a Reminder List

1 Click **New List** (+).

Note: You can also click **File** and then click **New List**, or press ⌘ + L.

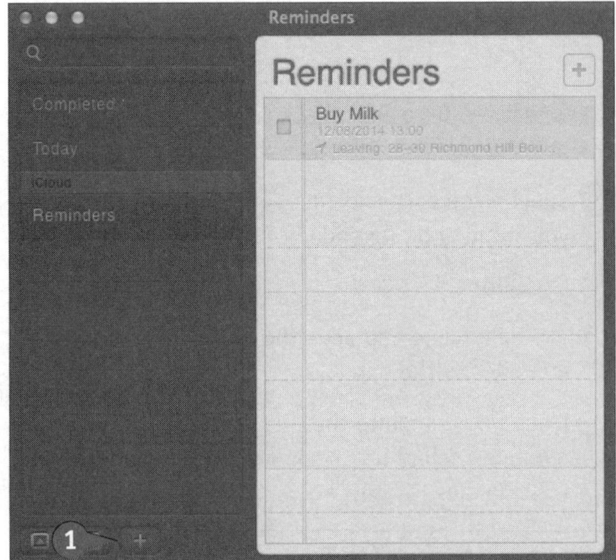

A The Reminders app adds the new list to the sidebar.

2 Type the list name and press Return.

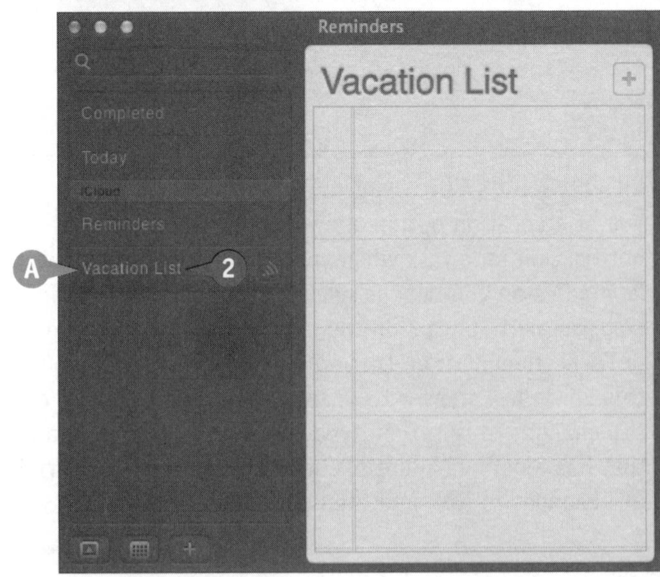

Move a Reminder to a Different List

1. Click the list that contains the reminder you want to move.
2. Click and drag the reminder and drop it on the destination list.

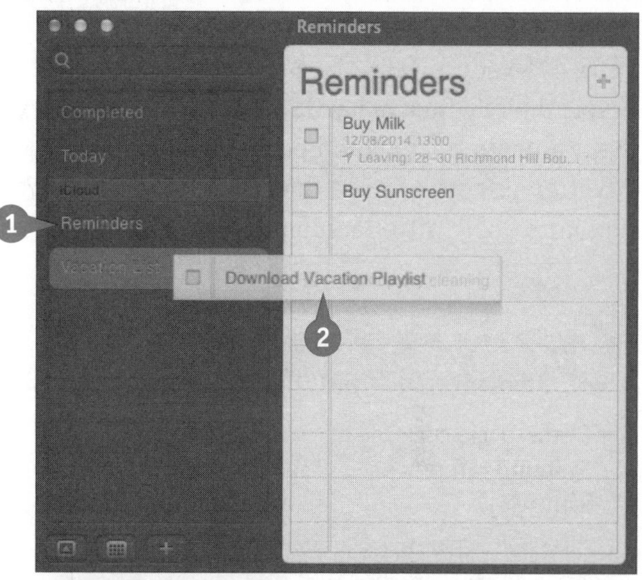

3. Click the destination list.

   B The reminder now appears in the destination list.

Note: You can also right-click the reminder, click **Move to List**, and then click the destination list.

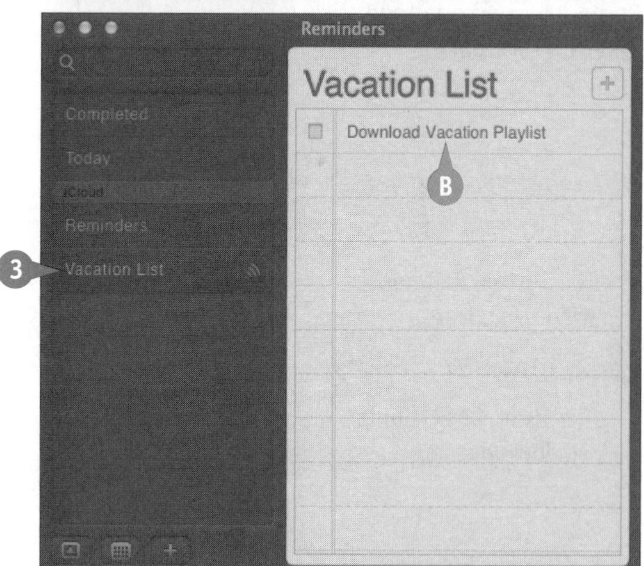

TIPS

Why does my Reminders app not have a Completed list?

The Reminders app does not show the Completed list when you first start using the program. When you mark a reminder as complete by selecting its check box (☐ changes to ☑), Reminders creates the Completed list and moves the task to that list.

Can I change the order of the lists in the sidebar?

Yes. By default, the Reminders app displays the new lists in the order you create them. To move a list to a new position, click and drag the list up or down in the sidebar. When the horizontal blue bar shows the list to be in the position you want, release the mouse button.

Sign In to Your Twitter Account

If you have a Twitter account, you can use it to share information with your followers directly from OS X Mavericks. OS X Mavericks comes with built-in support for Twitter. This enables you to send tweets directly from many OS X apps. For example, you can send a link to a web page from Safari or tweet a photo from Photo Booth. OS X also displays notifications if you are mentioned on Twitter or if a Twitter user sends you a direct message. Before you can tweet or see Twitter notifications, you must sign in to your Twitter account.

Sign In to Your Twitter Account

1. In the Dock, click the **System Preferences** icon (⚙).

Note: You can also click the **Apple** icon () and then click **System Preferences**.

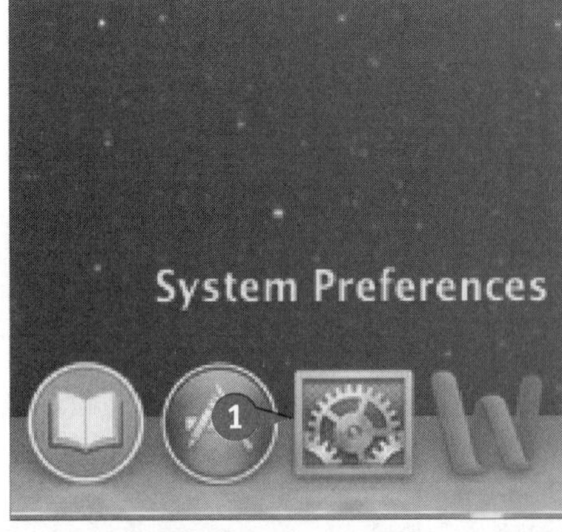

The System Preferences window appears.

2. Click **Internet Accounts**.

The Internet Accounts window appears.

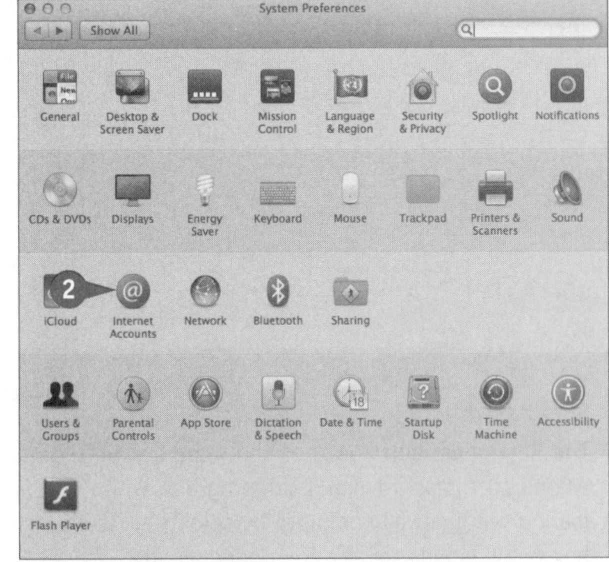

3 Click **Twitter**.

System Preferences prompts you for your Twitter username and password.

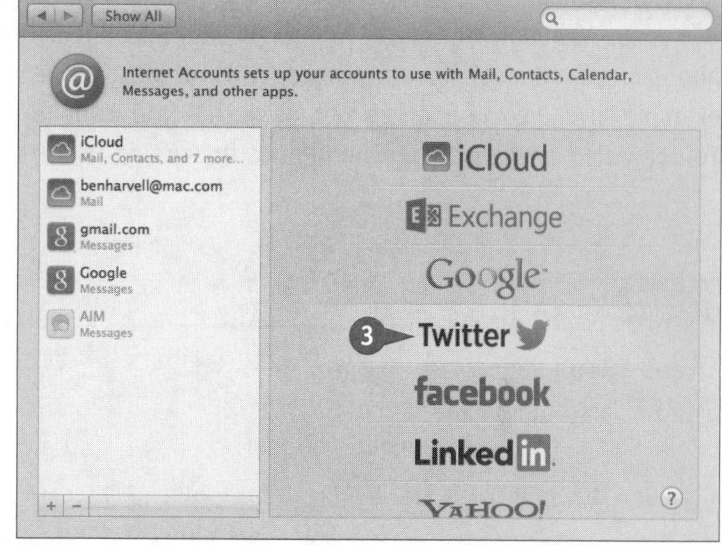

4 Type your Twitter username.

5 Type your Twitter password.

6 Click **Next**.

OS X signs in to your Twitter account.

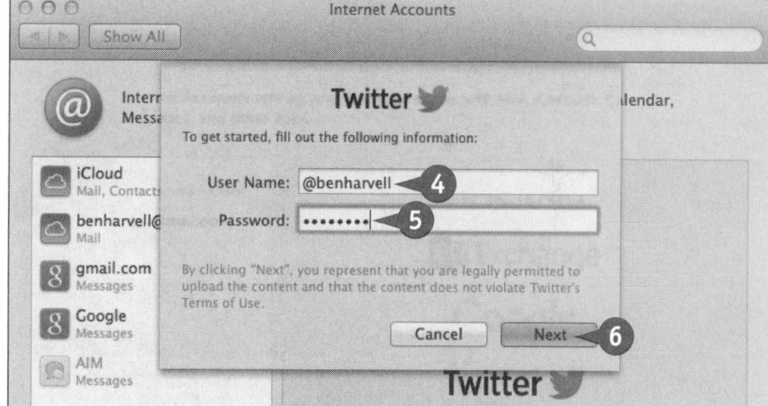

TIP

Some of the people on my contacts list are on Twitter. Is there an easy way to add their Twitter usernames to the Contacts app?

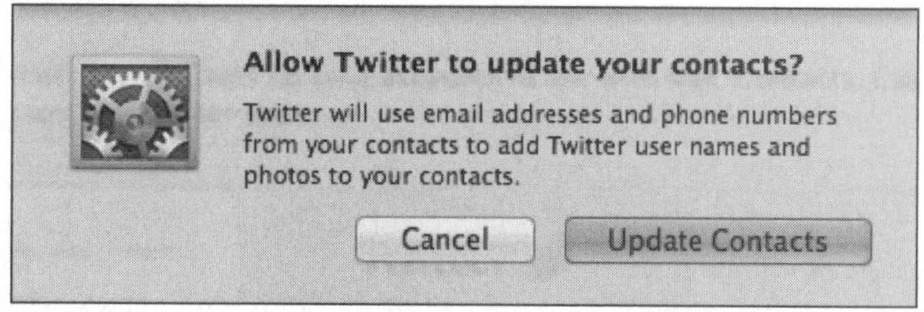

Yes, OS X Mavericks enables you to give permission for Twitter to update your contacts. Twitter examines the e-mail addresses in the Contacts app, and if it finds any that match Twitter users, it updates Contacts with each person's username and account photo.

Follow steps **1** and **2** to open the Internet Accounts window, click your Twitter account, and then click **Update Contacts**. When OS X asks you to confirm, click **Update Contacts**.

Send a Tweet

After you sign in to your Twitter account in OS X Mavericks, you can send tweets from various OS X apps. Although signing in to your Twitter account is useful for seeing notifications that tell you about mentions and direct messages, you will mostly use it for sending tweets to your followers. For example, if you come across a web page that you want to share, you can tweet a link to that page. You can also take a picture using Photo Booth and tweet that picture to your followers.

Send a Tweet

Tweet a Web Page

1. Use Safari to navigate to the web page you want to share.
2. Click **Share** (📤).
3. Click **Twitter**.

OS X displays the Twitter share sheet.

A The attachment appears as a link inside the tweet.

4. Type your tweet text.

B This value tells you how many characters you have remaining.

5. Click **Send**.

Twitter sends your web page.

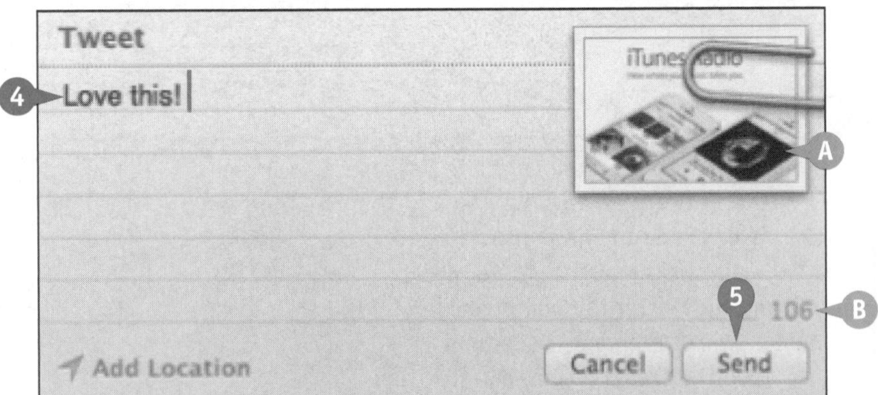

Tweet a Photo Booth Photo

1. Use Photo Booth to take a picture.
2. Click the picture you want to share.
3. Click **Share** (📤).
4. Click **Twitter**.

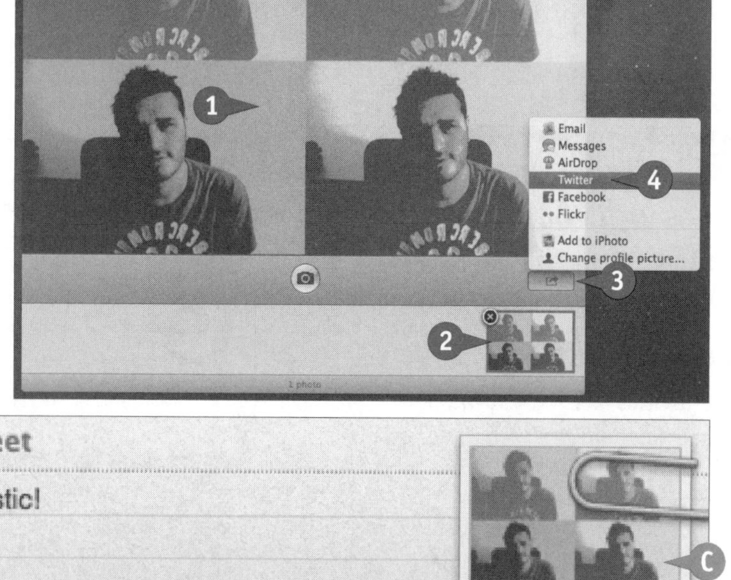

OS X displays the Twitter share sheet.

C The attachment appears as a link inside the tweet.

5. Type your tweet text.

D This value tells you how many characters you have remaining.

6. Click **Send**.

Twitter sends your photo.

TIP

Are there other apps I can use to send tweets?
Yes. If you open a photo using Quick Look (click the photo in Finder and then press Spacebar), you can click **Share** (📤) and then click **Twitter**. Similarly, you can open a photo in Preview, click 📤, and then click **Twitter**. Also, with your permission, many third-party apps are able to use your sign-in information to send tweets from the apps without requiring separate Twitter logins for each program.

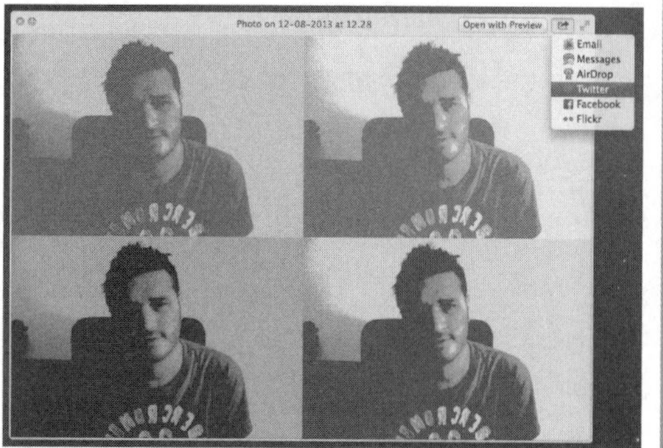

Share Information with Other People

You can use OS X Mavericks to share information with other people, including web pages, notes, pictures, videos, and Photo Booth photos. OS X Mavericks was built with sharing in mind. In previous versions of OS X, it was often difficult or tedious to share information such as web pages, images, and videos. OS X Mavericks implements a feature called the *share sheet*, which makes it easy to share data using multiple methods, such as e-mail, instant messaging, and Twitter.

Share Information with Other People

Share a Web Page

1. Use Safari to navigate to the web page you want to share.
2. Click **Share** (📤).
3. Click the method you want to use to share the web page.

Share a Note

1. In the Notes app, click the note you want to share.
2. Click **Notes Share** (📤).
3. Click the method you want to use to share the note.

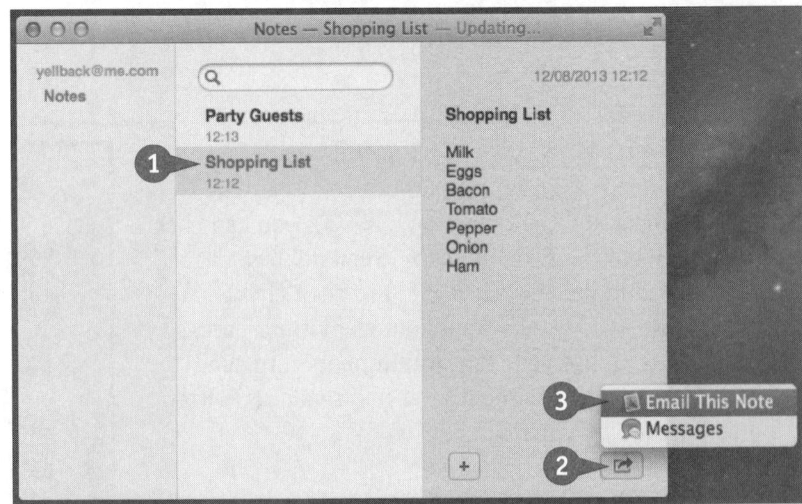

Share a Picture

1. In iPhoto, click the picture you want to share.
2. Click **Share** ().
3. Click the method you want to use to share the picture.

Share a Video

1. In QuickTime Player, open the video you want to share.
2. Click **Share** ().
3. Click the method you want to use to share the video.

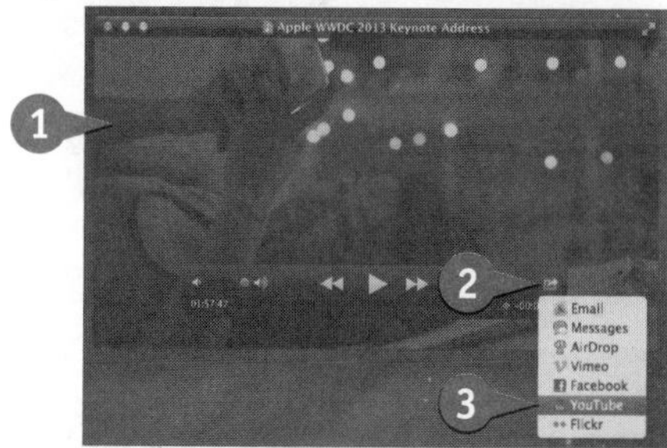

Share a Photo Booth Photo

1. Use Photo Booth to snap a photo.
2. Click the photo.
3. Click **Share** ().
4. Click the method you want to use to share the photo.

TIP

Do I need to configure OS X to use some of the sharing methods?

Yes. You cannot use the Email method unless you configure Mail with an e-mail account, and you cannot use the Message method until you configure Messages with an account. Flickr, Facebook, LinkedIn, and Vimeo must be configured in System Preferences. Click **System Preferences** () in the Dock, click **Internet Accounts**, and then click the type of account you want to add.

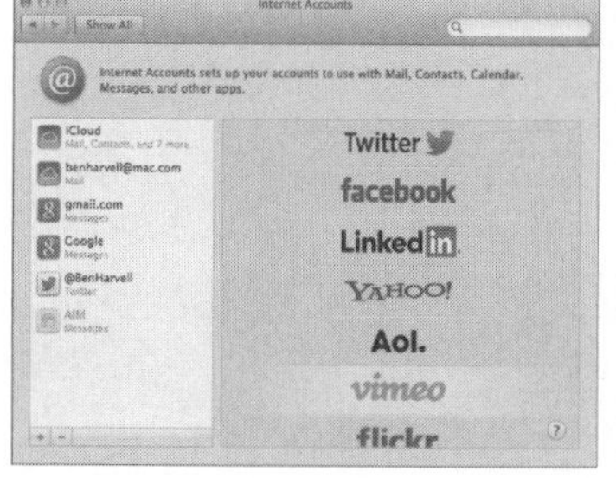

Work with the Notification Center

You can keep on top of what is happening while you use your Mac by taking advantage of the Notification Center. Several OS X Mavericks apps take advantage of a feature called *notifications,* which enables them to send messages to OS X about events and alerts that are happening on your Mac. For example, the App Store uses the Notification Center to let you know when there are OS X updates available. There are two types of notifications: a banner that appears on the desktop temporarily and an alert that stays on the desktop until you dismiss it. You can also open the Notification Center to view your recent notifications.

Work with the Notification Center

Handle Alert Notifications

An alert notification displays one or more buttons.

1. Click a button to interact with the notification.
2. Click the alert to view more information in the corresponding app.

The app that the notification came from opens.

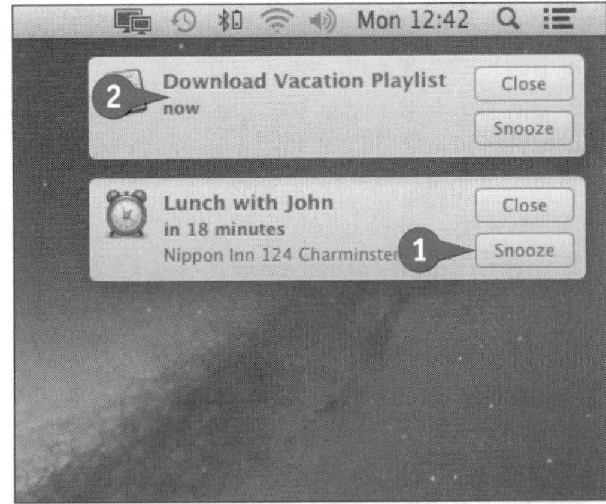

Handle Banner Notifications

A A banner notification does not display any buttons.

Note: The banner notification stays on-screen for about 5 seconds and then disappears.

View Recent Notifications

1. Click **Notification Center** (☰).

Note: If your Mac has a trackpad, you can also open the Notification Center by using two fingers to swipe left from the right edge of the trackpad.

Ⓑ OS X displays your recent notifications.

2. Click a notification to view the item in the original application.

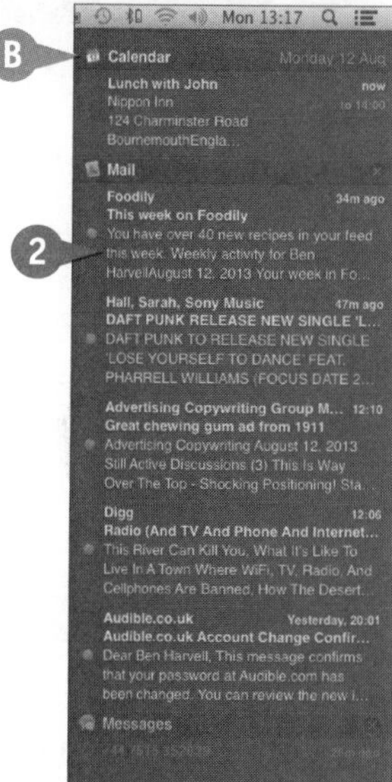

TIP

Can I control which apps use the Notification Center, and how they use it?

Yes. Click **System Preferences** (⚙) in the Dock and then click **Notifications**. Click an app on the left side of the window, and then click a notification style. To control the number of items the app can display in the Notification Center, click the **Show in Notification Center** option menu and select a number. To remove an app from the Notification Center, deselect the **Show in Notification Center** check box (☑ changes to ☐).

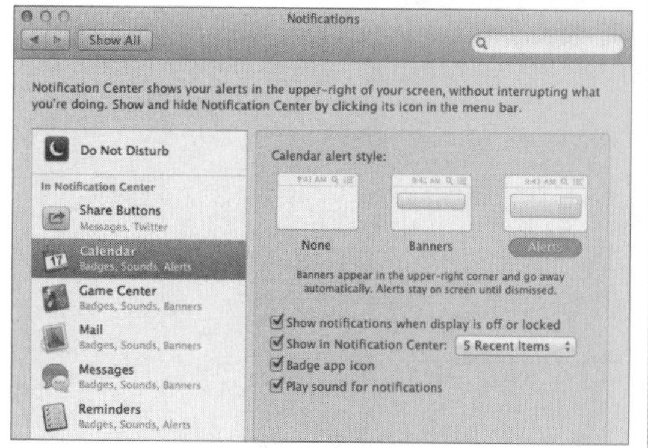

View the OS X Screen on Your TV

If you have an Apple TV, you can use it to view your OS X screen on your TV. If you want to demonstrate something on your Mac to a group of people, it is difficult because most Mac screens are too small to see from a distance. However, if you have a TV or a projector nearby and you have an Apple TV device connected to that display, you can connect your Mac to the same wireless network and then send the OS X screen to the TV or projector. This is called *AirPlay mirroring*.

View the OS X Screen on Your TV

Mirror via System Preferences

1. In the Dock, click the **System Preferences** icon (▣).

   The System Preferences window appears.

2. Click **Displays**.

   The display preferences appear.

3. Click the **AirPlay mirroring** ⬍ and then click your Apple TV.

   OS X displays your Mac's screen on your TV.

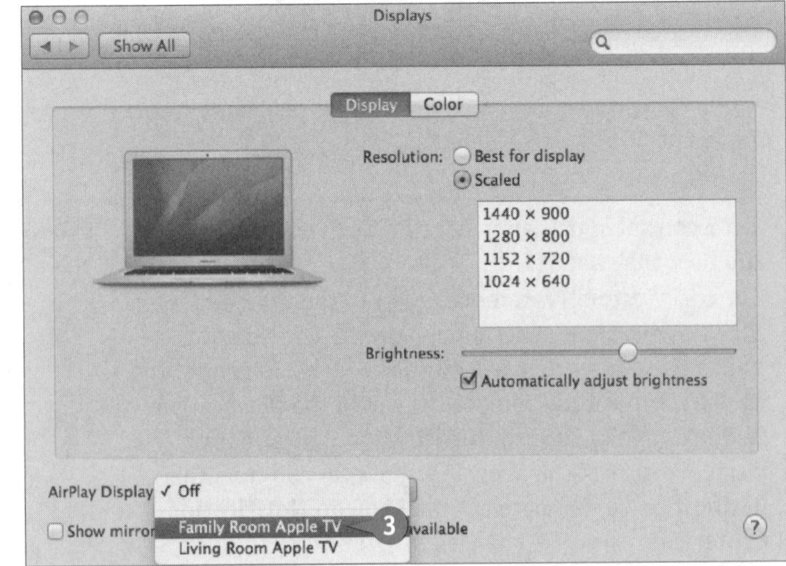

Mirror via the Menu Bar

Follow steps 1 and 2 to open the display preferences.

1. Select the **Show mirroring options in the menu bar when available** check box (☐ changes to ☑).

A. OS X adds the AirPlay Mirroring icon to the menu bar.

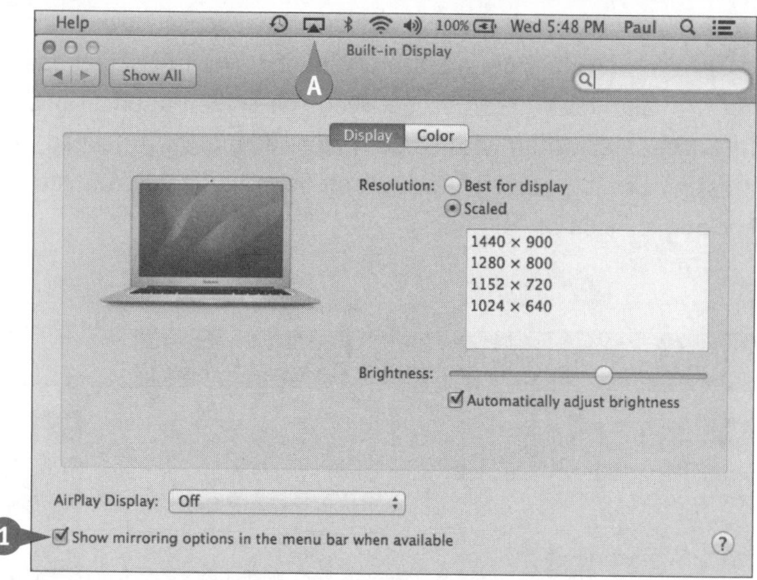

2. Click the AirPlay Mirroring icon.
3. Click your Apple TV.

OS X displays your Mac's screen on your TV (the icon changes).

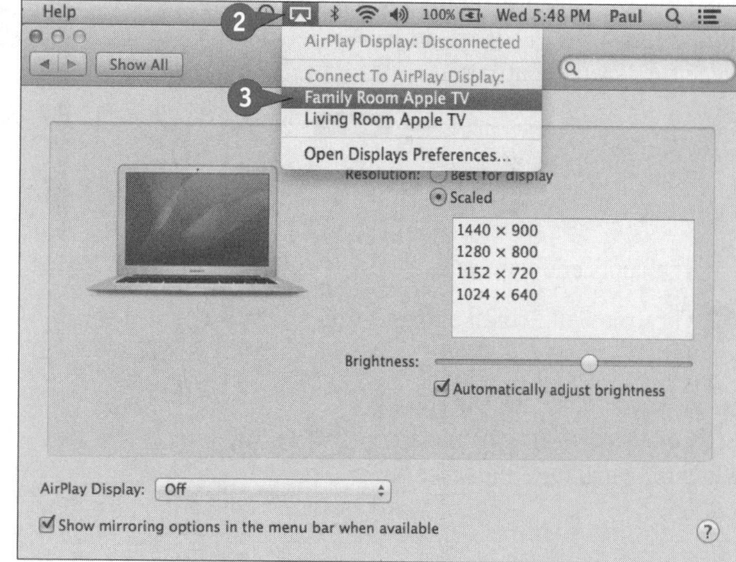

TIP

Is there an easy way to make my Mac's screen fit my TV screen?

Yes. Sometimes, the OS X screen might look a bit small on your TV. To fix that, click the AirPlay Mirroring icon and then in the Match Desktop Size To section of the AirPlay Mirroring menu, click your Apple TV.

View an Application in Full-Screen Mode

Many applications you use on your Mac can be viewed in full-screen mode, which provides you with a much larger area to work with. The full-screen view takes up an entire space Mission Control, and you can switch between full-screen applications and desktops using the Mission Control interface, by swiping with three fingers across the trackpad, or by holding the Control key and pressing the left and right arrows on your keyboard. You can also jump to a full-screen application by clicking its icon on the Dock.

View an Application in Full-Screen Mode

1. Launch an application compatible with full-screen mode.

Note: Almost all of the applications that come with OS X offer a full-screen mode, as do some third-party applications.

The application appears.

2. Click the **Full Screen** button (▣).

Note: If you don't see the Full Screen button (▣), look under the View menu for a full-screen option.

The application appears in full-screen mode.

3 Move the cursor to the top of the screen.

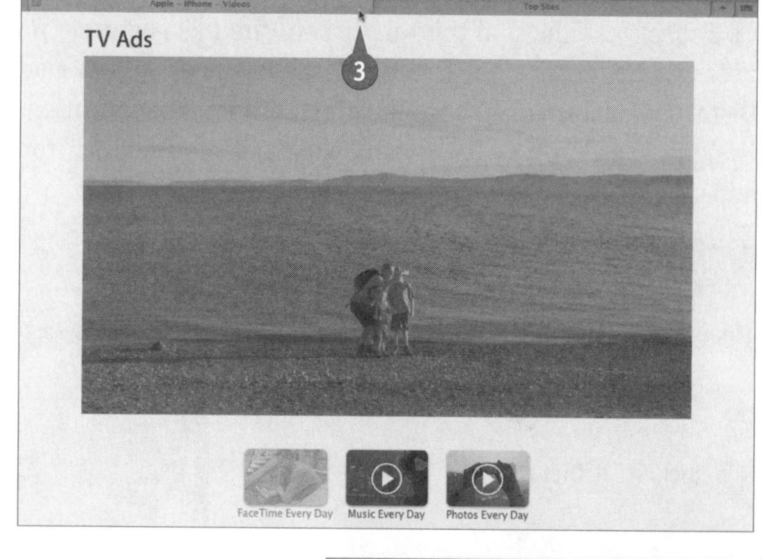

The menu bar for the application appears.

4 Click the **Full Screen** button again (▣).

The application exits full-screen mode.

TIPS

Is there a quicker way to exit full-screen mode?
Yes. Simply press Esc to exit full-screen mode in the selected application.

Can I take a single window of an application full screen?
Yes. Many applications, including Pages and Preview, allow you to open multiple documents or files in separate windows. You can then choose to use a full-screen view for all of them or only those you select using the Full Screen button (▣).

Dictate Text into an Application

You can dictate text into most applications that allow you to type, such as the Notes application, Pages, TextEdit, and third-party software like Microsoft Word. Once turned on, dictation can be accessed by pressing the Function key, marked as Fn on modern Apple keyboards, twice. The Start Dictation command can also be accessed from an application's Edit menu. Dictation listens to speech through your Mac's built-in microphone and then sends it to Apple to convert it to text. The results appear on-screen in a matter of seconds.

Dictate Text into an Application

1. Click within a text field or an open text document.
2. Click **Edit.**
3. Click **Start Dictation**.

A message appears asking if you want to enable Dictation.

4. Click **OK.**

Note: You are also asked if you want to use Enhanced Dictation, which allows for offline use and live feedback. If so, select the **Enhanced Dictation** check box (☐ changes to ☑). This feature requires a large file to be downloaded, so an Internet connection is required.

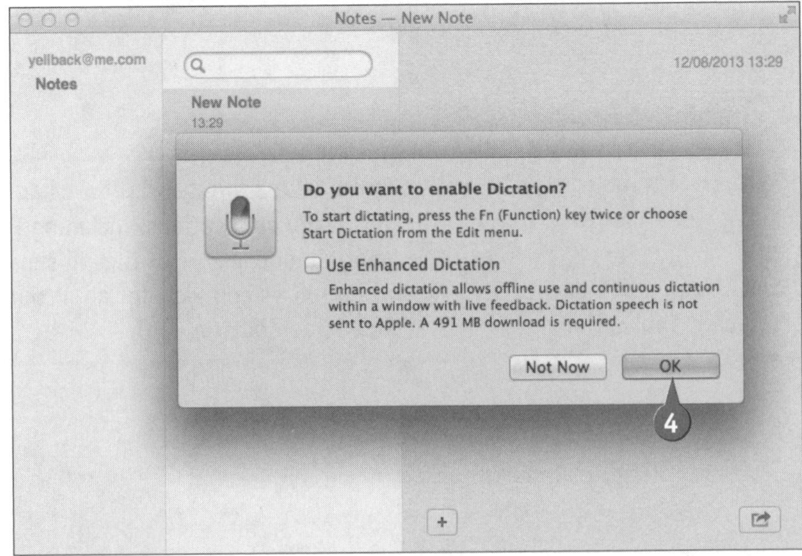

Another message appears explaining the dictation process.

5 Click **Enable Dictation**.

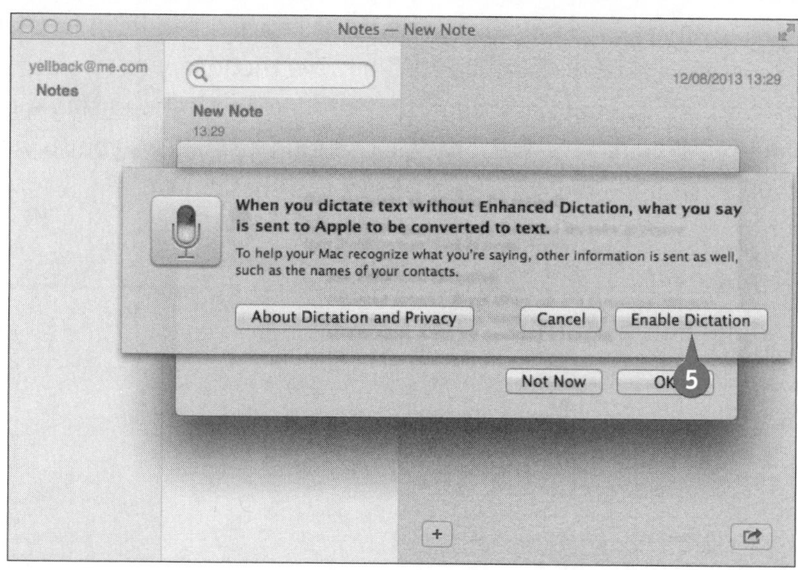

Dictation is enabled and the microphone icon appears.

6 Begin speaking your text and press Fn or click **Done** when you are finished.

OS X displays your speech as text.

Note: Once Dictation is enabled, you can select **Start Dictation** from the Edit menu or press Fn twice to begin dictation immediately.

TIPS

How do I add punctuation to text I dictate?
When you speak your text, you can also say the name of common punctuation marks such as "period," "comma," or "exclamation point." You can also say "new line" or "new paragraph" while dictating to add gaps between passages of text.

Why is my dictation sent to Apple?
Apple converts your speech to text on its own servers; therefore, you need an Internet connection when using Dictation. Other information such as your contacts is also sent to Apple to help make the conversion from speech to text more accurate.

Define Words with the Dictionary

You can access the Dictionary application that is built in to OS X in a number of ways to quickly define a word or check its spelling. The Dictionary can be accessed from the Applications folder, as a widget on your Dashboard, or within an application using a gesture on your trackpad or via a contextual menu. The Dictionary application also allows you to view word definitions from different sources such as Wikipedia, and to access a thesaurus.

Define Words with the Dictionary

Define Words with the Dictionary Application

1. Click the **Spotlight** icon (🔍).
2. Type **Dictionary** in the Spotlight field.
3. Click **Dictionary** under Applications.

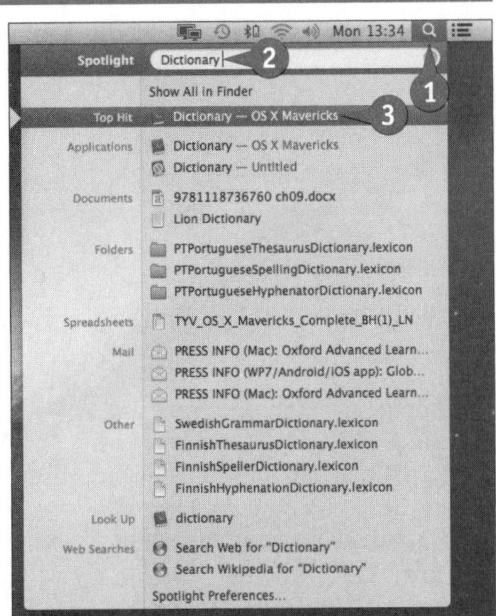

The Dictionary application appears.

4. Type a word into the search field.

A. The definition of the word you typed appears here.

B. Click **All** to show definitions from all sources or Thesaurus, Apple, or Wikipedia to filter definitions.

C. Click different word variations in the left-hand pane to see alternate definitions.

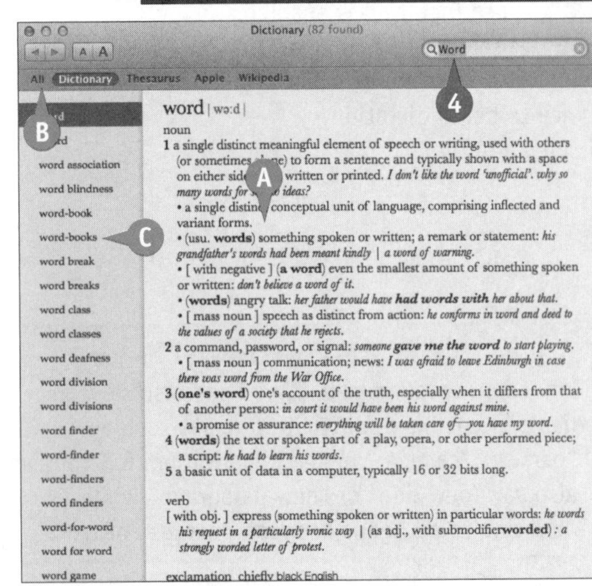

Define a Word Within a Document or Application

1. Highlight a word within an application or text document.
2. Right- or Ctrl+click the selection or tap two fingers on the trackpad.
3. Click **Look Up**.

Note: You can also tap on the word using three fingers on the trackpad to define a word.

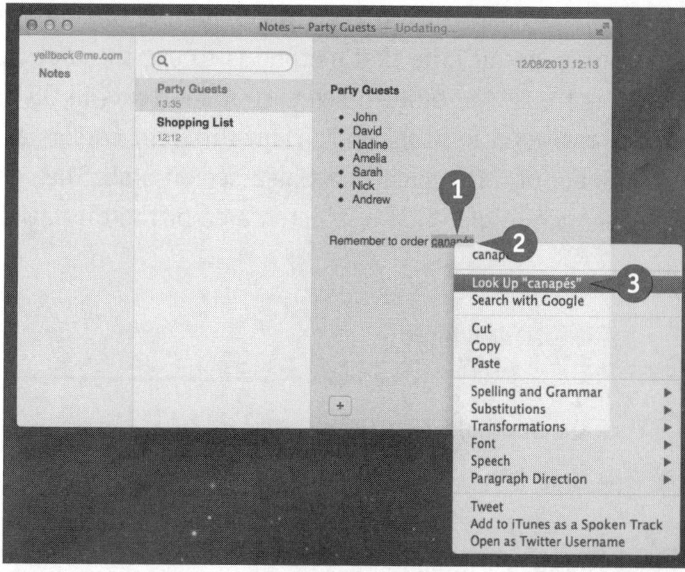

A definition of the word is displayed.

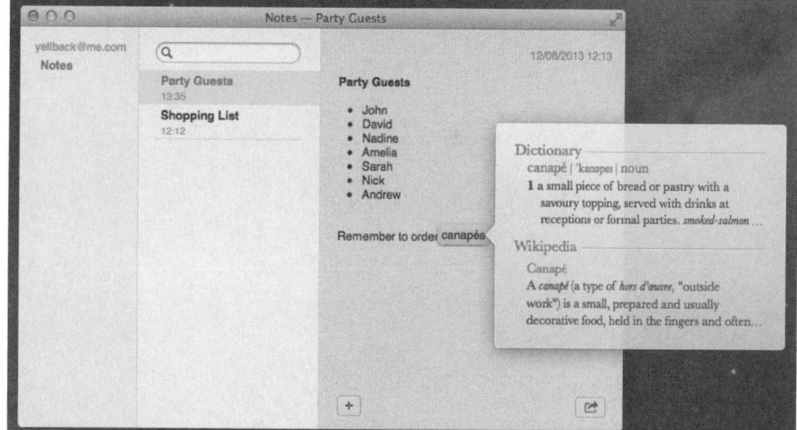

TIP

How do I access the Dictionary from the Dashboard?

On the Dashboard, click **Add** (⊕) and then click the **Dictionary** icon. The Dictionary is now loaded on the Dashboard and you can type your search into the field provided. You can also switch between dictionary definitions and thesaurus suggestions by clicking ⇕ to show the pop-up menu.

Take a Screenshot

There are a number of ways to take a picture of your screen in OS X Mavericks and save the picture as an image file. The first method is to use the Grab application that comes with OS X, and the second is to use the built-in screenshot shortcuts in OS X. A screenshot shows everything on your screen, and you can use Grab to show different cursors as well. Grab allows you to take screenshots in a number of ways, such as a timed screen grab. The screenshot shortcuts also provide different options, such as grabbing a selected area of the display rather than the whole screen.

Take a Screenshot

1. Click the **Spotlight** icon (🔍).
2. Type **Grab** into the Spotlight field.
3. Click **Grab** under Applications.

   The Grab application opens.

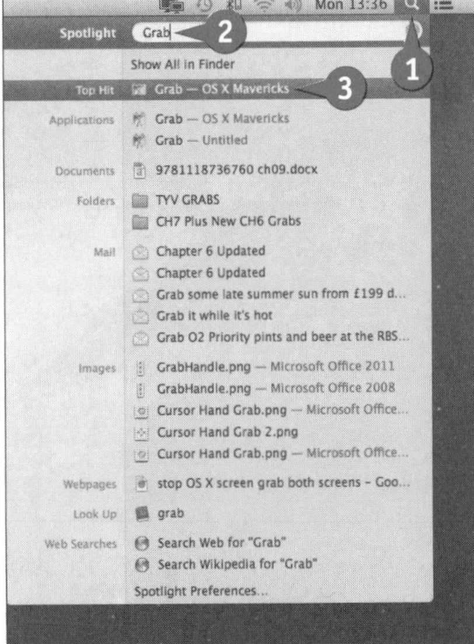

4. Click **Capture**.
5. Click a screenshot option from the menu.

   A. Click **Selection** to select an area of the display to screenshot.

   B. Click **Window** to take a screenshot of a single window.

   C. Click **Screen** to take a screenshot of the whole display.

   D. Click **Timed Screen** to take a screenshot of the whole display after a short delay.

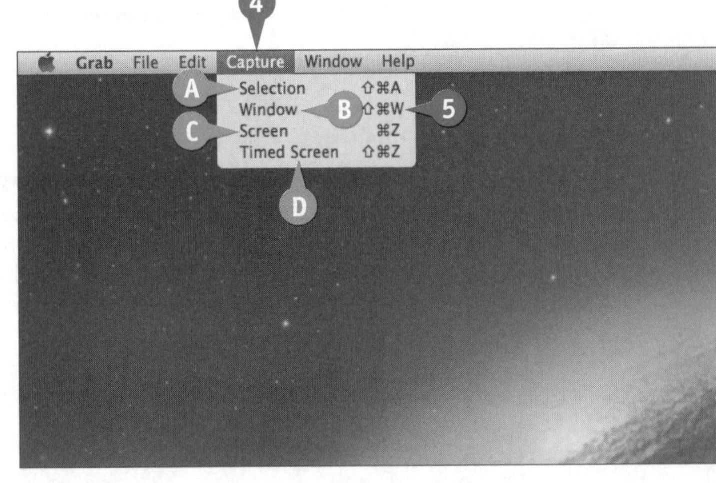

The screenshot is taken and a preview appears.

6 Click **File**.

7 Click **Save**.

The Save dialog appears.

8 Type a name for the screenshot in the Save As: field.

9 Select a save location on your Mac.

10 Click **Save**.

The image is saved to your chosen location.

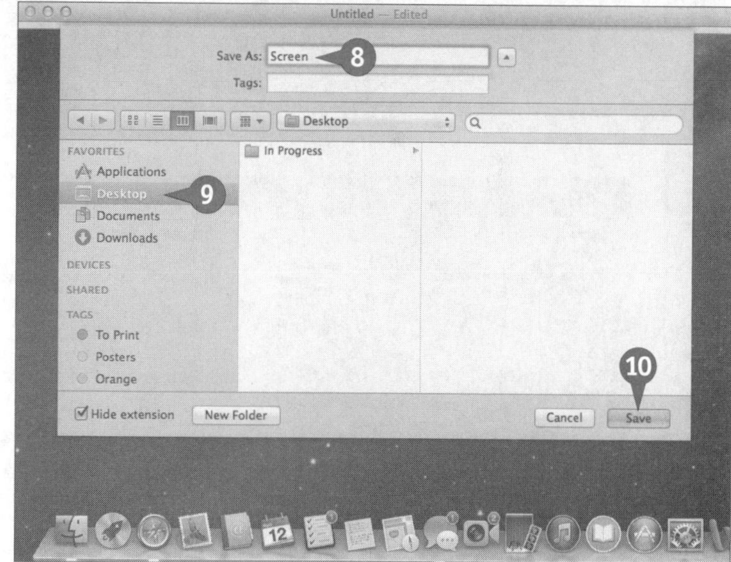

TIP

How do I take a screenshot using keyboard shortcuts?

You can press Shift+⌘+3 to take a picture of your whole screen, or Shift+⌘+4 to drag the cursor over the area of the screen you want to capture. You can also press ⌘+Shift+4 and then press Spacebar to change the cross hair to a camera icon. You can then click a single window or menu, the Dock or Menu bar to capture it. All screenshots taken using these shortcuts appear on the OS X desktop.

CHAPTER 10

Viewing and Editing Photos

Whether you just want to look at your photos, or you want to edit them to crop out unneeded portions or fix problems, iPhoto is a great tool for this purpose. The application comes with all new Macs or can be purchased from the Mac App Store.

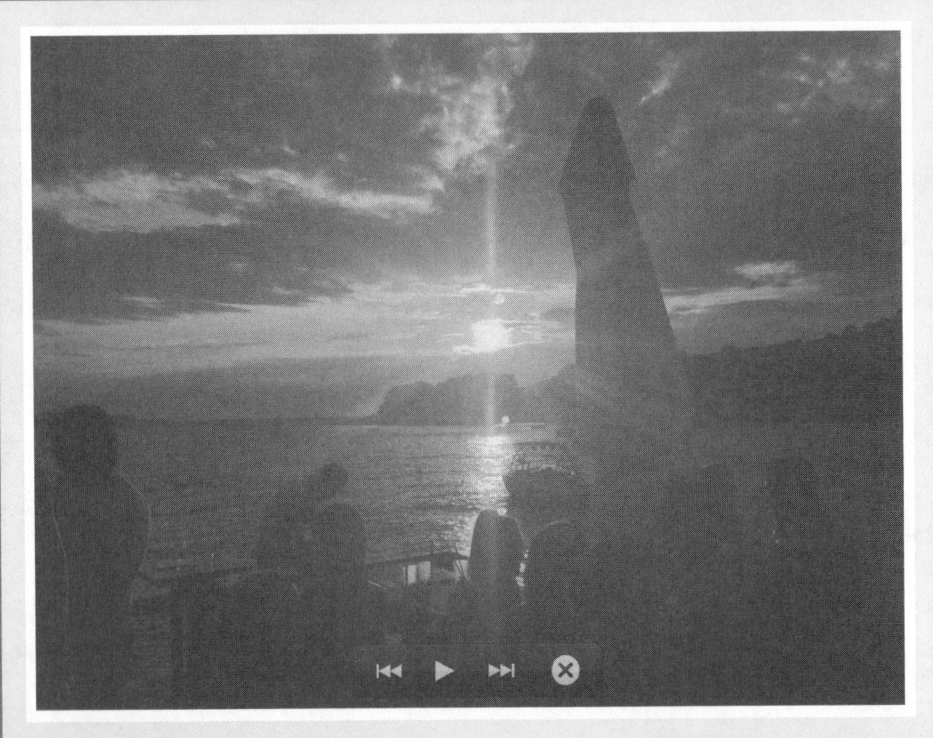

View a Preview of a Photo

OS X offers several tools you can use to see a preview of any photo on your Mac. The Finder application has a number of methods you can use to view your photos, but here you learn about the two easiest methods. First, you can preview any saved image file using the OS X Quick Look feature; second, you can see photo previews by switching to the Cover Flow view. You can also preview photos using the Preview application.

View a Preview of a Photo

View a Preview with Quick Look

1. In the Dock, click the **Finder** icon (Finder icon).
2. Open the folder that contains the photo you want to preview.
3. Click the photo.
4. Click **Quick Look** (Quick Look icon).

   You can also right-click the photo and then click **Quick Look**, or press Spacebar.

A. Finder displays a preview of the photo.

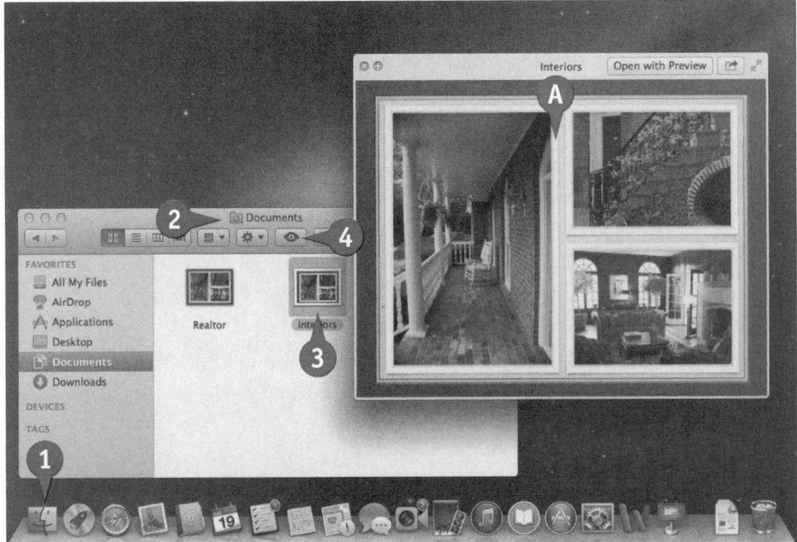

View a Preview with Cover Flow

1. In the Dock, click the **Finder** icon (Finder icon).
2. Open the folder that contains the photo you want to preview.
3. Click the photo.
4. Click **Cover Flow** (Cover Flow icon).

B. Finder displays a preview of the photo.

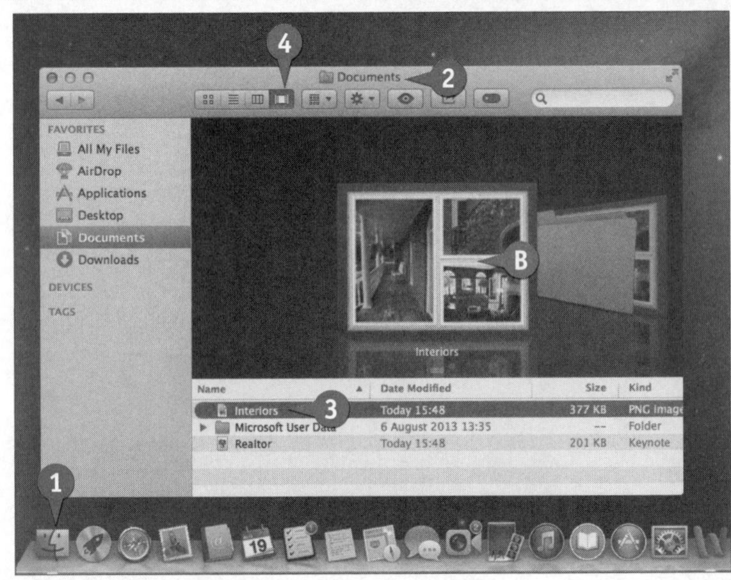

View a Preview in the Preview Application

1. In the Dock, click the **Finder** icon (🖼).
2. Open the folder that contains the photo you want to preview.
3. Click the photo.
4. Click **File**.
5. Click **Open With**.
6. Click **Preview**.

Note: In many cases, you can also simply double-click the photo to open it in the Preview application.

The Preview application opens and displays the photo.

7. Use the toolbar buttons to change how the photo appears in the Preview window.

(C) More commands are available on the View menu.

8. When you finish viewing the photo, click **Close** (◉).

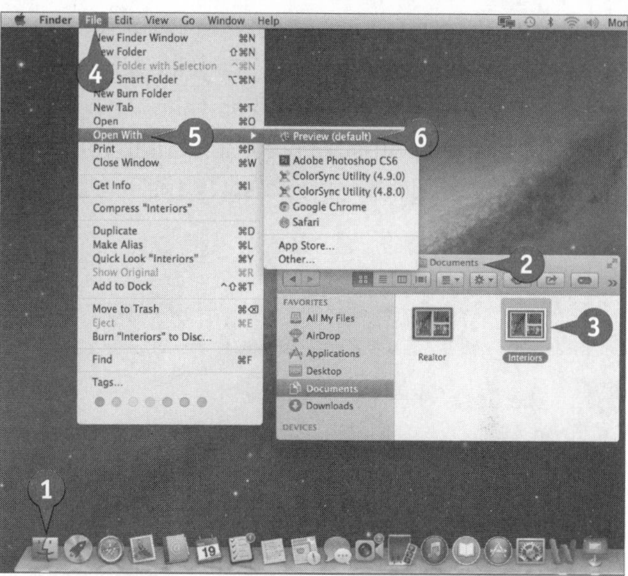

TIPS

Is there an easier way to preview multiple photos using the Preview application?

Yes. In Finder, navigate to the folder that contains the photos, and then select each file that you want to preview. Either click and drag the mouse (↖) over the photos or press and hold ⌘ and click each one. In Preview, click **Next** and **Previous** to navigate the photos.

Is there a way that I can zoom in on just a portion of a photo?

Yes. In Preview, click **Tools** and then click **Select Tool** (or either press ⌘ + 3 or click **Select** in the toolbar). Click and drag your mouse (↖) to select the portion of the photo that you want to magnify. Click **View** and then click **Zoom to Selection** (or press ⌘+*).

View a Slide Show of Your Photos

Instead of viewing your photos one at a time, you can easily view multiple photos by running them in a slide show. You can run the slide show using the Preview application. The slide show displays each photo for a few seconds, and then Preview automatically displays the next photo. Quick Look also offers several on-screen controls that you can use to control the slide show playback. You can also configure Quick Look to display the images full-screen.

View a Slide Show of Your Photos

1. In the Dock, click the **Finder** icon (▣).
2. Open the folder that contains the photos you want to view in the slide show.
3. Select the photos you want to view.
4. Click **File**.
5. Click **Open With**.
6. Click **Preview**.

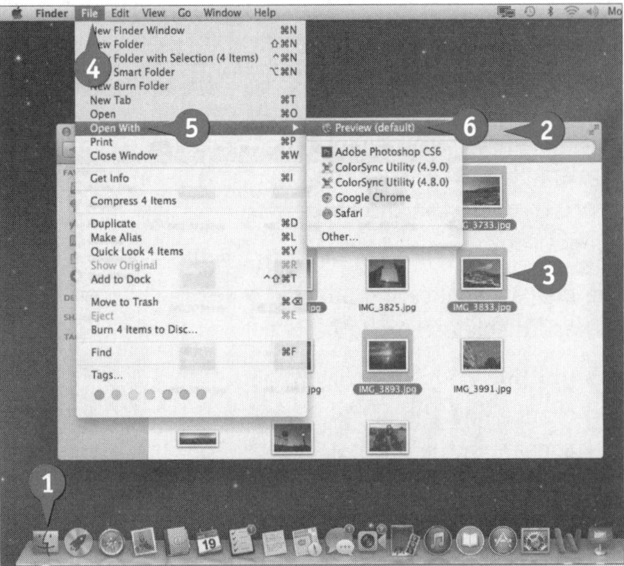

The Preview window appears.

7. Click **View**.
8. Click **Slideshow**.

   You can also select Slideshow by pressing Shift + ⌘ + F.

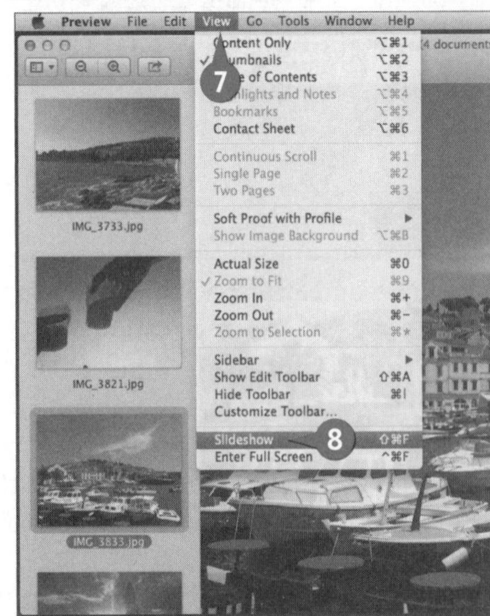

Preview opens the slide show window.

Ⓐ Preview displays the slide show controls when you move the cursor.

9 Click **Play** (▶).

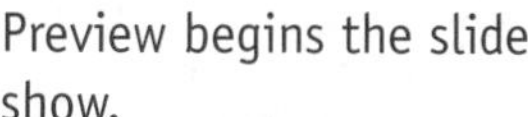

Preview begins the slide show.

Ⓑ Click **Next** (⏭) to move to the next photo.

Ⓒ Click **Back** (⏮) to move to the previous photo.

Ⓓ Click **Pause** (⏸) to suspend the slide show.

10 When the slide show is over or when you want to return to Finder, click **Close** (⊗) or press Esc.

TIPS

Can I jump to a specific photo during the slide show?
Yes. With the slide show running, press Return to stop the show. Use the arrow keys to select the photo that you want to view in the slide show, and then press Return. Preview returns you to the slide show and displays the selected photo. Click **Play** to resume the slide show.

What keyboard shortcuts can I use when viewing a slide show?
Press → or ↑ to display the next photo, and press ← or ↓ to display the previous photo. Press Esc to end the slide show.

Open and Close iPhoto

Your Mac came with iLife installed, and the suite includes the iPhoto application, which offers special tools for viewing, managing, and editing your photos. You can also purchase iPhoto separately through the App Store if the iLife suite is not installed on your Mac. With iPhoto, you can import photos from a digital camera, view and organize the photos on your Mac, and edit and repair photos. To begin using the program, you must first learn how to find and open the iPhoto window. When you finish using the program, you can close the iPhoto window to free up computer processing power.

Open and Close iPhoto

Open iPhoto

1. In the Dock, click the **iPhoto** icon (▣).

The iPhoto window appears.

iPhoto suggests ways to import new photos into your library.

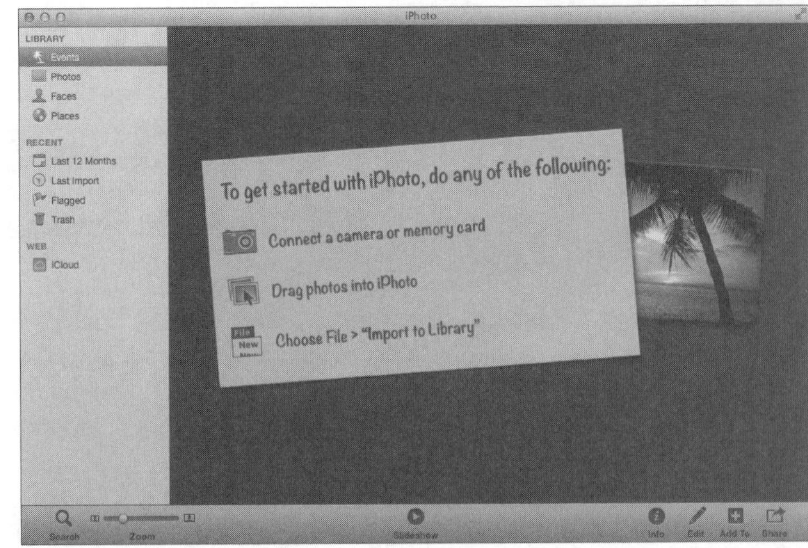

Close iPhoto

1 Click **iPhoto**.

2 Click **Quit iPhoto**.

iPhoto closes.

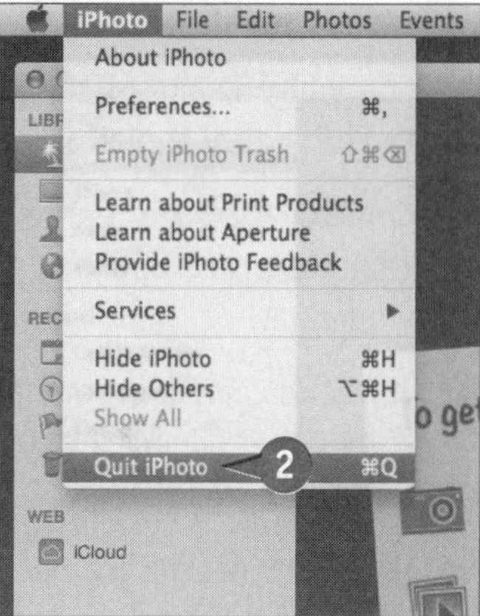

TIPS

Are there other methods I can use to open iPhoto?

Yes. If you have used iPhoto recently, click the **Apple** icon (), click **Recent Items**, and then click **iPhoto** to open iPhoto. Alternatively, click **Spotlight** (), type **iphoto**, and then click **iPhoto** in the search results.

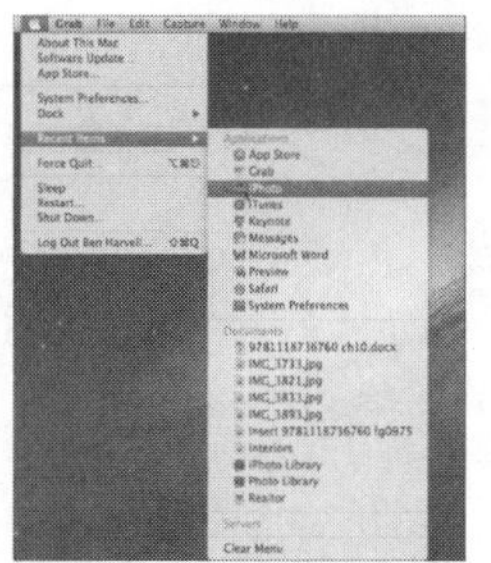

Are there faster methods I can use to close iPhoto?

Yes. Probably the fastest method you can use to quit iPhoto is to click **Close** (). Alternatively, right-click the **iPhoto** icon () and then click **Quit**. Finally, you can quit iPhoto by switching to the application and pressing ⌘+Q.

Import Photos from a Digital Camera or iOS Device

You can import photos from a digital camera or iPhone, iPad, or iPod touch and save them on your Mac. If you have the iLife suite installed on your Mac, you can use the iPhoto application to handle importing photos. iPhoto is also available separately through the App Store. iPhoto enables you to add a name and a description to each import, which helps you to find your photos after the import is complete. To perform the import, you need a cable to connect your digital camera or iOS device to your Mac. Most digital cameras come with a USB cable.

Import Photos from a Digital Camera or iOS Device

Import Photos from a Digital Camera

1. Connect one end of the cable to the digital camera.
2. Connect the other end of the cable to a free USB port on your Mac.
3. Turn the camera on and put it in either playback or computer mode.

Note: iOS devices do not need to be put in playback or computer mode, simply turn them on and connect them to your computer.

Your Mac launches the iPhoto application.

- A Your camera or iOS device appears in the Devices section.
- B iPhoto displays previews of the camera's photos.

4. Use the Add event name text box to type a name for the group of photos you are going to import.

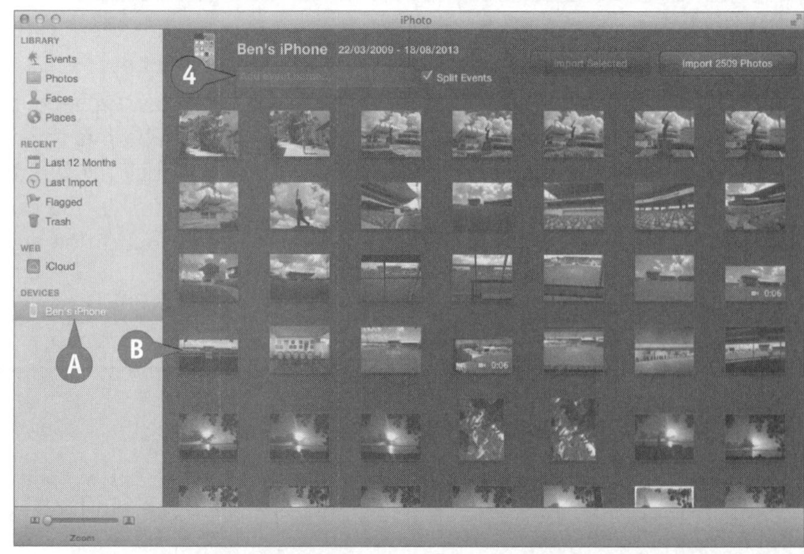

5. Press and hold ⌘ and click each photo you want to select.

6. Click **Import Selected**.

C. To import all the photos from the digital camera, click **Import *X* Photos**, where *X* is the number of photos stored in the camera.

iPhoto imports the photos from the digital camera.

iPhoto asks if you want to delete the original photos from the digital camera.

7. If you no longer need the photos on the camera, click **Delete Photos**.

D. To keep the photos on the camera, click **Keep Photos**.

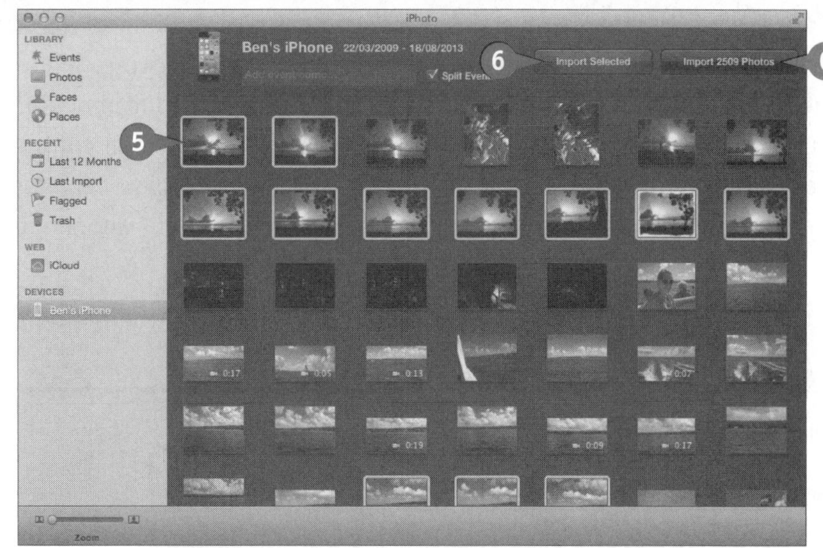

View the Imported Photos

1. Click **Events**.

2. Double-click the event name that you specified in step 4.

The photos you imported are shown.

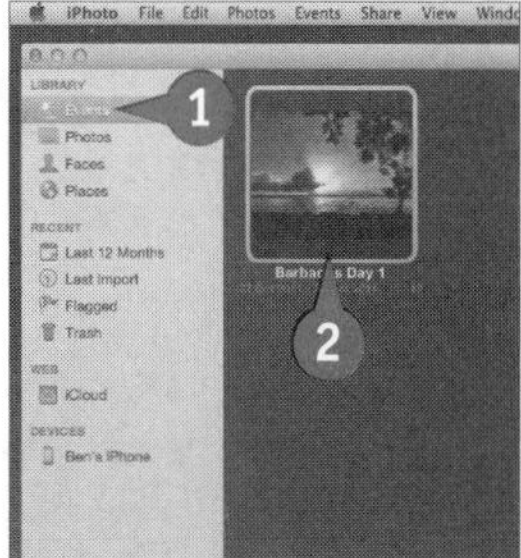

TIP

Why are my photos split into different events when I import them from a camera or iOS device?

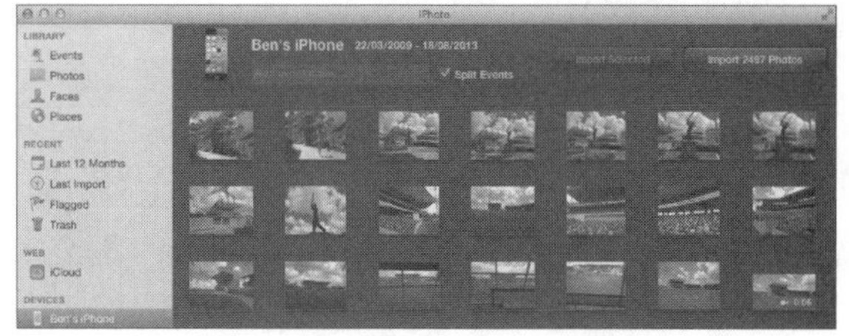

iPhoto looks for the time and date information embedded in most digital photos and groups your images by day when you import them. If you import a number of images across different days, they appear as separate groups of photos, one for each day. To prevent this from happening, deselect the **Split Events** check box (☑ changes to ☐) when importing your photos to group them into a single event.

View Your Photos

If you want to look at several photos, you can use the iPhoto application, which is available as part of the Apple iLife suite or separately via the App Store. iPhoto offers a feature called full-screen mode, which hides everything else and displays your photos using the entire screen. Once you activate full-screen mode, iPhoto offers several on-screen controls that you can use to navigate backward and forward through the photos in a folder. Full-screen mode also shows thumbnail images of each photo, so you can quickly jump to any photo you want to view.

View Your Photos

1. In iPhoto, click **Events**.
2. Double-click the event that contains the photos you want to view.

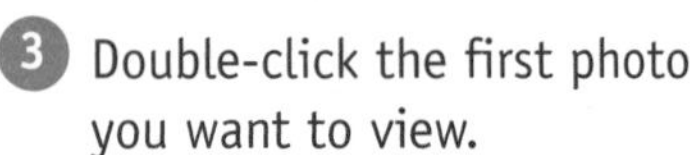

3. Double-click the first photo you want to view.

iPhoto displays the photo.

4 Click **Next** (→) to view the next photo in the event.

A You can also click **Previous** (←) to see the previous photo in the event.

Note: You can also navigate photos by pressing → and ←.

5 When you are done, click the name of the event.

TIP

Is there a way that I can jump quickly to a particular photo when in full-screen mode?

Yes. Move the mouse ↖ to the thumbnails at the bottom of the iPhoto window so that the thumbnails increase in size, and then click the photo you want to jump to.

Create an Album

You can use the iPhoto application to organize your photos into albums. You can get iPhoto either as part of the iLife suite, which is installed on all new Macs, or via the App Store. In iPhoto, an *album* is a collection of photos that are usually related in some way. For example, you might create an album for a series of vacation photos, for photos taken at a party or other special event, or for photos that include a particular person, pet, or place. Using your iPhoto library, you can create customized albums that include only the photos that you want to view.

Create an Album

Create the Album

1. Click **File**.
2. Click **New Album**.

Note: You can also start a new album by pressing ⌘+N.

iPhoto asks you to confirm that you want to create an empty album.

3. Click **Continue**.
4. Type a name for the new album and Press Return.

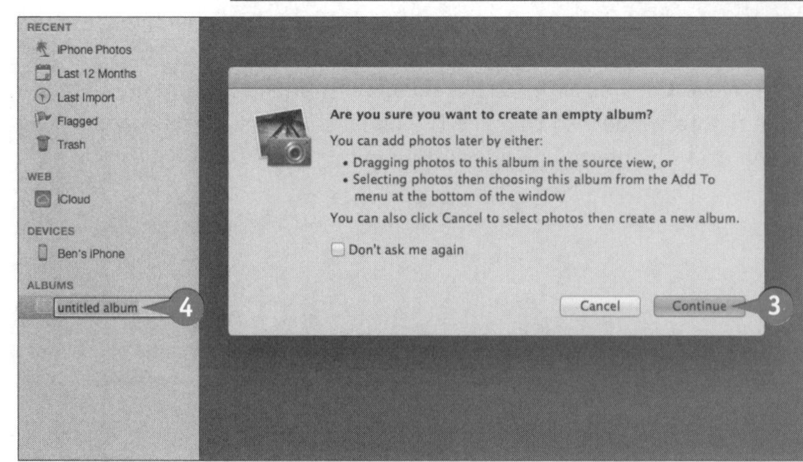

Add Photos to the Album

1. Click **Photos**.
2. Click the right-pointing arrow beside an event that contains photos you want to work with (the right-pointing arrow changes to a downward-pointing arrow).
3. Click and drag a photo and drop it on the new album.
4. Repeat steps 2 and 3 to add other photos to the album.
5. Click the album.

Ⓐ iPhoto displays the photos you added to the album.

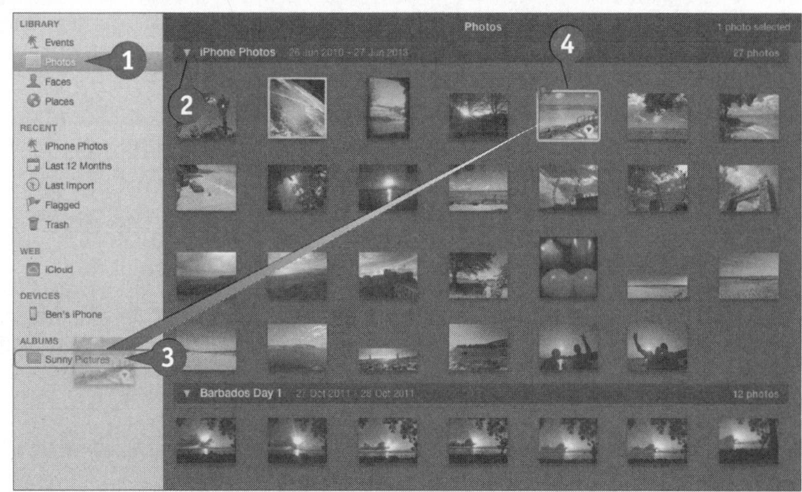

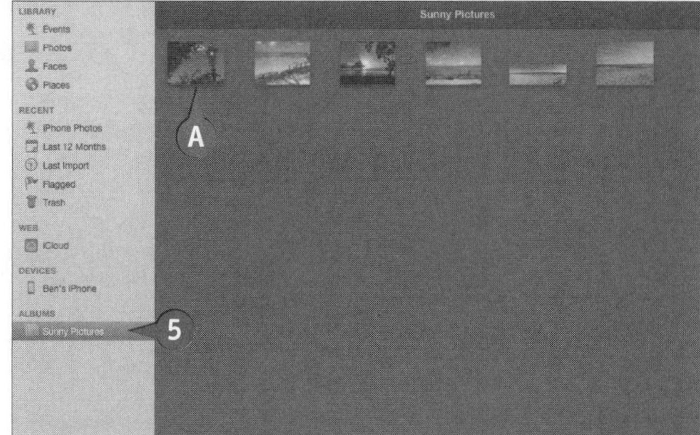

TIP

Is there any way to make iPhoto add photos to an album automatically?

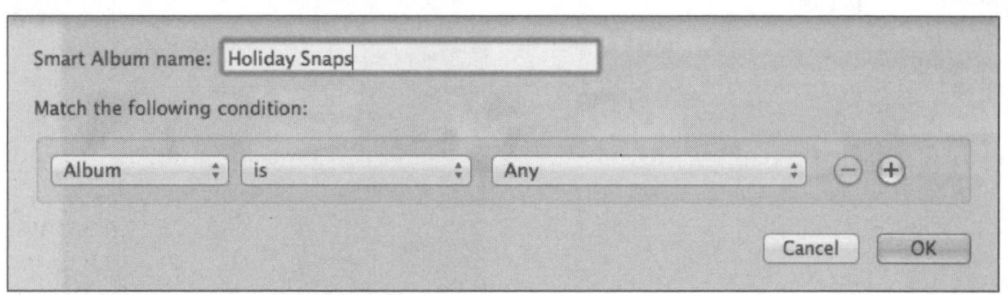

Yes, you can create a *Smart Album*, where the photos that appear in the album have one or more properties in common, such as the description, rating, date, or text in the photo title. Click **File** and then click **New Smart Album** (you can also press Option + ⌘ + N). Use the Smart Album dialog to create one or more rules that define which photos you want to appear in the album.

Crop a Photo

If you have a photo containing elements that you do not want or need to see, you can often cut out those elements. This is called *cropping*, and you can do this with iPhoto, which comes in the iLife suite or via the App Store. When you crop a photo, you specify a rectangular area of the photo that you want to keep. iPhoto discards everything outside of the rectangle. Cropping is a useful skill to have because it can help give focus to the true subject of a photo. Cropping is also useful for removing extraneous elements that appear on or near the edges of a photo.

Crop a Photo

1. Click the photo you want to crop.
2. Click **Edit** (✎).

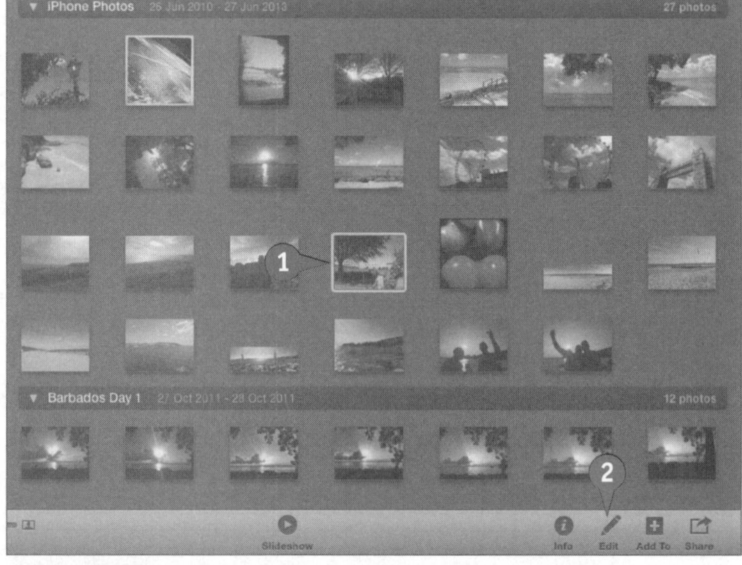

iPhoto displays its editing tools.

3. Click **Crop** (⧉).

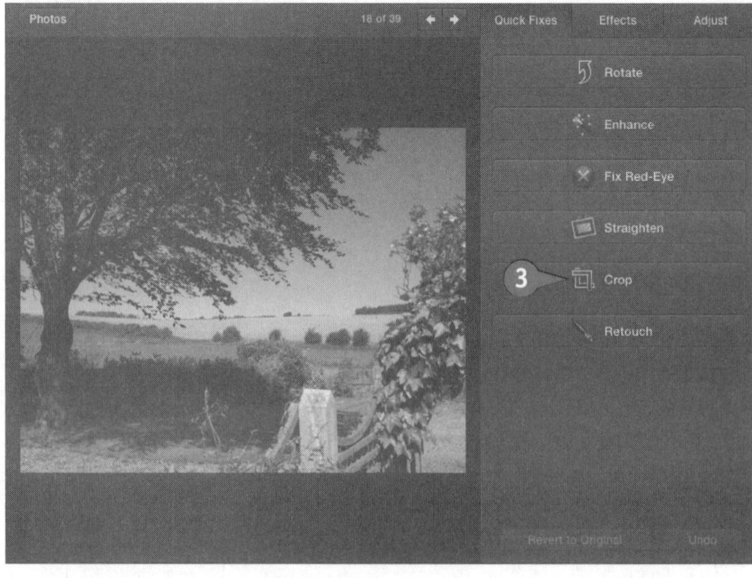

iPhoto displays a cropping rectangle on the photo.

4 Click and drag a corner or side to define the area you want to keep.

Note: Remember that iPhoto keeps the area inside the rectangle.

5 Click **Done**.

iPhoto saves the cropped photo.

6 Click **Edit** (✎).

iPhoto exits edit mode.

TIP

Is there a quick way to crop a photo to a certain size?

Yes, iPhoto enables you to specify either a specific size, such as 640 × 480, or a specific ratio, such as 4 × 3 or 16 × 9.

1 Follow steps 1 to 3 to display the Crop tool.

2 Select the **Constrain** check box (☐ changes to ☑), and then click ⬍ (not shown).

3 Click the size or ratio you want to use.

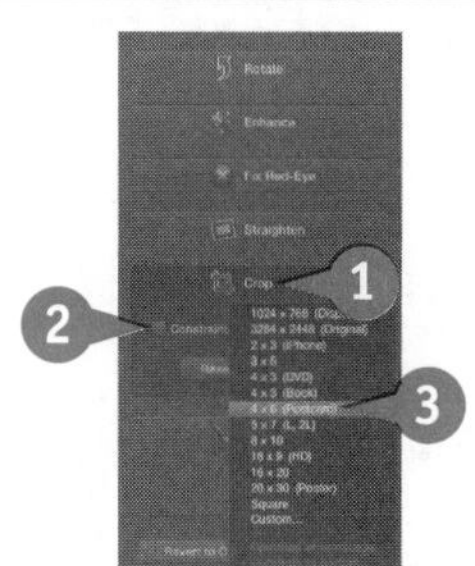

Rotate a Photo

You can rotate a photo using the iPhoto application, which comes with all new Macs as part of iLife and is also available separately via the App Store. Depending on how you held your camera when you took a shot, the resulting photo might show the subject sideways or upside down. This may be the effect you want, but more likely this is a problem. To fix this problem, you can use iPhoto to rotate the photo so that the subject appears right-side up. You can rotate a photo either clockwise or counterclockwise.

Rotate a Photo

1 Click the photo you want to rotate.

Note: A quick way to rotate a photo is to right-click the photo and then click **Rotate**.

2 Click **Edit** (✏).

iPhoto displays its editing tools.

3 Click **Rotate**.

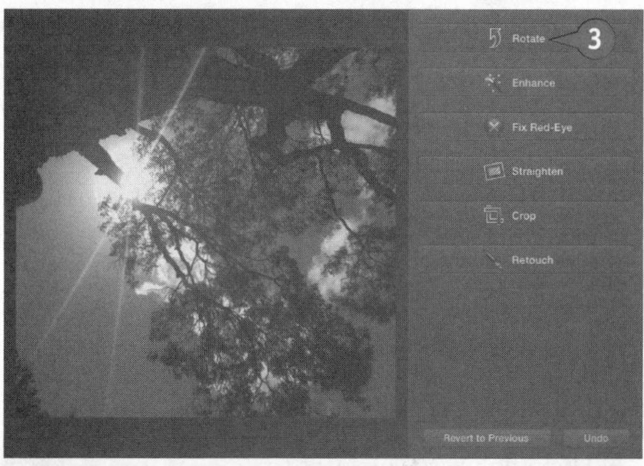

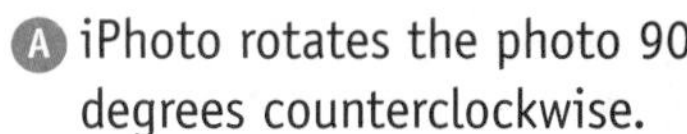

A iPhoto rotates the photo 90 degrees counterclockwise.

Note: You can change the default rotation direction to clockwise in iPhoto Preferences. This also reverses the rotation direction, as explained in the tip in this section.

4 Repeat step 3 until the subject of the photo is right-side up.

5 Click **Edit** (✎).

iPhoto exits edit mode.

TIP

Can I rotate a photo clockwise instead?

Yes. With the editing tools displayed, press and hold Option. The Rotate icon changes from a counterclockwise arrow to a clockwise arrow. Option+click **Rotate** to rotate the photo clockwise by 90 degrees. You can also right-click the photo and then click **Rotate Clockwise**.

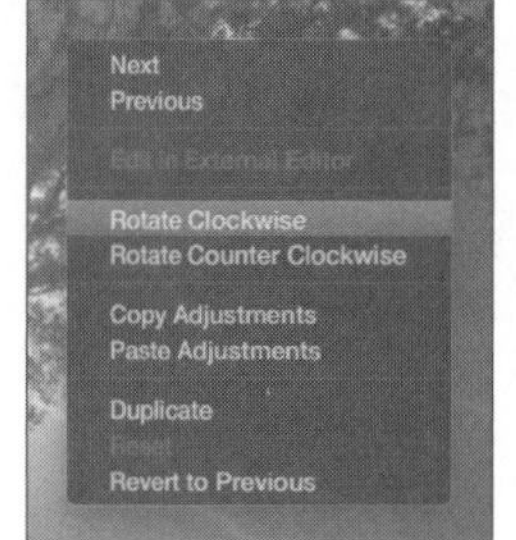

Straighten a Photo

You can straighten a crooked photo using the iPhoto application, which comes with all new Macs as part of iLife and is also available separately via the App Store. If you do not use a tripod when taking pictures, getting your camera perfectly level when you take a shot is very difficult and requires a lot of practice and a steady hand. Despite your best efforts, you might end up with a photo that is not quite level. To fix this problem, you can use iPhoto to nudge the photo clockwise or counterclockwise so that the subject appears straight.

Straighten a Photo

1. Click the photo you want to straighten.
2. Click **Edit** (✎).

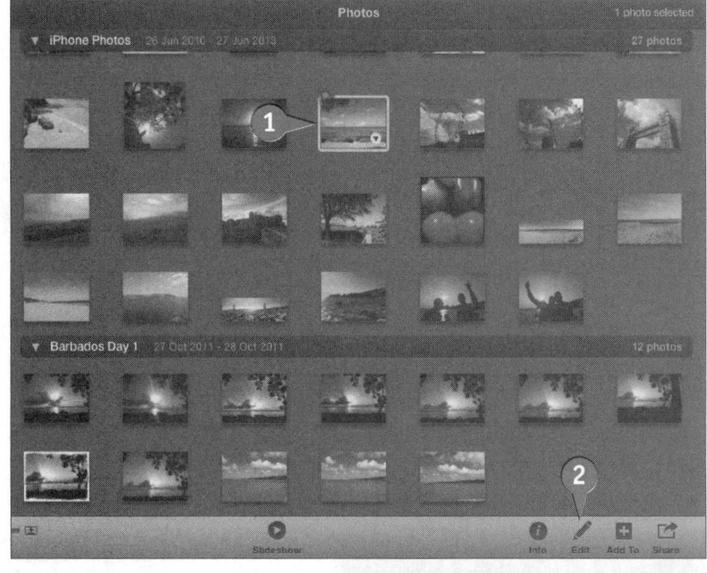

iPhoto displays its editing tools.

3. Click **Straighten** (▣).

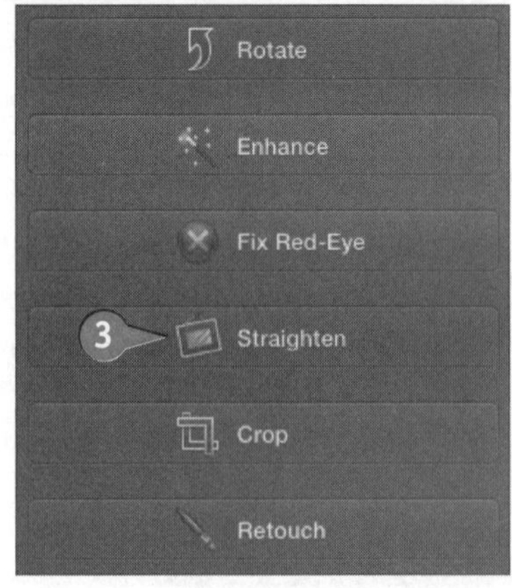

iPhoto displays a grid over the photo.

4 Click and drag the **Angle** slider.

Drag the slider to the left to angle the photo counterclockwise.

Drag the slider to the right to angle the photo clockwise.

5 Click **Done**.

The photo is adjusted according to your settings.

6 Click **Edit** ( ).

iPhoto exits edit mode.

TIP

How do I know when my photo is level?

Use the gridlines that iPhoto places over the photo. Locate a horizontal line in your photo, and then rotate the photo so that this line is parallel to the nearest horizontal line in the grid. You can also match a vertical line in the photo with a vertical line in the grid.

Remove Red Eye from a Photo

You can remove red eye from a photo using the iPhoto application, which comes with all new Macs as part of iLife and is also available separately via the App Store. When you use a flash to take a picture of one or more people, in some cases the flash may reflect off the subjects' retinas. The result is a common phenomenon called *red eye*, where each person's pupils appear red instead of black. If you have a photo where one or more people have red eyes due to the camera flash, you can use iPhoto to remove the red eye and give your subjects a more natural look.

Remove Red Eye from a Photo

1. Click the photo that contains the red eye.
2. Click **Edit** (✎).

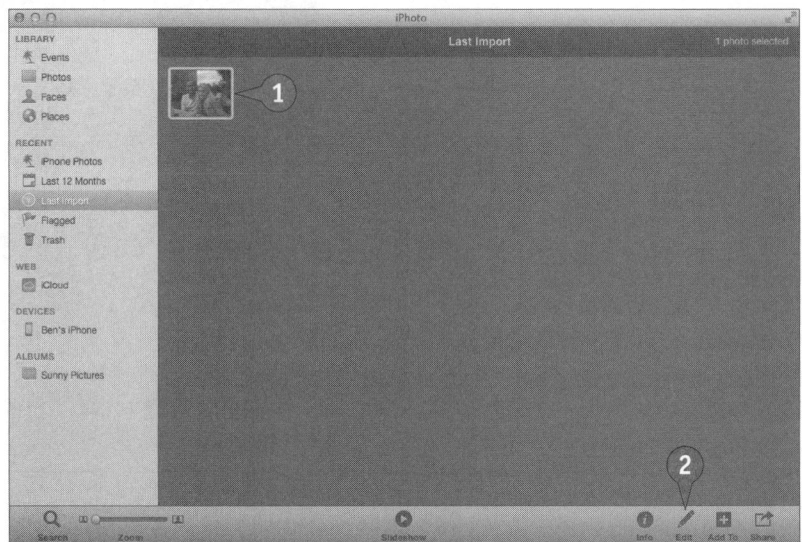

iPhoto displays its editing tools.

A. If needed, you can click and drag this slider to the right to zoom in on the picture.

B. You can click and drag this rectangle to bring the red eye into view.

3. Click **Fix Red-Eye** (✖).

iPhoto displays its Red-Eye controls.

C You may be able to fix the red eye automatically by selecting the **Auto-fix red-eye** check box (☐ changes to ☑). If that does not work, continue with the rest of these steps.

4 Move the red eye pointer over a red eye in the photo.

5 Click the red eye.

D iPhoto removes the red eye.

6 Repeat steps 4 and 5 to fix any other instances of red eye in the photo.

7 Click **Done**.

8 Click **Edit** (✎).

iPhoto exits edit mode.

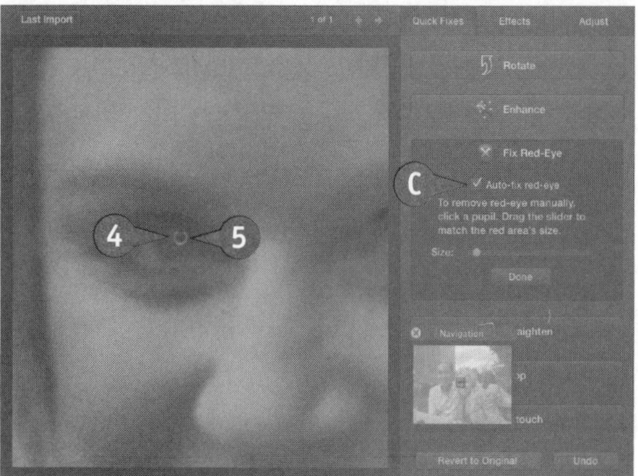

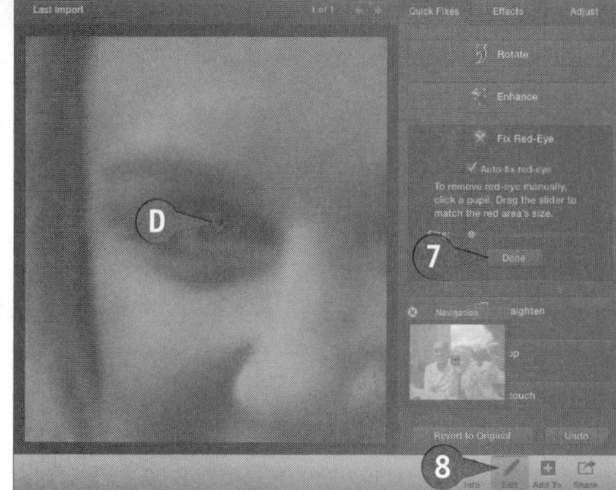

TIP

Why does iPhoto remove only part of the red eye in my photo?

The Red-Eye tool may not be set to a large enough size. The tool should be approximately the same size as the subject's pupil. Click and drag the Size slider until the Red-Eye tool is the size of the red-eye area. Use your mouse to move the circle over the red eye, and then click to remove red eye.

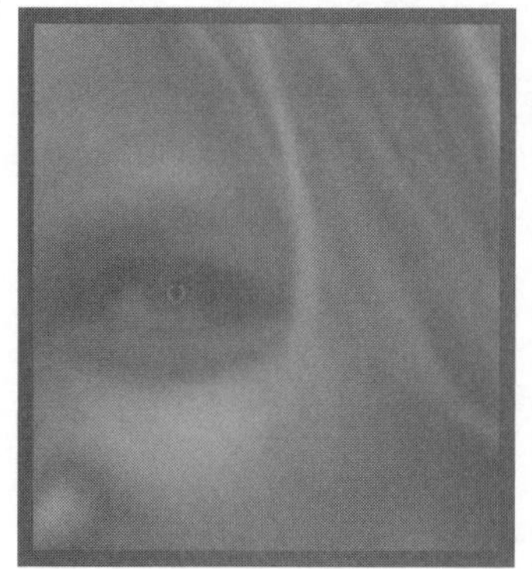

Add Names to Faces in Your Photos

You can make your photos easier to manage and navigate by adding names to the faces that appear in each photo. This is sometimes called *tagging*, and it enables you to navigate your photos by name. For example, you can view all your photos in which a certain person appears.

To add names to the faces in your photos, you must be using iPhoto '09 or later. To check this, click **iPhoto** in the menu bar and then click **About iPhoto**.

Add Names to Faces in Your Photos

1 Click the photo that you want to tag.

2 Click **Info** (■).

3 Click ***X* unnamed** (where *X* is the number of faces iPhoto identifies in the photo).

iPhoto displays its naming tools.

4 Click **unnamed**.

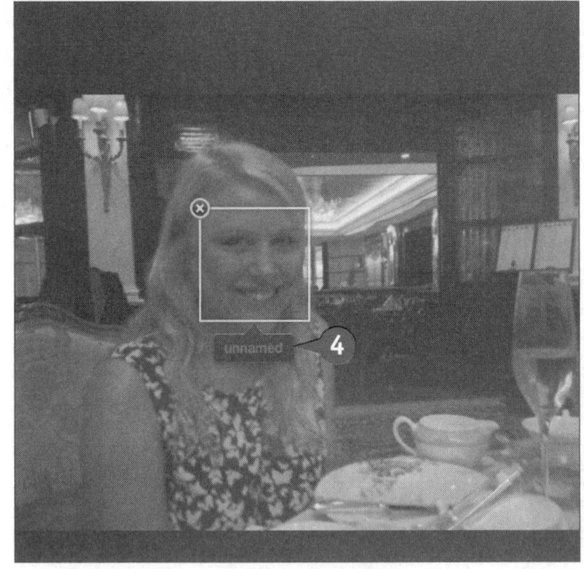

5 Type the person's name and press Return.

A If iPhoto did not mark a face in the photo, click **Add a face**, size and position the box over the face, and then type the name in the **click to name** box.

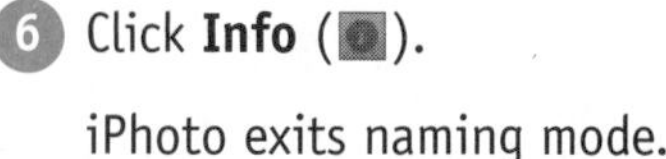

6 Click **Info** (■).

iPhoto exits naming mode.

TIP

How do I view all the photos that contain a particular person?

You can open a photo, click **Info** (■), and then click the **Show All** arrow (■) beside the person's name. You can also follow these steps:

1 Click **Faces** in the iPhoto sidebar.

A iPhoto displays the names and sample photos of each person you have named.

2 Double-click the person you want to view.

iPhoto displays all the photos that contain the person.

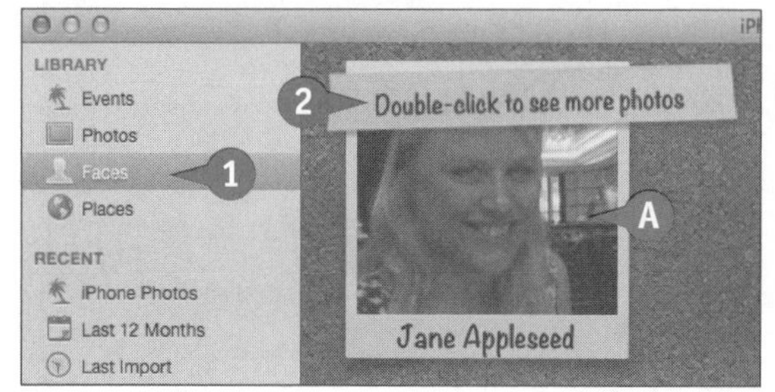

Map Your Photos

You can use *geotagging* to view your photos by location if you edit each photo to include the location where you took the image. If your camera does not add location data automatically, you can tell iPhoto the locations where your photos were taken, and then display a map that shows those locations. This enables you to view all your photos taken in a particular place.

To map your photos, you must be using iPhoto '09 or later. To check this, click **iPhoto** in the menu bar and then click **About iPhoto**.

Map Your Photos

1. Click the event that you want to map.

   If you want to map a single photo, open the event and then open the photo.

2. Click **Info** (●).
3. Click **Assign a Place**.
4. Type the location.

   A. iPhoto displays a list of locations that match what you typed.

5. When you see the place you want to use, click it.

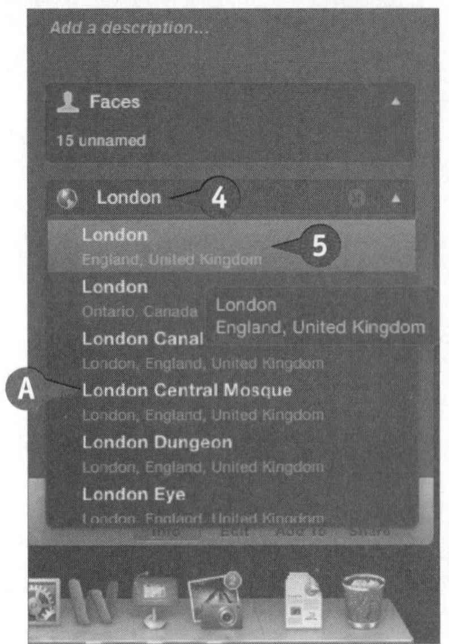

iPhoto displays the location on a map.

6 Click and drag the pin to the correct location, if necessary.

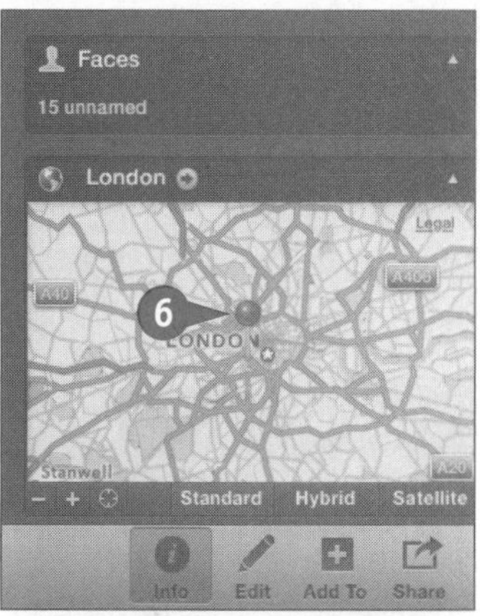

7 Click **Info** (ⓘ).

iPhoto closes the info window.

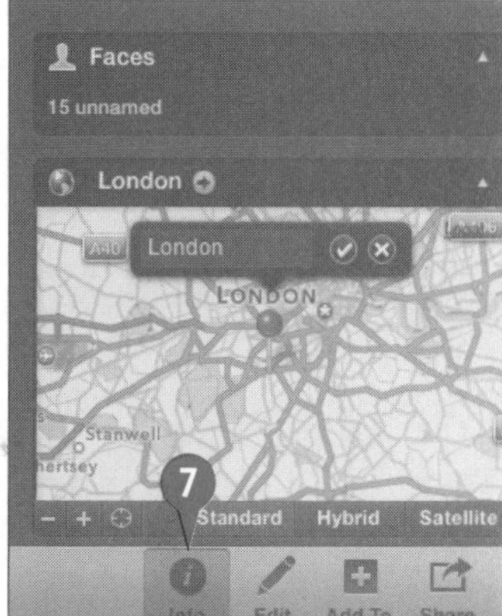

TIPS

Is there a way to have the location data added automatically?

Yes. If you have a GPS-enabled camera, iPhoto automatically picks up location data from the photos; however, you must activate this feature. Click **iPhoto** in the menu bar, click **Preferences**, and then click the **Advanced** tab. Click the **Look up Places** ⇕ and then click **Automatically**. Note that you may still have to add or edit location names for your photos.

How do I view all the photos that were taken in a particular place?

Click **Places** in the iPhoto sidebar to see a map of the world with pins for each of your photo locations. Position the mouse ↖ over the location's pin, and then click the **Show All** arrow (›). iPhoto displays all the photos that were taken in that location.

E-mail a Photo

You can use the iPhoto application to create a message to send a photo to another person via e-mail. iPhoto comes with all new Macs as part of iLife, and it is also available separately via the App Store. If you have a photo that you want to share with someone, and you know that person's e-mail address, you can send the photo in an e-mail message. Using iPhoto, you can specify which photo you want to send, and iPhoto creates a new message. Even if a photo is very large, you can still send it via e-mail because you can use iPhoto to shrink the copy of the photo that appears in the message.

E-mail a Photo

1. Click the photo you want to send.
2. Click **Share** (📤).
3. Click **Mail**.

A preview of the e-mail is created.

4. Type the e-mail address of the recipient you want to send the picture to in the To: field.
5. Type a subject in the Subject: field.
6. Click a theme from the list on the right of the screen.

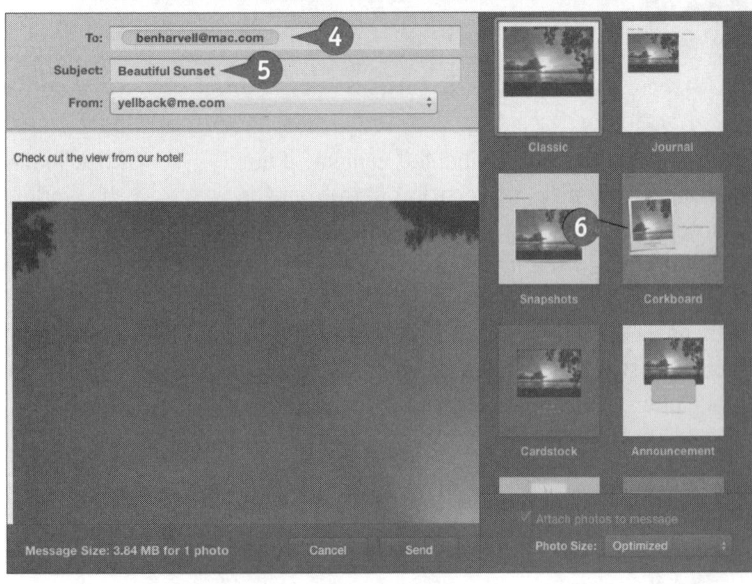

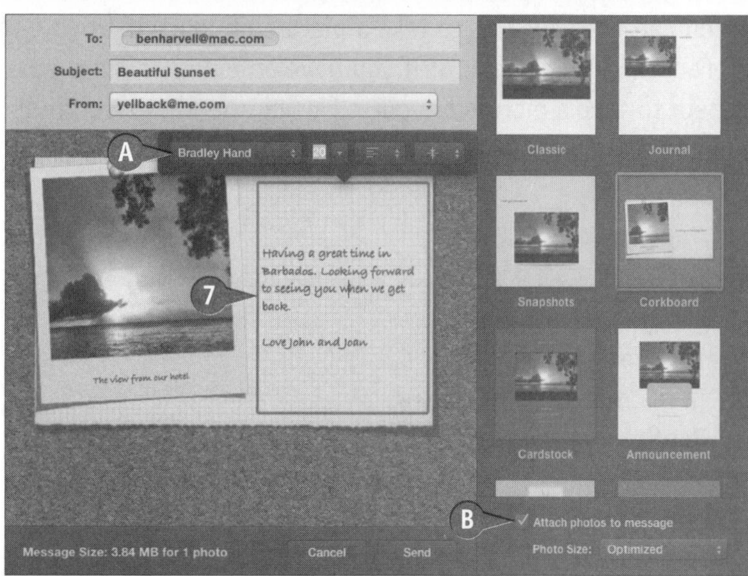

7 Add text to any of the fields in the theme.

A You can adjust the font using the menu that appears when you click a field.

B Select this check box (☐ changes to ☑) to attach the original image or images to the e-mail.

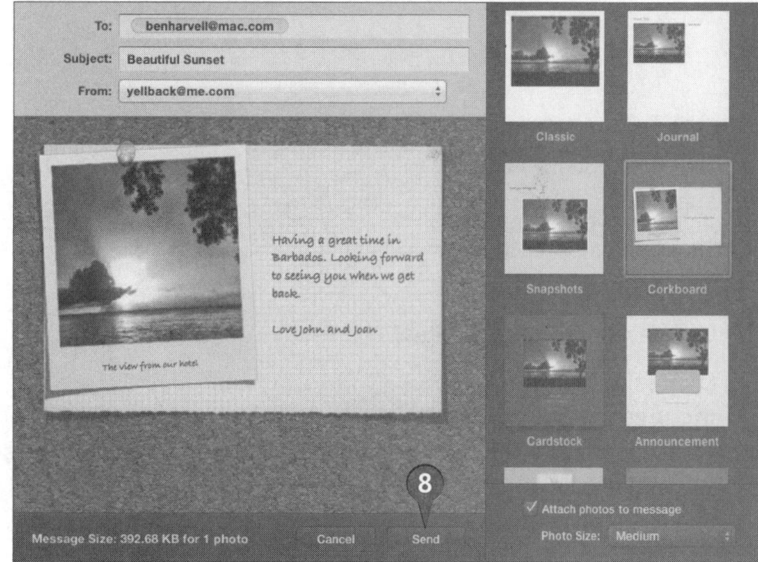

8 Click **Send**.

iPhoto sends the message.

TIP

How do I change the size of the photo?

You need to be careful when sending photos because a single image can be several megabytes in size. If your recipient's e-mail system places restrictions on the size of messages it can receive, your message might not go through.

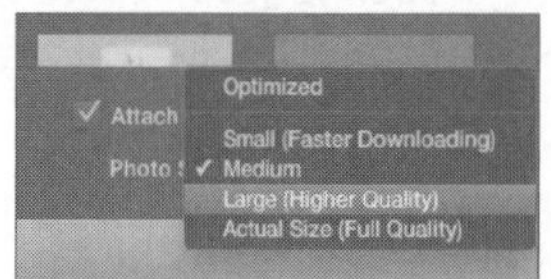

To change the size of the photo, click the **Photo Size** ⬍ and then click the size you want to use for the sent photo, such as Small or Medium. Note that this does not affect the size of the original photo, just the copy that is sent with the message.

Take Your Picture

You can use your Mac to take a picture of yourself. If your Mac comes with a built-in iSight or FaceTime HD camera, or if you have an external camera attached to your Mac, you can use the camera to take a picture of yourself using the Photo Booth application. After you take your picture, you can e-mail that picture, add it to iPhoto, or set it as your user account or iChat buddy picture.

Take Your Picture

Take Your Picture with Photo Booth

1. In the Dock, click the **Photo Booth** icon ( ).

The Photo Booth window appears.

A. The live feed from the camera appears here.

2. Click **Take a still picture** ( ).

B. Click **Take four quick pictures** ( ) if you want Photo Booth to snap four successive photos, each about 1 second apart.

C. Click **Take a movie clip** ( ) if you want Photo Booth to capture the live camera feed as a movie.

3. Click **Take Photo** ( ).

Note: You can also press ⌘+T or click **File** and then click **Take Photo**.

Photo Booth counts down 3 seconds and then takes the photo.

Note: When the Mac is taking your picture, be sure to look into the camera, not into the screen.

Work with Your Photo Booth Picture

D Photo Booth displays the picture.

1 Click the picture.

2 Click **Share** (share icon).

E Click **Add to iPhoto** to add the photo to iPhoto.

F Click **Change profile picture...** to set the photo as your user account picture.

G Click any of the sharing options to send the photo via e-mail, AirDrop, Messages, or to social media accounts.

TIP

Can I make my photos more interesting?

Definitely. Photo Booth comes with around two dozen special effects. Follow these steps:

1 Click **View**.

2 Click **Show Effects**.

3 Click an icon to select a different page of effects.

A You can also use the arrow buttons to change pages.

4 Click the effect you want to use.

Set Up Photo Stream

Photo Stream provides a convenient way to view and access photos you take on your iOS devices or Mac in OS X. With Photo Stream switched on on all of your devices, you can view the last 30 days of photos on any connected device in iPhoto on your Mac or in the Photos app on an iPhone, iPad, or iPod touch.

Set Up Photo Stream

1. In the Dock, click the **iPhoto** icon (▣).

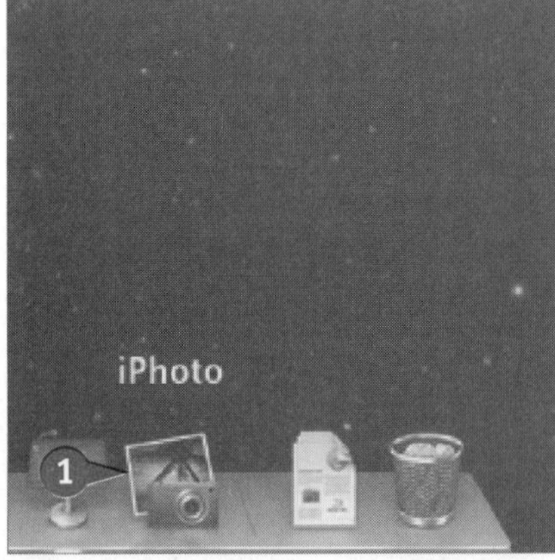

iPhoto appears.

2. Click **iCloud**.

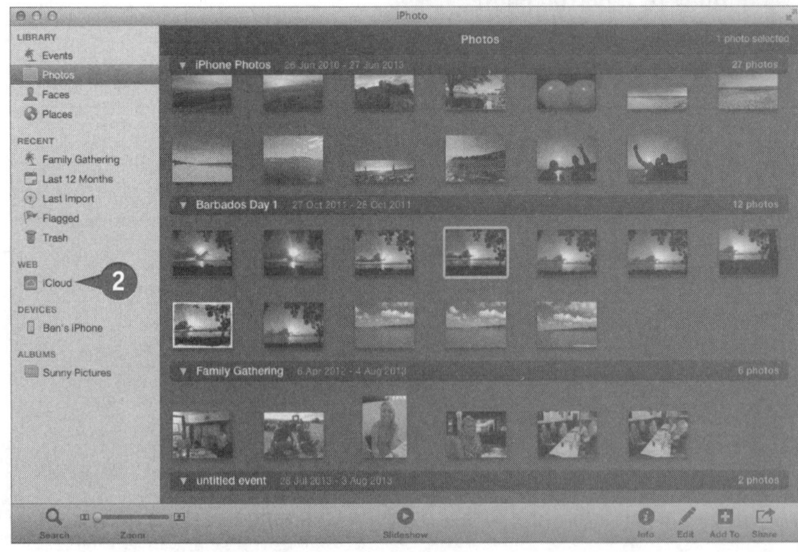

3 Click **Use iCloud**.

Photo Stream is turned on.

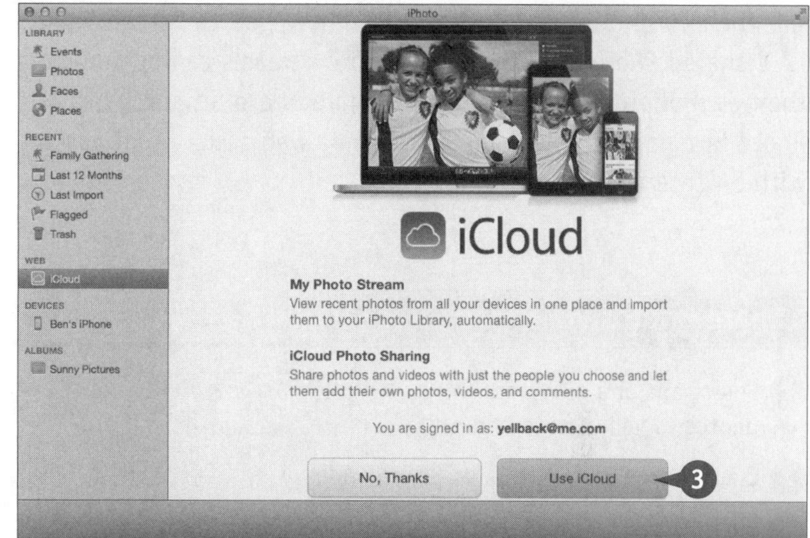

A Photos from your connected devices appear in My Photo Stream.

B Shared Photo Streams you have created also appear in the Photo Stream view.

4 Click **My Photo Stream**.

Your recent photos are shown.

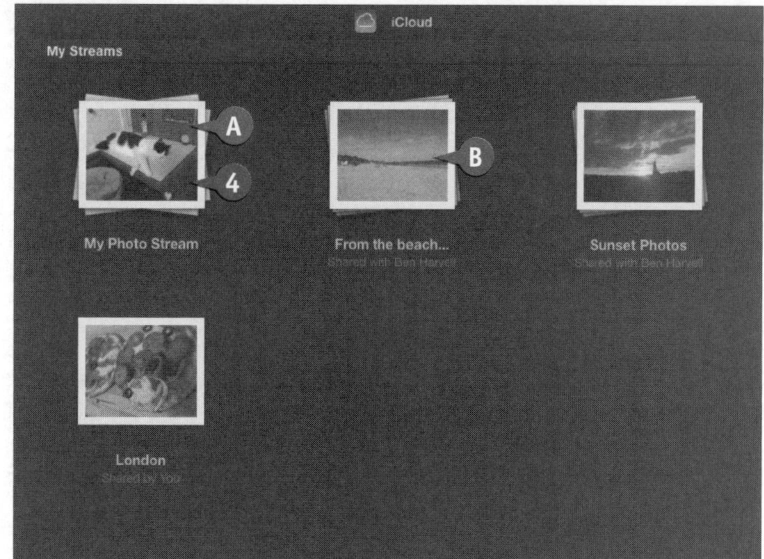

TIP

How do I set up Photo Stream on my iOS devices?

On an iPhone, iPad, or iPod touch, tap the **Settings** icon and then tap **iCloud** on the screen that appears. Sign in to your iCloud account with your Apple ID and password if you have not done so already. Now tap on **Photo Stream** and set the My Photo Stream and Shared Photo Streams switches to the ON position.

Share Photos Via Photo Stream

When you set up Photo Stream in iPhoto you can share images with other iCloud users via a shared Photo Stream. Shared Photo Streams can be collaborative, allowing other users to add their own photos, and you can also share Photo Streams with non-iCloud users by creating a public Photo Stream that also creates an online web gallery that can be viewed from any computer or device with an Internet connection.

Share Photos via Photo Stream

1. Select one or a group of photos in your iPhoto library.
2. Click **Share** ( ).
3. Click **iCloud**.

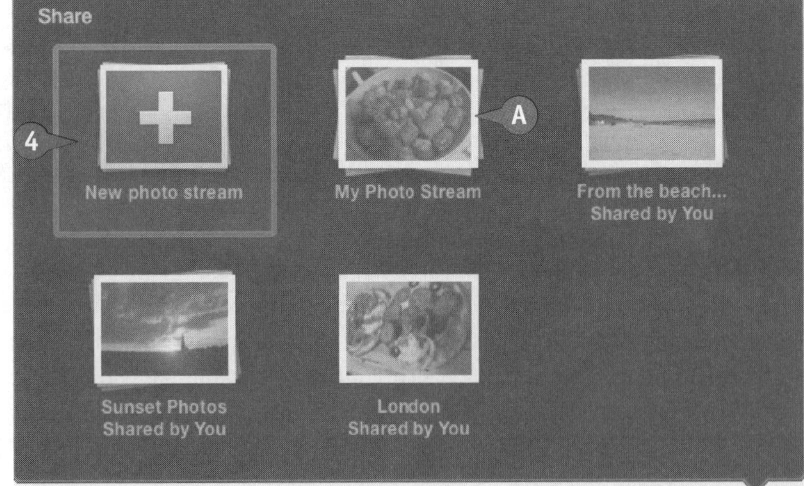

A. To add photos to an existing Photo Stream, click its name.

4. Click **New photo stream**.

5 Type the e-mail addresses of those with whom you want to share the Photo Stream.

6 Type a name for your Shared Photo Stream.

B Add a comment in this field if you want to.

C Select this check box to allow subscribers to the photo stream to add their own photos and videos to the photo stream (☐ changes to ☑).

D To make the Photo Stream public and allow non-iOS users to view it, select the **Public Website** check box (☐ changes to ☑).

7 Click **Share**.

Your shared Photo Stream is sent to the recipients you selected and appears in the Photo Stream section of iPhoto and on your iOS devices.

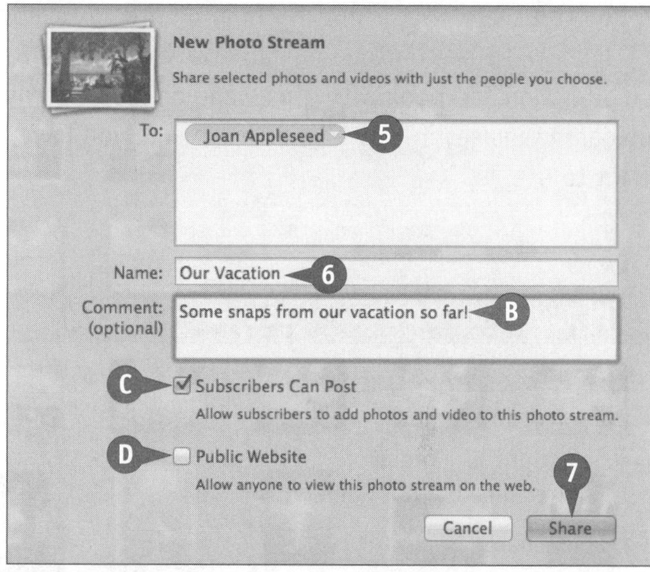

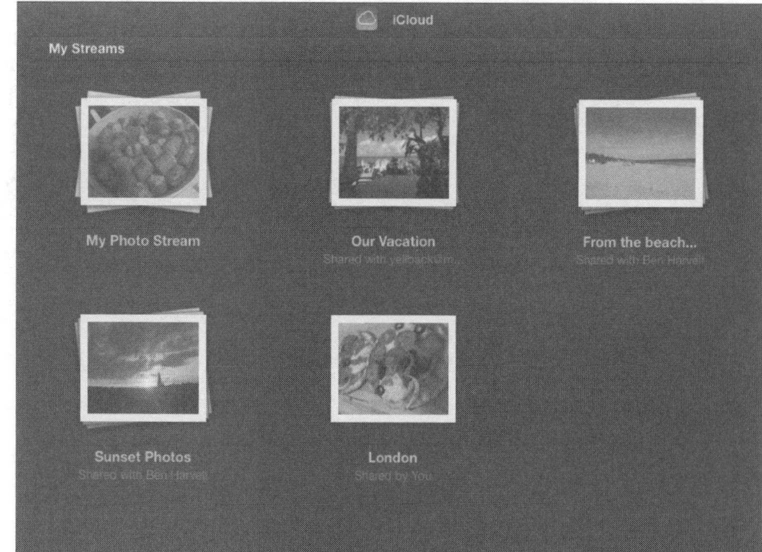

TIP

What do I do when I receive a shared Photo Stream?

If you receive an invitation to a Shared Photo Stream on an iOS device, you can automatically subscribe to it within the Photos app. On your Mac, you will receive an e-mail inviting you to a Photo Stream. Click the **Join this Photo Stream** button in the e-mail you received and, when prompted, click the **Join** button.

Upload Photos to Facebook and Twitter

You can share photos directly from iPhoto to Facebook, Twitter, and Flickr with just a few clicks. From the Share button you can attach an image to a tweet or send a group of photographs to an album on Facebook with a message or caption. You are required to type your login details when uploading images in this way, so make sure you have an account already set up with the service you want to use.

Upload Photos to Facebook and Twitter

Share Photos to Social Media Accounts

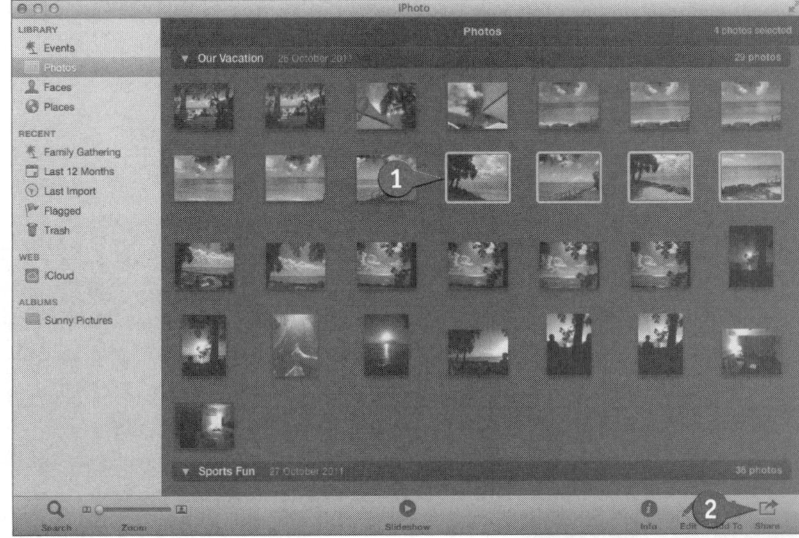

1. Select one or a group of photos in your iPhoto library.
2. Click **Share** (Share icon).

The Share menu appears.

3. Click the social network on which you want to share photos.

Ⓐ Click **Twitter** to share the photo in a tweet.

Note: You can only share one photo at a time when uploading to Twitter.

Ⓑ Click **Facebook** to upload photos to Facebook.

Ⓒ Click **Flickr** to upload photos to Flickr.

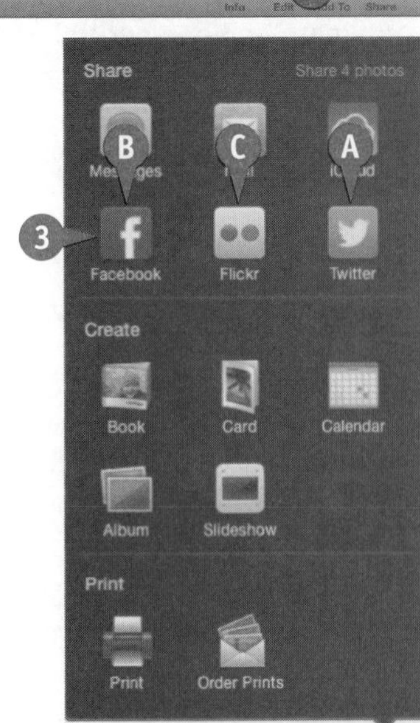

Upload Photos to Twitter

1. Type a short message to accompany your photo.
2. Click **Send**.

Note: If you have not set up Twitter within the Internet Accounts section of System Preferences you may need to sign in to your account.

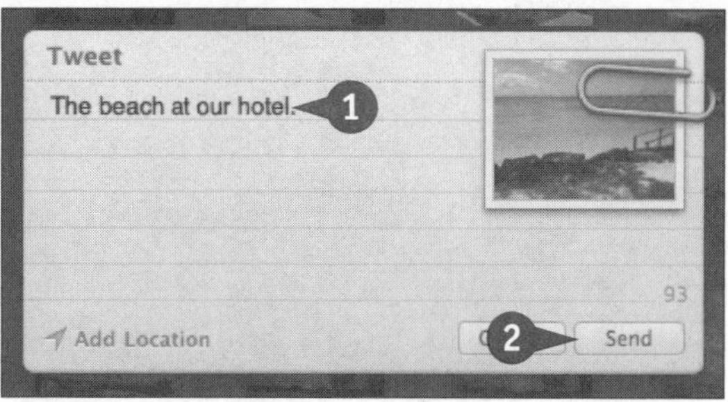

Upload Photos to Facebook

1. Type your e-mail address and password to log in to Facebook.
2. Select the check box to agree to Facebook's terms and conditions (☐ changes to ☑).
3. Click **Login**.
4. Click the Facebook photo album you want to upload your photos to.

D You can also create a new album by clicking **New Album**.

Your photos are uploaded to Facebook.

Note: If you have not set up Facebook within the Internet Accounts section of System Preferences you may need to sign in to your account.

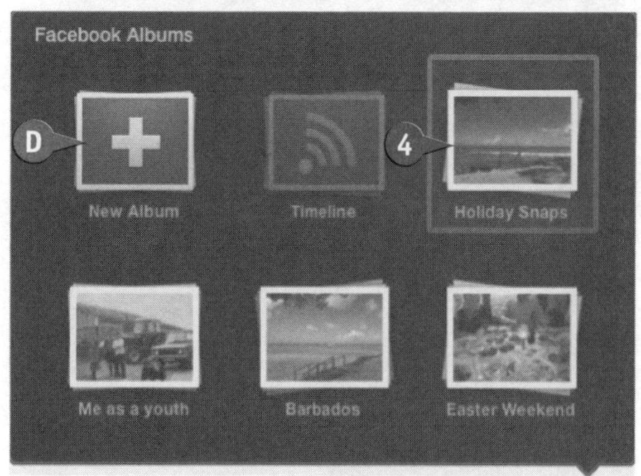

TIP

Do I have to add Facebook photos to an album?

No. You can click the **Timeline** option to upload photos directly to your Facebook Timeline so others can see them in their News Feeds. When you next log in to Facebook, you can edit photo descriptions or share them with other Facebook users or all of your friends in one go.

CHAPTER 11

Playing and Creating Digital Video

Your Mac comes with the tools you need to play movies and digital video as well as to create your own digital video movies.

Play a DVD Using DVD Player

If your Mac has a DVD drive, you can insert a DVD movie into the drive and then use the DVD Player application to play the movie on your Mac. You can either watch the movie in full-screen mode, where the movie takes up the entire Mac screen, or play the DVD in a window while you work on other things. DVD Player has features that enable you to control the movie playback and volume.

Play a DVD Using DVD Player

Play a DVD Full-Screen

1. Insert the DVD into your Mac's DVD drive or external device if your Mac doesn't have a built-in option.

   DVD Player runs automatically and starts playing the DVD full-screen.

2. Move the cursor to the bottom of the screen to display the playback controls.

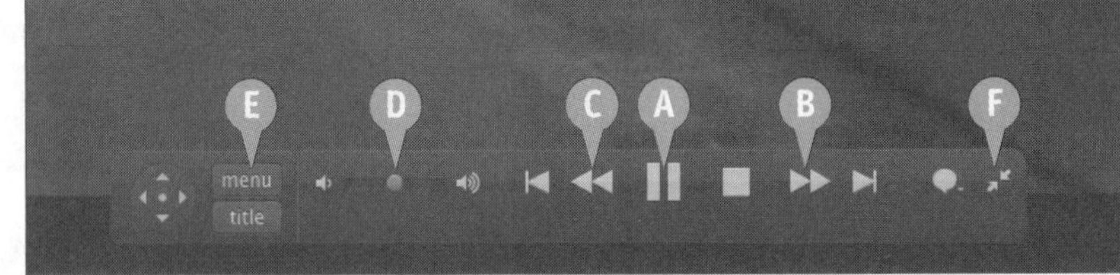

A. Click the **Pause** button (⏸) to pause the movie.

B. Click the **Fast-Forward** button (⏩) to fast-forward the movie.

C. Click the **Rewind** button (⏪) to rewind the movie.

D. Click and drag the **Volume** slider to adjust the volume.

E. Click **menu** to display the DVD menu.

F. Click the **Full-Screen mode** button to exit full-screen mode.

Play a DVD in a Window

1. Insert the DVD into your Mac's DVD drive.

   DVD Player runs automatically and starts playing the DVD full-screen.

2. Press ⌘+F.

Note: You can also press Esc or move the pointer to the bottom of the screen and then click **Exit full screen.**

   DVD Player displays the movie in a window.

- G DVD Player displays the Controller.

3. When you get to the DVD menu, click the **Play** button (▶) to start the movie.

- H Click the **Pause** button (⏸) to pause the movie.
- I Click and hold the **Fast-Forward** button (⏩) to fast-forward the movie.
- J Click and hold the **Rewind** button (⏪) to rewind the movie.
- K Click and drag the **Volume** slider to adjust the volume.
- L Click **menu** to display the DVD menu.
- M Click the **Stop** button (⏹) to stop the movie.
- N Click **eject** to eject the DVD.

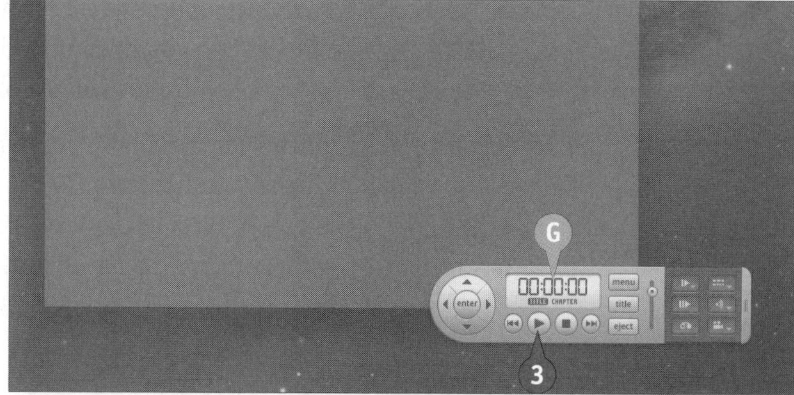

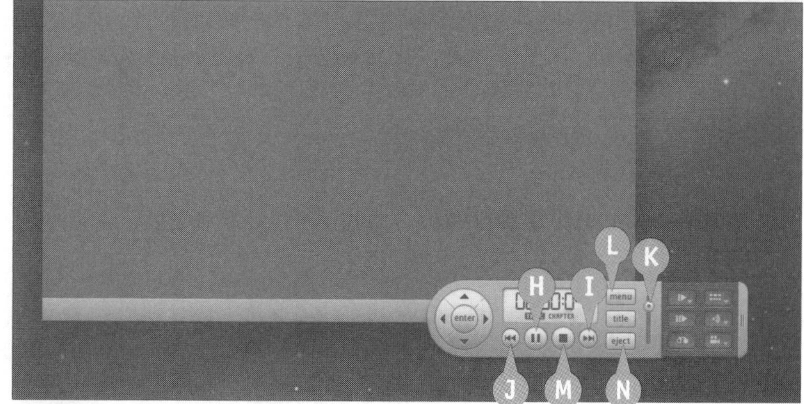

TIP

How can I always start my DVDs in a window?

1. Press ⌘+F to switch to the window view.
2. Click **DVD Player** in the menu bar.
3. Click **Preferences** to open the DVD Player preferences.

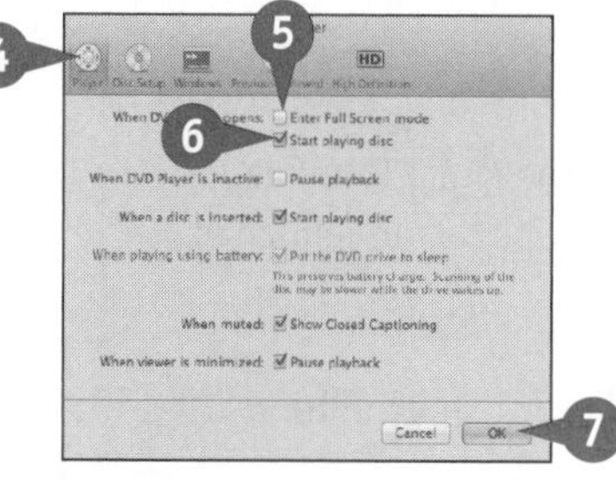

4. Click the **Player** tab.
5. Deselect the **Enter Full Screen mode** check box (☑ changes to ☐).
6. To manually control when the playback starts, deselect the **Start playing disc** check box (☑ changes to ☐).
7. Click **OK** to put the new settings into effect.

Play Digital Video with QuickTime Player

Your Mac comes with an application called QuickTime Player that can play digital video files in various formats. You will mostly use QuickTime Player to play digital video files stored on your Mac, but you can also use the application to play digital video from the web.

QuickTime Player enables you to open video files, navigate the digital video playback, and control the digital video volume. Although you learn only how to play digital video files in this section, the version of QuickTime that comes with OS X 10.9 (Mavericks) comes with many extra features, including the ability to record movies and audio and to cut and paste scenes.

Play Digital Video with QuickTime Player

1. In the Dock, click the **Finder** icon ().
2. Click **Applications**.
3. Double-click **QuickTime Player**.

Note: If you see the QuickTime Player icon in the Dock, you can also click that icon to launch the program.

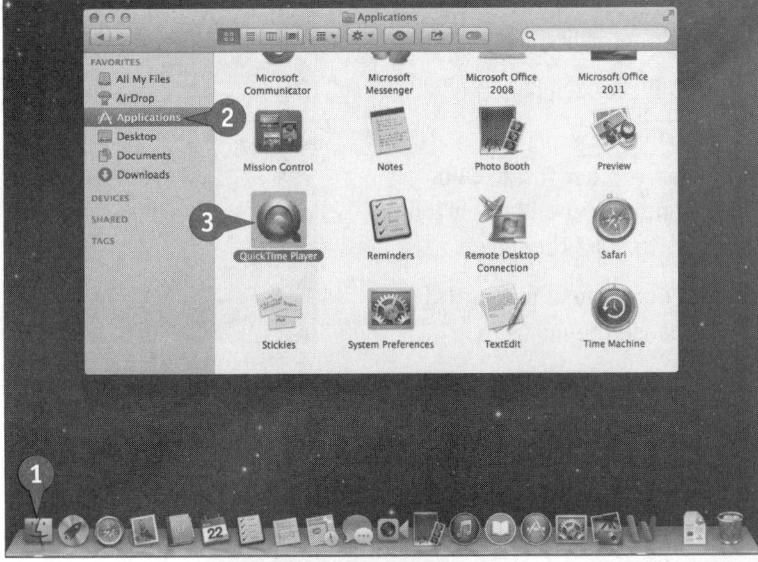

The QuickTime Player application launches.

4. Click **File**.
5. Click **Open File**.

Note: You can also press ⌘+O.

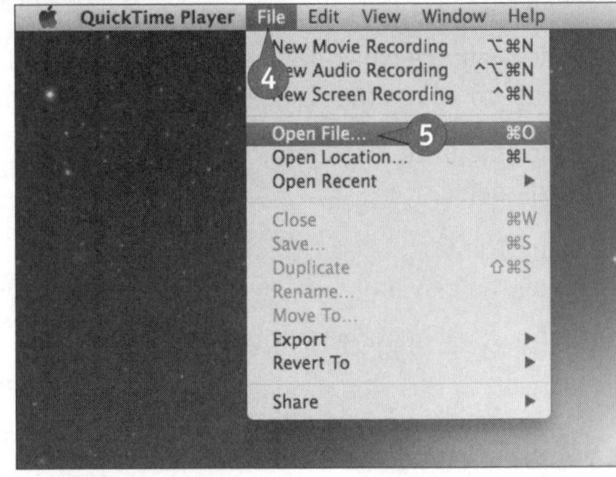

The Open dialog appears.

6 Locate and click the video file you want to play.

7 Click **Open**.

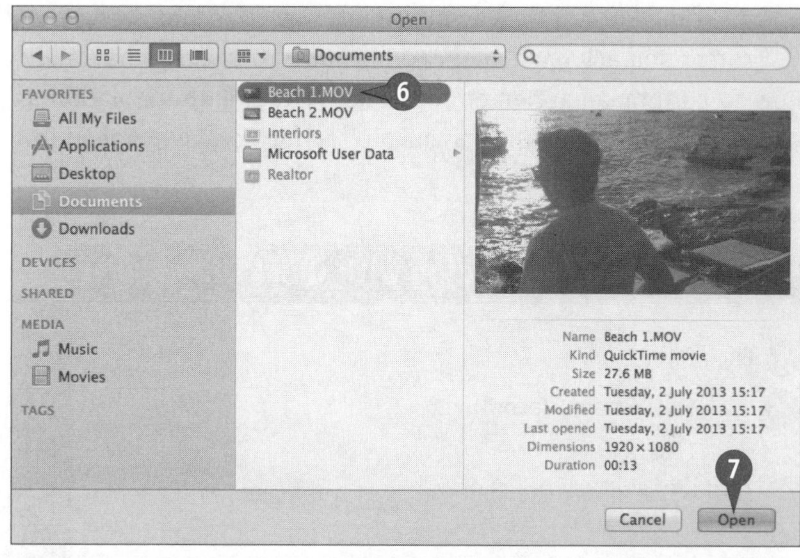

QuickTime opens a new player window.

8 Click **Play** (▶).

A Click the **Fast-Forward** button (▶▶) to fast-forward the video.

B Click the **Rewind** button (◀◀) to rewind the video.

C Click and drag the **Volume** slider to adjust the volume.

If you want to view the video in full-screen mode, press  ⌘+F.

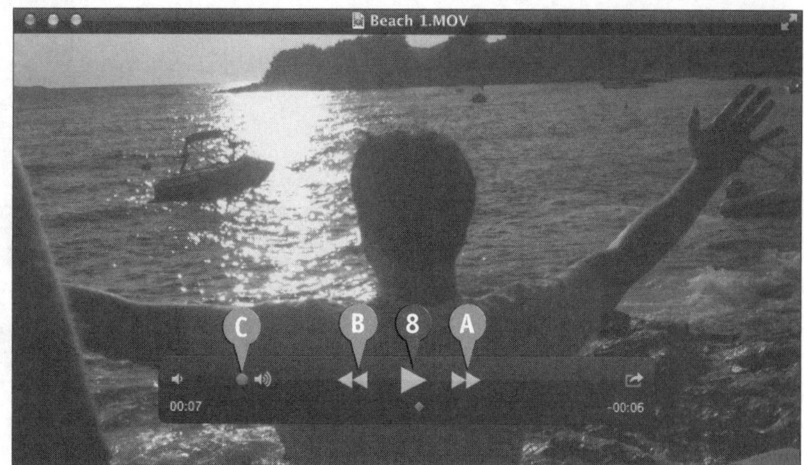

TIP

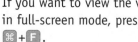

Can I use QuickTime Player to play a video from the web?

Yes. As long as you know the Internet address of the video, QuickTime Player can play most video formats available on the web. In QuickTime Player, click **File** and then click **Open Location** (or press ⌘+U). In the Open URL dialog, type or paste the video address in the **Movie Location** text box, and then click **Open**.

Create a Screen Recording with QuickTime Player

QuickTime Player offers a convenient way to record everything on your Mac's screen, including the cursor and any open application windows. This can be a handy tool if you need to show somebody how to perform an action on his or her Mac, share information as part of a presentation, or for any other purpose that requires a video of actions on your screen to be created.

Create a Screen Recording with QuickTime Player

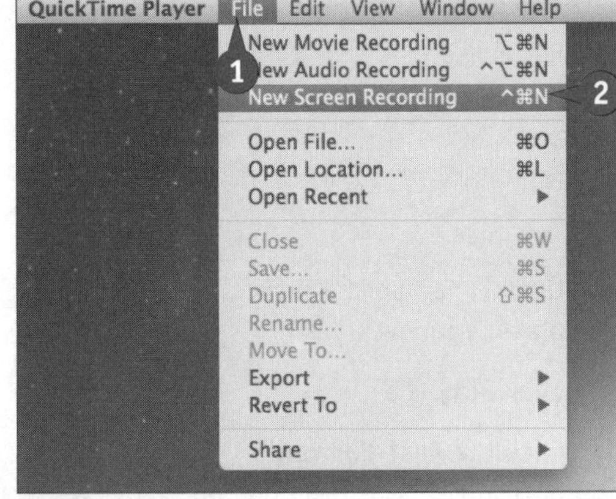

1 Click **File**.

2 Click **New Screen Recording**.

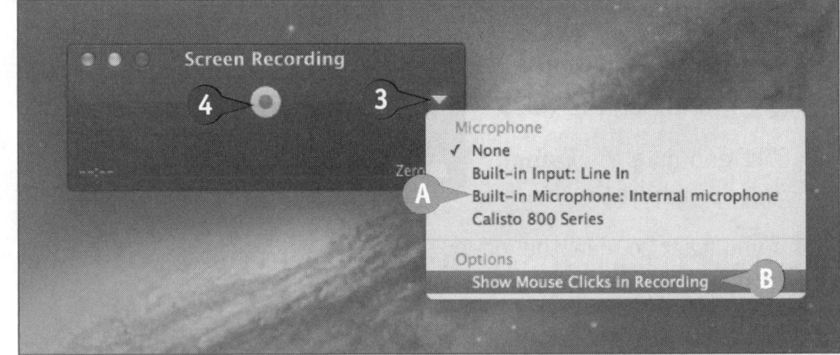

The QuickTime Screen Recording controls appear.

3 Click the **QuickTime Player** menu button (▾).

A Select a microphone for recording audio by clicking the microphone name.

B Determine whether mouse clicks are shown during recording by clicking here.

4 Click the **Record** button (●).

5 Click anywhere to begin recording.

C You can also click and drag over an area of the screen to record a specific section.

6 To finish recording, click the **Stop** button (■).

QuickTime loads your video.

D Preview your recording using the playback controls.

E Click the **Share** button (▣) to share your video via e-mail, Messages, AirDrop and social media.

7 Click **Close** (◉) to close the preview and save your recording.

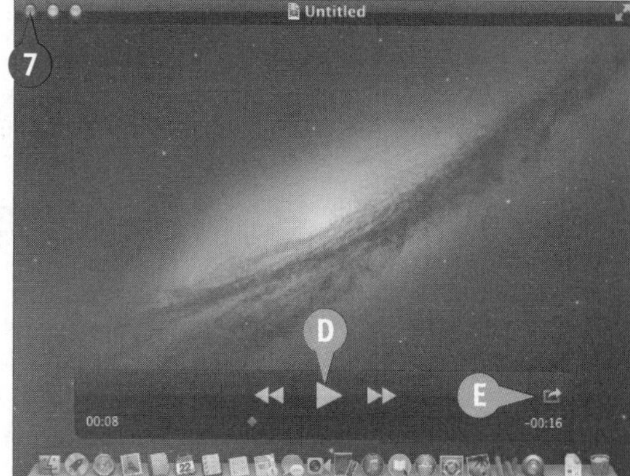

TIP

In what formats can I save my recording?

When you save your recording you can choose from a range of encoding options depending on how you want to use and share your video. First, you can set the resolution of the video to 480p, 720p, or 1080p, with the latter being the highest resolution and therefore the clearest, but it also produces the largest file size. You can also opt to store the video in an ideal format for iOS devices or for use on Macs and PCs.

Record a Video with QuickTime Player

QuickTime allows you to record a video of yourself to share with others using the camera built in to your Mac or with an external webcam. The video recording feature of QuickTime allows you to record both audio and video, which makes it useful for recording video messages to send to friends and family.

Record a Video with QuickTime Player

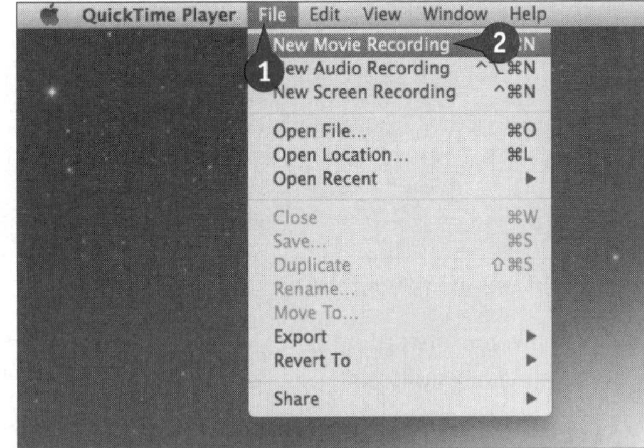

1 Click **File**.

2 Click **New Movie Recording**.

The QuickTime Movie Recording window appears.

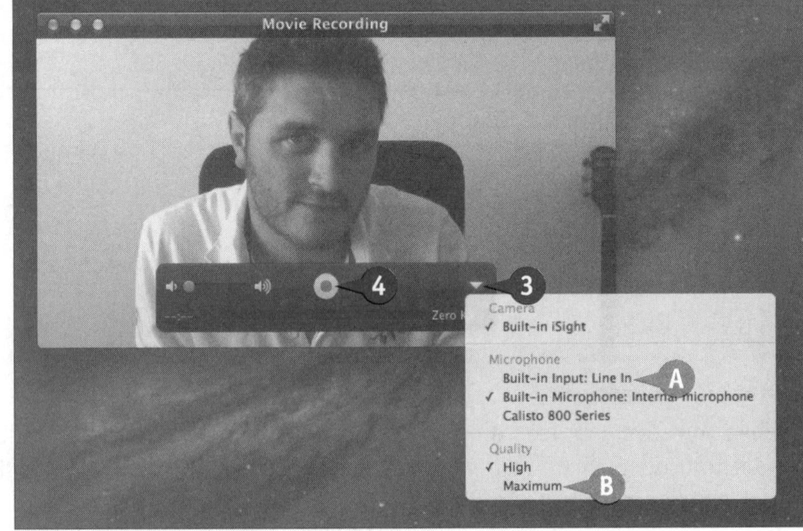

3 Click the **QuickTime Player** menu button (▼).

A Select a microphone for recording audio by clicking the microphone name.

B Select the quality of the video by clicking an option.

4 Click the **Record** button (●).

QuickTime begins recording video and audio.

5 Click the **Record** button again to stop recording.

QuickTime shows your recording.

C Preview your recording using the playback controls.

D Click the **Share** button (share icon) to share your video.

6 Click **Close** (close icon) to close the preview and save your recording.

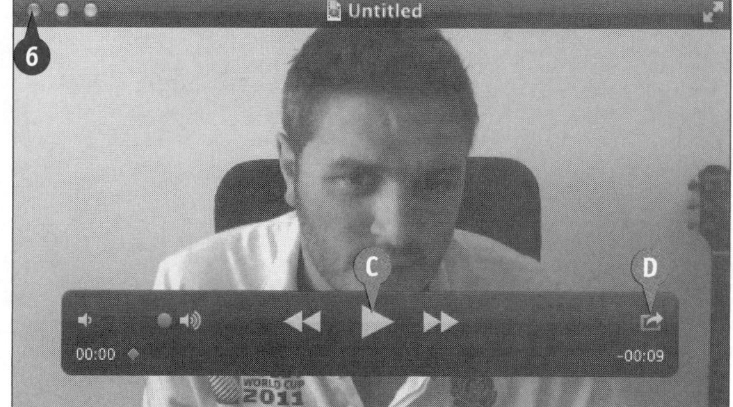

TIP

Where can I share my recorded video?

By clicking the **Share** button (share icon) you can send your recording via e-mail, as a message using the Messages app, or via AirDrop. You can also upload the video to Facebook, YouTube, Vimeo, or Flickr. Bear in mind that longer recordings with a larger file size may take a while to upload or be too large to upload to some services.

Record Audio with QuickTime Player

If you want to record an audio message as a reminder or to share with others, QuickTime offers an audio-only recording feature that allows you to do just that. You can choose an audio input from which to record, including your Mac's built-in microphone or an external microphone you have attached to your Mac.

Record Audio with QuickTime Player

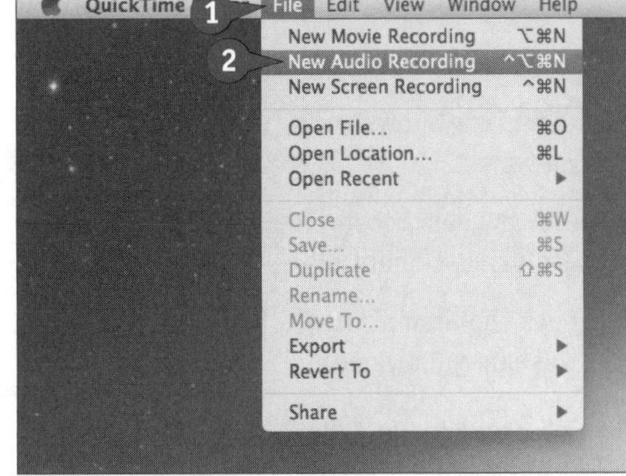

1. Click **File**.
2. Click **New Audio Recording**.

The QuickTime Audio Recording controls appear.

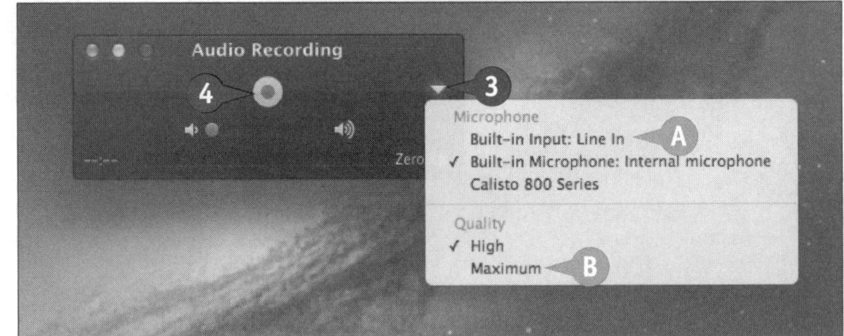

3. Click the **QuickTime Player** menu button (▾).

A. Select a microphone for recording audio by clicking the microphone name.

B. Select the quality of the audio by clicking an option.

4. Click the **Record** button (●).

QuickTime begins recording audio.

5. Click the **Record** button again to stop recording.

Note: The audio level indicators will move according to the volume of the sound you are recording.

QuickTime shows your recording.

C. Preview your recording using the playback controls.

6. Click **Close** (◉) to close the preview and save your recording.

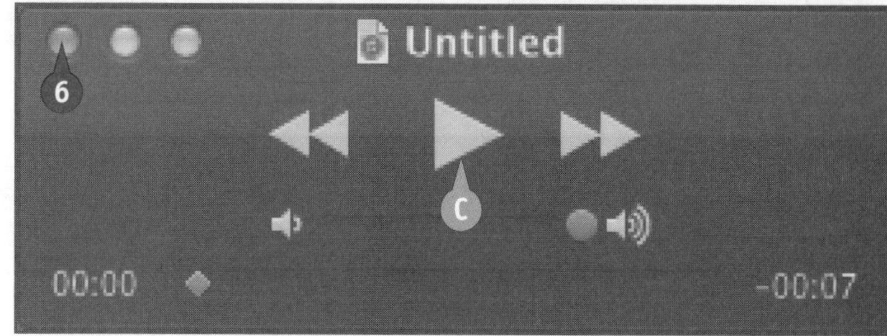

TIPS

Why can't I hear anything in my recording?
Check that you selected the correct microphone from the QuickTime menu and that you are close enough to it before you begin recording. While you record, look out for the audio level indicators that appear as sound is recorded. The wider the indicators appear, the louder the recording will be.

How can I see how long my recording is?
When you have finished recording, the length of the recording is shown to the right of the playback controls. As you play back the recording, the length of time reduces to show the playback time remaining.

Trim Video and Audio with QuickTime Player

Video or audio files opened in QuickTime Player can be edited using the Trim feature. This allows you to select a section of a file and remove the rest of it using handles to determine the area of the file you want to keep. This technique can be handy if you want to cut out periods of silence or noise at the beginning of a file or, alternatively, you can cut out a section and save it as a new file.

Trim Video and Audio with QuickTime Player

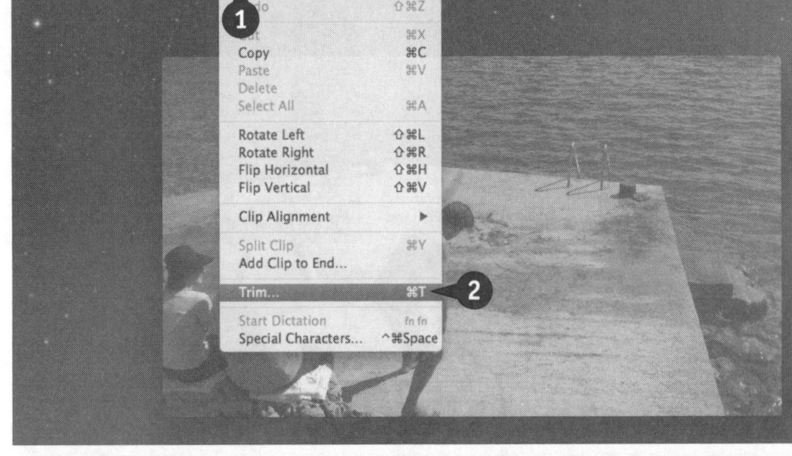

1. Click **Edit.**
2. Click **Trim.**

The Trim handles appear with a timeline.

3. Click and drag the left handle to the point where you want your video or audio file to start.

Note: You can view or listen to where your file will begin by clicking the **Play** button (▶) once you position the trim handle.

4. Click and drag the right handle to the point where you want your video or audio file to end.
5. Click **Trim.**

The file is trimmed to your selection.

Ⓐ Click the **Play** button (▶) to view your trimmed file.

6 Click **Close** (●).

The Save dialog appears.

Ⓑ Type a name for the new file in the Export As: field.

Ⓒ Click ⇕ and select a location on your Mac to save the file.

7 Click **Save**.

QuickTime saves your file.

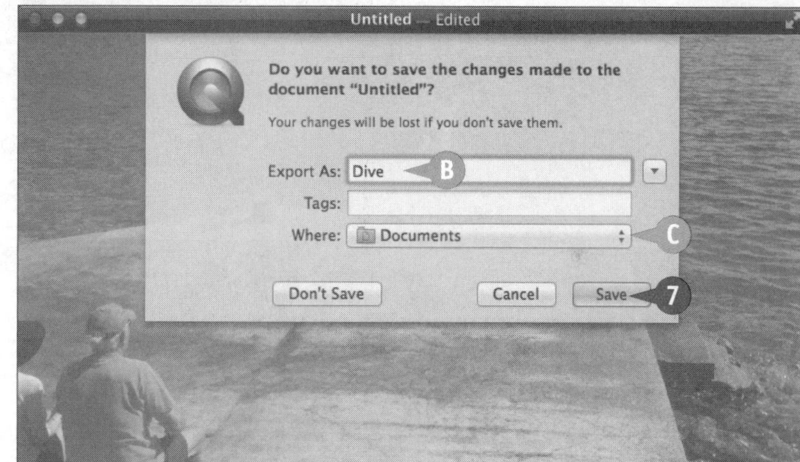

TIP

I made a mistake. Can I undo the trim I made?

Yes. You can undo the selection you made using the Trim tool by clicking **Edit** and then **Undo Trim**. If you want to make adjustments to the trim you made, click **Edit** and then click **Trim**. The Trim interface reappears and allows you to adjust the trim handles to new positions as required.

Open and Close iMovie

The iLife suite installed on your Mac includes iMovie, which enables you to import video from a digital camcorder or video file and use that footage to create your own movies. You do this by first creating a project that holds your video clips, transitions, titles, and other elements of your movie.

Open and Close iMovie

Open iMovie

1. In the Dock, click the **iMovie** icon (☆).

iMovie appears.

Close iMovie

1. Click **iMovie**.

2. Click **Quit iMovie**.

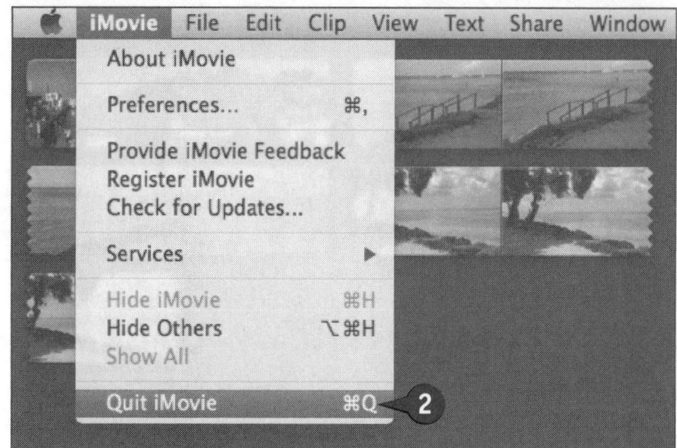

TIP

Are there other methods I can use to open iMovie?

If you have removed the iMovie icon ( ) from the Dock, there are a couple of other quick methods you can use to start iMovie. If you have used iMovie recently, click the Apple icon ( ), click **Recent Items**, and then click **iMovie**. You can also click **Spotlight** ( ), type **iMovie**, and then click **iMovie** in the search results.

Create a New Movie Project

When you first start iMovie, the program creates a new project for you automatically. Follow the steps in this section to create subsequent projects. Note that iMovie is also available from the App Store.

Create a New Movie Project

1. In the Dock, click the **iMovie** icon (![]).

The iMovie window appears.

2. Click **File**.
3. Click **New Project**.

Note: You can also press ⌘ + N.

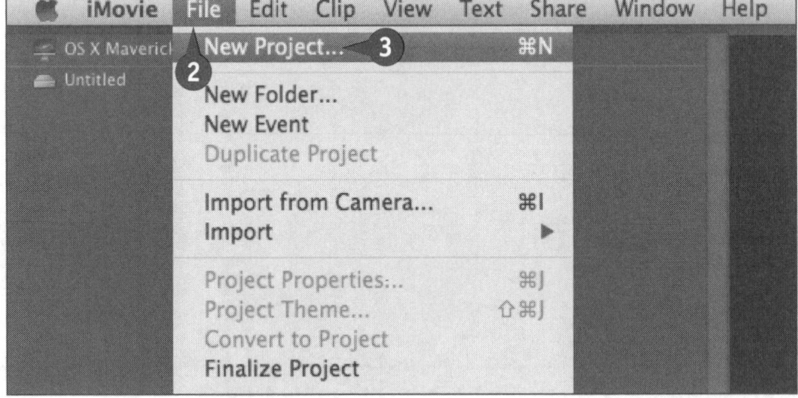

The New Project dialog appears.

4 In the Name text box, type a name for your project.

5 Click the **Aspect Ratio** ⬍ and then click the ratio you prefer: Widescreen (16:9) or Standard (4:3).

6 To apply a theme to your project, click the one you want in the Project Themes list.

Note: See the first tip in this section to learn more about themes.

7 To automatically insert transitions between all your clips, select the **Automatically add** check box (☐ changes to ☑) and then click ⬍ to choose the type of transition.

If you chose a theme in step 6, the check box changes to **Automatically add transition and titles** by default.

8 Click **Create**.

iMovie creates your new project.

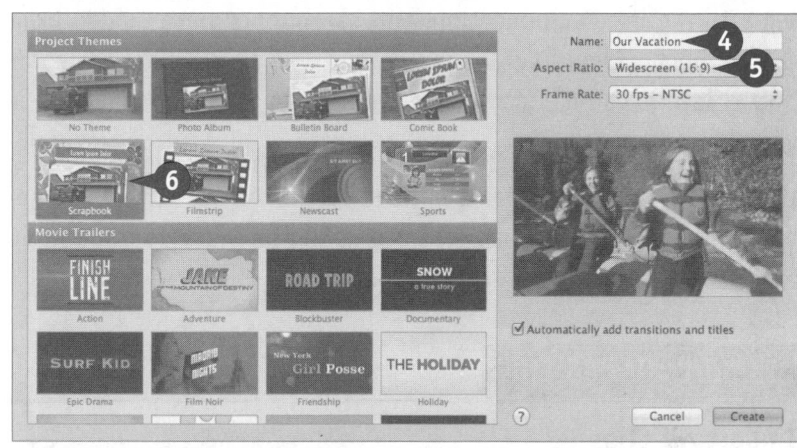

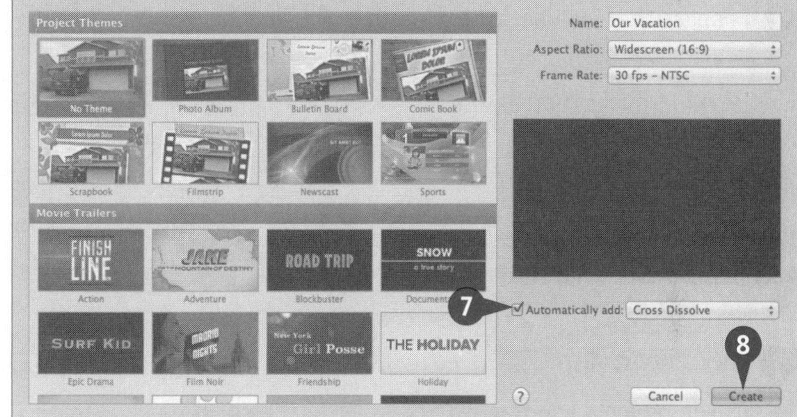

TIPS

What are the iMovie themes?
iMovie offers several themes that you can apply to a project. Each theme comes with its own set of titles and transitions that are added automatically, saving you a lot of work. There are seven themes in all, including Photo Album, Bulletin Board, Comic Book, and Scrapbook. If one of them is suitable for your project, applying it cuts down on your production time.

How do I switch from one project to another?
You use the Project Library, which is a list of your movie projects. To display it, click **Window** and then click **Show Project Library**. You can also click the **Project Library** button in the top-left corner of the iMovie window. In the Project Library, double-click the project you want to work with.

Import a Video File

With the iMovie application, you can import digital video from a camera for use in your movie project. If you have video content on a USB digital camcorder or smartphone (such as an iPhone 3GS or later), you can connect the device to your Mac and then import some or all of the video to your iMovie project.

If your Mac or monitor has a built-in iSight or FaceTime HD camera, you can also use iMovie to import live images from that camera to use as digital video footage in your movie project.

Import a Video File

Import All Clips

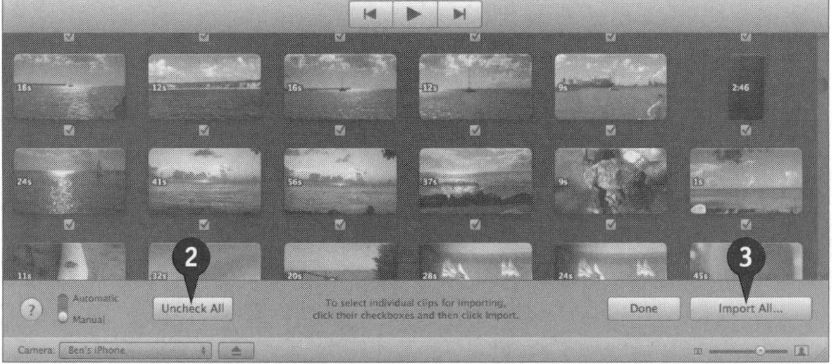

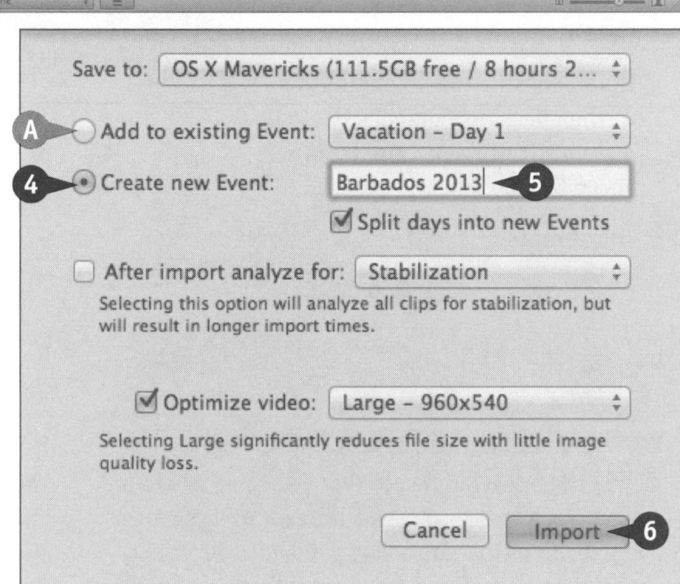

1. Connect the video device to your Mac.

   iMovie displays its Import From dialog.

2. Click **Check All.**

Note: The **Check All** button becomes **Uncheck All** once clicked.

3. Click **Import All.**

   iMovie prompts you to create a new event.

4. Click **Create new Event** (◯ changes to ◉).

5. Use the Create new Event text box to type a name for the import event.

A. If you want to add the video to an existing event, click **Add to existing Event** (◯ changes to ◉) and then choose the event from the pop-up menu.

6. Click **Import.**

Import Selected Clips

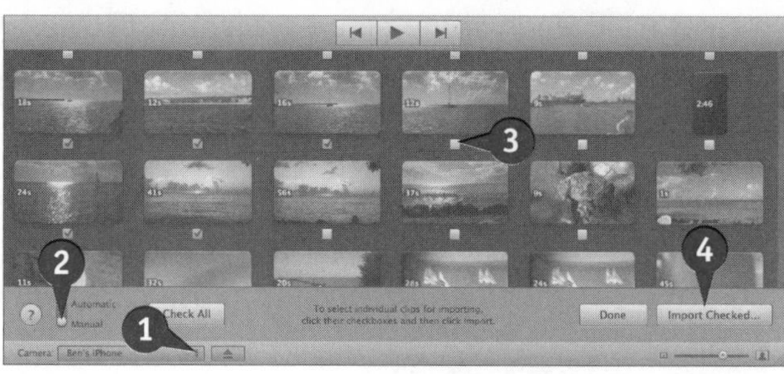

1. Connect the video device to your Mac and place it in playback mode, if necessary.

   iMovie displays its Import From dialog.

2. Click **Manual.**
3. Deselect the check box under each clip you do not want to import (☑ changes to ☐).
4. Click **Import Checked**.

   iMovie prompts you to create a new event.

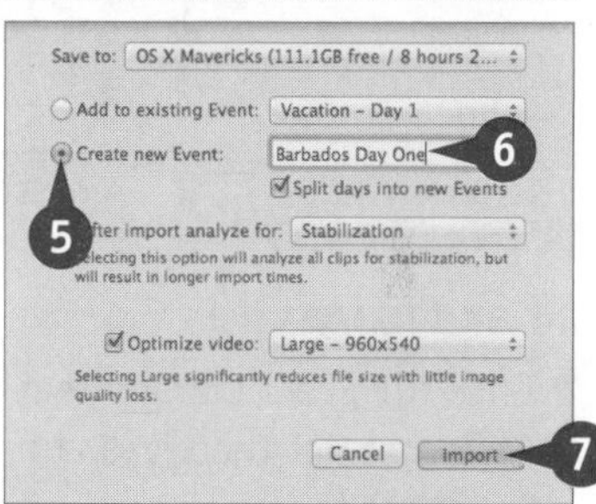

5. Click **Create new Event** (○ changes to ◉).
6. Use the Create new Event text box to type a name for the import event.
7. Click **Import**.

   iMovie begins importing the clips.

8. Click **OK.**
9. Click **Done.**

TIP

How do I import digital video from my iSight or FaceTime HD camera?

Click **File**, then **Import From Camera**. Select **Built-in iSight** or **FaceTime HD** from the Camera menu on the Import screen. You can now click **Capture** and record video directly into iMovie. When you finish recording, click **Done** to import the footage you recorded.

Add Video Clips to Your Project

To create and work with a movie project in iMovie, you must first add some video clips to that project. A *video clip* is a segment of digital video. You begin building your movie by adding one or more video clips to your project.

When you import digital video, as described in the "Import a Video File," iMovie automatically breaks up the video into separate clips, with each clip being the footage shot during a single recording session. You can then decide which of those clips you want to add to your project, or you can add only part of a clip.

Add Video Clips to Your Project

Add an Entire Clip

1. Click the Event Library item that contains the video clip you want to add.
2. Press and hold Option and click the clip.

A iMovie selects the entire clip.

3. Click and drag the selected clip and drop it in your project at the spot where you want the clip to appear.

B iMovie adds the entire video clip to the project.

C iMovie adds an orange bar to the bottom of the original clip to indicate that it has been added to the project.

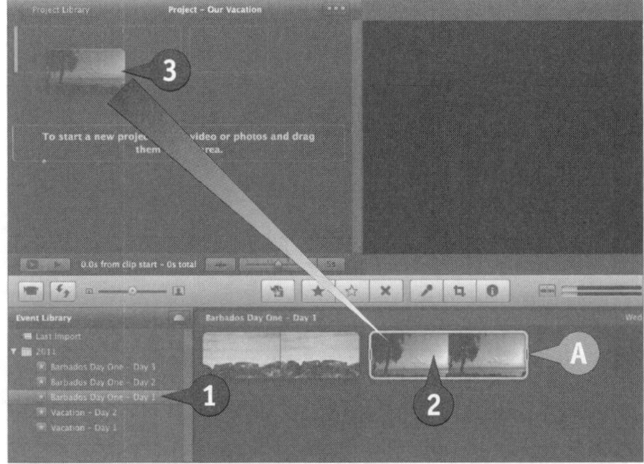

Add a Partial Clip

1. Click the Event Library item that contains the video clip you want to add.
2. Click the clip at the point where you want the selection to begin.
3. Click and drag the right edge of the selection box to the point where you want the selection to end.
4. Click and drag the selected clip and drop it in your project at the spot where you want the clip to appear.

- D iMovie adds the selected portion of the video clip to the project.
- E iMovie adds an orange bar to the bottom of the original clip to indicate that it has been added to a project.
- F If you opted to have transitions added automatically, they are included in the clips you add.

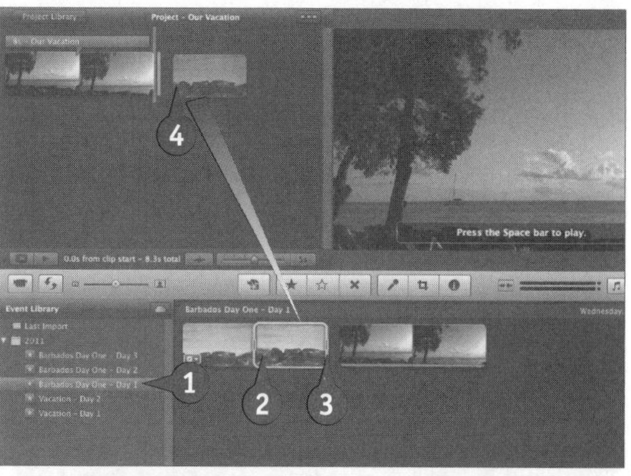

TIPS

Is it possible to play a clip before I add it?
Yes. The easiest way to do this is to click the clip at the point where you want the playback to start and then press Spacebar. iMovie plays the clip in the Viewer in the top-right corner of the window. Press Spacebar again to stop the playback.

I added a clip in the wrong place. Can I move it?
Yes. In your project, click the added clip to select it. Use your mouse to click and drag the clip and then drop the clip in the correct location within the project. If you want to delete the clip from the project, click it, click **Edit**, and then click **Delete Entire Clip** (or press Option + Delete).

Trim a Clip

If you have a video clip that is too long or contains footage you do not need, you can shorten the clip or remove the extra footage. Removing parts of a video clip is called *trimming* the clip.

Trimming a clip is particularly useful if you recorded extra, unneeded footage before and after the action you were trying to capture. By trimming this unneeded footage, your movie will include only the scenes you really require.

Trim a Clip

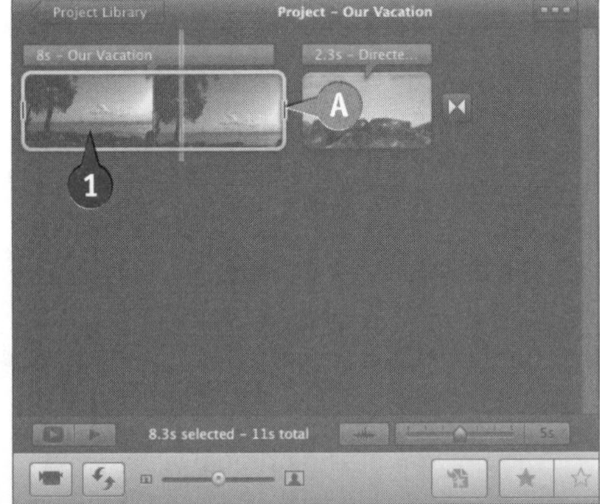

1. In your project, click the clip you want to trim.

A. iMovie selects the entire clip.

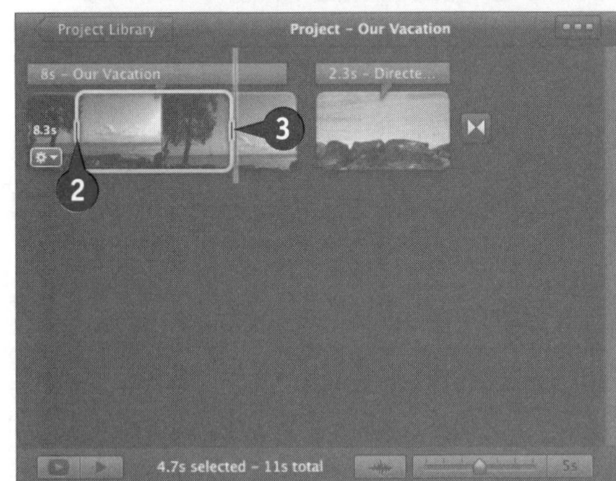

2. Use your mouse to click and drag the left edge of the selection box to the starting position of the part of the clip you want to keep.

3. Use your mouse to click and drag the right edge of the selection box to the ending position of the part of the clip you want to keep.

4 Click **Clip**.

5 Click **Trim to Selection**.

Note: You can also press ⌘ + B.

B iMovie trims the clip.

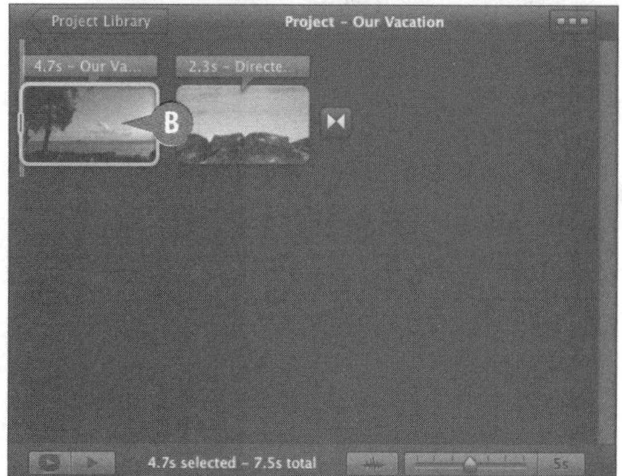

TIP

Is it possible to trim a certain number of frames from a clip?

Yes. iMovie enables you to trim one frame at a time from either the beginning or the end of the clip. Follow these steps:

1 In your project, click the clip you want to trim.

2 Click **Clip**.

3 Click **Trim Clip End**.

4 Select the trim direction by clicking **Move Left** or **Move Right**.

5 Repeat step **4** until you reach the number of frames that you want to trim.

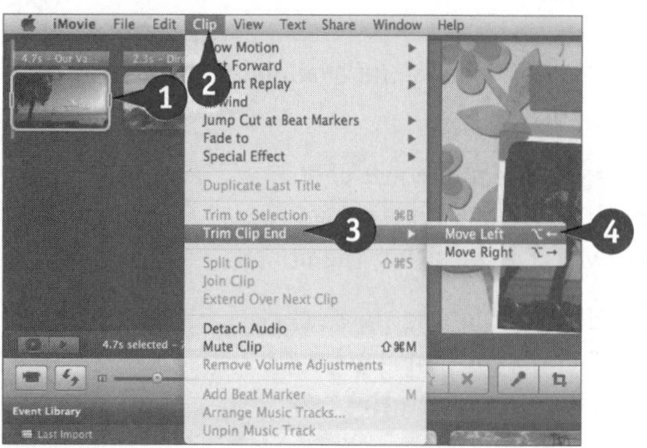

Add a Transition Between Clips

You can use the iMovie application to enhance the visual appeal of your digital movie by inserting transitions between some or all of the project's video clips. By default, iMovie jumps immediately from the end of one clip to the beginning of the next clip, a transition called a *jump cut*. You can add more visual interest to your movie by adding a transition between the two clips.

iMovie offers 24 transitions, including various fades, wipes, and dissolves. More transitions are available if you apply a theme to your iMovie project.

Add a Transition Between Clips

1 Click the **Transitions Browser** button (⧓).

Note: You can also press ⌘ + 4.

A iMovie displays the available transitions.

Note: To see a preview of a transition, position your mouse over the transition thumbnail.

2 Use your mouse to click and drag a transition and drop it between the two clips.

B iMovie adds an icon for the transition between the two clips.

3 Position your mouse over the beginning of the transition and move the to the right.

C iMovie displays a preview of the transition.

TIP

Can I change the duration of the transition?

Yes. The default length is half a second, but you can increase or decrease the duration by clicking the transition and selecting **Transition Adjustments** from the menu that appears. When the Inspector pane appears you can adjust the duration of the transition by adding a new value to the Duration field. You can also select the check box next to the field (☐ changes to ☑) to apply this change to all transitions in your project.

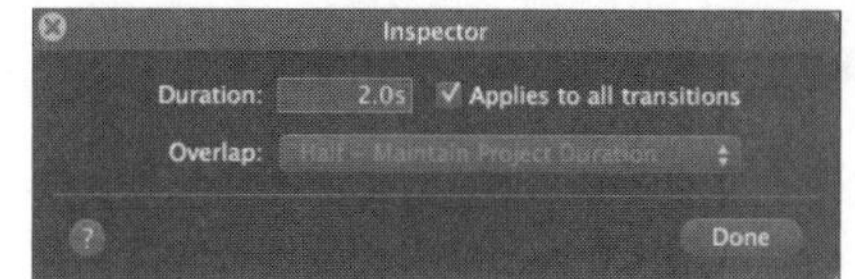

Add a Photo

You can use the iMovie application to enhance your movie projects with still photos. Although most movie projects consist of several video clips, you can also add a photo to your project. By default, iMovie displays the photo for 4 seconds.

You can also specify how the photo fits in the movie frame: You can adjust the size of the photo to fit the frame, you can crop the photo, or you can apply a Ken Burns effect to animate the static photo, which automatically pans and zooms the photo.

Add a Photo

1. Click the **Photos Browser** button (📷).

Note: You can also press ⌘ + 2.

A. iMovie displays the available photos.

2. Click the event or album that contains the photo you want to add.
3. Click and drag the photo and drop it inside your project.

B. iMovie adds the photo to the movie.

4. Click the photo.
5. Double-click the **Crop** button (⊡).

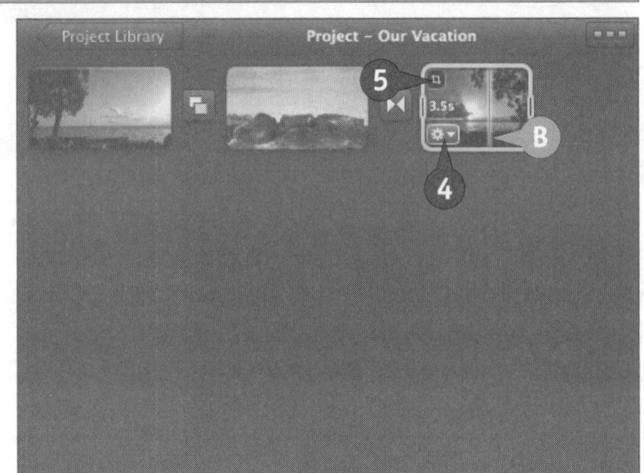

iMovie displays the cropping options for the photo.

6 Click **Ken Burns**.

C You can click **Fit** to have iMovie adjust the size of the photo to fit the movie frame.

D You can click **Crop** and then click and drag the cropping rectangle to specify how much of the photo you want to appear in the movie frame.

7 Click and drag the green rectangle to set the start point of the Ken Burns animation.

8 Click and drag the red rectangle to set the end point of the Ken Burns animation.

Note: Click and drag the corners and edges of the rectangle to change the size; click and drag the interior of the rectangles to change the position.

E The arrow shows the direction of motion.

9 Click **Done**.

TIP

Can I change the length of time that the photo appears in the movie?

Yes. The default length is 4 seconds, but you can increase or decrease the duration by double clicking the photo in the project and changing the value in the Duration field on the Inspector pane that appears.

Add a Music Track

Using the iMovie application, you can enhance the audio component of your movie by adding one or more songs that play in the background. With iMovie you can also add sound effects and other audio files that you feel would enhance your project's audio track.

To get the best audio experience, you can adjust various sound properties. For example, you can adjust the volume of the music clip or the volume of the video clip. You can also use iMovie to adjust the time it takes for the song clip to fade in and fade out.

Add a Music Track

1. Click the **Music and Sound Effect Browser** button (♫).

Note: You can also press ⌘ + 1.

- A iMovie displays the available audio files.

2. Click the folder, category, or playlist that contains the track you want to add.
3. Use your mouse (↖) to click and drag the song and drop it on a video clip.

- B iMovie adds the song to the movie.

Note: iMovie treats the song like a clip, which means you can trim the song as needed, as described in the section "Trim a Clip."

4. Double-click the music clip.

iMovie displays the Inspector.

5 Click the **Audio** tab.

6 Use the Volume slider to adjust the volume of the music clip.

7 If you want to reduce the video clip volume, select the **Ducking** check box (☐ changes to ☑) and then click and drag the slider.

8 To adjust the fade-in time, select the **Fade In: Manual** check box (☐ changes to ☑) and then click and drag the slider.

9 To adjust the fade-out time, select the **Fade Out: Manual** check box (☐ changes to ☑) and then click and drag the slider.

10 Click **Done**.

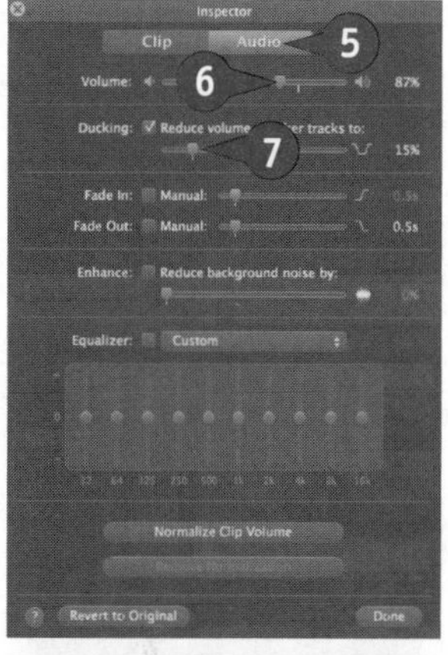

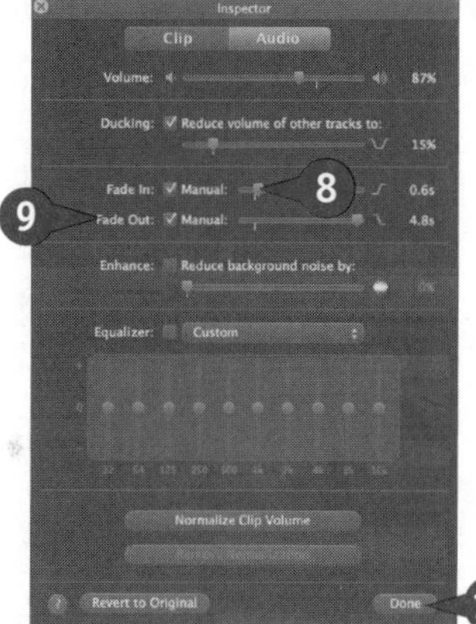

TIP

When I add a video clip before the music clip, the music does not play with the new video clip. How can I work around this?

You need to add your song as a background track instead of a clip.

1 Click the **Music and Sound Effect Browser** button (♫).

2 Click and drag a song onto the project background, not on a clip or between two clips.

A The background turns green when the song is positioned correctly.

Record a Voiceover

You can use the iMovie application to augment the audio portion of your movie with a voiceover. A *voiceover* is a voice recording that you make using audio equipment attached to your Mac.

A voiceover is useful for explaining a video clip, introducing the movie, or giving the viewer background information about the movie. To record a voiceover, your Mac must have either a built-in microphone, such as the one that comes with the iSight or FaceTime HD camera, or an external microphone connected via an audio jack, USB port, or Bluetooth.

Record a Voiceover

1. Click the **Voiceover** button (🎤).

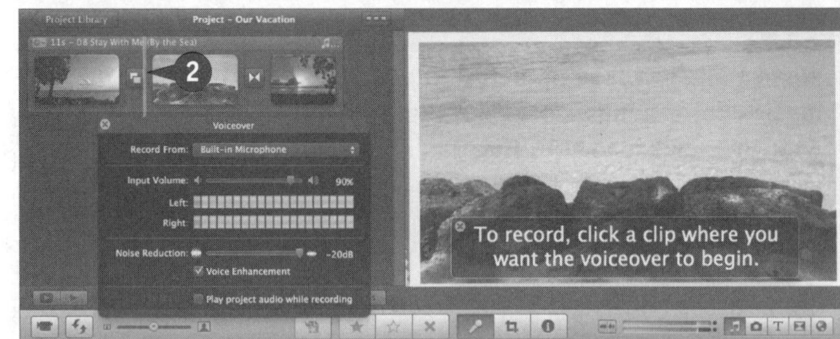

The Voiceover dialog appears.

2. Click the spot in the movie at which you want the voiceover to begin.

iMovie counts down and then begins the recording.

3. Speak your voiceover text into the microphone.

A. The progress of the recording appears here.

4. When you finish, click **Recording**.

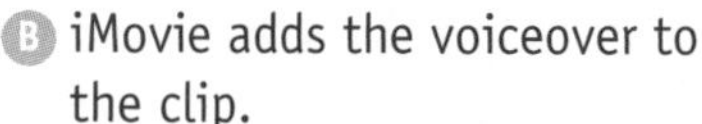

B. iMovie adds the voiceover to the clip.

You can double-click the voiceover to adjust the audio, as described in the section "Add a Music Track."

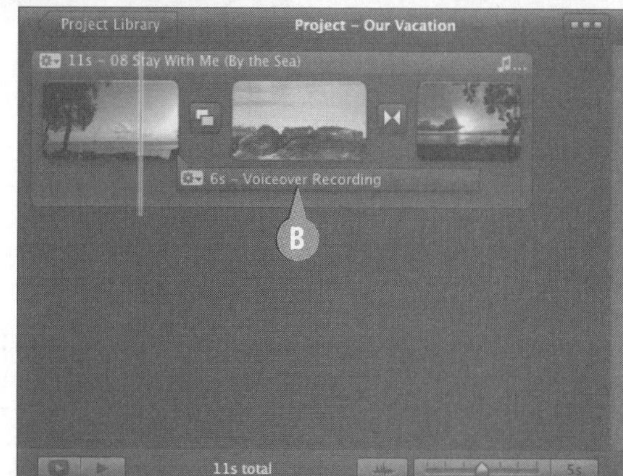

TIP

Is there a way to tell if my voice is too loud or too soft?

Yes, you can use the controls in the Voiceover dialog to check your voice level by talking into the microphone and then watching the Left and Right volume meters. Use the Input Volume slider to adjust the voice level up or down, as needed.

Add Titles and Credits

You can use the iMovie application to enhance your movie project with titles and scrolling credits. You can get your movie off to a proper start by adding a title and a subtitle at or near the beginning of the movie. iMovie offers a number of title styles from which you can choose, and you can also change the title font.

You can also enhance your movie with *scrolling credits*. This is a special type of title that you place at the end of the movie and that scrolls the names of the people responsible for the project.

Add Titles and Credits

1 Click the **Titles Browser** button (T).

A iMovie displays the available title types.

2 Use your mouse to click and drag a title and drop it where you want the titles to appear.

Note: To see just the titles, drop the title thumbnail at the beginning of the movie or between two clips. To superimpose the titles on a video clip, drop the title thumbnail on the clip.

B If you want to add credits, click and drag one of the **Credits** thumbnails and drop it at the end of the movie.

C iMovie previews the clip for the title.

3 Replace this text with the movie title.

4 Click to choose a background style.

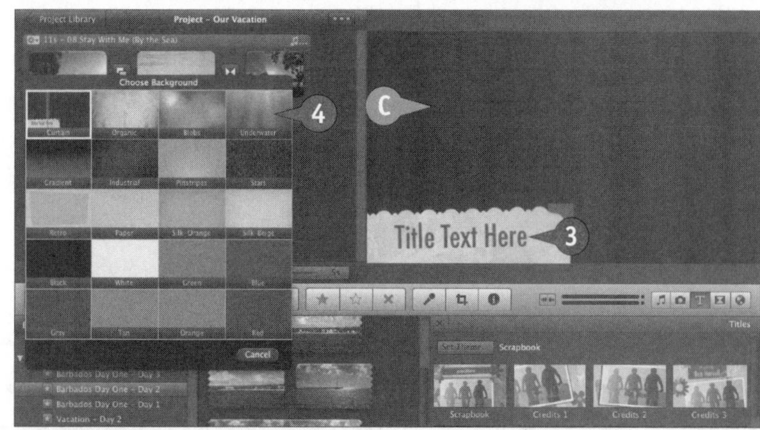

5 Click **Done**.

The titles or credits are added to your project.

Note: iMovie treats the title like a clip, which means you can lengthen or shorten the title duration by clicking and dragging the beginning or end, as described in the section "Trim a Clip."

TIP

How do I change the font of the titles?

The Text menu offers several font-related commands, including Bold, Italic, Bigger, and Smaller. You can also click the **Show Fonts** command to display the Choose Font dialog. If you do not see the Choose Font dialog shown here, you can switch to iMovie's predefined fonts by clicking **iMovie Font Panel**. You can then click a typeface, font color, and type size; click **Done** to close the dialog.

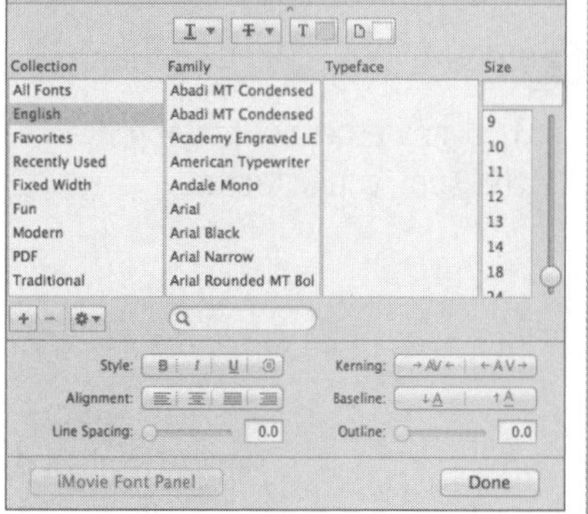

Play the Movie

The iMovie application offers the Viewer pane, which you can use to play your movie. While you build your iMovie project, it is a good idea to occasionally play some or all of the movie to check your progress. For example, you can play the entire movie to make sure the video and audio are working properly and are synchronized correctly. You can also play parts of the movie to ensure that your transitions appear when you want them to.

Play the Movie

Play from the Beginning

1. Click **View**.
2. Click **Play from Beginning**.

Note: You can also press \ or click the **Play Project from beginning** button (▶).

The movie plays from the beginning.

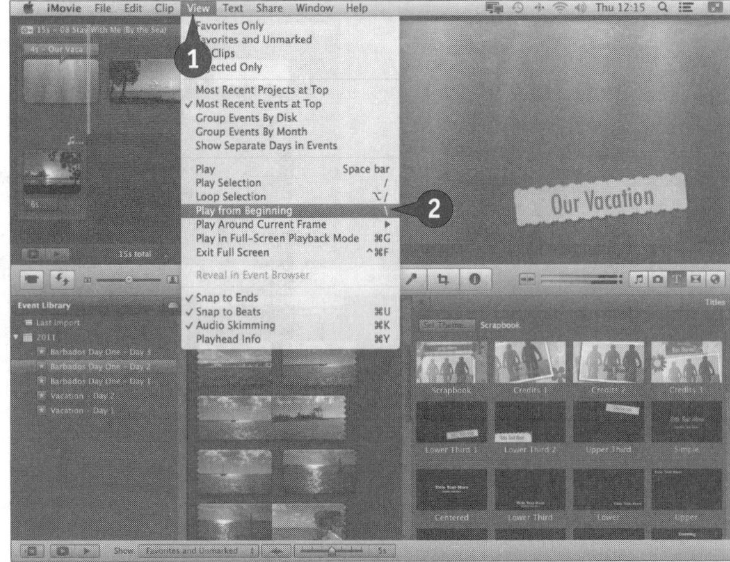

Play from a Specific Location

1. Position the mouse over the spot where you want to start playing the movie.
2. Press Spacebar.

The movie begins playing at the spot you selected.

Play a Selection

1. Select the video clips you want to play.

Note: See the first tip in this section to learn how to select multiple video clips.

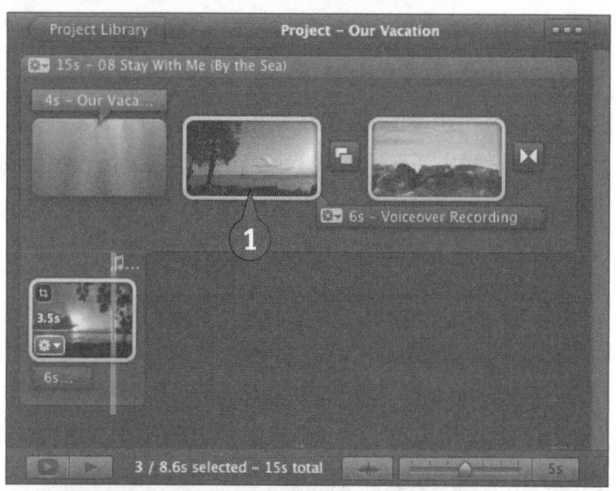

2. Click **View**.
3. Click **Play Selection**.

Note: You can also press /.

iMovie plays the clips you selected.

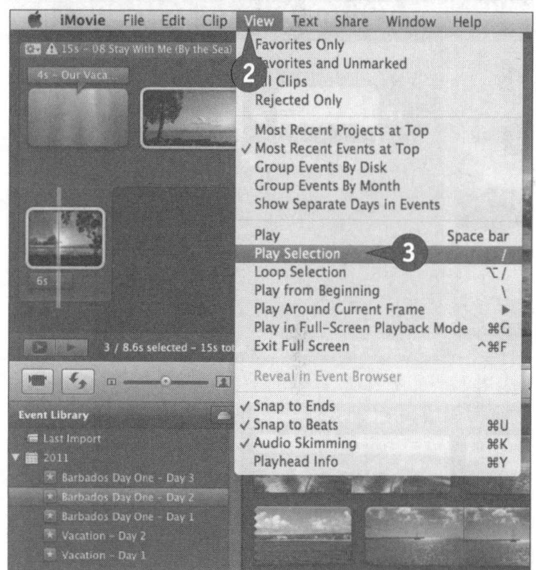

TIPS

How do I select multiple video clips?

To select multiple video clips, press and hold ⌘ and then click anywhere inside each clip you want to select. If you select a clip by accident, ⌘+click it again to deselect it. If you want to skip just a few clips, first press ⌘+A to select all the clips, then press and hold ⌘ and click the clips you do not want in the selection.

Can I enlarge the size of the playback pane?

Yes, you can play your movie in full-screen mode. To do this, click **View** and then click **Play in Full-Screen Playback Mode**. You can also press ⌘+G or click the **Play Project full screen** button ( ).

Publish Your Movie to YouTube

When your movie project is complete, you can send it to YouTube for viewing on the web. To publish your movie to YouTube, you must have a YouTube account, available from www.youtube.com. You must also know your YouTube username, which you can see by clicking your account icon on YouTube and then clicking **Settings**. Before you can publish your movie, you must select a YouTube category, such as Entertainment or Pets and Animals, provide a title and description, and type at least one tag, which is a word or short phrase that describes some aspect of the movie's content. It's worth noting that there are limits to the size and length of a video you upload. YouTube will inform you if your video is over this limit when you begin uploading.

Publish Your Movie to YouTube

1. Click **Share**.
2. Click **YouTube.**

3. Click **Add**.

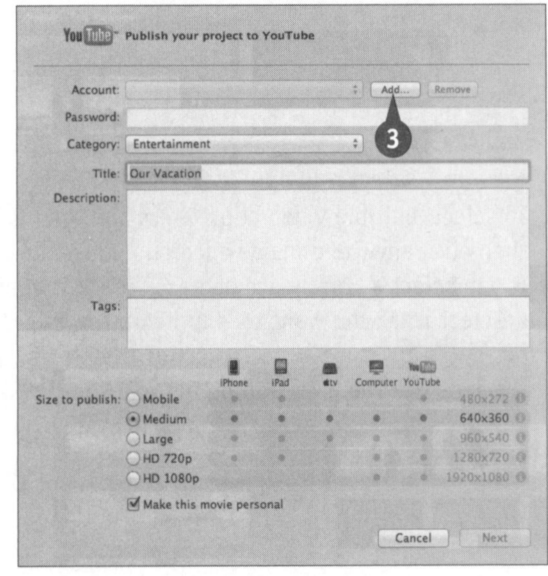

iMovie prompts you for your YouTube username.

4 Type your username.

5 Click **Done** (not shown).

6 Type your YouTube password.

7 Select a category.

8 Type a title.

9 Type a description.

10 Type one or more tags for the video.

11 If you do not want to allow anyone to view the movie, deselect the **Make this movie personal** check box (☑ changes to ☐).

12 Select a size for the uploaded movie.

13 Click **Next**.

iMovie displays the YouTube terms of service.

14 Click **Publish**.

iMovie prepares the movie and then publishes it to YouTube.

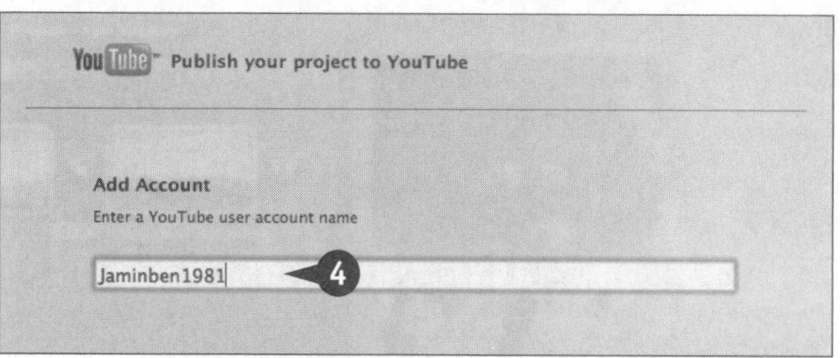

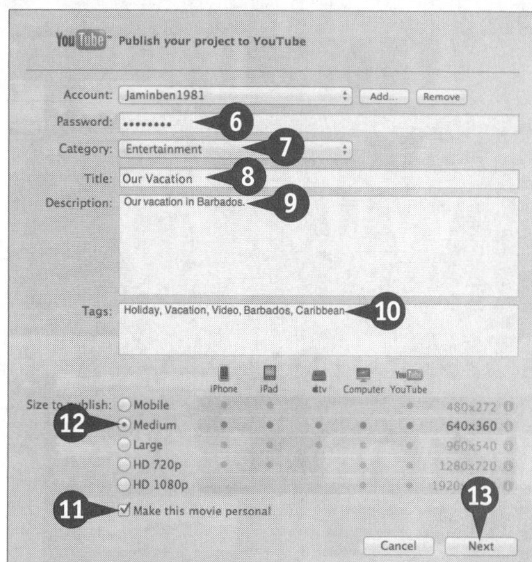

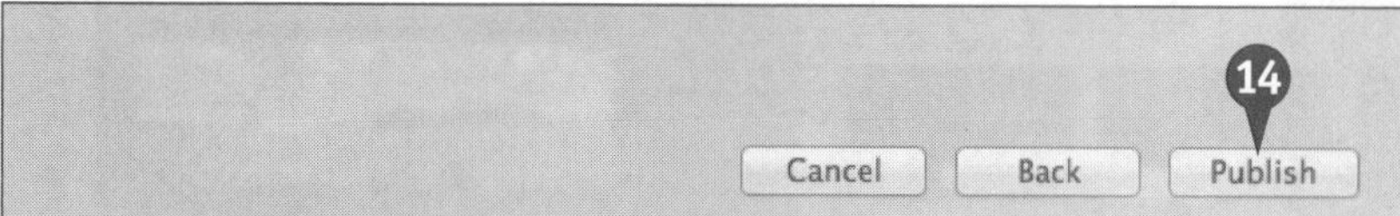

TIPS

How do I publish my movie to Facebook?
If you have a Facebook account, click **Share** and then click **Facebook**. Click **Add**, type your Facebook e-mail address, and then click **Done**. Type your Facebook password. Use the **Viewable by** pop-up to choose who can see the video, such as Only Friends or Everyone. Type a title and description, select a size, click **Next**, and then click **Publish**.

How do I view my movie outside of iMovie?
Beyond viewing it on YouTube or Facebook, you need to export the movie to a digital video file. Click **Share** and then click **Export Movie** (or press ⌘+E). Type a title for the movie, and then click a **Size to Export** option, such as Large or HD 720p (○ changes to ◉). Click **Export**.

CHAPTER 12

Viewing and Editing Documents with Preview

The Preview application comes preinstalled on your Mac and allows you to view and edit a number of file types including images and PDFs. Preview also allows you to annotate documents, highlight them, and export them in different formats.

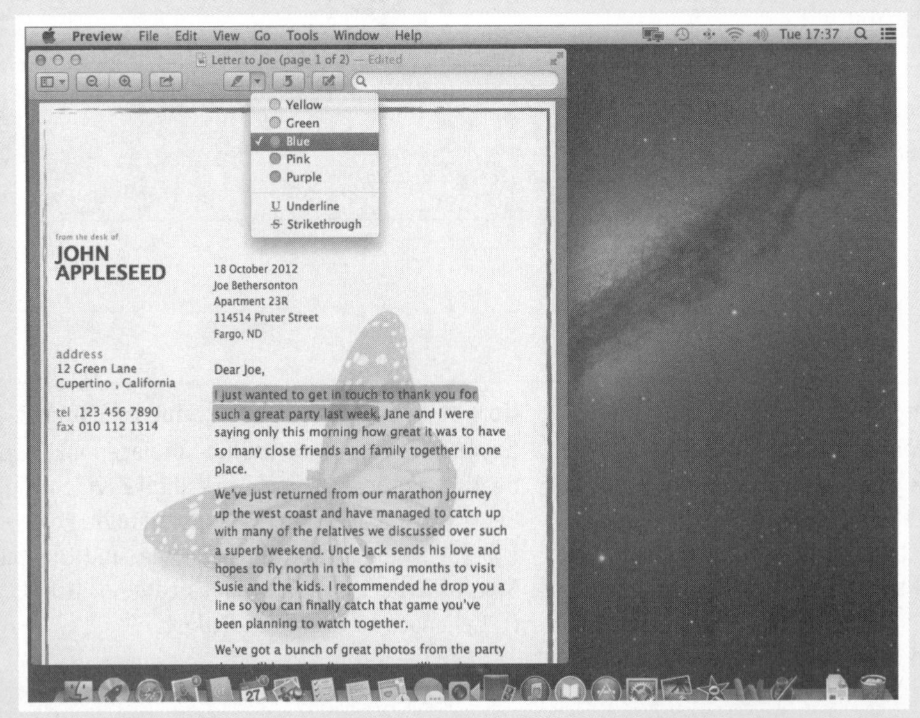

Open and Close Preview

The Preview application appears in the Dock in OS X, while the application can also be found in the Applications folder or in Launchpad. Preview can be launched by dragging a compatible file onto its app icon in the Dock, by double-clicking a compatible file in the Finder, by double-clicking the **Preview** icon in the Applications folder or in Spotlight, or by clicking its icon in the Dock.

Open and Close Preview

Open Preview

1. In the Dock, click the **Preview** icon (▣).

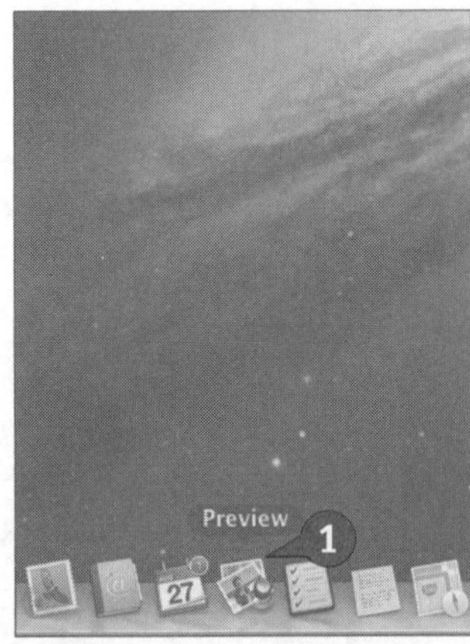

The Preview file browser opens.

Close Preview

1 Click **Preview**.

2 Click **Quit Preview**.

Preview closes.

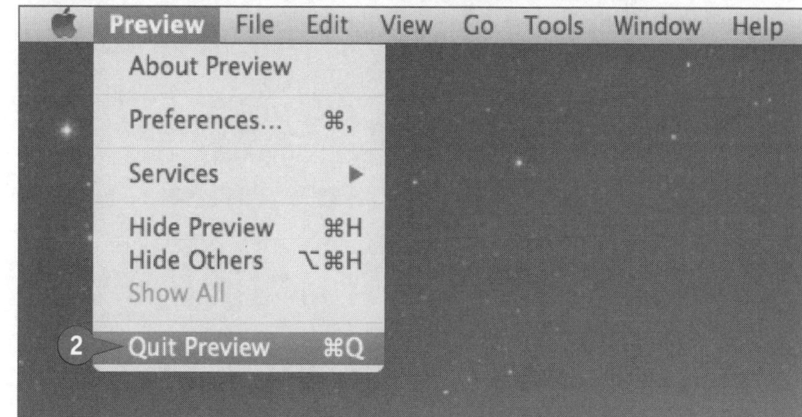

TIP

Are there other methods I can use to open and close Preview?

Yes. If you have hidden the Dock (as described in Chapter 13) or removed the Preview icon from the Dock, you can click **Spotlight** (🔍) and type **Preview**. You can then click **Preview** in the search results. Alternatively, you can double-click the **Preview** icon in the Applications folder or click its icon in Launchpad.

Open a Document in Preview

You can open a document in Preview in a number of ways, including launching the application by dragging a compatible document onto the Preview icon in the Dock or using the file browser that appears when you launch Preview. Alternatively, you can use the Open command to search for a file to open in Preview. Preview opens a wide range of image formats including JPEG and PNG files plus PDF files.

Open a Document in Preview

Using the File Browser

1 In the Dock, click the **Preview** icon (▣).

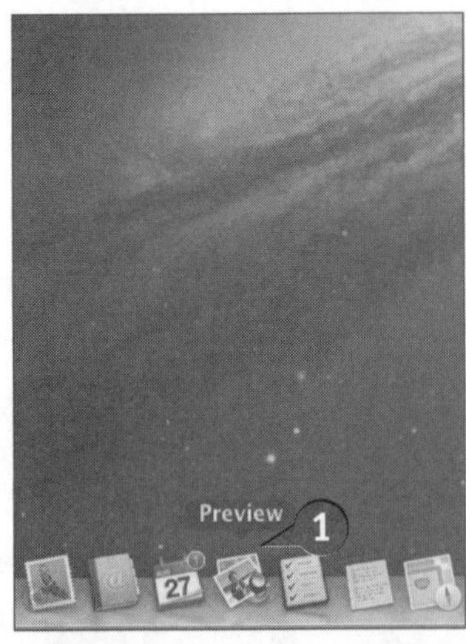

The Preview file browser appears.

A Click **iCloud** to view Preview documents stored in iCloud.

B Click **On My Mac** to locate documents stored on your Mac.

2 Click the file you want to open.

3 Click **Open**.

The file opens in Preview.

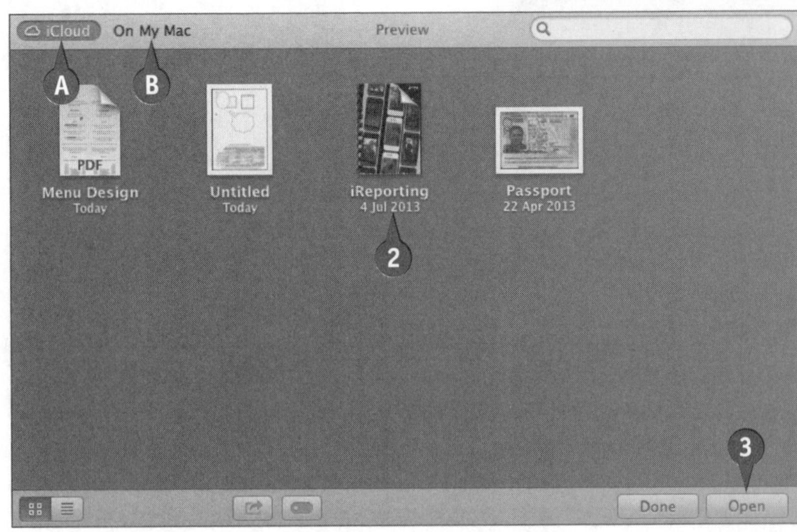

Open a File with Drag and Drop

1. Locate the file you want to open in Preview in the Finder.
2. Click and drag the file onto the Preview icon () in the Dock.

The file opens in Preview.

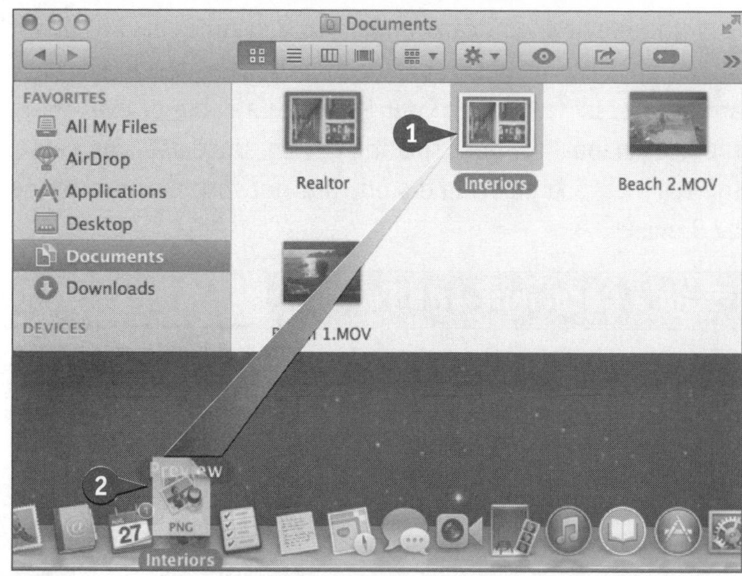

Using the Open Command

1. Click **File**.
2. Click **Open**.

- C Click **iCloud** to view Preview documents stored in iCloud.
- D Click **On My Mac** to browse files stored on your Mac.

3. Click the file you want to open.
4. Click **Open**.

The file opens in Preview.

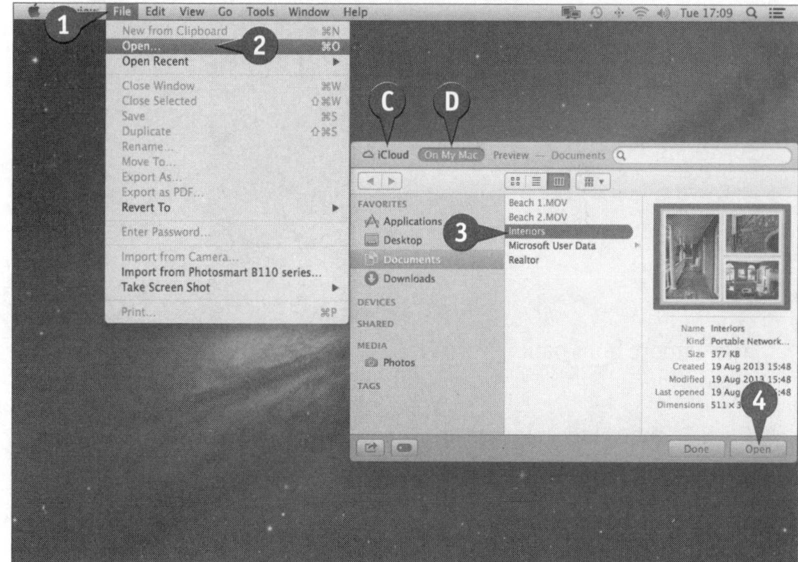

TIP

Is there another way to launch a file in Preview?

Yes. If Preview is set as the application to launch a specific file type, such as a PDF or PNG, by default in OS X, you can locate the file in the Finder and double-click it to launch Preview and open the file. See Chapter 13 to learn how to set default apps for specific file types.

Scan a Document with Preview

Using Preview, you can connect to a scanner or printer with a scanning function and import copies of physical images or documents directly into Preview. You first need to connect your computer and printer or scanner to your Mac with a cable or over Wi-Fi. This information is normally found in the user manual for your specific device. Once set, you can use the Import From command to access the scanner. Shared scanners on your network that are connected to other computers are not found by Preview.

Scan a Document with Preview

1. Click **File**.
2. Click **Import from *XYZ*** (where *XYZ* is the name of your scanner or printer).

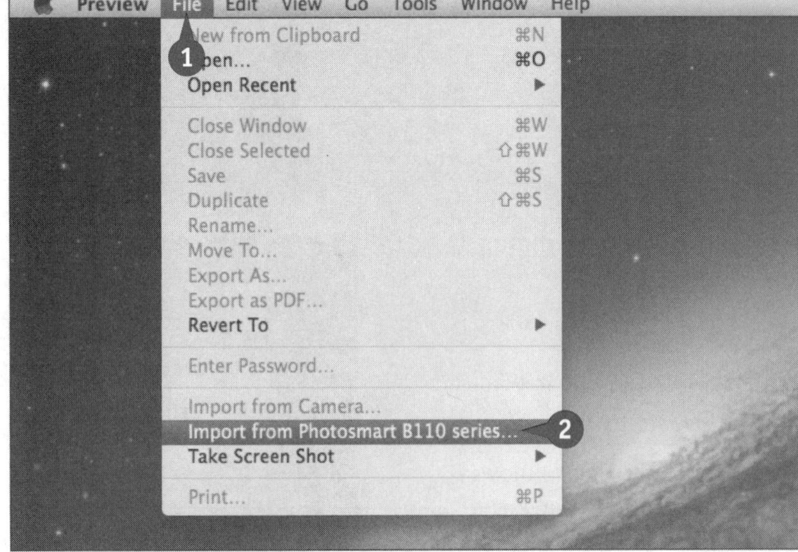

The Import from pane appears.

A. Click ⬍ and select paper size and image detection options.

3. Place your document or image in the scanner and click **Scan**.

The scanner warms up and scans your document.

B The scanned image opens in Preview.

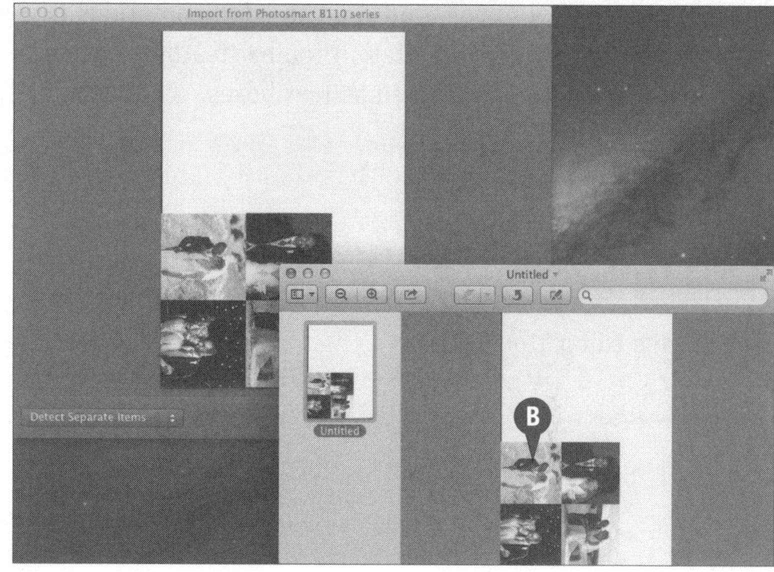

TIPS

What do the Detect Separate Items and Detect Enclosing Box options mean?

When you select Detect Separate Items, Preview attempts to locate different areas of the scanned image, such as different sections in a text document or a page with two images on it. The Detect Enclosing Box option looks for a box surrounding the content you are scanning and selects it.

Why don't I see my scanner when I choose Import from the File menu?

If your scanner doesn't appear, make sure it is connected to your Mac via Wi-Fi or USB and click **Import from Scanner** from the **File** menu, followed by **Include Networked Devices**. Your scanner should now appear when you click the **File** menu.

Annotate a Document with Preview

Using the Preview Application you can add annotations to a document or image using basic tools and text editing. The annotation toolbar features options that allow you to add lines, shapes, and arrows to a document as well as text boxes, speech bubbles, and thought bubbles in a range of colors.

Annotate a Document with Preview

1 Click the **Edit** button (![Edit]).

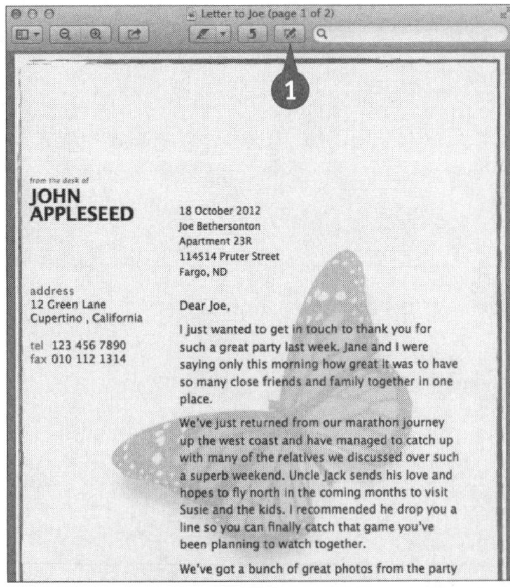

The Edit toolbar appears.

A Click a shape from the toolbar to apply it to the document.

2 Click and drag across the document to add the shape.

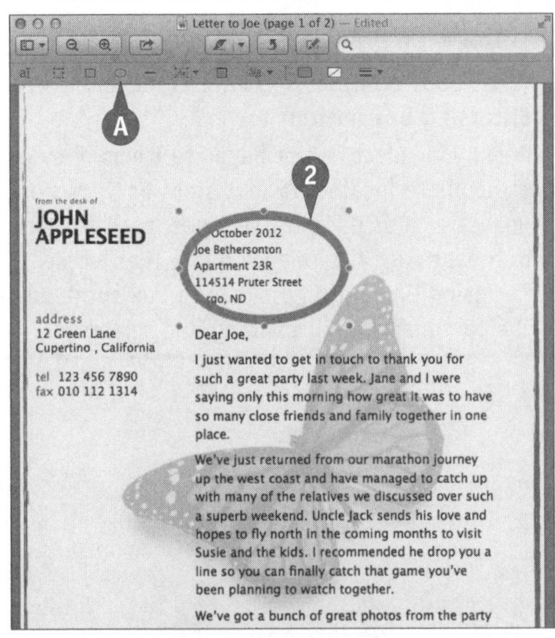

3 Click and drag the control handles that appear around the shape to adjust its size.

B Click the **Line Attributes** button (☰▾) to adjust the size of the lines in the shape.

C Click the **Colors** button (▢) to select a color for the shape.

4 Click the **Text Tools** button (Aa▾) to edit the look of your text.

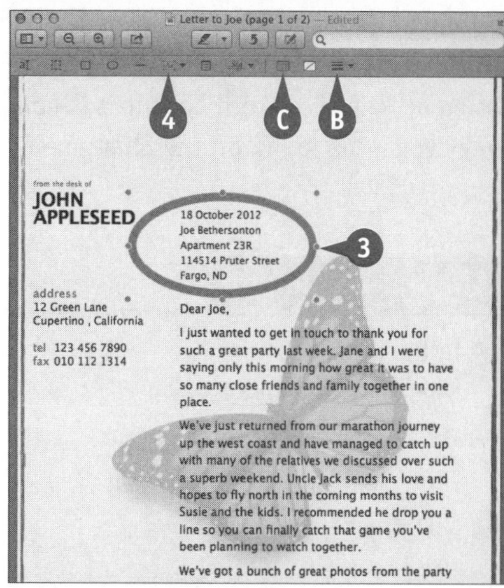

5 Click and drag across the document to add a text box.

6 Type text into the text box you created.

D Edit the size, style, and font in your text box with the font tools on the toolbar.

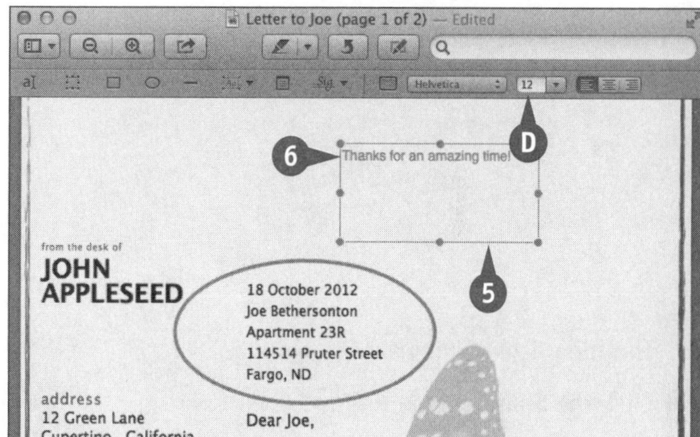

TIP

How do I use the speech and thought bubbles and outlined text in Preview?

Click the **Text Tools** button (Aa▾) from the Edit toolbar and select the text style you want to use. Drag a shape over your document. Now type text into the shape you created and use the font tools in the toolbar to adjust the style and size of the text within it. You can also adjust the size of your shape by clicking it to select the shape and then dragging the control handles that appear.

Share a Document

You can share documents opened with Preview in a number of ways, such as via AirDrop, E-mail, or Messages or by uploading the document to Twitter, Facebook, and Flickr. You also have the option to import the file into iPhoto if it is compatible with the application. All of the sharing options in Preview can be found on the Share menu that appears when you click the **Share** button (⎘).

Share a Document

1. In the Dock, click the **Preview** icon (▣).

   The Preview File Browser appears.

2. Click the file you want to share.
3. Click **Open**.

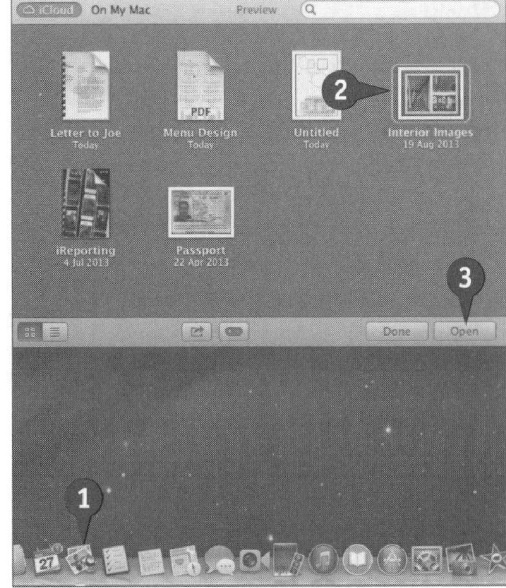

   The file opens in Preview.

4. Click the **Share** button (⎘).

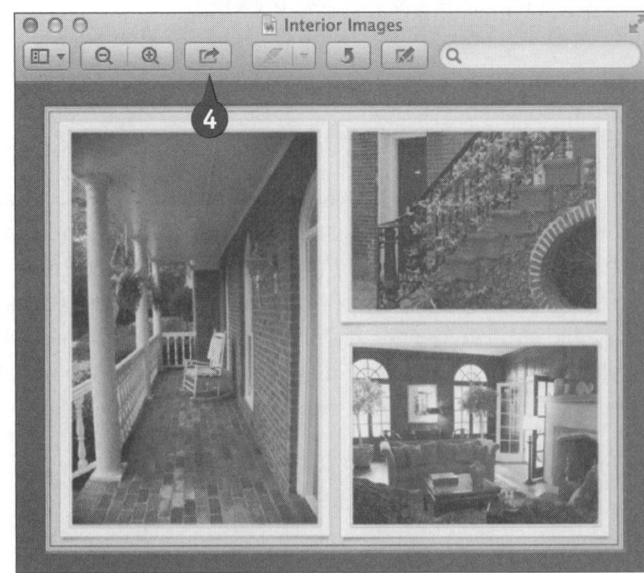

The Share menu appears.

5 Click one of the options on the menu to share your document.

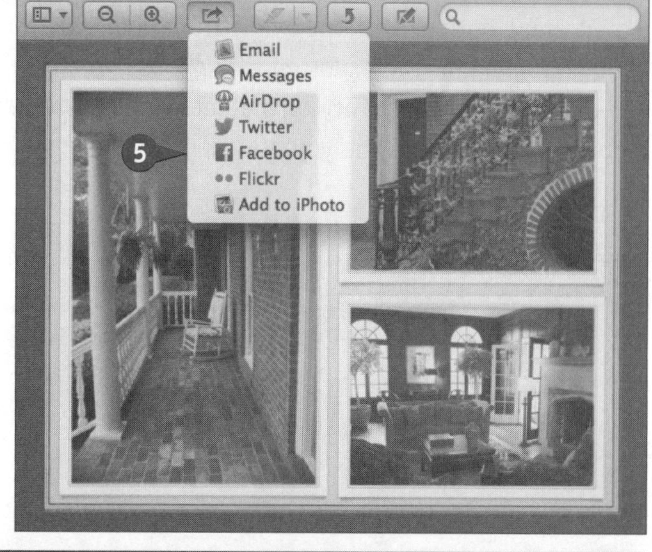

A If you choose to share your document via Messages, Flickr, Facebook or Twitter, a new window appears allowing you to add a message.

B If you choose to share your document via Mail or iPhoto, the corresponding application opens.

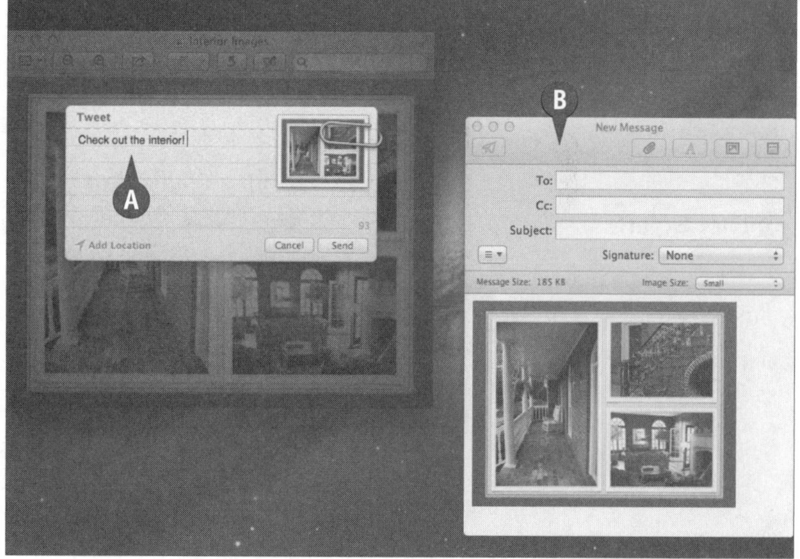

TIP

How do I share a document using AirDrop?

Click the **Share** button (⎘) and then click **AirDrop**. The Preview interface becomes grayed out and a new pane appears with a preview of your document clipped to it. Make sure that the computer you want to share to is turned on, is connected to the same network as your Mac, and has AirDrop open in the Finder. Select the computer you want to share the document to and click **Send**. Note, however, that AirDrop does not appear if you are using an older Mac that lacks the required hardware.

Export a Document

Exporting a document in Preview is similar to saving it but allows you to perform a number of different options without overwriting your existing document. From the Export dialog you can choose a name for the exported file, choose where to export it, and change the document format. You can also change the quality of the document to make it look clearer, or choose a lower quality level to reduce the size of the file you are exporting.

Export a Document

1 Click **File**.

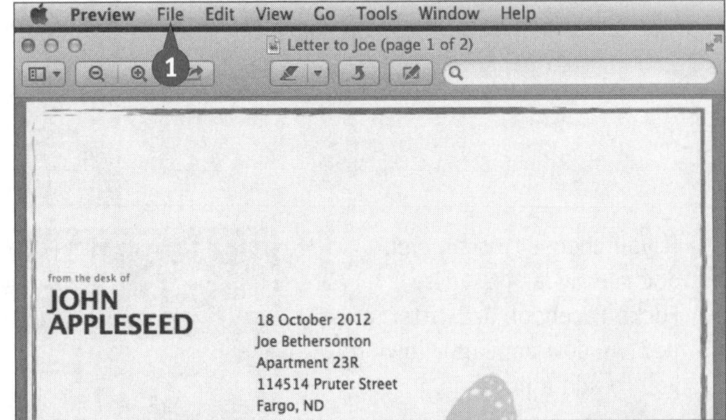

2 Click **Export**.

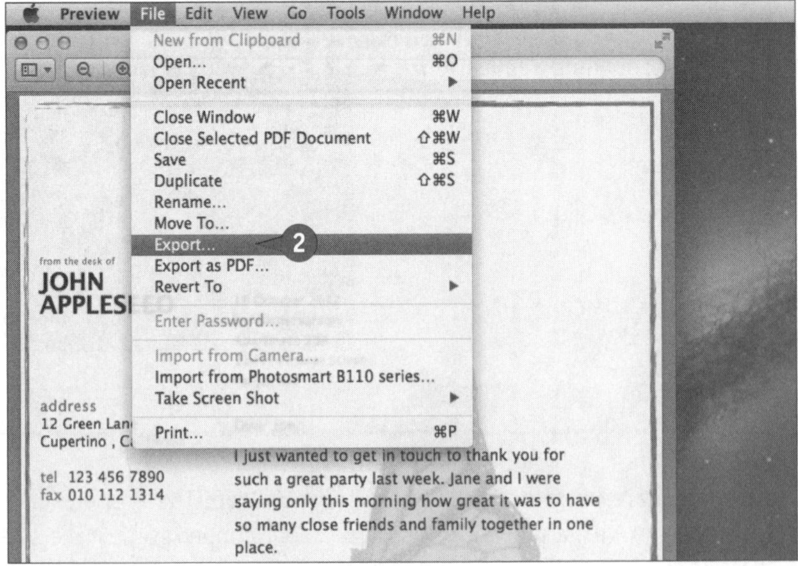

The Export dialog appears.

3 Type a name for your exported document in the Export As: field.

4 Click ⬍ and select a location to export the document to.

A Click ⬍ next to Format and select a new format for your file if required.

B Additional options may appear here depending on the file format you are exporting.

5 Click **Save**.

Preview exports your document.

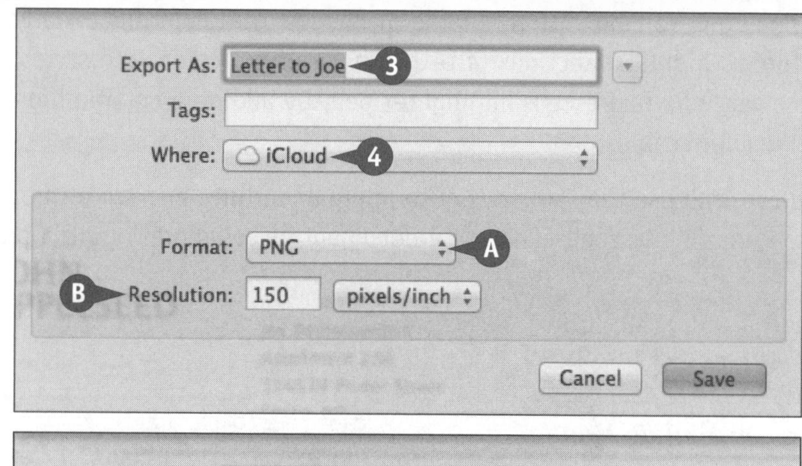

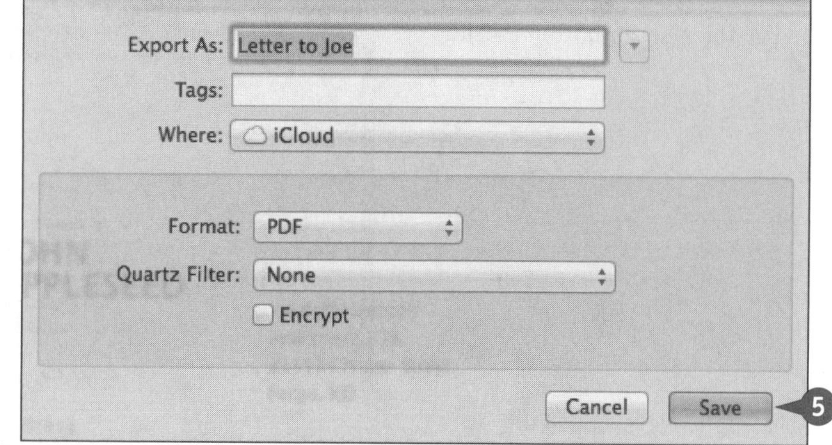

TIP

What difference does the Quality slider make to the exported document?

By setting the Quality of your exported document to best, the text and images within it will appear at the highest resolution possible so they will look clearer when printed or viewed on-screen. This will also result in a larger-sized file. Conversely, setting the lowest quality level will produce a lower-resolution document at a smaller file size.

Mark Up a Document

If you are working with a PDF file in Preview that contains text, you can use the in-built Markup tool to highlight sections of text in a variety of colors and styles. The Markup tool works in the same way as a fluorescent highlighter pen, by adding a colored highlight to text to make it stand out but remain visible.

You can also use the Markup tool to apply underlines and strikethroughs to text, which can be useful when proofing or spell-checking a document or collaborating on a project.

Mark Up a Document

Turn On Markup Mode

1. Click the **Markup** button ( ).

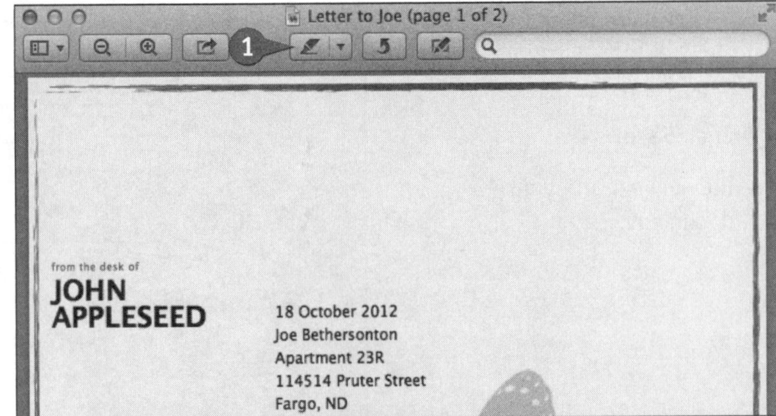

Markup mode is turned on.

Highlight Text in a Document

1. Click the arrow next to the Markup button.
2. Click the color you want to use for highlighting.
3. Click and drag over a section of text to highlight it.

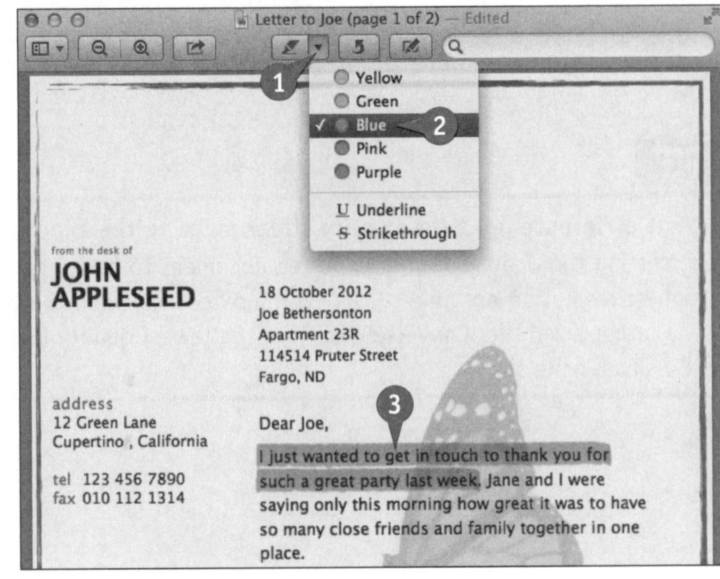

Underline Text in a Document

1. Click the arrow next to the Markup button.
2. Click **Underline**.
3. Click and drag over a section of text to underline it.

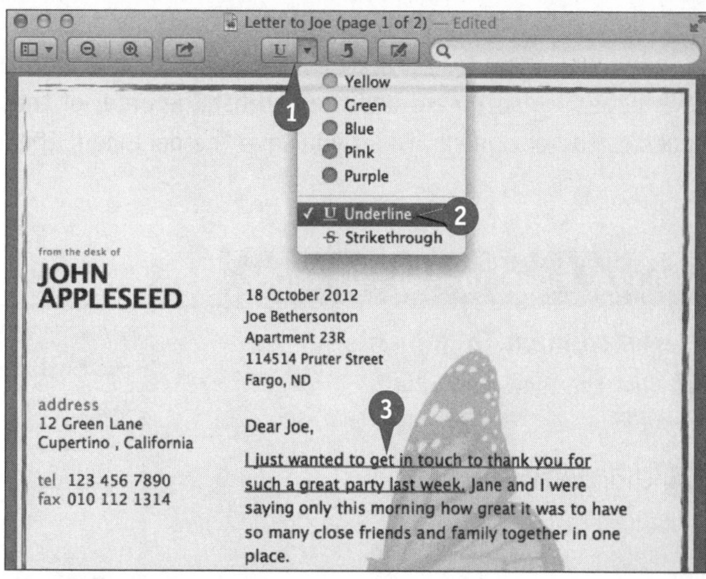

Strike Through Text in a Document

1. Click the arrow next to the Markup button.
2. Click **Strikethrough**.
3. Click and drag over a section of text to strike through it.

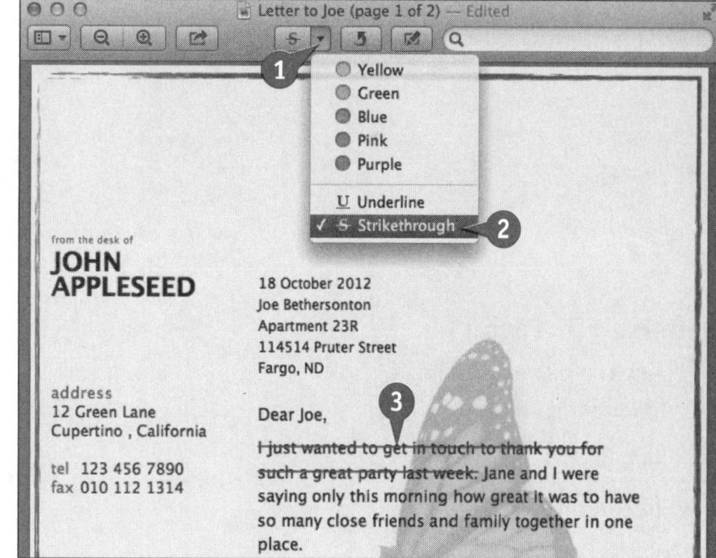

TIP

Can I add comments to sections of text I mark up?

Yes. Click **Tools** and then click **Annotate**. Click **Note** on the submenu that appears. Now, when you click the highlight or section of your document you want to add a comment to, a note appears and allows you to type text. Type your text and click another section of the document to add the note.

Delete, Move, or Add PDF Pages

If you are working with a PDF file that contains multiple pages, you can delete, move, or add individual pages from the document in Preview. Using the Thumbnails view in Preview you can view each page in a document and then adjust the order of those pages, delete specific pages, or add new pages to the document. When you save the document these changes are preserved in the original file.

Delete, Move, or Add PDF Pages

View Document Thumbnails

1. Click the **View Menu** button ( ).
2. Click **Thumbnails**.

   Thumbnails for your document appear in a pane.

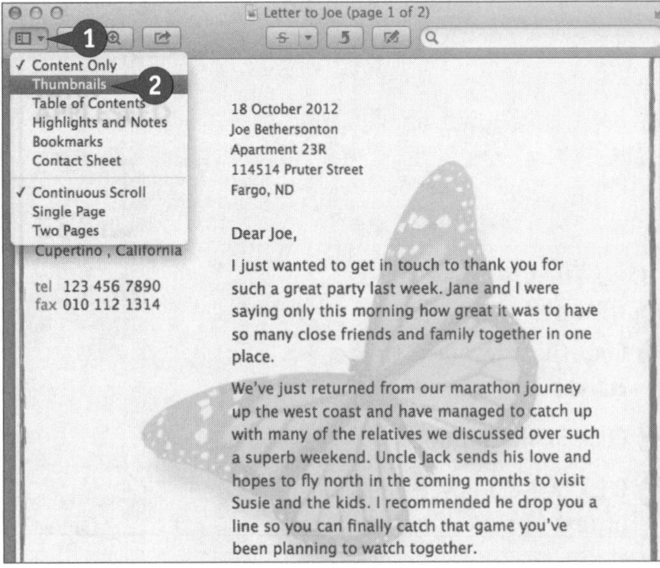

Delete a PDF Page

1. Click the page you want to delete.
2. Click **Edit**.
3. Click **Delete**.

   The page is deleted.

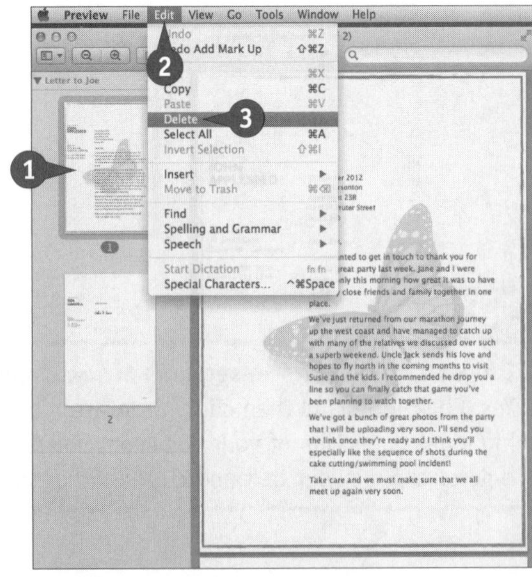

Move a PDF Page

1. Click the page you want to move.
2. Click and drag the page to a new location in the thumbnail pane.

   The page moves to the new location.

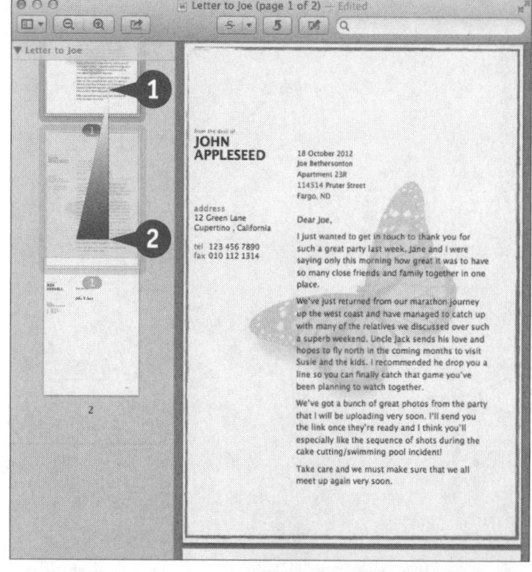

Add a PDF Page

1. Locate the page or pages you want to add to your PDF file in the Finder.
2. Click and drag the page or pages to the point in your document you want to add them.

   The pages are added to your document.

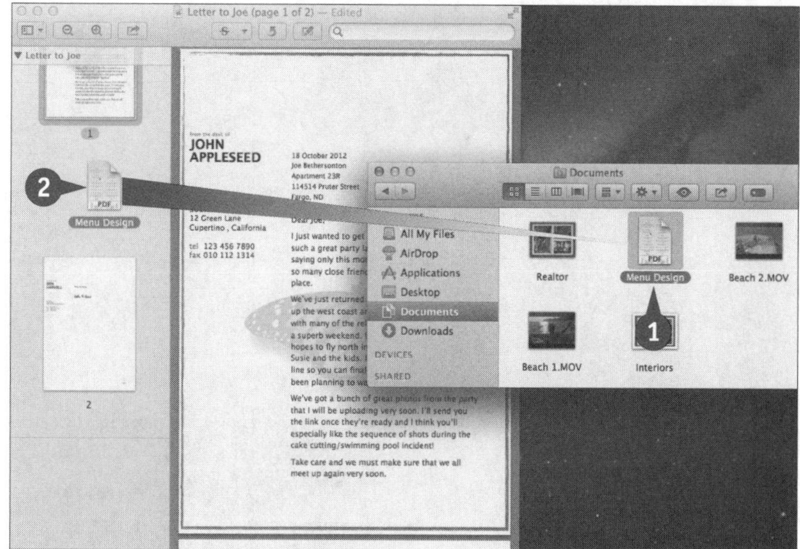

TIP

Is there another way to add pages to a PDF file in Preview?
Yes. Open the document to which you want to add a page and then click **Insert** on the Edit menu. Click **Page From File...** on the submenu that appears and locate the page you want to add. Select the page and click **Open**. The page is added to your open document below the page you are currently viewing.

CHAPTER 13

Customizing OS X

OS X comes with a number of features that enable you to customize your Mac. For example, you might not like the default desktop background or the layout of the Dock. Not only can you change the appearance of OS X to suit your taste, but you can also change the way OS X works to make it easier and more efficient for you to use.

Display System Preferences

You can find many of the OS X customization features in System Preferences, a collection of settings and options that control the overall look and operation of OS X. You can use System Preferences to change the desktop background, specify a screen saver, set your Mac's sleep options, add user accounts, and customize the Dock, to name some of the tasks that you learn about in this chapter. To use these settings, you must know how to display the System Preferences window.

Display System Preferences

Open System Preferences

1. In the Dock, click the **System Preferences** icon (☐).

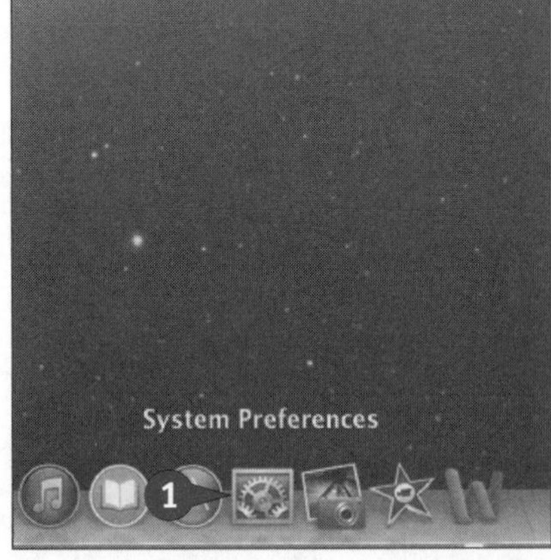

The System Preferences window appears.

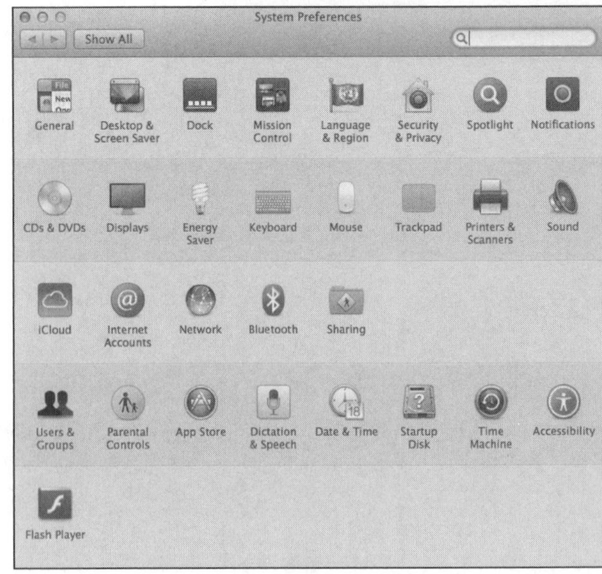

Close System Preferences

1. Click **System Preferences.**

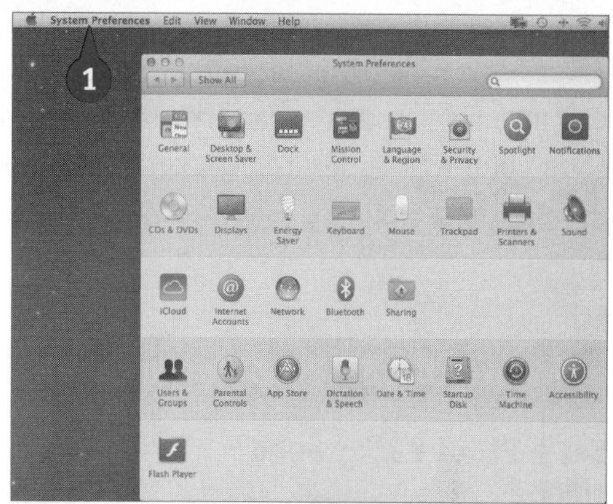

2. Click **Quit System Preferences.**

   System Preferences closes.

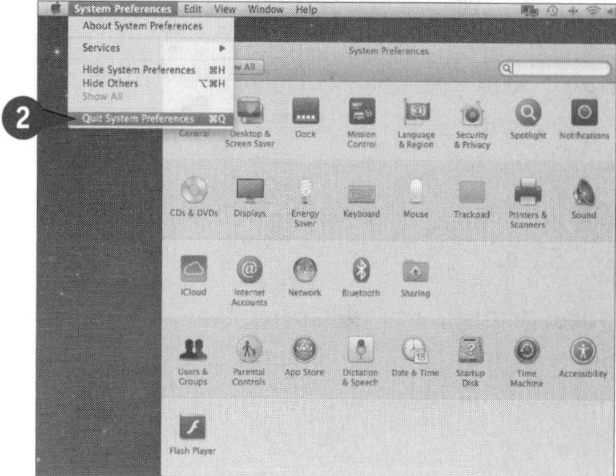

TIPS

Are there other methods I can use to open and close System Preferences?

Yes. If you have hidden the Dock (as described in the section "Hide the Dock") or removed the System Preferences icon from the Dock, you can click the **Apple** icon ( ) and then click **System Preferences.** To quit System Preferences, either press ⌘+Q or right-click and then click **Quit.**

Sometimes when I open System Preferences, I do not see all the icons. How can I restore the original icons?

View | Window | Help
Back ⌘[
Forward ⌘]
Show All Preferences ⌘L
Customize...
✓ Organize by Categories
Organize Alphabetically
Search ⌘F

When you click an icon in System Preferences, the window changes to show just the options and settings associated with that icon. To return to the main System Preferences window, click **View** and then click **Show All Preferences** (or press ⌘+L), or click the **Show All** button on the System Preferences pane.

Change the Desktop Background

To give OS X a different look, you can change the default desktop background. OS X offers a wide variety of desktop background options. For example, OS X comes with several dozen images you can use, from abstract patterns to photos of plants and other natural images. You can also choose a solid color as the desktop background, or you can use one of your own photos. You can change the desktop background to show either a fixed image or a series of images that change periodically.

Change the Desktop Background

Set a Fixed Background Image

1. Open System Preferences.

Note: See the section "Display System Preferences" in this chapter.

2. Click **Desktop & Screen Saver**.

Note: You can also right-click the desktop and then click **Change Desktop Background**.

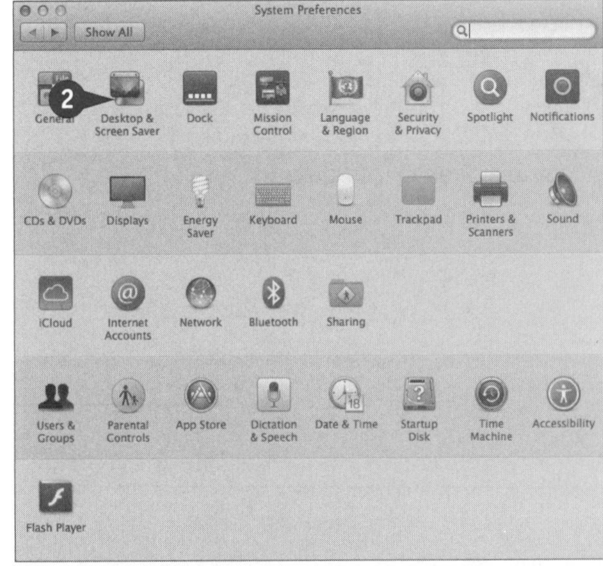

The Desktop & Screen Saver preferences appear.

3. Click **Desktop**.
4. Click the image category you want to use.

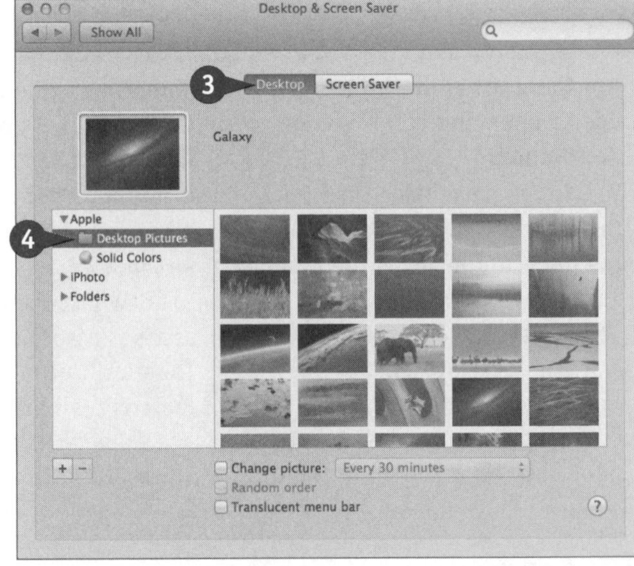

5 Click the image you want to use as the desktop background.

Your Mac changes the desktop background.

Note: You can also select a photo in iPhoto, click **Share**, and then click **Set Desktop**.

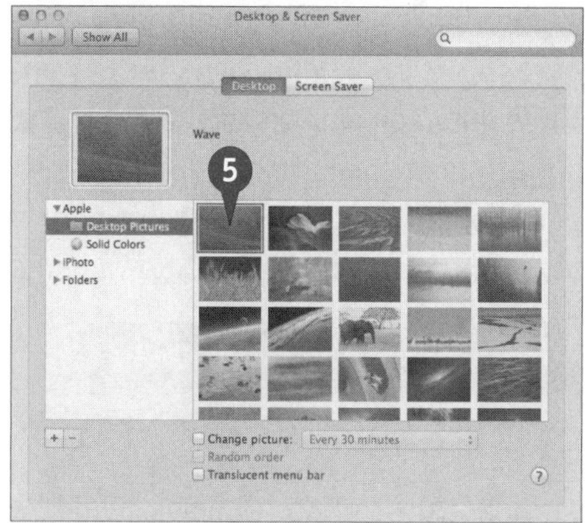

Set a Changing Background Image

1 Select the **Change picture** check box (☐ changes to ☑).

2 Click ⬍ in the pop-up menu and then click how often you want the background image to change.

3 If you want your Mac to choose the periodic image randomly, select the **Random order** check box (☐ changes to ☑).

Your Mac changes the desktop background periodically based on your chosen interval.

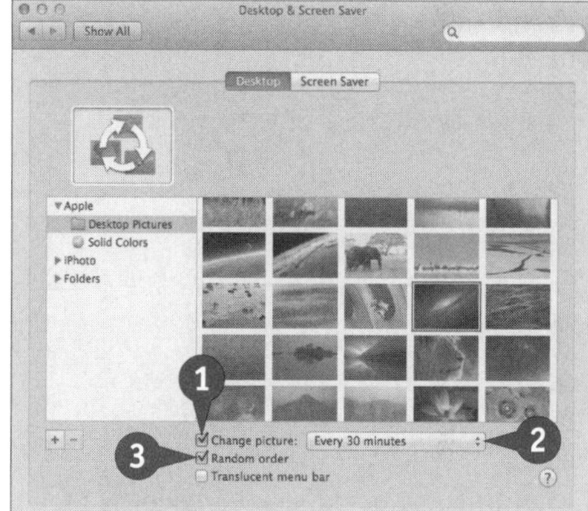

TIP

When I choose a photo, how do the various options differ for displaying the photo?

Your Mac gives you five options:

- **Fill Screen** expands the photo by the same percentage in all four directions until it fills the entire desktop. This option can cause some edges of the photo to be cropped out.
- **Fit to Screen** expands the photo in all four directions until the photo is either the same height as the desktop or the same width as the desktop.
- **Stretch to Fill Screen** expands the photo in all four directions until it fills the entire desktop. Because the photo is usually expanded more either vertically or horizontally, this option can cause the photo to appear distorted.
- **Center** displays the photo at its actual size and places the photo in the center of the desktop.
- **Tile** repeats your photo multiple times to fill the entire desktop.

Activate the Screen Saver

You can set up OS X to display a *screen saver*, a moving pattern or series of pictures. The screen saver appears after your computer has been idle for a while. If you leave your monitor on for long stretches while your computer is idle, a faint version of the unmoving image can endure for a while on the screen, a phenomenon known as *persistence*. A screen saver prevents this by displaying a moving image. However, persistence is not a major problem for modern screens, so for the most part you use a screen saver for visual interest. You can also download a range of screen savers from the Internet.

Activate the Screen Saver

1. Open System Preferences.

Note: See the section "Display System Preferences" in this chapter.

2. Click **Desktop & Screen Saver**.

The Desktop & Screen Saver preferences appear.

3. Click **Screen Saver**.
4. Click the screen saver you want to use.

A A preview of the screen saver appears here.

5. Click the **Start after** ⬍ and then click a time delay until the screen saver begins.

Note: The interval you choose is the number of minutes or hours that your Mac must be idle before the screen saver starts. If you set an interval greater than the sleep time you have set for your Mac, the screen saver will not appear before your Mac goes to sleep.

B If the screen saver is customizable, click **Screen Saver Options** to configure it.

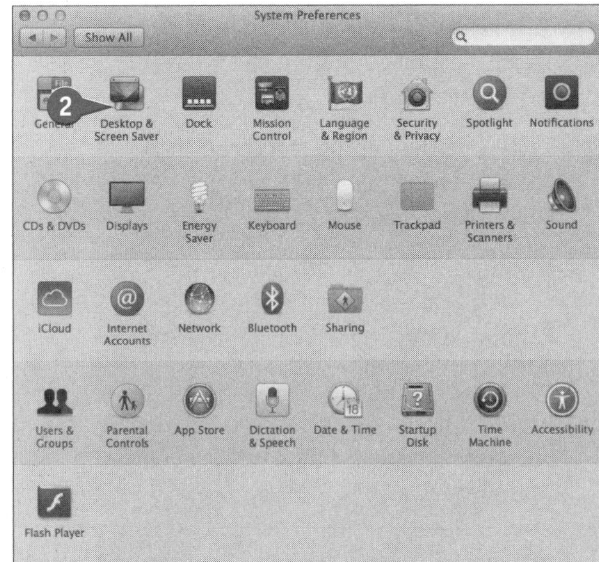

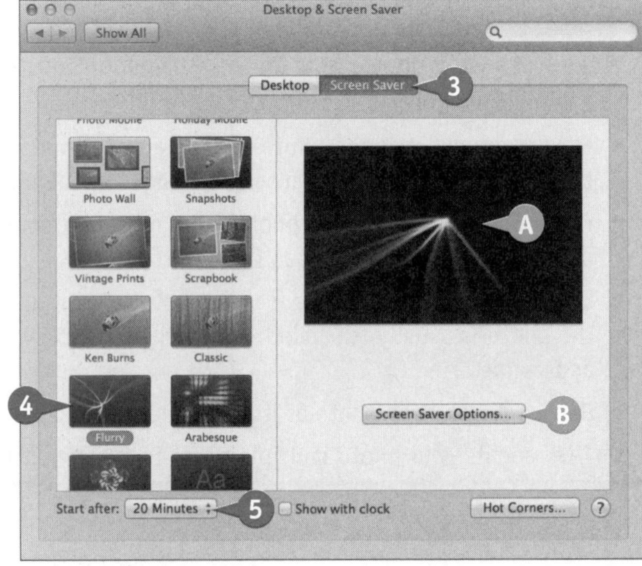

C If you choose a slide show instead of a screen saver, click the **Source** ⁝ to select an image collection.

D If you want to see the current time when the screen saver is active, select the **Show with clock** check box (☐ changes to ☑).

TIP

What are hot corners and how do I configure them?

A *hot corner* is a corner of your Mac's screen that you have set up to perform some action when you move the mouse ↖ to that corner. To configure hot corners, follow these steps:

1. Follow steps 1 to 4 in this section to select a screen saver.
2. Click **Hot Corners.**
3. Click ⁝ and then click the action you want to perform when you move the mouse ↖ to the top-left corner of the screen.
4. Click ⁝ and then click the action you want to perform when you move the mouse ↖ to the top-right corner of the screen.
5. Click ⁝ and then click the action you want to perform when you move the mouse ↖ to the bottom-left corner of the screen.
6. Click ⁝ and then click the action you want to perform when you move the mouse ↖ to the bottom-right corner of the screen.
7. Click **OK.**

Set Your Mac's Sleep Options

You can make OS X more energy efficient by configuring parts of your Mac to go into sleep mode automatically when you are not using them. *Sleep mode* means that your display or your Mac is in a temporary low-power mode. This saves energy on all Macs and also saves battery power on a notebook Mac. For example, you can set up OS X to put the display to sleep automatically after a period of inactivity. Similarly, you can configure OS X to put your entire Mac to sleep after you have not used it for a specified amount of time.

Set Your Mac's Sleep Options

Open the Energy Saver Preferences

1. Open System Preferences.

Note: See the section "Display System Preferences" in this chapter.

2. Click **Energy Saver**.

The Energy Saver preferences appear.

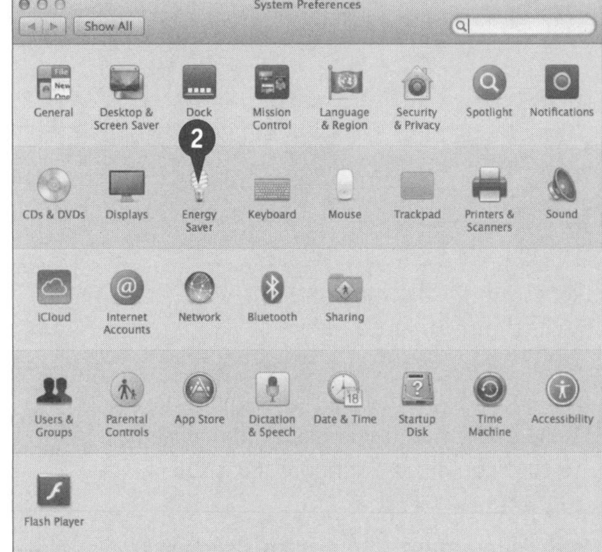

Set Sleep Options for a Desktop Mac

1. Click and drag ▽ to set the Computer sleep timer to specify the period of inactivity after which your computer goes to sleep.

2. Click and drag ▽ to set the Display sleep timer to specify the period of inactivity after which your display goes to sleep.

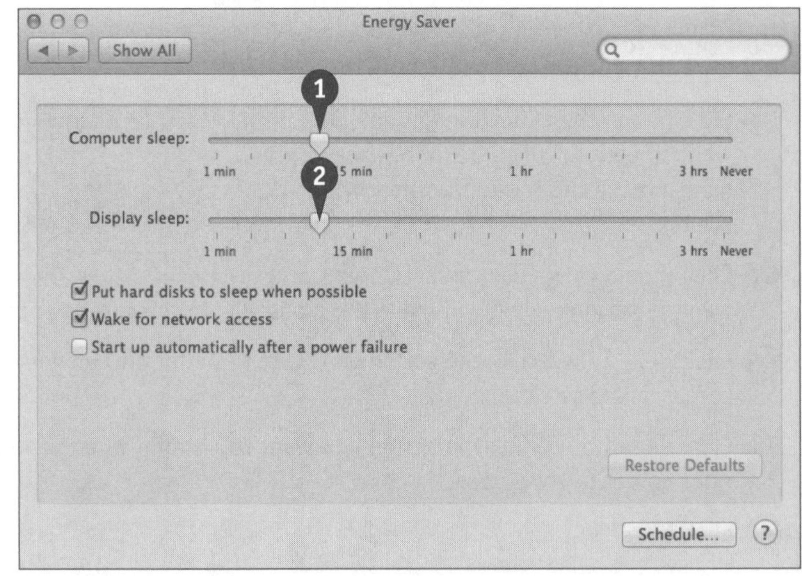

Set Sleep Options for a Notebook Mac

1. Click **Battery**.
2. Click and drag ▽ to set the Computer sleep timer for when your Mac is on battery power.
3. Click and drag ▽ to set the Display sleep timer for when your Mac is on battery power.

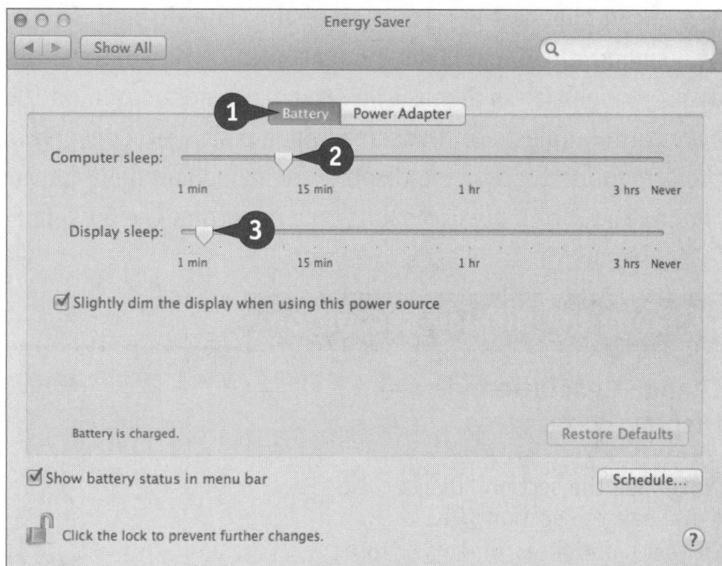

4. Click **Power Adapter**.
5. Click and drag ▽ to set the Computer sleep timer for when your Mac is plugged in.
6. Click and drag ▽ to set the Display sleep timer for when your Mac is plugged in.

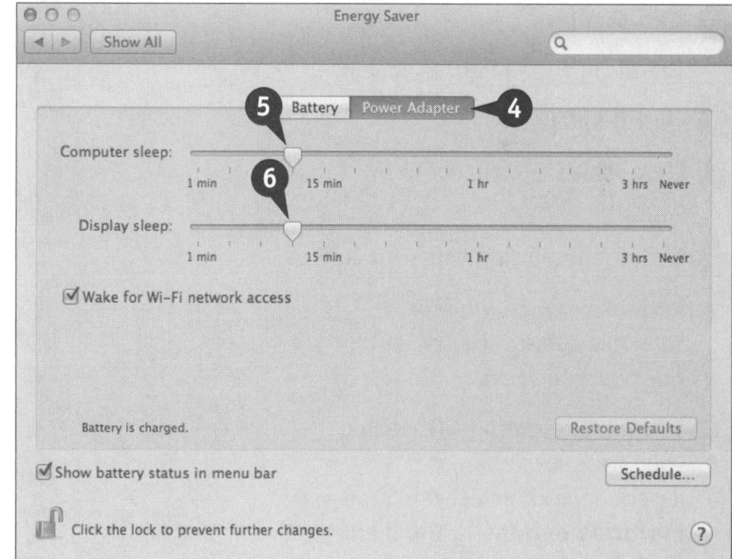

TIPS

How do I wake up a sleeping display or computer?
If your Mac's display is in sleep mode, you can wake up the display by moving your mouse or sliding your finger on the trackpad. You can also wake up the display or your entire Mac by pressing any key on the keyboard.

I changed the display sleep timer, and now I never see my screen saver. Why?
You have set the display sleep timer to a time that is less than your screen saver timer. Suppose you have configured OS X to switch on the screen saver after 15 minutes. If you then set the display sleep timer to a shorter interval, such as 10 minutes, OS X will always put the display to sleep before the screen saver appears.

Change the Display Resolution

You can change the resolution of the OS X display. This enables you to adjust the display for best viewing or for maximum compatibility with whatever application you are using. Increasing the display resolution is an easy way to create more space on the screen for applications and windows, because the objects on the screen appear smaller. Conversely, if you are having trouble reading text on the screen, decreasing the display resolution can help, because the screen objects appear larger. You can change the OS X display resolution using either the System Preferences window or the menu bar.

Change the Display Resolution

Change Resolution via the Display Preferences

1. Open System Preferences.

Note: See the section "Display System Preferences" in this chapter.

2. Click **Displays**.

   The Displays preferences appear.

3. Click **Display**.
4. Click **Scaled** (☐ changes to ☉).
5. Click the resolution you want to use.

   Your Mac adjusts the screen to the new resolution.

A. To control mirroring when using your Mac's menu bar, as described next, select the **Show mirroring options in the menu bar when available** check box (☐ changes to ☑).

Note: Older Macs may not display this option if their hardware does not support mirroring.

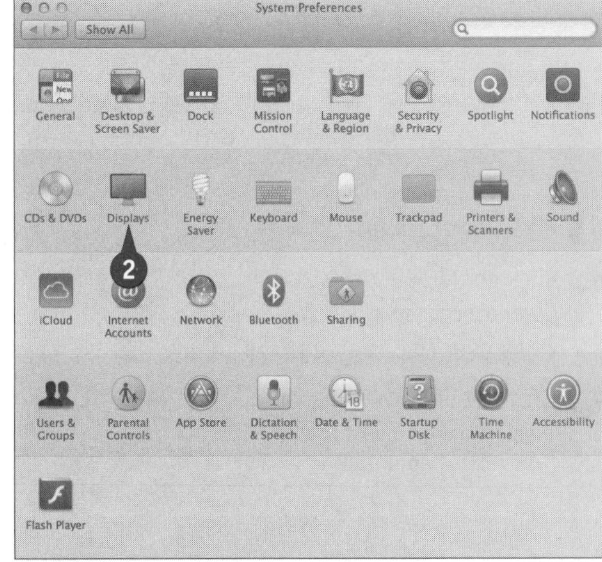

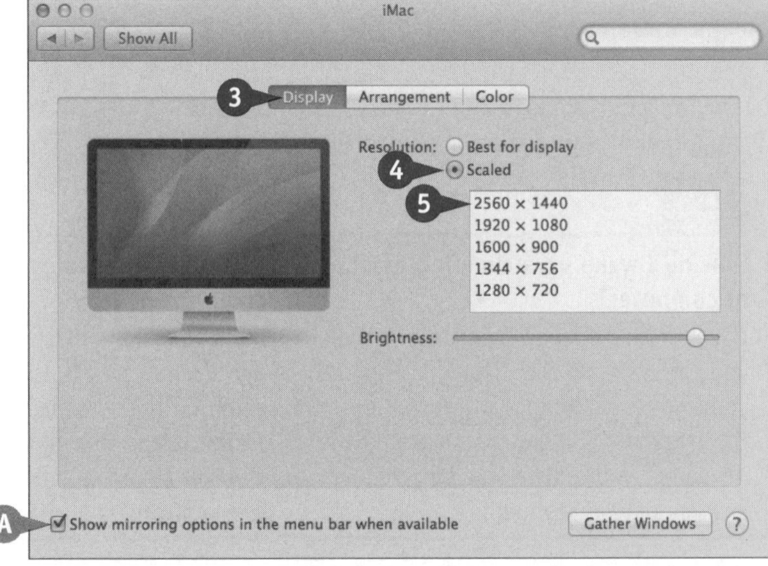

Turn On Display Mirroring via the Menu Bar

1. Click the **Mirroring Options** icon (▣).

2. Click **Turn Display Mirroring On.**

Ⓑ Click **Open Displays Preferences** to view display settings in System Preferences.

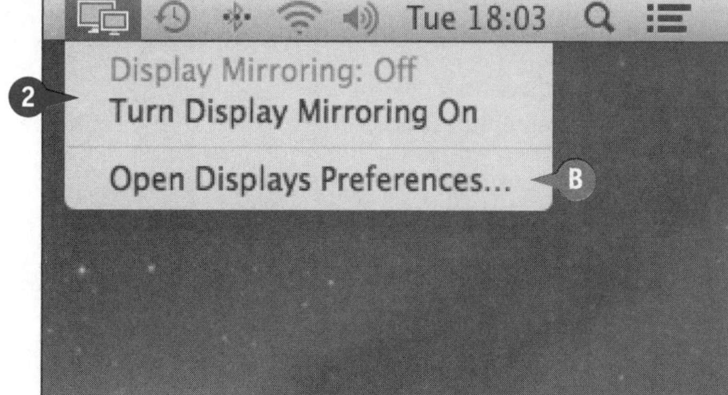

TIPS

What do the resolution numbers mean?
The resolution numbers are expressed in *pixels*, short for picture elements, which are the individual dots that make up what you see on your Mac's screen. The pixels are arranged in rows and columns, and the resolution tells you the number of pixels in each row and column. So a resolution of 1024 × 768 means that the display is using 1,024 pixel rows and 768 pixel columns.

Why do some resolutions also include the word stretched?
Most older displays are made with the ratio of the width to the height — this is called the *aspect ratio* — set at 4:3. However, most new Mac displays are made with an aspect ratio of 16:10, which is called *widescreen*. Resolutions designed for 4:3 displays — such as 800 × 600 and 1024 × 768 — take up only part of a widescreen display. To make them take up the entire display, choose the *stretched* version of the resolution.

Create an App Folder in Launchpad

You can make Launchpad easier to work with by combining two or more icons into a single storage area called an *app folder*. OS X Mavericks displays the Launchpad icons in a configuration of rows depending on your screen resolution. Also, if you have configured your Mac with a relatively low display resolution, you might see only partial app names in the Launchpad screens.

All of this can make it difficult to locate the app you want. However, by creating app folders, you can organize similar apps and reduce the clutter on the Launchpad screens.

Create an App Folder in Launchpad

1. In the Dock, click the **Launchpad** icon (![]).

   A Launchpad displays icons for each installed application.

2. Click the dot for the Launchpad screen you want to work with.

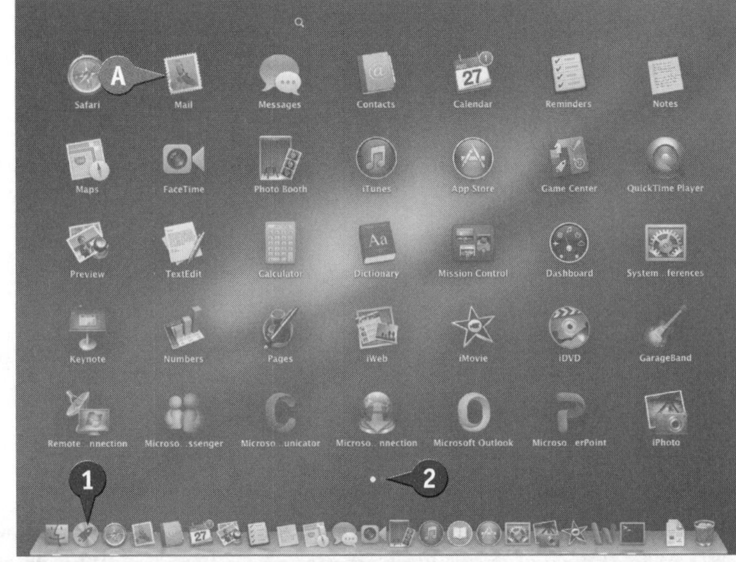

3. Use the mouse (![]) to click and drag an icon that you want to include in the folder, and drop it on another icon that you want to include in the same folder.

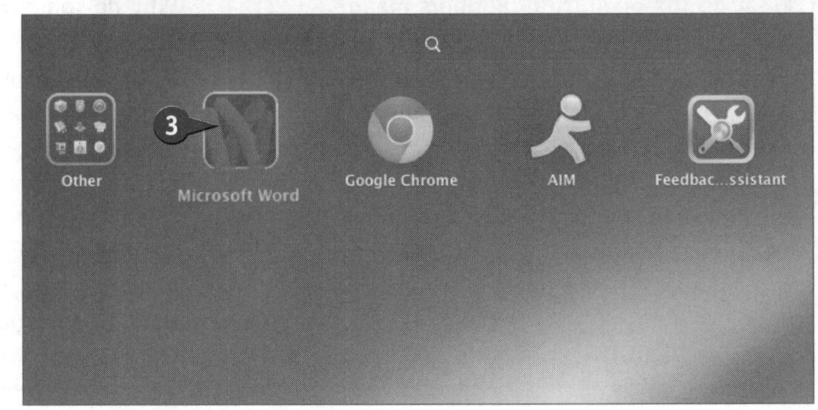

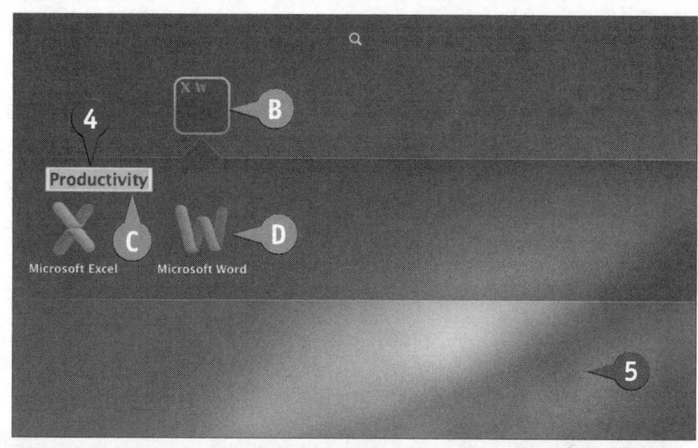

Ⓑ Launchpad creates the app folder.

Ⓒ Launchpad applies a name to the folder based on the type of applications in the folder.

Ⓓ Launchpad adds the icons to the app folder.

4 To specify a different name, click the name and then type the one you prefer.

5 Click the Launchpad screen, outside of the app folder.

Ⓔ Launchpad displays the app folder.

6 To add more icons to the new app folder, use the mouse to click and drag each icon and drop it on the folder.

Note: To launch a program from an app folder, click , click the app folder to open it, and then click the program's icon.

TIPS

Can I make changes to an app folder once it has been created?

Yes. Click to open Launchpad, and then click the app folder to open it. To rename the app folder, click the current name, type the new name, and then press Return. To rearrange the icons, use the mouse to drag and drop the apps within the folder. When you are done, click outside the app folder to close it.

Can I remove an icon from an app folder?

Yes. Click to open Launchpad, and then click the app folder to open it. To remove an app from a folder, click and drag the app out of the folder. Launchpad closes the folder, and you can then drop the icon within the Launchpad screen. Note that if you remove all the icons from an app folder, Launchpad deletes the folder.

Add a User Account

You can share your Mac with another person by creating a user account for that person. This enables the person to log on to OS X and use the system. The new user account is completely separate from your own account. This means that the other person can change settings, create documents, and perform other OS X tasks without interfering with your own settings or data. For maximum privacy for all users, you should set up each user account with a password.

Add a User Account

1 Open System Preferences.

Note: See the section "Display System Preferences" in this chapter.

2 Click **Users & Groups**.

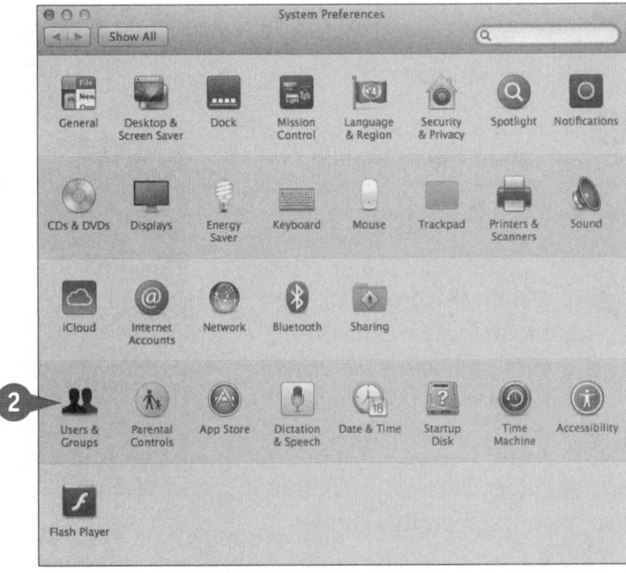

A In most OS X systems, to modify accounts you must click the **Lock** icon (🔒) and then type your administrator password (🔒 changes to 🔓).

3 Click **Add** (+).

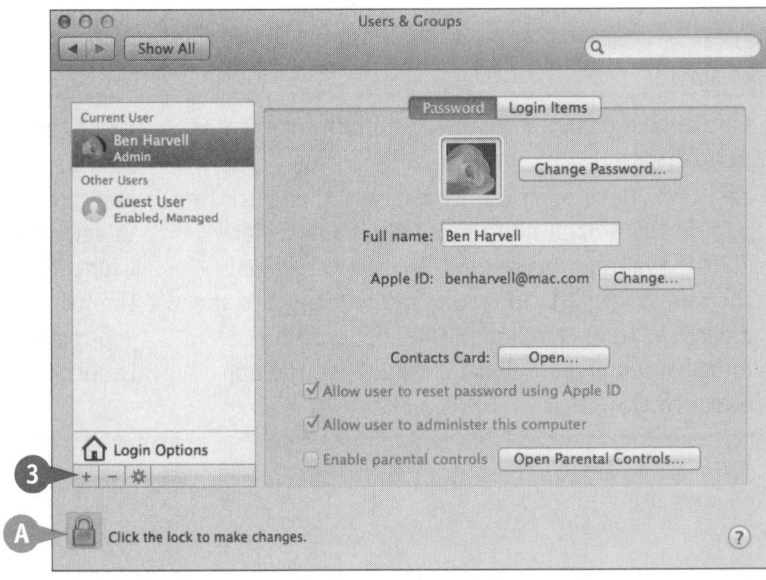

The New Account dialog appears.

4 Click ⬍ and then click an account type.

5 Type the user's name.

6 Edit the short username that OS X creates.

7 Type a password for the user.

8 Retype the user's password.

9 As an option, type a hint that OS X will display if the user forgets the password.

10 Click **Create User**.

B OS X adds the user account to the Users & Groups preferences window.

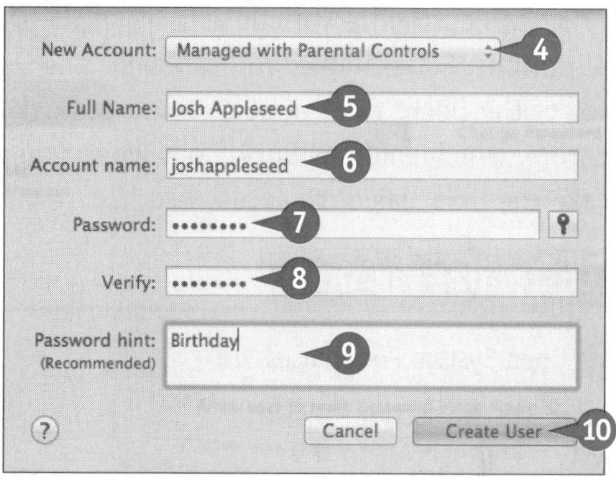

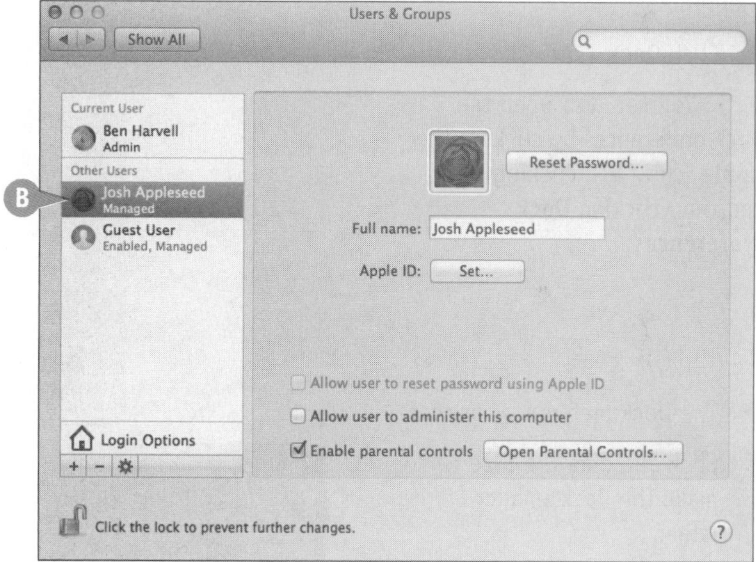

TIPS

Which account type should I use for the new account?

The Standard account type is a good choice because it can make changes only to its own account settings. Avoid the Administrator option because it is a powerful account type that enables the user to make major changes to the system. If the user is a child, consider the Managed with Parental Controls account type.

How do I change the user's picture?

In the Users & Groups preferences, click the user and then click the picture. OS X displays a list of the available images. If you see one you like, click it. If your Mac has a camera attached and the user is nearby, you can click **Camera** and then click the **Camera** icon to take the user's picture. Click **Done** to set the picture.

Customize the Dock

You can customize various aspects of the Dock by using System Preferences to modify a few Dock options. For example, you can make the Dock take up less room on the screen by adjusting the size of the Dock. You can also make the Dock a bit easier to use by turning on the Magnification feature, which enlarges Dock icons when you position the mouse pointer over them. You can also make the Dock easier to access and use by moving it to either side of the screen.

Customize the Dock

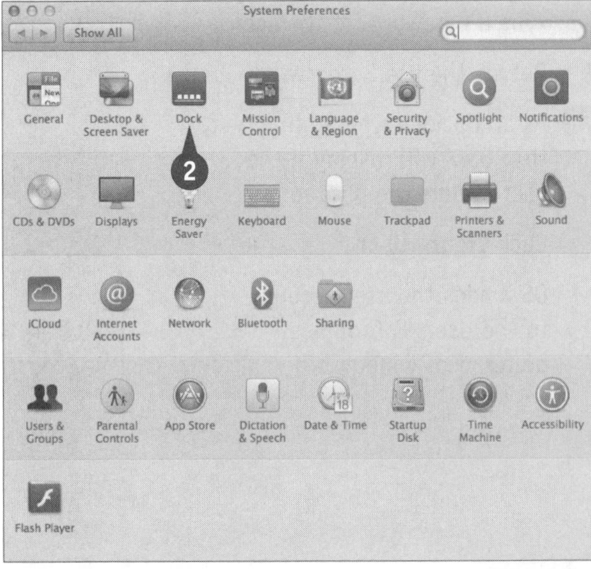

1 Open System Preferences.

Note: See the section "Display System Preferences" in this chapter.

2 Click **Dock**.

Note: You can also open the Dock preferences by clicking the **Apple** icon (), clicking **Dock**, and then clicking **Dock Preferences**.

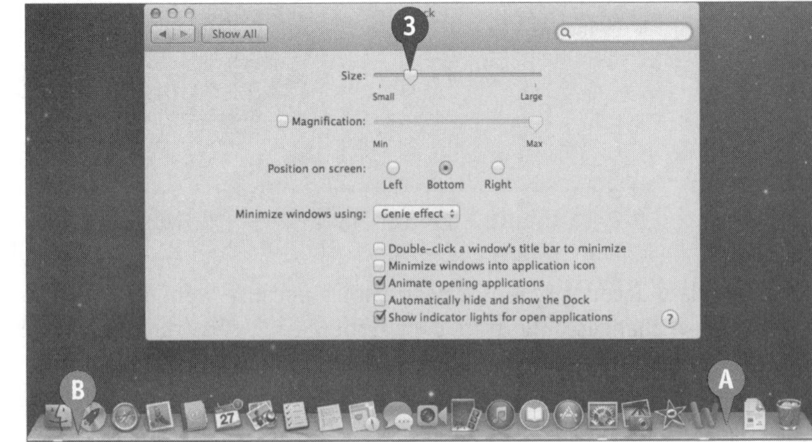

The Dock preferences appear.

3 Click and drag the **Size** to make the Dock smaller or larger.

A You can also click and drag the Dock divider: drag up to increase the Dock size, and drag down to decrease the Dock size.

B System Preferences adjusts the size of the Dock.

Note: If your Dock is already as wide as the screen, dragging the Size slider to the right (toward the Large value) has no effect.

4. Select the **Magnification** check box (☐ changes to ☑).
5. Click and drag the **Magnification** ▽ to set the magnification level.

C When you position the mouse ↖ over a Dock icon, your Mac magnifies the icon.

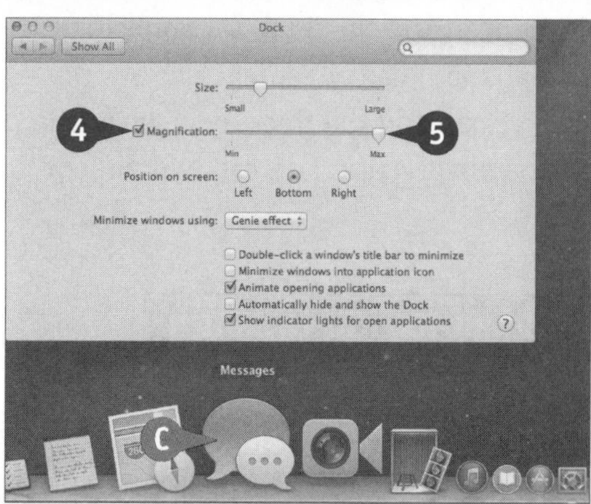

6. Use the **Position on screen** options to click where you want the Dock to appear, such as the **Right** side of the screen (○ changes to ◉).

D Your Mac moves the Dock to the new position.

7. In the **Minimize windows using** pop-up menu, click ⬍ and then click the effect you want your Mac to use when you minimize a window.

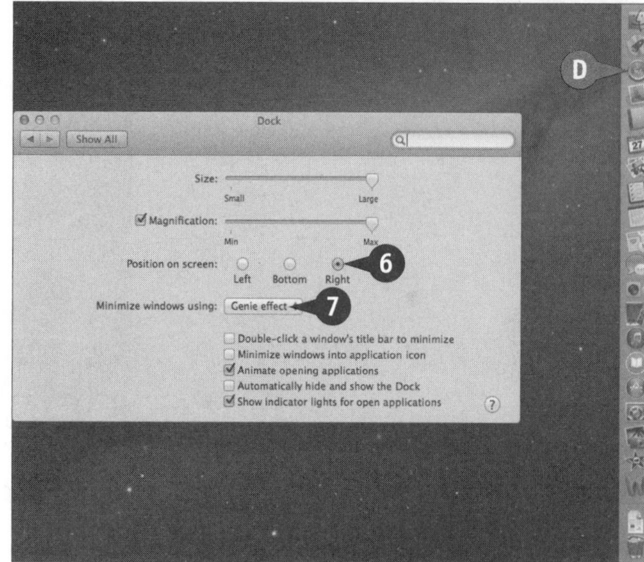

TIP

Is there an easier method I can use to control some of these preferences?

Yes. You can control these preferences directly from the Dock. To set the Dock size, click and drag the Dock divider left or right. For the other preferences, right-click the Dock divider. Click **Turn Magnification On** to enable the magnification feature; click **Turn Magnification Off** to disable this feature. To change the Dock position, click **Position on Screen** and then click **Left**, **Bottom**, or **Right**. To set the minimize effect, click **Minimize Using** and then click either **Genie Effect** or **Scale Effect**. You can also click **Dock Preferences** to open the Dock pane in System Preferences.

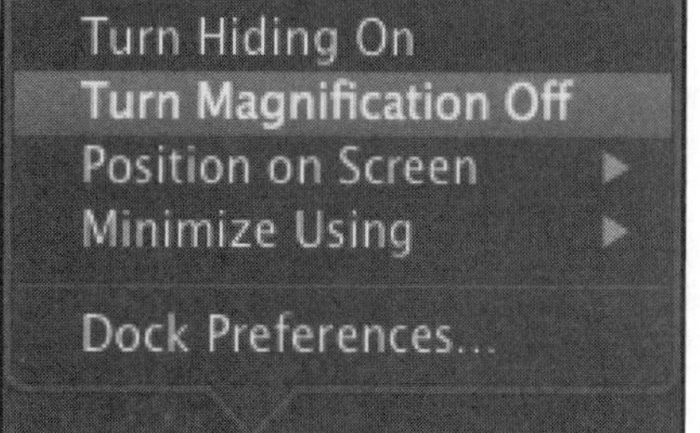

Add an Icon to the Dock

The icons on the Dock are convenient because you can open them with just a single click. You can enhance the convenience of the Dock by adding an icon for an application you use frequently. The icon remains in the Dock even when the application is closed, so you can always open the application with a single click. You can add an icon to the Dock even if the program is not currently running.

Add an Icon to the Dock

Add an Icon for a Nonrunning Application

1. In the Dock, click the **Finder** icon (![Finder icon]).
2. Click **Applications**.

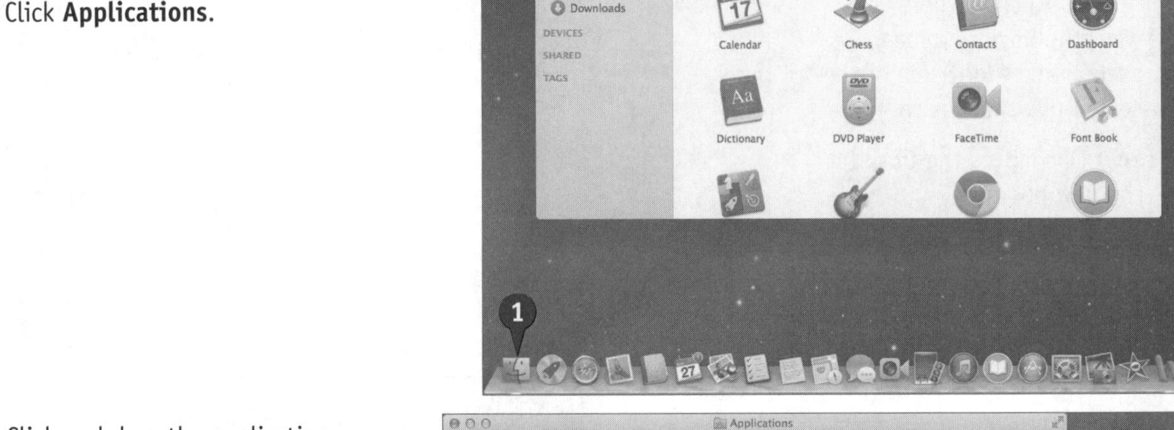

3. Click and drag the application icon, and drop it inside the Dock.

   Ⓐ Be sure to drop the icon anywhere to the left of the Dock divider.

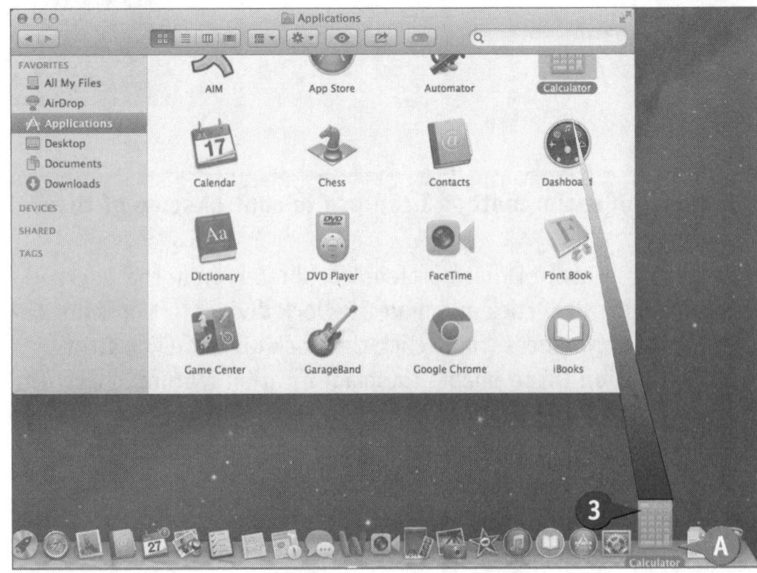

B OS X adds the application's icon to the Dock.

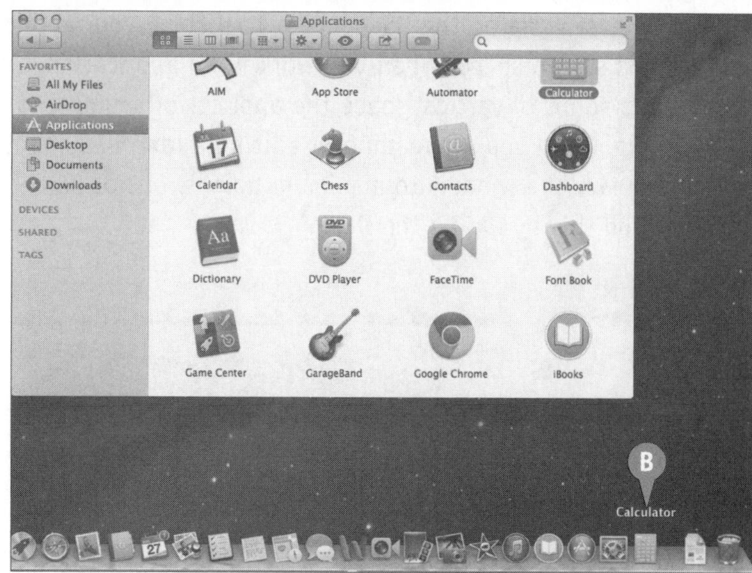

Add an Icon for a Running Application

1. Right-click the application icon in the Dock.
2. Click **Options**.
3. Click **Keep in Dock**.

   The application's icon remains in the Dock even after you close the program.

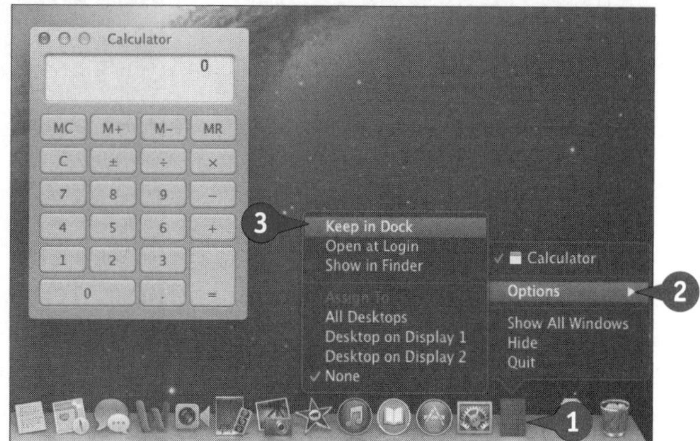

TIPS

Is there a way to get my Mac to start the application automatically each time I log in to the computer?

Yes. Your Mac maintains a list of *login items*, which are applications that run automatically after you log in. You can configure your application as a login item, and your Mac opens it automatically each time you log in. Right-click the application's Dock icon, click **Options**, and then click **Open at Login**.

How do I remove an icon from the Dock?

Right-click the application's Dock icon, click **Options**, and then click **Remove from Dock**. If the application is currently running, OS X removes the icon from the Dock when you quit the program. You can remove any application icon except Finder ( ) and Launchpad ( ). Note that removing an application's Dock icon does not delete the actual application.

Hide the Dock

If you want more room on the OS X screen to display your applications, you can hide the Dock to free up some screen space. When you work in an application, you might find that you need to maximize the amount of vertical space the application window takes up on-screen. This might come up, for example, when you are reading or editing a long document or viewing a large photo. In such cases, you can size the window to maximum height, but OS X will not let you go past the Dock. You can work around this by hiding the Dock.

Hide the Dock

Turn On Dock Hiding

1. Click the **Apple** icon (🍎).
2. Click **Dock**.
3. Click **Turn Hiding On**.

Note: You can also right-click the Dock divider and then click **Turn Hiding On**.

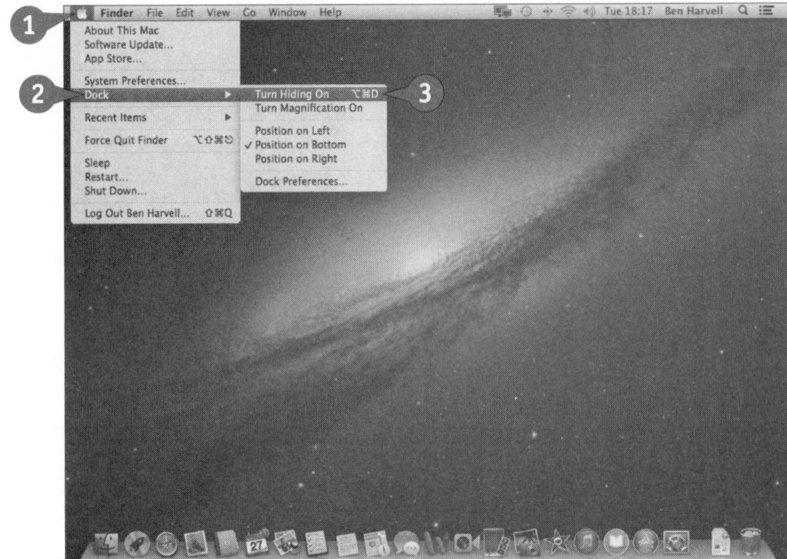

Ⓐ OS X removes the Dock from the desktop.

Display the Dock Temporarily

1. Move the mouse ↖ to the bottom of the screen.

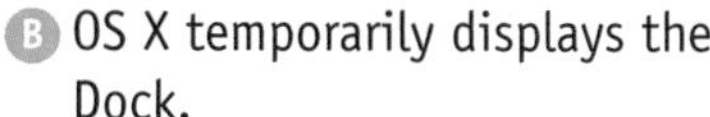

B OS X temporarily displays the Dock.

Note: To hide the Dock again, move the mouse ↖ away from the bottom of the screen.

TIPS

Is there a faster way to hide the Dock?

Yes. You can quickly hide the Dock by pressing Option + ⌘ + D. This keyboard shortcut is a toggle, which means that you can also turn off Dock hiding by pressing Option + ⌘ + D. When the Dock is hidden, you can display it temporarily by pressing Control + F3 (on some keyboards you must press Fn + Control + F3).

How do I bring the Dock back into view?

When you no longer need the extra screen space for your applications, you can turn off Dock hiding to bring the Dock back into view. Click , click **Dock**, and then click **Turn Hiding Off**. Alternatively, display the Dock, right-click the Dock divider, and then click **Turn Hiding Off**.

Add a Widget to the Dashboard

The Dashboard is an OS X application that you use to display widgets. You can customize the Dashboard to include any widgets that you find useful or informative. A widget is a mini-application, particularly one designed to perform a single task, such as displaying the weather, showing stock data, or providing sports scores. OS X comes with 16 widgets, which include a clock, a calculator, a tile game, and a unit converter. Many widgets are also available online.

Add a Widget to the Dashboard

1. In the Dock, click the **Finder** icon (![icon]).
2. Click **Applications**.
3. Double-click **Dashboard**.

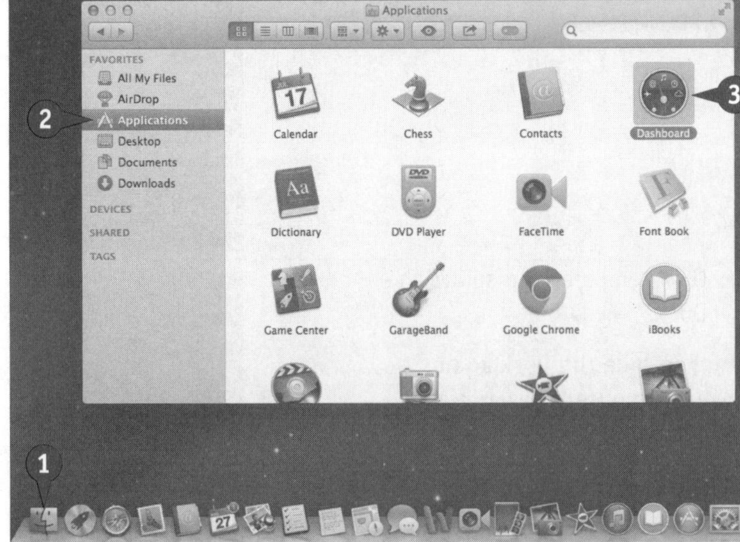

Your Mac displays the Dashboard and its current set of open widgets.

4. Click **Add** (⊕).

OS X displays its collection of widgets.

5 Click the widget you want to add.

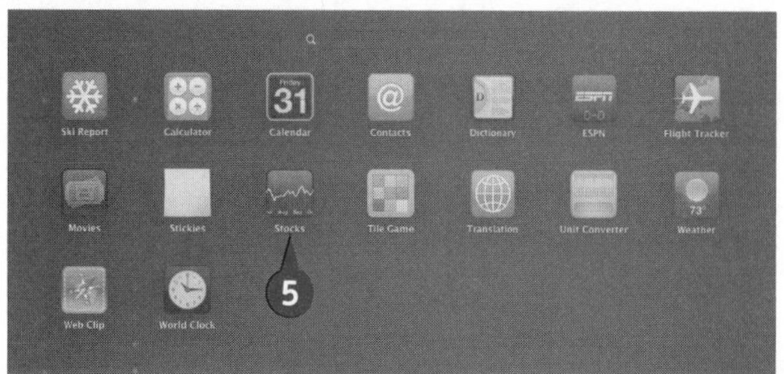

A Your Mac adds the widget to the Dashboard.

6 Use the mouse to click and drag the new widget or existing widgets to the position you prefer.

B If the widget is configurable, it displays an *i* when you position the mouse over it.

7 Click the ***i***.

8 Configure the widget as needed.

9 Click **Done**.

10 Click **Exit** (⊝).

Your Mac closes the Dashboard.

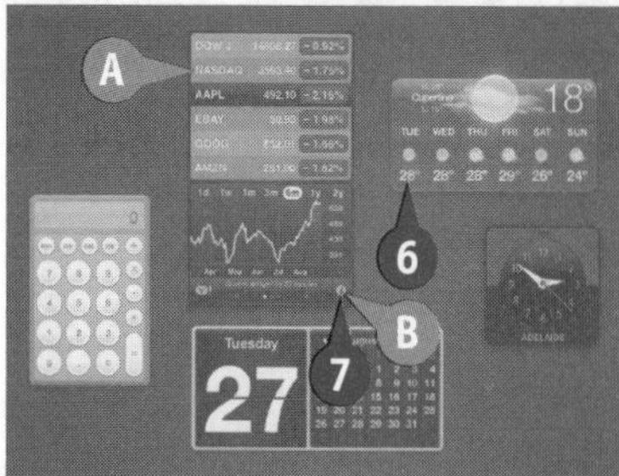

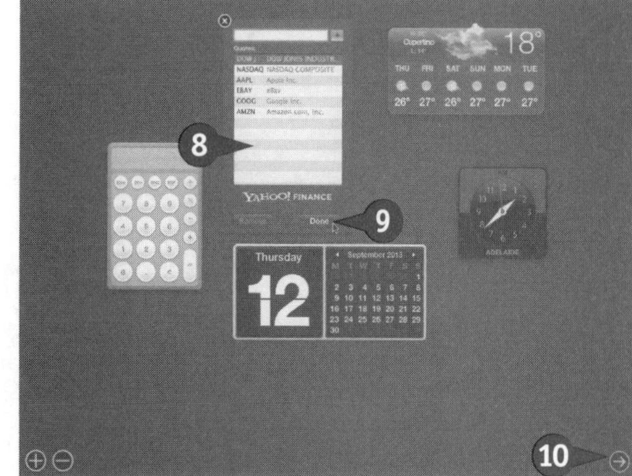

TIPS

Are there other methods I can use to open the Dashboard?
Yes. You can display the Dashboard quickly on most Macs by pressing F12. On some keyboards, you must press Fn+F12 instead. You can also press F12 (or Fn+F12) to close the Dashboard. On most Apple keyboards, you can also press F4 to open and close the Dashboard.

How do I remove a widget from the Dashboard?
If you just want to remove a single widget, press and hold Option, position the mouse over the widget, and then click the **Close** button (⊗) that the Dashboard displays in the upper-left corner of the widget. If you want to remove more than one widget, click ⊖ and then click ⊗ in each widget that you want to remove.

Using Do Not Disturb

The Do Not Disturb feature in OS X allows you to turn off all notifications and alerts from applications for 24 hours or until you turn Do Not Disturb off. This feature can be handy if your computer is left turned on overnight and you don't want to be woken by incoming alerts, if you need to focus on work and don't want to be distracted, or if you are giving a presentation on your Mac and don't want alerts getting in the way of your slides.

Using Do Not Disturb

1 Click **Notification Center** (☰).

Notification Center appears.

2 Scroll up on the Notification Center display and click **Do Not Disturb**.

Do Not Disturb is turned on and all alerts and notifications are stopped for 24 hours.

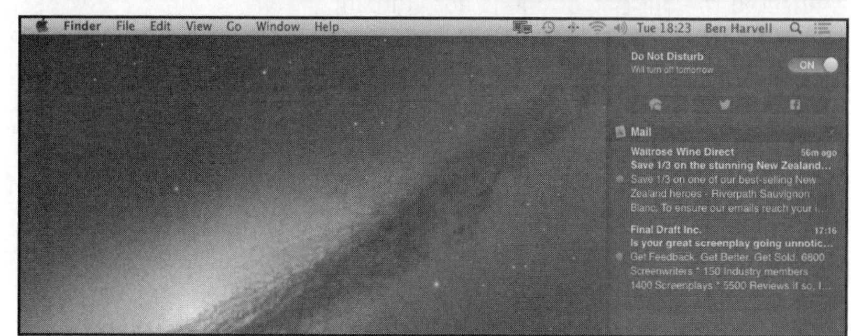

TIP

How do I turn Do Not Disturb off?

Do Not Disturb turns off automatically after a day, but if you want to turn it off sooner you can follow the previous steps and turn it back on using the toggle at the top of the Notification Center pane.

Set Trackpad Gestures

By default, OS X is set to respond to various gestures performed on a connected trackpad. These gestures can include pinching to zoom, swiping multiple fingers to move between apps and windows, and twisting two fingers to rotate windows and objects. There are also alternative gestures you may want to switch on or edit that can be found in the System Preferences pane.

Set Trackpad Gestures

Note: If you do not have a trackpad connected to your Mac or one is not built in, you will not be able to access the Trackpad section of System Preferences.

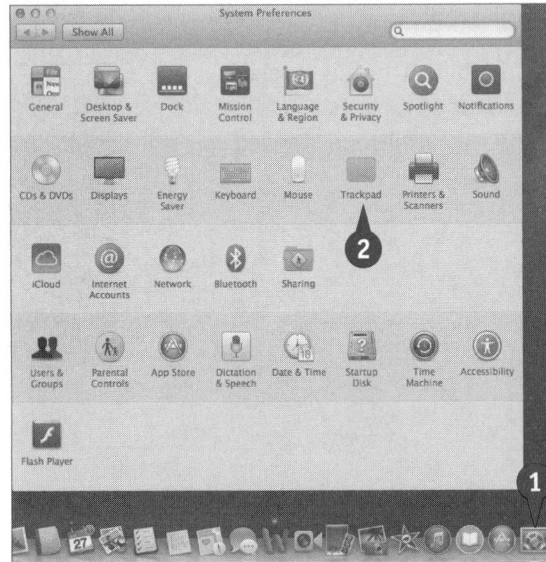

Access the System Preferences Trackpad Pane

1. In the Dock, click the **System Preferences** icon (▣).
2. Click **Trackpad.**

Set Point & Click Gestures

1. Click **Point & Click.**
2. Select the **Tap to click** check box (☐ changes to ☑) to select objects with a tap.
3. Select the **Secondary click** check box (☐ changes to ☑) to perform a Control+click when tapping or clicking with two fingers.
4. Select the **Look up** check box (☐ changes to ☑) to define a word when tapped with three fingers.
5. Select the **Three finger drag** check box (☐ changes to ☑) to move objects by tapping and dragging three fingers.

A. Click and drag the **Tracking speed** slider to adjust the speed of the cursor when using a trackpad.

Set Scroll & Zoom Gestures

1. Click **Scroll & Zoom**.
2. Select the **Scroll direction** check box (☐ changes to ☑) to make content follow your fingers when scrolling.
3. Select the **Zoom in or out** check box (☐ changes to ☑) to turn on two-finger pinching to zoom.
4. Select the **Smart zoom** check box (☐ changes to ☑) to enable zooming into content with a two-fingered double tap.
5. Select the **Rotate** check box (☐ changes to ☑) to enable rotation of images and objects using two fingers.

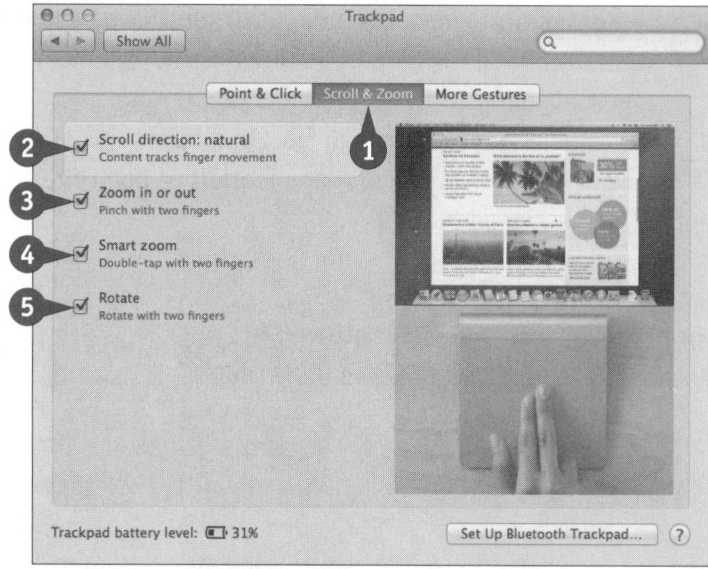

Set More Gestures

1. Click **More Gestures**.
2. Select the box next to the gesture you wish to turn on (☐ changes to ☑).

Note: A description of each gesture appears below the action, and a video shows how to use the gesture when you hover the cursor over the description text.

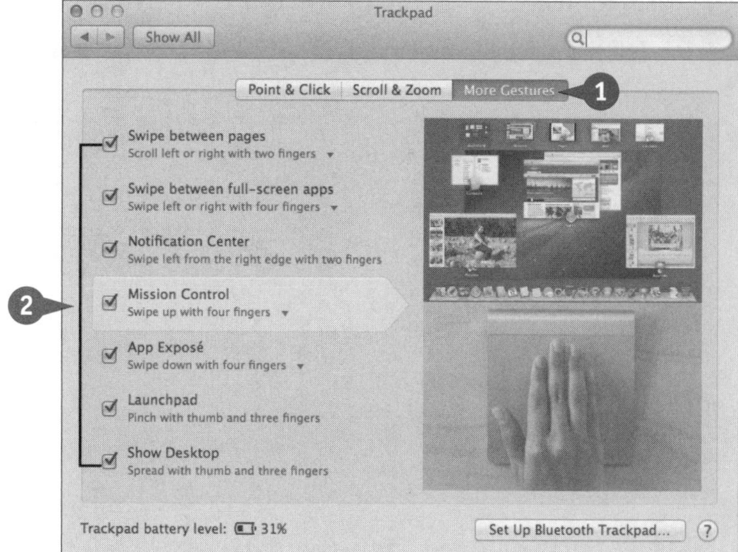

TIP

Can I change the type of gesture for a particular action?

Yes. Some of the actions that appear in the Trackpad section of System Preferences have an arrow next to them which, when clicked, shows a list of alternate gestures to use. Click a different gesture from the list to set it. Bear in mind, however, that changing the default gesture for an action may change the gesture for another action if the gesture you choose is already in use.

Set the Default Apps for File Types

OS X automatically chooses an application to open a specific file type on your Mac. For example, by default a PDF file will open in Preview. You can change the application in which a file or all files of a specific type open by using the OS X Info pane. From this pane, you can select the application to open a file and make it the default application to open all files of that type. This can be useful if you want to use a third-party application to open files of a specific type rather than the default application assigned by OS X.

Set the Default Apps for File Types

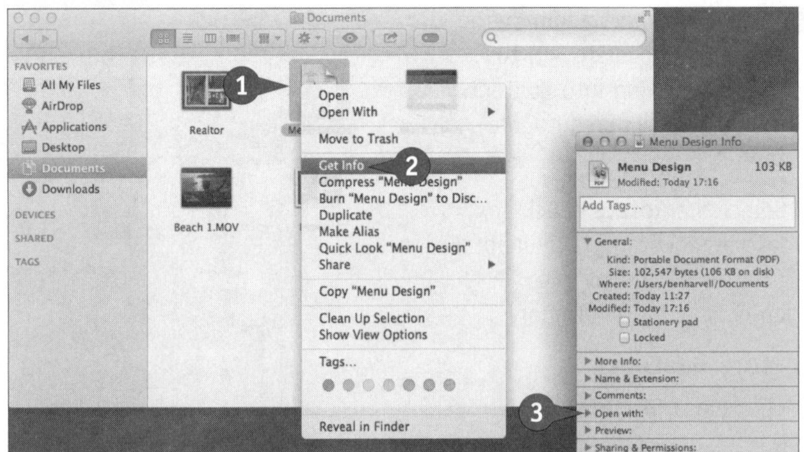

1. Click a file you want to open in a specific app and Control +Click or right-click it.
2. Click **Get Info**.

   The Info pane for the file appears.
3. Click the triangle (▶) next to Open with:.

   The Open with: section appears.

   Ⓐ The application that currently opens the file is shown here.
4. Click ⬍.

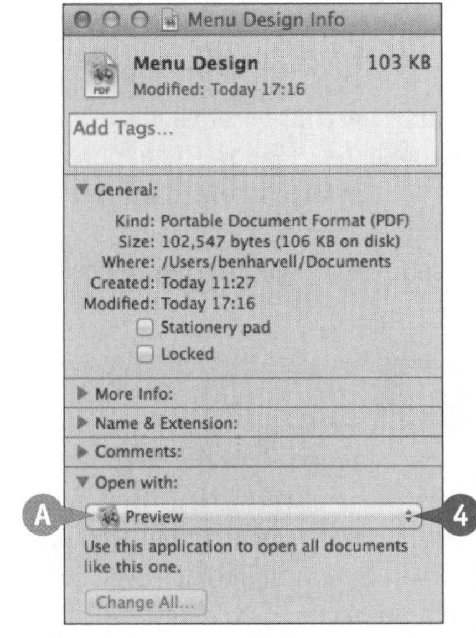

5 Click an option from the list of suggested applications.

B You can also click **App Store** to view suggested applications available for download from the Mac App Store.

C To set all files of this type to open using the application you set, click **Change All**.

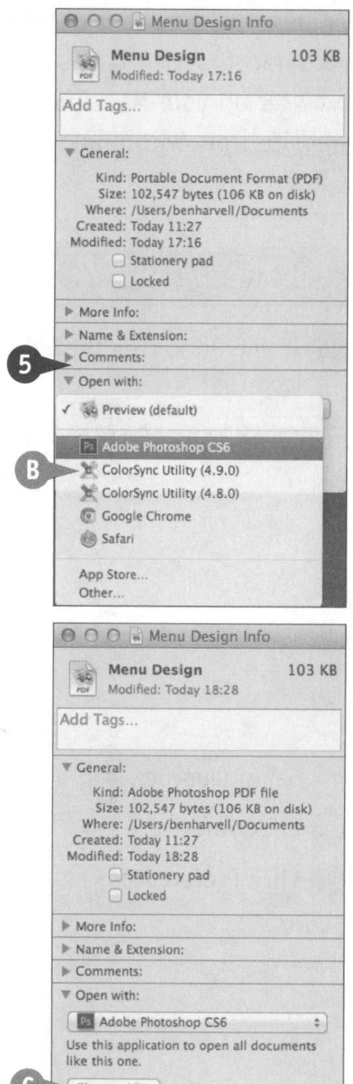

TIP

Why is the application I want to use not listed?

Applications associated with the type of file you have chosen are shown by default, but you can select a specific application by clicking **Other** on the Open with: pop up menu and browsing your Applications folder or another location on your Mac. OS X shows recommended applications in each folder you browse unless you click ⬍ and select **All Applications** from the pop-up menu that appears. Click the application you want to use and click **Add**.

Set the Default Web Browser

There are a number of web browser applications that can be installed in OS X alongside the default Safari browser. If you prefer using another browser over Safari, you can set one as the default browser on your Mac. The browser you set will open each time you click a link or are taken to a website from within another application.

Set the Default Web Browser

1. In the Dock, click the **Safari** icon ( ).

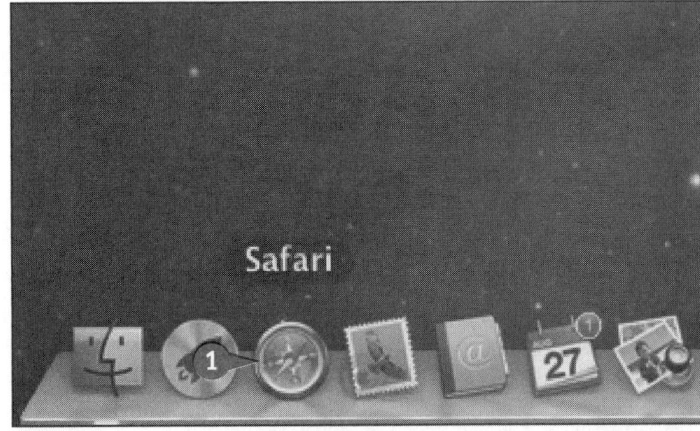

Safari launches.

2. Click **Safari**.
3. Click **Preferences**.

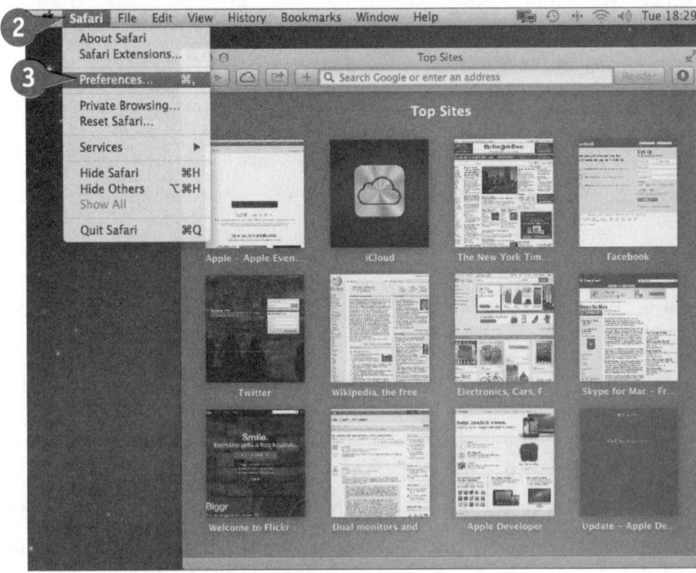

4 Click **General**.

5 Click ⬍ next to Default web browser:.

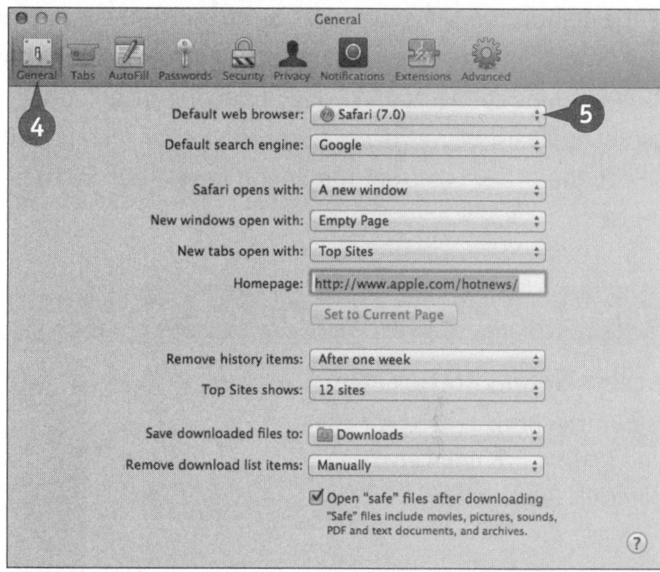

6 Select the application you want to set as the default web browser.

A If the web browser you want to use isn't shown, click **Select...** to choose an application from a location on your Mac.

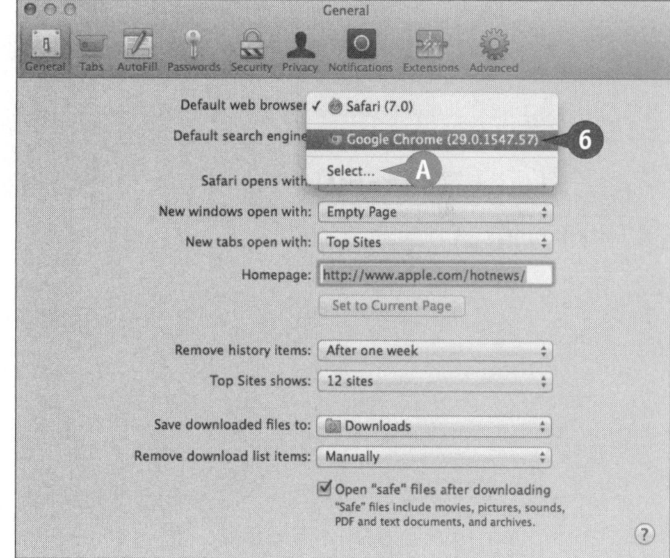

TIP

What web browsers can I use with OS X?

There are a number of free web browser applications available for Macs that can be used instead of or alongside Safari. Google provides its Chrome browser, which is useful for those who use Gmail and other Google services. Firefox and Opera are other popular options.

Choose Audio Input and Output Devices

By default, your Mac uses its built-in speakers to play audio and its built-in microphone to record input. You can use other devices with Mac OS X, however, such as headphones, speakers, and microphones connected via USB, FireWire, or wirelessly. You can also choose an AirPlay device such as an Apple TV or AirPlay speaker to stream system audio to. Once connected and installed you can select these devices from the Sound section of System Preferences.

Choose Audio Input and Output Devices

Access Sound Preferences

1. In the Dock, click the **System Preferences** icon (⚙).

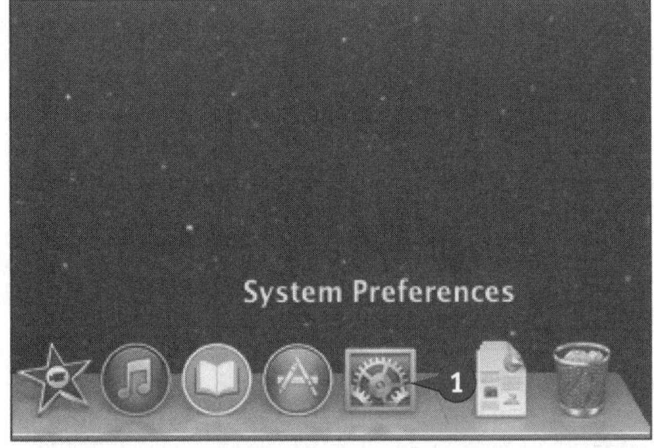

2. Click **Sound**.

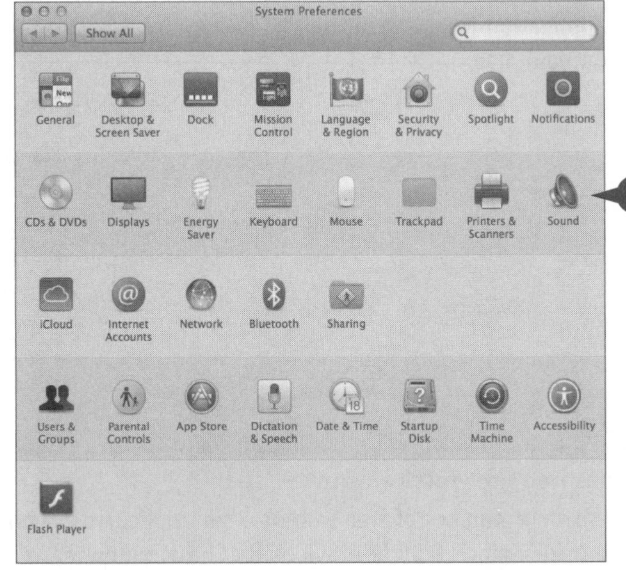

Set the Audio Output Device

1. Click **Output**.
2. Click the device you want to use.

A. Some stereo speaker devices allow you to set the audio balance using this slider.

B. You can set the output volume for the device you have chosen using this slider.

C. Select this box (☐ changes to ☑) to show the volume control in the menu bar.

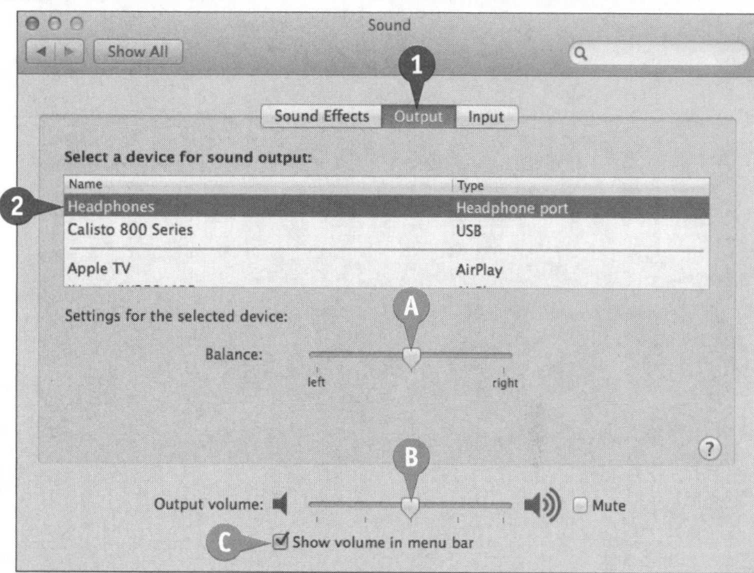

Set the Audio Input Device

1. Click **Input**.
2. Click the device you want to use.

D. Use this slider to set the input volume of your microphone.

E. This display shows the input level of your device.

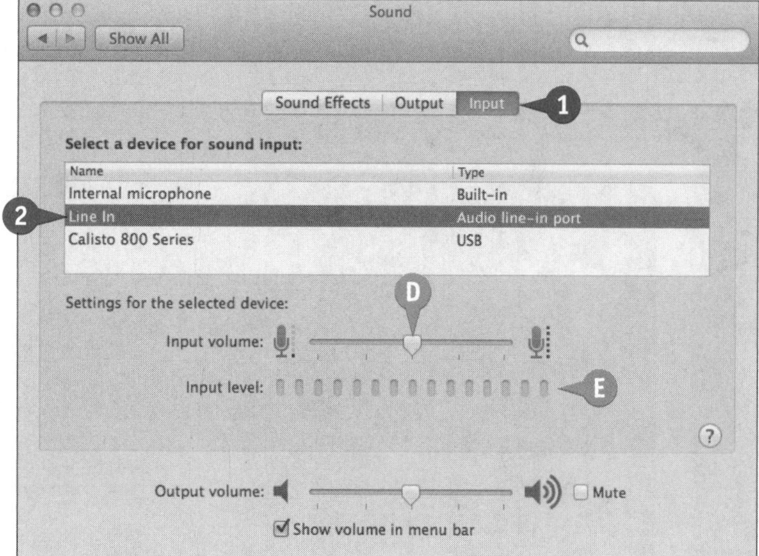

TIP

Is there a faster way to select audio input and output devices?

Yes. If you selected the **Show volume in menu bar** check box (☐ changes to ☑), you can click the volume control icon in the menu bar while pressing and holding the Alt key. A menu appears on which you can quickly select an input or output device to use or jump straight to the Sound System Preferences pane.

CHAPTER 14

Maintaining OS X

To keep OS X running smoothly, maintain top performance, and reduce the risk of computer problems, you need to perform some routine maintenance chores. This chapter shows you how to empty the Trash, delete unnecessary files, uninstall applications, update applications, back up your files, recondition your notebook battery, and more.

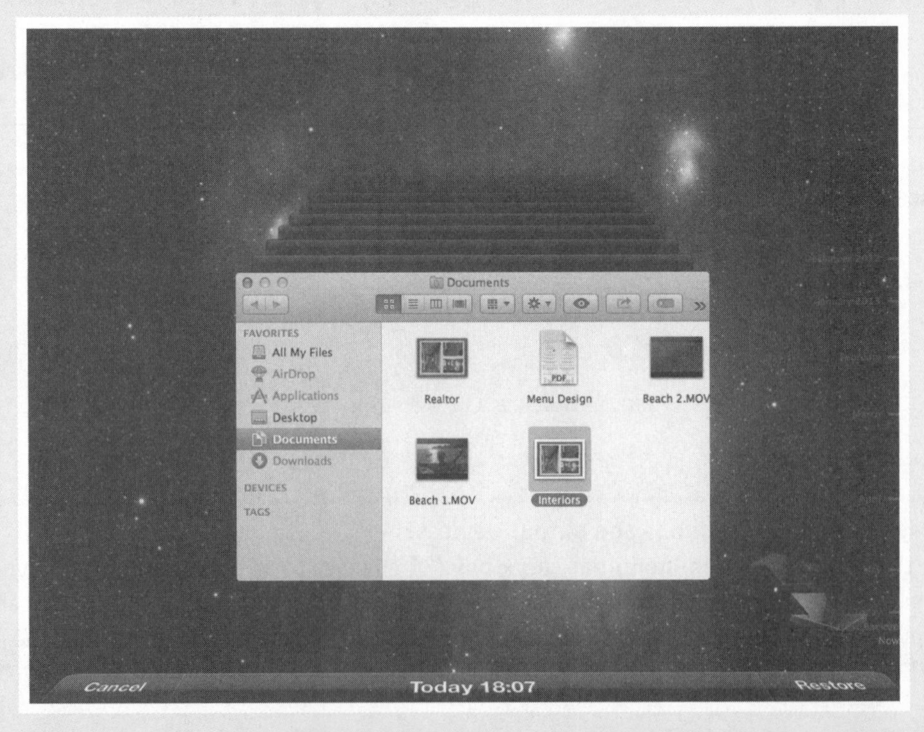

Empty the Trash

You can free up hard drive space on your Mac by periodically emptying the Trash. When you delete a file or folder, OS X does not immediately remove the file from your Mac's hard drive. Instead, OS X moves the file or folder to the Trash. This is useful if you accidentally delete an item, because it means you can open the Trash and restore the item. However, all those deleted files and folders take up hard drive space, so you need to empty the Trash periodically to regain that space. You should empty the Trash at least once a week.

Empty the Trash

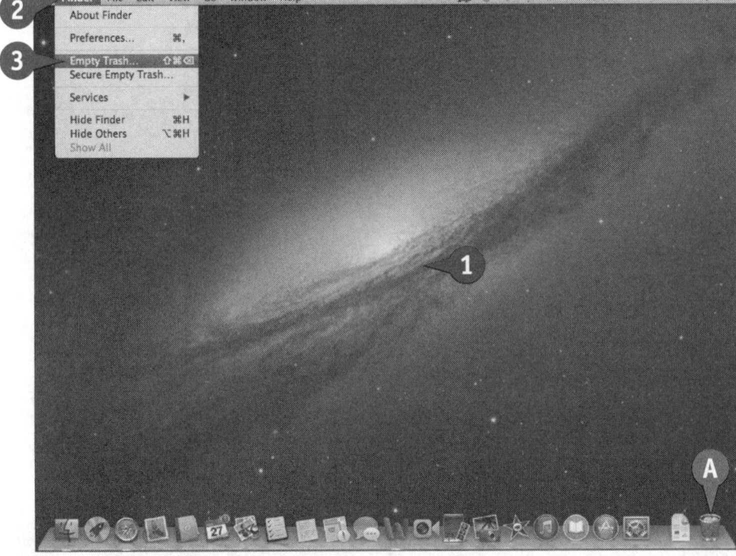

1. Click the desktop.
2. Click **Finder** from the menu.
3. Click **Empty Trash.**

   A. You can also right-click the **Trash** icon (🗑) and then click **Empty Trash.**

Note: Another way to select the Empty Trash command is to press Shift + ⌘ + Delete.

OS X asks you to confirm the deletion.

Note: OS X will not ask for you to confirm deletion if you have turned off this setting in Finder Preferences.

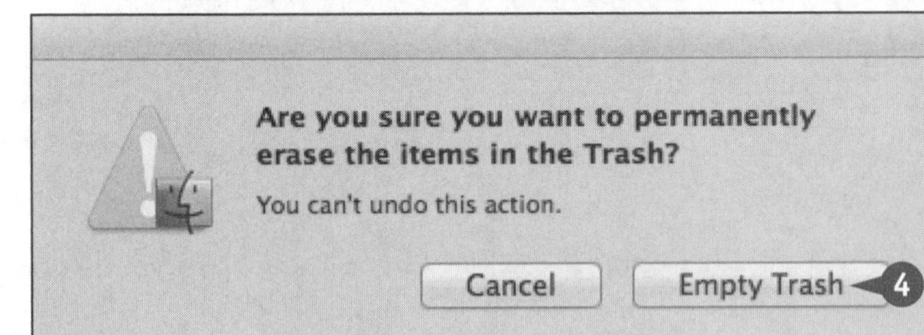

4. Click **Empty Trash.**

   OS X empties the Trash (🗑 changes to 🗑).

CHAPTER

14

Organize Your Desktop

You can make your OS X desktop easier to scan and navigate by organizing the icons. The OS X desktop automatically displays icons for objects such as your external hard drives, inserted CDs and DVDs, disk images, and attached iPods. The desktop is also a handy place to store files, file aliases, copies of documents, and more. However, the more you use your desktop as a storage area, the more the desktop can become disarrayed, making it hard to find the icon you want. You can fix this by organizing the icons.

Organize Your Desktop

1. Click the desktop.
2. Click **View**.
3. Click **Clean Up By**.
4. Click **Name**.

   You can also right-click the desktop, click **Clean Up By**, and then click **Name**, or press Option + ⌘ + 1.

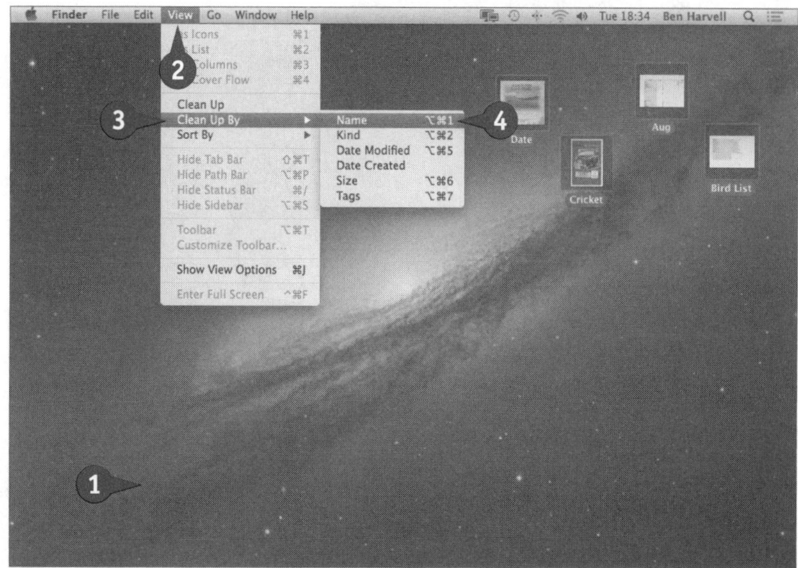

Ⓐ Your Mac organizes the icons alphabetically and arranges them in columns from right to left.

Check Hard Drive Free Space

To ensure that your Mac's hard drive does not become full, you should periodically check how much free space it has left. If you run out of room on your Mac's hard drive, you will not be able to install more applications or create more documents, and your Mac's performance will suffer. To ensure your free space does not become too low — say, less than about 20 or 25GB — you can check how much free space your hard drive has left. You should check your Mac's hard drive free space about once a month. If you frequently install programs, create large files, or download media, you should check your free space every couple of weeks.

Check Hard Drive Free Space

Check Free Space Using Finder

1. In the Dock, click the **Finder** icon ( ).
2. Click your user account.

Note: You can also click any folder on your Mac's hard drive.

3. Press ⌘ + / to display the status bar.
4. Read the available value, which tells you the amount of free space left on the hard drive.

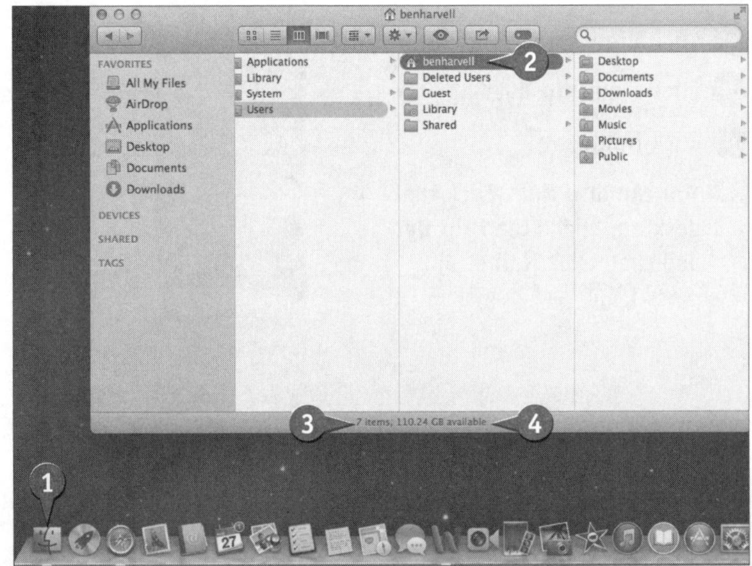

Display Free Space on the Desktop

1. Display your Mac's HD (hard drive) icon on the desktop, as described in the first Tip.
2. Click the desktop.
3. Click **View**.
4. Click **Show View Options**.

Note: You can also run the Show View Options command by pressing ⌘+J.

The Desktop dialog appears.

5 Select the **Show item info** check box (☐ changes to ☑).

A Your Mac displays the amount of free hard drive space under the Macintosh HD icon.

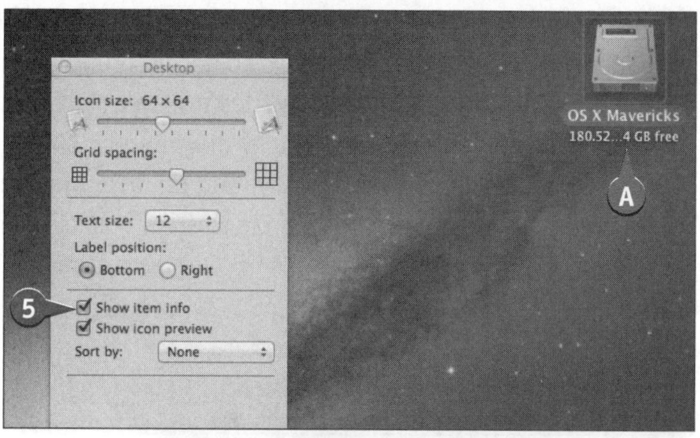

6 Drag the Icon size ▽ until you can read all the icon text.

7 If you still cannot read all the text, click the **Text size** ⬍ and then click a larger size.

8 Click **Close** (●).

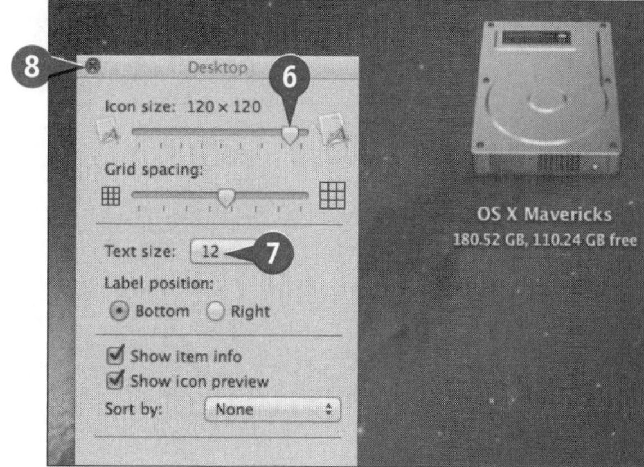

TIPS

My Mac's hard drive icon does not appear on the desktop. How do I display it?

If you do not see the Macintosh HD icon on your desktop, click the desktop, click **Finder** in the menu bar, and then click **Preferences**. Click the **General** tab, select the **Hard disks** check box (☐ changes to ☑), and then click **Close** (●).

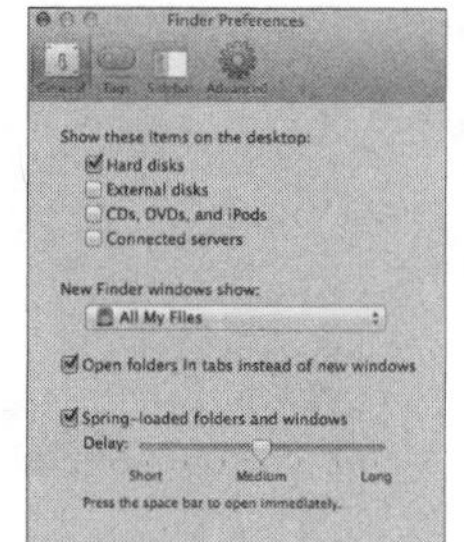

What should I do if my Mac's hard drive space is getting low?

First, you should empty the Trash, as described in the section "Empty the Trash." Next, uninstall applications that you no longer use, as described in the section "Uninstall Unused Applications." If you have any documents that you are sure you no longer need — particularly large media files — you should move them to an external hard drive USB flash drive, burn them to a disc, or send them to the Trash and then empty the Trash folder.

Uninstall Unused Applications

If you have an application that you no longer use, you can free up some hard drive space and reduce clutter in the Applications folder by uninstalling that application. When you install an application, the program stores its files on your Mac's hard drive, and although most programs are quite small, many require hundreds of megabytes of hard drive space. Uninstalling applications you do not need frees up the space they use and removes their icons or folders from the Applications folder. In most cases, you must be logged on to OS X with an administrator account to uninstall applications. Bundled applications that come with your Mac cannot be removed, even if you don't use them.

Uninstall Unused Applications

1. In the Dock, click the **Finder** icon (![]).

2. Click **Applications**.

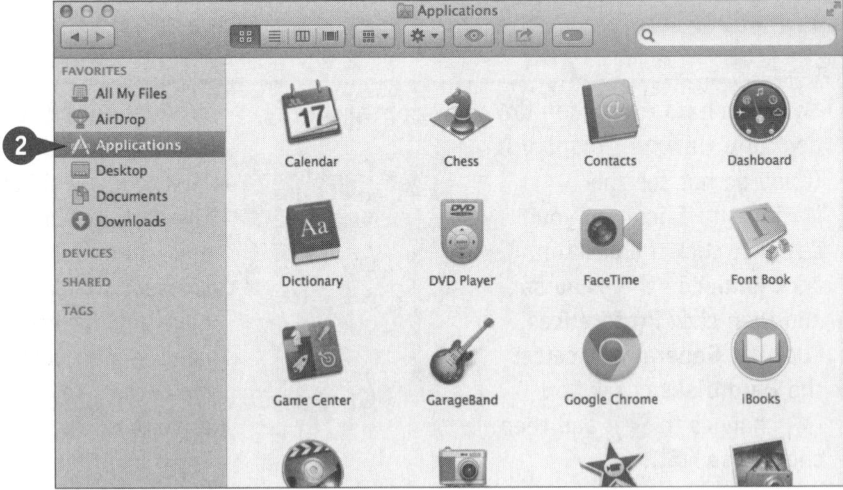

3 Click and drag the application or its folder and drop it on the **Trash** icon (🗑).

If your Mac prompts you for an administrator password, type the password, and then click **OK**.

A Your Mac uninstalls the application.

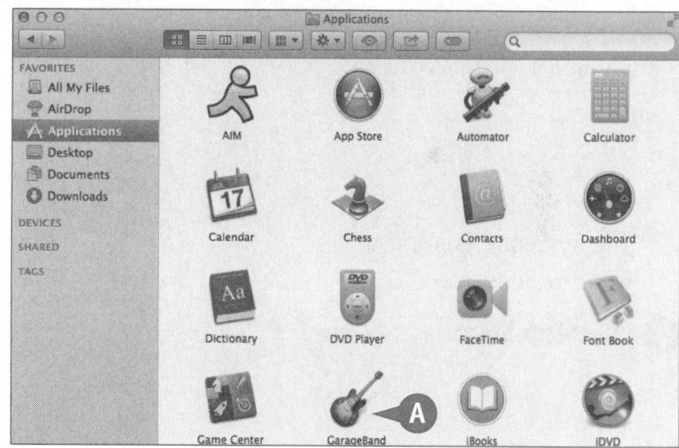

TIPS

Is there another way to uninstall an application?

A few Mac applications come with a separate program for uninstalling the application. Double-click the uninstaller program's icon and then follow the on-screen instructions.

How can I restore an uninstalled application?

If you used the application's uninstall program, you must reinstall the application. If you sent the application to the Trash, and that was the most recent operation you performed, click **Finder** (🖥), click **Edit**, and then click **Undo Move of *Application*** (where *Application* is the name of the application you want to restore). Otherwise, click **Trash** (🗑), and then use the Trash folder to drag the application back to Applications.

Set a Software Update Schedule

You can ensure that your Mac and the applications that come with OS X are up to date with the latest features and fixes by setting OS X to automatically download and install updates to software. Apple makes OS X updates available from time to time. These updates fix problems, add new features, and resolve security issues. You can reduce computer problems and maximize online safety by setting up OS X to download and install these updates automatically.

Set a Software Update Schedule

1 Click the **Apple** icon ().

2 Click **System Preferences**.

Note: You can also click the **System Preferences** icon () in the Dock.

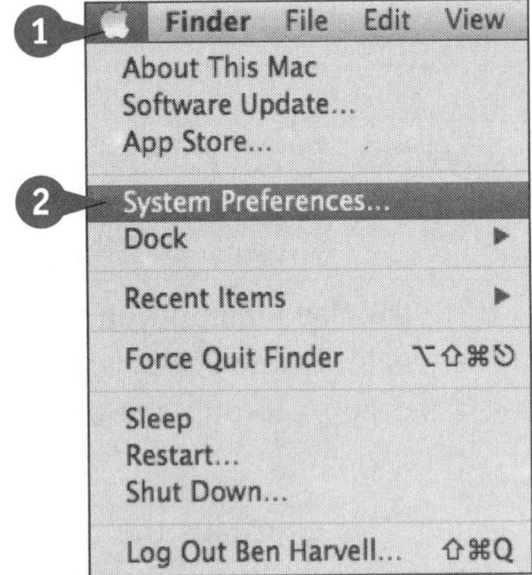

The System Preferences window appears.

3 Click **App Store**.

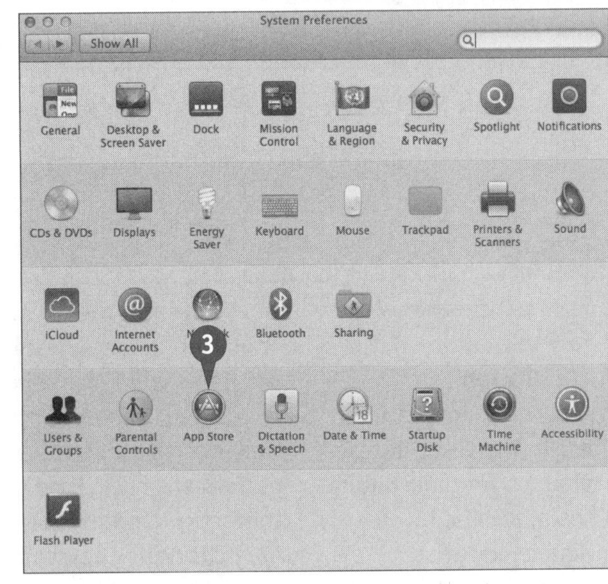

The App Store preferences appear.

4. Select the **Automatically check for updates** check box (☐ changes to ☑).

5. Select the **Download Newly available updates in the background** check box (☐ changes to ☑).

6. Select the **Install app updates** check box (☐ changes to ☑).

7. Select the **Install system data files and security updates** check box (☐ changes to ☑).

8. Select the **Automatically download apps purchased on other Macs** check box (☐ changes to ☑).

Your Mac automatically checks for updates and downloads them when available.

TIP

Do I have to let the App Store do the checking automatically?

Technically, no, you do not have to rely on automatic checking. Instead, you can check for software updates manually by deselecting all check boxes on the App Store preferences pane and clicking **Check Now** when you want to check for updates. However, this is not a good idea because you should always keep your Mac software up to date, and this might not happen if you have to remember to check for updates.

Update Software Manually

To make sure that your Mac and the applications that come with OS X are currently up to date with the latest features and fixes, you can update the software manually. By default, OS X checks for new software updates automatically on a regular schedule. If you turned off this feature or configured it to be less frequent, you can still keep OS X up to date by checking for — and if necessary, installing — updates yourself. See the section "Set a Software Update Schedule" to learn how to configure the Software Update schedule.

Update Software Manually

1. Connect to the Internet, if you have not already done so.
2. In the Dock, click the **App Store** icon ( ).

The App Store appears.

3. Click **Updates**.

OS X connects with the Apple servers and checks for new updates.

Ⓐ If you want to install all the available updates, click **Update All**.

4 To install individual updates, click **Update**.

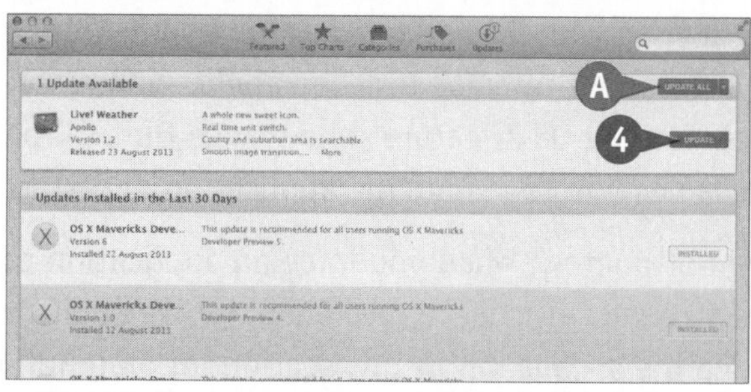

Ⓑ The App Store displays the update download and install progress.

The updates you selected install and are added to the list of recent updates.

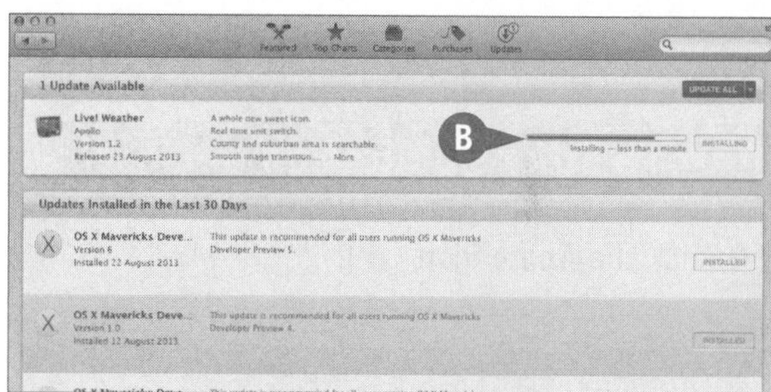

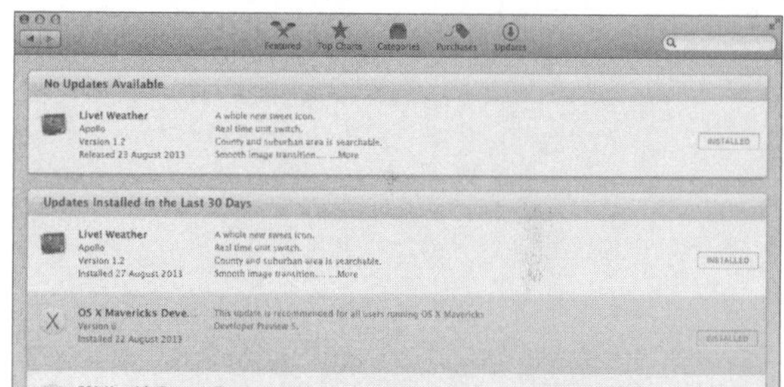

TIPS

Should I always install every available update?
As a general rule, yes. However, some exceptions exist. For example, if an update is available for an application that you never use, you can safely skip that update. Also, if your Internet connection is slow, you may prefer to install the updates one at a time.

Is the Mavericks Update important?
Yes, any update named Mavericks Update is very important. These are major updates to your Mac's operating system, and they generally improve system stability and security. Because such an update affects your entire Mac and is usually quite large — often several hundred megabytes — it is best to install this update on its own.

Force a Stuck Application to Close

When you are working with an application, you may find that it becomes unresponsive and you cannot interact with the application or even quit the application normally. In that case, you can use an OS X feature called Force Quit to force a stuck or unresponsive application to close, which enables you to restart the application or restart your Mac.

Unfortunately, when you force an application to quit, you lose any unsaved changes in your open documents. Therefore, you should make sure the application really is stuck before forcing it to quit. See the second Tip in this section for more information.

Force a Stuck Application to Close

1. Click the **Apple** icon ().

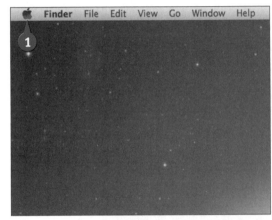

2. Click **Force Quit**.

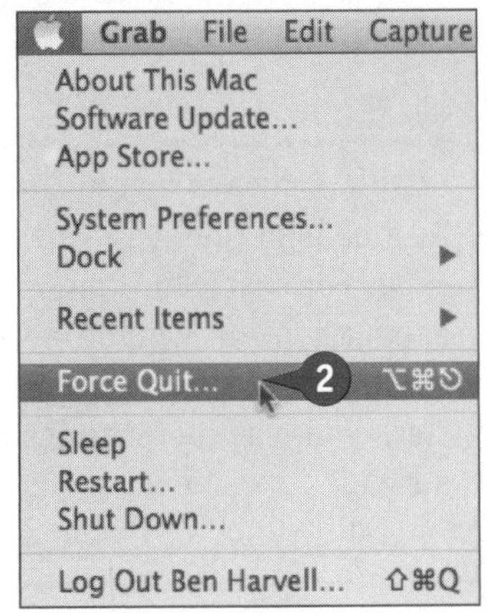

The Force Quit Applications window appears.

3 Click the application you want to shut down.

4 Click **Force Quit**.

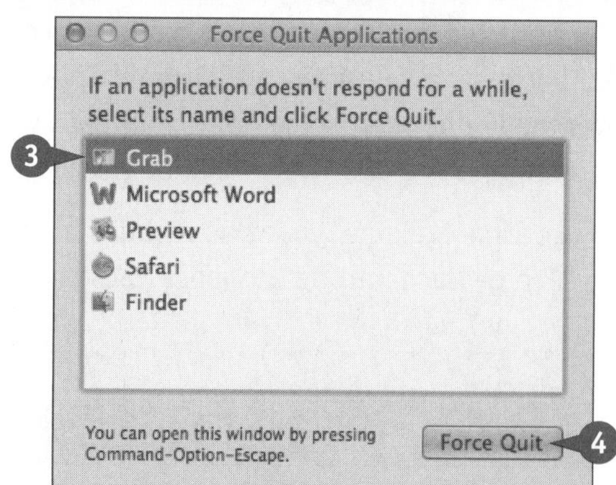

Your Mac asks you to confirm that you want to force the application to quit.

5 Click **Force Quit**.

Your Mac shuts down the application.

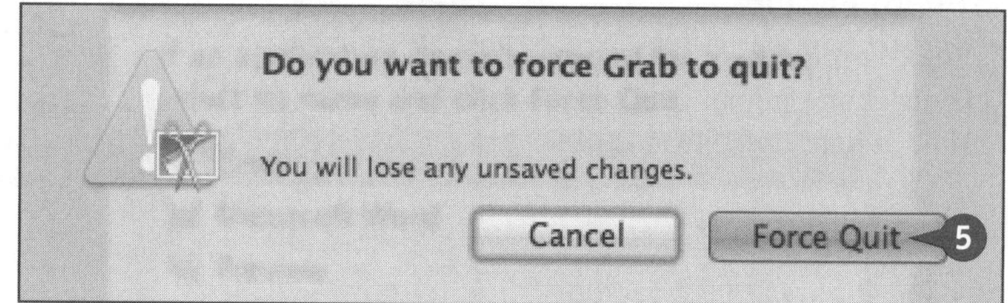

TIPS

Are there easier ways to run the Force Quit command?

Yes. From the keyboard, you can run the Force Quit command by pressing Option + ⌘ + Esc. If the application has a Dock icon, press and hold Control + Option and then click the application's Dock icon. In the menu that appears, click **Force Quit**.

If an application is not responding, does that always mean the application is stuck?

Not necessarily. For example, some application operations — such as recalculating a large spreadsheet or rendering a 3-D image — can take a few minutes, and during that time the application can appear stuck. Similarly, your Mac may be low on memory, which can also cause an application to seem stuck. In this case, try shutting down some of your other applications to free up some memory.

Configure Time Machine Backups

One of the most crucial OS X maintenance chores is to configure your system to make regular backups of your files. Macs are reliable machines, but they can crash and all hard drives eventually die, so at some point your data will be at risk. To avoid losing that data forever, you need to configure the OS X Time Machine feature to perform regular backups.

To use Time Machine, your Mac requires a second hard drive. This can be a second internal disk on a Mac Pro or Mac mini, but on most Macs the easiest course is to connect an external hard drive.

Configure Time Machine Backups

Configure Backups Automatically

1. Connect an external USB, Thunderbolt, or FireWire hard drive to your Mac.

   OS X asks if you want to use the hard drive as your backup disk.

2. Click **Use as Backup Disk**.

Note: If OS X does not ask to use the hard drive, continue with the following steps.

Configure Backups Manually

1. In the Dock, click the **System Preferences** icon (▣).

2. Click **Time Machine**.

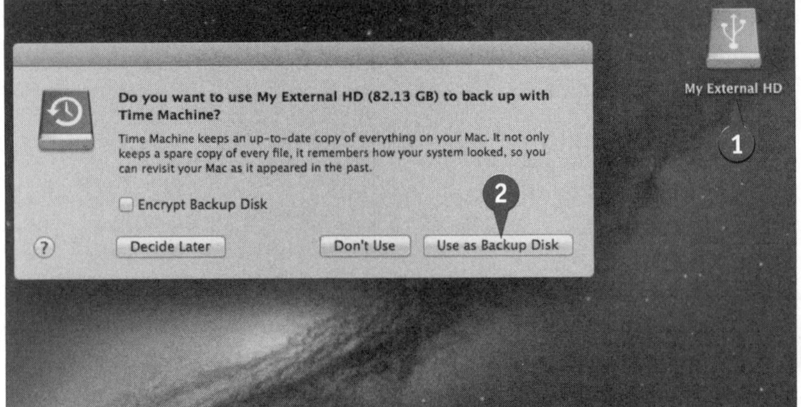

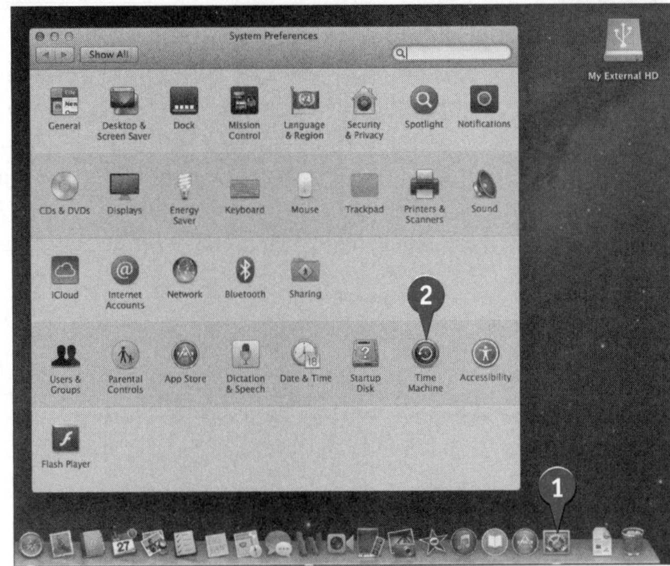

The Time Machine preferences appear.

3 Click **Select Backup Disk**.

Time Machine displays a list of available backup devices.

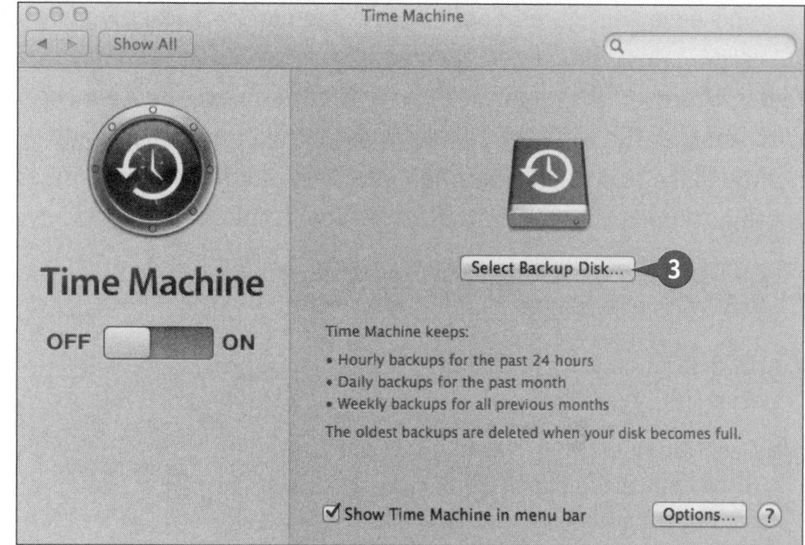

4 Click the external hard drive.

5 Click **Use Disk**.

Time Machine enables backups and prepares to run the first backup automatically in 2 minutes.

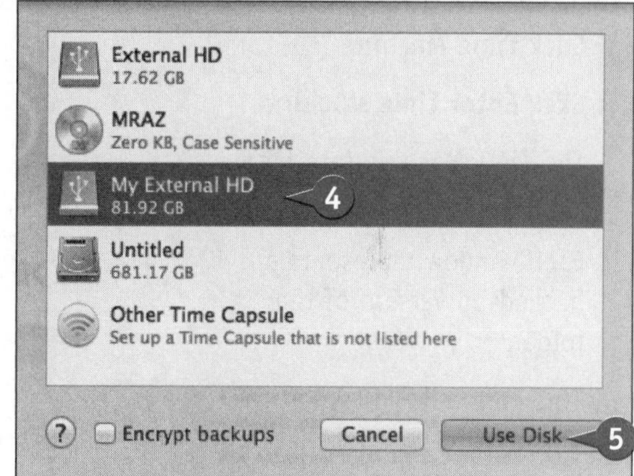

TIP

How do Time Machine backups work?

Time Machine makes backing up your Mac easy because backups are handled automatically on the following schedule:

- The initial backup occurs 2 minutes after you configure Time Machine for the first time. This backup includes your entire Mac.
- Time Machine runs another backup every hour. These hourly backups include just those files and folders that you have changed or created since the most recent hourly backup.
- Time Machine runs a daily backup that includes only those files and folders that you have changed or created since the most recent daily backup.
- Time Machine runs a weekly backup that includes only those files and folders that you have changed or created since the most recent weekly backup.

Restore Files Using Time Machine

If you have configured OS X to make regular Time Machine backups, you can use those backups to restore a lost file. If you accidentally delete a file, you can quickly restore it by opening the Trash folder. However, that does not help you if you have emptied the Trash folder, if you overwrite a file with another file with the same name, or if you improperly edit a file. Because Time Machine makes hourly, daily, and weekly backups, it stores older copies and older versions of your data. You can use these backups to restore any file that you accidentally delete, overwrite, or improperly edit.

Restore Files Using Time Machine

1. In the Dock, click the **Finder** icon ( ).
2. Open the folder you want to restore, or the folder that contains the file you want to restore.
3. Click **Time Machine** ( ).
4. Click **Enter Time Machine**.

   The Time Machine interface appears.

- A Each window represents a backed-up version of the folder.
- B This area tells you when the displayed version of the folder was backed up.
- C You can use this timeline to navigate the backed-up versions.

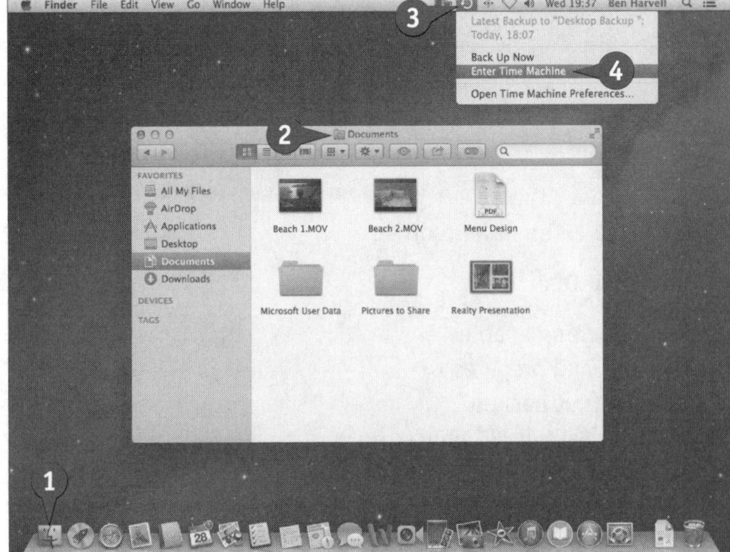

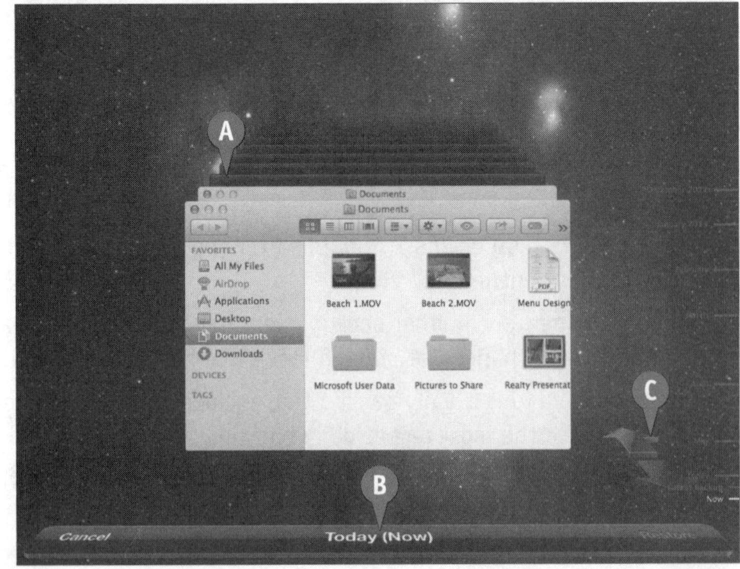

5 Navigate to the date that contains the backed-up version of the folder or file.

Note: See the Tip in this section to learn how to navigate the Time Machine backups.

6 If you are restoring a file, click the file.

7 Click **Restore**.

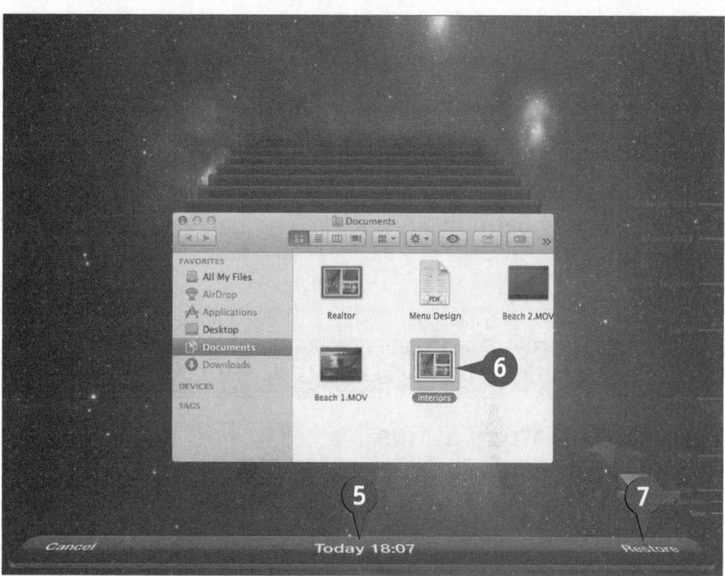

If another version of the folder or file already exists, Time Machine asks if you want to keep it or replace it.

8 Click **Replace**.

Time Machine restores the folder or file.

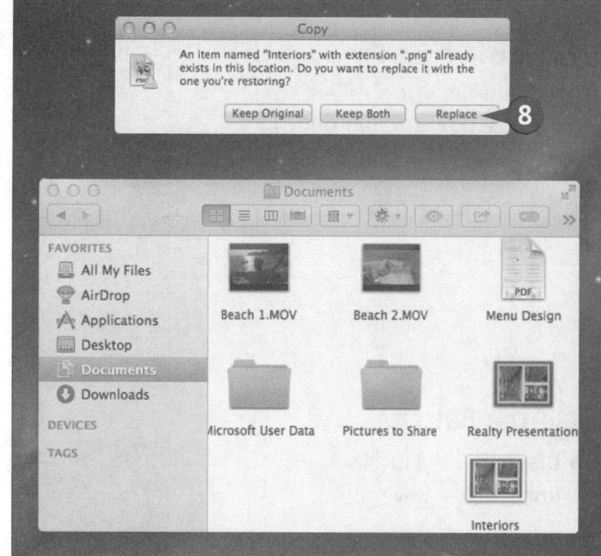

TIP

How do I navigate the backups in the Time Machine interface?

Here are the most useful techniques:

- Click the top arrow to jump to the earliest version; click the bottom arrow to return to the most recent version.
- Press and hold ⌘ and click the arrows to navigate through the backups one version at a time.
- Use the timeline to click a specific version.
- Click the version windows.

Recondition Your Mac Notebook Battery

To get the most performance out of your Mac notebook's battery, you need to recondition the battery by cycling it. *Cycling* a battery means letting it completely discharge and then fully recharging it again. Most Mac notebook batteries slowly lose their charging capacity over time. For example, if you can use your Mac notebook on batteries for 4 hours today, later on you'll only be able to run the computer for 3 hours on a full charge. You cannot stop this process, but you can delay it significantly by periodically cycling the battery. You should cycle your Mac notebook battery once a month or so.

Recondition Your Mac Notebook Battery

Display the Battery Status Percentage

1. Click the **Battery status** icon (▭).
2. Click **Show Percentage**.

   Your Mac shows the percentage of available battery power remaining.

Cycle the Battery

1. Disconnect your Mac notebook's power cord.

   A. The Battery Status icon changes from ▭ to ▭.

2. Operate your Mac notebook normally by running applications, working with documents, and so on.

3. As you work, keep your eye on the Battery Status percentage.

87%
Tue 11:12 AM
Paul
3

When the Battery Status reaches 4%, your Mac warns you that it is now running on reserve power.

4. Click **OK**.

5. Reattach the power cord.

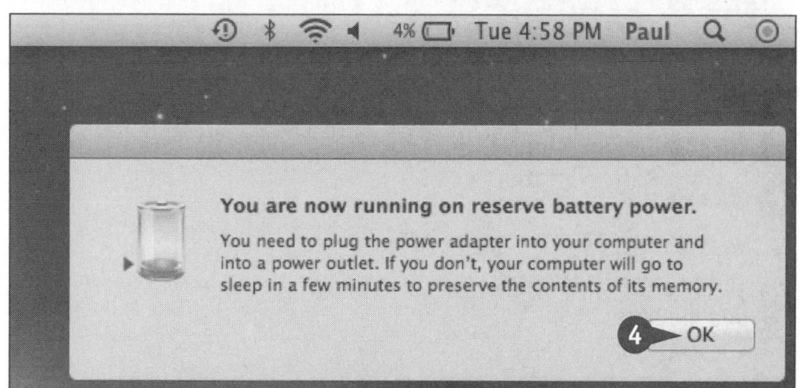

4%
Tue 4:58 PM
Paul
You are now running on reserve battery power.
You need to plug the power adapter into your computer and into a power outlet. If you don't, your computer will go to sleep in a few minutes to preserve the contents of its memory.
4
OK

Your Mac restarts and the Battery Status icon changes from ▭ to ▭.

6. Leave your Mac plugged in at least until the Battery Status shows 100%.

100%
Tue 9:16 PM
Paul
6

TIPS

I do not see the battery status in my menu bar. How do I display it?
Click **System Preferences** (▭) in the Dock to open System Preferences, and then click the **Energy Saver** icon. In the Energy Saver window, click **Battery** and then select the **Show battery status in the menu bar** check box (☐ changes to ☑).

Do Mac notebooks suffer from the memory effect?
Not anymore. Older portable computers used rechargeable nickel metal hydride (NiMH) or nickel cadmium (NiCad) batteries. The NiMH and NiCad types were phased out because they can suffer from a problem called the *memory effect*, where the battery loses capacity if you repeatedly recharge it without first fully discharging it. All the latest Mac notebooks have rechargeable lithium-ion (Li-ion) or lithium-polymer (Li-Po) batteries, which do not suffer from the memory effect.

Restart Your Mac

If a hardware device is having a problem with some system files, it often helps to restart your Mac. By rebooting the computer, you reload the entire system, which is often enough to solve many computer problems.

For a problem device that does not have its own power switch, restarting your Mac might not resolve the problem because the device remains powered up the whole time. You can *power cycle* — shut down and then restart — such devices as a group by power cycling your Mac.

Restart Your Mac

Restart Your Mac

1. Click the **Apple** icon (🍎).
2. Click **Restart.**

   Your Mac asks you to confirm and begins counting down one minute until it automatically restarts.

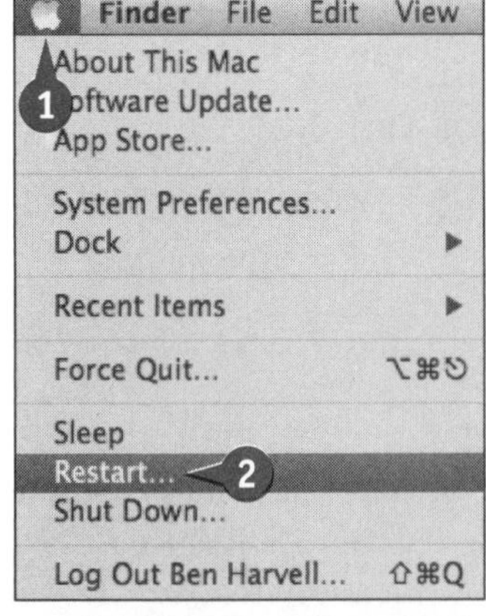

A. Select the **Reopen windows when logging back in** check box (☐ changes to ☑) to reopen any windows currently open when your Mac is restarted.

3. Click **Restart.**

Note: To bypass the confirmation dialog, press and hold Option when you click the **Restart** command.

Power Cycle Your Mac

1. Click the **Apple** icon (🍎).
2. Click **Shut Down**.

   Your Mac asks you to confirm.

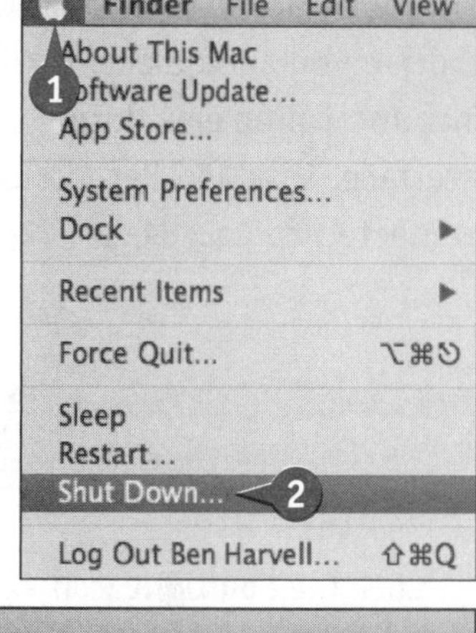

B Select the **Reopen windows when logging back in** check box (☐ changes to ☑) to reopen any windows currently open when your Mac is restarted.

Note: To bypass the confirmation dialog, hold down Option when you click **Shut Down**.

3. Click **Shut Down**.

   Wait 30 seconds to give all devices time to spin down before restarting your Mac.

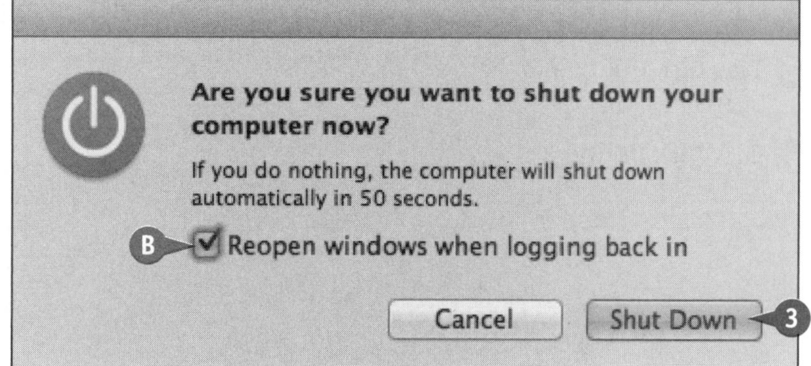

TIP

What other basic troubleshooting techniques can I use?

Here are several you can try:

- Make sure that each device is turned on, that cable connections are secure, and that insertable devices (such as USB devices) are properly inserted.
- If a device is battery powered, replace the batteries.
- If a device has an on/off switch, power cycle the device by turning it off, waiting a few seconds for it to stop spinning, and then turning it back on again.
- Close all running programs.
- Log out of your Mac — click 🍎; click **Log Out *User***, where *User* is your Mac username; and then click **Log Out** — and then log back in again.

Check and Repair a Hard Drive

If your Mac isn't performing as it should or you suspect there may be a problem with the hard drive you can quickly verify the disk and its permissions using the Disk Utility application. If you encounter problems during verification you can the repair the disk or its permissions using the same interface. Disk and Permissions verification and repair can be performed on any drive or partition connected to your Mac.

Check and Repair a Hard Drive

Access Disk Utility

1. Click the **Spotlight** icon (🔍).
2. Type **Disk Utility** into the Spotlight field.
3. Click **Disk Utility**.

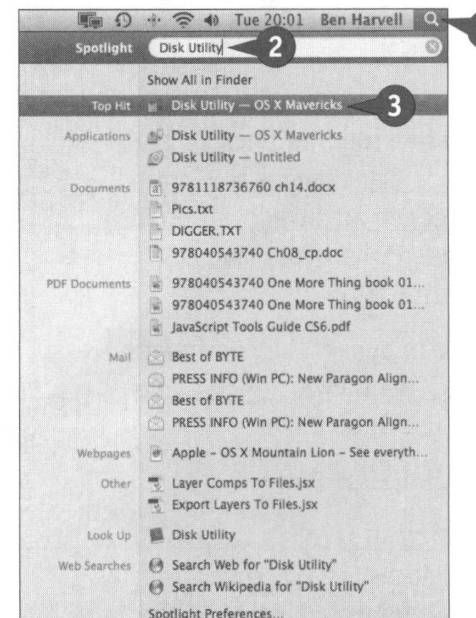

Disk Utility appears.

Verify and Repair a Disk

1. Click the drive you want to verify or repair in the source pane.
2. Click **First Aid**.
3. Click **Verify Disk**.

   Disk Utility verifies the disk and reports any problems.

Ⓐ If verification uncovers errors, click **Repair Disk**.

Note: You cannot repair the startup disk on your Mac.

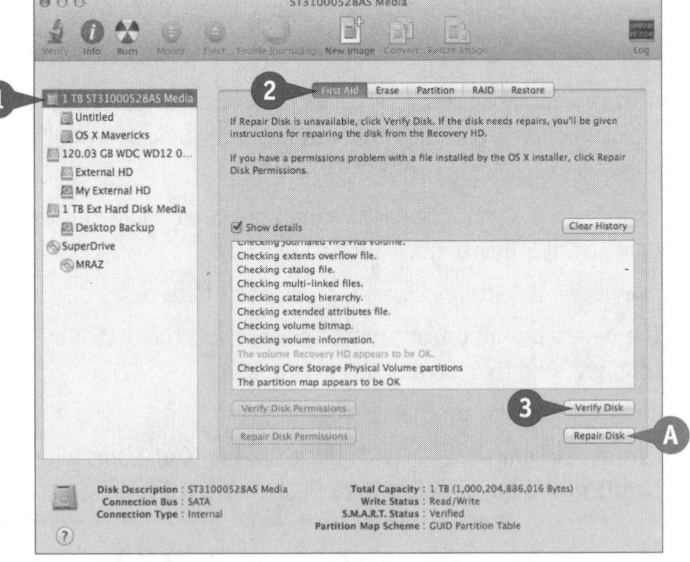

Verify and Repair Disk Permissions

1. Click the drive you want to verify or repair the permissions for in the source pane.
2. Click **First Aid**.
3. Click **Verify Disk Permissions**.

   Disk Utility verifies permissions on the disk.

   B If permission verification uncovers errors, click **Repair Disk Permissions.**

4. Click **Close** (◉).

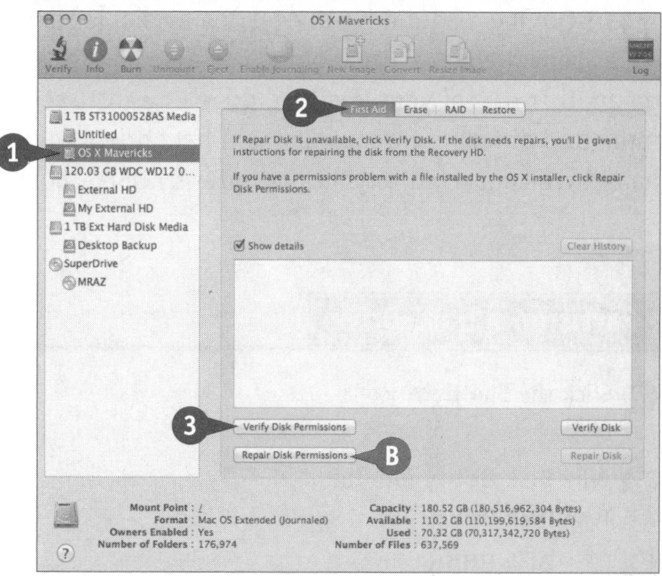

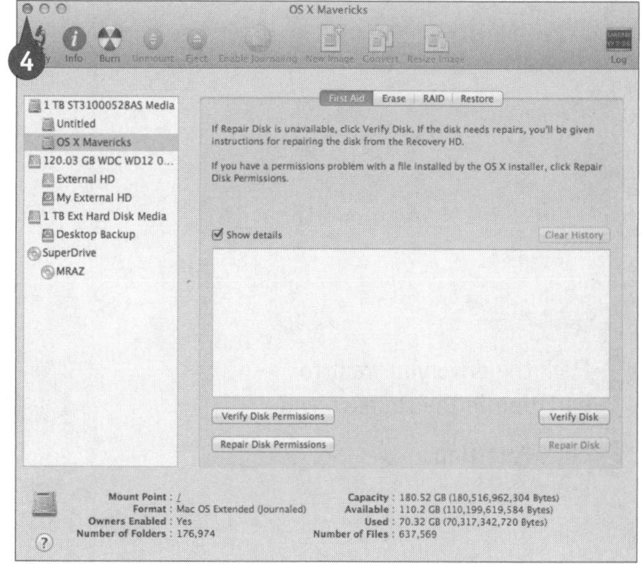

TIP

What type of problems can repairing a disk solve?

Using the Repair Disk tool in Disk Utility can help to solve a number of problems including applications that quit unexpectedly, external devices that are not working, and corrupted files. Try running Verify Disk first to determine if there are any problems before repairing the disk.

Partition a Hard Drive

Partitioning a hard drive divides the available space on the disk into sections, which appear as separate disks. Partitioning can be useful if you want to install another operating system on another part of your Mac hard drive or want a separate section of your main hard drive that is formatted differently from your main hard drive. You can also use Disk Utility to partition an external hard drive connected to your computer by USB, Thunderbolt, or FireWire cable.

Partition a Hard Drive

1. Click the **Spotlight** icon (🔍).
2. Type **Disk Utility** into the Spotlight field.
3. Click **Disk Utility**.

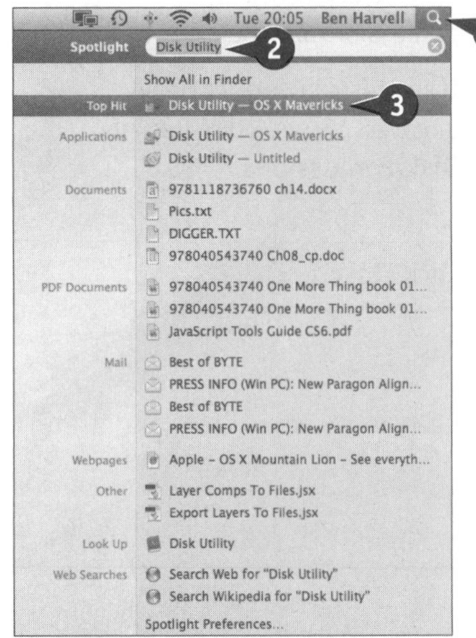

4. Click the drive you want to partition in the source menu.
5. Click **Partition**.

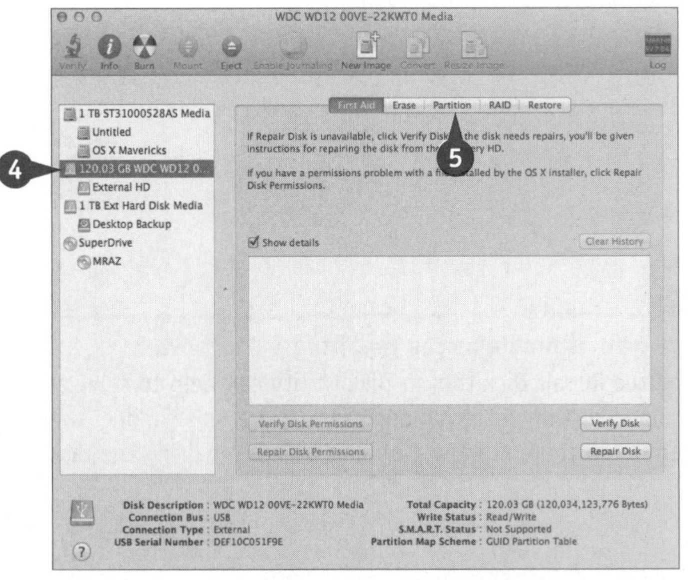

The current partition layout of your chosen drive is shown.

A Click and drag the lower right corner of an existing partition to adjust its size.

6 Click the **Add** button (+) to add a new partition.

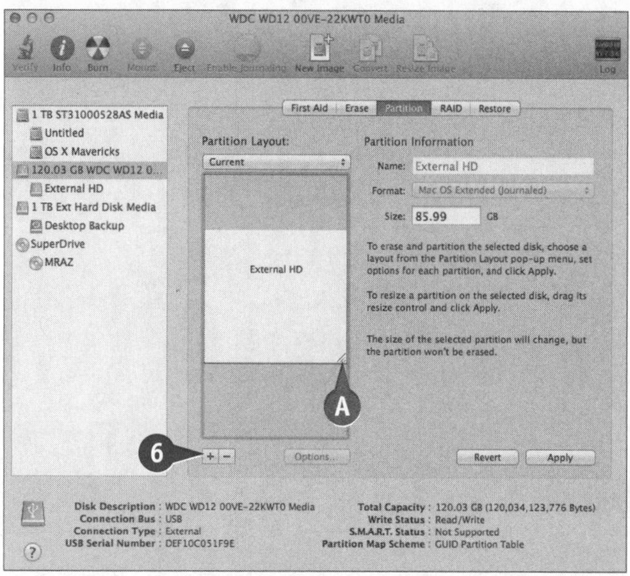

A blank partition is added.

7 Type a name for your new partition.

B If you want to use a different format for your new partition select it from this menu.

C If you want to set a specific size for your partition, enter it here.

8 Click **Apply**.

Your new partition is created.

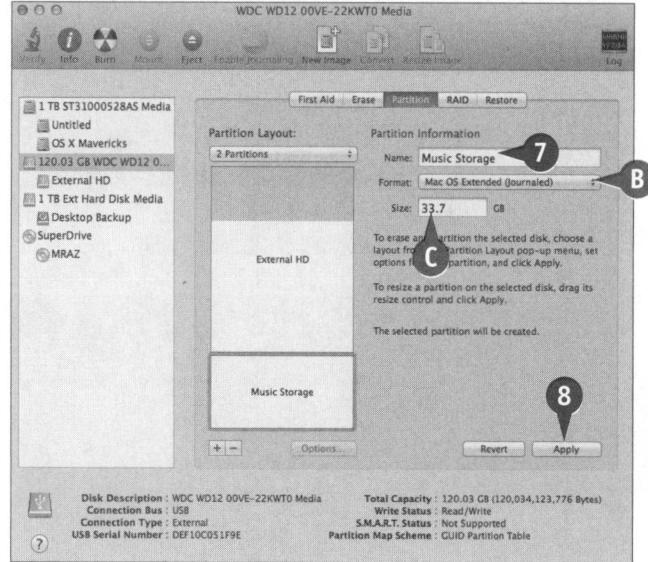

TIP

Why can I not make my new partition larger than a certain size?

The partitions you create can only add up to a total capacity that is less or equal to the maximum capacity of the hard drive that contains them. For example, if you have a 250GB partition on a 500GB hard drive, you will only be able to create a new partition up to 250GB to fit within the total amount of available storage.

CHAPTER 15

Working with Your iCloud Account

You can get a free iCloud account, which is a web-based service that gives you e-mail, an address book, and a calendar. You can also use iCloud to automatically synchronize data between iCloud and your Mac (as well as your iPhone, iPad, or iPod touch).

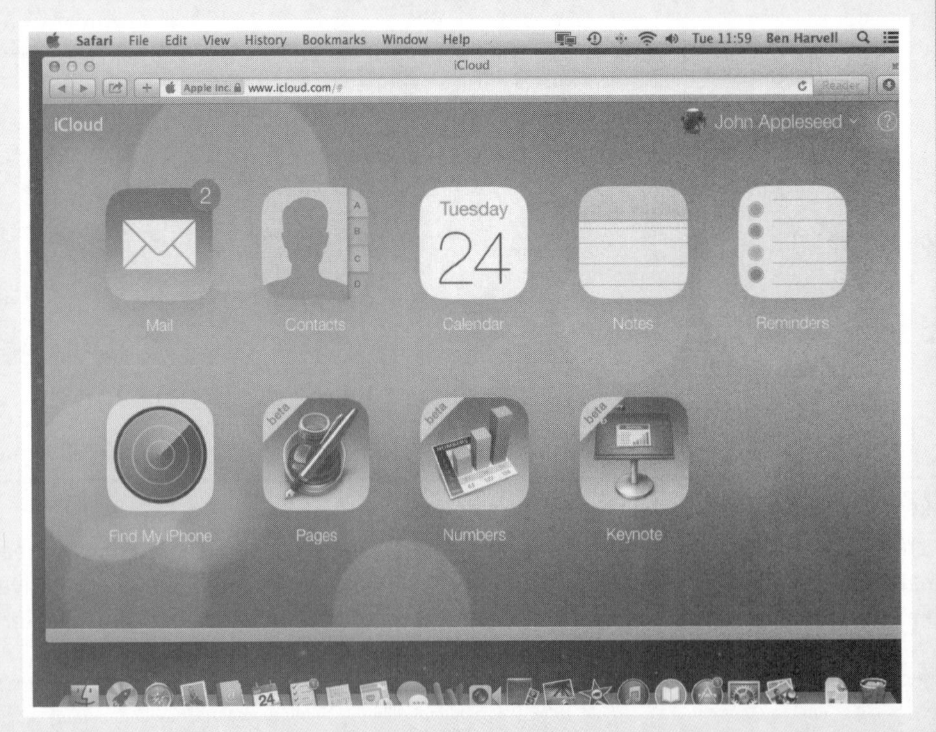

Create an Apple ID

To use iCloud, you need to create a free Apple ID, which you use to sign in to iCloud on the web and to synchronize your Mac and other devices. An Apple ID is an e-mail address. You can use an existing e-mail address for your Apple ID, or you can sign up for a new iCloud e-mail address, which uses the icloud.com domain name. If you use an existing e-mail address, you are required to verify via e-mail that the address is legitimate.

Create an Apple ID

1. In the Dock, click the **System Preferences** icon ( ).

   The System Preferences window appears.

2. Click **iCloud**.

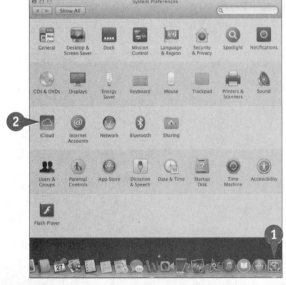

   The iCloud preferences appear.

3. Click **Create new Apple ID**.

The Create an Apple ID dialog appears.

4 Use the **Location** pop-up menu to choose your country.

5 Use the three **Birthday** pop-up menus to choose your month, day, and year of birth.

6 Click **Next.**

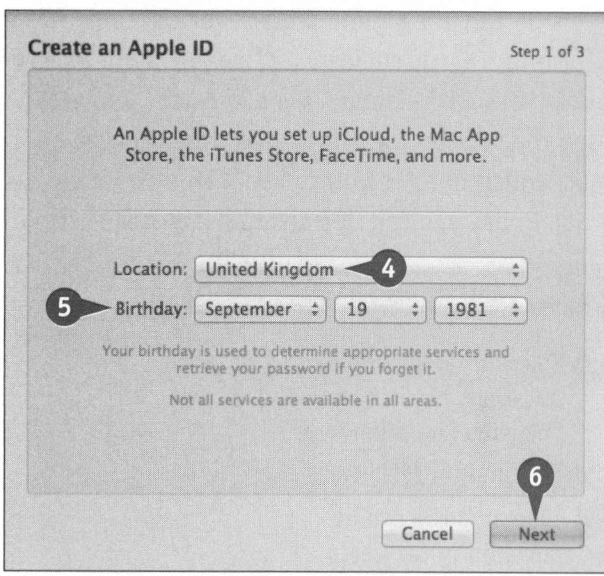

7 Select **Get a free iCloud email address** (◯ changes to ◉).

A If you prefer to use an existing address, select **Use an existing email address** (◯ changes to ◉) instead.

8 Type the e-mail address.

9 Type your name.

10 Type the password.

11 Verify your password.

12 Click **Next.**

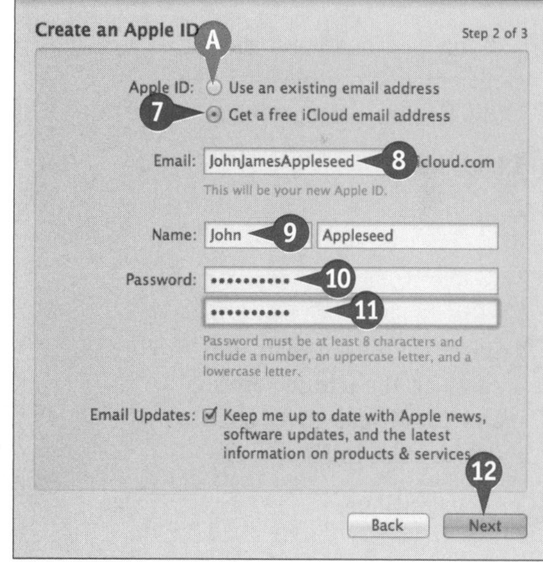

TIP

If I do not want to create a new iCloud address, can I use any e-mail address?

Yes, as long as the address belongs to you. Also, you need to be able to retrieve and read messages that are sent to that address, as this is part of the verification process. To learn how to verify an existing address that you typed in step 8, see the tip at the end of this section.

continued ►

As part of the signup process for an Apple ID, you must specify which iCloud services you want to use. First, decide whether you want to synchronize data such as contacts, calendars, and bookmarks with iCloud. If you are not sure, you can turn this feature off for now, and decide later (see the section "Set Up iCloud Synchronization"). Second, decide whether you want to use Find My Mac, which enables you to use iCloud to locate your Mac if it is lost or stolen. If you are not sure what to do, you can decide later (see the section "Locate a Lost Mac, iPod touch, iPhone, or iPad").

Create an Apple ID (continued)

13 Select three security questions by clicking ⇕ and choosing an option from each pop-up menu.

14 Type an answer to each question in the fields provided.

B If you have another e-mail address, you can type it in this field as a rescue e-mail.

15 Click **Next**.

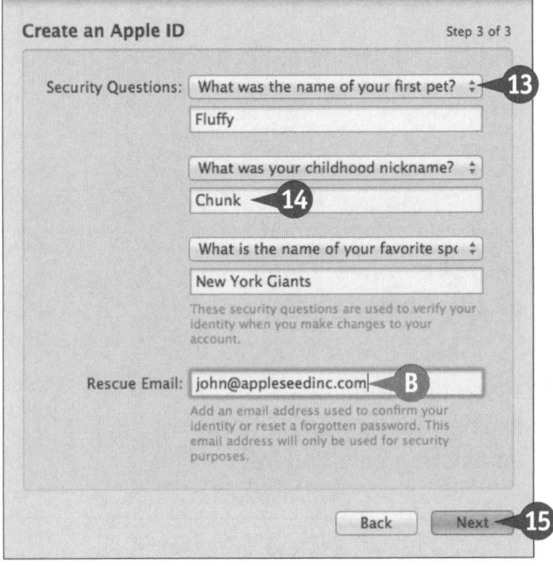

16 Select the **I have read and agree to the iCloud Terms and Conditions** check box (☐ changes to ☑).

17 Click **Continue**.

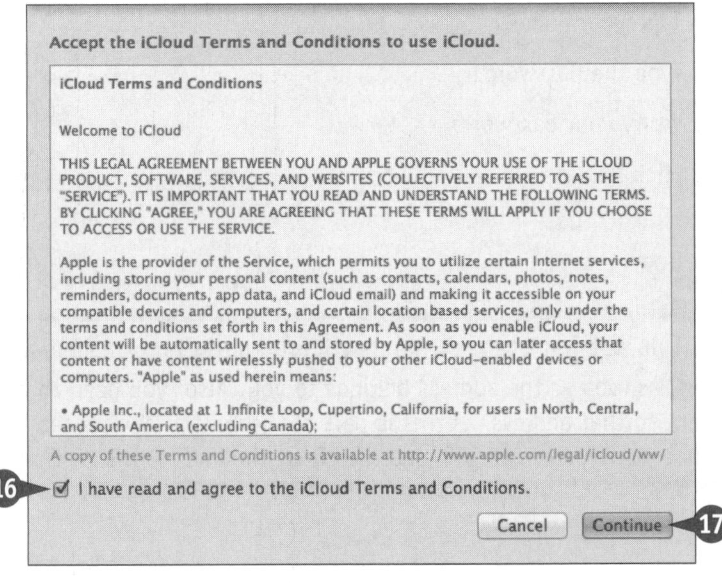

OS X prompts you to choose which iCloud services you want to use.

18 If you do not want to use iCloud for mail, contacts, calendars, reminders, notes, and Safari, deselect this check box (☑ changes to ☐).

19 If you do not want to use iCloud to locate your Mac, deselect the **Use Find My Mac** check box (☑ changes to ☐).

20 Click **Next**.

21 Type your Apple ID password into the iCloud Keychain password field.

22 Click **OK**.

23 Type four digits to use as an iCloud security code.

24 Click **Next**.

Note: You are asked to verify the code you entered and provide a phone number.

Your iCloud account is set up.

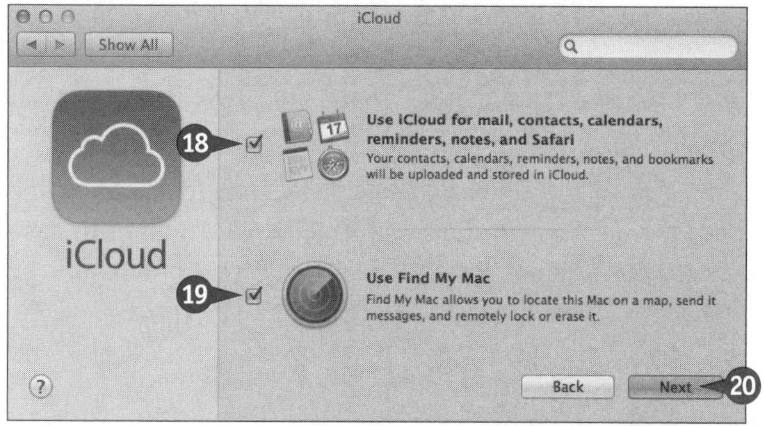

TIP

What happens after I create my Apple ID from an existing address?

After you agree to the terms of service, Apple sends an e-mail message to the address you typed in step 8. When that message arrives, open it and click the verification link. In the web page that appears, type your Apple ID (that is, the e-mail address from step 8), type your password, and then click **Verify Address**. Return to the iCloud preferences, click **Next**, and then follow steps 15 to 21.

Sign In to iCloud

Before you can use any of the features associated with your iCloud account, you must sign in to the service. iCloud is a web-based service, so you access it using a web browser. Most modern browsers should work fine with iCloud, but Apple recommends that you use at least Safari 5, Firefox 5, Internet Explorer 8, or Chrome 12.

You can also sign in to iCloud using a Mac, and for that you must be using OS X Lion 10.7.2 or later. You can also access iCloud using a Windows PC, and in this case the PC must be running Windows 8, Windows 7, or Windows Vista with Service Pack 2 or later.

Sign In to iCloud

1. In your web browser, type **www.icloud.com** and press Return.

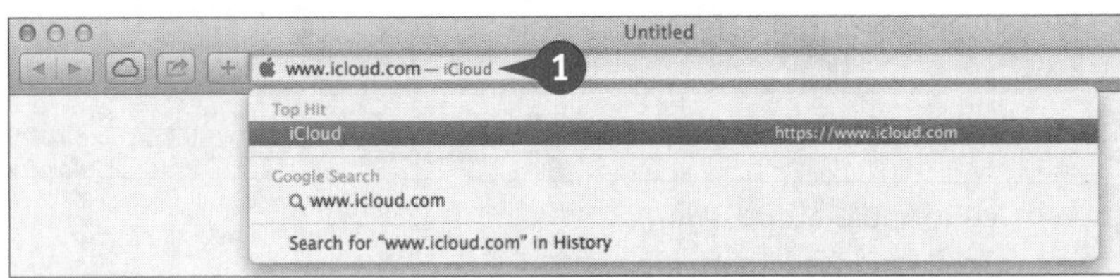

The iCloud Login page appears.

2. Use the Apple ID text box to type your Apple ID.
3. Use the Password text box to type the password for your Apple ID.

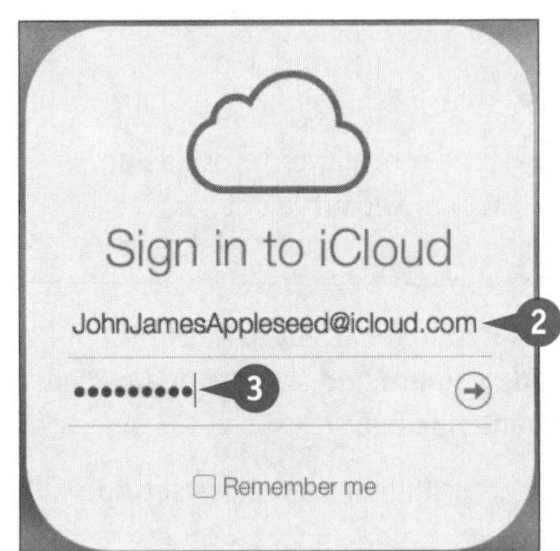

Ⓐ If you want iCloud to sign you in automatically in the future, select the **Remember me** check box (☐ changes to ☑).

4 Click **Sign In** (➔).

The first time you sign in, iCloud prompts you to configure some settings.

5 Click **Add Photo**, drop a photo on the dialog that appears.

6 Click **Done**.

7 Click **Language** and then click the language you prefer to use.

8 Click **Time Zone** and then click your time zone.

9 Click **Start Using iCloud**.

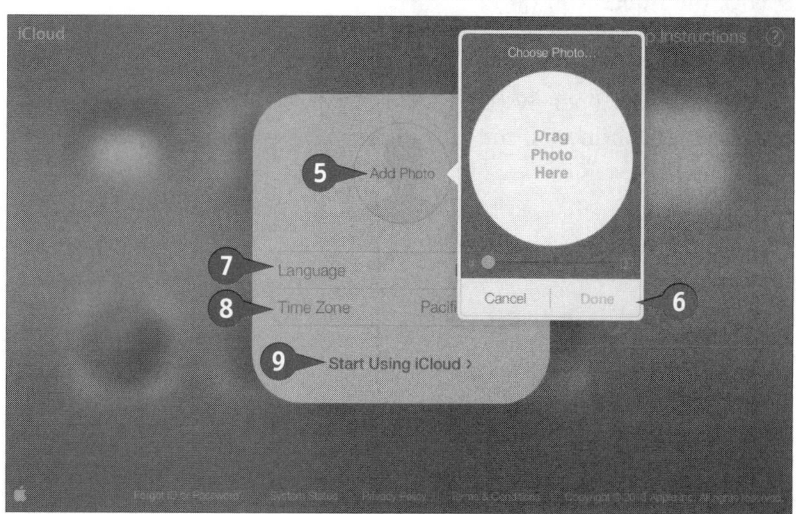

TIPS

Can I sign in from my Mac?

Yes. Click the **System Preferences** icon (⚙) in the Dock, or click the **Apple** icon () and then click **System Preferences**. Click **iCloud**. Type your Apple ID and password and then click **Sign In**.

How do I sign out from iCloud?

When you finish working with your iCloud account, if you prefer not to remain signed in to your account, click the **Sign Out** link beside your account name in the upper-right corner of the iCloud page.

Set Up iCloud Synchronization

You can ensure that your Mac and your iCloud account have the same data by synchronizing the two. The main items you will want to synchronize are Mail e-mail accounts, contacts, calendars, reminders, and notes. However, there are many other types of data you may want to synchronize to iCloud, including Safari bookmarks, photos, and documents. If you have a second Mac, a Windows PC, or an iPhone, iPad, or iPod touch, you can also synchronize it with the same iCloud account, which ensures that your Mac and the device use the same data.

Set Up iCloud Synchronization

1. Click the **Apple** icon ().
2. Click **System Preferences.**

Note: You can also open System Preferences by clicking its icon (⚙) in the Dock.

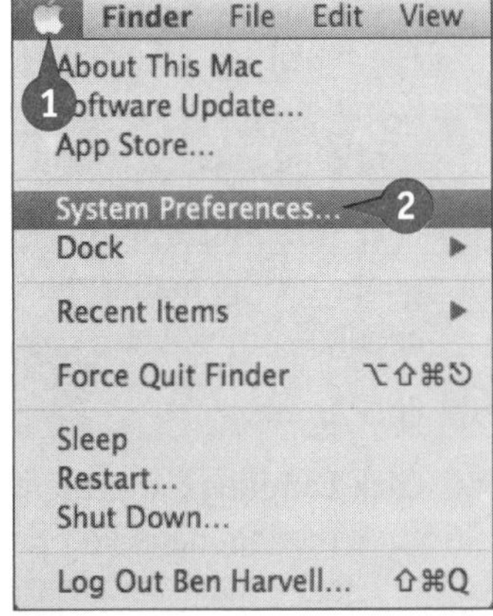

The System Preferences window appears.

3. Click **iCloud**.

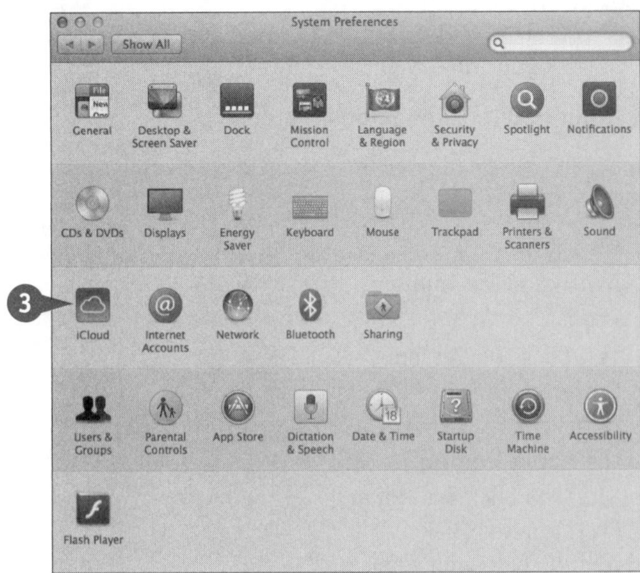

The iCloud preferences appear.

4 Select the check box beside a type of data you want to sync (☐ changes to ☑).

A OS X sets up the sync.

5 Repeat step **4** for each type of data you want to sync.

6 If you do not want to sync a type of data, deselect its check box (☑ changes to ☐).

OS X asks if you want to keep or delete the iCloud data that you are no longer syncing.

7 Click **Cancel** to keep the data on your Mac.

B If you do not want to keep the data, click **Delete from Mac** instead.

Your Mac synchronizes the data with your iCloud account.

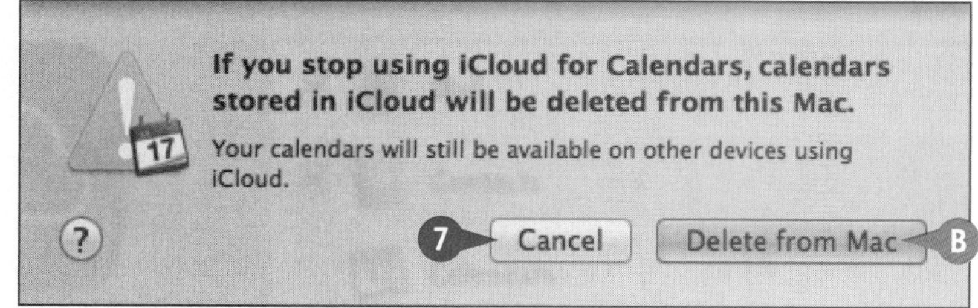

TIP

What happens if I modify an appointment, contact, bookmark, or other data in iCloud?

The synchronization process works both ways. That is, all the Mac data you selected to synchronize is sent to your iCloud account. However, the data on your iCloud account is also sent to your Mac. This means that if you modify, add, or delete data on your iCloud account, those changes are also reflected in your Mac data.

Send and Receive iCloud Mail

You can use the iCloud Mail feature to work with your iCloud e-mail account online. Using either your Mac or any computer or device with web access, you can access iCloud using a web browser and then perform your e-mail tasks. These include checking for incoming messages, replying to messages you receive, forwarding a received message, and composing and sending a new message. You can also configure iCloud Mail to send blind courtesy copies and to automatically send vacation messages.

Send and Receive iCloud Mail

Display iCloud Mail

1. Sign in to your iCloud account.

Note: See the section "Sign In to iCloud."

2. Click **Mail** (✉).

Get Incoming Messages

1. Click **Get Mail** (↻).

A. iCloud Mail checks for incoming messages and, if there are any, displays them in the Inbox folder.

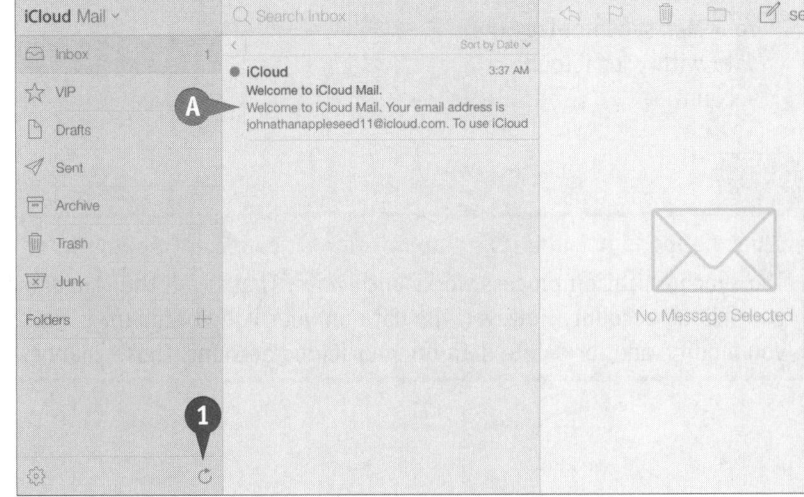

Reply to a Message

1. Click the message.
2. Click **Reply, Reply All, Forward** (⬅).
3. Click **Reply**.

   B To reply to the sender and all the recipients of the original message, click **Reply All**.

   C To pass the message to another person, click **Forward**.

4. In the message window that appears (not shown), type your message and then click **Send**.

   iCloud Mail sends your message.

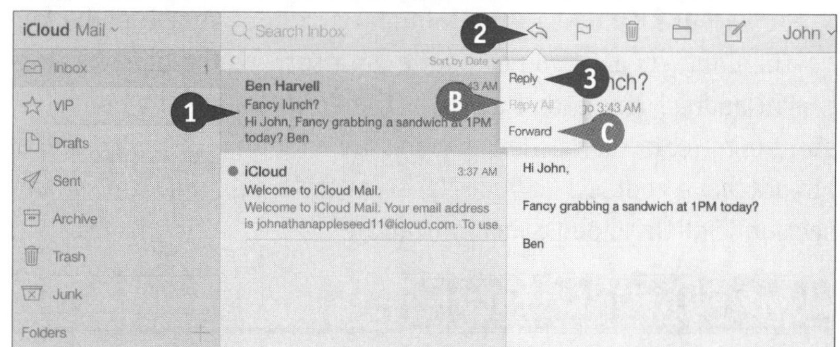

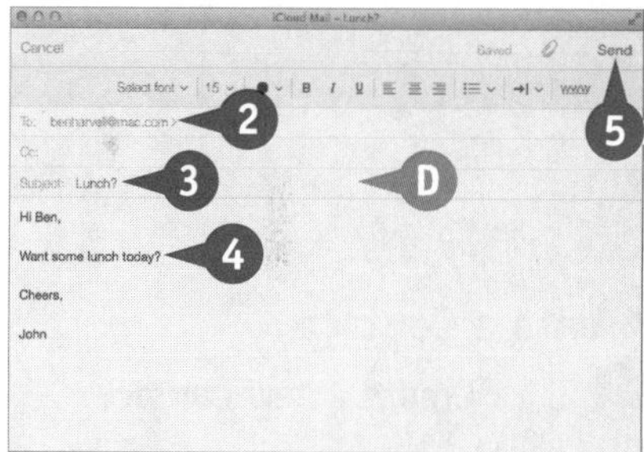

Send a New Message

1. Click **Compose new message** (✎).

   The New Message window appears.

2. Use the To text box to type the recipient's e-mail address.

   D If you want another person to see a copy of the message, type that person's address in the Cc text box.

3. Use the Subject text box to type the subject of the message.
4. Type your message.
5. Click **Send**.

   iCloud Mail sends your message.

TIP

Can I use iCloud to send a message to a person without other recipients knowing?

Yes. You can send that person a blind courtesy copy (Bcc), which means that he or she receives a copy of the message, but the other message recipients do not see that person's name or address in the recipient fields. To activate this feature, open iCloud Mail, click **Actions** (⚙), click **Preferences**, and then click the **Composing** tab. Select the **Show Bcc field** check box (☐ changes to ☑) and then click **Done**.

Work with iCloud Contacts

You can use iCloud to store information about your friends, family, colleagues, and clients. Using the Contacts app, you can store data such as the person's name, company name, phone numbers, e-mail address, and street address. The Contacts app also enables you to write notes about a contact, store extra data such as the person's job title and birthday, and assign a picture to a contact. If you already have contacts in your Mac's Contacts app, you can synchronize them with iCloud. See the section "Set Up iCloud Synchronization."

Work with iCloud Contacts

Display iCloud Contacts

1. Sign in to your iCloud account.

Note: See the section "Sign In to iCloud."

2. Click **Contacts**.

Create a Contact

1. Click **Create a new contact** (⊞).
2. Type the person's first name.
3. Type the person's last name.
4. Type the person's company's name.
5. Click here and then click a phone number category.
6. Type the phone number.
7. Click an e-mail category.
8. Type the person's e-mail address.

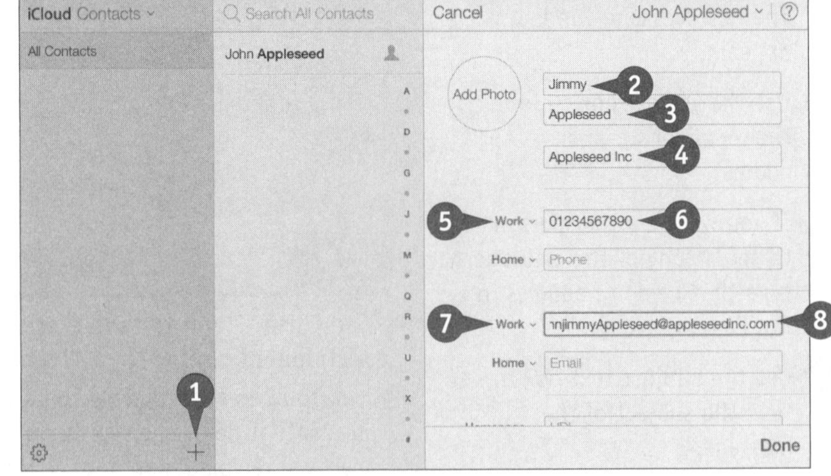

9. Click **Add New Address.**
10. Click a street address category.
11. Use the text boxes in this section to type the person's street address.
12. Type a note about the person's address.
13. Click **Done.**

    iCloud saves the contact.

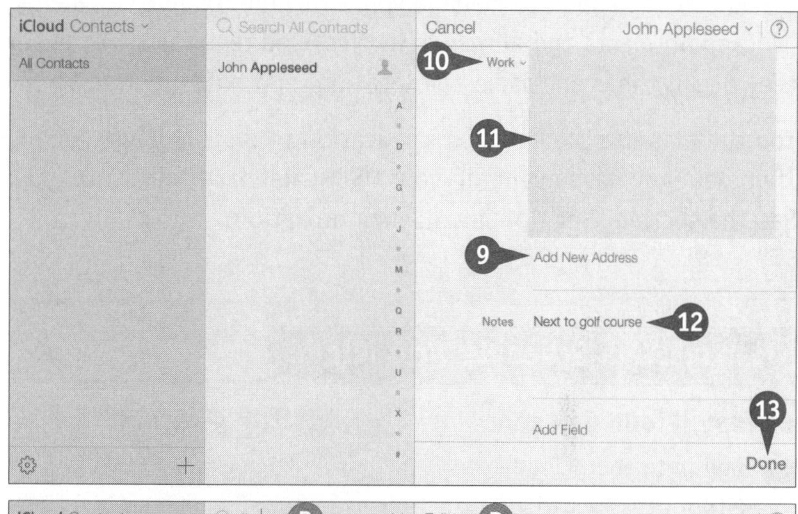

Display a Contact

1. Click the contact.

A. iCloud displays the contact's details.

B. You can also type part of the contact's name in the Search box.

C. To e-mail the contact, click the address.

D. To make changes to the contact, click **Edit**.

Note: To remove the contact, click **Edit** and then click **Delete Contact.**

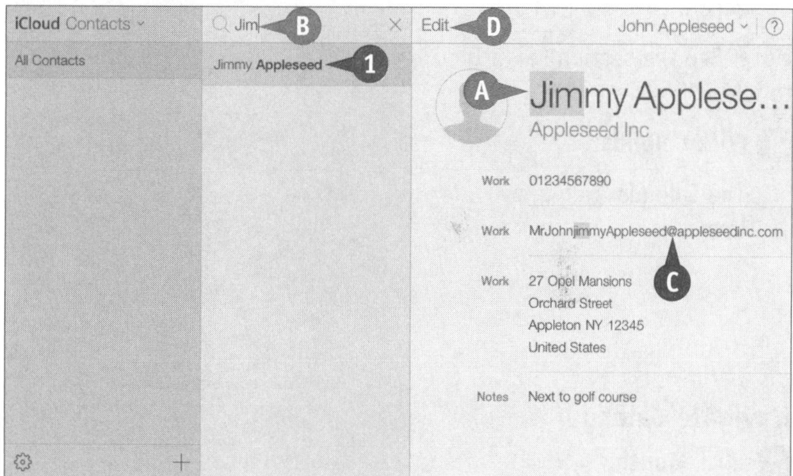

TIPS

How do I add a photo for a contact?

To add a photo to an existing contact, click the contact and then click **Edit.** Click **add photo** and then drag a photo to the dialog that appears. Alternatively, click **Choose**, click the photo you want to use, and then click **Choose**. Click **Done**. Note that you can use only GIF, JPEG, or PNG files that are no larger than 1MB.

Is there any way to store data such as the person's birthday or job title?

Yes. The Contacts app offers a number of other fields, including Birthday, Job Title, Nickname, Prefix, and Suffix. To add a field to an existing contact, click the contact and then click **Edit.** Click **Add Field**, click the field you want, and then edit the field data. Note that you can also add more instances of some fields by clicking the **Add Field** icon to the left of a field.

Manage Your Schedule with iCloud

You can use iCloud to manage your schedule. Using the Calendar application, you can add events (appointments and all-day activities) and reminders. For events, you can specify the date and time they occur, the event name and location, and notes related to the event.

You can also use the Calendar application to display your schedule by day, by week, or by month. If you already have events in your OS X Calendar application, you can synchronize them with iCloud. See the section "Set Up iCloud Synchronization."

Manage Your Schedule with iCloud

Display iCloud Calendar

1 Sign in to your iCloud account.

Note: See the section "Sign In to iCloud."

2 Click **Calendar**.

The Calendar web app launches.

Navigate Calendar

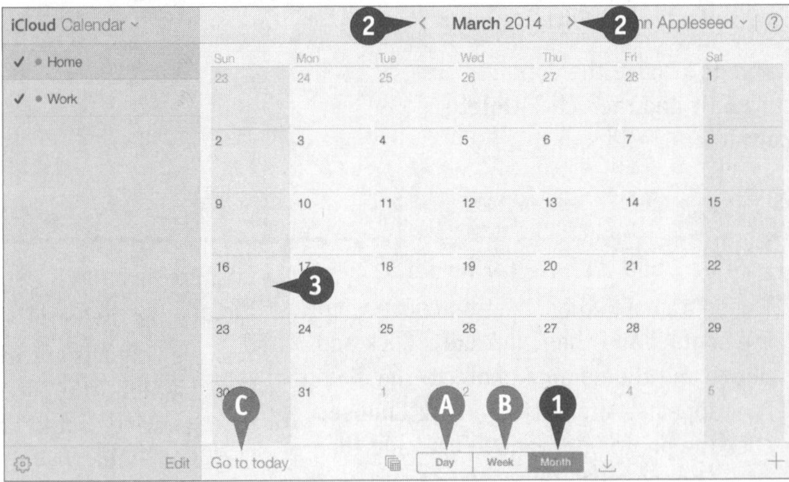

1 Click **Month**.

2 Click the Next Month and Previous Month arrows to select the month you want.

3 Click the date.

A To see just that date, click **Day**.

B To see the date in the context of its week, click **Week**.

C To return to today's date, click **Go to today**.

Create an Event

1 Navigate to the date when the event occurs.

2 Click the calendar you want to use.

3 Click **Week**.

4 Position the mouse pointer (↖) at the time when the event starts.

5 Click and drag the mouse ↖ down to the time when the event ends.

D Calendar adds the event.

6 Type the event name.

7 Type the event location.

E If the event lasts all day, select the **all-day** check box (☐ changes to ☑).

8 Adjust the start time, if necessary.

9 Adjust the end time, if necessary.

10 Fill in the other event details.

11 Click **OK**.

Note: To edit the event, double-click it.

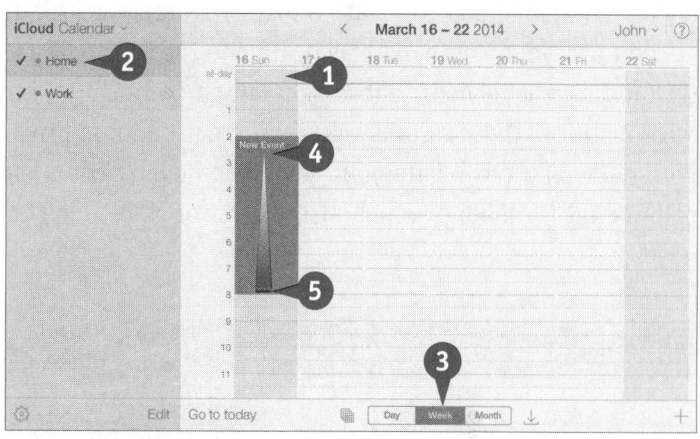

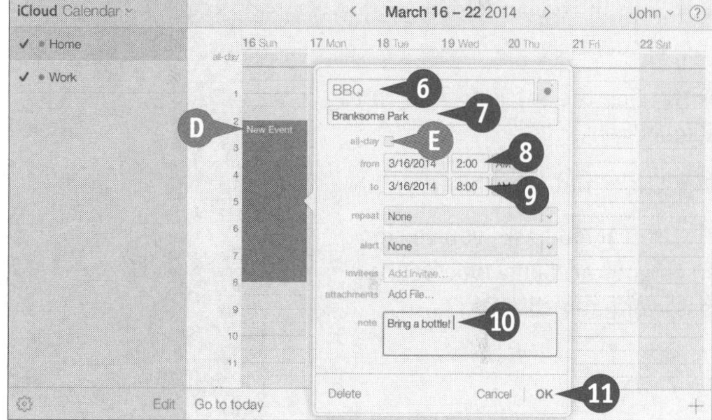

TIP

How do I create a reminder?

1 In Reminders, click **New Item**.

2 Type the reminder name.

3 Click the **priority** ⇕ and then click **None**, **Low**, **Medium**, or **High**.

4 Fill in the rest of the reminder details as needed.

5 Click **Done**.

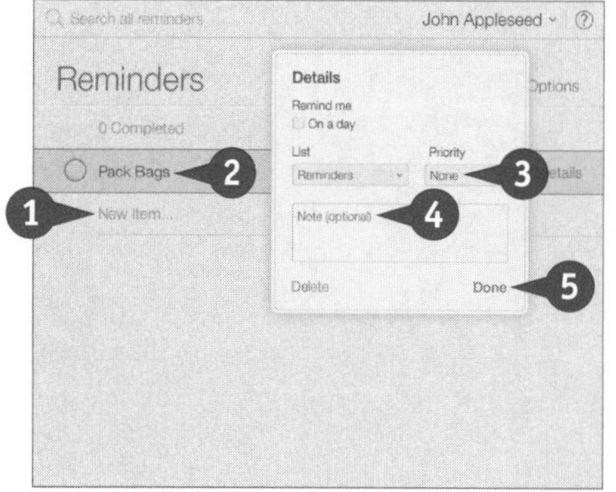

Locate a Lost Mac, iPod touch, iPhone, or iPad

You can use iCloud to locate a lost or stolen Mac, iPod touch, iPhone, or iPad. Depending on how you use your Mac, iPod touch, iPhone, or iPad, you can end up with many details of your life residing on the device. That is generally a good thing, but if you happen to lose your device, you have also lost those details, plus you create a large privacy problem because anyone can now see your data. You can locate your device and even send a message to the device using an iCloud feature called Find My iPhone, which also works for Macs, iPod touches, and iPads.

Locate a Lost Mac, iPod touch, iPhone, or iPad

Locate a Device on a Map

1 Sign in to your iCloud account.

Note: See the section "Sign In to iCloud."

2 Click **Find My iPhone**.

Note: If iCloud asks you to sign in to your account, type your password and click **OK**.

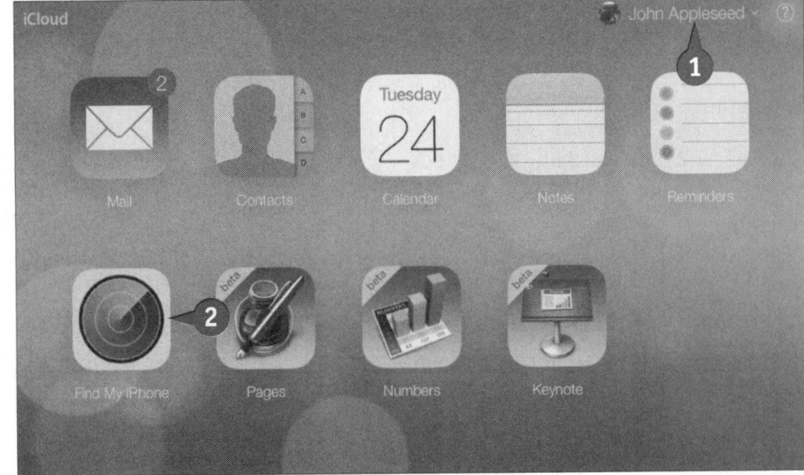

3 In the My Devices list, click the device you want to locate.

A iCloud displays the device location on a map.

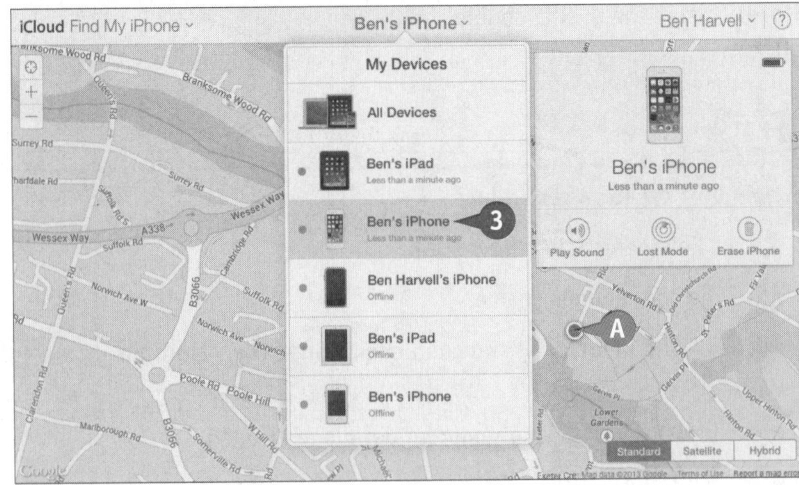

Play a Sound on a Device

1. Click the **Play Sound** button.

   A sound plays on your device.

Put a Device in Lost Mode

1. Click the **Lost Mode** button.
2. Type a code for your device and add a phone number if you wish.
3. Click **Next**.

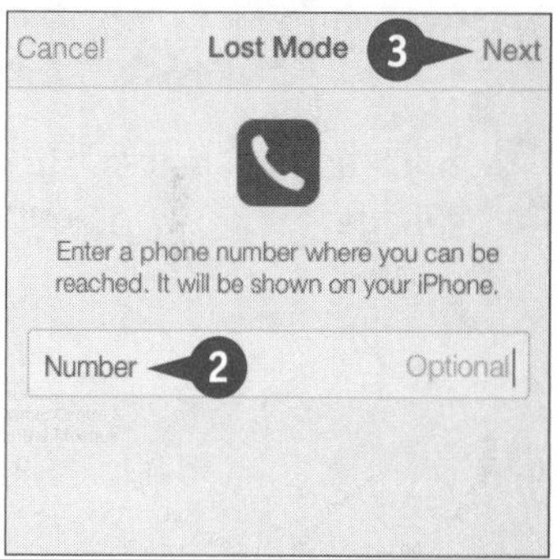

4. Type a message to show on your device.
5. Click **Done**.

   iCloud sends the message, which then appears on the device screen. The device is also locked with the code you set.

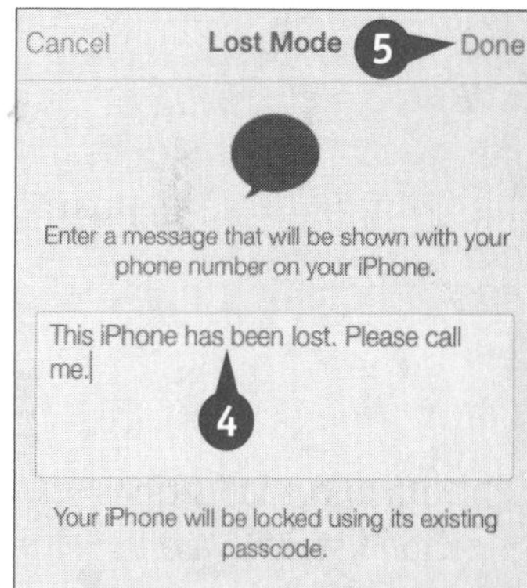

TIPS

I tried to enable Find My Mac, but OS X would not allow it. How can I enable Find My Mac?

You first need to enable location services. To do this, click the **System Preferences** icon (▣) in the Dock. Click **Security & Privacy**, click the **Lock** icon (▣), type your OS X administrator password, and then click **OK** (▣ changes to ▣). Click **Location Services** and then select the **Enable Location Services** check box (☐ changes to ☑).

Is there a way to completely erase my device remotely?

Yes. Click the **Erase *Device*** button (where ***device*** is the name of your device). This wipes the contents of your device.

Manage iCloud Storage

Each iCloud account comes with 5GB of free online storage for data such as backups, Mail messages, iWork documents, and photos. A number of applications on both your Mac and iOS devices can also use iCloud storage, and you may find you run out of space after a while. You can use System Preferences to manage your iCloud storage in order to reduce the amount of space taken up by specific data or, alternatively, you can pay for extra storage.

Manage iCloud Storage

1. In iCloud preferences, click **Manage**.

A. Data and applications using iCloud storage are listed in order of size.

2. Click an item or application to show more details.

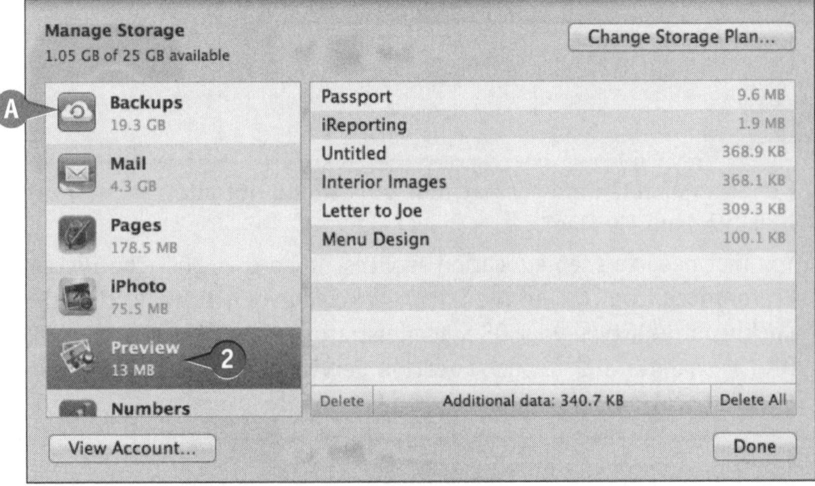

Details for the item or application you selected are shown.

3 Click a stored item.

4 Click **Delete** to remove the selected item.

B Click **Delete All** to delete all stored items for this application.

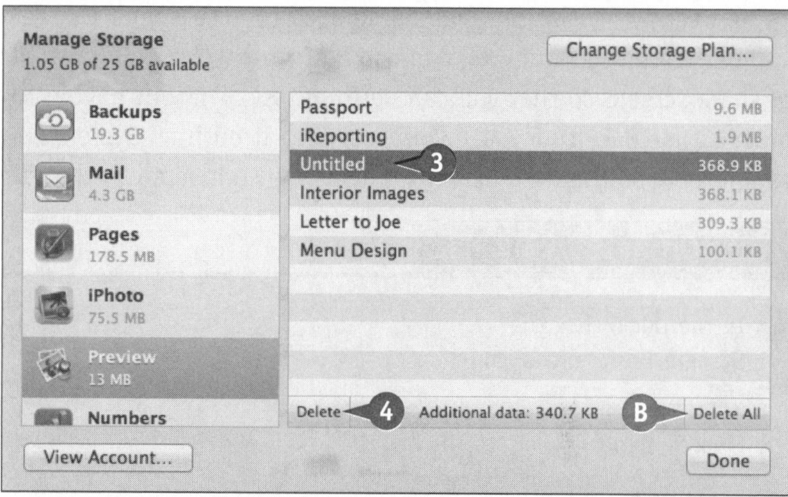

5 Continue to remove items from iCloud storage until you free the amount of space required.

6 Click **Done**.

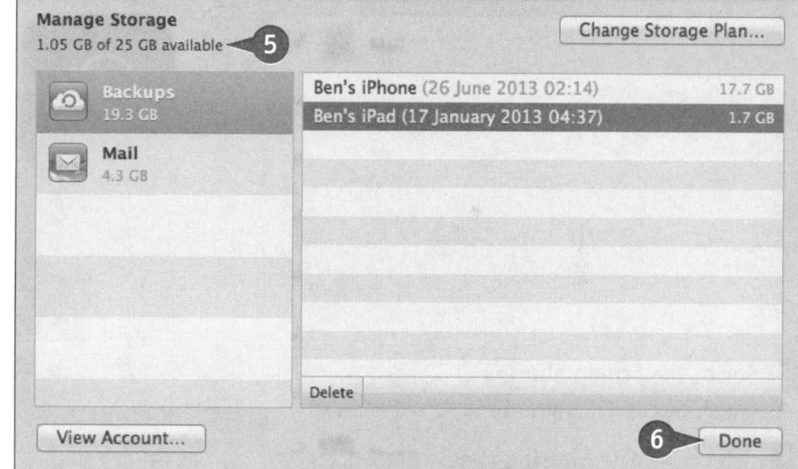

TIP

How do I buy more iCloud Storage?

If you want to add more iCloud storage you can pay an annual fee for an additional 20 or 50GB of storage. This amount is added to your existing free storage amount. On the Manage Storage screen, click the **Change Storage Plan** button, select the amount of storage you want to buy, and then follow the instructions to confirm your purchase.

Turn On Back to My Mac

The Back to My Mac feature can be used to access your Mac remotely from another computer using your iCloud account. You can use Back to My Mac to access files stored on the target computer or share screens so that you can perform tasks without having to physically be at your computer. In order to use Back to My Mac you must turn it on from System Preferences and make sure that both computers you use with Back to My Mac are connected to the same iCloud account.

Turn On Back to My Mac

1. In the Dock, click the **System Preferences** icon (⚙).
2. Click **Sharing**.

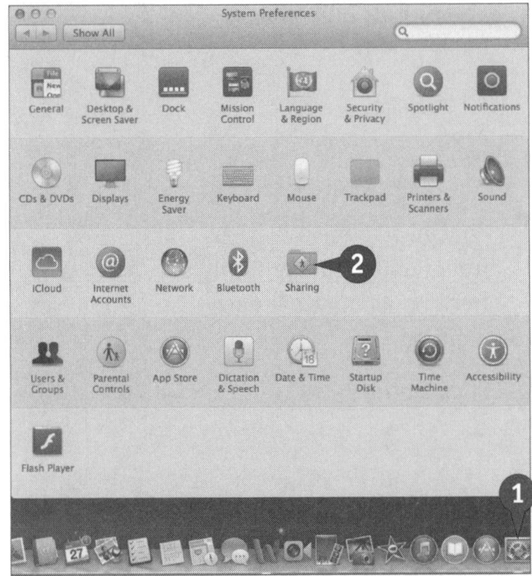

3. Select the **Screen Sharing** check box (☐ changes to ☑).
4. Select the **File Sharing** check box (☐ changes to ☑).
5. Click **Show All**.

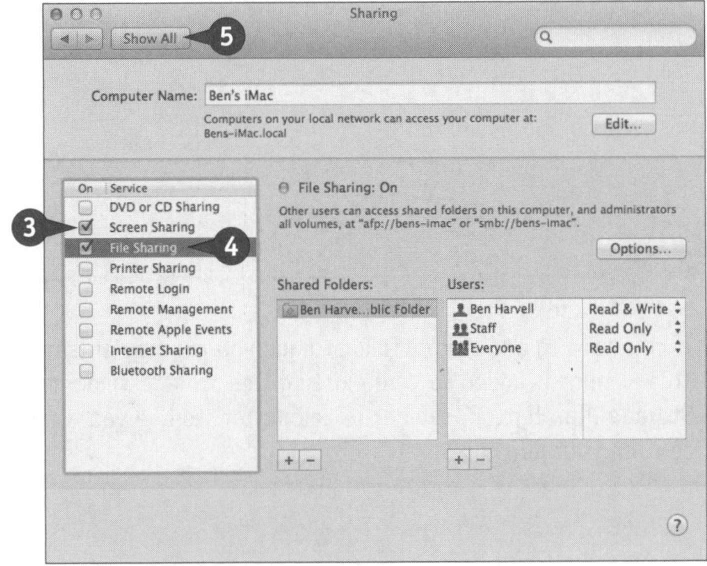

6 Click **iCloud.**

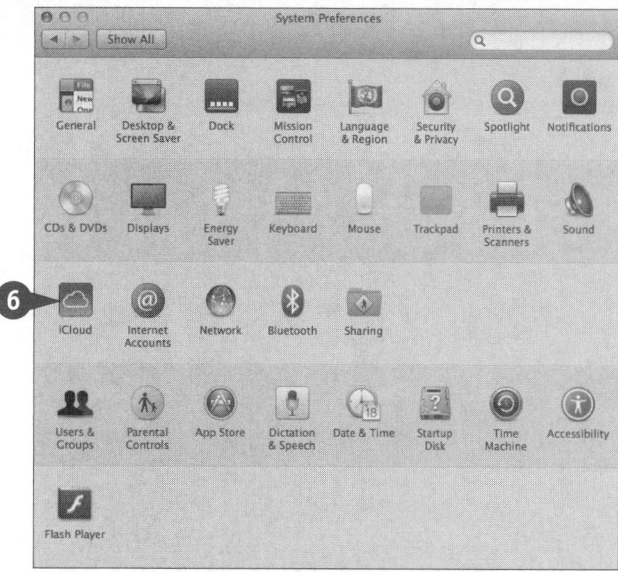

7 Select the **Back to My Mac** check box (□ changes to ☑).

Back to My Mac is turned on.

TIP

How do I view computers that are available for use with Back to My Mac?

Click the **Finder** icon (▣) in the Dock and then click the **Finder** menu. Select **Preferences** and then click the **Sidebar** tab. Select the **Back to My Mac** check box in the **Shared** section of Finder Preferences (□ changes to ☑). All of your available computers with Back to My Mac turned on now appear in the sidebar of any Finder window within the Shared section.

CHAPTER 16

Networking with OS X

If you have multiple computers in your home or office, you can set up these computers as a network to share information and equipment. This chapter gives an overview of networking concepts and shows you how to connect to a network, how to work with the other computers on your network, and how to share your Mac's resources with other network users.

Understanding Networking

A *network* is a collection of computers and other devices that are connected. You can create a network using cable hookups, wireless hookups, or a combination of the two. In both cases, you need special networking equipment to make the connections.

A network gives you a number of advantages. For example, once you have two or more computers connected on a network, those computers can share documents, photos, and other files. You can also use a network to share equipment, such as printers and optical drives.

Share Files

Networked computers are connected to each other, and so they can exchange files with each other along the connection. This enables people to share information and to collaborate on projects. OS X includes built-in security so that you can control what files you share with other people.

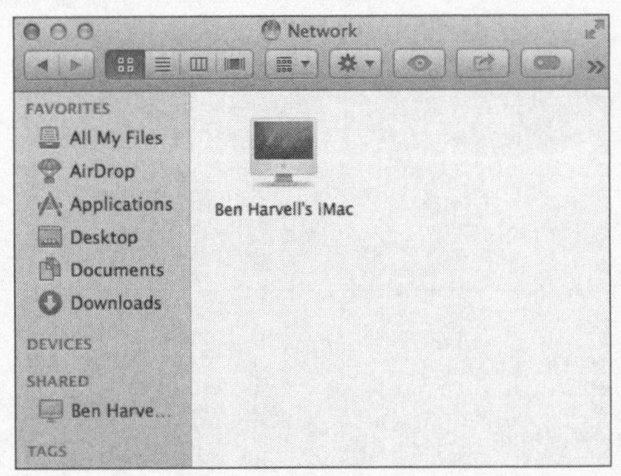

Share Equipment

Computers connected over a network can share some types of equipment. For example, one computer can share its printer, which enables other network users to send their documents to that printer. Networked computers can also share hard drives, optical drives, and document scanners.

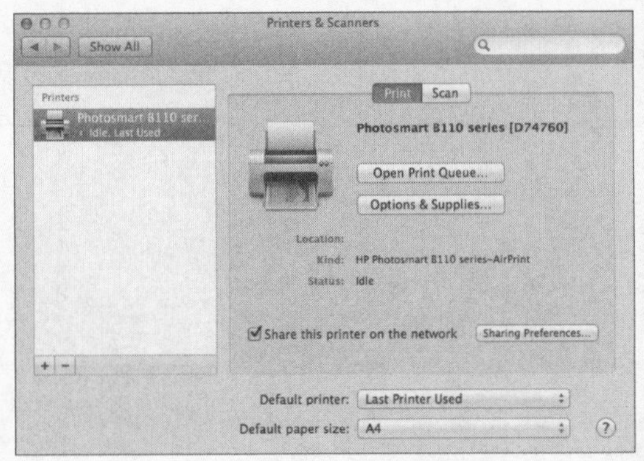

Wired Networking

Network Cable

A *network cable* is a special cable designed for exchanging information. One end of the cable plugs into the Mac's network port. The other end plugs into a network connection point, which is usually the network's router (discussed next), but it could also be a switch, hub, or even another Mac. Information, shared files, and other network data travel through the network cables.

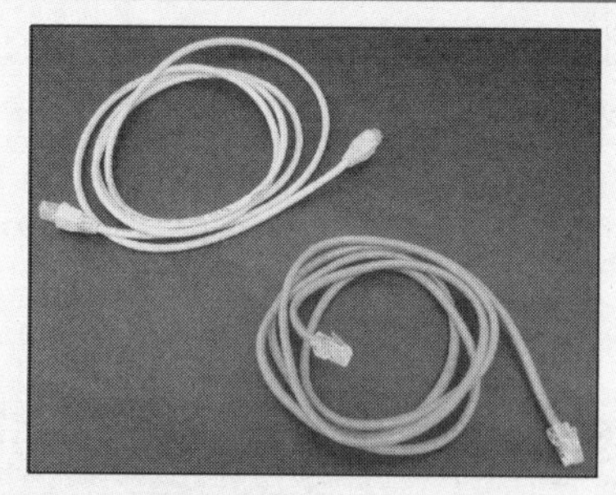

Router

A *router* is a central connection point for all of the computers on the wired portion of the network. For each computer, you run a network cable from the Mac's network port to a port in the router. When network data travels from computer A to computer B, it first goes out through computer A's network port, along its network cable, and into the router. Then the router passes the data along computer B's network cable and into its network port.

Wireless Networking

Wireless Connections

A *wireless network* is a collection of two or more computers that communicate with each other using radio signals instead of cable. The most common wireless technology is Wi-Fi (rhymes with hi-fi), or 802.11. There are four main types — 802.11b, 802.11g, 802.11n, and 802.11ac — each with its own range and speed limits. The other common wireless technology is Bluetooth, which enables devices to communicate directly with each other.

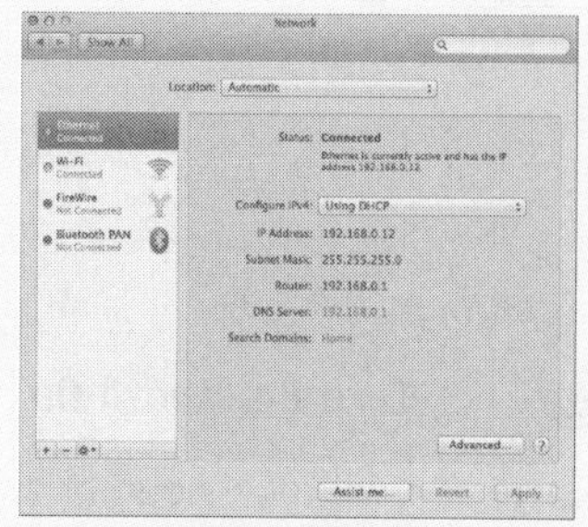

Wireless Access Point

A *wireless access point* (WAP) is a device that receives and transmits signals from wireless computers to form a wireless network. Many WAPs also accept wired connections, which enables both wired and wireless computers to form a network. If your network has a broadband modem, you can connect the modem to a type of WAP called a *wireless gateway,* which includes a built-in router that extends Internet access to all of the computers on the network.

Connect a Bluetooth Device

You can make wireless connections to devices such as mice, keyboards, headsets, and cell phones by using the Bluetooth networking technology. The networking tasks that you learn about in the rest of this chapter require special equipment to connect your computers and devices. However, with Bluetooth devices, the networking is built in, so no extra equipment is needed. For Bluetooth connections to work, your Mac must support Bluetooth (all newer Macs do) and your device must be Bluetooth-enabled. Also, your Mac and the Bluetooth device must remain within about 30 feet of each other.

Connect a Bluetooth Device

Connect a Bluetooth Device without a Passkey

1. In the Dock, click the **System Preferences** icon (▣).
2. Click **Bluetooth**.

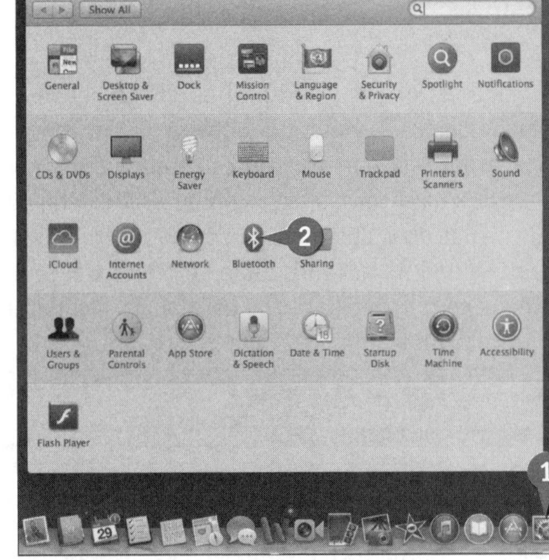

The Bluetooth preferences appear.

3. Click **Turn Bluetooth On**.

Note: You will now need to turn on your Bluetooth device and set it to Discoverable. Consult the device's product manual for how to do this.

OS X searches for discoverable Bluetooth devices.

A Discovered devices are listed here.

4 Click **Pair** next to the device you want to connect.

Your Mac connects with the device.

5 Click **Close** (◉) to close Bluetooth preferences.

TIPS

What does "discoverable" mean?

This means that you configure the device to broadcast that it is available for a Bluetooth connection. Controlling the broadcast is important because you usually want to use a Bluetooth device such as a mouse or keyboard with only a single computer. By controlling when the device is discoverable, you ensure that it works only with the computer you want it to.

What does pairing mean?

As a security precaution, many Bluetooth devices do not connect automatically to other devices. This prevents strangers with a Bluetooth device from connecting to your cell phone or your Mac. Most Bluetooth devices require you to enter a password before the connection is made. This is known as *pairing* the two devices.

continued ►

A Bluetooth mouse and a Bluetooth headset do not require any extra pairing steps, although with a headset you must configure OS X to use it for sound output. However, pairing devices such as a Bluetooth keyboard and a Bluetooth cellphone does require an extra step. In most cases, pairing is accomplished by your Mac generating a 6- or 8-digit *passkey* that you must then type in to the Bluetooth device (assuming that it has some kind of keypad). In other cases, the device comes with a default passkey that you must type in to your Mac to set up the pairing.

Connect a Bluetooth Device (continued)

Connect a Bluetooth Device with a Passkey

1. Turn your device on and, if required, turn on the switch that makes the device discoverable.
2. Follow steps 1 and 2 from earlier in this section.
3. Click **Pair** next to your Bluetooth device in the Devices section.

The Bluetooth Setup Assistant displays a passkey.

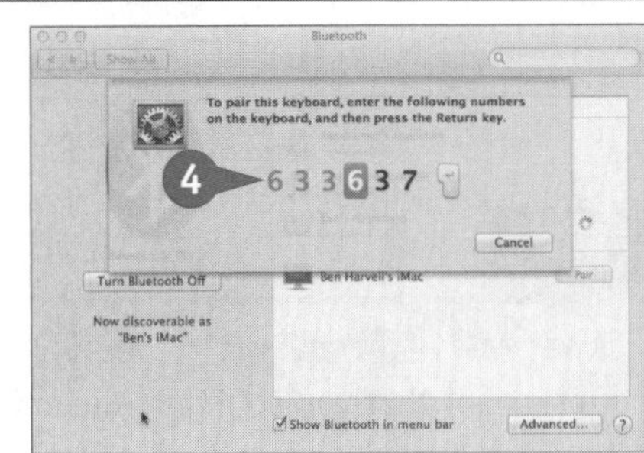

4. Use the Bluetooth device to type the displayed passkey.
5. Press Return.

The devices are now paired.

Listen to Audio through Bluetooth Headphones or Speakers

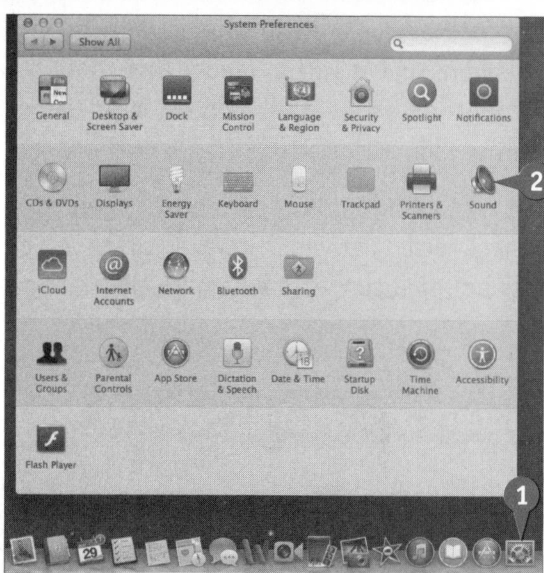

1. In the Dock, click the **System Preferences** icon (![]).
2. Click **Sound**.

The Sound preferences appear.

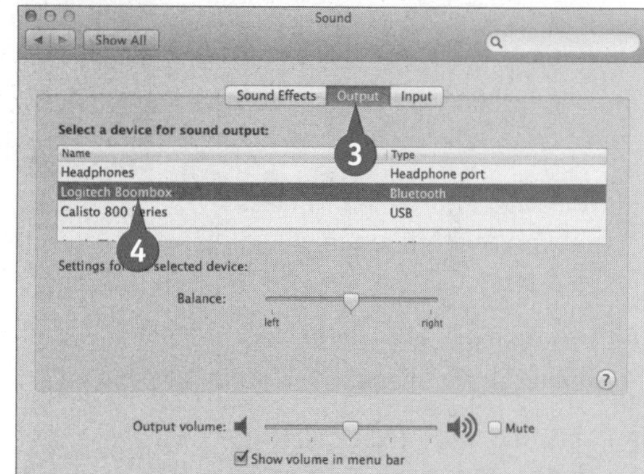

3. Click **Output**.
4. Click the Bluetooth headphones or speakers.

Your Bluetooth device is set as the audio output.

TIP

How do I remove a Bluetooth device?

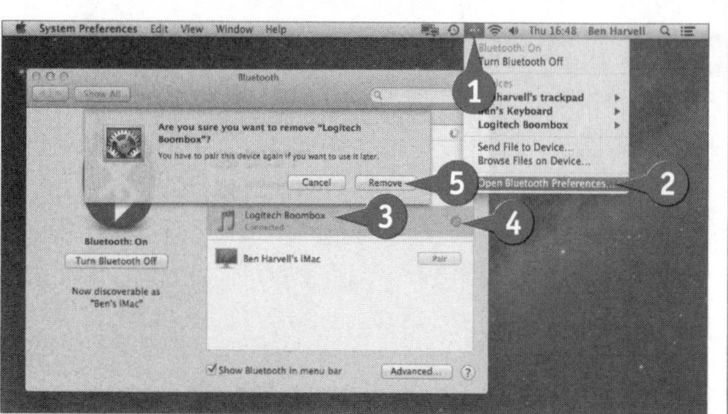

1. Click the **Bluetooth status** icon (![]) in the menu bar.
2. Click **Open Bluetooth Preferences**.

Note: You can also click the **Apple** icon (![]), click **System Preferences**, and then click **Bluetooth**.

3. Click the device you want to remove.
4. Click the X next to the device name.

   Your Mac asks you to confirm.

5. Click **Remove**, and your Mac removes the device.

Connect to a Wireless Network

If your Mac has built-in wireless networking capabilities, you can use them to connect to a wireless network that is within range. This could be a network in your home, your office, or a public location such as a coffee shop. In most cases, this also gives you access to the wireless network's Internet connection.

Most wireless networks have security turned on, which means you must know the correct password to connect to the network. However, after you connect to the network once, your Mac remembers the password, and connects automatically the next time the network comes within range.

Connect to a Wireless Network

1 Click the **Wi-Fi status** icon (☐) in the menu bar.

Your Mac locates the wireless networks within range of your Mac.

A The available networks appear in the menu.

B Networks with a Lock icon (☐) require a password to join.

2 Click the wireless network you want to join.

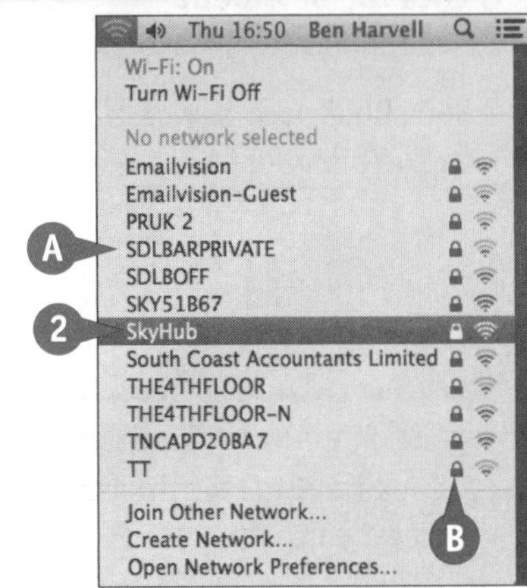

If the wireless network is secure, your Mac prompts you for the password.

3 Use the Password text box to type the network password.

C If the password is very long and you are sure no one can see your screen, you can select the **Show password** check box (☐ changes to ☑) to see the actual characters instead of dots. This helps to ensure you type the password correctly.

4 Click **Join**.

Your Mac connects to the wireless network.

D The Wi-Fi status icon changes from ☐ to ☐ to indicate the connection.

TIPS

I know a particular network is within range, but I do not see it in the list. Why?

As a security precaution, some wireless networks do not broadcast their availability. However, you can still connect to such a network, assuming you know its name and the password, if one is required. Click ☐ and then click **Join Other Network**. Use the Network Name text box to type the name of the network, click the **Security** ☐, and then click the network's security type. Follow steps 3 and 4 to join the network.

I do not see the Wi-Fi status icon on my menu bar. How do I display the icon?

You can do this using System Preferences. Click the **System Preferences** icon (☐) in the Dock, or click the **Apple** icon (☐) and then click **System Preferences** to open the System Preferences window. Click **Network**, click **Wi-Fi**, and then select the **Show Wi-Fi status in menu bar** check box (☐ changes to ☑).

Connect to a Network Resource

To see what other network users have shared on the network, you can use the Network folder to view the other computers and then connect to them to see their shared resources. To get full access to a Mac's shared resources, you must connect with a username and password for an administrator account on that Mac. To get access to the resources that have been shared by a particular user, you must connect with that user's name and password. Your Mac can also connect to the resources shared by Windows computers.

Connect to a Network Resource

1. Click the desktop.
2. Click **Go**.
3. Click **Network**.

Note: Another way to run the Network command is to press Shift + ⌘ + K.

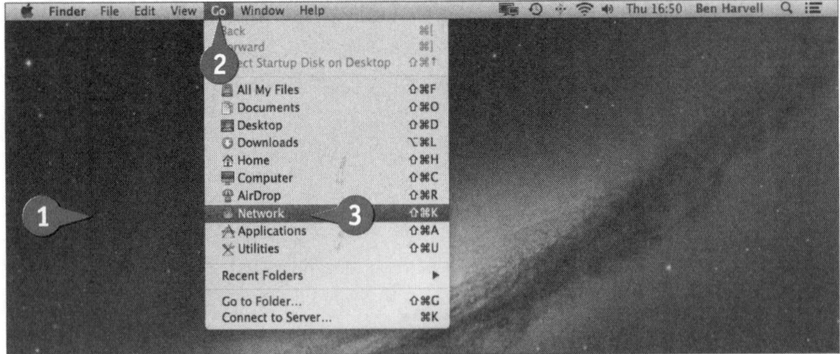

The Network folder appears.

A Each icon represents a computer on your local network.

4. Double-click the computer you want to connect to.

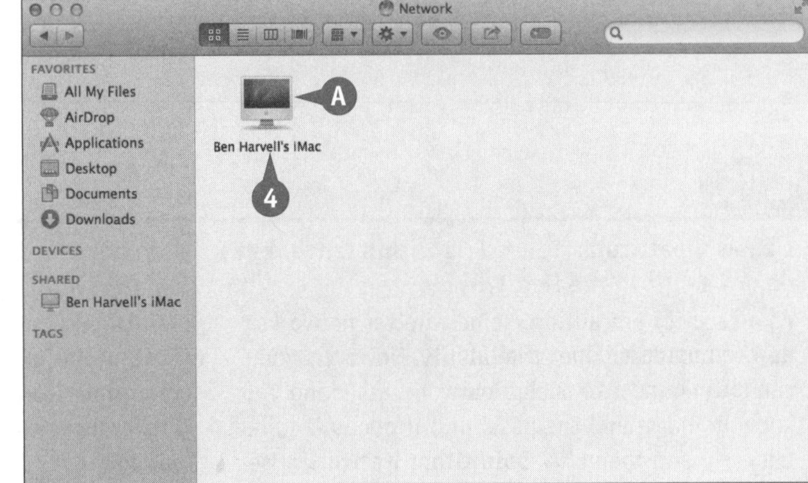

Your Mac connects to the network computer using the Guest account.

Note: The Guest account has limited access to the network computer.

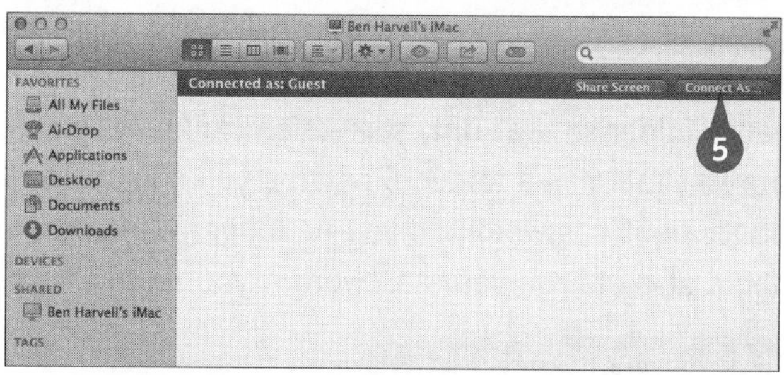

5 Click **Connect As.**

Your Mac prompts you to connect to the network computer.

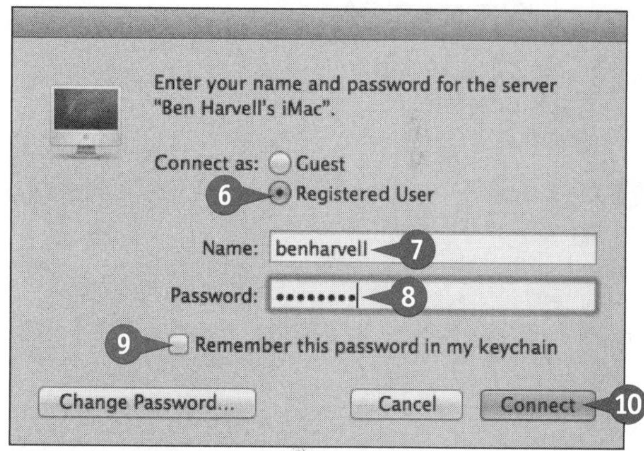

6 Click **Registered User** (☐ changes to ◉).

7 Use the Name text box to type the username of an account on the network computer.

8 Type the password of the account.

9 To store the account data, select the **Remember this password in my keychain** check box (☐ changes to ☑).

10 Click **Connect.**

Your Mac connects to the computer and shows the shared resources that you can access.

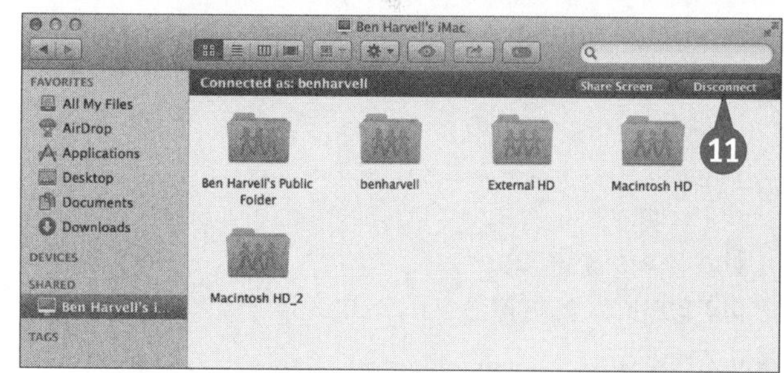

11 When you are done, click **Disconnect.**

TIP

Is there a faster way to connect to a network computer?
Yes. In the Shared section of Finder's sidebar area, click the computer you want to connect with (A) and then follow steps 5 to 10 to connect as a registered user.

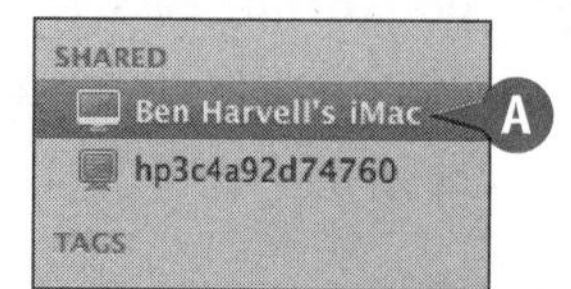

Change Your Password

You can make your Mac and your shared folders more secure by changing your password. For example, if you turn on file sharing, as described in the next section, you can configure each shared folder so that only someone who knows your user account password can get full access to the data in that shared folder. Similarly, you should change your password if other network users know your current password and you no longer want those users to have access to your shared folders. You should also change your password if you feel that your current password is not secure enough.

Change Your Password

1. In the Dock, click the **System Preferences** icon ( ).
2. Click **Users & Groups**.

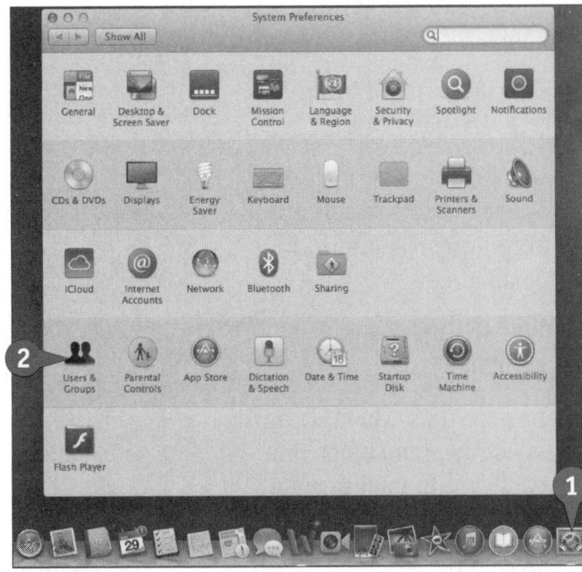

The Users & Groups preferences appear.

A. Your user account is selected automatically.

B. If you want to work with a different user account, click the **Lock** icon ( ) and then type your administrator password (changes to).

3. Click **Change Password**.

The Change Password dialog appears.

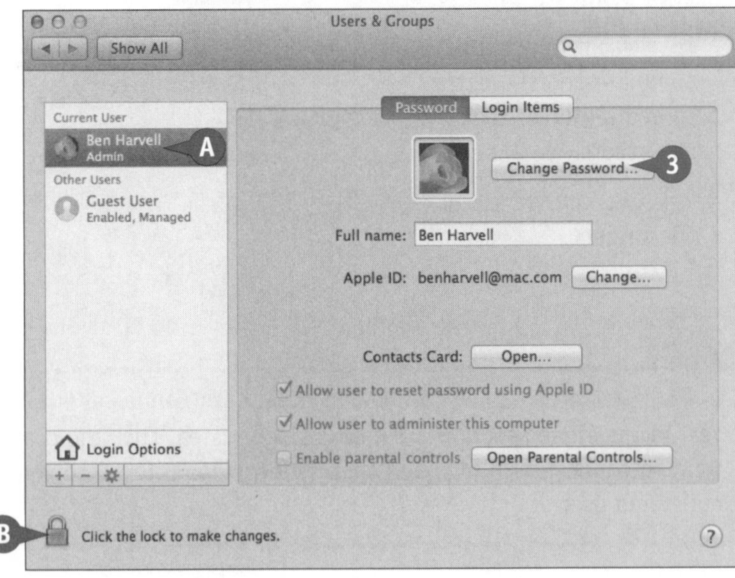

4. Type your current password.
5. Type your new password.
6. Retype the new password.
7. Type a hint that OS X will display if you forget the password.

Note: Construct the hint in such a way that it makes it easy for you to recall the password, but hard for a potential snoop to guess the password.

8. Click **Change Password**.

   OS X changes your password.

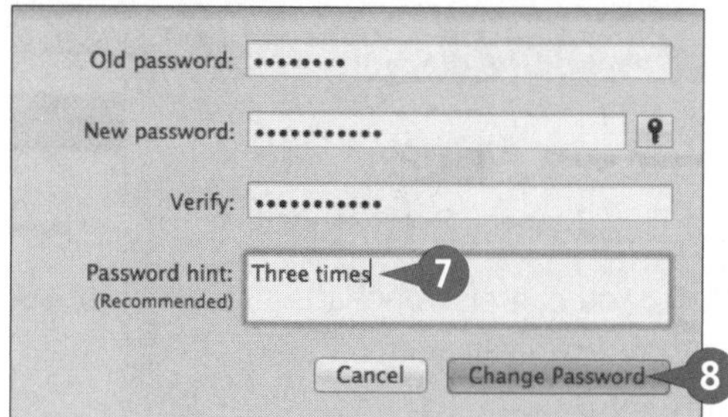

TIP

How do I create a secure password?

A secure password requires only two characteristics. First, it must be relatively long — at least eight characters — and second, it must include characters from at least three of the following four sets: lowercase letters, uppercase letters, numbers, and nonalphanumeric symbols such as $ and @. If you want OS X to create a secure password for you, follow these steps:

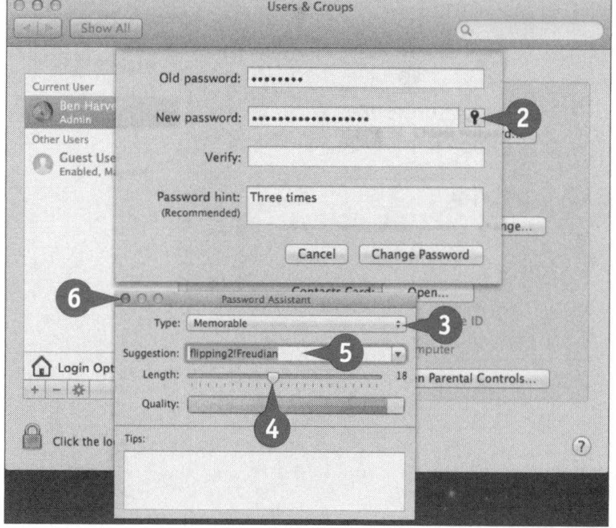

1. Follow steps **1** to **4** in this section.
2. Click the **Password Assistant** icon (🔑).

   The Password Assistant dialog appears.

3. Click the **Type** ⬍ and then click a password type.
4. Click and drag the **Length** slider to set the password length you want to use.
5. Click the **Suggestion** down arrow and then click the password you want to use.
6. Click **Close** (●).

Turn On File and Printer Sharing

You can share your files with other network users. This enables those users to access your files over the network. Before you can share these resources, you must turn on your Mac's file-sharing feature. To learn how to share a particular folder, see the section "Share a Folder." You can also share your printer with other network users. This enables those users to send print jobs to your printer over the network. Before this can happen, you must turn on your Mac's printer-sharing feature. To learn how to share a particular printer, see the section "Share a Printer."

Turn On File and Printer Sharing

1. Click the **Apple** icon ().
2. Click **System Preferences**.

Note: You can also click the **System Preferences** icon () in the Dock.

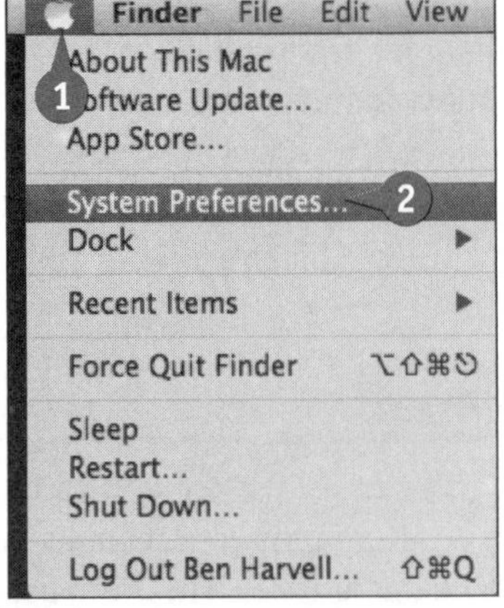

The System Preferences window appears.

3. Click **Sharing**.

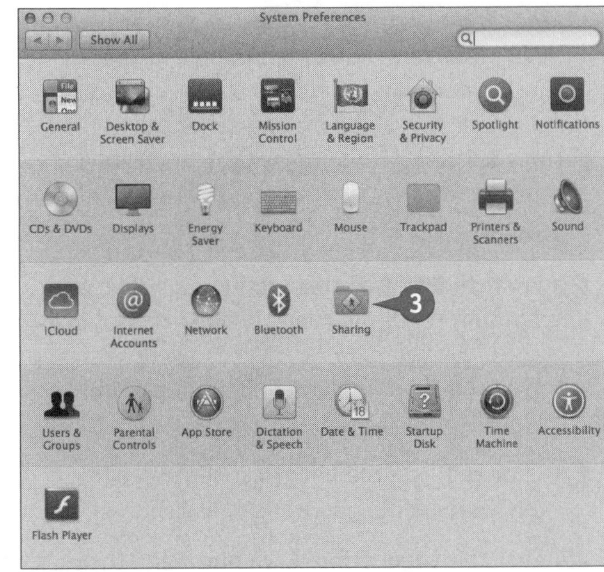

The Sharing preferences appear.

4. Select the **File Sharing** check box (☐ changes to ☑).

   You can now share your folders, as described in the next section.

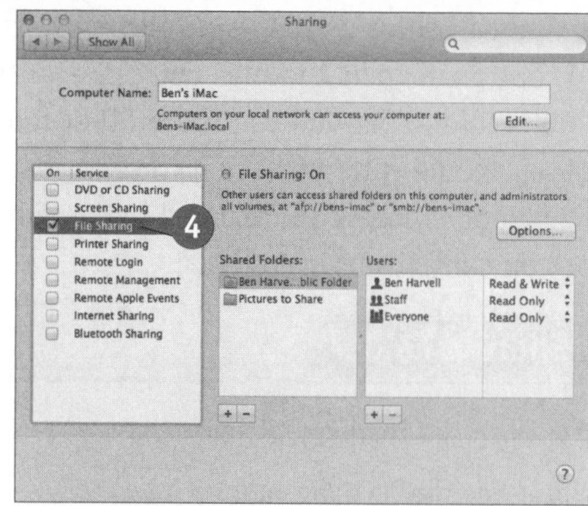

5. Select the **Printer Sharing** check box (☐ changes to ☑).

   You can now share your printers, as described in the section "Share a Printer."

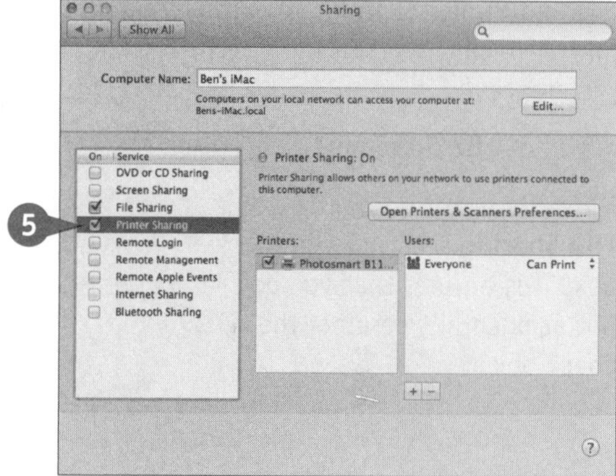

TIPS

Another user has asked me for my Mac's IP address. How do I look that up?
Your Mac gives you a couple of ways to do this. Follow steps 1 to 3 in this section, and then click **File Sharing** (click the name, not the check box); the series of digits after afp:// is your IP address (such as 10.0.1.13). Alternatively, open System Preferences, click **Network**, click **Ethernet** (or click **Wi-Fi** if you have a wireless network connection), and then read the IP Address value.

What is the Public folder and how do I access it?
Your user account's Public folder is a special folder that you use to share files with other people on the network or on your Mac. If someone connects to your Mac using your username and password, he or she has full access to the Public folder. Everyone else can only read the contents of the folder or add files to the Drop Box folder. To access the folder, click **Finder** (), click your username, and then open the Public folder.

Share a Folder

You can share one of your folders on the network, enabling other network users to view and optionally edit the files you place in that folder. OS X automatically shares your user account's Public folder, but you can share other folders. Sharing a folder enables you to work on a file with other people without having to send them a copy of the file. OS X gives you complete control over how people access your shared folder. For example, you can allow users to make changes to the folder, or you can prevent changes.

Share a Folder

1 Open the Sharing preferences.

Note: See the section "Turn On File and Printer Sharing" to learn how to display the Sharing preferences.

2 Click **File Sharing**.

Note: Be sure to click the **File Sharing** text, not the check box. This ensures that you do not accidentally deselect the check box.

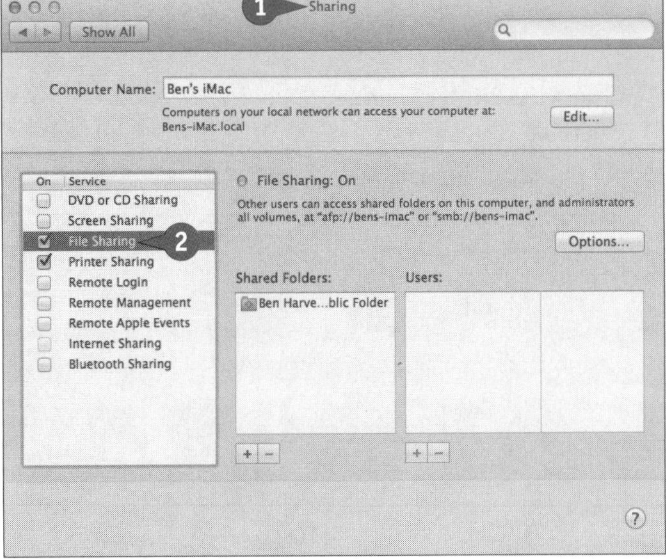

3 Under Shared Folders, click +.

An Open dialog appears.

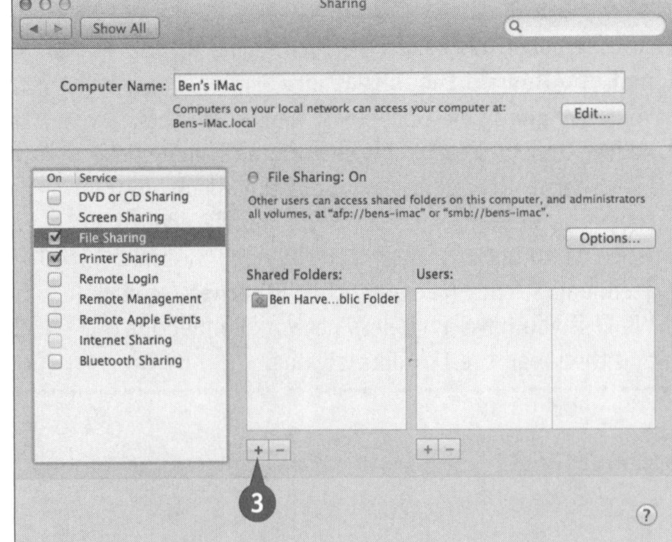

4 Click the folder you want to share.

5 Click **Add**.

Your Mac begins sharing the folder.

A The folder appears in the Shared Folders list.

6 Click the folder.

7 For the Everyone user, click the current permission and then click the permission you want to assign.

B The current permission is indicated with a check mark.

OS X assigns the permission to the user.

C You can also click ⊞ under the Users list to add more users.

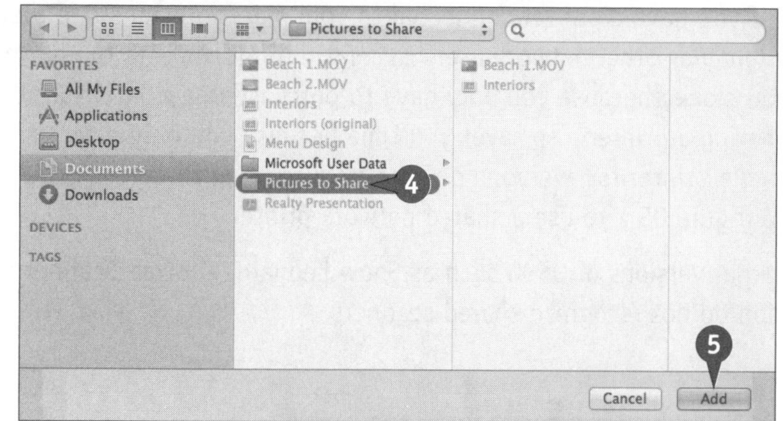

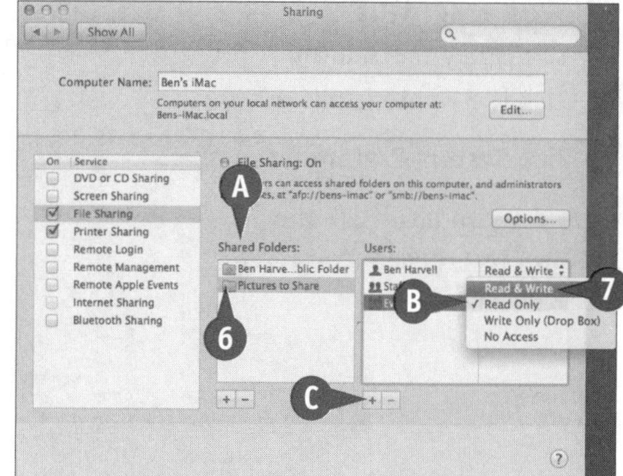

TIPS

What are the differences between the various types of permissions I can assign to users?

Permissions define what users can and cannot do with the shared folder:

- **Read & Write.** Users can open files, add new files, rename or delete existing files, and edit file contents.
- **Read Only.** Users can open files, but cannot add, delete, rename, or edit files.
- **Write Only (Drop Box).** Users can add files to the folder as a Drop Box, but cannot open the folder.
- **No Access.** Users cannot open (or even see) the folder.

Can I share folders with Windows users?

Yes. In the Sharing window, click **Options** and then select the **Share files and folders using SMB (Windows)** check box (☐ changes to ☑). Select your user account (☐ changes to ☑), use the Password text box to type your account password, click **OK**, and then click **Done**. Windows users must type your username and password to see your shared folders.

Share a Printer

If you have a printer connected to your Mac, you can share the printer with the network. This enables other network users to send their documents to your printer. Sharing a printer saves you money because you only have to purchase one printer for all the computers on your network. Sharing a printer also saves you time because you only have to install, configure, and maintain a single printer for everyone on your network. See the section "Add a Shared Printer" to learn how to configure OS X to use a shared network printer.

Earlier versions of OS X, such as Snow Leopard, allowed Scanner Sharing. OS X Mavericks and Mountain Lion do not recognize shared scanners.

Share a Printer

1. Click the **Apple** icon (■).
2. Click **System Preferences.**

Note: You can also click the **System Preferences** icon (■) in the Dock.

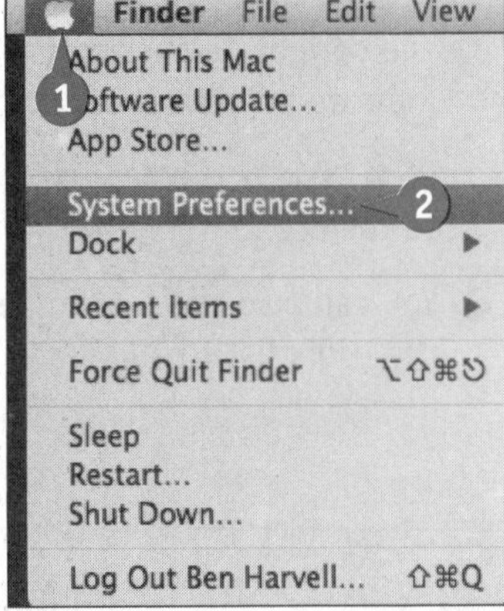

The System Preferences window appears.

3. Click **Sharing.**

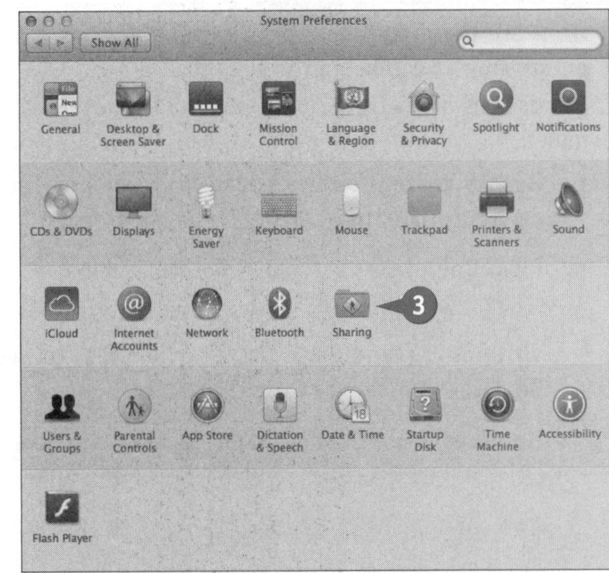

4 Click **Printer Sharing**.

Note: Be sure to click the **Printer Sharing** text, not the check box. This ensures that you do not accidentally deselect the check box.

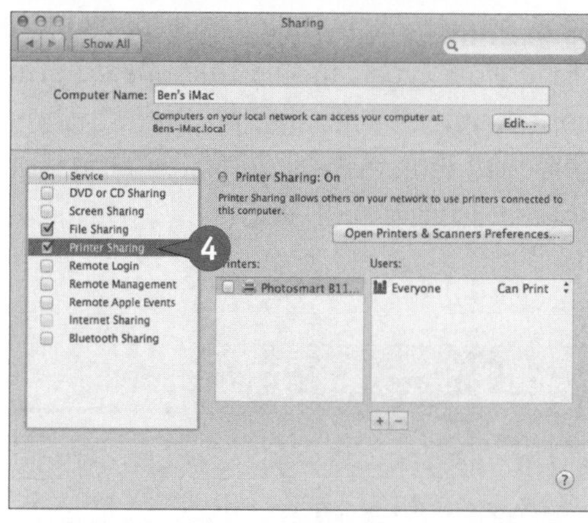

5 Select the check box beside the printer you want to share (☐ changes to ☑).

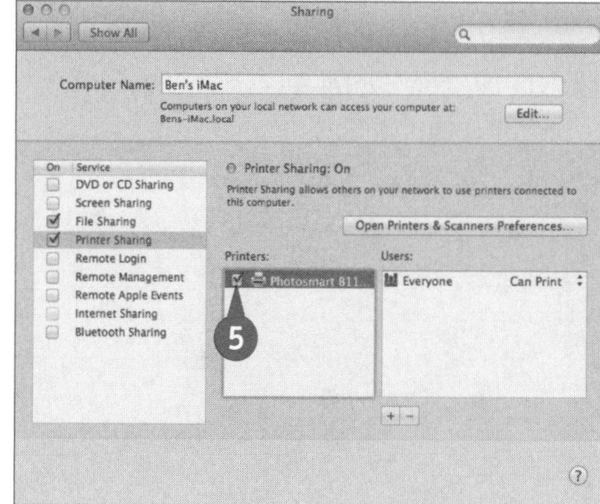

TIP

Is there another method I can use to share a printer?

Yes, you can follow these steps:

1. Click the **Apple** icon ().
2. Click **System Preferences**.
3. Click **Printers & Scanners** (not shown).
4. Click the printer you want to share.
5. Select the **Share this printer on the network** check box (☐ changes to ☑).

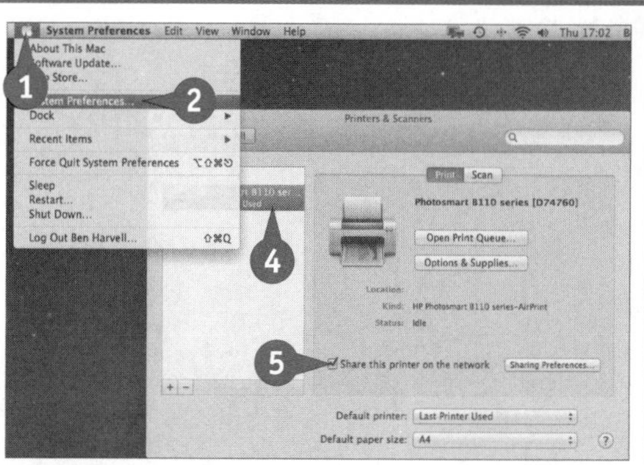

Add a Shared Printer

If another computer on your network has an attached printer that has been shared with the network, you can add that shared printer to your Mac. This enables you to send a document from your Mac to that shared printer, which means you can print your documents without having a printer attached directly to your Mac. Before you can print to a shared network printer, you must add the shared printer to OS X.

Add a Shared Printer

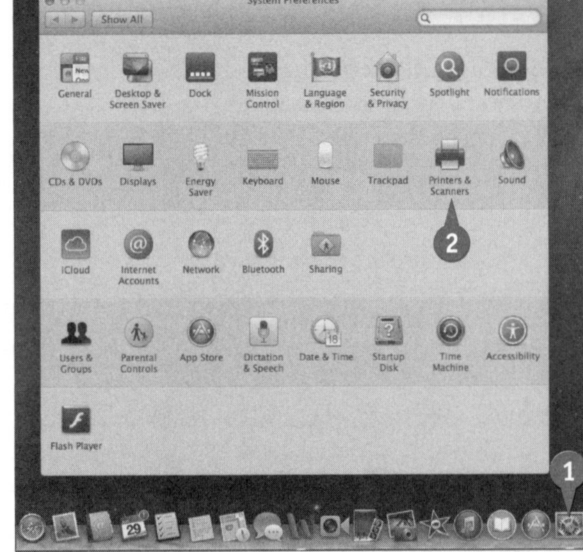

1 In the Dock, click the **System Preferences** icon (▣).

The System Preferences window appears.

2 Click **Printers & Scanners.**

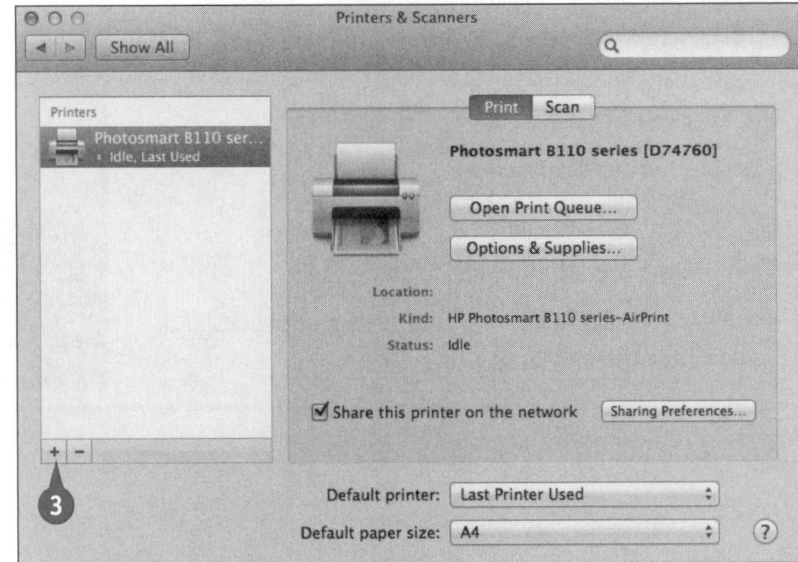

3 Click [+].

4 Click **Default**.

5 Click the shared printer.

6 Click **Add**.

Note: If OS X alerts you that it must install software for the printer, click **Install**.

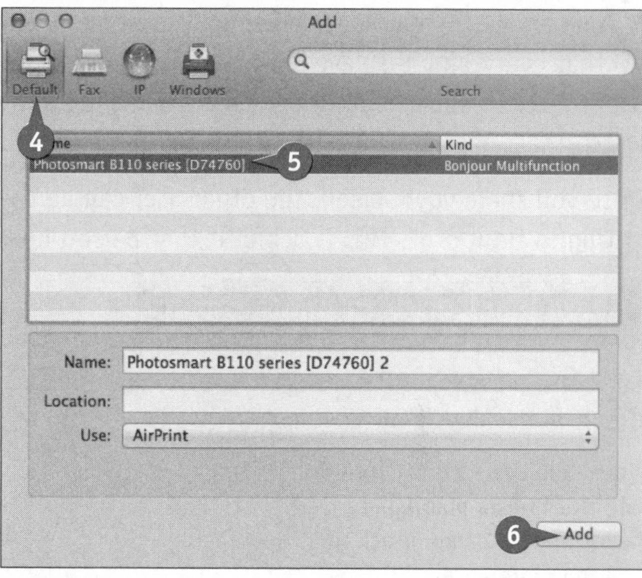

A OS X adds the printer.

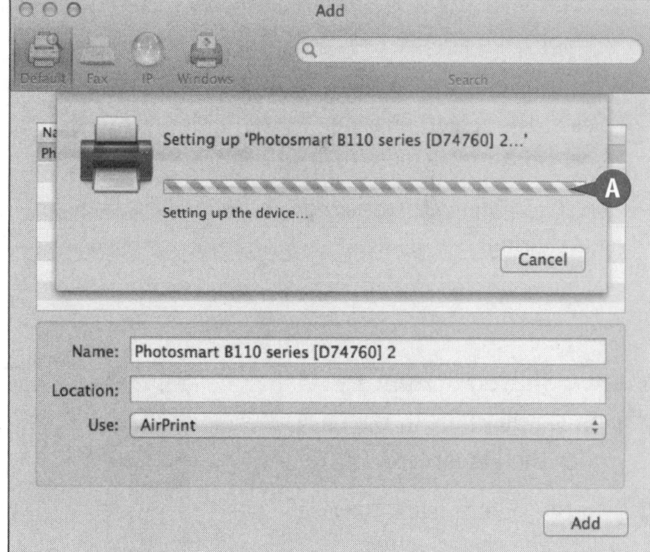

TIP

Can I add a shared Windows printer?

Yes. If you have Windows computers on your network, you can connect to any printers that they share. Follow steps 1 to 4 and then click the **Windows** tab. Click the Windows workgroup, click the computer with the shared printer, log on to the Windows computer, and then click the shared printer you want to use. In the Print Using list, click [+], click **Other**, and then click the printer in the list that appears. Click **Add**.

Share a Screen with Another Mac

You can share your Mac's screen with other computers on your network. Sharing your screen means that everything displayed on your Mac's desktop is also displayed inside a window on the other user's Mac. This is useful for demonstrating something on the screen, because the other user can watch the demonstration without having to be physically present in front of your Mac.

Once you share your screen, the other user can also work with your Mac just as though he or she was sitting in front of it. This is useful if that person needs to troubleshoot a problem.

Share a Screen with Another Mac

Turn On Screen Sharing

1 Open the Sharing preferences.

Note: See the section "Turn On File and Printer Sharing" to learn how to display and unlock the Sharing preferences.

The Sharing preferences appear.

2 Select the **Screen Sharing** check box (☐ changes to ☑).

OS X configures the desktop for sharing.

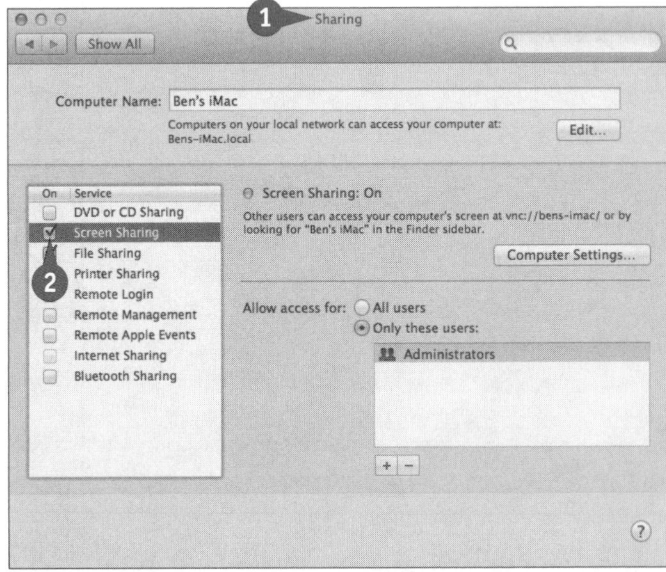

View a Shared Screen

1 On another Mac, in the Dock, click the **Finder** icon (▣).

2 In the sidebar, click the Mac with the shared screen.

3 Click **Share Screen**.

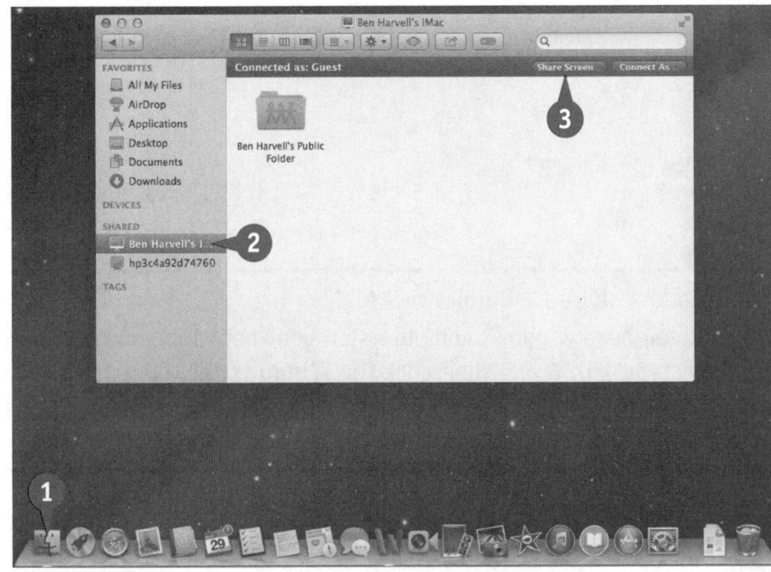

OS X prompts you to log in to the remote computer.

4. Type the password for an administrative account on the Mac that is sharing the screen.

5. Click **Connect**.

A. OS X displays the shared screen in a window.

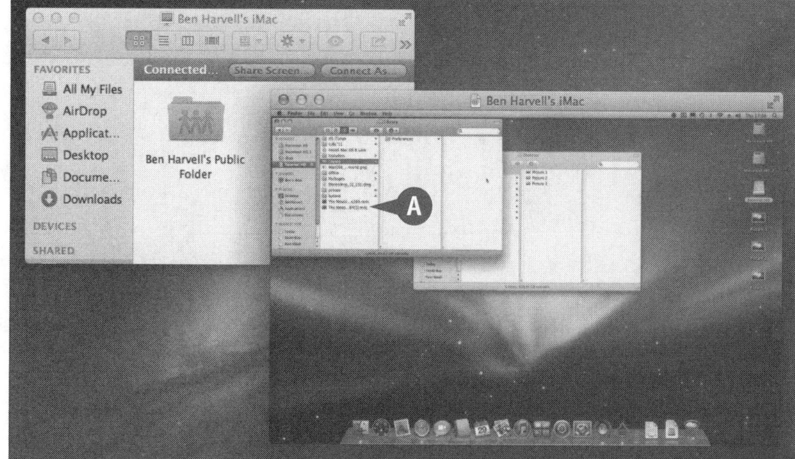

TIP

Is it possible to copy data either from or to the Mac with the shared screen?

Yes, you can copy data either way. This is useful if you have text or an image on one Mac and you need to use it on the other. If you want to send data to the Mac with the shared screen, copy the data that you want to send, click **Edit**, and then click **Send Clipboard**. If you want to receive data from the Mac with the shared screen, use that Mac to copy the data that you want to receive. In the Screen Sharing window, click **Edit**, and then click **Get Clipboard**.

CHAPTER 17

Downloading New Software

New software can be installed on your Mac via download from a website or via the Mac App Store, which offers the safest and most convenient buying experience, although not always the best value compared to some online retailers. Most software requires payment in order to install it; however, free applications and trials are available.

Open and Close the Mac App Store

The Mac App Store is an application that allows you to browse, purchase, and download software for your Mac in a similar way to buying music on iTunes. Purchases through the Mac App Store are charged to your Apple ID or iTunes account and can be downloaded on all of your computers that are connected to that account. Updates to software purchased from the Mac App Store are also handled within the app.

Open and Close the Mac App Store

Open the Mac App Store

1. In the Dock, click the **App Store** icon (![]).

The Mac App Store opens.

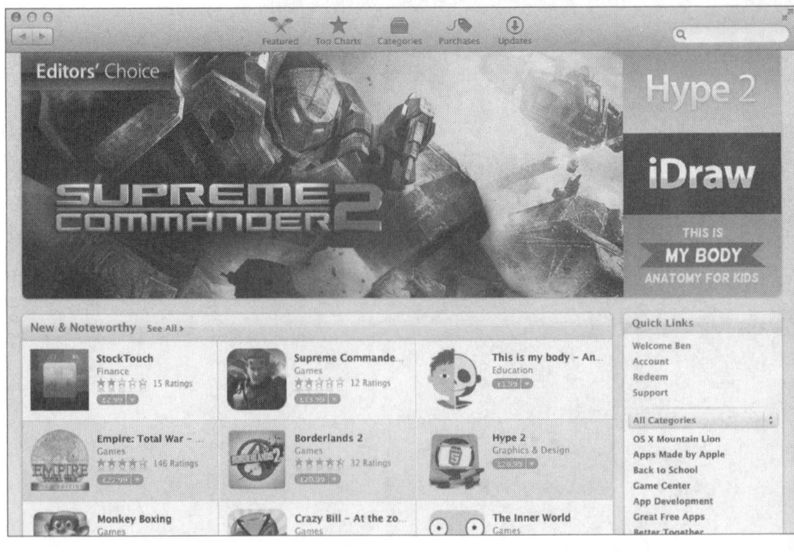

Close the Mac App Store

1. Click **App Store**.

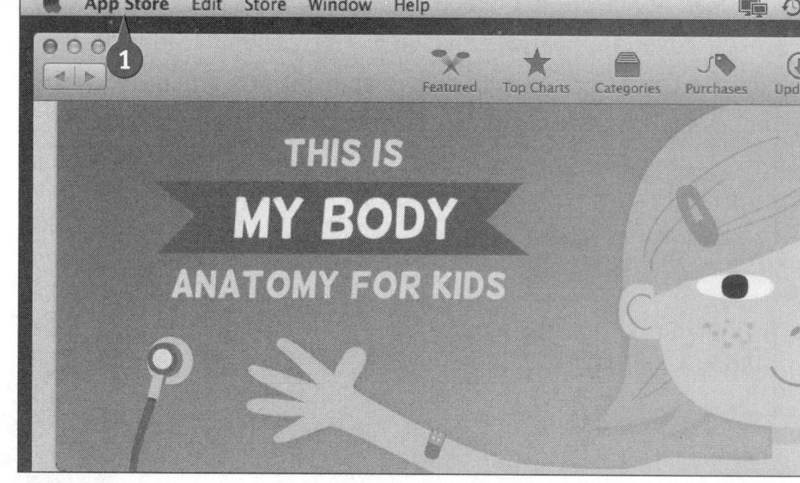

2. Click **Quit App Store**.

   The Mac App Store closes.

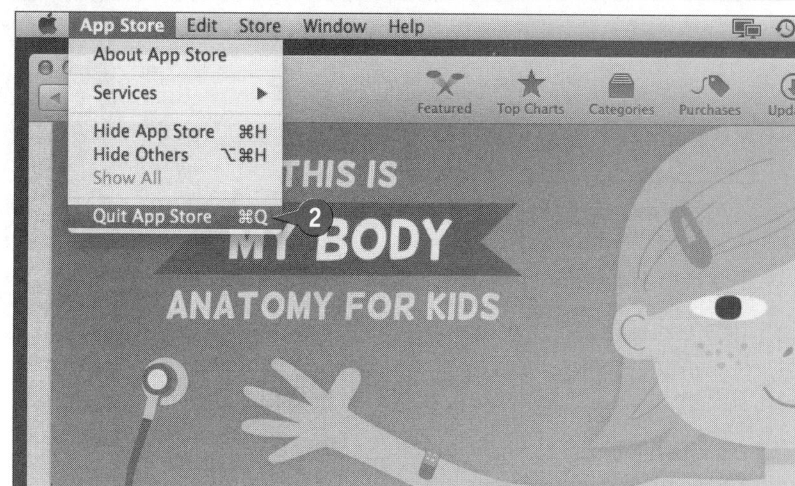

TIP

Are there other methods I can use to open and close the Mac App Store?

If you have hidden the Dock (as described in Chapter 13) or removed the App Store icon from the Dock, you can click **Spotlight** (🔍) and type **App Store**. You can then click **App Store** in the search results. Alternatively, you can double-click the **App Store** icon in the Applications folder.

Browse Software

The Mac App Store is divided into sections to help you quickly find the software you are looking for or discover applications that may interest you. The Featured section shows new and featured apps, while the Categories section shows applications broken down by type. You can also view the most popular applications ranked by download numbers using the Top Charts feature.

Browse Software

1. In the Dock, click the **App Store** icon ().

The Mac App Store appears.

A New and featured apps are shown on the Featured screen.

B Click these boxes to show curated selections of apps.

C Type into this field to search for a specific app.

2. Click **Top Charts**.

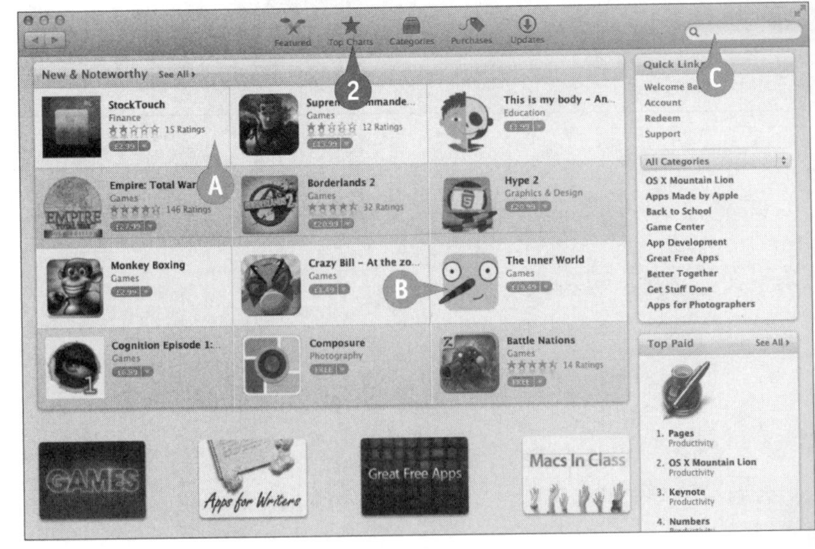

The Top Charts screen appears.

D The top 12 paid apps are shown here.

E The top 12 free apps are shown here.

F Click a link to see charts within a particular software category.

Note: You can click **See All** next to the title of any chart to see the full list.

3 Click **Categories**.

The Categories screen appears.

G Click the name of a category to view corresponding apps.

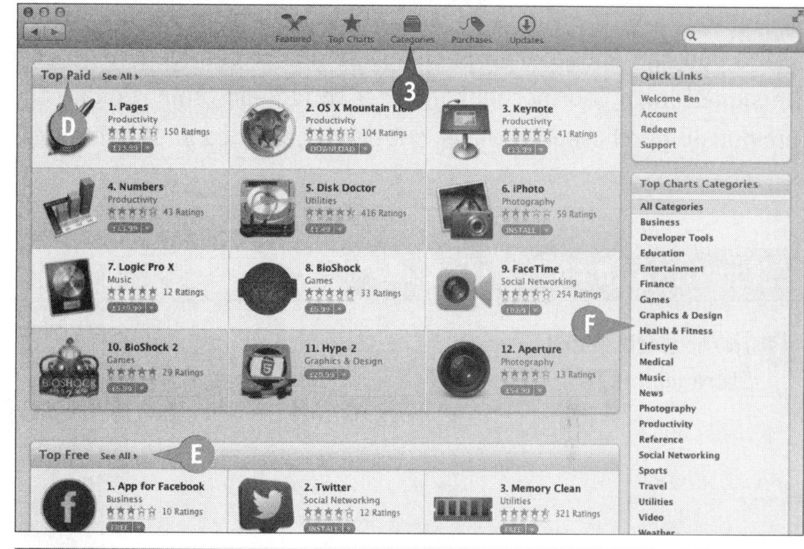

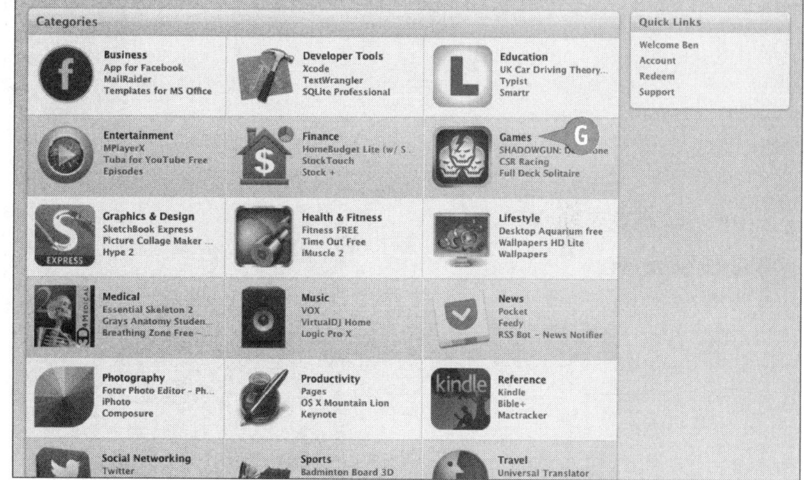

TIP

How do I quickly see the best-selling apps?

On the Mac App Store main screen, click **See All** next to the Top Paid chart that appears on the right of the screen. This takes you to a list of the most popular apps for sale on the App Store. You can do the same for the Top Free chart that appears below Top Paid on the Mac App Store main screen.

Sign In to the Mac App Store

Signing in to the Mac App Store allows you to make purchases and access your account information so you can update your payment details or change any other information. You will need to be signed in to your account in order to redeem promotional codes or access software you have previously purchased but have not downloaded to your computer.

Sign In to the Mac App Store

1. In the Dock, click the **App Store** icon ().

The Mac App Store appears.

2. Click **Sign In**.

The Sign In dialog appears.

3 Type your Apple ID.

4 Type your password.

5 Click **Sign In**.

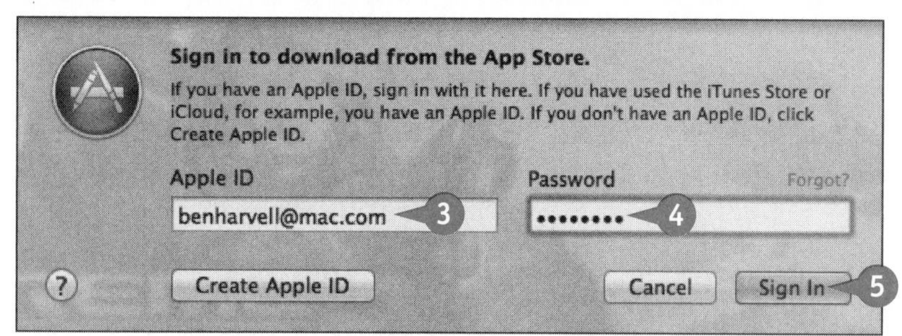

You are signed in to the Mac App Store.

A Sign in changes to a welcome message.

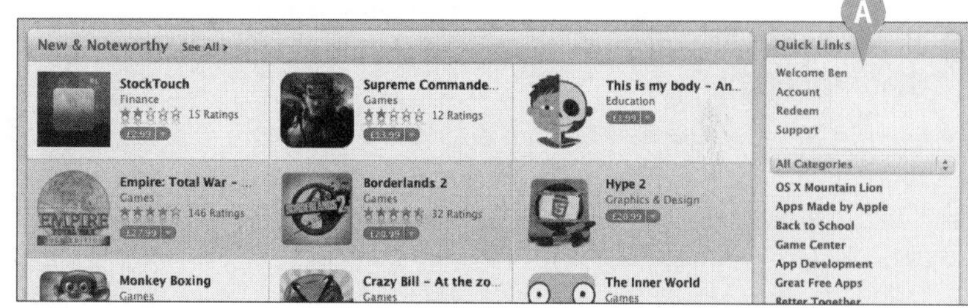

TIPS

How do I redeem a gift card or promo code in the Mac App Store?

If you have a Mac App Store gift card or a promo code to download an application or add credit to your account, you can use the Redeem section to access your gift or app. Click **Redeem**, which appears under Quick Links on most App Store pages, and then type the promo code or gift card code. If your gift card has a box around the code, you can use your Mac's built-in camera to redeem the code by holding it up to the screen.

How do I sign out of the Mac App Store?

To sign out of the Mac App Store, click the **Account** link under Quick Links that appears on most pages of the store. The Sign In dialog appears, and you can click the **Sign Out** button to sign out of your account. The Welcome message under Quick Links changes back to Sign In. Click this link to sign back in to the Mac App Store.

Update Software from the Mac App Store

Software installed via the Mac App Store is also updated through the Mac App Store. You may notice that a red badge sometimes appears on the App Store icon in the Dock. This means that one or more updates are available to software you have installed. Software updates can be installed from the Updates section of the Mac App Store or set to download automatically.

Update Software from the Mac App Store

1. In the Dock, click the **App Store** icon (icon).

The Mac App Store appears.

2. Click **Updates**.

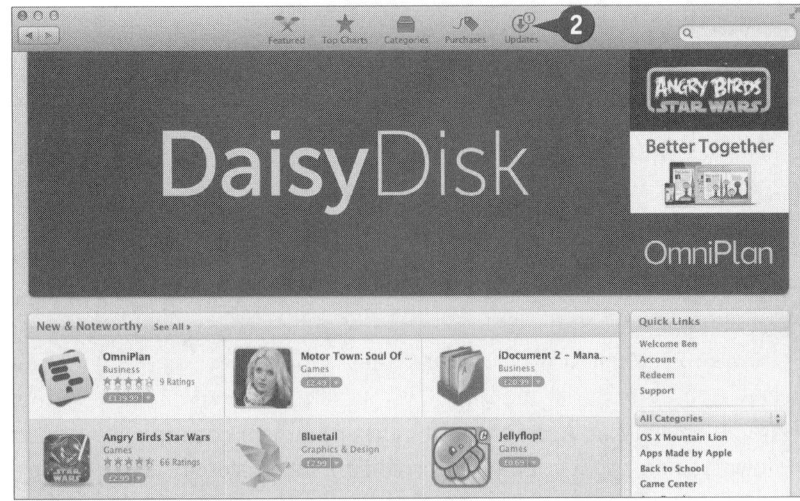

All available updates are shown.

A Click **Update All** to download and install all updates.

3 Click **Update** next to the application you want to update.

OS X downloads and installs the update.

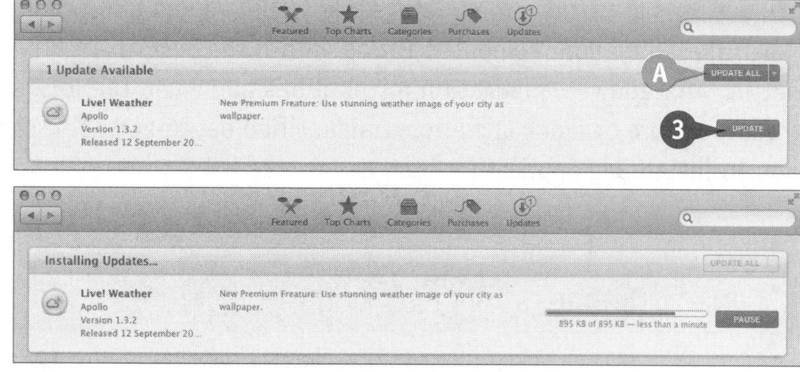

TIPS

How can I tell when there are software updates available?
OS X notifies you about software updates in a number of ways; with a badge on the App Store icon showing how many updates are available, with a badge on the Updates button within the Mac App Store application, and, in the case of system software updates, through notifications that appear at the top right of your screen.

Does all software update through the Mac App Store?
No. Some software needs to be updated from within the application itself, while other programs have a separate "update manager" utility that checks for and downloads updates.

Set Which Application Types Can Be Installed

OS X uses a feature called Gatekeeper to help avoid potentially malicious software from being installed on your computer. Found within the Security & Privacy System Preferences pane, settings for allowed application installations allow you to block any apps not downloaded from the Mac App Store or block apps from unidentified developers. You can also turn off all blocking to allow you to install any application from any source.

Set Which Application Types Can Be Installed

1 In the Dock, click the **System Preferences** icon ( ).

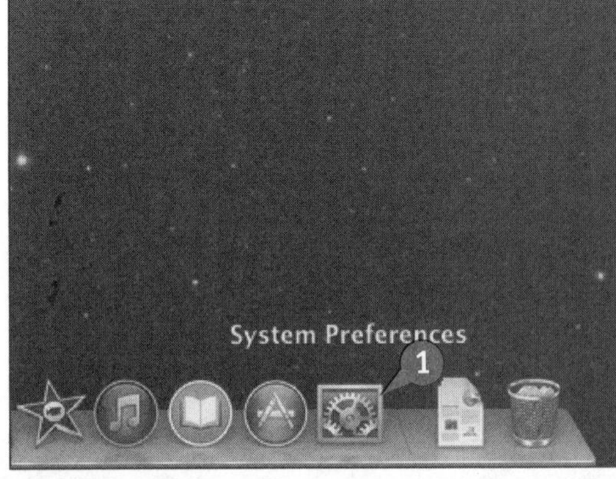

System Preferences appear.

2 Click **Security & Privacy**.

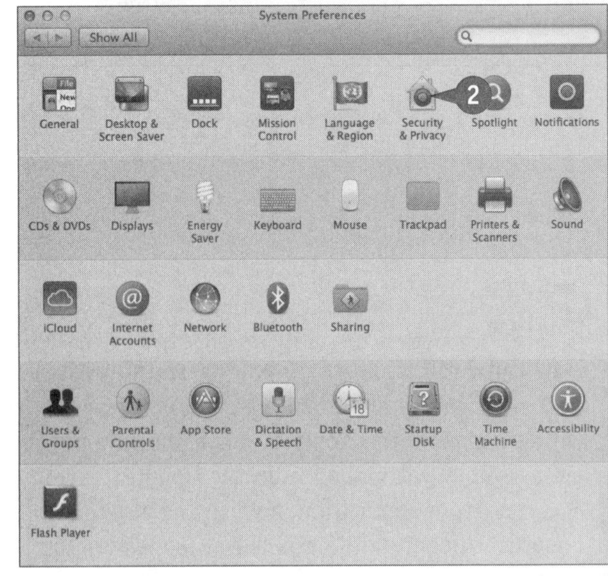

3. Click **General**.

A. Click **Mac App Store** (◯ changes to ◉) to only allow installations from the Mac App Store.

B. Click **Mac App Store and identified developers** (◯ changes to ◉) to allow Mac App Store downloads and applications built by approved developers.

C. Click **Anywhere** (◯ changes to ◉) to allow any app to be installed.

Note: In order to make changes on this pane, you may need to click the lock icon and type your system password.

4. Click **Close** (●).

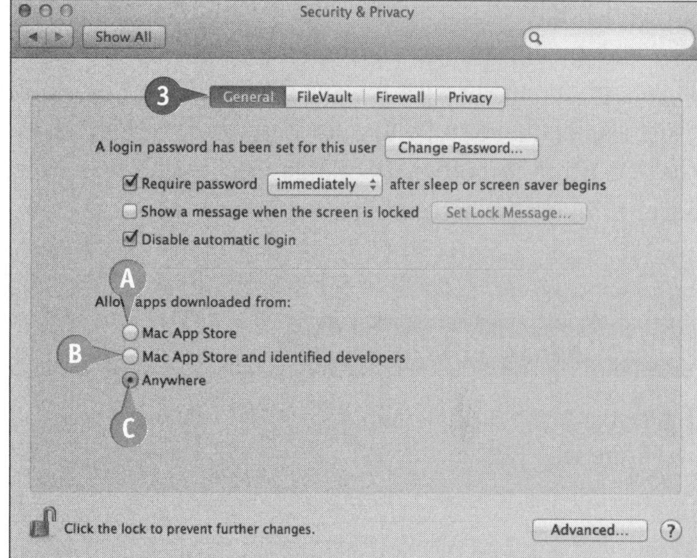

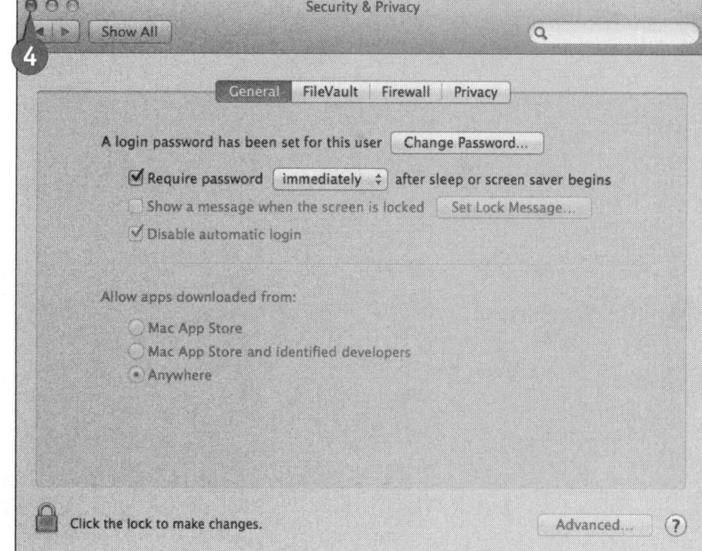

TIP

What are identified developers?

An identified developer is a software maker that has been approved by Apple. Software created by these developers includes a special certificate that is recognized by OS X and, if you are using the identified developers Gatekeeper option, approved for installation. This feature helps prevent malicious apps designed to look like legitimate software from being installed and potentially harming your computer or breaching security.

Install Previous Purchases

Applications that you have previously downloaded from the Mac App Store and uninstalled or you have purchased and installed on other Macs can be downloaded again via the Mac App Store. If you are logged in with the same Apple ID, all previous purchases you have made on the Mac App Store are available to be downloaded from the Purchases section as long as the software remains in the App Store inventory. The Purchases section lists every purchase you have made from the Mac App Store through the account you are using.

Install Previous Purchases

1. In the Dock, click the **App Store** icon ().

The Mac App Store appears.

2. Click **Purchases**.

Your previous software purchases are shown.

Ⓐ Software already installed on your Mac is shown as Installed.

Note: Installed software with updates available have an Update button next to them.

Ⓑ Previously purchased applications not installed on your Mac have an Install button next to them.

❸ Click **Install** next to the application you want to download.

OS X downloads and installs the software you selected.

TIP

Why is some of the software installed on my Mac not shown in the Purchases list?

Only software installed through the Mac App Store is shown in the list and available to be downloaded again. If you did download the software on your Mac from the Mac App Store, make sure you are signed in to the Mac App Store with your Apple ID and that you are using the same Apple ID you used to purchase and download the software.

Install Software from the Internet

In addition to the Mac App Store, there are a number of sources online from which to download software. Many developers sell their software via their own websites or online stores and there is a wide range of download sites that feature software from a number of developers. Always be careful when downloading software from the Internet, however, and try your best to ensure that it comes from a reputable source.

Install Software from the Internet

Download Software

1. In Safari, locate the page that contains a link for the software you want to download.
2. Click the download.

The software downloads.

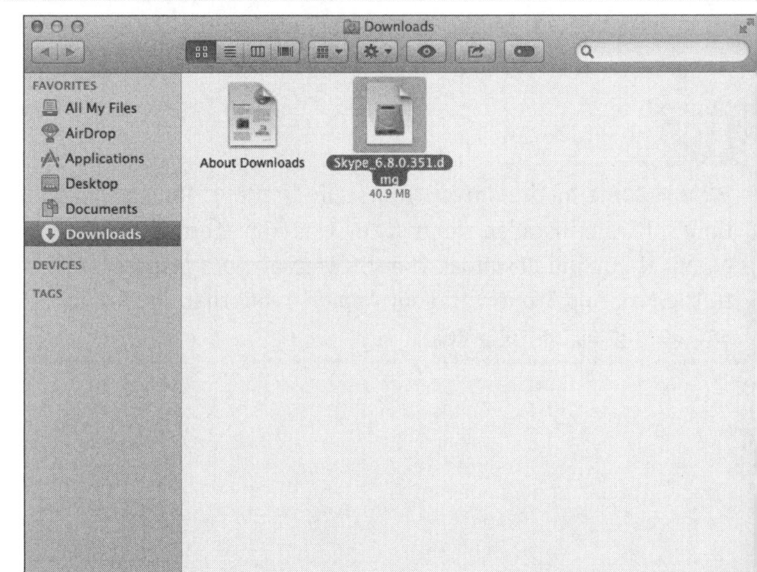

When the download is complete, the software is ready to be installed.

3 Double-click the downloaded file.

Note: In many cases, the downloaded application automatically opens a window when it finishes downloading. If this is the case, skip step **3**.

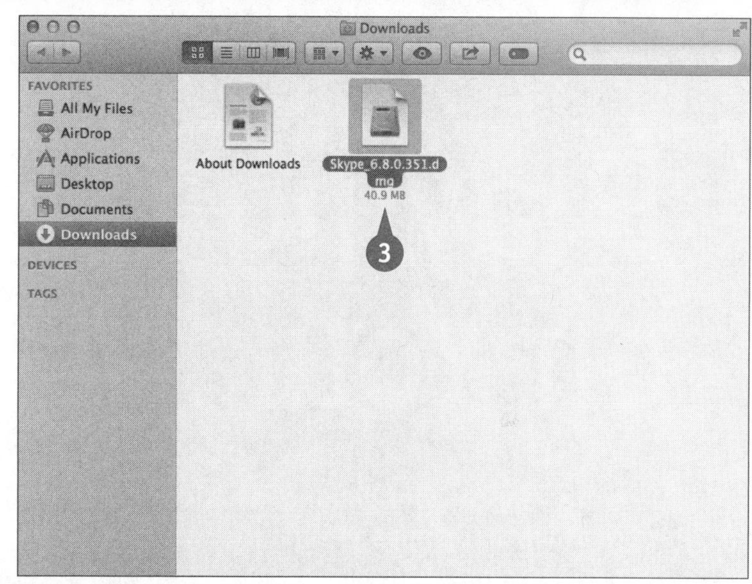

The application now normally shows an installer or prompts you to drag the application to your Applications folder. If not, see the following Tips.

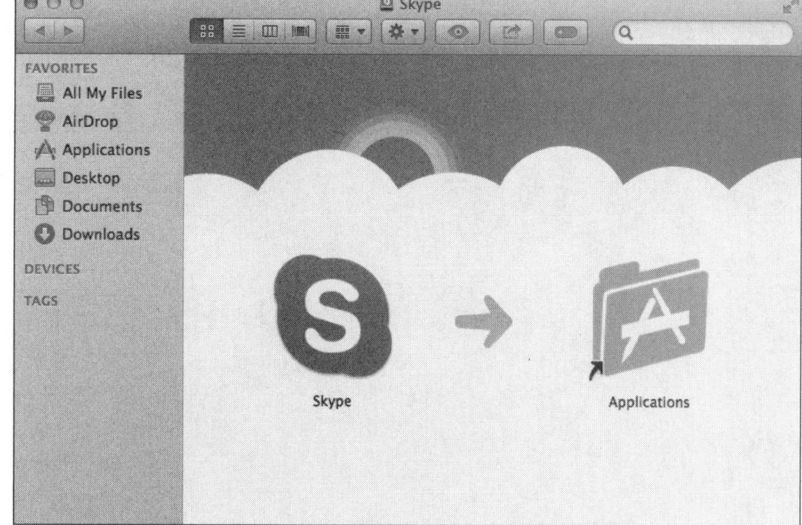

TIPS

I didn't receive any instructions; an app just downloaded. What do I do next?

If an app simply downloaded without any instructions or an installer, click and drag it from your Downloads folder to your Applications folder and launch it from there.

My download appeared as a DMG or ZIP file. What do I do with it?

A DMG file is a disk image that behaves like a hard drive or external disk. Simply double-click it to mount it and then follow the instructions that appear or drag the application within it to your Applications folder. A ZIP file is a compressed folder. Double-click the file to have OS X unzip it for you, and then follow the instructions for DMG files above.

CHAPTER 18

Playing Games on Your Mac

Macs are very capable gaming machines. With the Game Center application that comes preinstalled with OS X, you can play games with friends and challenge them to beat your best scores as well as discover new games to play.

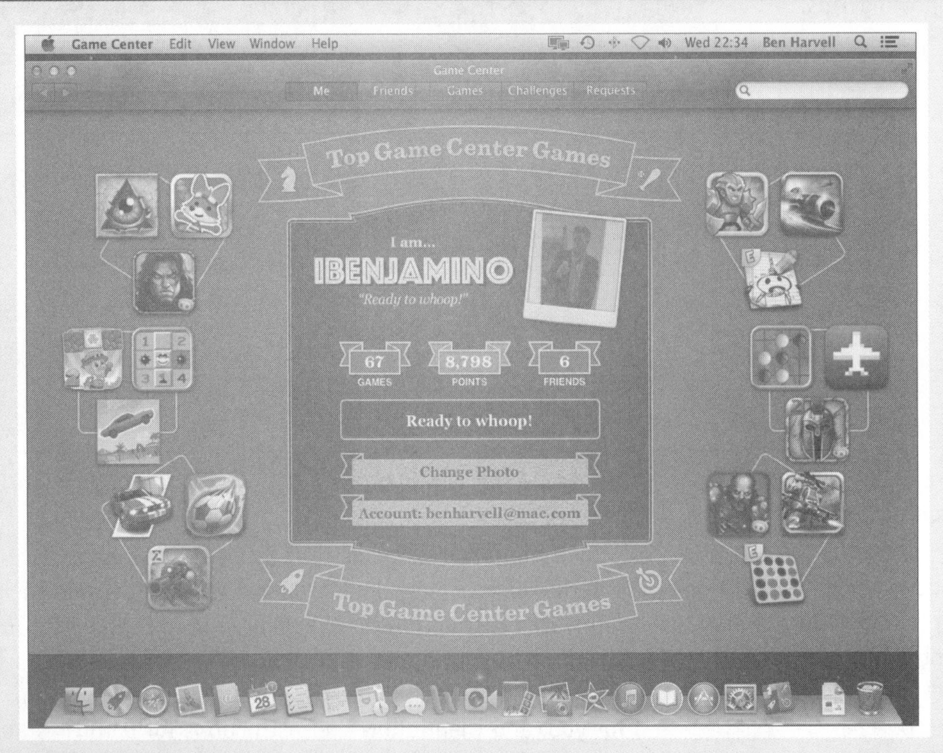

Open and Close Game Center

Game Center allows you to discover games and play and share your experiences with friends, right from your Mac. The app stores your high scores and achievements as well as a list of the games you are playing and allows you to share this information with friends. You can also challenge friends to games or to attempt to beat your high scores in games you have in common.

Open and Close Game Center

Open Game Center

1. Click **Spotlight** (🔍).
2. Type **Game Center**.
3. Click **Game Center**.

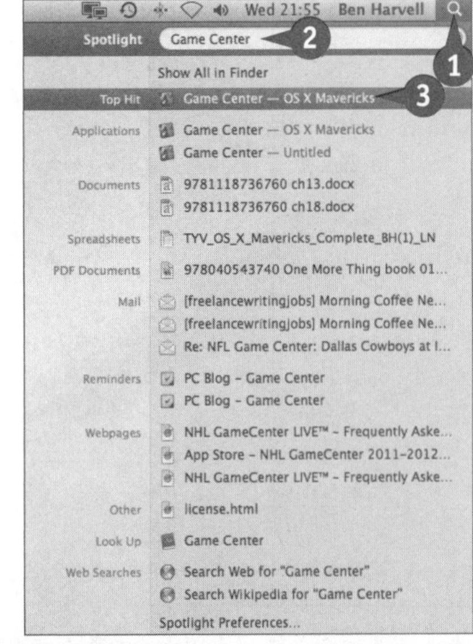

Game Center opens.

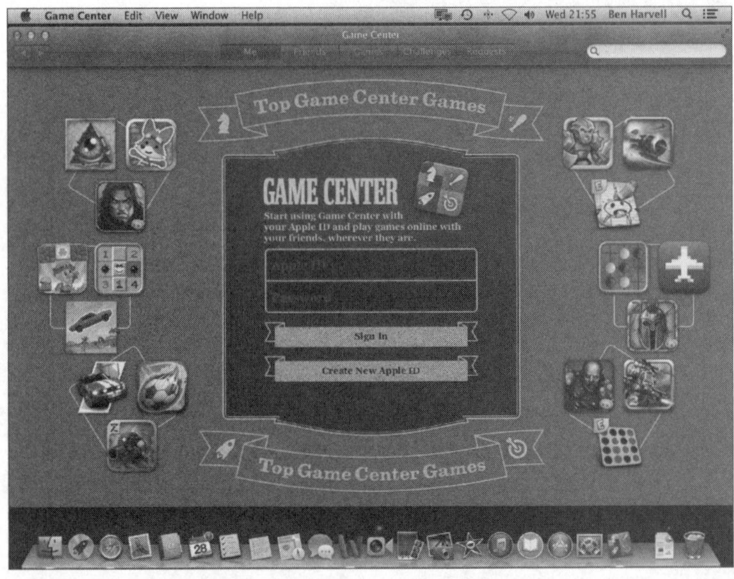

Close Game Center

1 Click **Game Center**.

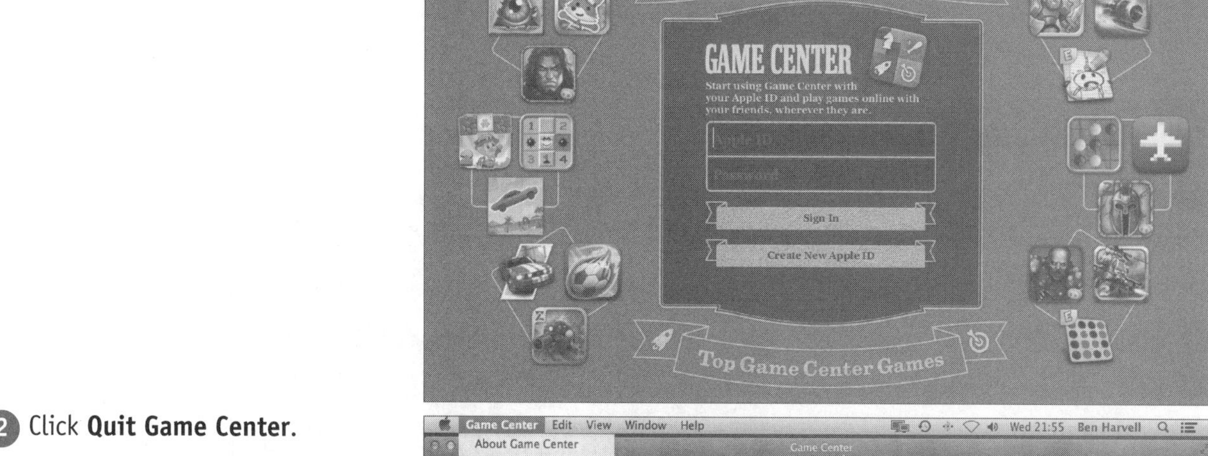

2 Click **Quit Game Center**.

Game Center closes.

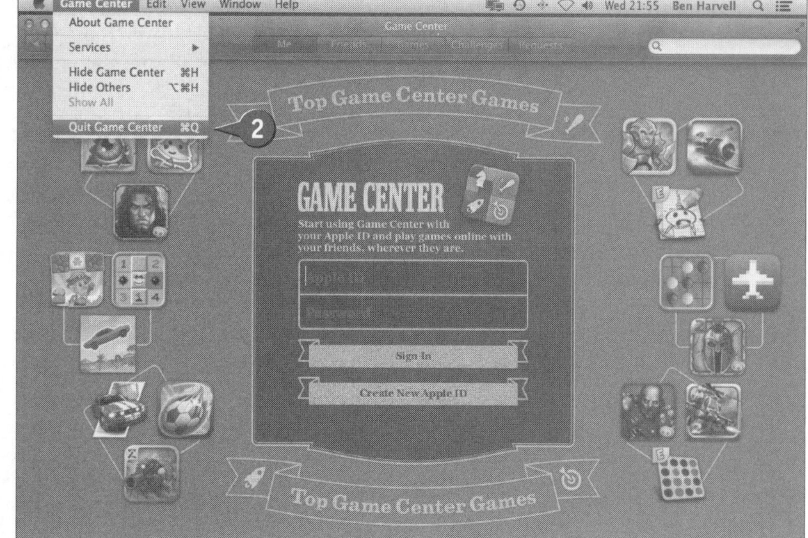

TIP

Is there another way to open Game Center?

Yes. You can open a Finder window and click Applications in the sidebar. From here you can locate the Game Center icon in the Finder window and double-click it to launch the application. You can also use Spotlight to search your Mac for the Game Center application and launch it.

Create a Game Center Account

In order for your friends to find you on Game Center and for you to interact with them, you need to create an account and personalize it. You can sign in to Game Center with your Apple ID and then add information. Games you have purchased with your Apple ID are added to Game Center automatically when you create an account.

Create a Game Center Account

1. Launch Game Center.

Note: See the section "Open and Close Game Center."

2. Type your Apple ID.
3. Type your password.
4. Click **Sign In**.

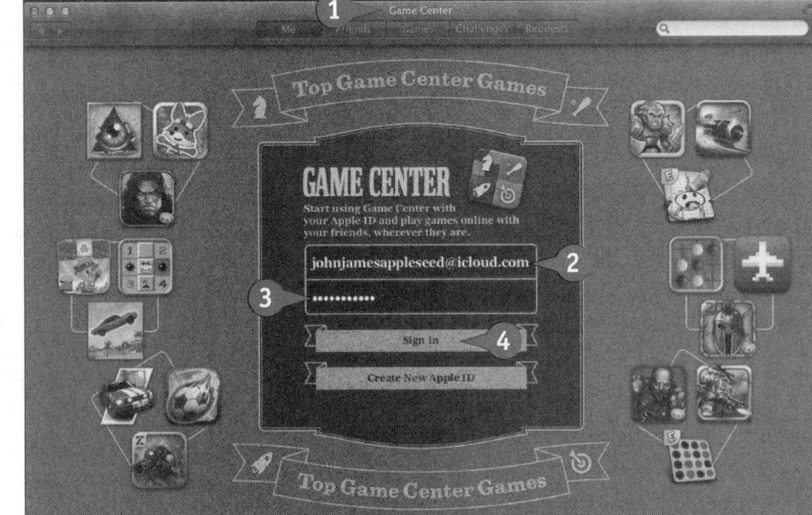

5. Select the **I have read and agree to these terms & conditions** check box (☐ changes to ☑).
6. Click **Accept**.

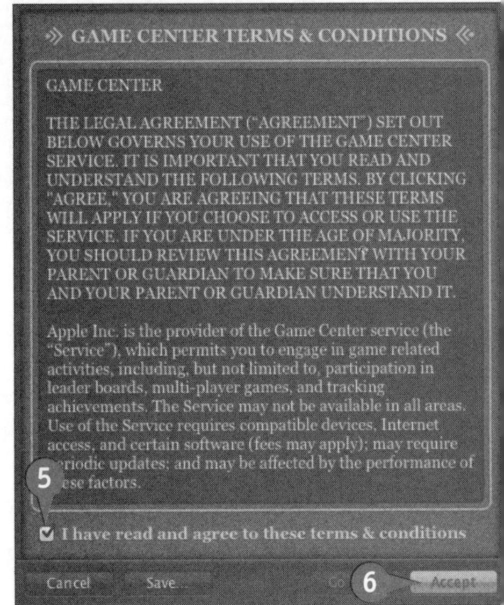

7. Type a nickname.

A. To make your profile public, select the **Public Profile** check box (☐ changes to ☑).

B. To upload your contacts to match you with friends on Game Center, select the **Use Contacts for Friend Suggestions** check box (☐ changes to ☑).

8. Click **Continue**.

Note: Game Center also asks if you want to find friends on Facebook. Click **Later** to do this another time or click **Allow** to grant Game Center access to your Facebook friends list.

C. Click the status area and type a message for your friends to see.

D. Click **Change Photo** and select a photo from your Mac or take a photo with your Mac's camera.

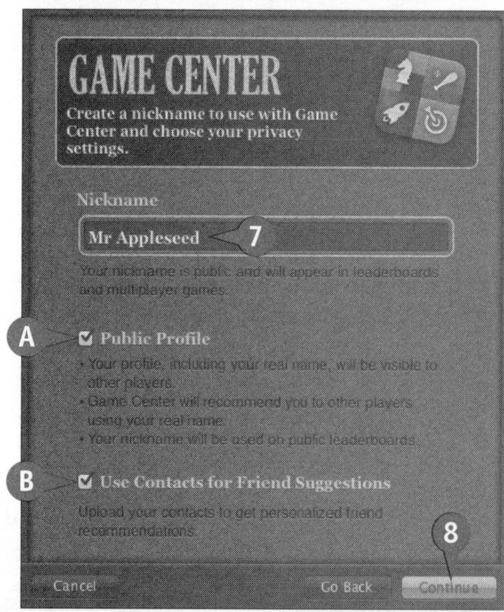

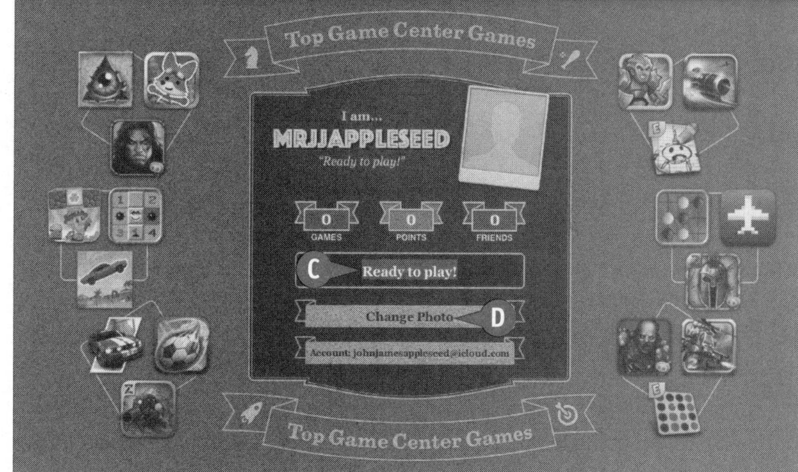

TIP

What's the difference between a public and a private Game Center profile?

If you select a Private profile, you are only able to see and be contacted by friends who add you as a Game Center friend or that you have added. A Public profile suggests you to other Game Center users you may not know but who have a similar taste in games.

Find Friends to Play Games With

Game Center lists all of the friends you have already connected with through Game Center, be it on a Mac or iOS device, and also suggests friends you might like to play with. Friends you connect with through Game Center can play games with you and send you challenges, and you can also view the games you have in common with your friends.

Find Friends to Play Games With

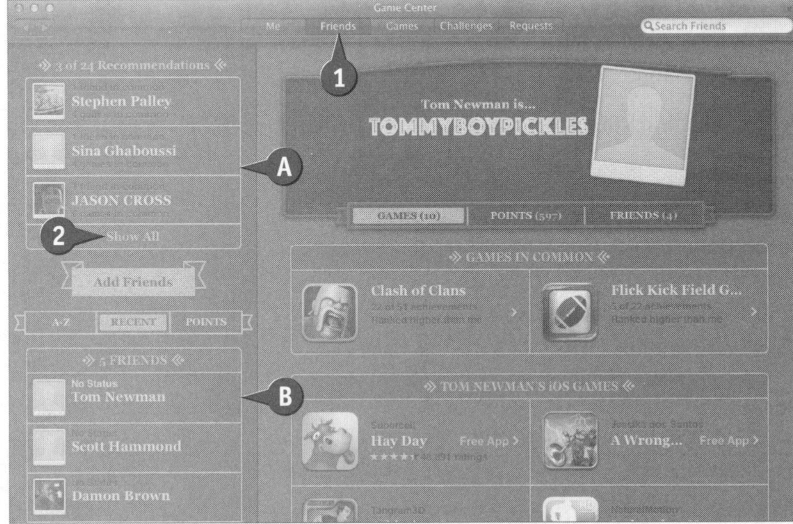

1. Click **Friends**.

   A Recommended friends are shown here.

   B Accepted friends are shown here.

2. Click **Show All**.

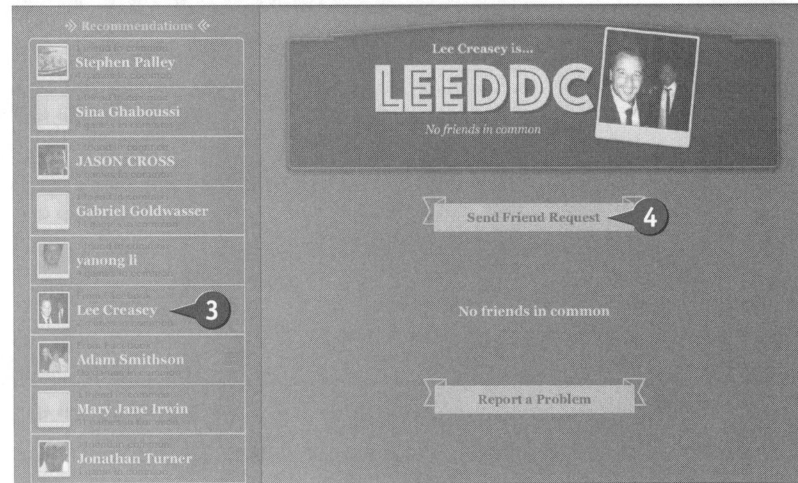

All suggested Game Center friends are shown.

3. Click the name of a suggested friend.
4. Click **Send Friend Request**.

C Edit the message in your friend request.

5 Click **Send**.

Your friend request is sent.

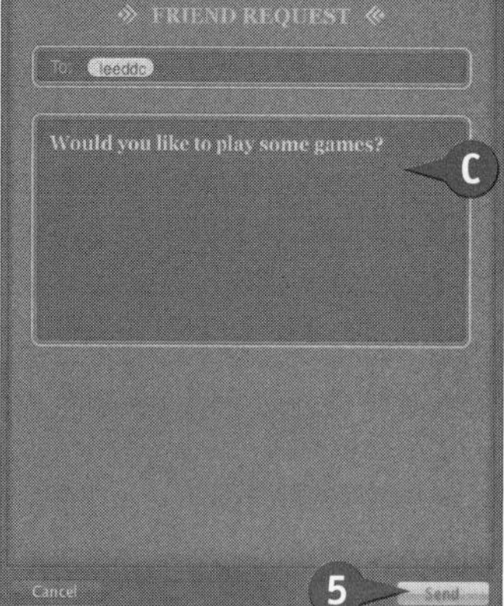

6 Click **Close** (●).

Game Center closes.

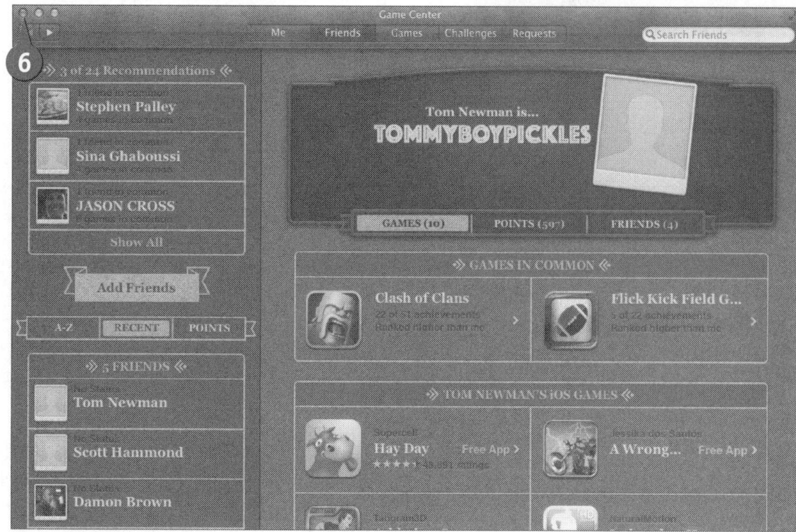

TIP

A friend has requested to add me as a friend. How do I accept?

Click the **Requests** tab at the top of the Game Center screen. All requests you have been sent are shown here. On this screen you can also send a request to a friend via e-mail if you do not know his or her Game Center username.

Challenge Friends to Beat Your Scores

If you earn a high score or a particular achievement in a game, you can challenge your friends to beat you through Game Center. Clicking the achievement or score gives you the choice to share the achievement with friends to see if they can match your skill. Anyone you are friends with on Game Center can be sent a challenge, even if they do not have the game you are playing.

Challenge Friends to Beat Your Scores

1. Click **Games.**
2. Click the game from which you want to share a score or achievement.

3. Click **Achievements.**
4. Click the achievement you want to share.
   - A. Click the **Share** button (📤) to share the achievement via e-mail, Messages, or on Twitter or Facebook.
5. Click **Challenge Friends.**

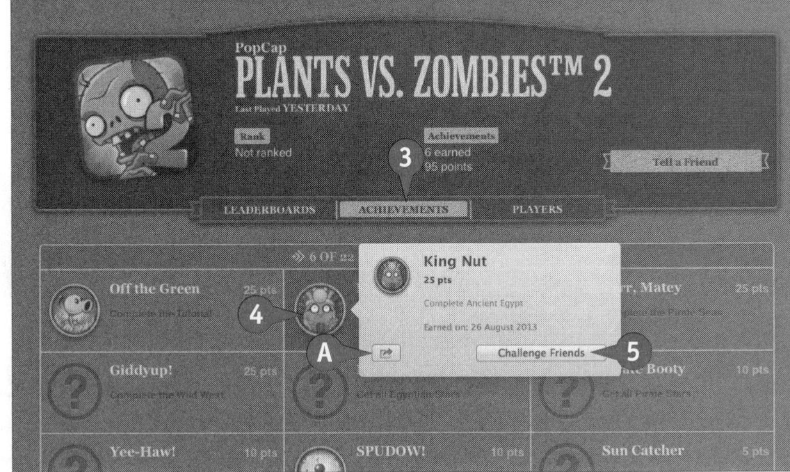

6 Select the check box next to each friend you want to challenge (☐ changes to ☑).

7 Click **Next**.

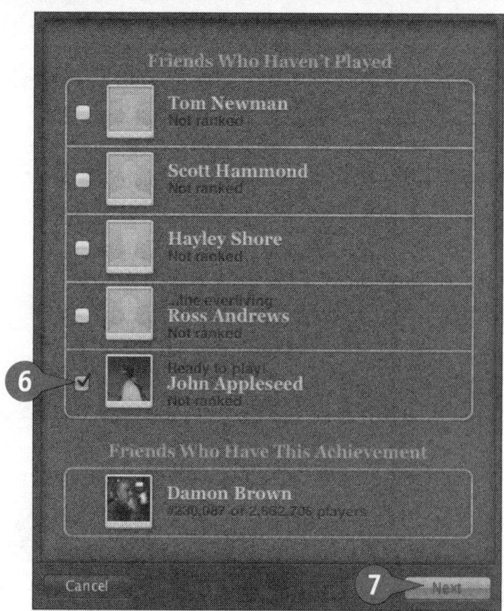

B Type an optional message as part of your challenge.

8 Click **Send**.

Your challenge is sent.

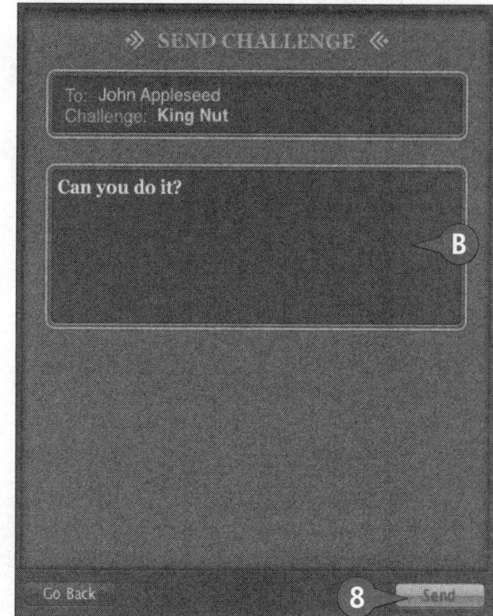

TIPS

Can I challenge friends to beat scores and achievements I have not yet managed?

Yes. Click an achievement you do not have and follow steps **5** to **8**. A notification is sent if any of the friends you challenge manage to obtain the achievement.

How can I see my friend's achievements and scores?

Click the **Friends** tab at the top of the screen and then click your friend's name in the Friends panel. View his games until you find the game you are looking for and click it. The achievements and scores of your friend are shown.

Discover New Games

It is easy to find new games to play through Game Center and download them to your Mac. The Me tab shows the most popular Game Center games being played, and you can also get recommendations from the Games tab based on the rating of the game or the number of your friends playing them. You can then click the game you want to play to open its page in the App Store.

Discover New Games

1. Launch Game Center.

Note: See the section "Open and Close Game Center."

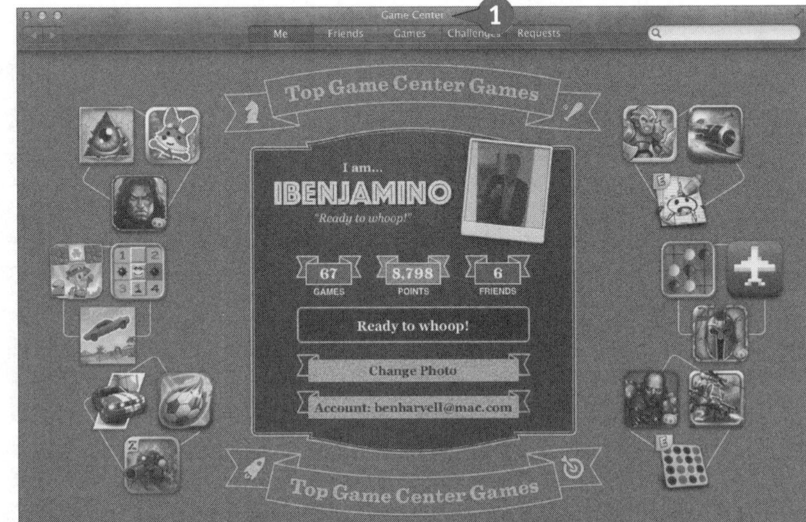

2. Click **Me**.
3. Click any of the icons listed under Top Game Center Games.

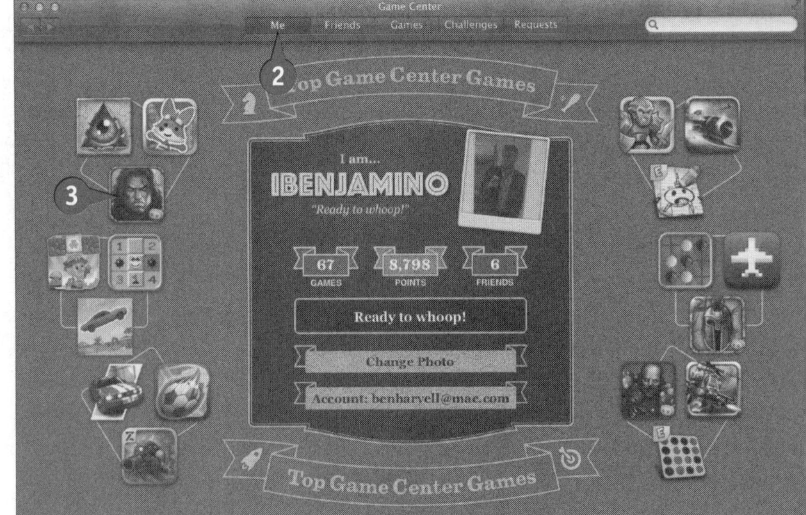

The App Store shows the game's page.

4 Click **Games**.

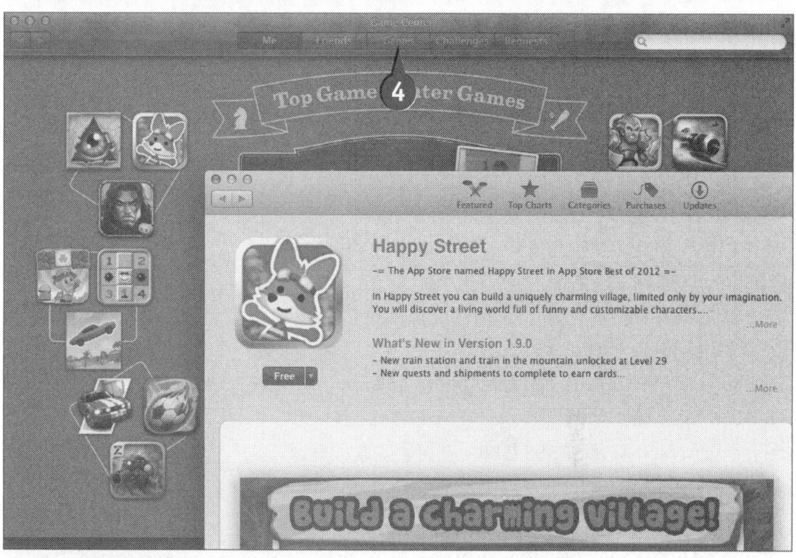

A Games recommended for you are shown in the recommendations section.

5 Click a game to be taken to the Game Center page.

TIPS

How do I see more game recommendations?
Click the **Show All** link to show more game recommendations under the Games tab. The games listed are based on popularity, and you can receive even more suggestions if you add more friends to Game Center or install more games.

How do I see if my friends are playing a recommended game?
Click the name of the game in the Recommendations screen to view the page for that game. Click **Leaderboards**, and all of your friends, if any, who are also playing the game are listed.

Index

A

B

E

F

G

H

J

K

L

M

N

T

U

V

Y

Z

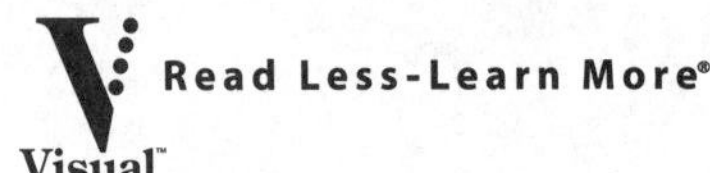

There's a Visual book for every learning level...

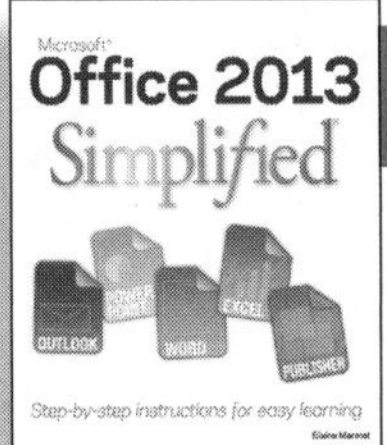

Simplified®

The place to start if you're new to computers. Full color.

- Computers
- Creating Web Pages
- Digital Photography
- Excel
- Internet
- Laptops
- Mac OS
- Office
- PCs
- Windows
- Word

Teach Yourself VISUALLY™

Get beginning to intermediate-level training in a variety of topics. Full color.

- Access
- Adobe Muse
- Computers
- Digital Photography
- Digital Video
- Dreamweaver
- Excel
- Flash
- HTML5
- iLife
- iPad
- iPhone
- iPod
- Macs
- Mac OS
- Office
- Outlook
- Photoshop
- Photoshop Elements
- Photoshop Lightroom
- PowerPoint
- Salesforce.com
- Search Engine Optimization
- Social Media
- Web Design
- Windows
- Wireless Networking
- Word
- WordPress

Top 100 Simplified® Tips & Tricks

Tips and techniques to take your skills beyond the basics. Full color.

- Digital Photography
- eBay
- Excel
- Google
- Office
- Photoshop
- Photoshop Elements
- PowerPoint
- Windows